W9-BUY-050

Andrew Watt and Jonathan Watt
with Jinjer Simon and Jim O'Donnell

SAMS
Teach Yourself

JavaScript™

in 21 Days

SAMS

201 West 103rd St., Indianapolis, Indiana, 46290 USA

Sams Teach Yourself JavaScript™ in 21 Days

Copyright © 2002 by Sams Publishing

All rights reserved. No part of this book shall be reproduced, stored in a retrieval system, or transmitted by any means, electronic, mechanical, photocopying, recording, or otherwise, without written permission from the publisher. No patent liability is assumed with respect to the use of the information contained herein. Although every precaution has been taken in the preparation of this book, the publisher and author assume no responsibility for errors or omissions. Neither is any liability assumed for damages resulting from the use of the information contained herein.

International Standard Book Number: 0-672-32297-8

Library of Congress Catalog Card Number: 2001092863

Printed in the United States of America

First Printing: May 2002

04   03   6   5   4

Trademarks

All terms mentioned in this book that are known to be trademarks or service marks have been appropriately capitalized. Sams Publishing cannot attest to the accuracy of this information. Use of a term in this book should not be regarded as affecting the validity of any trademark or service mark.

Warning and Disclaimer

Every effort has been made to make this book as complete and as accurate as possible, but no warranty or fitness is implied. The information provided is on an "as is" basis. The authors and the publisher shall have neither liability nor responsibility to any person or entity with respect to any loss or damages arising from the information contained in this book.

ACQUISITIONS EDITOR
Betsy Brown

DEVELOPMENT EDITOR
Jonathan Steever

MANAGING EDITOR
Charlotte Clapp

PROJECT EDITOR
Tony Reitz

COPY EDITOR
Karen Whitehouse

INDEXER
Larry Sweazy

PROOFREADER
Cindy Long

TECHNICAL EDITOR
Jim O'Donnell

TEAM COORDINATOR
Amy Patton

INTERIOR DESIGN
Gary Adair

COVER DESIGN
Aren Howell

PRODUCTION
Ayanna Lacey

Contents at a Glance

Contents

About the Authors

Andrew Watt is an independent consultant and author with expertise in XML and Web technologies including SVG. He is author of *Designing SVG Web Graphics* (New Riders) and *XPath Essentials* (Wiley). He is co-author of *XML Schema Essentials* (Wiley) and contributing author to *XHTML, XML & Java 2 Platinum Edition* (Que), *Professional XSL, Professional XML 2nd Edition,* and *Professional XML Meta Data* (Wrox).

Jonathan Watt has been working with JavaScript for two years and has been Webmaster of the Strathclyde University Skills Society Web site, as well as a number of his own Web sites such as dsvg.com. His primary expertise is in the application of JavaScript in the client-side environment, but he also has used ASP and PHP to create database-driven Web sites. He is currently in the third year of a master's degree in engineering at Strathclyde.

Jinjer Simon has been actively involved in the computer industry for the past 17 years. Her involvement in the industry has included programming, providing software technical support, end-user training, developing written and online user documentation, creating software tutorials, developing Internet Web sites, and writing technical books. Jinjer and her husband currently live in Coppell, Texas, with their two children where she currently works as a consultant for MillenniSoft Inc. by providing Web site development and online documentation development.

Jim O'Donnell was born on October 17, 1963, in Pittsburgh, Pennsylvania (you may forward birthday greetings to `jim@odonnell.org`). After a number of unproductive years, he went to Rensselaer Polytechnic Institute for 11 years earning three degrees. He now lives in Washington, DC, and spends most of his time building spacecraft. He has been writing and editing books for eight years. When he isn't working, he collects comic books and PEZ dispensers and plays ice hockey for the DC Nationals. Go, Nats!

Dedication

I would like to dedicate my contribution to this book to the memory of my late father George Alec Watt—a very special human being.
—**Andrew Watt**

To my immediate and extended family, all of whom I love very much.
—**Jonathan Watt**

To Ryan Miller. Italy in 2006!
—**Jim O'Donnell**

Acknowledgments

Andrew Watt and Jonathan Watt

We would first like to thank Shelley Johnston, who assisted in getting this project off the ground. We also would like to sincerely thank Betsy Brown whose ingenuity, practical suggestions, and almost limitless patience steered this project to a successful conclusion.

We would also like to thank Jim O'Donnell, whose knowledge of JavaScript ideally fitted him to be technical editor for the book and who helped pick up those small errors that are so easy to overlook as an author.

Jon Steever did his usual thorough and perceptive editing job on the submitted manuscript. Thanks, Jon.

Finally, thanks to our fellow authors Jinjer Simon and Jim O'Donnell, without whose efforts the book would not have been completed.

Jinjer Simon

I would like to thank Betsy Brown for giving me the opportunity to work on this book. I would also like to thank Karen Whitehouse, Tony Reitz, and Jon Steever—the editors at Sams who pulled everything together on the book. I would also like to thank the Technical Editor on this book, Jim O'Donnell. He did a great job of identifying changes that needed to be made to enhance the content of the book. Finally I would like to thank my husband and two children for their patience while I worked to meet the deadlines on this book.

Jim O'Donnell

I would like to acknowledge Betsy Brown, Jon Steever, and all of the other fine editors I've worked with over the years.

Tell Us What You Think!

As the reader of this book, *you* are our most important critic and commentator. We value your opinion and want to know what we're doing right, what we could do better, what areas you'd like to see us publish in, and any other words of wisdom you're willing to pass our way.

You can e-mail or write me directly to let me know what you did or didn't like about this book—as well as what we can do to make our books stronger.

Please note that I cannot help you with technical problems related to the topic of this book, and that due to the high volume of mail I receive, I might not be able to reply to every message.

When you write, please be sure to include this book's title and author as well as your name and phone or e-mail address. I will carefully review your comments and share them with the author and editors who worked on the book.

E-mail: webdev@samspublishing.com

Mail: Mark Taber
Associate Publisher
Sams Publishing
201 West 103rd Street
Indianapolis, IN 46290 USA

Introduction

JavaScript has become the most important client-side scripting language on the Web. It provides the Web developer with the functionality to create rollover effects, move objects around the browser screen, check the validity of data entered into HTML and XHTML forms, and much, much more. *Sams Teach Yourself JavaScript in 21 Days* will give you an understanding of JavaScript that will help you carry out the day-to-day tasks that you will use JavaScript to accomplish. As you master more and more of the important aspects of JavaScript, you will be able to add functionality to your existing Web pages, improving their impact on the experience of your Web site visitors.

JavaScript has come a long way since it was first introduced in version 2 of the Netscape browser. While JavaScript, currently at version 1.5, is still produced by Netscape, there is an internationally recognized, standardized scripting language, ECMAScript, which is made available to developers on a more open basis. Both Netscape's JavaScript and Microsoft's JScript are based on ECMAScript, although both extend its functionality.

In the late 1990s, incompatibilities among JavaScript versions were a major problem for Web developers. Many of those problems are disappearing as users upgrade to more modern versions of browsers, which have been introduced since the ECMAScript standardization process started. With the advent of Netscape version 6, the Netscape browser is making fuller use of standards such as the Document Object Model and Cascading Style Sheets. Unfortunately the first release, Netscape 6.0, had a number of problems that are being progressively ironed out as the Netscape browser transitions through versions 6.1 and later. As users discontinue use of browsers such as Netscape 3 and Internet Explorer 3, the need to support outdated implementations of client-side scripting becomes less. This makes writing cross-browser JavaScript code a much less frustrating and demanding task than it was only a few years ago. Both Microsoft and Netscape genuinely seem to attach importance to standards as they relate to JavaScript. Hopefully many of the remaining problems will be ironed out in the near future.

The future for JavaScript is an exciting one.

How This Book Is Organized

Sams Teach Yourself JavaScript in 21 Days is organized into 21 chapters, and they are written in such a way that you can work through one chapter a day and complete the book in three weeks, if you have the time available to do so. The book has been written so that you can work through chapters in the order in which they are presented. If you decide to dip into a particular chapter that interests you, then you may need to refer back to earlier chapters to fully understand the code and how you can further develop it for your own use.

Week 1

Day 1, "Getting the Basics Right," introduces you to JavaScript and helps you to understand what kind of language JavaScript is. The tools you need to create and view JavaScript are discussed, and how to correctly create a JavaScript script within an HTML/XHTML file is covered.

Day 2, "Working with Data," introduces you to how JavaScript handles data. Day 2 also shows you how to store data in variables, and then how to change the value of that data, as well as how to create constants that can be used unchanged throughout a script are discussed.

In Day 3, "Functions and Statements," you are shown how to create code, stored in functions, which you can re-use as often as needed in your scripts. You also are shown how to create code that executes depending on conditions you define, and how to create code that loops through a process as often as you specify.

Day 4, "JavaScript Is Object-Based," introduces you to the important topic of JavaScript objects by discussing what an object is, and how you can use objects to write efficient scripts.

Day 5, "An Introduction to Arrays," teaches you what an array is, and how to create and use them.

Collecting information from users is a hugely important part of the interactive Web. Day 6, "HTML Forms and the `String` Object," introduces you to using JavaScript with HTML/XHTML forms to collect data from visitors to the Web sites you have created. Strings of characters are commonly collected when using forms, and Day 6 will show you how strings are handled in JavaScript.

Day 7, "Numbers and Math," introduces the JavaScript `Number` and `Math` objects and teaches you how numbers are handled in JavaScript as well as how to use the built-in mathematical functions which the JavaScript interpreter makes available to a scripter.

Week 2

Day 8, "The Browser Issue," tells you about the differences in the variety of browser versions and how they handle JavaScript. It also shows you how to produce JavaScript code that will run on commonly used modern browsers.

Day 9, "Date and Time Manipulation," introduces you to the JavaScript `Date` object and shows you how to create code that will handle dates and times.

Day 10, "Events and Events Handling," presents the important topic of events. You are shown what an event is and how to create your code to run in response to appropriate events, which take place within a Web browser.

Day 11, "Dynamic HTML," introduces Dynamic HTML, often referred to as DHTML. DHTML makes use of Cascading Style Sheets and layers, which allow interactive and dynamic Web pages to be created, taking Web pages to a new level.

Day 12, "Windows and Frames," tells you how JavaScript can be used in association with Web pages which use multiple frames, and how JavaScript can be used to create new windows.

Day 13, "Regular Expressions Make It Easier," introduces the JavaScript regular expressions that give the scripter enormous control over the patterns of string characters a user is allowed to enter into an HTML/XHTML form, for example.

Day 14, "Advanced Array Management," takes you deeper into the use of the JavaScript Array object, building on the knowledge you gained in Day 5.

Week 3

Day 15, "Debugging and Error Handling," shows you how to diagnose and correct errors that you may create as you build longer and more complex JavaScript scripts.

Day 16, "Cookies: Storing Persistent Data," introduces cookies, files JavaScript creates and stores on a user's machine that can be used from one browser session to another.

Day 17, "Privacy and Security," introduces you to the important topic of security in JavaScript, and then discusses how Web developers and users are affected by JavaScript's security model.

Day 18, "Plugins and Applets," demonstrates how JavaScript can be used with browser plugins and Java applets.

Day 19, "Creating Your Own Objects," shows you how to create custom objects that can be used with the built-in objects that JavaScript provides.

Day 20, "JavaScript in E-Commerce," discusses the use of JavaScript in e-commerce and shows you how to use JavaScript in the creation of an online shopping basket.

Day 21, "JavaScript and SVG," takes you beyond the world of HTML/XHTML to show you a little of how JavaScript will be used with the exciting new Web graphics format SVG—Scalable Vector Graphics.

Who Should Read This Book

This book is designed to meet the needs of Web developers who want to add intelligence and interactivity to their Web pages using JavaScript.

What This Book Assumes

We assume that you are comfortable using the World Wide Web, and that you are familiar with creating HTML and/or XHTML pages—so, there will not be an explanation of the basics of HTML and XHTML as JavaScript is applied to the fairly straightforward Web pages shown as examples in the book. If you are not confident that you are fully comfortable creating HTML/XHTML, perhaps you might want to have an introductory HTML or XHTML book at hand as you work through this book. *Sams Teach Yourself HTML and XHTML in 24 Hours* by Michael Morrison is a book you might consider as a reference to keep at hand.

We also assume that you are either new to JavaScript or have very limited experience trying it out. As you are introduced to the individual parts of JavaScript, we won't assume that you already know that material, but we will assume that you are a fairly quick learner and that you have seen many of JavaScript's effects and know its capabilities.

Conventions Used in This Book

This book uses the following conventions:

Text that you type or see on screen appears in `monospace`.

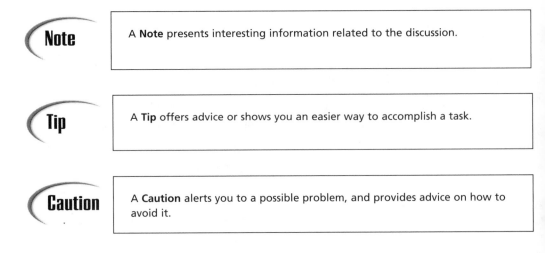

Note   A **Note** presents interesting information related to the discussion.

Tip   A **Tip** offers advice or shows you an easier way to accomplish a task.

Caution   A **Caution** alerts you to a possible problem, and provides advice on how to avoid it.

What's on the Web Site?

On the Web site, you will find the code for all the full code listings that we will create in the book. These will be useful to you if you receive error messages that you can't solve when you run code that you have typed in.

Great care has been taken to eliminate errors in the book but any reported errors will be listed on the Web site too.

To get to the Web site, point your Web browser to `http://www.samspublishing.com/`. In the Search box, type in `javascript in 21`. Find this book from the list presented, and click on the link. On the book's main page, find and click the link called `Related Materials` to get to the files.

WEEK 1

A Sound Foundation

WEEK 1

DAY 1

Getting the Basics Right

JavaScript is a scripting language that allows you to add interactivity to HTML or XHTML Web pages. XHTML, the Extensible HyperText Markup Language, is HTML 4 rewritten in XML syntax. JavaScript is the scripting language of choice when it comes to adding interactivity and functionality to your Web pages that HTML or XHTML alone cannot provide.

This book will introduce you to many of the most useful characteristics and features of JavaScript. At times, some of the topics may seem a bit abstract when they are introduced. For now, know that JavaScript works most powerfully when you use several of its aspects together. So initially you may need to learn some features of JavaScript through step-by-step examples in order to understand the explanation. As you get further into the book, you will gain the confidence in your own ability to combine these techniques, and begin to create JavaScript scripts that work and, with practice, perform exactly as you want on a Web page. If you work through the examples you will, by the time you finish this book, be a competent author of JavaScript scripts, applying its power to bring your site to life.

In this introductory chapter, we will introduce you to both the applications and the basic structure of the JavaScript language. This will provide you with a solid foundation on which to build your knowledge of JavaScript throughout the rest of the book.

Today you will learn

- What JavaScript is
- The foundations of JavaScript syntax including datatypes and a number of JavaScript functions

Introducing JavaScript

The primary questions you need to ask yourself when you start to learn something new is "what is it?" and "what does it do?" So let's begin there.

What Is JavaScript?

To state some commonly heard jargon, JavaScript is a cross-platform, object-based scripting language that most commonly is used on the Web. If you are new to programming, that definition may not mean too much to you. So let's look at each of its features.

Cross-Platform

In computer terminology, the term platform is used as shorthand for operating system platform. Examples of operating systems that commonly run on desktop computers today include Windows (various flavors), Linux, and the MacOS. What we mean when we say that JavaScript is cross-platform is that it will (for the most part) run happily and produce the same results on a wide variety of different computer operating systems.

The cross-platform nature of JavaScript is a very important aspect of the language. People use all sorts of different operating systems on the computers they use to connect to the Internet. Without JavaScript's ability to behave consistently across platforms, it would be much more difficult for you to write scripts that would allow Internet users who use a variety of platforms to benefit from the JavaScript-based enhancements you might want to add to your Web pages.

One of the central aims of JavaScript's inventors was to create a cross-platform scripting language, which has been a key factor in its success. Without it, JavaScript wouldn't have been nearly so appealing to Web designers—most of whom want to reach the widest audience possible.

Object-Based

Up until now, the language you most likely would have used was HTML—which means you already know it is a markup language. Markup languages use tags to surround pieces of text. The tags tell the browser how that text should be treated.

JavaScript is quite different. It requires that a data structure such as the structured information on a Web page already exist. It then treats the data on a page as a series of hierarchically structured objects that it can use. If the phrase "hierarchically structured objects" doesn't mean too much to you, don't worry, we will come back to that topic. In fact, we will be dedicating the whole of Chapter 4, "JavaScript Is Object-Based," to investigating JavaScript's object-based nature, as well as describing and using objects in many of the later chapters. For the moment, it is enough that you appreciate that objects allow you to more easily organize and manipulate Web pages.

Scripting Language

JavaScript is also a scripting language. It is important to note that there are significant differences between scripting languages and standalone programming languages (for example, C++ or Visual Basic). Among the differences between scripting languages such as JavaScript and the many other computer languages are that scripting languages are interpreted and they usually require significantly less code.

If a language is an interpreted language it simply means that the code you write does not need to be compiled into binary computer code before it can be used. Instead scripting languages are turned into instructions that a computer understands by parsing them with an interpreter each time the code is run.

Another important difference is that a scripting language runs within another program or application, such as a Web browser. A typical client-side JavaScript script is contained within an HTML/XHTML Web page. Languages such as C++ and Java can be run independently, although Java also allows programs (called applets) to run within Web pages too.

The JavaScript interpreter is the software that is built into the browser, which then takes your JavaScript code and follows the instructions within the code step by step.

All major browsers that are version 3.0 and higher, support JavaScript.

Note JavaScript can be run on the client side—within a Web browser—or it can be run on a Web server or Web-application server. In this book we will be covering client-side JavaScript only.

An important practical difference you will notice when using a scripting language is that when you write a JavaScript script you tend to write a lot less code than for a standalone program. This is because the Web browser provides a lot of useful functionality that supports JavaScript.

Scripts are easier to write but run more slowly than code which is compiled. The advantage of the scripting code is that it is often easier to write and demands less complex and expensive tools than some compiled languages.

What Does JavaScript Do?

JavaScript "does" a number of things. Its main use, however, is for the enhancement of Web pages. It enables you to program a Web page so that it has motion or other interactivity which HTML alone cannot provide. JavaScript also can provide error checking of information collected from forms on your Web page.

JavaScript in Context

Before we begin our study of the JavaScript language for real, let's take a brief look at the need for JavaScript and how it fits in with other popular Web technologies.

A Requirement for More Than Just HTML

Over the past decade a typical computer user has experienced a vast increase in the quality and functionality of the programs they use. Advances in software and hardware have contributed to improvements in both functionality and appearance. Computer users have grown accustomed to colorful, dynamic, and engaging programs. And they are now far less willing to settle for information presented in a bland and non-interactive format. Adding JavaScript to the Web browser makes Web pages more immediately interactive than was possible using interactivity that depended on server-side processing.

Things are no different on the Web. Although originally intended as a way to make static text without any graphics accessible over a network, the Web has changed considerably over the years since its conception. Advances in HTML and the addition of CSS (Cascading Style Sheets) have come a long way in enabling the addition of color and images to Web pages to make them more visually pleasing. However, by itself HTML is still very much a static presentation format. The most it can offer in terms of user interaction is the use of hyperlinks or perhaps some form elements for a user to fill out. Even then, HTML can't perform these useful tasks (such as checking the validity of information entered into a form) without the aid of another technology.

1

Competition among a growing number of Web sites puts increasing pressure on Web developers to find ways of attracting people to their sites, and keeping them coming back for further visits. This has led to the development of a wide variety of new and sometimes exciting technologies being developed to augment the simple but useful functionality provided by HTML. Some of these new technologies are intended to enhance the user experience with dynamic and interactive pages, and others are aimed at enabling the development of useful business functionality and other services.

The JavaScript language is one of the key Web-enhancing technologies available. Its difference is underscored by its ability to bring otherwise static HTML pages to life.

Server-Side or Client-Side?

Broadly speaking, Web-enhancing technologies can be split into two camps: server-side technologies and client-side technologies. Server-side and client-side simply describe where a technology runs—that is, which computer is used to do the processing.

Confused? Okay, in a computer network, whether it is the Internet or a company intranet, there are two types of computers: clients and servers. A server's job is to store documents (in our case Web documents) and send them to any other computers that ask for them. A computer that makes a request to a server (asks for a file which is held on the server) is called a client. Therefore if a technology is a "server-side" technology, it simply means that it uses the server to run and process data. Similarly, if a technology is a "client-side" technology, then it processes data on the client machine, most often within or in association with Web-browser software. This is an important distinction to make as it can make a big difference to the way things work.

Server-Side

Technologies such as CGI (Common Gateway Interface), ASP (Active Server Pages), and JSP (JavaServer Pages) are examples of server-side technologies with which you might be familiar. When you use a Web site you may see fairly frequently within a URL (Uniform Resource Locator) the letters "cgi" or the filename endings ".asp" or ".jsp". Quite likely you regularly make use of their functionality for a variety of different purposes. For example, every time you submit a search to a search engine you're making use of server-side processes. In the case of search engines, an HMTL form is used to collect your search criteria, which are then sent to the server for processing. After the programs or scripts on the server have finished doing their job, the results are turned into HTML and returned by the Web server to your browser.

The problem with server-side processing is the time it takes for the desired results to appear. The reasons for this are twofold. First there is the submit-and-wait aspect of the Internet. It takes time for data to reach the server and be processed, and for the results to be passed back. This can be especially frustrating for the many users who are connected to the Internet by means of a dial-up connection.

A second reason for possible delays is the fact that server-side technologies load the server with the job of processing. This isn't too much of a problem if the server is required to handle only a limited number of requests at a time. However, all computers have limited processing power. On busy servers handling perhaps many thousands of requests an hour and coping with dozens if not hundreds of requests at once, everything can very noticeably slow down, and in some cases can stop altogether. If you have used the Web frequently, you will almost certainly have seen those error messages in the browser which indicate that a Web site isn't responding at that time and suggesting you try again later. Very likely at the time you made your request the capacity of the server was stretched and it simply couldn't accept a further request for information.

The wait for pages to load due to network transit time and server processing time inherent in server-side technologies is undesirable. It also makes running the scripts on the server side for some applications (such as DHTML, Dynamic HTML) simply unfeasible, since the whole process would become too slow and unresponsive to allow real-time interaction between the user and the Web page. Dynamic HTML, by the way, is a term used to describe various combinations of HTML, JavaScript, and CSS which allow additional interactivity or animation within Web pages.

You should carefully weigh the pros and cons of using the server to do the processing. The original objective of improving interactivity and providing new applications should not be negated by excessive waiting times.

Client-Side

When using server-side technologies the client computer—and often the human user—sits idle waiting for pages to arrive, while at the other end the server may be struggling to keep up with its workload. An obvious solution to this problem is to carry out at least some of the processing on the client computer.

The first benefit of moving some of the load to the client-side is that it reduces the number of times the user has to load a page and thereby incur the inevitable time penalty of data traveling the Internet. When, for example, the validation of data entered on a form on an HTML Web page is conducted client-side using JavaScript, network delays are avoided altogether, at least until the point where the data has been validated and is ready to be sent to the server for definitive processing.

1

An important advantage of client-side scripting is that it enables the Web page itself to be programmed. In effect, this enables dynamic Web pages which can respond to user actions as they view and interact with the page.

In addition to the direct benefit of removing a load from the server, whenever a new page must be requested the server can respond to requests a lot faster because it isn't bearing the load of processing multiple scripts. Consequently, requests aren't queued at all or for such a long time. By reducing the time spent waiting for pages to download from the server, this approach can greatly enhance a user's browsing experience.

Reality

Of course, in reality, a client computer cannot do everything. All sorts of Web-based services require that data be sent to the server to be stored or processed. For example placing an order on an e-commerce site simply wouldn't be possible if the order never left your computer. At the same time, there's no point using up server resources (its processing power) and incurring the inevitable time lag of sending data to the server when a task can be done perfectly adequately, or maybe even better on the client-side.

In practice both client- and server-side technologies are used. Both are important for the diverse functioning of modern Web pages.

When a task requires that information be sent to the server, for example for permanent storage, then it should be sent. Though, if possible, the load of processing data and ensuring its validity should be carried out on the client-side using scripts. By spreading the load between client and server computers, it is more likely that the best results can be obtained.

Selecting the Right Technology

There are other client-side technologies, for example Flash, which are used mainly to enhance the look and feel of the user experience. Typically there is no built-in support in mainstream browsers simply because it is practical to support only a limited number of data formats so a Flash plug-in has to be used. The major browsers have a JavaScript interpreter built in, but to add a whole range of additional functionality would make the browser even larger (and they are already pretty bloated).

To solve this problem, software plug-ins were developed and they first appeared in Netscape Navigator 2. By allowing users to choose which plug-ins they needed for the data they wanted to access, part of the bloated-browser problem could be removed. Plug-ins also allow the data to be blended into the document seamlessly rather than the browser opening up an application to display it. Animation also can be integrated into part of a page; and audio or video can be downloaded and played or streamed for live content.

The downside of Web technologies that use plug-ins is that not everyone who views your Web page will have the necessary plug-in installed. For Flash this isn't too great a problem now since the plug-in is widely distributed. For the newer Scalable Vector Graphics format (which we will look at in Chapter 21, "JavaScript and SVG"), fewer users will have an SVG plug-in and therefore care has to be taken to provide an alternate viewing experience for users who can't yet view SVG. A link to a download can be provided, but some users may prefer, for whatever reason, not to bother. JavaScript support on the other hand has been provided in all the major browsers for a number of years now.

JavaScripts can be very compact although you can make them as long and complex as you choose. However, keep in mind that the large file size often associated with Flash data is off-putting to many users, especially if they use a dial-up Internet connection. So, strive to keep your JavaScript as succinct as possible.

There are occasions when a developer will require more power on the client-side than HTML and the other "popular" Web technologies can provide. Java in the form of Java applets was designed to address this problem. Applets are small Java applications (hence the name) written specifically for use within the context of a Web browser. Java is a full programming language that can run cross-platform and which can, for example, delete or overwrite files, therefore Java applets are designed to be limited (so as not to be used to create a security risk). Java is often a logical choice in environments (such as in some intranets) where you can be sure all visitors will have Java capabilities in their browsers. However, it can be problematic using Java applets on the Internet since not everyone chooses to allow Java applets to function in their browser.

Java applets can be integrated seamlessly into a Web page. For example Java applets are commonly used as Web-based chat clients because Java can maintain a connection to a server listening for any new messages, unlike most scripting technologies. Java's streaming ability also makes it popular with sites providing instant updates on news and stock prices.

The downside of Java applets is similar to that for plug-ins in that they can take longer to download than some users are willing to wait. Not all browsers are able to handle Java, and some users also decide to turn it off. Java also has the problem of complexity, at least for those unfamiliar with using a full programming language. It is a full programming language in its own right. This prevents it from being a viable option for many casual or part-time developers. A language with Java's power but a simpler syntax, and that made fewer demands on programmers, could offer many advantages.

1

In 1995, Brendan Eich, inspired by Apple's HyperCard, was developing just such a language. Netscape originally released the language under the name LiveScript, which was intended to run on both the client and server-sides. At the time, Netscape's browser had the major share of the browser market and so LiveScript—with its ability to move some of the work previously done by the server to the client—caught on very quickly.

By the time Navigator 2 was released in early 1996, LiveScript had been renamed JavaScript. Unfortunately this association with Java has caused, and still causes, a lot of confusion to those who are new to the Web development community. JavaScript is not Java! JavaScript is not a cut-down version of Java. Despite syntactic and structural similarities there are also some significant differences between the two.

Java was developed as a full programming language capable of creating its own GUI (Graphical User Interface). JavaScript on the other hand was designed simply to work within a Web browser with HTML elements already in existence.

In JavaScript there is a lot to learn about, but it is still simpler to learn than a full programming language, and it can be used productively almost from the word go. It also can be just about as complex or as simple as you want it to be. For some applications, you may only want to use it to place the cursor in the first element of a form so the user can start typing when the page loads. For another, you might use it to create a complex and dynamic image-based navigation menu. As you acquire JavaScript skills working through this book, you will be able to make your own choices about how you want to use JavaScript.

As we said earlier, JavaScript can be used server-side and for a number of other applications. However, its most common use is on the client-side in HMTL pages where it is downloaded and run on the client (on the computer of the person viewing the Web page). It is here where it has the ability to turn static HMTL and images into a lively interactive user experience that has made it the widely used phenomenon it is today.

JavaScript allows you to move objects around on a Web page and respond to various user actions.

JavaScript isn't the solution to every Web project. It is, however, the natural choice for checking forms, detecting user input (even down to detecting the position of the mouse on the screen), manipulating the Web page, and processing data that doesn't need to be sent to the server.

JavaScript doesn't have any inherent graphics capabilities, but it is increasingly being used to script vector graphic formats such as Flash and Scalable Vector Graphics (SVG). You will be introduced to the use of JavaScript with SVG in Chapter 21, "JavaScript and SVG."

JavaScript, Jscript, and ECMAScript

JavaScript has several "flavors" so when you begin learning JavaScript certain terms may confuse you. More experienced developers often will refer to JavaScript, Jscript, and ECMAScript. So what exactly are these scripting languages? And what are the differences?

JavaScript

JavaScript, as mentioned earlier, was the term Netscape, who invented JavaScript, chose to use for what was originally a proprietary scripting language. In fact, Netscape owned the name JavaScript. Version 1.0 of JavaScript originated in the Netscape browser version 2.0. In Netscape 3, JavaScript version 1.1 followed.

JScript

It wasn't long before Microsoft acknowledged the potential of JavaScript and integrated its implementation into Microsoft Internet Explorer 3. Microsoft then created JScript, since using the term JavaScript would have acknowledged Netscape's ownership of the technology. Although it uses its own interpreter and varies from JavaScript, in some ways JScript has many similarities to JavaScript. From the developer's perspective, once you have learned one, you know most of the other. Although Microsoft might at one time have preferred that VBScript be used in preference to JavaScript, JavaScript has remained the client-side scripter's language of choice—partly because the Netscape browser was more popular initially, but even more so because JavaScript is available on a larger range of browsers than JScript. VBScript is now uncommonly found in mainstream Web pages because only Microsoft browsers support it. Strangely enough as JavaScript's popularity with the server-side scripter waned, VBScript became ever more popular in the server-side scripting technology ASP.

On the client side, however, there were sufficient differences between JavaScript and JScript so that writing cross-platform scripts was far from easy. The JavaScript standard was passed to the European Computer Manufacturers Association, ECMA, in order to create a "standard" version of what had been JavaScript. Enter ECMAScript.

ECMAScript

With the advent of version 4 of Netscape Navigator and Internet Explorer both browsers attempted to implement a standards-based version of JavaScript, ECMAScript. Arguably Internet Explorer did a better job of implementation than Netscape, and this may have been one minor factor in Internet Explorer's expansion to become the dominant force in the Web browser market.

ECMA (European Computer Manufacturers Association) is an international industry association. It has developed a number of standards for the computer industry, most of which can be downloaded free from their Web site at http://www.ecma.ch. ECMAScript is the name that has been adopted for the ECMA-262 standard that came about after Netscape proposed JavaScript 1.1 as a standard. ECMAScript is the *de facto* international standard for JavaScript. At the time of writing, it was in its third iteration, which is roughly equivalent to JavaScript 1.5 and JScript 5.5.

It is important to realize that ECMAScript is a standard for the core JavaScript language. By "core" we mean the language features that exist independent of which environment JavaScript is being used in (Web browser, PDF, and so on). This includes features such as those used for doing math or handling dates. These parts of the language do not interact with or depend on the presence of a browser.

The parts that enable JavaScript to communicate with and manipulate its host environment are covered by a different standard known as the World Wide Web Consortium Document Object Model (or W3C DOM for short). This standard is important to HTML so you already may have come across it. As well as describing how HTML should be written, it specifies how JavaScript can access and manipulate parts of HTML documents. We will be looking at that aspect of the language later in the book.

In practice, ECMAScript is not a language for JavaScript scripters to learn from. It is intended for browser developers so that their implementation of JavaScript will have the same functionality as other browser developers.

ECMAScript has done a good job of bringing more uniformity to the JavaScript language. JavaScript will always include features that are not part of the ECMAScript specification, partly in order to provide backwards compatibility for older versions of browsers. JavaScript is compatible with ECMAScript, while providing additional features.

We have spent quite a bit of time describing JavaScript's background; now let's begin to look at how to use the language itself.

Let's Get Started

To become a JavaScript author you are going to need two tools: a text editor and a browser.

Choosing a Text Editor and Web Browser

You may well be used to using a WYSIWYG (What You See Is What You Get) editor such as Adobe GoLive, Microsoft FrontPage, or NetObjects Fusion for creating your

Web pages. However, when it comes to scripting you will have to get used to typing code out by hand, although HTML editors such as Adobe GoLive and Macromedia DreamWeaver provide some pre-packaged JavaScripts, which you can use without necessarily understanding the code that such programs produce. Typically WYSIWYG editors will produce some nice effects but if you don't understand the JavaScript that underlies those effects, you won't be able to modify the effects to produce exactly the effect you want.

The examples throughout this book have been included on the CD-ROM for your convenience. You will remember a lot more if you type out the scripts yourself, so we would encourage you to do so. Even the times when you make mistakes in typing will help you really grasp the details you need to master to become an efficient scripter.

Whatever you decide, you will still need a means of writing scripts when it's time to write your own. To do this you will need a text editor.

When you save text in a word processor it is saved in files that include many formatting codes, which browsers aren't designed to handle. It is possible to use a word processor but you must remember to save a file as plain (ASCII) text, and often it's really more trouble than it's worth. A text editor on the other hand saves files in ASCII format without adding proprietary codes that browsers cannot read. It is also relatively simple to get text editors to save files with an `.htm` or `.html` extension.

Note

> In this book we will consistently use the `.htm` file extension. A browser on a 32-bit Windows platform will treat a file with `.htm` the same as a file with `.html`. Some platforms only allow three-letter file extensions. If you are using such a platform, then you will be able to use only the `.htm` file extension.

For the Windows user, you likely have a version of Notepad already installed. Look for Notepad in the Start menu, under Programs, Accessories. Notepad will be adequate for creating many JavaScript scripts, but once your files start to get large you may want to use WordPad or download a version of a more fully featured shareware editor such as TextPad. For MacOS users, SimpleText will be adequate to begin with, but an editor with more features, such as BBEdit, will be useful as you advance to creating longer and more complex scripts.

Most of the screen shots in this book have been taken using Notepad and Netscape 6 on the Windows platform. You may be working on a different operating system such as the MacOS or one of the flavors of Unix so the output to your screen may look slightly different. If it does look a little different, don't worry too much about it. Different browsers on different platforms do display things slightly differently but the underlying data is the same.

Once you have created your scripts you will, of course, need to view them to make sure that they work, and also that they work as you intended them to work. If you are interested in learning JavaScript, you are more than likely already familiar with using a Web browser such as Microsoft Internet Explorer or Netscape Navigator. As long as your browser is able to understand JavaScript and has JavaScript turned on, then, for the moment, it doesn't matter which browser you choose. Either Netscape 6 or any recent version of Internet Explorer will enable you to view the results of your scripts.

When learning JavaScript it is useful to have access to several Web browsers so you can test your code on all of them. It is often useful to know the differences in the visual appearance of a Web page and the behavior of its interactive parts when viewed in different browsers. Being aware of those differences will give you an insight into what some of your users are seeing when they visit your Web pages.

Here is a list of some of the more important Web browsers currently available, together with a URL where you can download them from if you don't already have them on your machine.

- Internet Explorer is currently at version 6.0 and can be downloaded from `http://www.microsoft.com/windows/ie/`. If you have an earlier version of Internet Explorer and want to update, then open Internet Explorer, go to the Tools menu, and choose Windows Update to begin upgrading your version of Internet Explorer. If you have never done this before, it can be a slow process as you will be required to download various "critical" updates, quite possibly before you can download the new version of Internet Explorer.

- Netscape Navigator 4.7 can be downloaded from `http://home.netscape.com/browsers/`. A variety of Netscape browser versions can be accessed from that page.

- Netscape Navigator 6.2 can be found at `http://home.netscape.com/browsers/`.

- The Mozilla browser can be downloaded from `http://mozilla.org/releases/`.

- Opera 6 can be downloaded from `http://www.opera.com/download/`.

Note

You do not need an Internet connection to use a browser. Web pages stored on your computer can be loaded for viewing locally.

Basic Things to Remember

In this section we will cover some basic rules which you will need to keep in mind when you write any JavaScript. In time they will become second nature, but at first you may need to consciously think of them as you are writing your scripts.

Case Sensitivity

JavaScript is case sensitive. So you have to be very careful to be consistent when using upper and lower case for any name of a JavaScript variable or constant which you create. It is a very common error among those just starting out to find that they have given a variable or function a name and then later write it out again using one or more characters with a different case. In a short script that can be easy to spot but in long scripts it can be very difficult to pin down from where the error is coming. Therefore if you give something the name "myElement" you must always refer to it with exactly the same case—not using the same case can produce either an error or cause unexpected effects.

Semicolons

It is good practice to routinely use a semicolon at the end of each JavaScript statement. However, JavaScript doesn't actually require that lines be finished with a semicolon. When you do need a semicolon is when two or more JavaScript statements need to be written on the same line. This is often used when you are creating a looping construct in JavaScript using a FOR loop, which will be described in a later chapter.

Line Breaks

Line breaks can be used to help make your code more readable. The longer your scripts become the more important readability of code becomes.

Whitespace

Whitespace characters (tabs, spaces, and new lines) are given their name due to the fact that they aren't seen except in the way they create space within your code. Apart from the spaces necessary to separate certain elements of JavaScript code, the JavaScript interpreter will ignore extraneous whitespace. Therefore

```
x = y + z
```

can also be written as

```
x   =   y   +   z
```

Although writing code like this is acceptable to the JavaScript interpreter, it makes it more awkward for most people to read and understand the code. The idea behind JavaScript ignoring extraneous whitespace is to allow us to write out code in a way that

1

makes it easy to see the major parts of its structure. By using whitespace to structure our code, we can make it far more readable. For example if we have some code written between a pair of curly brackets:

```
{code
code
code}
```

we are able to use whitespace to make this easier to read:

```
{
    code
    code
    code
}
```

The fact that the opening and closing curly braces are written on their own line and at the beginning of a line makes it easy to see where such a block of code starts and ends. This helps our eyes recognize what belongs to what as we scan through a large piece of JavaScript code.

Where Does JavaScript Go?

JavaScript, like HTML, is simply text that can be typed directly into a text editor such as Notepad. However, for the JavaScript interpreter to recognize and correctly process your code, you must place your JavaScript code in a place where the JavaScript interpreter in the Web browser is expecting to find it.

There are three places where you can put JavaScript code when you are using JavaScript in your HTML pages. Each of these will be explained in more detail below:

- In a script block typed into the HMTL
- In its own JavaScript file
- Inside the opening tag of many HMTL elements

Script Blocks

Typing your JavaScript into the HTML of your Web page using a script block is the simplest way to insert JavaScript. But what is a script block?

A script block simply put is a piece of JavaScript code surrounded by a pair of HTML `<script>` tags—an opening `<script>` tag before the JavaScript and a closing `</script>` tag after the end of the JavaScript. The `<script>` tag can be used in HTML to mark up an area of JavaScript just as the `<p>` tag can be used to mark up a paragraph or the `<form>` tag can be used to mark up a form. Listing 1.1 shows an example of how it could be used.

LISTING 1.1   A Skeleton for JavaScript Code (`skeleton.htm`)

```
<html>
<head>
<title>Title of Document</title>

<script>

// ALL YOUR JAVASCRIPT CODE
// GOES IN HERE BETWEEN THE
// OPENING AND CLOSING
// SCRIPT TAGS.

</script>

</head>
<body>

The content of
your page here.

</body>
</html>
```

You can place script blocks almost anywhere between the opening and closing HTML tags of your Web page. However, unless it is necessary to place it at a particular place in the body of the HTML page, it is best to put the script block between the opening and closing <head> tags and after the title and any meta tags you may be using. This ensures that your scripts are fully downloaded into the browser before the page is displayed. By doing so, you avoid all sorts of errors that can occur when user actions call scripts that haven't loaded yet.

Lets take a look at the effect different placement of your script can have on the way your page runs. Type the following code from Listing 1.2 into the text editor you have chosen to use.

LISTING 1.2   Creating an Alert Box Using JavaScript (`firstAlert.htm`)

```
<html>
<head>

<script>

alert("Do you see the page heading?");
```

LISTING 1.2   continued

```
</script>

</head>
<body>

<h1>Page heading</h1>

</body>
</html>
```

This should produce an appearance on screen like that in Figure 1.1.

OUTPUT

FIGURE 1.1

A JavaScript alert displayed by a script block in the head of the page.

Now try shifting the script block to a point after the page heading, as in Listing 1.3.

INPUT

LISTING 1.3   An Alert Box Created by JavaScript Within the HTML Body (secondAlert.htm)

```
<html>
<head>

</head>
<body>

<h1>Page heading</h1>

<script>

alert("Do you see the page heading?");
```

LISTING 1.3   continued

```
</script>

</body>
</html>
```

Now you should see something like Figure 1.2:

OUTPUT

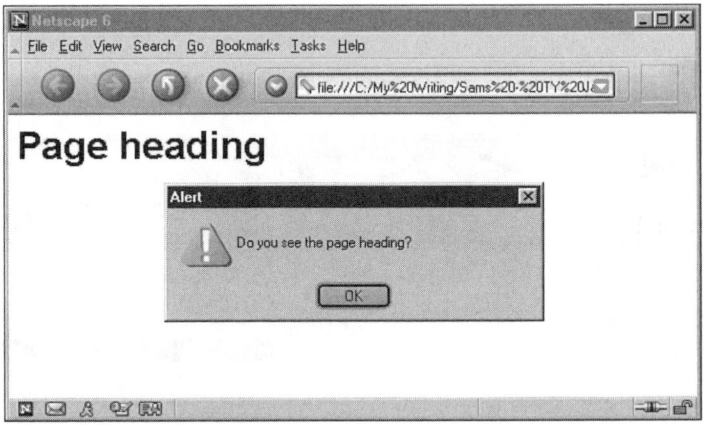

FIGURE 1.2

*The alert box dis-
played by a script
block in the body of
the HTML page.*

ANALYSIS   Notice the difference the placement of the script block made. When the script
block was in the document head it brought up the alert box before the words
"Page heading" had loaded into the browser window. By moving the script block within
the body of the HTML page, below the <h1> tags, the words "Page heading" had loaded
into the browser and was displayed on the page by the time the JavaScript alert box was
shown.

Note

The lines of an HTML document are loaded from top to bottom, and each
line is loaded from left to right. Therefore whatever you put first will be
loaded first.

Caution

Always remember that the <script> tags are an HTML or XHTML tag pair.
You should always remember to include the closing </script> tag.

External JavaScript Files

Any JavaScript code placed between the `<script>` tags also can be stored in a separate text file. However, although it is a text file, you must avoid giving it a `.txt` file extension. It needs to have a `.js` file extension to be correctly recognized by the JavaScript interpreter. As long as it is given a `.js` extension the whole script then can be used in an HTML page, as if it was actually typed into the page itself, by including the external JavaScript file.

To include a JavaScript file you simply add a `src` attribute to the opening `<script>` tag.

So the opening `<script>` tag would look something like this:

```
<script src="MyFirstExternalScript.js">
```

Nothing should be written between the opening and closing tag, so it is best to place the closing `</script>` tag immediately after the opening tag, like this:

```
<script src"MyFirstExternalScript.js"></script>
```

Caution

In XHTML you have the option of writing an empty script tag like this: `<script/>`. Unfortunately this can cause errors in some browsers, so it is safer to use a `<script></script>` tag pair.

Listing 1.4 is an example. There isn't an external file to link at present. The code is simply to demonstrate the syntax in place.

LISTING 1.4 An HTML Page That Accesses an External JavaScript File

INPUT (external.htm)

```
<html>
<head>
<title>Title of Document</title>

<script src="path/to/file/fileName.js"></script>

</head>
<body>

The content of
your page goes here.

</body>
</html>
```

Most of the code in this book will be shown in script blocks—since that is easier when teaching a new topic. In practice, however, there are good reasons for using external files for storing your scripts once you get to the stage of writing serious code. We'll talk about those reasons shortly in the "Reusing Code" section, but for the moment we need to cover a few more things you need to know about using the `<script>` tags.

Within an HTML Start Tag

Placing JavaScript inside the opening tag of an HTML element is a special case. The only part of the JavaScript language ever used in this way is event handlers. Event handlers are quite an advanced topic, which we will look at in Chapter 10, "Events and Events Handling." For the moment, we will just ignore this aspect until later in the book after you have become more familiar with JavaScript.

Specify the Script Language

Currently, JavaScript is the default script language for all browsers so HTML desktop Web browsers will understand your code without you telling the browser that it's being given JavaScript. However, there is good reason to specify the language that you are using. The default script language could change in the future. In fact, there could be profound changes in browsers over the next few years as the Extensible Markup Language, XML, becomes more widely used, and as mobile browsers become more common too. For the moment at least, it looks unlikely that the default will change for any of the browsers.

To cover the possibility of the default scripting language changing, for at least some browsers, you should routinely specify two attributes in your opening `<script>` tag: the `language` attribute and the `type` attribute.

Until recently, the language attribute has been the recognized way of telling a browser that a script is JavaScript. Although it is no longer the approved way of doing so, it is the only method which version 4 browsers and below will understand. Therefore, for backward compatibility, it is still necessary to use the `language` attribute in an opening `<script>` tag whenever you begin a piece of script.

The `language` attribute is written in the same way you would write other HMTL attributes such as the `bgColor` attribute. For JavaScript it is simply given the word `"javascript"` as its value.

In this case the J and S of JavaScript are not capitalized. This will allow you to use your scripts in XHMTL documents. XHTML, like JavaScript, is case sensitive and therefore `"javascript"` (all lowercase) is the only version acceptable for use in XHTML.

> **Note**
>
> XHTML stands for eXtensible HyperText Markup Language. XHTML 1.0 is HTML 4.0, which has been rewritten in XML rather than in SGML syntax (in which all HTML is actually written).

Assuming you used all lowercase, this is how your opening script tags should now look:

```
<script language="javascript">
```

Or in the case of including an external file:

```
<script src="path/to/file/fileName.js" language="javascript">
```

New browsers, such as Microsoft Internet Explorer version 5 and above and Netscape Navigator version 6 and above, will continue to support the `language` attribute for some time, but eventually it is likely that it will fade out.

The `Type` Attribute

The specifications for HTML 4.0 and XHTML 1.0 use a different attribute within the opening `<script>` tag, called the `type` attribute. The reason for changing to this attribute is to standardize the way of describing the type of content contained in a variety of files accessible across the Web. The types of files are called "media types" and each has its own standard way of being described. When the media type is `"text/javascript"` a browser, or other Web application, knows that it is dealing with JavaScript, and then can work out whether or not it knows how to process the content of the file by simply accessing the `type` attribute.

When using JavaScript, the `type` attribute for the script tag takes the value `"text/javascript"`.

To achieve maximum cross-browser version acceptance, it is best to use both the `language` and `type` attributes. This ensures not only that your scripts will be understood by old browsers but also that you won't need to go back and add the `type` attribute at some future time.

If we go back to the example code for a script block, it now should look like this:

```
<script language="javascript" type="text/javascript">
// ALL YOUR JAVASCRIPT CODE
// GOES IN HERE BETWEEN THE
// OPENING AND CLOSING
// SCRIPT TAGS.
</script>
```

Old Browsers

To achieve compatibility with very old browsers, we still have one last thing we probably should add, especially when we use script blocks in Web pages that may be viewed using such old browsers. We need to add comments to the JavaScript code to prevent really old browsers that don't understand the code from displaying the code in your Web page—which, almost certainly, isn't what you want.

The problem stems from the fact that some very old browsers don't understand the <script> tag. Take a quick look at what happens when a browser doesn't understand a tag. Type the HTML shown in Listing 1.5 and after you've saved it, take a look at it in your browser.

LISTING 1.5 A Listing Illustrating What Happens When a Browser Doesn't
INPUT Recognize a Tag (nonExistentTag.htm)

```
<html>
<head>
<title>Title of Document</title>

<nonExistentTag>

TYPE OUT LOTS AND LOTS OF TEXT HERE. IT DOESN'T MATTER WHAT IT IS AS LONG AS
THERE IS PLENTY OF IT.

AS YOU WILL NOTICE THIS TEXT IS IN THE HEAD OF THE DOCUMENT. YOU WOULDN'T REALLY
WANT THIS STUFF SHOWING UP ON YOUR PAGE WOULD YOU?

</nonExistentTag>

</head>
<body>

<h1>Title of Document</h1>

<p>Maybe write some more stuff in here.</p>

</body>
</html>
```

If you ran this script you would see an appearance like the one shown in Figure 1.3.

1

OUTPUT

FIGURE 1.3

The content of unrecognizable tags displayed in a Web page.

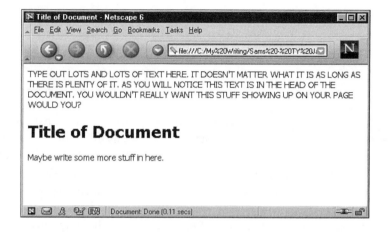

ANALYSIS As you can see, the browser displayed the text that was between the unrecognized start and end tags. The same thing happens in older browsers that don't understand the `<script>` tag. The `<script>` tags are ignored, and the browser renders the script on the Web page in the browser. Clearly, this could make a mess of a page that would otherwise have looked fine—even if the scripts hadn't run.

Luckily, there is a little trick involving HTML comments which you can use to make sure this doesn't happen. Take a look at the following code in Listing 1.6:

INPUT

LISTING 1.6 Using HTML Comments to Avoid Errors in Older Browsers (hideScript.htm)

```
<html>
<head>
<title>Hide scripts using comments.</title>
<script language="javascript" type="text/javascript">

<!--

lines of JavaScript code here
...

//-->

</script>

</head>
<body>
```

LISTING 1.6   continued

```
Page content here...

</body>
</html>
```

ANALYSIS   If you look closely you will notice that there are a pair of HTML comments
nested inside the script tags. This means that if the script tags are ignored (by
browsers that don't understand them), then all the code between them will be hidden by
the comment just as a browser knows not to display an HTML comment. This seems
quite clever, but what about the JavaScript being interpreted by a more modern browser
that does understand how `<script>` tags are used? Is there the possibility that the HTML
comments could cause errors if they were inside the script block? The answer is no. The
JavaScript interpreter knows that it is not to try and render the "open comment" mark,
and the two forward slashes before the HTML "close comment" mark prevent it from
being interpreted (and you'll see why shortly).

So if you include HTML comments inside `<script>` and `</script>` tags, your code will
work normally and be prevented from displaying on the page.

Reusing Code

Before we go on to look at some example JavaScript, let's take a quick look at the
reasons why you might want to store your JavaScript code in an external `.js` file and
include it into your page.

For small pieces of code that are specific to an individual Web page, it is likely best to
keep the JavaScript code inside the page itself. By keeping everything together in one
file, when your code listings are short, it makes finding and maintaining your scripts
simpler.

However, when the same piece of code possibly could be used in more than one
document it is better to store the JavaScript code in an external file.

The first benefit of doing this is that if you need to modify the script (as is almost bound
to happen at some time); then you don't need to make repeated changes on every page
that uses the script. This can save you a lot of time opening, pasting, saving, and then
uploading every file. It also avoids the necessity of making exactly the same changes in
each version.

The second benefit is not as immediately obvious. Because some browsers cache external .js files for the duration of a browser session, then by placing the code in an external JavaScript file your visitors only have to download it once for that browser session. So, for example, if you have several files in a directory that use the same JavaScript navigation menu, then you only need to download the code once but can use it on several pages. While the majority of users are still using modems to connect to the Internet this cuts down the time it takes them to download your pages.

Documenting Your Code

Once you start to develop more involved JavaScript applications you will find that your code can become large and complex.

If you don't document your code, this can make it very difficult for someone else to understand how the code works without spending a great deal of time analyzing it line by line. You may even find that you don't understand it yourself if you need to go back to it and make changes some time after it was written. Writing comments at key places in the code can go a long way to making the code more easily understood, possibly saving you a lot of frustration and wasted time.

JavaScript provides two methods to insert comments into your code in order to document what it does: One method comments out a single line and the other method comments out multiple lines.

To comment out an individual line, you simply need to type two consecutive forward slashes (//). The JavaScript interpreter will ignore everything that follows the forward slashes to the end of the line. The forward slashes can be placed at the beginning of a line or later in the line after some code. Examples of this style of commenting are below:

```
// This entire line has been commented out!
var dynMenuWidth = 10 // This comment follows some code.
```

There are times when you will need more than just a line or two of text to adequately comment a section of your code. You could, of course, place a couple of forward slashes at the beginning of each line, but that can become pretty tedious. JavaScript has another method to save us the trouble.

To begin comments which span several lines we type a forward slash followed by an asterisk (/*). This time the comment does not end with the end of the line. The JavaScript interpreter treats everything on the page as a comment until it comes to an asterisk followed by a forward slash (*/). The following code demonstrates this for you:

```
/* All of the text in
a comment block like
this is ignored. */
```

This method is also very useful when you need to temporarily comment out large sections of your code. Much easier than typing and later removing two forward slashes from the beginning of every line!

Be careful to avoid nesting comments. If you have comments like this:

```
/*
x = 1;
y = 2; /* this comment will close the outer comment */
z = 3;
*/
```

then the */ that ends the second comment will also end the first comment. So when the JavaScript interpreter finds the */ on the final line an error can be expected.

To make it easier to see where these comments start and end, you may find it useful to add a row of characters such as the hyphen at the top and bottom of the comment. As long as they are within the comment marks, the JavaScript interpreter will ignore them too.

```
/* ----------------------------------
   All of the text in a comment block
   like this as well as the lines
   above and below are ignored.
   ----------------------------------

*/
```

Although you shouldn't skimp on your comments, try to keep them concise. Remember that they're downloaded with the rest of the script every time someone requests one of your pages.

Reserved Words

JavaScript has a number of words that are set aside for giving instructions to the JavaScript interpreter. These are listed here:

abstract	final	public
boolean	finally	return
break	float	short
byte	for	static
case	function	super
catch	goto	switch
char	if	synchronized
class	implements	this
const	import	throw
continue	in	throws
debugger	instanceof	transient
default	int	true
delete	interface	try
do	long	typeof
double	native	var
else	new	void
enum	null	volatile
export	package	while
extends	private	with
false	protected	

At the moment don't worry about how these keywords are used. As we progress through the book, they will be introduced when we need them. The point in giving the list to you now is to make you aware from the start that some words are reserved and can't be used in your code except in the ways prescribed in JavaScript.

Caution

JavaScript is case sensitive. In theory, by capitalizing one of the letters of a reserved word you could use it to name something. However, this is very bad practice, creating all sorts of potential confusion.

Data Types

This final part of the chapter will conclude with coverage of the different types of valid JavaScript data, and the requirement for data type conversion in JavaScript.

Data, the name given to information, which is used by a computer, can come in several different forms. For example, numbers, dates, and text readily spring to mind. Depending on the computer language used to process the data, data that contains different types of information is likely to be treated differently. It is important to know just how the language you are using will treat the data you will use in it.

Some programming languages are strongly typed, which means that when a piece of data is included in the program being written its data type must be declared first. The data then must be treated according to strict rules which apply to that particular data type if an error is not to be caused. For example, if you tried to add a number to the end of a statement while using a strongly typed language, the computer wouldn't know what to do. Most conventional programming languages such as C or C++ are strongly typed.

JavaScript is what's called a dynamically typed language. JavaScript is also weakly typed. You might guess, correctly, that when data is given to a JavaScript script you don't need to specify its data type. The other aspect of a dynamically typed language is that it allows pieces of data to change types during run time (from the time when the script starts up to when it finishes).

However, this doesn't mean that we can just ignore data types, but JavaScript is more flexible than some other languages. Unless you understand how JavaScript treats data types, things can still turn out to have unexpected results. For example,

```
10 + 0
```

is treated by JavaScript as the number 10

but

```
10 + "0"
```

is processed by JavaScript as "100". We will discuss why later.

Numbers

Fully featured languages such as Java and C++ have several different data types for numbers that are used depending on its size and nature. The program then knows how much memory to set aside for it.

In JavaScript the priority is on ease of writing code. Therefore distinctions between different types of numbers are not made, which removes one source of possible coding errors.

JavaScript understands numbers in two forms: integers (whole numbers such as the number 10), and floating point numbers (numbers with a fractional part, such as 1.55). Our lives are made easier by the fact that most of the time JavaScript treats all numbers as floating point numbers so we don't need to worry about number types. Because JavaScript applications are usually small, the difference in performance is not noticeable.

JavaScript can handle positive and negative numbers between -2^{1024} and 2^{1024} (approx. -10^{307} to 10^{307}).

As well as understanding the decimal (base 10) numbers we use, JavaScript also understands octal (base 8) and hexadecimal (base 16) numbers. This can be useful when you want to manipulate an object's color for example, as colors are commonly expressed in hexadecimal in HTML and XHTML.

Unless you specifically tell JavaScript that the number you are giving it is an octal or hexadecimal number it will assume it is a decimal number. To designate a number as octal, you simply start with a zero. To designate a hexadecimal number, it needs to start with a zero and an "x". Note that while you can give JavaScript octal and hexadecimal numbers to work with, it will always give back the result in decimal form. For example, the following code

```
alert(10 + 10);
```

returns 20 as you would expect. But

```
alert(010 + 010);
```

will alert as 16. This is because octal 10 is equivalent to decimal 8, and eight plus eight is 16 (remember it returns numbers in decimal form). For the same reason the following, which adds hexadecimal 10 to hexadecimal 10 (decimal 16 to decimal 16) will alert as 32.

```
alert(0x10 + 0x10);
```

Caution   Whenever you collect decimal numbers from a user you must strip out any leading zeros otherwise JavaScript will assume it is an octal number.

There are three special values that can occur when using numbers. These are as follows:

```
Infinity
```

```
-Infinity
```

```
NaN
```

Positive and negative infinity can result from either of two conditions: if the numbers you are working with exceed the maximum amount that JavaScript can handle, or if you divide a number by 0. In the case of dividing by 0, Infinity (positive infinity) is produced if the number was positive, and –Infinity (negative infinity) if the number was negative.

NaN is short for "Not a Number." NaN can be produced if you attempt to do something inappropriate with a number, such as divide it by a string of characters. If, for example, you tried to divide 100 by "kangaroo"

```
100 / "kangaroo"
```

the result would be NaN.

Boolean

Often when writing your scripts you will make decisions as to whether JavaScript should do something or not. For example, say you have a Web page that allows a user to fill out an online form to send you an e-mail. Before the user is allowed to submit the form, you may want to check that the return e-mail address that was entered is valid. For the moment, let's ignore the script you would create in order to accomplish this (it will be dealt with later in the book). The outcome from your test would be either "yes, it is a valid e-mail address" and the form would be sent, or "no, that isn't an e-mail address" and you would ask again for a valid one.

In this case you have been looking for a `true` or `false` condition. This scenario is so common in coding that the `Boolean` data type was created. Boolean data has two and only two possible values: `true` or `false`. There is no "maybe," "perhaps," or "could be." JavaScript can only make decisions when given a decisive "yes" or "no" in the form of Boolean logic.

Strings

A more obvious data type we might want to use in our scripts is the `string` data type. However, because JavaScript code itself is written in text, without some means of distinguishing between the text, which is code, and the text that is a string things could become confusing. To solve this problem quote marks can be used to surround a line of text or sequence of characters to indicate it is "not code." This makes sure that when the

JavaScript interpreter is run the text is treated just as a series of characters strung together and not as a piece of code.

The name given to data when it is put into the form where it is to be treated as a series of characters "strung" together one after another is, naturally, a "string." Strings are not limited to only storing letters of the alphabet; you also can store any other characters simply by enclosing them in quote marks.

JavaScript is happy for you to use either double quotes or single quotes. Hence `"I am a string"` and `'I am also a string'` are equally acceptable ways of turning data into a string. Care should be taken however that you do not mark the beginning of a string with one type of quote marks and then end it with the other. If you write `"I am a string'` or `'I am also a string"`, you will cause an error. So, remember, whichever type of quote mark you use to begin the string must also end the string.

You might think that if both double and single quotes can be used to indicate the beginning and end of a string, then it really shouldn't matter if you start with one and then end with the other. However, if you stop a moment to think, you might wonder how you would then put quote marks into a string. The solution is that when you start a string with one of the quote marks the JavaScript interpreter waits until it finds one of the same type before says to itself "okay, that's the end of the string, what follows now is code." With this setup, if you want to put one type of quote marks into a string all you need to do is surround the quotation with the other type of quote marks.

You likely will need to include—sooner rather than later—both types of quotes within a string. This is usually required for coding itself, but for the moment we will demonstrate it by imagining we need to make a string out of the following sentence:

Ian called out "Hey, pass me Andrew's football!".

If you were to enclose the sentence with double quotes

```
"Ian called out "Hey, pass me Andrew's football!"."
```

JavaScript would think that the string was merely "Ian called out." After it passed this point to "Hey," which doesn't mean anything to it, an error would occur. The same thing would happen if you enclosed it in single quotes. As soon as JavaScript got as far as "Andrew'" it would fail because the apostrophe in Andrew's would be interpreted as the closing single quote mark for the string.

JavaScript has set aside the backslash character (\)to solve this problem. Whenever you use a backslash in JavaScript it means that the next character is special. For the quote marks, preceding them with a backslash simply means that they do not indicate the end of a string. For example you could write:

'That is Andrew\'s football'

Or if you want to store five double quote marks in a string you would write:

```
"\"\"\"\"\""
```

And for single quotes you would write:

```
'\'\'\'\'\''
```

When a character has a backslash placed in front of it, it is referred to as being "escaped." There are several other characters that can be escaped to produce special characters. These are shown below:

\b	Backspace
\f	Form feed
\n	New line
\r	Carriage return
\t	Tab
\'	Single quote
\"	Double quote
\\	Backslash
\xNN	A character in the Latin-1 character set (x is just an "x" and NN is a hexadecimal number)
\uNNNN	A character in the Unicode character set (u is just a "u" and NNNN is a hexadecimal number)

Suppose you wanted to include the copyright symbol in a string. In Latin-1 and Unicode respectively you would write:

```
"Copyright \xA9 2002 by Sams Publishing"
```

```
"Copyright \x00A9 2002 by Sams Publishing"
```

Both of the above strings will give you the following:

Copyright © 2002 by Sams Publishing

As you may have noticed, Unicode seems to use the same hexadecimal number with a couple of extra zeros in front. In fact it is the same, but the extra two characters give it many extra possible characters. To see the full range of Unicode characters visit the Unicode Web site at http://www.unicode.org.

> **Caution** Although Unicode gives you far more characters to work with, it is a more recent character set that isn't supported by version 4 browsers and below. In fact, some of the characters aren't supported by even the latest browsers.

Some Useful Tools

In the next couple of chapters, you will learn how to use three JavaScript tools that will enable you to show output, make decisions, and collect input respectively. The proper names for these tools are "functions," but for the moment, if you don't know what functions are, don't worry about it. We will be taking a closer look at functions in Chapter 3, "Functions and Statements."

The `alert()` Function

We have already used the `alert()` function several times in this chapter to bring up what's called an alert box. You have probably seen these small boxes that pop up many times before on Web sites to warn you, or "alert" you, to the consequences of an action.

To bring up an alert box on your Web page, you need to use the JavaScript `alert()` function. When you use this function you only need to provide the function with a message in order for it to display. The JavaScript interpreter does all the construction of the alert box behind the scenes. Here is an example:

```
alert("Hello all!");
```

This alert function could be placed on a line of code anywhere in a script block and it would bring up an alert box.

There are two things to notice about the `alert()` function. The first is that the message to show on the page has to be enclosed within a pair of parentheses. In addition to that, because the contents are a string, they have to be enclosed within quote marks. If, for example, the message had been simply a number, then we would have written it without the quote marks (but still within the parentheses) like this:

```
alert(55);
```

We will use the `alert()` function quite extensively in the next couple of chapters to show the results of some of our scripts. For example if we wanted to check what JavaScript would do with the sum 5+5, we might write:

```
alert(5+5);
```

The result, 10, would then be shown in the alert box so that we could be sure that 10 was indeed what JavaScript would return.

The `confirm()` Function

The `confirm()` function is a bit more advanced than the `alert()` function. Rather than simply providing a user with information, it allows a user to make a choice between two options. Again, you already may have seen the small box that this function brings up in visits to Web sites. It is similar to the alert box, but in addition to a message and an "OK" button, it also has a "Cancel" button.

For the moment we won't take too close a look at the `confirm()` function. This is because, to be of any use, we need to use it in conjunction with pieces of code called "control statements" that allow us to make decisions. In simple terms, the button that the user clicks determines which of the two values is sent back to the script. These two values are the values `true` and `false`, which we have already seen. They can be thought of as the computer equivalent of "yes" and "no." Whichever value is sent back by the user enables the script to determine whether or not to take a particular action.

The `confirm()` function is written in a way that is similar to the alert box, and it also can be placed on a line of code anywhere in a script block. Here is an example:

INPUT

```
confirm("Are you sure you want to reset the form?");
```

When this confirm function is executed, it will display the confirm box shown in Figure 1.4.

OUTPUT

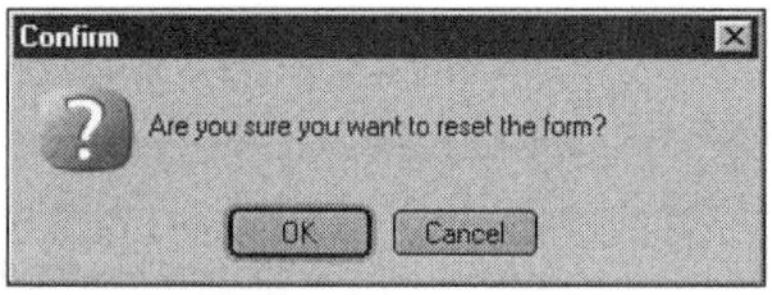

FIGURE 1.4

Our first confirm box.

To see the `true` or `false` values that are returned from confirm boxes we can actually place the `confirm()` function inside an `alert()` function. Whichever value the confirm box sends back will be shown in the alert box that pops up. Here is how we would write this:

```
alert(confirm("Are you sure?"));
```

The part of this line that will be evaluated first is the confirm function. Once the confirm box displays and the user clicks "OK" or "Cancel," then the value `true` or `false` will be given back and placed inside the parentheses of the alert function. The `alert()` function then will bring up an alert showing this value. Try it out and see for yourself.

In the following chapters you will see how to use the value returned by a `confirm()` function to make decisions in your scripts.

The `prompt()` Function

The `prompt()` function is the last of the three functions we will look at for the present. This is the function that pops up a box that "prompts" you to enter some text for a script to use. For example you could be asked to enter your name and then the script could write your name into the HTML of the Web page to personalize it for you.

The `prompt()` function is a little bit more complex than the previous two functions, but it is still fairly straightforward. It requires two strings to be written between the parentheses of the function. The first of these is the message that is shown in the `prompt()` box, and the second is used to pre-fill the area where you type in your input (pre-fill works in Internet Explorer only). To separate these strings, a comma is used, as shown in the following line of code:

INPUT

```
prompt("Please enter your name.", "Write it here.");
```

This will bring up the prompt box in Figure 1.5.

OUTPUT

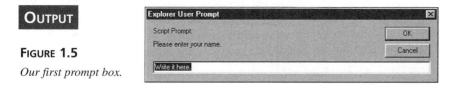

FIGURE 1.5

Our first prompt box.

ANALYSIS The text that the user enters into the box is returned in the same way as a `true` or `false` value is given back from a confirm box.

Note that if you don't want to fill out the input area of the prompt box, you don't leave out the second string in the function. You have to use what is called an "empty string" instead, which is simply an opening and closing quote mark that doesn't surround any characters at all.

```
prompt("Please enter your name.", "");
```

These three functions enable us to take three actions that we will need over the next few chapters as we work our way through various parts of the fundamentals of JavaScript. Using alert functions we can find out the results of a piece of code we have written; with confirm boxes we can make decisions; and with a prompt box we can provide external input for some of our scripts.

Summary

This chapter introduced you to what JavaScript is, and it discussed a little about its place among other Web technologies. You have learned how the desire of Web authors to interact with their users led to the development of many new technologies, and how the cross-platform nature of JavaScript made it ideal for use on the Web. After learning how to insert JavaScript into your pages using script blocks or external files, you also learned some basic features of the language itself, such as that we can, and should, use whitespace to make our code more readable. You also learned about more key topics such as the five data types that JavaScript understands: numbers, boolean values, strings, null, and undefined.

You also were introduced to some basic JavaScript and shown some simple code.

Workshop

In the workshops, you will find a quiz and exercises that will conclude each chapter. We will ask some questions that you might ask yourself, together with possible answers to each question, as well as exercises to help you further explore chapter material for yourself.

Q&A

Q. I created code that looked like this:

```
Alert("Hello I am learning JavaScript");
```

but it didn't work. Why?

A. JavaScript is case sensitive. To get the code to work you would need to write,

```
alert("Hello I am learning JavaScript");
```

Q. How would I ask the user for their location?

A. You could use a prompt box, which uses the JavaScript `prompt()` function. For example, you could write

```
prompt("Where do you live?", "Enter your location here.");
```

Quiz

1. The JavaScript entities `alert()`, `confirm()`, and `prompt()` are all functions or statements?

2. Is JavaScript that follows "Hello World!" called a data type or a string?

3. What does NaN mean? Does it mean "not a number" or "nearly a number"?

Quiz Answers

1. The `alert()`, `confirm()`, and `prompt()` entities are all JavaScript functions.

2. "Hello World!" is a string. In JavaScript strings must be enclosed in pairs of either single or double quotes.

3. NaN means "Not a Number" and is returned by, for example, a function when something is wrong with a mathematical operation you have attempted.

Exercises

1. Create an alert box that tells the user, "This is Teach Yourself JavaScript in 21 Days."

2. Create a confirm box that asks the user, "Are you enjoying learning about JavaScript?".

3. Create a prompt box that asks the user, "What is your name?" and then gives the user the prompt, "Enter your name here."

DAY 2

Working with Data

After reading Chapter 1, "Getting the Basics Right," you should be clear about what JavaScript is and have a general idea of how it fits into the range of technologies available for use on the Web. Today, after having looked at the data types recognized by JavaScript, you will see how the data that you define as a Web-page author or collect from a user can be stored and processed.

First, we are going to take a look at some simple methods of data storage followed by a study of operators, JavaScript's basic data manipulation tools.

This chapter will teach you

- What variables are
- How variables are created and used
- What constants are
- How constants are created and used
- What operators are
- How JavaScript's operators are used

Simple Data Storage

In most JavaScript applications some data is used more than once or it is used at some time after the page has loaded. In these situations it is useful to have some means to temporarily store data. To allow you to do so, JavaScript provides several facilities that can be used to store data for re-use.

Variables

The JavaScript storage facility for an individual piece of data is called a *variable*. Variables are effectively small containers which are given a name, and then filled with a piece of data that is in the form of one of the data types discussed in Chapter 1, "Getting the Basics Right."

Variables will be your primary method of data storage in JavaScript programs, although there are other containers (such as arrays), which are used for data storage. Arrays, which can be used for storing lists of information, will be covered in later chapters.

Creating Variables

To create a variable, the first thing you must do is "declare" it. This simply lets the computer know that it has to set aside some memory for the storage of a new variable and, optionally, tells the computer about the data it will store. To declare a variable, simply write the var keyword followed by the name you wish to give to the variable. So, for example, to declare a variable called myFirstVar, without defining the value to be stored in it, you would write the following:

```
var myFirstVar;
```

The next step is to give the variable some data to store. When a variable initially is given some data to store, the variable is referred to as "initialized." More generally—that is, after the first time—this process of giving the variable a (new) value is known as "assigning" data to the variable. To do this, the variable name is written on a new line followed by the equal sign and the data to be stored. In the following code the first line declares the variable myFirstVar and the second line assigns a particular string to myFirstVar:

```
var myFirstVar;
    myFirstVar = "I'm a string stored in a variable.";
```

 Caution

Note that the var keyword is only used once for each variable at the time you first declare it. Once a variable has been declared, don't use the var keyword again with the same variable.

Every time you use the variable `myFirstVar` you will actually be using the data it contains. To demonstrate this, write the two lines of code above into the template which you saw earlier in Listing 1.6 and add a third line to bring up an alert box containing the value of the variable, as shown below in Listing 2.1.

INPUT   **LISTING 2.1**   Variable Demo (`variableDemo.htm`)

```html
<html>
<head>
<title>Variable Demo</title>

<script language="javascript" type="text/javascript">
<!--

var myFirstVar;
myFirstVar = "I'm a string stored in a variable.";
alert(myFirstVar);

//-->
</script>

</head>
<body>

<h1>Variable Demo</h1>

</body>
</html>
```

Save the file and load it into your browser. The alert box brought up by the third line of code will contain the value of `myFirstVar`, as shown in Figure 2.1.

OUTPUT

FIGURE 2.1
Displaying the value of `myFirstVariable`.

Congratulations! You have just stored data in your very first JavaScript variable.

ANALYSIS   The way the variable `myFirstVar` was created and assigned a value is actually longer than it needs to be. It was created in two steps simply to demonstrate the difference between setting aside some memory for a variable and actually filling the memory with data. There is a shortcut that allows you to use a single line of code for the declaration of a variable and the assignment of data to it. To do that for the above example you would write the following:

```
var myFirstVar = "I'm a string stored in a variable.";
```

There is no difference between the two in terms of the way your scripts will run so you can use either method. Although it is sometimes useful to declare your variables before you assign data to them, the second method commonly is used simply because it is shorter.

Omitting the var Keyword

If you have ever looked at scripts created by other people, you may have noticed in some scripts that the var keyword was not used to create variables. As long as you assign some data to a variable on the same line as you write the variable name, the JavaScript interpreter will accept this (if you omit the var keyword and also fail to assign it a value that will cause an error).

The syntax you can use to declare and assign a value to a variable without using the var keyword is

```
myFirstVar = "I'm a string stored in a variable.";
```

and it works correctly.

However, as we will see later in the book, once you start using variables in functions and omit the var keyword, it can have a very undesirable effect. The omission of the var keyword should be a deliberate choice, and until we have taken a closer look at the reasons for using or omitting it, it is best to get into the habit of using it every time you declare a new variable.

Naming Variables

JavaScript has naming rules so variables can't always be given the first name that comes to mind. It is important that certain simple naming rules be followed if errors are not to occur in your scripts. The rules for naming your JavaScript variables are the same as those for naming HTML elements. Names may only consist of alphanumeric characters (letters and numbers), the underscore character (_) and the dollar sign ($). There is a further rule that the first character of a name is not permitted to be a number. As we will see throughout the book, these rules are the same no matter what the item is you're naming in JavaScript.

Caution

Remember that the JavaScript keywords listed in Chapter 1 can be used only for their designated purpose. They can't be used for naming variables or other names. Remember too that JavaScript, unlike HTML, is case sensitive.

Version 1.5 of JavaScript now allows variable names to include letters from the ISO-8859-1 and Unicode character sets, such as å and ü in addition to the letters of the English alphabet. Just remember that some of the users of your Web pages still may be using version 4 browsers or below, which don't support the use of such characters. Also, note that Internet Explorer 5.5 will not accept these new characters as the first character of a variable name.

Acceptable variable names include:

```
myFirstVar, bob, max_width, total_$s, _1st_answer_
```

However, the following variable names will cause JavaScript errors and, depending on where they are used, they could possibly prevent your entire script from running at all.

```
var             // It uses a key word as a variable name
2nd_var         // It begins with a number
101_dalmatians  // It begins with a number
@home           // The '@' character is not allowed in a name
first#          // The '#' character is not allowed in a name
```

The reason var will cause an error is because it is a keyword. 1st_var and 101_ dalmatians are unacceptable because they start with a numeric character, and @home and first# will fail because they use characters which aren't allowed in JavaScript names.

Tip

Give your variables names that indicate their purpose. When multiple variables with nondescript names are used in a complex piece of code things can become very confusing. Using meaningful names helps you to follow the flow of code, particularly if you wrote it some time ago.

To adequately describe the purpose of a variable, it may be necessary to use more than one word in its name. Because a space character isn't allowed in variable names there are two conventions which are commonly used to make the words within multiword variable names more readable. One method strings the words together and capitalizes the first letter of all but the first word; the second method separates the words with underscores. For example you might write the following:

```
multiWordVariable

phoneNumber

faxNumber
```

or,

```
multi_word_variable

phone_number

fax_number
```

The method you choose is completely up to you. The JavaScript interpreter accepts both methods just described. In this book we will usually use the first method purely because of personal preference. If you prefer the latter, feel free to use it instead. When looking at JavaScript code on the Web you will probably see both naming conventions used.

Caution   In theory you can use non-alphabetic characters in JavaScript names, such as * and +, or a period, but it is wiser to avoid these since they may cause confusion with JavaScript operators or object-related syntax that uses the period character.

Changing a Variable's Contents

As is implied by the name variable, the contents of variables can change. To change the data contained in a variable all you have to do is write the variable name followed by an equal sign and the new data. This process "reassigns" to the variable a new value. For example:

```
var myVariable = 10; //Creates myVariable and assigns it the value 10
    myVariable = 5;  //Reassigns myVariable the value 5
```

To see this process working, try running the following code shown in Listing 2.2.

LISTING 2.2   Reassigning Variables (reassignVariables.htm)

```
<html>
<head>
<title>Reassigning Variables</title>

<script language="javascript" type="text/javascript">
<!--
```

LISTING 2.2 continued

```
var myNum = 3;
alert("Variable myNum contains the value: " + myNum);
myNum = 2;
alert("Variable myNum contains the value: " + myNum);
myNum = 1;
alert("Variable myNum contains the value: " + myNum);
myNum = "Go!";
alert("Variable myNum contains the value: " + myNum);

//-->
</script>

</head>
<body>

<h1>Reassigning Variables</h1>

</body>
</html>
```

Not only does the data change in value, but for the final assignment, it also changes data type from number to string.

Constants

Constants are a new type of data container, which were introduced with JavaScript 1.5. They are declared in the same way as JavaScript variables but with the const keyword.

As their name suggests, once you've given a constant a value it doesn't change. In fact it cannot be changed. This rule is stricter than you might think. It is not possible to declare a constant and then assign it some data later, as we initially did to create a variable. If you were to try to do that the constant would simply take the value undefined at the time of the declaration, and then remain unchanged by any subsequent attempt made to assign it a value. For example, try the following three lines:

INPUT
```
const TEST_CONST;
      TEST_CONST = 10;
alert(TEST_CONST);
```

This displays the following alert box, which shows that the value of constant testConst has remained undefined, even after attempting to assign it the value 10 (see Figure 2.2).

OUTPUT

FIGURE 2.2

The value of
TEST_CONST.

ANALYSIS To assign testConst the value 10, you have to make the assignment on the same line as the declaration of the variable. Therefore we would have to change the previous lines of code as follows:

```
const TEST_CONST = 10;
alert(TEST_CONST);
```

Also note that you can't re-declare a constant as a variable in an attempt to change its value. The following will produce an error:

```
const TEST_CONST = 10;
var TEST_CONST = 20;
```

When you declare constants the const keyword must be used. It is not an option in the way that the var keyword is optional. The default data container is the variable, so if the const keyword is omitted, then a variable will be created, which may not be what you intended.

Caution At the time of writing, Internet Explorer, version 5.5, does not support constants.

It is traditional, although not required, in JavaScript to name constants with all uppercase letters, using an underscore to create any spaces between words. As you will see later in the book, this is also how the predefined JavaScript constants are written. It simply reminds us not to try to change the data they contain later in a script.

Operators

You have learned about the types of data JavaScript understands, and you are able to use variables as a simple means of data storage. The next step is to learn about some of the different methods available to you for working with your data.

To begin with, we will examine operators, which are JavaScript's basic data manipulation tools, many of which you will use regularly. JavaScript also has several other ways of processing data, including some built-in functions and powerful regular expressions (which we will look at in later chapters).

Understanding Operators

"Operators" may sound a bit abstract, but you shouldn't let their name put you off. You will find that you are already familiar with some of them, and many of them are intuitive to use.

The term "operator" came about because in programming when you perform a simple action on a piece of data you are said to perform an "operation" on it. It is quite logical then that the JavaScript tools provided to perform this task—an operation—are called operators.

Operators can operate on all of the data types that JavaScript understands. Take a look at an example of an arithmetic (mathematical) operation, with which you will undoubtedly be familiar:

```
1 + 2
```

In the simple arithmetic calculation above, a very common operation (addition) is performed using the numbers 1 and 2 and an operator (the plus sign). The plus sign is an operator you will have seen many times before, but quite possibly didn't realize it could be called an operator. As you can see, this really is very simple. The thing most likely to cause confusion in this chapter is the terminology, so let's quickly review some of the terms we will be using.

Terminology

In addition to "operator" and "operation," there are three other words that will come up regularly as we look at JavaScript operators: operands, expressions, and evaluation. Let's clarify what each means in the context of JavaScript.

Operands

Okay, so the plus sign was called an operator, but what about the other parts of the calculation—the numbers 1 and 2? Because the types of data used with operators will not always be numerical data, we can't always call the data numbers. Instead, data in this context is given the general term "operand." Therefore the numbers 1 and 2 in the above addition are called the + operator's "operands." So, if we want to add two numbers, we could, in tech-speak, say that we want to add the operand 1 to the operand 2 using the + operator.

For many of the operators, operands can be any of the JavaScript data types or they can be a data container containing some valid data.

Expressions

For the same reason (that is, not all operations are arithmetical), we don't use the word "calculation" to describe a typed-out sequence of operators and operands. Instead we call this an "expression."

So, the code

```
1 + 2
```

could be described as an expression in which we use the + operator on the operand 1 and the operand 2. The process is simple, although the terminology may not be. So don't let terminology that is unfamiliar make you uncomfortable.

In JavaScript as with other languages, an expression is any combination of data, data containers, and operators that will evaluate to a single value. For example 1 + 2 evaluates to (it becomes) 3. In this expression there are two pieces of data and a mathematical operator, but expressions can consist of many more than two operands and one operator.

You can use such expressions to assign a value to a variable. Thus, the following code adds the operand 1 to the operand 2, and assigns the resulting value to the variable mySecondVariable.

```
mySecondVariable = 1 + 2
```

Evaluation

Finally, we need a word that expresses what happens to an expression when the JavaScript interpreter processes it. For this process we use the words "evaluation" or "evaluates." For example we would say that 1 + 2 evaluates to the value 3.

Although this example simply evaluates to a value (and therefore would need to be used immediately), expressions can also assign a value to a data container such as a variable or constant when they are evaluated. For example, the following is an expression, which in this case will assign the value 3 to a variable called myVar on evaluation:

```
var myVar = 3;
```

Most of the time your JavaScript expressions will evaluate to one of the three data types shown in Table 2.1.

TABLE 2.1   Data Types to Which Expressions Commonly Evaluate

Data type	Example
Number	For example, 15 or 3.14
String	For example, "Alan" or "3.14"
Logical	true or false only

They can also evaluate to something called an "object," but we'll leave the explanation of what an object is and how you use it for a later chapter.

JavaScript Operators

With the terminology out of the way, let's get down to business. JavaScript has a very wide range of operators that can be broken up into the types shown below:

- Arithmetic operators
- Comparison operators
- Logical operators
- String operators
- Assignment operators
- Bitwise operators
- Special operators

We will examine all of the operators in each of the types except for the special operators, which we will only look at briefly. The special operators will be discussed later in the book at the points when they are most relevant.

Arithmetic Operators

Arithmetic operators (also called mathematical operators) can be used to perform calculations with numbers or data containers that hold numerical values. In addition to the operators for the four basic mathematical processes (addition, subtraction, multiplication, and division), and an operator to reverse the sign of a number, there are three operators provided as shortcuts for some commonly used processes.

Table 2.2 lists the mathematical operators along with a brief description of what they do.

TABLE 2.2   Arithmetic Operators in JavaScript

Operator	Name	Description
+	Addition	Adds two operands together
-	Subtraction	Subtracts the second operand from the first operand
*	Multiplication	Multiplies two operands together
/	Division	Divides the first operand by the second operand
%	Modulo (or Remainder)	Returns the remainder of dividing the first operand by the second operand
++	Increment	Adds 1 to its operand
- -	Decrement	Subtracts 1 from its operand
-	Negation	Reverses the sign of its operand

It is worth mentioning that the last three operators in Table 2.2 are commonly termed "unary" operators. This simply means that they only operate on one operand. Operators which operate on two operands, such as the simple addition calculations you saw earlier are called "binary" operators.

Caution

> Note that the division operator (/) returns a floating-point value (a number with a decimal point and a fractional part after the decimal point), and the modulo operator (%) returns an integer (whole number).

The first four arithmetic operators behave as you would expect:

```
4 + 8   // evaluates to 12
4 - 8   // evaluates to -4
4 * 8   // evaluates to 32
4 / 8   // evaluates to 0.5
```

As does the negation operator:

```
-5      // evaluates to -5
-(-5)   // evaluates to  5
```

In other words, the negation operator turns positive values negative and negative values positive. However, the use of the remaining three operators—Modulo, Increment, and Decrement—may not be immediately apparent to you at this point.

The Modulo Operator

The modulo operator finds the remainder after dividing its first operand by its second operand and it is written like this:

```
7 % 3
```

In this example, the expression would evaluate to 1 (7 divides by 3 twice before it leaves a number less than 3; for example, the remainder 1).

At first the modulo operator may seem strange. Surely you don't need to find the remainder of a division so often that a special operator had to be made to do the job. Well, maybe that is true, but it saves a lot of work for the times that we do need to find out what the remainder is.

Note

> The modulo operator is sometimes referred to as the "modulus" operator. The two terms mean the same.

The Increment and Decrement Operators

The increment and decrement operators are used extensively with variables in looping control statements (such statements will be dealt with more fully in the next chapter).

The increment operator x++ is simply a shorthand. The following two lines of code mean the same thing:

```
x++;
x = x + 1;
```

Basically, when you need to repeatedly go through a piece of code a set number of times, a variable is set at a value and then each time the code is run the variable is incremented (increased in value by 1) or decremented (decreased in value by 1). The value of the variable, after it has been incremented (or decremented), then can be tested to determine at what stage the code is running, and whether the loop should be run again.

You should note that one of the characteristics of these operators is that prefixing and postfixing the increment or decrement operator has different effects. The following code shows the prefix and postfix increment and decrement operators:

```
++x  // the prefixed increment operator
x++  // the postfixed increment operator
--x  // the prefixed decrement operator
x--  // the postfixed decrement operator
```

Let's look at an example to see just what we mean.

Assume that a variable x has the value 3. If the increment operator is prefixed to it (applied to its left-hand side), then ++x sets x to 4 and returns 4. This is demonstrated by the following code:

```
var x = 3;
alert(++x);  // alerts 4
alert(x);    // alerts 4
```

On the other hand if we postfix the increment operator to x, then x is not incremented to 4 until the next line of code. This can be shown with a similar piece of code using the postfix increment operator rather than the prefix increment operator:

```
var x = 3;
alert(x++);  // alerts 3
alert(x);    // alerts 4
```

At the moment we don't expect you to see why these techniques might be useful. Just bear it in mind for when we come to control statements later.

With the exception of the increment or decrement operators, boolean values and the null value can be used as the operands of arithmetic operators in JavaScript. The values false and null are treated as 0, whereas the value true is treated as 1.

Comparison Operators

Comparison operators are regularly used in JavaScript to test whether a condition is true or not. Although we may not consciously think in terms of comparison operators, we use this sort of evaluating process all the time in our day-to-day lives. For example, if you were to pass a shop and see something in the window that you liked, the first thing you might do is check in your purse or wallet to see if you have enough money (assuming you haven't brought your credit card). Effectively you are making a comparison by asking yourself, "is the money I have greater than the money I need to buy that item." These types of questions or comparisons always will result in a "yes" or "no" answer and are the basis of many decisions that we make. In this case, if the money you have is less than the money you need then you cannot buy the item.

Just as we make comparisons in our lives to help us make decisions, JavaScript provides comparison operators so that we can compare data in order to make decisions in our scripts. Comparison operators take two operands and compare them to see if a certain condition is true. If it is, the expression evaluates to the value true, but if it's not true, the expression evaluates to false. The values true and false are the JavaScript equivalent of "yes" and "no," and they are the only values a comparison expression will evaluate to. Comparison expressions always evaluate to one or other of these two logical values. A condition is either true or false and nothing in between. Comparisons, in JavaScript at least, cannot evaluate to "maybe."

Shortly we will look at how comparison expressions are used to make decisions, but for now let's take a look at a simple example to show expressions at work.

Imagine you have a variable called myVar and you want to check whether the number it contains is less than three. The less than and greater than operators in JavaScript are the same as they are in standard mathematical notation. Therefore to check this condition you would write the following:

```
myVar < 3
```

Try it out by adding some lines of code to the template as shown in Listing 2.3:

INPUT **LISTING 2.3** A Comparison Operator Demo (operatorDemo.htm)

```
<html>
<head>
<title>A Comparison Operator Demo</title>

<script language="javascript" type="text/javascript">
<!--

var myVar = 2.5;   // test different values
alert(myVar < 3);

//-->
</script>

</head>
<body>

<h1>A Comparison Operator Demo</h1>

</body>
</html>
```

OUTPUT If you change the value assigned to myVar you will see that when it contains a value less than three the expression evaluates to true, and when three or greater it evaluates to false.

A complete list of the comparison operators is shown in Table 2.3.

TABLE 2.3   Comparison Operators in JavaScript

Operator	Name	Description
>	Greater than	Checks whether the first operand is greater than the second operand
<	Less than	Checks whether the first operand is less than the second operand
>=	Greater than or equal to	Asks if the first operand is greater than or equal to the second operand
<=	Less than or equal to	Checks whether the first operand is less than or equal to the second operand
==	Equal to	Checks whether both operands are equal
!=	Not equal to	Checks whether both operands are unequal
===	Strict equal to	Asks if both operands are equal and of the same data type
!==	Strict not equal to	Checks whether both operands are unequal and/or not of the same data type

The first four operators are most likely to immediately make sense to you. There is a slight difference between the greater than (>) and greater than or equal to (>=) operators, and between the less than (<) and less than or equal to (<=) operators, as you most likely know. However, just in case math wasn't your favorite class, here are a couple of examples that show the difference:

```
3 <  3     // evaluates to false
3 <= 3     // evaluates to true
3 >  3     // evaluates to false
3 >= 3     // evaluates to true
```

As you can see, they act just as their names imply. With the greater than or less than operators, the first operand has to actually be greater than or less than the second operand for the expression to evaluate to true. The greater than or equal to and the less than or equal to operators on the other hand will also evaluate to true if the operands are equal.

The differences among some of the four equality comparison operators may not be quite so obvious however. The key to understanding how they work is to know that two of the comparison operators pay attention to data types and two of them don't. Let's look at some examples to demonstrate just what this means.

Caution

> It is a very common mistake to forget that there is a difference between the single equal sign that assigns a value to a variable and the double equal signs that compare its operands. If a comparison which checks for equality is causing errors check whether you have remembered to use a second equal sign.

2

```
3 ==  3    // evaluates to true
3 ==  "3"  // evaluates to true
```

but:

```
3 === 3    // evaluates to true
3 === "3"  // evaluates to false
```

Why have the second and fourth examples above not evaluated to the same logical value? The answer is that if the operands of the equal to (==) operator (and the not equal to operator) are of different data types, the JavaScript interpreter will try to convert one of them to the data type of the other to make a comparison. Therefore in the comparison 3 == "3" the second operand, a string containing the character 3, is converted to the number three which is equal to the first operand. Effectively the data types of the two operands have been ignored.

On the other hand in the fourth comparison which uses the strictly equal to comparison operator, the data type of the operands is also taken into account. Therefore, as the first operand is a number and the second operand is a string, the expression immediately evaluates to false. It doesn't matter that the character in the string is the character 3. The two operands aren't strictly equal because they are not of the same data type.

The problems with mistakenly using the assignment operator (=) instead of the equality operator (==) can arise when you have an expression like if (x==3). If, in error, you write if (x=3), then you have changed the value of the variable x to 3. Instead of checking whether the value of the variable x matches a certain value (the integer 3) you have, instead, changed its value to that numerical value. This won't cause an error but it may cause problems later in your script, depending on whether or not the code depends on the value of x.

These rules apply in the same way to the not equal to (!=) and the strictly not equal to (!==) comparison operators. Hence,

```
3 != 3     // evaluates to false
3 != "3"   // evaluates to false
```

but:

```
3 !== 3     // evaluates to false
3 !== "3"   // evaluates to true
```

> **Caution**
>
> Notice that the negation of the equal operator, ==, is !=, which has one less "=" than the operator it negates. Similarly, the negation of the strictly equal operator, ===, is !==, which again has one less "=" than the operator it negates.

The most obvious and frequently used application of comparison operators is to compare numeric values. However operands can also be string and logical values. If a logical value is used as an operand, the rule is very simple: true evaluates to 1 and false evaluates to 0.

Therefore:

```
true  > 0.5       // evaluates to true
```

and

```
false > 0.5       // evaluates to false
```

> **Caution**
>
> Be careful when comparing boolean (logical) values with numbers or strings, since different languages observe different rules for such comparisons, and it is easy to introduce a subtle error which could cause symptoms somewhere else in your code.

String comparisons are a bit more exciting and probably a lot more useful. The outcome of a string comparison is based on lexicographical ordering using the Unicode standard. That probably sounds pretty complicated but effectively it means that we can use the comparison operators to see if one string comes before another in the alphabet. Unfortunately this is not as simple as you might first think as Unicode separates uppercase letters from lowercase letters. The full set of uppercase letters, ABC...XYZ, comes before the lowercase letters, abc...xyz. For the moment, let's just see how the operators work when the strings aren't altered.

If one of the operands of a comparison expression is a string, then JavaScript compares the operands lexicographically. The less than operator checks whether the first operand comes before the second operand according to alphabetical ordering. If it does, then the expression evaluates to true. Let's take a look at a couple of examples:

```
"a" < "b"          // evaluates to true

"James" < "Alison" // evaluates to false
```

The greater than comparison operator acts in the opposite way, so it asks if a string comes after another string according to alphabetical ordering. Therefore:

```
"a" > "b"    // evaluates to false

"James" > "Alison" // evaluates to true
```

It is important to remember that the ordering is based on Unicode values. Therefore, uppercase letters come before lowercase letters:

```
"James" < "andrew" // evaluates to true
```

and

```
"James" > "andrew" // evaluates to false
```

To get around this when we want to put strings in alphabetical order, you can temporarily change all the letters in both strings to either uppercase or lowercase; then the comparisons work alphabetically in the way that you would expect. Don't worry about this for the moment though. For now let's continue our examination of JavaScript's comparison operators.

Conditional Operator

The conditional operator is the only special operator that we will cover in depth at this point in the book. We are going to examine it now so that we are better able to demonstrate the logical operators in the next section of this chapter.

The conditional operator is also the only JavaScript operator to take three operands. The operator consists of a question mark and a colon, which separate the three operands as shown below:

```
operand1? operand2: operand3
```

Any of the three operands can be just a simple value or an expression in its own right. Therefore you could use the conditional operator to create the following expressions:

```
true? 1: 0
myVariable? 5+5: 5-5
6>7? "it's greater": "it's less"
```

How the operator works is unlikely to immediately be apparent, so let's first look at a simple example where the operands are simple values. Type the following line into the template, and open it with your browser.

```
alert(true? 1: 0);
```

On opening the page, you should see an alert box with the value 1 in it. Now try changing the logical value true in the code to the value false. Save and refresh the page. This time you should see an alert box with the value 0.

What the operator is doing is this: The whole expression evaluates to the second or third operand depending on whether the first is (or evaluates to) true or false. If the first operand evaluates to true, then the whole conditional operator expression evaluates to the second operand. If, however, the first operand evaluates to false, then the whole expression evaluates to the third operand. In the case above, the whole operand evaluates to the value 1 or 0. The resulting value, in this case it is 1, is then taken by the alert function and displayed in an alert box.

The second and third operands can evaluate to any of the five data types, but the first operand will always evaluate to a logical value based on the following rules:

- Numbers are treated as true if they are not equal to 0.
- Strings are treated as true if they are greater than 0 characters in length.
- undefined is treated as false.
- null is treated as false.

Hopefully these rules should be fairly easy to remember. Think of it in these terms: Any number with a value of 0 is not positive, so it won't evaluate as true. In a similar sense, the empty string "" which contains no characters doesn't have any length, so it evaluates to false. The undefined and null values mean that something does not yet contain any useful data, so they also evaluate to false.

Let's now take a look at an example where the first operand is an expression:

```
alert(2<4 ? "The expression was true": "The expression was false");
```

As 2 is less than 4, the conditional operator will evaluate to the string "The expression was true". Try it and see for yourself.

The conditional operator is a very useful shortcut for passing one of two possible values to a variable. For example, let's take a look at an example with the help of the confirm() function. Type out, save, and view the following code from Listing 2.4:

LISTING 2.4 Conditional Operator Demo (`conditionalOp.htm`)

```
<html>
<head>
<title>Conditional Operator Demo</title>

<script language="javascript" type="text/javascript">
<!--

confirmVal = confirm("You will be told which button you click");
alertStr = confirmVal? "You clicked OK": "You clicked Cancel";
alert(alertStr);

//-->
</script>

</head>
<body>

<h1>JavaScript Test Page</h1>

</body>
</html>
```

OUTPUT This should bring up a confirm box followed by an alert. The value of the alert box depends on whether you click OK or Cancel. But how does it work?

ANALYSIS Well, first, the confirm box is displayed. The confirm function will evaluate to true if you click OK, or `false` if you click Cancel. This value is then stored in the variable `confirmVal`. The JavaScript interpreter then proceeds to the second line of code where it first evaluates the first operand of the conditional operator, which is the variable `confirmVal`. If it contains the value `true`, the whole expression evaluates to `"You clicked OK"`, and if it is `false` it evaluates to `"You clicked Cancel"`. The value of either the second or third operand (depending on what you clicked) is then assigned to the variable `alertStr` (before it is alerted by the third line of the script).

Logical Operators

Logical (boolean) values are a very important part of JavaScript. As we saw when we looked at conditional operators, they are the basis of JavaScript decisions. This was further demonstrated by the example of their use with the conditional operator. So far the examples you have seen demonstrated making decisions based on only one condition. There are some times when you want to make a decision based on more than just one condition, or you may want to reverse a condition. To do this JavaScript provides us with the three logical operators shown in Table 2.4.

TABLE 2.4   JavaScript Logical Operators

Operator	Name	Description
!	Logical NOT	Reverses a logical value.
&&	Logical AND	Asks if both of two conditions are true.
||	Logical OR	Asks if one or both of two conditions are true.

Let's look at three examples for each of these operators. Hopefully you will find them fairly easy to grasp. First, let's look at the ! (logical NOT) operator:

```
!false    // evaluates to true
!true     // evaluates to false
!(3<4)    // evaluates to false
```

As you can see, this operator simply reverses the boolean value that would otherwise have been returned. If the value would have been true, the logical NOT operator would have changed the value to false; and if the value would have been false, the logical NOT operator would have changed the value to true.

The following examples will use boolean values for simplicity. This is because the && and || operators actually can have a behavior when used with other data types that need some explanation. (We will look at that later in this chapter.)

For the && (the logical AND) operator:

```
false && false    // evaluates to false
true  && false    // evaluates to false
true  && true     // evaluates to true
```

And for the || (logical OR) operator:

```
false || false    // evaluates to false
true  || false    // evaluates to true
true  || true     // evaluates to true
```

As you can see, if both operands are logical values then logical values of the type you would expect are returned. An expression with the && operator will only evaluate to true if both its operands are true. But an expression using the || operator will evaluate to true even if only one of its operands is true.

However, in a similar way to how the first operand of the conditional operator need not be a logical data type, the logical operators can accept values other than boolean values. The rules are also the same as for the conditional operator. Numbers with the value zero, zero length strings, the null value, and the undefined value all evaluate as false, and everything else evaluates as true.

When we use non-boolean data types with the && and || operators something called *short-circuit evaluation* can cause some unexpected results. You may find yourself at a future time frequently using logical operators with non-boolean operands, so it is good to understand what happens, and why.

"Short-Circuit" Evaluation

The ! operator will always return a logical value no matter what type of data it is used on. However, the && and || operators will return the value of one of their operands—only if this operand happens to actually be a logical value will a logical value be returned. As we'll see, the operand that is returned depends on whether the first operand is equivalent to true (non-zero numbers and strings greater than zero characters in length) or equivalent to false (zero, zero length strings, undefined, and null).

In a logical expression the first operand is evaluated before the second. For certain values of the first operand with some logical operators the second operand does not need to be evaluated to know what the expression will return. For example, if the left-hand operand of the && operator is equivalent to false, it doesn't matter whether the right-hand operand is false or true—the expression will still evaluate to false. Similarly, if we use the || operator and its first operand is equivalent to true, it doesn't matter what the value of the righthand operand is—the expression will always evaluate to true.

This may seem pretty abstract and opaque to you, so let's look in the following examples at how this works in practice.

If, in the following examples, one of the above conditions is met then the first operand is returned, but if it isn't met, then the second operand is returned. Here are some lines of code to illustrate this. Let's look at the && operator first:

```
"water" && "fire"      // returns "fire"
1 && "fire"            // returns "fire"
true && "fire"         // returns "fire"
"" && "fire"           // returns ""
0 && "fire"            // returns 0
false && "fire"        // returns false
null && "fire"         // returns null
undefined && "fire"    // returns undefined
```

Notice that when the first operand is equivalent to true the second operand is returned, but when it is equivalent to false the first operand is returned. The rule is that the last operand to be checked is the one returned. Therefore, when the && operator has to check the second operand, as is the case in the first three examples, then it is the second operand which is returned. However, if the JavaScript interpreter knows that the expression will evaluate to the equivalent of `false` regardless of the value of the second operator, it doesn't even bother checking it. It short-circuits and simply returns the first operand.

Hopefully you have the idea, but let's look at some examples of using the || operator just to make sure:

```
"water" || "fire"      // returns "water"
1 || "fire"            // returns 1
true || "fire"         // returns true
"" || "fire"           // returns "fire"
0 || "fire"            // returns "fire"
false || "fire"        // returns "fire"
null || "fire"         // returns "fire"
undefined || "fire"    // returns "fire"
```

If, as in the first three examples, the first operand of the || operator is equivalent to `true`, then there is no need to evaluate the second. The expression is short-circuited and only the first operand is checked. Therefore, it is the one returned. However, in the other five the first operand is equivalent to `false`. Therefore, the second operand needs to be checked and it is the one returned.

Most of the time these effects won't be of any consequence to your scripts. The operators are usually used in conditional expressions to make decisions. Therefore, the action based on the decision is either taken or it isn't. The one time you may need to know about these effects is if one of your operands has a side effect such as incrementing a variable. If this is the case, then you should be very careful because as we have seen sometimes one of the operands of these expressions is not evaluated and the incrementing of the variable would never take place.

String Operators

There is only one operator for working with strings. It is called the *concatenation operator*. If you aren't familiar with this term, it simply refers to the action of joining something to the end of something else. In the case of the string operator, it enables us to join one string to the end of another to make a longer string. The symbol that is used for the concatenation operator is exactly the same as the one used for the addition operator: it's the plus sign (+).

To concatenate two strings, the operator is just placed between them as you might expect:

```
var concatStr = "string 1 " + "string 2";
alert(concatStr);
```

This code would bring up an alert box with the value `"string 1 string 2"`.

The only way to distinguish the concatenation operator from the addition operator is to examine whether one or both of its operands is a string. If one or both of the operands is a string, then the + sign acts as the concatenation operator, but if neither is a string then it acts as the addition operator. This is important when you have an expression that contains a mixture of numbers, strings, and plus signs. To know which + sign will act as the addition operator and which will act as the concatenation operator, it is important to know that evaluation in JavaScript is generally processed from left to right.

Let's look at some examples to demonstrate this:

```
1 + 2 + "string"   // evaluates to "3string"
1 + "string" + 2   // evaluates to "1string2"
"string" + 1 + 2   // evaluates to "string12"
```

In the first example, the first thing to be evaluated is the 1 + 2. The two numbers are added together. Only then does the result of that addition have the string "string" concatenated to it. In the second example, the number 1 and the string "string" are concatenated by the first expression evaluated. As "string" is a string, they are concatenated to produce the result in the string "1string". Because "1string" is a string, the final operand, 2, also is concatenated to produce another string, "1string2". In the third example, the leftmost operation is evaluated first. As one of the first two operands is a string, the + sign concatenates them. The result of the first operation is a string—so 2 is also concatenated to give the string "string12".

Note that the plus operator also will convert any of the other data types to a string for concatenation if one of the operands is a string. Therefore, in the following examples, since the first operand is a string, the second operand is converted to a string value and concatenated to the first string operand:

```
"Operand 2 = " + 1          // returns "Operand 2 = 1"
"Operand 2 = " + true       // returns "Operand 2 = true"
"Operand 2 = " + null       // returns "Operand 2 = null"
"Operand 2 = " + undefined  // returns "Operand 2 = undefined"
```

Each of the operands that were of the data types other than string—1 which is a number, true which is boolean, and null and undefined—is converted to string values, then concatenated to the string "Operand 2 =".

Assignment Operators

Assignment operators are used to tell the JavaScript interpreter to store a piece of data in a variable or some other data container, hence they "assign" data to something.

You already have come across the simplest JavaScript assignment operator, which is the equal sign. It simply does a straightforward assignment with no additional processes.

Everything to its right is evaluated and assigned to the data container on its left. Hence, as you know to store the number 2002 in a variable called `presentYear`, you would simply write:

```
var presentYear = 2002;
```

Frequently, you will want to add or subtract a number from the number contained within a variable. One way to do this is to recursively assign data to a variable using the variable name:

```
someVar = someVar + 10;
```

You will find yourself frequently using this kind of operation. To save yourself from typing out the variable name twice, as in the above example, JavaScript provides several shortcut assignment operators. These shortcut assignment operators are not only for addition and subtraction, but for many other operations as well.

Shortcut assignment operators require that the variable name isn't written a second time and that the operator in the right-hand expression is moved in front of the equal sign. Hence the shortcut for adding 10 to the variable `someVar` would look like this:

```
someVar += 10;
```

Both methods have exactly the same effect so you can forget about these shortcuts if you find them unintuitive or confusing. However, we would encourage you to get used to using the shortcuts as they can be useful time or space savers in large scripts. Table 2.5 shows the shortcut assignment operators you will most likely use.

TABLE 2.5   JavaScript Shortcut Assignment Operators

Operator	Equivalent To
x += y	x = x + y
x -= y	x = x - y
x *= y	x = x * y
x /= y	x = x / y
x %= y	x = x % y

These shortcut assignment operators usually act on numbers, but if one of the operands of the += operator is a string, it will act as a string operator. In other words, it will concatenate the two operands as if both were strings.

There are also shorthand operators for the bitwise operators that are discussed next, but you are far less likely to use them. They are listed in Table 2.6 for completeness.

TABLE 2.6   Shortcut JavaScript Bitwise Operators

Operator	Equivalent To
x &= y	x = x & y
x ^= y	x = x ^ y
x |= y	x = x | y
x <<= y	x = x << y
x >>= y	x = x >> y
x >>>= y	x = x >>> y

Bitwise Operators

Bitwise operators have been left to last in this chapter because—unless you already use them in another programming language—it is very unlikely that you will make use of them in JavaScript. This is because they take numeric operands (in the form of octal and hexadecimal as well as decimal numbers) and work on them at the binary level. This means that when bitwise expressions are evaluated they convert their operands to binary numbers (1's and 0's) to perform their operation. After they have finished, they then convert the result to a decimal value.

Manipulation of bits is used in such processes as encryption routines and data conversion to other programming languages. In client-side JavaScript, it is most commonly used with a bit of ingenuity to optimize scripts by making them work faster and more efficiently. It can be a very complex topic so if you don't already know of any reason why you really need them then feel free to skip this section.

In JavaScript bitwise operators accept operands as a set of 32 bits (zeros and ones). If one of the operands is larger than 32 bits when converted to binary form, then the additional bits are removed before the calculation proceeds. Of course, you need to make sure that the data you want to manipulate is not among the data that will be discarded.

Bitwise Logical Operators

Conceptually, the bitwise logical operators work as follows: The operands are converted to 32-bit binary integers. Each bit in the first operand is paired with the corresponding bit in the second operand; first bit to first bit, then second bit to second bit, and so on. The operator is applied to each pair of bits in turn, and the result is constructed bitwise.

Table 2.7 summarizes JavaScript's logical bitwise operators.

TABLE 2.7   JavaScript Bitwise Logical Operators

Operator	Name	Description
&	Bitwise AND	Returns 1 for each bit position where the corresponding operand bits are both ones
|	Bitwise OR	Returns 1 for each bit position where either of the corresponding operand bits is one
^	Bitwise XOR	Returns 1 for each bit position where only one of the corresponding operand bits is one
~	Bitwise NOT	Returns its operand bits inverted

For example, the binary representation of nine is 1001, and the binary representation of fifteen is 1111. So, when the bitwise operators are applied to these values, the results are as follows:

```
15 & 9   // evaluates to 9   (1111 & 1001 = 1001)
15 | 9   // evaluates to 15  (1111 | 1001 = 1111)
15 ^ 9   // evaluates to 6   (1111 ^ 1001 = 0110)
```

Or for bitwise NOT:

```
~9       // evaluates to -10
```

Bitwise Shift Operators

The bitwise shift operators take two operands. The first is converted to binary for shifting, and the second specifies the number of bit positions by which the first operand is to be shifted.

The shift operators are listed in Table 2.8.

TABLE 2.8   JavaScript Bitwise Shift Operators

Operator	Name	Description
<<	Left shift	Shifts to the left discarding bits shifted off to the left and moving zero bits in from the right
>>	Sign-propagating right shift	Shifts to the right discarding bits shifted off to the right. Moves in bits from the left with the value of the original left-most bit
>>>	Zero-fill right shift	Shifts to the right discarding bits shifted off to the right and moving zero bits in from the left

Operator Precedence

Until now, we have mostly ignored which parts of expressions that contain several operators are evaluated first. However, once you start to use larger and more complex expressions, it becomes increasingly important to know the order of evaluation. To help us describe this, we will refer to operators as having precedence over each other. The higher the precedence, the sooner it is evaluated. For example, you probably already know that in a sum, multiplication and division are carried out before addition and subtraction. Hence the sum

1 + 2 * 3

results in 7, even though the 1 + 2 came first reading from left to right. This is because multiplication has a higher operator precedence than addition.

Table 2.9 shows the operators from highest precedence to lowest (i.e., from the operators that evaluate first to the operators that evaluate last).

TABLE 2.9   Operator Precedence in JavaScript

Operator(s)	Operator Type(s)
. []	Member
() new	Call / create instance
! ~ - + ++ -- typeof void delete	Negation / increment / special
* / %	Multiply / divide / modulo
+ -	Addition / subtraction
<< >> >>>	Bitwise shift
< <= > >= in instanceof	Relational / special
== != === !==	Equality
&	Bitwise AND
^	Bitwise XOR
|	Bitwise OR
&&	Logical AND
||	Logical OR
?:	Conditional
= += -= *= /= %= <<= >>= >>>= &= ^= |=	assignment
,	comma

Special operators are included in this table, so if you don't recognize some of the operators shown in Table 2.9, don't worry about it. (They haven't been covered yet.)

If you find it difficult to remember even the simpler precedence rules within this table, you can override operator precedence by using parentheses. Hence in the expression

```
1 + 2 * 3
```

if you weren't sure which came first, multiplication or addition, you could use parentheses just to make sure:

```
1 + (2 * 3)
```

Alternatively, parentheses can be used to override operator precedence. For example, if you intended to add 1 and 2 before multiplying by 3, you would write:

```
(1 + 2) * 3
```

As you may have noticed in the table, some operators have the same precedence level. When this is the case the operators are evaluated as normal from left to right. For example

```
13 % 5 * 2
```

will evaluate to 6 because the remainder of 13 divided by 5 is 3, which multiplied by 2 equals 6.

Summary

In this chapter we have covered a lot of ground. We have seen how data can be stored in variables and constants, and how these are subsequently used. In addition, we have covered all the JavaScript operators, with the exception of a few of the special operators. This will enable us to work with data far more effectively in the coming chapters.

Don't be too concerned if you feel we have covered more rules than you can remember. When appropriate, we will remind you as we continue through the book. Gradually, as you work through the examples and exercises, you will pick up the rules for yourself and they will become second nature to you.

Workshop

This workshop asks only a few questions to test whether you are comfortable with the chapter material. Also, this workshop contains two exercises for you to try.

Q&A

Q. When will it be safe to use constants?

A. This varies depending on your audience. It will likely be years before all browsers in common use support them. Therefore it is up to you to decide when the number of visitors to your site using browsers that don't support constants has fallen below an acceptable level. If possible, use site logs to help you make this decision. If you don't have access to site logs, you can try to make an educated guess from the browser statistics published by other sites. In fact, if you create a variable and never change its value, it can function as a constant for your script.

Q. Will I need to use bitwise operators often?

A. Unless you need to carry out binary arithmetic, it is unlikely that you will need to know about the bitwise operators.

Quiz

1. How do you declare a variable called `Temp` and assign to it a value of `5`?
2. How do you declare a constant called `MY_FIVE` that has the numeric value of `5`?
3. Will the following expression evaluate to `true` or `false`?

   `true && true || false`

Quiz Answers

1. You can use the following code to declare the variable `Temp` and assign it a value of `5`:

   `var Temp = 5;`

2. You can declare the constant `MY_FIVE` with a numeric value of `5` using the following code:

   `const MY_FIVE = 5;`

3. The expression

   `true && true || false`

   will evaluate to `true`.

Exercises

1. Create a constant called `MY_CONST` and give it a value of `12` and a variable called `myVariable` and assign it a value of `10`. Alter the value of `myVariable` by adding to the value of `myVariable` the value of `MY_CONST`. Then display the new value of `myVariable` in an alert box.

2. Create two variables `firstVariable` and `secondVariable`. Assign the value of `10` to `firstVariable` and assign the value of `12` to `secondVariable`. Create an alert box that outputs the comparison of the two variables.

DAY **3**

Functions and Statements

This chapter begins by looking at how you can store code by creating your own functions, and how you can control the flow of a script. This will provide the other "half" of the basics you will need to create useful scripts (in addition to what you learned about variables in Chapter 2, "Working with Data"). You will also find out about some of the conveniently built-in pieces of code found in JavaScript.

In this chapter you will learn the following:

- What functions are
- How to create a function
- How to use a function
- About predefined global functions
- What statements are
- Conditional statements
- Loop statements

User Defined Functions

A user-defined function is a function that you create, as opposed to one of the built-in JavaScript functions. JavaScript provides both built-in functions and the tools to create your own. Both have their place, but for the moment, let's concentrate on learning what functions are and how we can build and use our own.

What Is a Function?

Chapter 2 started by looking at how variables and constants can be used to store data until it is needed or it can be used again. Although this is an essential part of programming, to create truly useful scripts you also need to be able to store code (as opposed to data). So far, the code we have worked with runs as soon as the page loads or is reloaded. Frequently, though, you may want to use the same piece of code multiple times or run it some time after the page has loaded in response to a user action. To do this, a function is used. Just as you can think of variables as data containers that can be used to store data, think of functions as code containers used to store pieces of code. Let's take a look at how they work.

Creating a Function

In much the same way as variables are declared with the `var` keyword, functions are declared using the function keyword followed by the name you wish to give to the function. However, when you declare a function you are required to include two additional items: a pair of parentheses and a pair of curly braces, as shown in the example below:

```
function functionName(){}
```

> **Tip**
>
> JavaScript functions are named according to the same rules that are used for naming variables. They can contain alphanumeric characters, the underscore character, and the dollar sign as long as you do not use a JavaScript keyword. The first character cannot be a number. Remember also to give your functions meaningful names.

We will discuss the function of the parentheses shortly, so let's concentrate on the curly braces for now. The curly braces (or "curly brackets" as they are sometimes called) act as code containers. All the code that is to be contained by the function (termed the *function body*) has to be placed between them. Essentially, the curly braces tell the JavaScript interpreter where the function body starts and where it ends. Here is an example of a function with some code:

```
function myFirstFunction(){ alert("I'm in a function!") }
```

As functions usually contain more than a single line of code, it is usual to break the curly braces over more than one line, as shown below:

```
function myFunction(){
    .
  code
    .
}
```

or sometimes the code is written like this:

```
function myFunction()
{
      .
    code
      .
}
```

> **Caution**
>
> Do not put a semi-colon (;) after the parentheses or after the curly braces. This will cause an error.

3

The JavaScript interpreter will treat both methods of code layout the same way. The JavaScript interpreter knows that functions aren't finished until it has reached a closing curly brace so it ignores the extraneous white space. The aim of spreading code across several lines and indenting statements is to make the start and end of your function stand out so that when you scan large sections of code you can immediately pick out function names and where their code begins and ends. Which method you use is up to you.

Let's create a page that contains a function that will greet a visitor by name. Use the template in Listing 1.6 and add to it the function in the following code. After you have created the page, save it, and load it into your browser. See Listing 3.1.

INPUT **LISTING 3.1** Creating a Function (`storedGreeting.htm`)

```
<html>
<head>
<title>Function Demo</title>

<script language="javascript" type="text/javascript">
<!--

function greetVisitor()
{
```

LISTING **3.1**   continued

```
            var myName = prompt("Please enter your name.", "");
            alert("Welcome " + myName + "!")'

}

//-->
</script>



</head>
<body>

<h1>Function Demo</h1>

</body>
</html>
```

ANALYSIS   As you will see, the page loads without an error but the JavaScript contained within the function body doesn't run. Hopefully this was what you expected. Remember, functions store code—we have yet to learn how to evaluate the code.

Using Functions

To evaluate the function's code (or as we are going to refer to it from now on, "to call the function"), we need to write out something termed a function call. To do this, simply write the function's name followed by opening and closing parentheses. The parentheses tell the JavaScript interpreter to call the function immediately and to run its code before it does anything else. Therefore to call the function in your page, simply write the following line under the function declaration:

```
greetVisitor();
```

If you load your page with these changes, the function should be called, and you then will be prompted for your name and greeted.

Caution   As with the var keyword for variables, the function keyword is only used one time—the first time you declare a function. It is not used when you call it.

Function calls can be placed anywhere in a script block (and can be placed in event handlers, as you will learn later in the book). For the moment, though, to call our functions, we are going to use the ability of anchor tags to execute JavaScript using their href attribute. To do this, simply write "javascript" followed by a colon and a JavaScript statement between the href's quote marks. To see this at work, add the following line to the body of an HTML document and click on the hyperlink it produces.

```
<a href="javascript:alert('You clicked on the link!')">Click Here!</a>
```

This can be used to call functions simply by replacing the alert function with a function call to one of your own functions.

Go back to your page for greeting a visitor and add a hyperlink that calls the function as shown in Listing 3.2. Resave the page, and then open it with your browser.

INPUT **LISTING 3.2** Creating a Function (storedGreeting2.htm)

```
<html>
<head>
<title>Calling a Function</title>

<script language="javascript" type="text/javascript">
<!--

function greetVisitor()
{
    var myName = prompt("Please enter your name.", "");
    alert("Welcome " + myName + "!");
}

//-->
</script>

</head>
<body>

<h1>Please click below and enter your name when prompted.</h1>

<p><a href="javascript:greetVisitor()">Click for a greeting</a></p>

</body>
</html>
```

As you will see, the page loads without the alert box displaying. Now try clicking on the hyperlink. This will call the function, and the prompt for your name should appear as shown in Figure 3.1.

OUTPUT

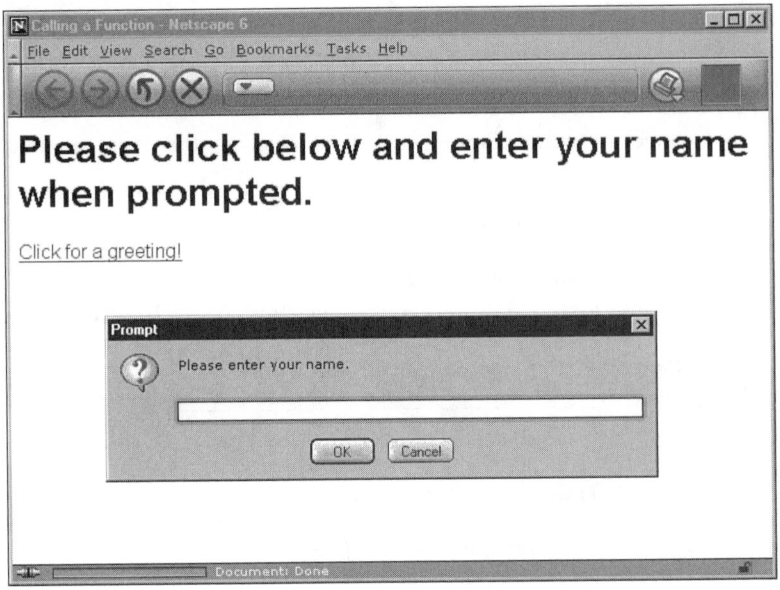

FIGURE 3.1

*A prompt box
requests your name.*

Fill in your name and an alert box will appear to greet you. You will see later in the chapter how to handle situations when someone may not fill in the prompt or they may click Cancel.

Hopefully you now see how simple functions are created and used, and you understand why they are so essential. Without functions JavaScript couldn't do anything after the page had loaded. With them, you can create countless interactive or useful enhancements.

Sending Data to Functions

Frequently, when creating a function you will want to give it some data on which to work. This allows you to perform the same process repeatedly on different sets of data. The process of sending data to a function is termed *passing* data to a function, which means that the data to be passed is written into the parentheses of the function call. For example, to send the numeric value 10 to a function called squareNum() you would write:

```
squareNum(10);
```

Sometimes you will need to extend this process so that more than one piece of data can be passed to a function. This can be accomplished by placing each piece of data to be passed to the function within the parentheses, and separating each of them with a comma. For example, if you wanted to send two different strings followed by the number 3 and the Boolean value true to a function called processThis(), you would write:

```
processThis("1st string", "2nd string", 3, true);
```

As you will see later, the order in which these pieces of data are written between the parentheses is important to the correct functioning of a function.

All these pieces of data that are sent to a function for use in the code that the function contains are known as *arguments* (or parameters) of the function. Now that you can pass arguments to a function, let's see how you can use them in the function body.

Using Arguments

There are two ways of grabbing the arguments that are passed to functions. For the moment, we will deal with the simpler and more popular of the two.

The usual method of accessing arguments is to write names into the parentheses of the function declaration that correspond to the arguments written into the function call. For example, say you have a function called numOddOrEven() that calculates whether the single numeric argument that is passed to it is odd or even. To call the function and send it the number 9, you would write the following:

```
numOddOrEven(9);
```

To use this number in the function, a name must have been written in the parentheses when the function was defined. For example, if the name theNum was used, it might look like this:

```
function numOddOrEven(theNum)
{
    numType = (theNum % 2)? "odd": "even";
    alert("The number " +theNum+ " is an " +numType+ " number.");
}
```

For the moment, you don't need to worry about how the function works. The important thing to note is the way that theNum is used repeatedly throughout the function block. Effectively, the name (or names) contained within the parentheses acts exactly like a variable. Wherever it is used in the function body, the theNum is replaced by the data that was sent to the function as an argument (in this case the number 9).

The method of separating arguments with commas is also used to separate the argument names in the function declaration's parentheses. To use two arguments in the function, you would declare it as shown below:

INPUT

```
function numsOddOrEven(num1, num2)
{
    numType1 = (num1 % 2)? "odd": "even";
    numType2 = (num2 % 2)? "odd": "even";
    alert("The number " +num1+ " is an " +numType1+ " number.");
    alert("The number " +num2+ " is an " +numType2+ " number.");
}
```

To call this function and send it the numbers 5 and 10, you would write the function call as shown below:

```
numsOddOrEven(5, 10);
```

This would result in the two alert boxes shown in Figures 3.2 and 3.3.

OUTPUT

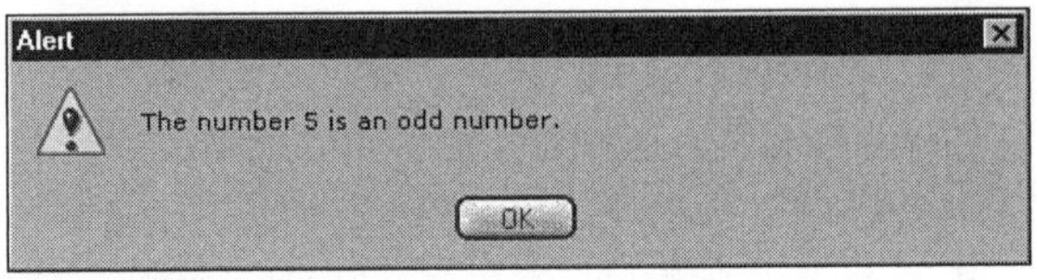

FIGURE 3.2

Alert showing the type of the first argument passed to the numsOddOrEven() *function.*

The number 5 is an odd number.

OK

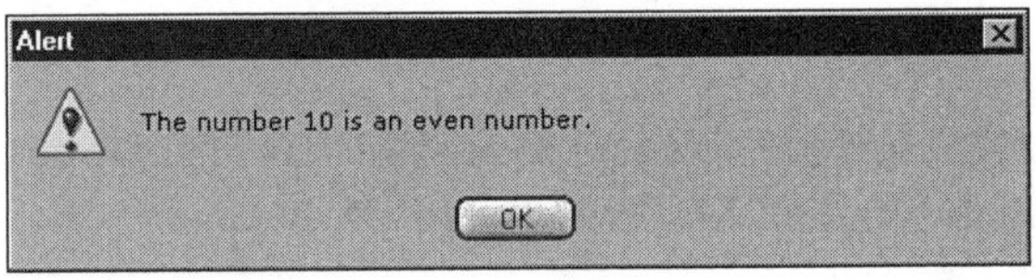

FIGURE 3.3

Alert showing the type of the second argument passed to the numsOddOrEven() *function.*

The number 10 is an even number.

OK

ANALYSIS Note the order in which the alert boxes appear. The argument name num1, which comes first in the parentheses of the function declaration, takes the value 5, which was given first in the function call. Likewise num2, which came second in the function declaration, takes the value 10, which came second in the function call.

Caution

Always be careful to provide data in the correct order. If you confuse the order in which you provide the arguments to a function, you will likely get an unexpected result or an error.

Another thing to note is that if you have declared your function with argument names in the parentheses, you do not necessarily have to send them data with the function call. If arguments aren't sent, then the argument names will simply have the value undefined. For example, try calling the following function both with and without an argument:

INPUT

```
function checkForArg(myArg)
{
     var msg  = "The function argument was "; // Start message
     // Add ending based on whether an argument has been sent
         msg += myArg? myArg: "not sent!";
     alert(msg);
}
checkForArg();
```

OUTPUT The conditional operator concatenates the argument passed to the function to the variable msg, if an argument has been passed to the function. If no argument has been passed to the function, then the string "not sent!" is concatenated to the msg variable.

ANALYSIS This feature can be useful if for some reason you want to code your function so it does not rely on being sent arguments. But that would be an unusual situation.

3

Caution

> Be careful about passing the correct number of arguments to a function, since most of your functions will only operate correctly if the correct number of parameters is passed to the function. With no parameters or an incorrect number passed to the function an unexpected result or an error may occur.

Returning Data from a Function

Very often you will want functions to give back data after they have processed the data that was sent to them. To do this we use the return statement. Take a look at this example before we walk through it:

INPUT

```
function getModulus(theNum)
{
     var theModulus = (theNum>=0)? theNum: -theNum;
     return theModulus;
}

var myNum = -12;
    myNum = getModulus(myNum);
alert(myNum);
```

Notice that the function call is on the right-hand side of an assignment to a variable called myNum, and that the function is sent the original value of myNum as an argument. The first line of the function processes the number to find its modulus (the number 12) prior to storing it in the variable theModulus.

> **Note**
>
> The modulus of a number is the same as the number if the number is greater than zero. If the number is less than zero, then its modulus is the negation of the number—that is, the modulus of -5 is 5. The modulus is sometimes referred to as the absolute value of the number.

It is the next line that is really of interest here. It uses the `return` keyword to return the value of the variable `theModulus` to the point in the code where the function call is situated. In this case, the function call was to the right of the = assignment operator. Therefore the value 12 is assigned to the variable `myNum` replacing its original value of -12. This is shown when the alert box displays `myNum`'s value (see Figure 3.4).

OUTPUT

FIGURE 3.4

An alert showing the value of `myNum`, *which is the value returned by the* `getModulus ()` *function.*

ANALYSIS The `return` statement does indeed return data from the function to wherever the function call was located. However, there is another characteristic of the `return` statement that the above example doesn't clearly demonstrate. When the `return` statement is evaluated it stops any further evaluation of the function body. Enter the following into the template from Listing 1.6 and try it out:

INPUT
```
function returnTest()
{
    alert("This will alert.");
    return;
    alert("This won't alert.");
    alert("Neither will this.");
    alert("Or this.");
}
returnTest();
```

OUTPUT In this example, the first alert would be the only one to be evaluated, and therefore displayed, because the `return` statement stops the function from continuing to the end of the function body.

ANALYSIS A `return` statement can have two effects. When a `return` keyword is encountered it always stops a function from further evaluation. If provided with some data, the `return` statement will return the data to the place in the code where the function call is situated. If the `return` statement is not provided with data, it will simply return `undefined`—just as a function without a return statement would.

Variable Scope

As promised in Chapter 2, let's now look more closely at the differences that including or omitting the `var` keyword during declaration of a variable would make on the variables in your JavaScript code. The reason for putting this examination off until now is because it is in functions that your choice of including or omitting the `var` keyword has the most significant effect.

Before we go on to find out more about the scope of a function, let's first take a look at the meaning of the word scope.

3

NEW TERM The word *scope* refers to the limits inside which something is applicable. For example, in the United States there are two types of law: federal law and state law. State law is only applicable in individual states and therefore due to its geographical limitation, it might be referred to as having "local" scope. Federal law, on the other hand, isn't limited by state boundaries. It governs the whole country, so it might be said that, as far as the United States is concerned, it has "global" scope.

The idea of local and global scopes also exists for JavaScript variables. When a variable is termed a global variable it means that it can be accessed and used by any part of any of the scripts in the same HTML document. In addition, you also can use global variables in scripts that are in a different frame or browser window (although we haven't covered that yet). All variables declared in the script block, but outside of functions, have global scope.

Variables defined inside a function are different. Their scope depends on whether you do or do not declare them with the `var` keyword. If a variable is declared within a function without the `var` keyword, then its scope is global. If a variable is declared within a function using the `var` keyword, then its scope is local.

The problem with creating global variables from inside a function may not be immediately apparent. What tends to happen is that functions use temporary variables that are of use only while the function is evaluating. Outside the function they aren't needed. It is easy in a long piece of code to forget some of the global variable names and give one or more of the variables inside a function the same name as a global variable which already exists. If you have not included the `var` keyword when a variable is declared within a function, then the variable is global in scope and the data in the global variable with the same name outside the function is overwritten. This can play havoc with your scripts, and it can be very hard to track down the problem, as error messages that may be generated won't tell you from where the problem stems. The JavaScript interpreter is doing what you told it to do, but it is doing something that you may well not have expected it to do.

Creating local variables enables you to eliminate the possibility that this type of problem will ever arise. If you happen to unintentionally use the same name for a variable in a function and a variable in the main script block, then as long as you used the var keyword an entirely different local variable is created inside the function.

 Note

> Local variables are not only limited to the function in which they were defined, but they also only exist for the time it takes for the function to execute. As soon as the function body has been evaluated, local variables cease to exist and the data they contained is discarded.

Here is an example that will show you the effect of declaring a variable within a function. Run it both with and without the var keyword in front of the variable testVariable in the function.

First, if you run it with the var keyword within the function, the value of the global variable will not be overwritten.

INPUT
```
var testVariable = "Global variable was NOT overwritten!";
function someFunction()
{
      var testVariable = "Global variable WAS overwritten!";
}
someFunction();
alert(testVariable);
```

However, if you run the following code with the var keyword omitted in the declaration of the variable within the function, then the global variable will be overwritten.

INPUT
```
var testVariable = "Global variable was NOT overwritten!";
function someFunction()
{
      testVariable = "Global variable WAS overwritten!";
}
someFunction();
alert(testVariable);
```

In summary, unless you specifically want the function to change the value of a global variable you should always declare variables inside of functions with the var keyword.

It may seem tedious, but if you get into this good habit of using the var keyword all the time, you will ensure that you don't accidentally overwrite an important global variable in a long complex script.

Caution

If you are using publicly available JavaScript code written by someone else with your own code, you need to be particularly careful. The way the other script author uses variables could be similar to your own, and one of your local variables could overwrite one of his global variables, causing problems that could be very difficult to track down.

Predefined Global Functions

3

JavaScript provides many predefined functions. Some of these functions, termed global functions, can be called from any part of a script—just as you can call the functions you have written. However, many predefined functions need to be treated as belonging to objects. This means that they can't be called in the same way that functions have been called so far (as you will learn later in the book). For the moment, let's look at global functions.

Note

JavaScript's predefined functions use native code (binary computer code) so you can call them but the code they contain cannot actually be seen. They are not written in JavaScript in the way that we write functions.

We have already come across and used some predefined functions such as the alert(), confirm(), and prompt() functions which bring up small dialog boxes to enable basic user interaction. These functions have been around for so long that the majority of browsers support them, although they are not actually part of core JavaScript. This means that in an environment other than a Web browser they may or may not be available. For the moment let's concentrate on the core JavaScript functions.

The predefined core JavaScript functions are listed below.

- decodeURI()
- decodeURIComponent()
- encodeURI()
- encodeURIComponent()

- escape()
- unescape()
- eval()
- isFinite()
- isNaN()
- Number()
- parseFloat()
- parseInt()
- toString()
- watch()
- unwatch()

With the exception of watch() and unwatch(), you have already learned enough to be able to make use of all these functions. The watch() and unwatch() functions work with things called "object properties" to help in debugging. (As object properties are quite an advanced topic, and we haven't yet covered objects; those functions will be discussed later in the book.)

All these built-in functions either check or modify data in some way or another. Let's take a look at them now, one by one, and see what they do and how they can make our lives easier.

URI Encoding and Decoding

NEW TERM   *URIs* (Uniform Resource Identifiers) is the most general name for the addresses used to access files on the Web. A "resource" is a unit of information that can be addressed. Not only can URIs be used to specify the address of a Web page, but they also can be used to send it information. You have probably seen Web sites where the address bar contains a question mark and lots of % symbols that are each followed by two numbers or letters. These are query strings used by sites, such as search engines, to send data from you to the server. The reason that much of the data is converted to what is called *hex form*, also called "escaped form"—when a character is converted to a % and the two characters of its hexadecimal value—is that some characters such as the space character can't be carried as they are in a URI.

When a form is used to submit data as a query string using the HTTP GET method, the browser automatically converts the characters that aren't allowed within a URI to their encoded hex values. To do this using JavaScript, you need to use built-in functions.

The original JavaScript functions for encoding and decoding URIs were the `escape()` and `unescape()` functions respectively. Let's look at an example to clarify just what they do:

INPUT

```
var priceRange = "$4 - $6";
var escapedRange = escape(priceRange);
alert(escapedRange);
```

Figure 3.5 shows the output from the code.

OUTPUT

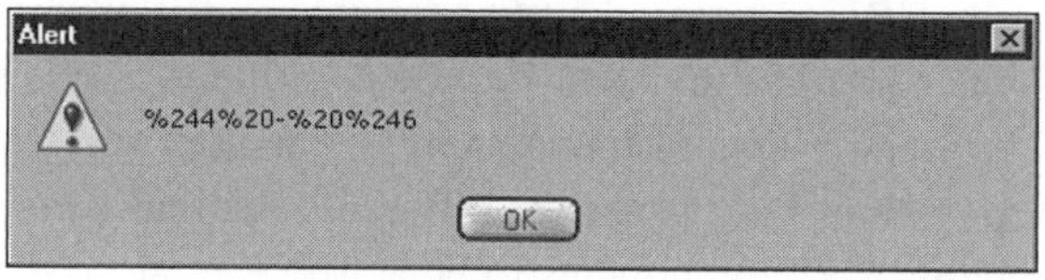

FIGURE 3.5

Contents of the `escapedRange` *variable after the* `escape()` *function has been applied to the* `priceRange` *variable.*

ANALYSIS The `escape()` function has replaced the $ and space characters with their escaped values, which are `%24` and `%20` respectively. The `unescape()` function acts in exactly the opposite way. When applied to the variable `escapedRange` the `unescape()` function will turn it back into text again.

Unfortunately the `escape()` and `unescape()` functions encode characters that do not need to be encoded. They are also slightly inconsistent from browser to browser in which characters they will encode. To remedy this, ECMAScript Edition 3 defined four new functions which are intended to replace the `escape()` and `unescape()` functions. These are the `encodeURI()`, `decodeURI()`, `encodeURIComponent()`, and `decodeURIComponent()` functions.

Caution | `encodeURI()`, `decodeURI()`, `encodeURIComponent()`, and `decodeURIComponent()` are only supported by Netscape 6+ and Internet Explorer 5.5+.

The `encodeURI()` function will encode all characters except for alphanumerical characters and the following characters which it *leaves* intact:

```
! # $ & ' ( ) * + , - . / : ; = ? @ _ ~
```

The encodeURIComponent() function is slightly different. It will encode all the characters that the encodeURI() function encodes but will also encode these characters:

```
# $ & + , / : ; = ? @
```

Therefore, it only leaves alphanumeric and the following characters intact.

```
! ' ( ) * - . _ ~
```

The reason for having two different encoding functions is that sometimes you may want to encode a whole URI including the http:// etc., and at other times you may want to only encode some data to be attached as a query string. Clearly, if you were to encode a complete URI with the encodeURIComponent() function, you would end up encoding the :// part of http:// too. Therefore, two different functions were created: One for thoroughly encoding URI components to be added as a query string; and another function for encoding the address before the query string.

The counterparts of these functions are the decodeURI() and decodeURIComponent() functions. The decodeURIComponent() function is similar to the unescape() function. It will decode all encoded characters. The decodeURI() function on the other hand will leave the following characters encoded:

```
# $ & + , / : ; = ? @
```

Evaluating Strings as Code

The eval() function is unusual in that it takes a string and processes it as code. Clearly, if this is not to cause an error, the string must be recognizable as JavaScript. To demonstrate this, try the code in Listing 3.3.

INPUT   **LISTING 3.3**   eval() Demo (evalDemo.htm)

```html
<html>
<head>
<title>eval() Demo</title>

<script language="javascript" type="text/javascript">
<!--

var myCode = "alert('I was a string!')";

//-->
</script>

</head>
<body>
```

LISTING 3.3 continued

```
<h1>eval() Demo</h1>

</body>
</html>
```

In the single line of JavaScript code, a string is stored in the variable `myCode`. Although you can see it is a piece of JavaScript, JavaScript itself doesn't realize this. As far as it is concerned, it is just a series of characters strung together that it has been asked to store in a variable. Now try adding the following line after the variable declaration:

INPUT   `eval(myCode);`

OUTPUT   The `eval()` function will force the string to be evaluated as JavaScript and the alert box should appear.

For the moment we haven't covered enough to make practical use of the `eval()` function, but take note of it as it comes in very useful as you will see in later chapters.

Arithmetic Functions

Often programming is about manipulating numbers. It is no surprise then that JavaScript has a number of built-in functions designed to complement the arithmetic operators you learned about in Chapter 2.

JavaScript provides functions that check whether a piece of data is a number or what type of number it is, as well as functions which enable the manipulation of the numbers.

Numerical Checks on Data

There are two conditions that commonly cause arithmetic scripts to fail in JavaScript. One is that a number is, or becomes, infinite (or too large for JavaScript to handle, in which case the JavaScript interpreter treats the number as having the value `Infinity`). The other is that one of the pieces of data in an arithmetic operation is not a number. To check for these conditions where they are likely to occur, JavaScript provides two functions: `isFinite()` and `isNaN()`.

Before examining these functions, it should be mentioned that there are three special values which have the data type `number`. These are `Infinity`, `-Infinity`, and `NaN`. `Infinity` and `-Infinity` represent, respectively, positive and negative numbers that have become too large for the JavaScript interpreter to handle or are genuinely infinite. They aren't of much practical use in an operation except to indicate that a number is too large for the JavaScript interpreter to reliably process. The other special value NaN, which stands for "**Not a** Number," indicates that an arithmetic operation could not be carried out:

```
alert("a" - 10);  //alerts NaN
```

As you already may have guessed, the isFinite() function checks to make sure that a number is not one of the special values Infinity or -Infinity. If the number is finite and calculations can be carried out, then the function returns true, otherwise false.

It is rare that numbers to be entered directly into JavaScript are too big for it to process. It usually occurs when numbers are raised to excessive powers or divided by zero or a number very close to zero. Special care must be taken when accepting user input that might be used in these ways.

The isNaN() function is a little more tricky. It checks that a value is *not* a number. This allows us to check for numbers without checking for all of the other four data types in turn. Unfortunately, the function can cause some confusion at first because it returns false if a value is a number and true otherwise (after all it is checking that a value is not a number). See for example, the following:

```
alert(isNaN("a"));  // alerts true
alert(isNaN(2));    // alerts false
```

If you really want it to return true for numbers, the logical NOT operator can be placed in front of the function thereby reversing the result.

Caution

Rather surprisingly NaN does not even evaluate as being equivalent to itself. Therefore:

```
NaN == NaN    // evaluates to false
NaN === NaN   // evaluates to false
```

To check for the value NaN, you must use the function isNaN():

```
isNaN(NaN)    // evaluates to true
```

The isNaN() function is especially useful when you collect numerical data from a visitor who is viewing your Web page. If the user enters non-numerical data either accidentally or intentionally then, without some appropriate error checking, your script will fail. It is always a good idea to use the isNaN() function to check any data you collect when you process it in any scripts. Let's look at Listing 3.4, where the getModulus() function we wrote earlier is improved:

LISTING 3.4   Safely Finding the Modulus (`getModulus.htm`)

```
<html>
<head>
<title>Finding the Modulus</title>

<script language="javascript" type="text/javascript">
<!--

function getModulus()
{
    var theNum = prompt("Please enter a number", "");
    var theModulus = (theNum>=0)? theNum: -theNum;
    var msg = (isNaN(theModulus))? "Numbers only please.":
                "The modulus of " + theNum + " is " + theModulus;
    alert(msg);
}

//-->
</script>

</head>
<body>

<h1>Finding the Modulus</h1>

<a href="javascript:getModulus()">Get Modulus</a>

</body>
</html>
```

ANALYSIS   When the link is clicked the function `getModulus()` is called. It prompts the user for a number and stores the input in the variable called `theNum`. The conditional operator is used on the following line to try to find the modulus (or absolute value) of the input. If this input is not numeric, then the result will be the value `NaN`. On the next line, the conditional operator is used again. This time the condition is the result from the function `isNaN()`.

If the result of finding the modulus was `NaN`, then the `isNaN()` function will return true and the conditional operator will evaluate to its second operand which is the string `"Numbers only please."`. Note that the end of this line is a colon and not a semicolon. A new line for the third operand was started because it is quite long. If the result of the function was false, then the conditional operator will evaluate to its third operand, which is an expression. This expression combines the values of `theNum` and `theModulus`. It generates a string that tells the user, in a user-friendly way, the modulus of the number that was entered. Whichever operand the conditional operator evaluates to is assigned to the variable called `msg`. This message is then alerted to the user using the code on the final line of the function body.

The `isNaN()` function enabled you to output a result that has some intelligence to the user. In combination with the powerful control statements that you will learn about later in the chapter, the `isNaN()` function can be a very useful tool. Try to get used to using the function to check the data you collect with HTML forms or prompt boxes when this data should be numerical. It will help you make more professional scripts and allow you to avoid a significant number of potential errors.

Conversion Between `String` and `Number`

There are good reasons for converting strings to numbers and vice versa. For example, numbers collected from user input are always in the form of a string. Most times if you perform an arithmetic operation with this data it will automatically be converted to the `number` data type, but sometimes it is necessary to do it manually. Most notably is when you wish to add two numbers that are stored as strings. If you try to do this without converting their data types, then the two strings will simply be concatenated.

Conversely, in other settings, if you do want to concatenate two numbers which are of the data type `number`, you will need to convert their data type to `string` first. If you don't, they will simply be added.

The `Number()` and `parseFloat()` functions both take a single argument (or *parameter* if you prefer) and treat it in a very similar way. If the argument is a number they will return it unaltered, but if it is a string they will convert its data type to `number` (if possible) so that it can be used in arithmetic operations. They also both leave the number's floating point intact (unless all the digits are zeros in which case they are removed). They differ in two respects: how they treat other data types, and how they treat strings starting with numerical characters followed by non-numeric characters.

The `parseFloat()` function will always evaluate to `NaN` if used on a data type other than `number` or on a string, except when it contains only arithmetic characters. The `Number()` function, on the other hand, is a bit more flexible about the data with which it will work. As you might expect, it will convert `false` and `null` to `0`, `true` to `1`, and only `undefined` will be converted to `NaN`. Most of the time your choice of either of these two functions won't make a difference, but sometimes you may need one effect rather than the other—depending on how you want the function to treat non-numeric or string data. As you progress through the book and learn more, you will become better equipped to make that decision.

If a string starts with numbers and they are followed by other characters, the `Number()` function will realize it is not a number and return the value `NaN`. The `parseFloat()` function, on the other hand, exhibits a special behavior. It removes the non-numeric characters from the end of the numbers and returns the numeric characters as a number. For example, the following code shows how the `Number()` and `parseFloat()` functions handle strings passed to them as arguments:

```
Number("1.12 is a number");      // returns NaN
parseFloat("1.12 is a number");  // returns 1.12
```

Sometimes you may want to round off a number to get rid of its fractional part. The `parseInt()` function allows you to do exactly that. It converts a value's data type to number and rounds it down to an integer in a single step. Here is an example:

```
parseInt("2.1");       // returns 2
parseInt("2.5");       // returns 2
parseInt("2.99999");   // returns 2
```

This is useful, but the `parseInt()` function also has another less well known ability. It can convert numbers with a base between 2 and 36 to a decimal number (base 10). It does this by taking the number as its first argument, and then it allows you to specify the number's base as a second argument. The values can be either the `string` or `number` data type. For example, see the following:

```
parseInt("1111", 2); // returns 15
```

In this case, the number is the value `"1111"`, and the base was specified as 2, which is binary. Therefore the first argument is converted from binary to its decimal equivalent, which is 15. Here are another few examples:

```
parseInt(20, 16);  // returns 32
parseInt("10", 8); // returns 8
parseInt("30", 4); // returns 12
```

Note that `parseInt()` still rounds down numbers before conversion:

```
parseInt("1111.1111", 2); // still returns 15
parseInt("ff.ffff", 16); // returns 255
```

> **Caution**
>
> The value you give to `parseInt()` must be a string if it is above base 10. This is because numbers above base 10 may include alphabetical characters.

If numerical data is collected from a user and the numbers after the decimal point are not required, it is a good idea to use the `parseInt()` function and specify the number's base as 10. This will prevent it being interpreted as an octal number if the user began the number with a 0. The parseInt() function behaves in the same way as the parseFloat() function if a string starts with a number but continues with other characters; it will return only the number.

The final function for string-number conversion is the toString() function. It behaves exactly opposite of the Number(), parseFloat(), and parseInt() functions. Instead of converting strings containing numeric characters to numbers, it converts numbers to strings. If you want to add one set of digits to another without them being summed, it can be done with this function.

The syntax for the toString() function is different from that used for the Number(), parseFloat(), and parseInt() functions. Instead of taking a value as an argument typed into its parentheses, it uses something called the dot notation. In this case, the value must be stored in a data container such as a variable. The variable is then joined to the function call with a dot. Here is an example:

```
var myVar = 2;
myVar.toString();  // returns the string "2"
```

The dot tells the JavaScript interpreter to apply the toString() function to the contents of the variable myVar, which causes its data type to be changed to the data type string. You will learn more about dot notation as it applies to objects and their functions (methods) later. Let's have a look at the effect this has on a few examples:

INPUT
```
var num1 = 12;
var num2 = 34;
alert(num1 + num2);
alert(num1 + num2.toString());
alert(num1.toString() + num2);
```

As you would expect, the expression on the third line sums the contents of the two variables num1 and num2. The toString() function causes the next two expressions to behave very differently though. Both functions would display the following alert box (see Figure 3.6).

OUTPUT

FIGURE 3.6

After the toString() *function is applied the numbers concatenate!*

ANALYSIS The toString() function has caused the operands of the + operator to concatenate rather than sum. Remember that in Chapter 2 you learned that if one of the operands of the + sign is a string, then it concatenates the two operands regardless of the data type of the other. Therefore there is no need to apply the toString() function to both operands. Applying it to one of them is enough.

It is probably the last thing you would expect, but the toString() function is also able to convert numbers between bases. It does exactly the opposite of the action taken by the parseInt() function. The difference is that rather than converting a number from a base between 2 and 36 to a decimal value, the toString() function takes decimal numbers and converts them to a base between 2 and 36. Of course JavaScript only outputs numbers as decimal values so the "numbers" the toString() function returns aren't of the data type number, but rather of the data type string. However, as they look like numbers to all intents and purposes, this doesn't usually matter.

To use toString() in this way, you simply give it the base you want to convert to as an argument:

INPUT
```
var y = 10;
y.toString(8);    // returns 12 (10 decimal expressed to base 8)
var x = 0.5;
x.toString(16);   // returns 0.8 (0.5 decimal expressed to base 16)
```

Note that as JavaScript accepts numbers in octal, decimal, or hexadecimal format, the toString() function converts from octal and hexadecimal numbers to the base you chose as well as from decimal.

By combining the parseInt() and toString() functions, it is possible to convert a number from any base between 2 and 36, to any other base between 2 and 36. As shown below, this can be written into a function so it can be used multiple times on the same page. Just remember that because the parseInt() function removes floating points the function won't be accurate with non-integers:

INPUT
```
function convertNum(theNum, fromBase, toBase)
{
    var numBase10 = parseInt(theNum, fromBase);
    alert(numBase10.toString(toBase));
}

convertNum(1100, 2, 16);
```

ANALYSIS In this example, the first line takes the 1100 from the argument theNum, and the argument fromBase specifies it as binary. The parseInt() function then converts it to decimal before it is stored in the variable numBase10. On the second line, the decimal value is converted using the argument toBase to specify the base as hexadecimal.

This then alerts the value c, which is the hexadecimal equivalent of the binary value 1100. Note that the alert could just as easily be replaced with a return keyword for more practical use.

What Is a Statement?

NEW TERM All JavaScript scripts are essentially a series of commands that are passed to the interpreter to be carried out sequentially. JavaScript usually requires that each one be placed on a separate line. So far, we have been referring to these lines simply as lines of code. It is more accurate to call them *statements*.

Already, you have come across several statements. For example, the method for adding comments into your code, which you learned in Chapter 1, uses the comment statements /* and */ or //. The // characters instruct the JavaScript interpreter to ignore all characters until the end of the line of code. Other examples include the following keywords: var, const, and function, which tell the interpreter to create a variable, constant, and function respectively. These are all statements.

It is important to realize that although the words "expression" and "statement" can occasionally be used interchangeably, there is a difference between the two. As you have seen, expressions use operators to manipulate data before they evaluate to a single value (with the possible exception of the assignment expressions that also assigns its value). This is great and an essential part of a programming or scripting language, but expressions can't do anything productive by themselves. Statements are the commands that decide what is done with the data that expressions return and, as you will see shortly, what is done with other statements. Expressions, on the other hand, are usually only a part of a statement, as shown in the example:

```
const MY_CONST = 72/9;
```

The 72/9 is a sub-expression of the assignment expression, which assigns the outcome of dividing 72 by 9 (the value 8) to the constant MY_CONST. However, the line, as a whole, is considered to be a const statement. It is the const keyword that causes the constant to be created, thereby doing something useful with the data that the expression to its right evaluates to.

Usually statements end with a line break, but if two statements are placed on the same line a semicolon must be used to separate each one. The semicolon tells the JavaScript interpreter that it has reached the end of a statement and should finish processing the code in front of the semicolon before it proceeds. In any case, it is helpful for the readability of your code to put no more than one statement on a line.

Let's study the type of statement that controls other statements.

Control Statements

Control statements are designed to allow you to create scripts that can decide which lines of code are evaluated, or how many times to evaluate them. There are two different types of control statements: *conditional* statements and *loop* statements.

Control statements make their decisions based on an expression that evaluates to the logical values `true` or `false` or their equivalents in other data types. As we will be using non-boolean data types extensively for the remainder of the chapter, here is a reminder of how the other data types are treated in logical conditions:

- Numbers are treated as `true` if not equal to 0, otherwise they are treated as `false`
- Strings are treated as `true` if greater than 0 characters in length, otherwise they are treated as `false`
- `undefined` is treated as `false`
- `null` is treated as `false`

Conditional Statements

NEW TERM *Conditional statements* are used to make decisions. In real life, we make all sorts of decisions based on criteria such as "am I being offered enough money to take this job?" If the answer is "yes," then the result is "take the job." If the answer is "no," then "don't take the job." In JavaScript, you need to make decisions about which sections of code to evaluate. For example, if you asked a user for input so you could perform a calculation, you will want to carry out the calculation if the input is numeric, but not if it isn't.

You already have come across a simple means of making a decision in the form of the conditional operator, `?:`. The conditional operator checks to determine if a condition is true or false, and uses the result to decide whether to evaluate to its second or third operand. Although this is a quick method of assigning one of two values to a variable, it is also very limited. If you want to choose between more than two options, the conditional operator is inadequate to do what you want.

The `if`, `else`, and `else if` Statements

NEW TERM The `if`, `else`, and `else if` statements allow you to make a choice among several options. First let's look at how to use the `if` statement to make a choice between two alternatives.

The if statement is the most frequently used decision-making statement. It checks a condition and if it evaluates to true, then the statement(s) that it governs are evaluated, but if it evaluates to false then the statement(s) are passed over. The syntax is as follows:

```
if (condition) statement
```

or

```
if (condition)
    statement
```

The condition is always surrounded by parentheses but the statement it governs can be on the same line or the following line. The JavaScript interpreter always associates the if statement with whatever statement follows it. Both code layouts work but some people prefer using separate lines because it makes their if statements easier to read. Here is an example that uses two if statements so you can get a feel for how the if statement works:

INPUT

```
var myVar1 = true;
var myVar2 = false;
if (myVar1 == true) alert("myVar1 is true");
if (myVar2 == true) alert("myVar2 is true");
```

This will display only one alert box. The final line in the code will not cause an alert box to be displayed because the variable myVar2 has the value of false. See Figure 3.7.

OUTPUT

FIGURE 3.7

The first if statement evaluates to true so the first alert box displays.

Remember that the comparison operator, ==, checks to see if the operands to its right and left are equal. If they are equal it returns true, and if they are not equal it returns false. In the above example, the condition for the first if statement evaluates to true because the value of myVar1 is true. The condition for the second statement evaluates to false because myVar2 does not equal true. As you can see, the if statement makes the decision as to whether the alert() function is called based on the evaluation of the condition.

NEW TERM Frequently, you will want the `if` statement (and the other conditional statements for that matter) to govern more than just one other statement. To do this, you need to use what is known as a *statement block*. The statement block consists of a pair of curly braces that surround the `if` statement's statements in the same way that curly braces surround the statements in the function body. For example:

```
if (condition) {
   statement1
   statement2
   ...
   statementN
}
```

Hopefully this feels familiar. If the condition in parentheses evaluates to `true`, then the statements within the curly braces are evaluated. If the condition in parentheses evaluates to `false`, then none of those statements is evaluated.

3

Tip It is useful to use curly braces even when the `if` statement has only one statement associated with it. Then if you later need to add other statements, you won't encounter errors caused by forgetting to add the curly braces.

Remember that conditional statements allow you to take one action if a condition is true and another if it isn't. This is where the `else` statement comes in. By placing the `else` statement after the `if` statement, it is linked to the `if` statement so that the statement(s) it governs is evaluated if the condition in the parentheses of the `if` statement turns out to be false. This saves writing out the condition again. In this way, either the statements the `if` statement governs will be evaluated, or the statements the `else` statement governs will be evaluated. After all a condition in JavaScript can only evaluate to `true` or `false`. Here are a couple of examples to demonstrate how you would write this:

INPUT
```
if (4 < 3)
   alert("4 is less than 3");
else
   alert("4 is greater than 3");
```

ANALYSIS Since 4 is greater than 3, the alert after the `if` statement is ignored; therefore, the `alert()` function after the `else` statement is evaluated. The `else` statement can also be used with a function block so you could write:

INPUT
```
if (4 < 3) {
  alert("The if statement's statement block was evaluated");
  alert("because 4 is less than 3");
}
else {
  alert("The else statement's statement block was evaluated")
  alert("because 4 is greater than 3")
}
```

Finally, when you need even more flexibility to check multiple conditions there is the `else if` statement. It is inserted between the `if` and `else` statements. Here's an example:

INPUT
```
var promptVal = prompt("Please enter a number", "");

if (promptVal > 0)
  alert("The number you entered was positive");
else if (promptVal == 0)
  alert("The number you entered was zero");
else
  alert("The number you entered was negative");
```

ANALYSIS In this example, the script accepts an inputted number and uses it along with the `if ... else if ... else` statements to choose among three possible alerts to evaluate. Note that only one of the control statements will be used. If the `if` statement's condition evaluates to `true`, then the `else if` statement and the `else` statement will be ignored. If the `if` statement evaluates to `false`, then the condition of the `else if` statement is checked. Likewise if the condition of the `else if` statement evaluated to `true`, then the `else` statement would be ignored. The `else` statement acts as the default if all the previous conditions evaluated to `false`. Sometimes you will not want anything to happen if none of your conditions evaluates to `true`, in which case you would not use an `else` statement.

Multiple `else if` statements can be placed between the `if` statement and `else` statement if you want to check for more than three conditions.

If you remember the discussion about the `isNaN()` function earlier, you may have realized that there is a problem with the example above—it doesn't allow for the fact that the user may enter a non-numeric value. To accommodate this situation, you would want to move the condition checking for a number greater than 0 to an `else if` statement and use the `if` statement to first check if the value entered is numeric. To do this you would use the `isNaN()`. Here's an example:

INPUT
```
var promptVal = prompt("Please enter a number", "");

if (isNaN(promptVal))
  alert("That wasn't a number!");
else if (promptVal > 0)
```

```
        alert("The number you entered was positive");
    else if (promptVal == 0)
        alert("The number you entered was zero");
    else
        alert("The number you entered was negative");
```

Note that statement blocks also can be used with the `else if` statement to control more than just one statement, such as the alerts in the earlier example.

Let's look next at an alternative control statement, the `switch` statement, that could have been used instead of the `if...else` statements in the above example.

The `switch` Statement

The `switch` statement allows you to choose one of several options. It has functionality which resembles that provided by the `if`, `else if`, and `else` statements. Let's look at how the `switch` statement works.

The `switch` statement has markedly different syntax from the `if...else` statements, but it works in a similar way. Its structure is shown below. Note that the lines that begin with `case` must end in a colon.

INPUT
```
switch (expression){
    case value:
        statements
    case value:
        statements
    case value:
        statements
}
```

Note

Case values in JavaScript do not need to be constants or the same data type.

The first thing a `switch` statement does is evaluate the expression contained within its parentheses to a single value. It then works its way down through the case statements checking if the value returned by the expression in parentheses after the switch keyword is matched by any of the values that follow the `case` keywords. If it finds a match, then it evaluates all the following statements that belong to that case statement.

Try the example in Listing 3.5, and see for yourself.

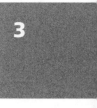

LISTING 3.5 Switch Statement Demo (switchDemo.htm)

```
<html>
<head>
<title>Switch Statement Demo</title>

<script language="javascript" type="text/javascript">
<!--

switch (1+1){
  case "a":
    alert(1);
  case 2:
    alert(2);
  case true:
    alert(3);
}

//-->
</script>

</head>
<body>

<h1>Switch Statement Demo</h1>

</body>
</html>
```

This page will result in the alert boxes shown in Figure 3.8.

OUTPUT

FIGURE 3.8

Two alert boxes are brought up because the second and third case statements each evaluate as true.

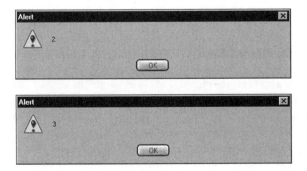

ANALYSIS This is because the 1+1 evaluates to 2. Therefore it should come as no surprise that the first case, the string "a", does not cause the associated alert() function to be evaluated. But the next case is the number 2, which is a match. As you can see from the screenshots in Figure 3.8, this causes not only the alert containing the number 2 to be evaluated, but, perhaps surprisingly, the alert containing the number 3 is also displayed. However, this may come as no surprise. We did say that if a match was found *all* the following statements would be evaluated up to the closing curly brace of the switch statement. Although this feature can occasionally be of use, generally you will want to evaluate only the statements between the matching case and the following one. To do this, you need to use the break statement. Replace the switch statement in Listing 3.5 with the following code:

INPUT

```
switch (1+1){
  case "a":
    alert(1);
    break;
  case 2:
    alert(2);
    break;
  case 3:
    alert(3);
    break;
}
```

Note

> The statements following each case are not enclosed in curly braces as in a statement block even if there are lots of them on multiple lines. Therefore, it is helpful to lay out your code as shown in the example above, to help you or someone else decipher your code.

ANALYSIS As you will see, using the break statement as the last statement in a case statement block breaks off evaluation of the switch statement, and execution of the script continues after the closing curly brace of the switch statement. This has the desired effect of preventing the statements belonging to the other case statements from being evaluated.

The switch statement is able, optionally, to run some code in the event that there are no matches—just as a concluding else statement works at the end of an if...else statement. To do this, you would include, following the case statements, the keyword default followed by a colon, as shown in the example below:

INPUT

```
switch ("Match this string."){
  case "This doesn't match.":
    alert("This would have alerted if it had!");
    break;
  case "Nor does this.":
    alert("This would have alerted if it had!");
    break;
```

```
        case "Or this.":
          alert("This would have alerted if it had!");
          break;
        default:
          alert("None of the cases matched so the default evaluated.");
          break;
      }
```

As none of the cases above are the string `"Match this string"`, their statements are ignored and the statements under the default are evaluated. See Figure 3.9.

OUTPUT

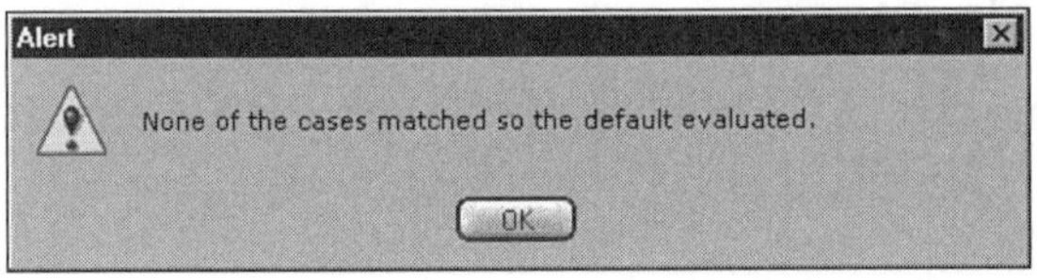

FIGURE 3.9

The default *statement is evaluated when none of the case statements match.*

ANALYSIS So which should be used: the `if...else` statement or the `switch` statement? The answer is that often either will do. The `switch` statement checks for a match to a single expression, and therefore is useful when you need to evaluate different statements based on the value of a single variable. It is also more efficient, so try to become accustomed to using it when possible. The `if...else` statement, on the other hand, can be given a new condition to check with each `else if` statement. This gives the `if` statement (and its associated `else if` statements) more flexibility, so the `if` statement tends to be used more than the `switch` statement.

Loop Statements

NEW TERM Sometimes you will need to repeat an operation multiple times until a certain condition is `true`. As you will see in Chapter 5, "An Introduction to Arrays," this is especially important when you need to work with data stored in arrays. The types of statements used to accomplish repetitive loops are called *loop statements*. An integral part of these statements is comparison and increment operators discussed in Chapter 2.

There are three types of loop statements: the `while` statement, the `do while` statement, and the `for` statement. Let's look at the `while` statement first.

The `while` Statement

The `while` statement is the easiest of the looping statements to understand and use. Although it performs a different task, its structure is similar to the `if` statement:

```
while (expression) statement
```

or

```
while (expression)
  statement
```

Like all the looping statements, the first thing the `while` statement does is evaluate the expression contained within its parentheses to see whether the expression evaluates to `true` or `false`. If the expression evaluates to `true`, the `while` statement evaluates its statement(s). Where it differs from the statements that you have seen before is that it then goes back to recheck its expression. If the expression is `true`, then the JavaScript interpreter will execute the statement(s) in the statement block and it will evaluate the expression in parentheses again. The JavaScript interpreter will continue to loop in this way until the expression evaluates to `false`.

Clearly, if the `while` statement isn't to loop infinitely something in the expression has to change. This is achieved by including a variable in the expression that is changed by one of the statements evaluated by the loop during each evaluation. For example take a look at the following code:

```
var loopCounter = 0;

while (loopCounter <= 3)
  alert(loopCounter++);
```

ANALYSIS This causes the display of four alert boxes in succession with the numbers 0, 1, 2 and 3 respectively. After the fourth alert has been displayed the variable `loopCounter` will contain a value of 4, so when the expression `loopCounter <= 3` is evaluated, it returns `false`. Therefore, the `while` loop is not executed again and control passes to the statement that follows the `while` statement.

In Chapter 2 you learned that increment and decrement operators (++ and -- respectively) can be used to increment or decrement the value of their operand by 1. As you can see, this is especially useful in loops such as the one above. Every time the above alert is evaluated the value of the variable `loopCounter` is increased by 1. Therefore, after four loops the value of `loopCounter` is no longer less than or equal to three. Hence the expression evaluates to `false`, causing the `while` statement to stop looping, at which point evaluation will continue at the code following the `while` statement.

It is uncommon to actually use a long variable name such as loopCounter because they are extensively used in the statements belonging to the loop statement. It is standard practice to give counter variables the names i, j, and k so as to keep the code as uncluttered as possible. But note this is the only time that it is considered acceptable to give variables such nondescript names.

> **Caution**
>
> You must be careful that the variable in the expression changes each time so eventually it will cause the expression to evaluate to false. If you don't change the variable in the expression, the while statement will loop infinitely preventing any other scripts from running and, in some older browsers, will cause the browser to crash. This can happen if you forget to include a statement that increments/decrements the variable, or if you increment/decrement it in the wrong direction!

Generally, when you use the while statement you will want it to loop through more than just one line of code. To do this, include the curly braces as usual to create a statement block belonging to the while statement. For example, you could have written the above example like this:

```
var loopCounter = 0;
while (loopCounter <= 3) {
  alert(loopCounter);
  loopCounter++;
}
```

The do while Statement

The do while statement is very similar to the while statement. The difference is that the expression is evaluated at the end of the statement. In other words, the statement block is always evaluated once before the expression is evaluated. The structure of a do while statement is shown below:

INPUT
```
do
   statement
while (expression);
```

ANALYSIS The major effect of having the expression at the end of the loop is that the statements contained by the do while statement will be evaluated at least once before the expression is evaluated to decide whether it should loop again. For example try out the following code:

INPUT
```
do
   alert("Statement evaluated!");
while (false);
```

As you will see, the alert box displays once regardless of the fact that the expression is simply the value `false`. Other than this, there is no difference between the way the `while` statement and the `do while` statement work.

If you want a `do while` statement to control multiple statements use a statement block, like this:

```
do {
    statement1
    statement2
    ...
    statement5
} while(condition);
```

> **Caution**
>
> Because the do while statement does not end with a closing curly brace, it requires a semicolon after the closing parenthesis. Forgetting to include the semicolon may cause an error.

The for Statement

The `while` and `do...while` statements have three essential elements: a statement that sets the initial value of a counter; an expression that tests a condition; and an expression that increments the counter. It can be easy to forget one or other of these when you are quickly typing out a piece of code, and you could end up with problems such as infinite loops. Fortunately, there is an alternative in the form of the `for` statement, which can contain all these elements in one place. It is written with the following structure:

```
for (setInitialCounterValue; testCondition; changeCounterValue)
  statement
```

Because all three of the essential parts of a `loop` statement are located between the parentheses, the `for` loop is much more popular than the other two methods because it is easier to follow the logic that controls the looping.

> **Note**
>
> The for statement can govern multiple statements by enclosing them in a statement block.

Here's a simple example that would display three alert boxes:

```
for (var i=0; i<3; i++) {
    alert(i);
}
```

ANALYSIS   The first statement in the parentheses declares and assigns to the variable i an initial value. It is this variable that then acts as the loop counter. Note that it is only evaluated at the beginning of the first loop. The second statement is the condition for the loop. Each time a loop finishes it is checked again to determine whether another loop should be made. Finally there is the third statement. It declares how the loop counter should be incremented (or decremented).

> **Note**
>
> Note that the three elements inside the parentheses are statements. Therefore, semicolons separate them and not commas. Remember this is how more than one statement can be placed on a single line.

> **Caution**
>
> The variable used for the loop counter in a for statement is inside the parentheses so it can only be incremented using the increment and decrement operators ++ and -- or the full syntax equivalent to increase the value of the loop counter.

To get some experience using the for statement, let's try to use it to create a page that will generate a simple multiplication table. First, we will ask a user which multiplication table he wants to see; then we will output the first 12 lines of that multiplication table in an alert box.

The first thing we will need to do is ask the user to enter the multiplication table that he wants. This can be done using a prompt box that assigns the value to a variable we will call multTable. See the following example:

```
var multTable = prompt("Please enter the table.", "");
```

What about generating the table? We could write out each of the 12 lines concatenating each one to a variable. But this would be very inefficient. A better way would be to use a loop statement. To do that let's choose the for statement.

For the moment, let's ignore the statement needed for the statement block and concentrate on the for statement itself. We probably want to start at 1 so this can be the initial value of our counter i, and we know when we want to stop once we get to 12. With this in mind our for loop will need to look something like this:

```
for (var i=1; i<=12; i++) {
  statement;
}
```

Okay, that's fairly easy so far, but what about the statement the for loop controls? Well, to help decide what it should look like, it is useful to take a look initially at the first few lines of a multiplication table. Let's take the 2 times table as an example:

```
1 x 2 = 2
2 x 2 = 4
3 x 2 = 6
```

Looking at the table, you can see that the first element of each line increments by 1. To recreate this with each iteration of the loop, you could quite easily use the counter i.

The next three characters are always the same. The x and the equal sign could be created simply by using two strings, but the number in between depends on which table the user asks for. It's not much of a problem though as that value can simply be found in the variable multTable. Let's take a look at how our statement looks so far:

```
i + " x " + multTable + " = "
```

We are just concatenating all the components of the line together. But how do we actually add the answer to the end? Well actually it isn't too hard if you think about it. What we have on the left-hand side of the equal sign is exactly what generates the answer: i multiplied by the variable multTable. This is all that is needed to finish the statement. Well, almost. We will also want to include a new line character to make sure each line of the table is actually displayed on a new line. This is done with the escaped character \n. Our statement now looks like this:

```
i+ " x " +multTable+ " = " +(i*multTable)+ "\n";
```

During each iteration through the for loop, you will need to concatenate the line to a variable, which builds up the table. Call this variable theTable and your completed statement will look like this:

```
theTable += i+ " x " +multTable+ " = " +(i*multTable)+ "\n";
```

With this statement in place within the loop, and an alert for theTable after the loop, a multiplication table will be generated. If you also store the entire piece of code within a function, it will allow users to request a different table as many times as they like. If you use a hyperlink to call the function, Listing 3.6 shows how your finished page might look:

INPUT   **LISTING 3.6**   Multiplication Table Generator (multTableGenerator.htm)

```html
<html>
<head>
<title>Multiplication Table Generator</title>
```

LISTING 3.6   continued

```
<script language="javascript" type="text/javascript">
<!--

function generateTable()
{
    var multTable = prompt("Please enter the table.", "");
    var theTable = "";
    for (i=1; i<=12; i++) {
      theTable += i+ " x " +multTable+ " = " +(i*multTable)+ "\n";
    }
    alert(theTable);
}

//-->
</script>

</head>
<body>

<h1>Multiplication Table Generator</h1>

<a href="javascript:generateTable()">Create New Table</a>

</body>
</html>
```

Try it yourself.

Before you finish, it is worth mentioning that a statement that is related to the loop statements is the `break` statement. Remember that the `break` statement allows you to prematurely `break` out of conditional statements. There is a similar statement for the loop statements called the `continue` statement. However, rather than breaking out of the loop altogether and carrying on evaluation further down the page, it simply prevents evaluation of any remaining statements in the statement block. The loop continues to check the condition at the top of the loop to see whether it should loop again. Later in the book you will learn just how this can be useful.

The `for in` Statement

A second use of the `for` loop is to loop through the properties and child objects of an object. Objects are the JavaScript entities that allow you to apply these tools to making a difference to your Web pages, and to a certain extent the browser. (Objects will be covered in the next chapter.)

Summary

In this chapter you have learned "the other half" of the basics for creating useful scripts. You have learned how to create your own functions and you have learned about most of JavaScript's built-in functions. You also have looked at how to control the flow of scripts through the use of control and loop statements. This prepares us to explore objects in Chapter 4, "JavaScript Is Object-Based."

Workshop

The workshop will test how much you have grasped of the topics discussed in this chapter.

Q&A

Q. I want to repeat a piece of code an exact number of times. Which JavaScript statement should I use?

A. The `for` statement is ideal to achieve that. You could achieve the same thing using a `while` loop, for example, but it is less convenient to use it.

Q. I want to be able to check the length of several strings of characters in my code. How can I do that?

A. You could create a short function which takes a single argument—the string you want to check. You may want to use array techniques within the function. Those will be described in Chapter 5.

Q. I want to check if more than one thing is true. Can I use a `switch` statement to do that?

A. You could use a `switch` statement, but not on its own. You could nest another function which uses a `switch` statement within a `case` statement. Often it will be at least as easy to use an `if` statement with a number of `else if` statements. Whichever technique you choose you need to be clear about the process of logic and which statements will be evaluated and which statements won't.

Quiz

1. List the looping statements that are present in JavaScript.
2. Is it possible to include multiple statements in my own functions?

3

Quiz Answers

1. The looping statements in JavaScript are the `while` statement, the `do while` statement, and the `for` statement.

2. Yes. You can include multiple statements in a function by enclosing them in curly braces, like this:

```
function myFunction()
{
    statement
    statement
    ...
    statement
}
```

Exercise

Modify the multiplication table generator so that it will respond appropriately if the user clicks Cancel or enters a non-numeric value.

Day 4

JavaScript Is Object-Based

In Chapter 1, "Getting the Basics Right," you learned that JavaScript is an object-based scripting language. At the time, we didn't look too deeply at what the term object-based meant. In this chapter, we are going to take a discovery tour of JavaScript objects and find out just what they mean for us as scripters. You then will be better placed to understand objects and their place in the scheme of things as they are explored in more detail in later chapters.

Now that you have been introduced to topics such as data types, variables, and functions you will be able to make more efficient use of JavaScript objects. By creatively combining objects with the basic techniques you have already learned, you will find yourself better able to make a real a difference to your Web pages.

This chapter will teach you the following:

- What objects are
- What object properties are
- What object methods are
- About the Global object and its children
- How to use objects, their methods, and properties

Understanding Objects

All of the elements of an HTML document and some parts of the browser are made available to JavaScript in the form of something called "software objects," or more simply "objects." In practical terms, objects enable you to *get* (find out about) and *set* (change) characteristics of a document. For example, you can use JavaScript to get (find out) something about an image object, such as its width; you also can set (change) things about the same object, such as assign an image a new width and thereby change its size.

Although the notion of objects can initially take a little time to grasp, once you understand what they are and how they're used it will enable you to use JavaScript considerably more effectively and efficiently. Objects really are the crux of almost everything done in JavaScript.

What Are Objects?

So what exactly are objects, and why are they helpful?

Before we get technical about what an object is it might help to look at the idea of an object simply as a thing. A car is an object. It has several properties. It may have red paint. It may have four wheels. Properties are individual pieces of information that describe a characteristic of the car. A car can do things. It can move forward. It can accelerate. It can brake. The things that a car does could be called its "methods."

NEW TERM   So a JavaScript object has many similarities to real-world objects (such as a car). It has one or more *properties*. For example, a browser window object in JavaScript has a width property. JavaScript objects also frequently have *methods*, which are pieces of code that enable the object to do things. For example, the window object has a `moveTo()` method which can be used to move the browser window to another part of the screen. Of course JavaScript objects and their properties and methods are much more abstract than the properties and methods of a motor car, but the analogy is a helpful one.

NEW TERM   In technical terms, objects are a *collection* of properties and methods. Very often a JavaScript object represents something—such as an HTML form or a link— which is to be displayed on a Web page. Properties of JavaScript objects contain information, or values, which tell you about some characteristic of the object. For example, the document object has a `title` property. You may be familiar with the following HTML/XHTML tag:

```
<title>Untitled</title>
```

The `<title>` tag defines what is to be displayed in the title bar of the browser window displaying a Web page. Using JavaScript you could access the value of this tag by using the expression `window.document.title`. The notation `window.document.title` indicates that the title property of the `document` object is being referenced. For the moment, though, don't worry about the syntax. It will be covered in detail soon.

As well as accessing information, you can change the value of properties. So, taking the `image` object as an example you could assign its width property, `image.width`, a new value so its display width on an HTML page would change.

Similarly, you can change the value of the text contained in the `<title>` element using the code in Listing 4.1.

LISTING 4.1   Changing the Document Title (`changeTitle.htm`)

```
<html>
<head>
<title>Untitled</title>

<script language="javascript" type="text/javascript">

function changeTitle()
{
    var newTitle = prompt("Please enter a new title.", "");
    window.document.title = newTitle;
}

</script>
</head>

<body>

<p>You can change <a href="javascript:changeTitle()">
the &lt;title&gt; element</a> on this page</p>

</body>
</html>
```

4

The methods of an object are very like functions. Methods provide tools to carry out a task on the object to which they belong.

Although you probably weren't aware of it at the time, you already have been using properties and methods in earlier chapters. However, when calling these properties and methods, we have been using variables and functions. When you have created a data container, such as a variable, it also has been the property of an object. Whenever you created a function it also has been a method of an object.

For the moment, don't worry too much about which object owns which variables and functions; it will be discussed a little later in the chapter. What is important is that you realize that properties are simply a special case of data containers; and, similarly, methods are simply a special case of functions.

Client-Side JavaScript Objects

All objects in JavaScript belong to an object called the `Global` object. When a document containing JavaScript is loaded or downloaded into an environment where JavaScript is understood, all subsequent objects, properties, and methods are built upon it.

The `window` Object

In the client-side browser environment, the `Global` object is called the `window` object. Whenever any other JavaScript object is accessed, it is done through the `window` object. This includes all objects that represent parts of the document, browser objects, and the Core JavaScript objects that you will learn about later. It is essential then that you know how to access the `window` object. Thankfully this is very simple. To access the `window` object, simply write the keyword `window`. The following alert demonstrates this:

```
alert(window);
```

See Figure 4.1.

FIGURE 4.1

The alert box shows that the window object is a JavaScript object.

As you can see, JavaScript recognizes the keyword `window` and responds by telling you that it is an object. By itself this isn't very useful, but once you know how to use the `window` object to get to its properties and methods, and the properties and methods of the objects that belong to it, then you will be well on your way to producing real and useful scripts. To learn how to think about these objects, properties, and methods, let's consider an analogy.

The Dot Notation

Imagine for a moment that you are at home and you want a friend to fetch you a soda. Also imagine that your home is all that exists in the whole universe—it is the `Global` object. Assuming the person you ask doesn't know where the soda is located, you will have to give him instructions. You might describe the route in these terms: "in this house, go to the first floor, into the kitchen, then open the fridge, look in the top shelf and you find the soda." This route to the soda also could be written in any of the following ways:

house - first floor – kitchen – fridge – top shelf - coke

house : first floor : kitchen : fridge : top shelf : coke

house > first floor > kitchen > fridge > top shelf > coke

The symbols between each location separate each step of the route. If you think about it, you might note that they describe a hierarchical route. The first floor belongs to the house; the kitchen belongs to the first floor; the fridge belongs to the kitchen; the top shelf belongs to the fridge; and the soda belongs on the top shelf.

JavaScript's structure is very similar to this. Objects own properties and methods, but they also own (and are owned by) other objects—just as the above example shows what real-world objects are. All JavaScript objects are structured hierarchically within the Global object, which in Web browsers is the window object. Although in the situation above you would most likely just say something like "grab me a soda from the fridge," object-based computing languages such as JavaScript usually need each step of the route spelled out.

4

To describe the path to the object, property, or method you want, you need to use the dot notation or the dot syntax, which requires that each successive object in the route be joined to a following object, property, or method with a period. This is similar to the way you might separate a route with hyphens, colons, or angled brackets as done above. Therefore, if you were telling JavaScript to fetch you a soda, you would write it like this:

```
house.groundFloor.kitchen.fridge.topShelf.coke.get()
```

This syntax must not contain spaces, so the names of each object have been joined together. Otherwise it is remarkably similar to the three possible ways to describe the path to the soda used earlier.

Hopefully this helps to make the syntax used in our first example slightly clearer. We wrote window.document.title to change the title of the document. The document (object) is an object belonging to the window object; and, as it happens, the title (property) is a property of the document object.

You will learn more shortly about how the dot notation can be used to access objects and their properties and methods, but for the moment let's consider just what properties and methods are.

Variable or Property? Function or Method?

Earlier it was hinted that there is a strong similarity between data containers (such as variables) and object properties, and between functions and object methods. The link is so strong in fact, that one is really just a special case of the other.

Properties are a special type of data containers. They are data containers that not only belong to an object, they give us information about the object. For example, there is a property of the `window` object called `status`. This property contains the value that is being shown in the status bar of the window at the time it is accessed. By default, once the page has loaded, the status bar doesn't contain a value, so if you were to write

```
alert(window.status);
```

you would get simply an empty alert box—or at least it would look like an empty alert box. In fact, it would contain an empty string.

Properties of the `window` object can also be changed using JavaScript. For example, you could write:

```
window.status = "JavaScript was used to place this text here!";
```

So the window's status bar would contain the message: "JavaScript was used to place this text here!"

Listing 4.2 shows a fuller example where a prompt box in a function is used to allow a user to enter text that will be shown in the status bar:

INPUT   **LISTING 4.2**   Placing Text in the Status Bar (`changeStatus.htm`)

```
<html>
<head>
<title>Status Bar Changer</title>

<script language="javascript" type="text/javascript">
<!--

function changeStatus()
{
    window.status=prompt("Enter some text for the status bar","");
}

//-->
</script>

</head>
<body>
```

LISTING 4.2   continued

```
<h1>Status Bar Changer</h1>

<p><a href="javascript:changeStatus()">Change Status</a></p>

</body>
</html>
```

Figure 4.2 shows an example of what the status bar might look like after the function has been called, and the user has entered some text into the textbox.

OUTPUT

FIGURE 4.2

The status bar in Internet Explorer has changed to show the text entered in the prompt box.

4

Unfortunately, Netscape 6.0 replaces the text when a link is clicked to call the function. Because the link takes back focus when the prompt box closes, then the contents of the `href` attribute immediately overwrite the text that our function writes to the status bar.

Methods are another special case. Method is the name given to functions that belong to an object, and (frequently) acts on that same object. One of the methods that belongs to the `window` object is the `scrollBy()` method. Assuming the document is large enough that the scrollbars have been activated, then this method will scroll the window by the number of pixels that have been specified (if the scrollbars haven't been activated, it will do nothing).

Note

> Methods are written with parentheses, just like functions. Because `window.scrollBy()` uses parentheses (as the final part of the dot notation), you can assume that `scrollBy()` is a method.

The `scrollBy()` method belongs to and acts on the `window` object. Listing 4.3 shows an example page which uses the `scrollBy()` method.

LISTING 4.3   Scrolling the Window (`scrollWindow.htm`)

```html
<html>
<head>
<title>Window Scroller</title>

<script language="javascript" type="text/javascript">
<!--

function scrollWin()
{
    var y = prompt("How many pixels should the window be scrolled?","");
    if (isNaN(y)) return alert("Numbers only please");
    window.scrollBy(0, y);
}

//-->
</script>

</head>
<body>

<h1>Window Scroller</h1>

<p><a href="javascript:scrollWin()">Scroll Window</a></p>

<p>
1<br />2<br />3<br />4<br />5<br />6<br />7<br />8<br />
9<br />10<br />11<br />12<br />13<br />14<br />15<br />16<br />
17<br />18<br />19<br />20<br />21<br />22<br />23<br />24<br />
25<br />26<br />27<br />28<br />29<br />30<br />31<br />32<br />
</p>

<p>THE END</p>

</body>
</html>
```

ANALYSIS   When you click on the link the function `scrollWin()` will be called and you will be prompted to enter the number of pixels by which the window should be scrolled. Notice that because you are asking for numeric input from a user, the `isNaN()` function has been used to stop errors from occurring should the value the user enters have non-numeric characters. Assuming the input is accepted, then it is passed to the `scrollBy()` method. This method accepts two parameters. The first is the number of pixels that the window should be scrolled across, and the second is the number of pixels it should be scrolled down. Because we only want the window to scroll down, `0` has been specified for the first parameter, and the variable `y` for the second.

If the number entered into the prompt box is larger than the number of pixels the window can be scrolled, then the `scrollBy()` method doesn't scroll the window beyond the end of the document. It simply stops at the end. Therefore if you were to enter the value `1000` into the prompt box, the window should scroll to the end of the document and you should see an appearance like that shown in Figure 4.3.

OUTPUT

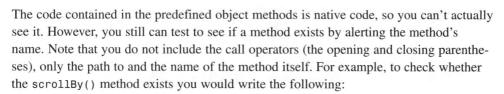

FIGURE 4.3

Window will scroll to the end after entering a large value in the prompt box.

The code contained in the predefined object methods is native code, so you can't actually see it. However, you still can test to see if a method exists by alerting the method's name. Note that you do not include the call operators (the opening and closing parentheses), only the path to and the name of the method itself. For example, to check whether the `scrollBy()` method exists you would write the following:

```
alert(window.scrollBy);
```

This would display an alert box like the one shown in Figure 4.4.

FIGURE 4.4

An alert box allows a check for the existence of the `window.scrollBy()` *method.*

As you can see, the alert shows that the `scrollBy()` function is supported, and also that the function body consists of native code.

As stated earlier, JavaScript objects can own other objects as well as have their own properties and methods. Shortly, you will learn about the objects that belong to the `window` object, but in the meantime, it is worth mentioning something about the variables and functions you have been writing and using so far.

You may have wondered where the variables and functions you created in previous chapters have been stored. Well, because they weren't assigned to any particular object, they were assigned to the Global object. Whenever you created a new data container, such as a variable or constant, it was assigned to the window object. This is true for your functions as well. Whenever you created a new function, it was assigned to the window object.

To demonstrate this, type the following lines of code into a page and load it:

INPUT

```
var myVar = "Variable myVar's value.";

function alertMyVar()
{
        alert(window.myVar);
}

window.alertMyVar();
```

Notice that you have used the window object both to call the function and to get to the value of the variable myVar. If the variable myVar and the function alertMyVar didn't belong to the window object, then this will cause an error. When you load the page, you should see an alert box something like the one in Figure 4.5.

OUTPUT

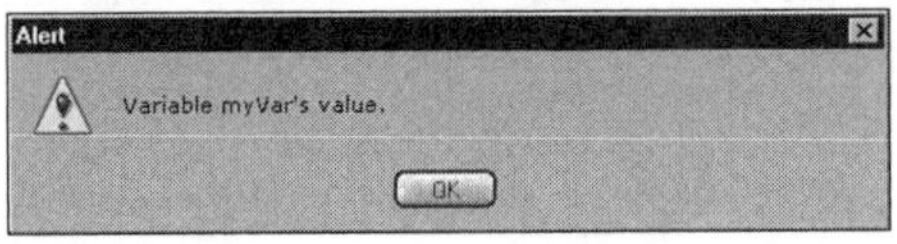

FIGURE 4.5

An alert box demonstrates that the myVar *variable is a property of the* window *object.*

ANALYSIS It works! The variable myVar was owned by the window object, which is the Global JavaScript object in a browser, as was the function alertMyVar().

Other functions that you have been using, such as the alert(), confirm(), and prompt() functions, also belong to the window object, as do the predefined global functions discussed in the previous chapter (yes, the word "global," meaning they belong to the Global object—the window object).

This, of course, raises the question as to why, if the variables and functions created and used belong to the window object, you have not always had to access them by writing the following:

```
window.variableName
```

and

```
window.functionName()
```

Everything to which client-side JavaScript has access is encompassed in the `window` object. It is the default. Therefore, if you omit the keyword `window` (and haven't used the name of some other object), the JavaScript interpreter knows to put it in for you. This means that you can start object paths with the objects next to the `window` object in the object hierarchy, and the JavaScript interpreter still will know what to do. This saves you from needlessly writing the word `window` at the beginning of the directions to an object.

Before we finish, note that we haven't, nor will we later, refer to our variables and functions as properties and methods of the `window` object. There are two reasons for this. One is that, in the case of properties, they do not give us information about the `window` object, and in the case of functions, they do not act on the `window` object. The second is that, because we can miss out the reference to the `window` object, we don't have to consciously treat our variables and functions as belonging to the `window` object.

For the rest of this chapter, when objects are accessed, properties and methods will include the `window` object in the object path. Although this isn't necessary (as you've just seen), it will help you get used to the syntax for accessing objects and remind you that the `window` object is the object at the top of the tree.

The `window` Object's Children

When one object belongs to another, it is said that it is a child of that object. Conversely, the object that owns the child object is said to be its parent object. The `window` object has several child objects, but in general they can be split into three types:

- The `document` object
- Environment objects
- Core JavaScript objects

It is important to distinguish between the three types of objects as they enable us to perform different tasks. The `document` object is the object by which you gain access to your HTML documents. Without the `document` object, no matter how many processes were performed behind the scenes, you would never be able to affect the Web page itself. All interactions with page elements such as forms, images, and layers must take place through the `document` object.

The environment objects enable you to find out details about such things as the browser and the user's screen. This enables you to accomplish such tasks as loading a different page or finding out whether one of your scripts is supported and can be run.

Finally, the Core JavaScript objects are the objects that are actually built into JavaScript itself. These always exist regardless of where JavaScript is used, whether it is in a Web browser, a PDF (Portable Document Format) file, or any other environment. These Core JavaScript objects provide a powerful means to create, sort, and otherwise manipulate data and data structures in your documents.

This chapter will take an overview of the objects in all three groups.

The document Object

Not too surprisingly, the document object provides access to the document that is currently loaded in the browser window. This means that it includes not only the elements contained between the body tags that are displayed in the window, but everything between the <html> and </html> tags.

Before going any further, if you need to convince yourself that the document object really does belong to the window object, type the following line into the HTML for a Web page and view it with your browser:

INPUT

```
alert(window.document);
```

This will display the following alert box which shows that the document object does indeed exist as a child object of the window object. See Figure 4.6.

OUTPUT

FIGURE 4.6

A check for the docu-ment *object as a child of the* window *object.*

The document object has many properties and methods as well as containing all the objects that make up the model that represents the document: the "Document Object Model." The document object model is so large that we will spend many chapters exploring its different parts. For the present, though, let's take a cursory look at the document object model to get a preliminary feel for what is there.

Properties

The standard set forth by the W3C Document Object Model (or DOM for short) describes a logical association of properties and methods to objects. This chapter will focus only on the properties that have been included in either the W3C DOM or browser-specific properties that have equivalent properties in other browsers.

> **Caution**
>
> Several of the properties that previously belonged to the document object are no longer approved for use. This is due to the fact that many of the properties that originally belonged to the document object should have been associated with other objects. It will be noted when this is the case.

A list of the properties of the document object in the W3C Document Object Model is given below:

```
charset
characterSet
cookie
domain
height
lastModified
referrer
title
URL
width
```

You already know about the `title` property of the `document` object and how you can use JavaScript to change the title displayed in the browser's title bar, so let's move on.

The `charset` and `characterSet` properties are browser-specific properties of Internet Explorer 4+ and Netscape 6+ respectively. They can be used to find out the character set that has been associated with the document. For example if the document contains the following meta tag:

```
<meta http-equiv="Content-Type" content="text/html; charset=iso- 8859-1">
```

Then in Internet Explorer the `document` object's `charset` property will have the value `"iso-8859-1"`, and in Netscape the `characterSet` property will have the value `"ISO-8859-1"`. The case of the letters in the meta tag doesn't make any difference to the case of the string returned by these properties. Internet Explorer will return it in lowercase, and Netscape will return it in uppercase, whichever way you happen to have written it.

The document object's `cookie` property gives you the ability to set a cookie using JavaScript. We will take a detailed look at this property later in the book.

The `domain` property is another property that we will leave until later for a detailed analysis. In brief, however, it allows you to access documents in other frames or windows that have been loaded from the same domain as the document in which the script resides, but from a different server. By default this is not possible for security reasons.

The `height` and `width` properties of the `document` object are both Netscape-specific. They contain an integer that represents in pixels the total height and width of the document at the point in time that they are checked. This includes the parts of the page that are out of sight due to page scrolling. These properties enable you to know how far a document can be scrolled. You can then use the `scrollBy()` method used earlier to create custom scrollbars, for example.

Internet Explorer has two equivalent properties to the Netscape `height` and `width` properties but they belong to the `body` object, so they will be discussed slightly later in the chapter.

The `lastModified` property of each document contains a string with the date and time that the document was last changed. It can be used to do such things as add an automatic "Last Updated" line to our pages, but also for more advanced things such as checking whether the document has been changed since the last time a user visited. This script would also require the use of cookies however, so we will discuss that later.

There are times that you will need to check that a visitor has only come from a designated page using the correct link. For example, you may require a user of your Web site to have checked a news page before entering another area. The document object's `referrer` property allows you to check exactly from where a visitor has come—but, only if the user clicked on a link to get to the present page. If a link was clicked to navigate to the present page, then the `referrer` property will contain the URI of the document in which that link was contained. If a link wasn't clicked, say the user entered the location directly into the location bar of her browser, then the property will simply contain an empty string. You can check for a certain URI and redirect the user, if she hasn't been there yet.

The document object's `URL` property provides the URI that was used to download the document as a string value. However, there are two other ways of finding this information. There is a `location` object that will provide this string and a lot more information. You will learn about the `location` object shortly.

> **Caution**
> You may have seen the properties bgColor, fgColor, alinkColor, linkColor, and vlinkColor used with the document object. These properties are now deprecated and should no longer be used. Because the document includes everything from the HTML tags down, and not just the displayed body, it is more appropriate to use either the style attribute, or the property equivalents that belong to the body object. You will see how to do that shortly.

Let's now continue our study of the document object by investigating some of its methods.

Methods

The document object has many methods, but for the moment we will only look at the methods that are most useful to us. A list of these is given below:

```
close()
getElementById()
getElementsByName()
getElementsByTagName()
open()
write()
writeln()
```

When a document begins to load into a browser the first thing that happens is that the browser opens a data stream to accept the data that makes up the file. After all the data has arrived, the data stream is closed.

The document object's open(), write(), writeln(), and close() methods are all closely related. These methods enable you to construct entirely new documents using JavaScript. What they do not do is enable you to add to an existing document that has already loaded into a browser window. You will see how to do that later.

The open() method allows you to open a new data stream to a browser window or frame. To construct a document in this window or frame, you then can use the write() or writeln() methods to add data to the data stream. After you have created a file and the data that makes up the file has been sent, you finish by using the close() method to close the data stream, indicating that the document content has ended.

As soon as the open() method is used, one of two things can happen. If the document in a window has already finished downloading, then it will be removed to make way for a new document. But if the method is written into a script block (rather than a function's body) so that it is called while a page is loading, then the open() method is ignored. After all, the data stream for that page is already open. Therefore the open() method is only of use when you need to create a new document.

Once a data stream to a window is opened, the next step is to send some data to the window concerned. Use either the write() method or the writeln() method. The two methods are identical except for the fact that the writeln() method adds a line break to the end of the string it is given. In client-side JavaScript, the difference is not noticeable because—even after the document has been constructed—you can't view the code that was used to make it by doing a view-source on the window in which it is contained. When you are constructing a document using server-side JavaScript the situation is different. Because the document is constructed on the server before being sent to the browser the source can be viewed and line breaks after each line of the page becomes useful. Because we are working client-side, we will only use the write() method in this book. Here is an example of how you might start constructing a new document:

```
document.open();
document.write("<html><head><title>Generated</title></head>...");
```

With the exception of Netscape 4, you can use as many calls to the write() method as needed to construct a document. In Netscape 4 there is a bug that prevents you from using more than one write() method per document. To get around that, you need to build up your page in a variable, and then write it all at once into the data stream. If you need to script for Netscape 4, then the existence of the bug isn't too much of a problem.

Caution

If images are to be included in the document that you generate, then you will need to set either their src attributes with absolute URIs or the <base> element. Without setting the <base> element, relative URIs will not be recognized by some browsers. In order to locate the image its absolute address must be known, either directly using an absolute URI or relative to a stated base URI.

Finally, finish constructing the document by using the document object's close() method to close the data stream:

```
document.close();
```

If the `write()` or `writeln()` methods are applied to a document that has finished loading without first using the `open()` method, then the browsers will automatically implement the `open()` method. Therefore, to a certain extent, the `open()` method is actually optional. However, you do need to use it if the document you are constructing is not an HTML document. This is because the default MIME type for the document that is created is `"text/html"`. If, say, for example, you wanted to create a page made purely from SVG, then you would have to specify the MIME type as `"image/svg+xml"`. To specify the MIME type of the document to be created, you need to declare it as a parameter of the `open()` method. For example, if your document is pure SVG then you would start with the following:

```
document.open("image/svg+xml");
```

Other commonly used MIME types include those listed here:

```
text/html      // the default
text/plain
image/gif
image/jpeg
```

SVG images are created from markup so using the document object's `write()` method is feasible, but it is less likely that you would want to write a GIF or JPEG (MIME type `"image/jpeg"`), which are pure binary. To generate a chart from user input would be relatively simple using SVG, but creating it from binary would be impractical.

Note

> If the image you were generating were to be part of an HTML document, the MIME type would be `"text/html"`. The MIME type specified is for the MIME type of the main document.

We will make extensive use of the `write()` method to construct parts of a document as it loads. Remember that the `write()` method will clear a document from the window if used after it has finished loading, but if the document is still in the process of loading (therefore the data stream is still open), then the `write()` method can be used to add HTML to the page without destroying the HTML that has already arrived. In general, we will not make a great deal of use of the `open()`, `write()`, and `close()` methods to create new documents. Although they can be invaluable in this respect on some occasions, this use is not very common.

By now, you probably would like a bit of variety from using alert boxes to display the output from JavaScript code. Although we won't banish alert boxes entirely, you'll be happy to know that this aspect of the `write()` method will now enable you to output the results from your scripts into the HTML of the document. Listing 4.4 is an example page.

INPUT **LISTING 4.4** Writing HTML to the Page Using `document.write` (`writingHTML.htm`)

```
<html>
<head>
<title>Writing HTML</title>

</head>
<body>

<script language="javascript" type="text/javascript">
<!--

document.write("<h1>Writing HTML</h1>");

var myPara  = "<p>This page was written using the ";
    myPara += "document object's write() method!</p>";

window.document.write(myPara);

//-->
</script>

</body>
</html>
```

The result from loading the page in Listing 4.4 is shown in Figure 4.7.

OUTPUT

FIGURE 4.7

Writing to an HTML page using docu-ment.write().

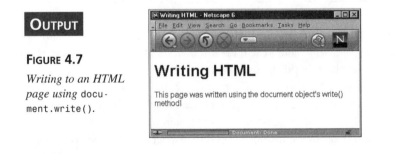

ANALYSIS As you can see, by applying the `write()` method of the `document` object as the document was loading, you were able to add HTML to the data stream and, therefore, to the page itself. The first time the `write()` method was used the argument it was given was the document header as a plain string, but for the longer paragraph it was built up in a variable first. By using control statements you will be able to selectively write different things into an HTML page rather than alerting it in alert boxes. Note that a `document.close()` call is not used after the script because there is still more HTML to come.

Let's now look at the other methods of the `document` object that were listed earlier.

The `document` object's methods that start with the word "get" are new and as such are only supported by Internet Explorer 5+ and Netscape 6+. These methods provide a cross-browser means of accessing any element or group of elements in the document.

The `getElementById()` method is our means of accessing any element in the document that has been assigned an `id` attribute in its opening tag. The `getElementById()` method returns a reference to the object which has the `id` attribute so that you are effectively taken straight to it without navigating the document tree. Note that the value assigned to an `id` attribute must be unique in the whole document. Assigning the same `id` to more than one element will simply mean that all duplicate `id`s after the first are ignored, and you won't be able to access those elements using the value of the `id` attribute.

The `getElementsByName()` and `getElementsByTagName()` methods play a similar role. Unlike the `getElementById()` method, they can return a collection of more than one object. In the case of the `getElementByName()` method, the element objects returned are only those elements that have the `name` attribute set to the value that was specified. The `getElementsByTagName()` method is similar but it returns the elements with the tag name that was specified.

You will learn more about collections in the next chapter on arrays. In JavaScript, collections are a type of array—so let's wait until after arrays have been discussed before exploring these methods in more detail.

Child Objects

You have learned about reaching objects through a hierarchically structured path of objects belonging to the `window` object. Therefore, you may expect that to access the contents of a `textarea` belonging to a form contained within a table, you would write something like this:

```
window.document.html.body.form.table.tr.td.textarea.contents
```

In the most recent browsers, it is indeed possible to access objects in a way similar to (although not exactly like) this. However, originally JavaScript didn't enable access and manipulation of all document parts.

Up until the release of Internet Explorer 4, the elements of a page that could be accessed were very limited. In earlier browsers, the `document` object was still the route to the document, but an HTML element could only be accessed if it belonged to a certain group of elements, or was a child element of one of these elements. As long as it was among this group, then it was possible to refer to it through a "collection." The accessible HTML elements were split into these collection groups by tag name. For example, all the forms on a page could be accessed through a collection known as the "forms collection." It didn't matter how far down the tree they were found, the collections made access to them only one step away.

NEW TERM Because the shortcuts provided by collections are such a useful feature, they have been included in the W3C DOM specifications. In fact, the W3C have added to the collections and provided methods that enable the creation of your own collections. However, collections don't give access to every part of the document. To enable this the structure of the `document` object has been changed so that you can traverse every part of it using *nodes*. Nodes not only give access to the objects representing document elements, they also give access to their attributes and the text contained within them.

NEW TERM There are pros and cons to both methods. Collections give quick and easy access to the elements you are most likely to want to access, but for the times you need more power to access other objects, then you will need to traverse the Document Object Model's treelike structure of nodes. The Document Object Model, or DOM for short, maps out and describes how a document is constructed in terms of the hierarchical structure of its objects. It also requires certain methods and *event handlers* to be present.

This chapter will take a quick look at the collections that are available to access the main parts of the document. We will cover the DOM way of doing things later in the book. Here is a list of the widely supported HTML collections and an important object that is the body object, which belongs to the `document` object:

```
all
applets
anchors
body
embeds
forms
frames
images
layers
```

```
links
```

`plugins` == embeds; seems to be being phased out

```
styleSheets
```

Before examining the body object, let's take a quick look at the collections so that you can get a feel for these objects, which will be examined in more detail at appropriate points later in the book.

Let's use the `forms` collection first. Once you have learned what arrays are and how they are used in the next chapter, you will see how the `forms` collection (a type of array) can be used to access the HTML forms on a Web page. In general, there are two way to do this: Use the name you give to the form, or use an integer representing the form's place among any other forms on the page. For example, if the first form on one of our Web pages is called `myForm`, you could access it using either of the following lines of code:

```
window.document.forms.myForm
```

or

```
window.document.forms[0]
```

Either will take you straight to the object representing that form.

4

> **Note**
>
> The individual parts of an array are numbered from zero—not from one.

Don't worry if you don't understand those lines—especially the second one. Once arrays have been covered, it should be a lot clearer.

The `all` and `layers` collections are specific to Internet Explorer and Netscape 4 respectively. Note that when we say Netscape 4, we really do mean only version 4. The `layers` object was removed in Netscape 6 and replaced by the W3C DOM way of doing things. These collections provide a shortcut to objects on the page if the objects possess a particular `name` or `id` attribute. In the case of the `all` object, you can access any object on a page, but with the `layers` object you can only access `layer` objects or `div` objects. To do this you usually would write the following:

```
window.document.all.nameOrId
```

or

```
window.document.layers.nameOrId
```

or use the same integer notation that was used for the `forms` collection.

The `applets`, `embeds`, and `plugins` collections can all be used to access the objects and information needed to insert other technologies into your pages. Collections will be covered in detail in Chapter 18, "Plugins and Applets."

When we do look at the `anchors` and `links` collections it is important to make clear the distinction between the two. Anchors are `<a>` tags that have been given a `name` attribute; whereas links are `<a>` tags that have been given an `href` attribute. As `<a>` tags can be given both, it is possible that some of the objects in the `anchors` and `links` collections will be present in both collections. Not that this is a problem, but is something of which you might want to be aware.

When looking at scripting between windows and frames in detail in a later chapter, you will learn how to make use of the `frames` collection.

As you may expect by now, the `images` collection gives access to all the images on a page. Again you can access the individual images by specifying a name or index using the syntax used for the `forms` collection. For example, if you have an image on your page and you specified the `name` attribute in its opening tag to be `"myImage"`, then you can change the image that is being shown by writing something similar to the following:

```
window.document.images.myImage.src = "path/to/new/image.gif";
```

The image being displayed on the page would now be replaced with the image you specified. This is because by changing the `src` property that corresponds to the `src` attribute of the `<img>` tag you force the image to change.

The final entry in the above list is the `styleSheets` collection, which provides access to the style sheets in the page. This object gives access to all the `<style>` tags on the page. Note that it does not give access to any external style sheets loaded using the `<link>` tag. Again, you will learn much more about the `styleSheets` collection later in the book.

There are other interesting objects belonging to the `document` object. Especially worth mentioning is the `documentElement` object, which gives access to the corresponding node of a document. The `document` object provides access to selected objects on the page mainly through the collections just mentioned. However with the `documentElement` object, you can get access to everything, as you shall see later.

The body Object

The `body` object, which is a child object of the `document` object, is available in both Internet Explorer 4+ and Netscape 6+. Surprisingly, it usually isn't used as a gateway to the elements of a page, but rather as a means to set the main colors of the Web page and the background image, if there is one. By changing properties of the `body` object, you can change these corresponding attributes that can be added to the opening <body> tag. The properties of the body object are listed below:

aLink

background

bgColor

link

text

vLink

These properties all have the same names as the attributes that can be added to the body tag, so if you are already fluent in HTML, hopefully it should be fairly easy for you to see how they are used. For example, you can change the background image of a page by writing this:

```
window.document.body.background = "path/to/new/image.gif";
```

Or you can change the color of links that have been visited by writing this:

```
window.document.body.vLink = "#4488ff";
```

The colors assigned also can be color names, just as they can be for the corresponding body tag attributes.

Caution

Remember that although the attribute names in HTML use the same letters as the JavaScript properties mentioned, you must use the correct case in JavaScript—whereas in HTML, attribute names are case-insensitive.

Internet Explorer also provides several properties that allow things such as the margin widths to be set. However, these properties are available in Internet Explorer only and are done better by using the style attribute or by adding style sheet rules, which you will learn about later.

Environment Objects

As well as working with the document, you also may want to know some things about the browser and where it has been. There are four objects that belong to the window object that provide this information. They are the following objects:

4

- The `location` object
- The `history` object
- The `navigator` object
- The `screen` object

The `location` and `history` objects provide access to the present URL and the browser history respectively. The `navigator` and `screen` objects provide information about the browser that is being used to view the document and the browser's position in the user's screen respectively.

The `location` Object

The `location` object gives you access to and control over the URL that the current document was downloaded from. Initially, this may not seem all that useful. After all, you know the URL of the site where your Web pages are kept. But what if you want to make the browser load another page? Or what if you want to access data from the URL query string? For these sorts of tasks, you will need the `location` object.

The `location` object has eight properties:

hash

host

hostname

href

pathname

port

protocol

search

The `location` object also has three methods:

assign()

reload()

replace()

You will use the `location` object most often for loading a new document, so first let's look at how this is done.

Loading a New Page

The usual way to load a new page into a window is to assign to its `href` property a string containing the new URL. To do this, you simply write something like the following:

```
window.location.href = "http://www.xmml.com/path/to/file.htm";
```

The `assign()` method enables you to assign a new URL to a window's or frame's location, and thereby load into the window or frame the Web page located at that URL. Although the `assign()` method still works in browsers, it is now deprecated—meaning it is no longer the approved way to do it. In any case, it is almost never used.

Caution

In some old browsers, the `location` object originally belonged to the `document` object rather than the `window` object. This is now deprecated, so if you ever see

```
window.document.location
```

or

```
document.location
```

don't be tempted to copy. At present, browsers support the `location` object as belonging to the `window` or `document` objects. However, in the future that may no longer be the case.

4

There are many times when it is beneficial to use JavaScript to load a new page. For example, you may wish to use an HTML select box as a way of navigating to different sections of your site.

It is very important to note that there are times when you should not load a new page using the `location` object's `href` property. One example is when filter pages are used to redirect a visitor to a different page based on which browser he is using. Frequently, you will see the `href` property being used to do the redirecting. This means that when a visitor hits the back button he is immediately bounced forward again. You may well have come across pages that act like this yourself. The problem is that the filter page is still in the browser's history, so when the back button is hit, it is reloaded and once again redirects to the page the user has come from. To solve this, you need to get the filter page to overwrite itself so that it isn't included in the browser history. This is accomplished by using the second of the `location` object's methods.

The `location` object's `replace()` method is an important alternative to assigning its `href` property with a new location. It replaces the page where it is used with a new URL, thereby preventing the browser from storing that page in the browser's history. This

means that when a visitor hits the back button, the page the replace method was on effectively doesn't exist, and the browser loads the previous page. This prevents the nasty
bounce effect associated with filter pages.

Note that relative URLs can also be used with the `location` object's `href` property and
the `replace()` method. To demonstrate, assume the document being navigated from is
located at the following URL:

```
http://www.xmml.com/path/to/file.htm
```

If you wanted to move to a Web page called `index.htm` located in the directory `/path/`,
you could write this:

```
location.href = "http://www.xmml.com/path/index.htm";
```

But you also could use a relative URL path to do the same thing. Therefore you could
just write:

```
location.href = "../index.htm";
```

Both are acceptable. Similarly, if you wanted to go to the page `index.htm` in the root
directory, instead of writing this:

```
location.href = "http://www.xmml.com/index.htm";
```

You could just write:

```
location.href = "/index.htm";
```

Both absolute and relative URLs can be used in the `href` attribute of an anchor tag to
make it a link, so you can use absolute and relative URLs with the `href` properties and
`replace()` method of the `location` object.

Accessing the URL

As well as using the `location` object's properties and methods to load a new page, you
may sometimes want to just find the URL of the document currently loaded in a window.
This could be the URL of the page the script is running on, or the URL of a page in
another frame or browser window. The simplest way to use a script to find out a page's
URL is to swap the `location.href` to the other side of an assignment statement to
assign the value of the `href` property to a variable. For example, by writing this:

```
var pageURL = location.href;
alert(pageURL);
```

The `location` object's `href` property contains the whole URL. So in the variable `pageURL`, you now will have everything including the protocol, hostname, and path to the file as well as the port number, query string, and hash, if they are present. Often, though, you will want one, or only some part of the URL. To make it easy for you to get this selectively, the `location` object has a number of other properties.

To demonstrate these properties, let's assume that the present URI of the page where the script can be found is the following:

```
http://www.xmml.com:80/path/to/file.htm?myVar=val#anchorName
```

The following show the values that would then be contained within the other properties of the `location` object for the page:

```
alert(location.hash)       // alerts "#anchorName"
alert(location.host)       // alerts "www.xmml.com:80"
alert(location.hostname)   // alerts "www.xmml.com"
alert(location.pathname)   // alerts "/path/to/file.htm"
alert(location.port)       // alerts "80"
alert(location.protocol)   // alerts "http:"
alert(location.search)     // alerts "?myVar=val"
```

Most of the time URIs do not contain many components, in which case some of these properties will contain just empty strings.

It can be helpful to use these properties instead of the `href` property. For example, when a hash (#) is used in a URL it is followed by the name of an anchor tag in the document. This causes the page to load prescrolled to the point in the document that the anchor tag is located. This is very useful for linking directly to a certain part of a long document.

If you use anchor tags like this, you may want to find out which part of a document a page has loaded. For example, if there is some important information at the top of a page, you might want to check for a hash and if it exists alert the reader to the information.

To find the name of an internal link, simply use the `hash` property of the `location` object. It contains the hash character itself followed by the name of the anchor to which it has been linked. Therefore, if we were on the page with the URL given earlier, and we wrote:

INPUT

```
var myHash = location.hash;
alert(myHash);
```

We would get the following alert box seen in Figure 4.8.

FIGURE 4.8

The hash *property of
the* location *object
is displayed.*

ANALYSIS If you wanted to test whether an internal document link had been used, then this
would be all you needed. If one wasn't used, then the hash property returns a
zero length string. As the zero length string " " evaluates as false in a logical context, you
could simply write:

```
var myHash = location.hash;

if (myHash) {
  alert("Please read the important information at the top.");
}
```

If on the other hand, you wanted to actually find out the name of the anchor that had
been linked to then you would need to remove the hash character. You will find out later
how to do this when we examine the String object and its properties and methods.

Reloading the Page

There are a few circumstances that will require reloading a page. For example, some uses
of <div> tags send the browser haywire if they are being viewed using Netscape 4, and
then the page is resized. The only solution is to detect when the browser is resized, and
then refresh the page to clean it up. There are other reasons you may want to reload the
page. For example, you may want to create your own navigation buttons. Regardless of
the reasons, the location object provides a method with which to do it.

To reload the current page, simply use the reload() method as shown below:

```
location.reload();
```

Note that the reload() method is similar to holding down the Shift key and hitting the
reload button. Simply clicking on refresh will leave data that has been entered into any
HTML form elements intact, but the Shift+Refresh key combination clears everything.
This is exactly what the reload() method of the location object does. It does a complete reload of the page, which normally should be from the browser's cache. We say
"should" because browser implementations frequently don't implement the reload()
method as they are supposed to do. For an even fuller refresh, add the logical value true
as an argument to the reload() method:

```
location.reload(true);
```

This should not only refresh the page but also go to the server to collect the most up-to-date version. Again, however, we say "should" because this isn't always what happens.

Hopefully in the future browsers will behave a bit more consistently, but for the moment there is a workaround for the times when you really need the newest version of a page to load. This involves adding a timestamp to the end of the page as a query string. We will look at how to generate a timestamp later when we deal with the Core JavaScript Date object in Chapter 9, "Date and Time Manipulation," but for the moment let's continue with our overview of JavaScript objects.

There is also a method that is designed to reload the page from the cache *and* leave form elements filled out. It belongs to the `window` object's `history` object.

The `history` Object

You likely are aware that Web browsers store a list of the pages you have visited in what is called the browser's history. This enables the browser to supply back and forward buttons to allow users to go backward and forward through the sites they have recently visited. You already have limited access to the browser's history through the `window` object's `history` object. Under normal conditions, it isn't possible to discover the URLs of the sites where a user has been; however, the `history` object allows you to do simple things such as move backward and forward within the browser's history.

The `history` object has the `length` property and the following methods:

`back()`

`forward()`

`go()`

Netscape provides an additional three properties—`current`, `next`, and `previous`—that provide the URIs of the current, next, and previous history entries respectively. They all require signed scripts, which we will cover in detail later in the book.

The `history` object's `length` property stores the number of history events in the browser's history. In reality, this is only of use in conjunction with signed scripts when history entries can be obtained. Without that information, you can't determine where you are in the history events and, thus, which of the other entries you may wish to move to.

It is really the methods of the `history` object that are the most useful. The back and forward buttons are fairly self-explanatory. They allow you to force the browser back to the last page that was loaded or forward to the next. If you wanted to create your own back and forward buttons, you could use hyperlinks with these methods to achieve the effect.

Just remember that there will need to be history entries for before and after the current page for the buttons to work! See Listing 4.5.

LISTING 4.5   Simulated Back and Forward Buttons (`backAndForward.htm`)

```
<html>
<head>
<title>Simulated Back and Forward Buttons</title>

</head>
<body>

<h1>Simulated Back and Forward Buttons</h1>

<p><a href="javascript:history.back()">Back</a> |
<a href="javascript:history.forward()">Forward</a></p>

</body>
</html>
```

To create more attractive buttons, simply wrap the <a> tags around some images instead of the text.

When moving forward or backward by one is not enough you can use the go() method. This allows you to specify how many steps backward or forward in the history the browser should go. For example to go back to the previous page, write this:

```
window.history.go(-1);
```

Or to go forward by two you would write this:

```
window.history.go(2);
```

If you overshoot the entries, even by one, then the go() method is ignored.

Using the go() method in this way is problematic as you most likely will need to have access to the history entries for your scripts to determine where to go. However, what the go() method is very useful for is refreshing a page without removing any data that a user may have entered into an HMTL form. This is opposed to the fuller refreshes provided by the location object's reload() method. To do this more limited type of refresh, you would write this:

```
window.history.go(0)
```

The 0 just means that it is the present history entry—that is, the present document—that should be loaded. Just "soft" refresh.

> **Caution**
>
> Note that it is the history object that is used to effect a soft refresh, and it is the location object that is used to do a hard refresh. Since the `back()` and `forward()`, and `go()` methods belong to the `history` object it is easy to forget that the `reload()` method belongs to the location object and thus make mistakes in your scripts.

The `navigator` Object

Netscape was the first company to provide a mechanism for finding out information about the browser being used to view a Web page. It was quite logical then that the object that was introduced to provide scripts with information about Netscape Navigator was given the name `navigator`. At the time, Netscape was king in the browser world and so other browser manufacturers gave the object in their browsers the same name so the JavaScript being used on the Web also would work in their browsers.

In Internet Explorer, the `navigator` object can also be accessed using the name `clientInformation`. However in Internet Explorer both names point (refer) to the same object. Because `clientInformation` works only in Internet Explorer but `navigator` works in both main browsers, the norm is to use the name `navigator` to access the `navigator` object. This ensures that your scripts will work on all browsers.

The `navigator` object has many properties. Because several of the `navigator` object's properties are specific to individual browsers, only cross-browser properties and some of the more useful proprietary properties are listed:

appCodeName

appName

appVersion

browserLanguage

cookieEnabled

language

platform

systemLanguage

userAgent

userLanguage

The main use of these properties is to provide our scripts with information that will enable them to determine whether the browser a visitor to our site is using will support certain pieces of code we may want to use. This information can be used in conjunction with the control statements that we saw in the previous chapter to control whether the code is executed or not. Unfortunately the information that some of these properties provide can be quite misleading and difficult to understand. We will discover how to use them later in Chapter 8, "The Browser Issue."

The `screen` Object

The `screen` object provides our scripts with useful information about the size and settings of the monitor that a visitor to our site is using. This can be useful when we want to move an existing or new window to a certain place on the screen, or when we need to know whether the screen has high enough resolution or color depth to support something we want to use. The properties that are widely supported are:

```
availHeight
```

```
availWidth
```

```
colorDepth
```

```
height
```

```
pixelDepth
```

```
width
```

There are also two other very useful properties, `availLeft` and `availTop`, which surprisingly are not supported by Internet Explorer.

A more in-depth study of the `screen` object will be discussed in Chapter 12, "Windows and Frames," where it is more applicable.

Core JavaScript Objects

Core JavaScript, the parts of JavaScript that exist in every environment in which it is used, is made up of several language elements. You have already learned about most of the operators and statements that are available, but just as important are the Core JavaScript objects. Without these objects, what you can do is severely limited.

There are 11 Core JavaScript objects, which have been listed below:

```
Array
```

```
Boolean
```

```
Date
```

```
Error
```

```
Function
```

```
Global
Math
Number
Object
RegExp
String
```

In the client-side environment the `Global` object is, of course, the `window` object. You have already used the `window` object to discover how objects are accessed and in so doing have seen some of its properties and methods. However, learning about the `window` object is a important topic, so we will take a closer look at it later, mostly in Chapter 12.

All the other Core JavaScript objects (which in the client-side browser environment belong to the `window` object) are also important topics in their own right, and much of the rest of this book will be spent discovering more about them. The remainder of this chapter will take an introductory look at what these objects are and how to make use of them.

The Core JavaScript objects are very different to the other objects that belong to the `window` object. For one thing, the majority of the time you will not use the Core JavaScript objects directly in the way you have used the other objects. More frequently, you will be using copies, or clones, of these objects that JavaScript has automatically created or that you have created for yourself.

In general, you can create a copy of one of the Core JavaScript objects using one of two ways. You can create it either by using literal notation or by using *constructor function* notation. You already have used literal notation on many occasions. For example, whenever you have created a string, it has been based on the `String` object. You didn't have to do anything special; you simply surrounded the characters for the string with quote marks and, seeing the quote marks, JavaScript automatically created a string literal. The same happens for boolean and numerical values. JavaScript recognizes them as keywords or values and knows automatically what object on which to base them (the `Boolean` and `Number` objects respectively).

When you use literal notation the result is usually a true literal, which means that it is not an object in and of itself. It simply gains access to the properties and methods of the object on which it was based. You can't give it any properties or methods of your own.

When you create an instance of an object using the constructor function notation it is quite different. Instances are full objects in their own right. They not only inherit the properties and methods of the object on which they were based, but your own properties or methods and, if you want, even your own child objects can be added.

So far you have learned how to create your own data (which as just discussed also can be called "literals") and some ways of working with that data in the form of operators and statements. What you haven't learned yet are ways of structuring or ordering your data. This is one of the useful purposes of creating instances of Core JavaScript objects.

It is possible to create your own objects from scratch, along with the properties and methods that will be needed for them. However this can be quite involved. To make the job a lot easier, use the Core JavaScript objects as prototypes or blueprints. They provide a way to easily make your own data structures that will have many useful management tools (methods) and properties already built in.

So what is constructor function notation, and how is it used to create instances of the Core JavaScript objects? Well, to understand this, you have to understand that all of the Core JavaScript objects are also functions. At first this may seem very strange. You probably have functions and objects as totally separate entities in your mind. Actually, though, it isn't too hard to understand. Functions can take on properties and methods (additional functions if you like) as belonging to them, as well as child objects of their own. You just haven't seen them used in that way yet. For example you can write this:

```
function myFunc()
{
    alert("hello");
}
```

and then write:

```
myFunc.myProp = "another hello";
```

If the function myFunc didn't already have the property called myProp, then it would immediately be created and assigned the string literal "another hello".

Functions are objects, and although they weren't signified by writing the call operators after their names in the list of Core JavaScript objects above, all those objects except the Math object are function objects (even the function object itself). In fact if you alert the names of these objects in an alert box, you will be told that they are functions. For example if you were to write the following:

INPUT
```
alert(Boolean);
```

you will see the alert box shown in Figure 4.9.

OUTPUT

FIGURE 4.9

The `alert()` *function showing the character of* `Boolean`.

ANALYSIS This is significant because you can call the Core JavaScript objects as functions and, when you do, they will create a copy of themselves. For example you could write this:

```
var myNum = Number();
```

This only creates a number literal; it doesn't create an instance of the `Number` object (a full copy that is a number object) and so isn't proper constructor function notation. To create an instance of one of the Core JavaScript objects, you have to use another of the operators, the `new` operator. Here is how to use it with the `Number()` function.

```
var myNum = new Number();
```

When a Core JavaScript object is called as a function like this using the `new` operator it is true constructor function notation and a new copy of the object is automatically created. That's it! You don't have to write any methods for it or assign it any properties of your own. Most of what you usually will need is already there. You simply have to add the data and you are ready to go.

4

Note

> Note that the `Math` object is the exception to this rule. You cannot make copies of the `Math` object at all, either literals or instances! The `Math` object is used directly.

Admittedly, you don't often have a reason to create an instance of the `Number` object so that you can add properties and methods to it (although sometimes it can be useful). The Core JavaScript object that you most often will want to make copies of is the `Array` object. The `Array` object is an extremely powerful way of creating a data structure, and its methods provide some extremely powerful tools for managing the data it contains. For this reason, it will be investigated in Chapter 5.

It is worth mentioning that when a page loads, the Core JavaScript objects are all constructed themselves. The original object is the `Function` object. It is then used as a constructor function to create all the Core objects except the `Math` object. The `Object` object, which has been created from the Function object, is used to construct the Math object. This helps to explain why some of the Core objects own some of the properties and methods that they do. Some don't seem applicable to the object they belong to, but it is because they inherit them from the Function object. Another thing to note from this is that you can use the Function object to create your own object constructor functions, which will be discussed in detail much later in the book.

As a final note on the Core JavaScript objects, each core object has its own notations for creating literals and full instances. Using constructor function notation will always result in a full instance, but literal notation will not always result in a literal. For example, when you use literal notation to create an Array or Object object, it will create a full instance anyway. This is because it is the nature of some of these objects that they can only create objects.

Exploring an Object

Before this chapter ends, let's look at two of the JavaScript operators that weren't discussed in Chapter 2. Both of these operators are useful once you start working with objects. One, the in operator, allows you to check whether a property or child of an object exists, and the other, the typeof operator, allows you to discover the type of data or object with which you are dealing.

When you use the in operator you are checking for the existence of a property, method, or child object in another object by name. For example, if you wanted to discover if there was a child object of the window object called "document" you could write this:

```
alert("document" in window);  // alerts true
```

Because the document object does contain an object with the name document the alert() function would display an alert box with the value true. Note that the name of the item we are checking for is written as a string. If we were to write its name as code, the result will simply be false.

As it happens, this use of the in operator is not supported in browser versions before Internet Explorer 5 and Netscape 6. Originally, it was limited to use in a for loop. To demonstrate how it can be used in this way, let's look at an example. For this example assume that an object called bike was created, and you assigned it two properties. One of the properties has the name color and the value green and the other has the name age and the value 5. If you wanted to show all of the bike's properties and their values, you could use the for loop with the in operator as shown here:

INPUT
```
var props = "";
for (var prop in bike) {
  props += "The bike's " + prop + " is " + bike[prop] + "\n";
}
alert(props);
```

This would bring up an alert box with the result shown in Figure 4.10.

OUTPUT

FIGURE 4.10

Using a for *loop to display all the properties of the* bike *object.*

ANALYSIS At first how this form of the for loop works may seem hard to understand. There is no counter variable, no increment of a loop counter, and no condition. However, it isn't actually too complicated. Basically when you use a for in loop like this, during each loop that is made the variable called prop contained within the for loop parentheses is assigned the name of a new property belonging to the object to the right of the in operator. The for statement will continue to loop until the variable prop has been assigned the names of all the properties once. Then it will stop. JavaScript manages internally the assigning of the variable names and the ending of the loop.

In the one statement that the for loop governs in our example above, the variable prop is used to build up a string containing information about the bike object. This string starts out with the value "The bike's " to which the property name contained in the variable prop is concatenated. To this, you then concatenate the string " is " before finally concatenating the value of the property to the string and a line break. The method used to obtain the value of the property is not one you have come across yet. You will learn more about this use of square brackets in the next chapter, but for now just accept that it retrieves the value of the property.

As the for loop loops through the properties of the bike object, it builds up a string stored in the props variable before that string finally is alerted when the loop ends.

Of course you could change the statements in the for loop so that it cycles through the properties of an object performing any process you want. Now let's find out about our second operator.

The `typeof` operator is another useful operator. It is invaluable when you need to take different actions on a piece of data depending on its data type. When applied to a piece of data this operator will return one of six strings. The possible values of these strings are listed below:

```
boolean
```

```
function
```

```
number
```

```
object
```

```
string
```

```
undefined
```

Notice that, even though functions are a type of object, the `typeof` operator will distinguish functions from other types of objects that may exist. Here are some examples of the `typeof` operator applied to some objects and literals:

```
alert(typeof window.document);    // alerts "object"
alert(typeof 3);                  // alerts "number"
alert(typeof document.scrollBy);  // alerts "function"
alert(typeof true);               // alerts "boolean"
```

All these alerts return the string that you would hopefully expect them to. The only result that may surprise you is that if applied to the value `null`, then the `typeof` operator will return the string `"object"`. Although it is not often that that you will need to know this, it is worth bearing in mind.

To see both the `in` and `typeof` operators in action in a real script, let's look at a full example. In Listing 4.6, the `for in` loop and the `typeof` operators were used to expose the properties of the `navigator` object and to discover the values and types of these properties.

INPUT **LISTING 4.6** The `navigator` Object Exposed (`objectExplorer.htm`)

```html
<html>
<head>
<title>Object Explorer</title>

<style type="text/css">
td             {padding: 0.05em 1em}
</style>

</head>
<body>
```

LISTING 4.6   continued

```
<h1>Object Explorer</h1>

<table>
  <tr>
    <th>Property</th><th>Data Type</th><th>Value</th>
  </tr>

<script language="javascript" type="text/javascript">
<!--

var obj = window.navigator;

for (var prop in obj) {
  document.write("<tr>");
  document.write("  <td>" + prop + "</td>");
  document.write("  <td>" + typeof obj[prop] + "</td>");
  document.write("  <td>" + obj[prop] + "</td>");
  document.write("</tr>");
}

//-->
</script>

</table>

</body>
</html>
```

4

ANALYSIS   The first thing we have done in this example is to start a table and give it three headings. This has been done outside the script block because we will not be repeating this process.

In the first line of script, a reference to the navigator object to a variable called obj was assigned. This saves you from writing out window.navigator three times in the for loop that follows the variable. The for loop was set up like the previous example, but this time the variable called obj was placed to the right of the in operator so that it is the navigator object that the for loop will loop through. In the statement block of the for loop, write out a new row for each loop. The first of the cells is given the name of the property that is stored in the variable prop. The second cell is a little more complex. The typeof operator was applied to the value contained within the property referred to by the variable prop. This will tell you the type of data or if it is an object contained within the property. Finally, the value of the property itself was assigned to the third cell. When loaded the page should contain a table similar to the one shown in Figure 4.11.

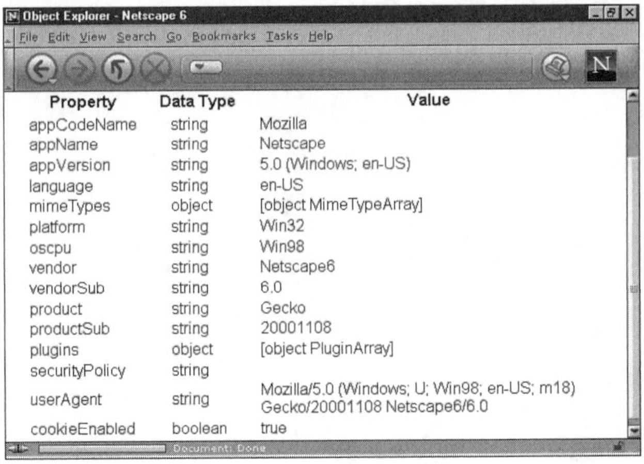

FIGURE 4.11

Using a for in *loop to explore the properties of the* navigator *object.*

Note that the properties that belong to the navigator object vary from browser to browser so when you run the code you may be missing some of the properties shown in Figure 4.11 or have additional ones.

By changing the object assigned to the variable obj you can use this page to discover the properties belonging to other objects. However when a for in loop is used to explore an object it will reveal the names of all child objects, properties, and event handlers. Therefore, if you change the above example to explore other objects, you may see names that you don't expect. Event handlers always start with the word "on". So for example, if you see the name onclick, what you are seeing is the name of an event handler. We will discover what event handlers are used for and how they are used in Chapter 10, "Events and Event Handling."

Note that using the for in loop will only reveal the methods of an object if it is an object that you have created yourself. When used to explore a predefined object such as the window object they will not show up.

Summary

This chapter took a big step toward giving you the tools you will need to make a real difference to your Web pages. You have learned how JavaScript models everything it can work with as objects with properties and methods, as well as providing you with Core objects of its own. When used in the client-side browser environment you gain access to some of the browser and all of the document through the DOM.

Workshop

In this workshop, questions and exercises will be used to review what you have learned in this chapter about objects.

Q&A

Q. In object terminology, what is equivalent to a function?

A. An object has *methods*, which are equivalent to a function.

Q. Does the `window` object always need to be used in the object path when we navigate to one of its child objects?

A. No. From this chapter forward, you will cease to explicitly navigate to objects through the `window` object. Remember that because it is the default it does not need to be included in our object paths. It was used in this chapter simply to help familiarize you with navigating to objects through the hierarchy tree.

Quiz

1. Which Core JavaScript object can you not create a copy of?
2. What is the `Global` object called in client-side JavaScript?
3. The `document` object is a child of which object?

Quiz Answers

1. You can't create a new copy of the `Math` object. It must be used directly.
2. The `window` object is the `Global` object on the client side.
3. The `document` object is a child of the `window` object.

Exercises

1. Display a message such as "Welcome to the world of JavaScript" in the status bar of the browser window.
2. Create an HTML page which contains JavaScript, which uses the `document.write()` method to write the values of the properties of the document object to the Web page.

4

DAY 5

An Introduction to Arrays

Arrays are the first JavaScript objects that we will look at in detail. This chapter will introduce the concept of arrays in JavaScript and how arrays are used, and it will show you how they are useful both in terms of structured data storage and in accessing document objects.

This chapter will teach you

- What arrays are
- How arrays are created
- How arrays are used
- The difference between indexed and associative arrays

What Is an Array?

An array is a special type of object that uses numbers to access each characteristic of the object—in much the same way as property names are used. If you remember what has been said about naming rules in JavaScript, you are probably thinking that this goes fully against the naming conventions discussed earlier, and you would be right. When saying the numbers are like property names, we don't mean that they are exactly the same. Each number does refer to a unique piece of data belonging to the `array` object, but each number also is referred to as an *index* of the array—not a property name. This comparison between property names and indexes was made simply to help you grasp the concept of an array index. Indexes, like property names, are simply the means of accessing an array's data containers.

Since array indexes are not, technically speaking, the same as property names, you can't use the dot notation that you would use for property names. If JavaScript names are not allowed to start with a number, then they certainly aren't allowed to be only a number. Because the indexes of an array are numerical they have to be written in a special way. What you need to do is wrap the index (number) in square brackets. So, the code to access three individual indexes of an array would look like the following:

```
myArray[2]
```

```
myArray[3]
```

```
myArray[4]
```

In the table of operator precedence in Chapter 2, "Working with Data," you might remember that the two operators at the top of the table were the period and a set of square brackets. Each of those was referred to as being a "Member" operator. Hopefully now you can see why.

One member operator is the pair of square brackets, `[ ]`, and it is used to access the indexes of an array.

The other member operator is the period (the full stop), and it is used to describe properties of an object like this:

```
myObject.color
```

```
myObject.size
```

```
myObject.price
```

The period tells JavaScript to consider its right-hand operand as belonging to its left-hand operand. So

```
document.title
```

tells JavaScript that the `title` property belongs to the `document` object. The square brackets mean exactly the same thing. Similarly, when we write

```
myArray[2]
```

JavaScript is referred to the piece of data belonging to the array object `myArray` that has the index 2.

By now you may be wondering why we would want to refer to the pieces of data belonging to an object by number. Well, one of the benefits of doing so is that you can use loop statements to loop through all the indexes of the array to perform the same process on each piece of data.

Looping through the indexes of an array is possible because the indexes of an array are ordered! For example, myArray[2] comes immediately before myArray[3] which comes immediately before myArray[4]. The fact that array indexes are ordered makes looping and other uses of arrays possible.

As you will see in the examples to follow, the numbering of an array starts from zero. Thus the first index in an array is written as

myArray[0]

not, as you might expect:

myArray[1]

Caution

Arrays are numbered from zero. Forgetting that can cause errors because if you refer to myArray[1] thinking it is the first member of an array (when it is the second), the result you will get is not likely to be the result you want.

Arrays are primarily used to structure data in JavaScript. By grouping pieces of data together under one object name, the data can be structured in a way that makes it much easier to use. In addition to having the ability to refer to each piece of data by number and therefore have the capability to use loop statements to get at the data, the Array object also has some very powerful methods for data management.

5

Note

If you find the concept of arrays difficult to grasp, then you might try thinking of them as a single column table or database. The column has a name (the array name), and each of the cells in the column is referred to by row number (the array's index numbers).

Okay, enough theory; let's actually make and use some arrays.

Creating an Array

NEW TERM Usually arrays are created using one of JavaScript's Core Objects which, as you may have realized from Chapter 4, "JavaScript Is Object-Based," is the `Array` object. This object also is referred to as one of JavaScript's *constructor functions*, so called because they can be used to construct new objects.

> **Caution**
>
> The first letter of the name of an `Array` object is capitalized, as is the case with all the other Core JavaScript objects. A common error is forgetting to capitalize the first letter. That simple mistake can cause some puzzling errors in your code.

When you use a constructor function to create a new object it is used in conjunction with the `new` keyword, as you may remember from the end of Chapter 4. The `new` operator acts on the `Array()` function (as it does when used with any other constructor function). It ensures that the function returns an object and not just a piece of data (some of the constructor functions always return an object, but some can return a piece of data or an object). Here is an example of how you would create an array using this method:

```
var myArray = new Array();
```

The first thing you may notice about this example is that it uses the `var` statement to create a variable, called `myArray`, and then assigns it the new `Array` object. This is because arrays are stored in variables—or at least a reference is stored in the variable so that it looks as if the array is stored in the variable. Arrays don't actually have a name of their own. They can only be accessed using data containers that store a reference to them. If that doesn't make sense at the moment don't worry about it. For now just think of the variable name as loosely being the name of the array. You will see how important the distinction is later.

Providing Individual Arguments

Although the use of the constructor function above creates a new `Array` object, it has not been given any data to store in the *array elements* (which, put simply, is what the data containers are called that belong to an array and are accessed using index numbers). When the `Array()` constructor function is used to create an array there are two methods that can be used to create elements and store data in them. When only a small array is needed, it is common to pass each piece of data as an argument to the `Array()` constructor function. So, to create an array with three pieces of data `"a"`, `"b"`, and `"c"`, you would write:

```
var myArray = new Array("a", "b", "c");
```

When this method is used the function takes the data that is passed to it through the arguments and places each piece of data into the first elements of the array it creates. Note that the pieces of data are stored in the elements in the order that you write them. Therefore the array declaration above will create an array where the value of element 0 is "a", the value of element 1 is "b" and the value of element 2 is "c". Remember, the first element of an array is given the index 0, and the index of each subsequent element increases by 1.

> **Note**
>
> The reason arrays begin at index 0 is that computers (and therefore programmers) commence their counting from zero. Although this can initially take some time to become accustomed to, hopefully you will find it becomes second nature as you progress through the book.

Creating an Empty Array and Populating It

Another method involves creating the array, and then populating (filling) its elements with data separately. To do this, you declare the array first, then on separate lines use the assignment operator to assign each piece of data to an array element one by one. The elements are written as you might expect. Just as you would use the property name of an object's property to assign data to that property, like so:

```
object.propertyName = "data";
```

You can use an element's index to assign data to array elements, like this:

```
arrayName[index] = "data";
```

So, if you rewrote the previous example using this second method for creating an array, you would write it like this:

```
var myArray = new Array();
myArray[0] = "a";  // remember the first element index is 0!
myArray[1] = "b";
myArray[2] = "c";
```

Listing 5.1 creates an array that writes each of its elements back to the screen using a for loop.

INPUT

LISTING 5.1   Creating an Array, Populating It, and Displaying the Contents of Each Array Element (arrayContents.htm)

```
<html>
<head>
<title>Writing an Array</title>
```

5

LISTING 5.1   continued

```
</head>
<body>

<h1>Writing an Array</h1>

<p>

<script language="javascript" type="text/javascript">
<!--

var myArray = new Array();
myArray[0] = "-- First Element --";
myArray[1] = "-- Second Element --";
myArray[2] = "-- Third Element --";
for (var i=0; i<myArray.length; i++) {
  document.write("Element " +i+ " contains: " +myArray[i]+ "<br />");
}

//-->
</script>

</p>

</body>
</html>
```

Figure 5.1 shows the output when you run Listing 5.1.

OUTPUT

FIGURE 5.1

Displaying the elements that are contained in a newly created array.

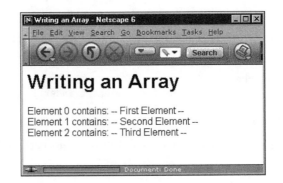

ANALYSIS   This method and the one shown earlier are simply different ways of doing the same thing. When only a small number of short pieces of data are needed to fill an array, the former is a quicker way to write it. But when you have a large number of longer pieces of data the first method becomes cumbersome and difficult to read. It is then better to use the second method just presented to individually assign each piece of data to an element after the array has been declared.

For example, when you created an array earlier using

```
var myArray = new Array()
```

the length of the new array was undefined. Sometimes you may want to create an array of a particular length, say 10 elements, at a time when you don't necessarily know the data (or all of the data) with which the array is going to be populated. So, a new array of a particular length can be declared like this:

```
var myArray = new Array(10);
```

The above code causes an array with 10 elements to be created, although each element is presently empty. The number in parentheses tells the function how many elements the array should be created with. It makes no perceivable difference to the speed with which you can create the array, nor does it prevent you from adding more elements later. When it comes in useful is if you need an array to be a certain size but don't yet want to populate its elements.

Remember that when the length is 10, the first element in the array is `myArray[0]`, and the final element in the array is `myArray[9]`.

Note

Just as you can assign and reassign different types of data to a variable, all of the array elements need not have the same data type. Unlike more fully featured programming languages, JavaScript allows you to change the data type of array elements.

5

Array Literals

As mentioned at the end of Chapter 2, in addition to using constructor function syntax, you also can create copies of objects using a literal notation.

To achieve the same result as in the examples shown above, you could use array literals to declare the array, like this:

```
var myArray = ["a", "b", "c"];
```

This third way of declaring an array hasn't been commonly used until recently because it was introduced with version 4 browsers. Now that the vast majority of browsers are version 4 and above, it is fairly safe to use this method unless you know that you must cater to earlier browser versions.

When you use literal notation to create an array you do not need to use the `Array()` constructor function. Simply list the pieces of data in the order that you want to place them into the array's elements, and then enclose this list within square brackets.

The JavaScript interpreter knows that the square brackets are indicating that it should create a new array and use the list of data to fill the elements.

When using literal notation to create an array, the array that is created is no different than the array that would have been created had the `Array()` constructor function been used. Therefore you can use any of the three methods without worrying about the differences.

However, for the remainder of this chapter, let's concentrate on using the constructor function notation because it is the only general way of guaranteeing—with other Core JavaScript objects—that the objects we want to create are actually objects. For arrays, using the constructor notation is one of several useful forms of syntax. For other objects, it will be essential for you to use the constructor function. So using the constructor function to create arrays will help you become accustomed to using the constructor function notation.

Accessing Arrays

To use the data in the elements of the arrays shown above, simply reference them as you would when accessing a variable, object property, or any other data container. Just be careful to specify the index of the element whose data you want. For example, if you wanted to obtain the data from the second element in the examples above, you would write:

```
// Remember the second element has the index 1!
var myVal = myArray[1];
alert(myVal);//  alerts "b"
```

Let's look at something a bit more interesting, looping through the elements of an array. By structuring data in arrays, you can use loop statements to loop through the elements. Any time you have a repeated process where the only change is a piece of data, a combination of loop statement(s) and array(s) is ideal.

In the following example (Listing 5.2), let's write out some phone numbers to an HTML table. This could be done directly, but to demonstrate how we can combine arrays and `loop` statements let's use JavaScript. Note that because you will be writing HTML in the body of the document, you will have to place the script block into the body of the page.

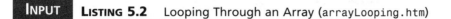

LISTING 5.2 Looping Through an Array (`arrayLooping.htm`)

```html
<html>
<head>
<title>Table of Phone Numbers</title>

</head>
<body>

<h1>Table of Phone Numbers</h1>

<table border="1">

<script language="javascript" type="text/javascript">
<!--

var phoneNos     = new Array();
    phoneNos[0] = "31 20 305355";
    phoneNos[1] = "49 30 20670 0";
    phoneNos[2] = "44 020 4562 2929";
    phoneNos[3] = "01 518 463 5622";
    phoneNos[4] = "02 9663 0551";

for (var i=0; i<5; i++) {
  document.write("<tr><td>Phone Number " + i + " is:</td>");
  document.write("<td>" + phoneNos[i] + "</td></tr>");
}

//-->
</script>

</table>

</body>
</html>
```

5

As the `for` statement loops through the array plucking data from each element and writing it to the page into the table's rows and cells, the table is populated, and when the page loads you should see something like Figure 5.2.

OUTPUT

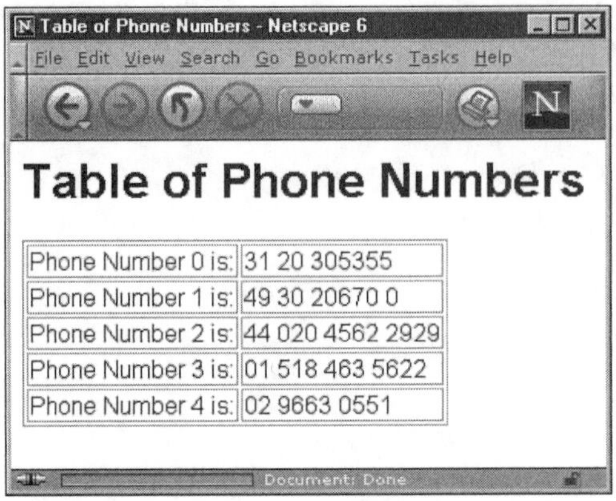

FIGURE 5.2

Tabulated phone numbers.

As you can see, even before you begin the script block you have already written the opening tag of the table. It shouldn't be included in the script block because it is only written once. However, the process used to produce each row needs to be repeated, and so fits well within the functionality of a `for` loop.

So to recap, the first thing you have done in your script is to store the phone numbers in an array called `phoneNos`. You then set up a loop statement. In this example, we used a `for` loop.

The first thing you need to think about when designing the loop is what the three statements will consist of (the three statements are contained within the parentheses of the `for` statement). The index of the first element of the array is 0. So you will need to set the initial value of the counter variable `i` to 0. As there are five pieces of data in the array, the index of the array's last element is 4. Therefore set the condition of the array so that it will continue to loop while `i` is less than 5, which means that 4 will be the last value of `i` that will be processed by the `for` loop. Lastly, of course, set `i` to be incremented because you will want to iterate through the elements. Now let's look at the statement block.

The statements that the `for` loop governs clearly need to contain the document object's `write()` method if the contents of our array elements are to be written to the page. It is the code contained within the parentheses of the `write()` methods that may be a little more tricky to devise.

In the first line of the statement block, start a new table row and write out the first cell. Concatenate the string `"<tr><td>Phone Number "` with `i` and another string `"is:</td>"`. With each loop the value of `i` will be different, so you will end up with a different string in the first cell of each row of the table with the format:

```
Phone Number X is:
```

where X is the value of i during the loop that wrote the row in which the cell is contained.

In the second line of the statement block, write out the table cell that will hold the appropriate phone number. Of course this time you will need to extract a phone number from the array phoneNos.

The clever thing here is that you do not specify an index in the square brackets. Instead you use the counter variable i. Since i is the looping variable the index for each loop is different. On the first loop the value of i is zero, and so the phone number stored in phoneNos's first element, phoneNos[0], will be written to the page. The second time through the value of i is 1 and the contents of phoneNos's second element, phoneNos[1], will be written to the page. The looping continues until the data contained in all of the elements of the phoneNos array has been written to the HTML page.

Although in this example it would have been just as quick to write out the table as HTML without the use of JavaScript, using arrays can often save space. The Array object's powerful methods also allow you to organize and change this data before it is outputted.

Before looking at the Array object's properties and methods, let's first look at using arrays in parallel.

Parallel Arrays

There are times when you may want to work with two or more related sets of data. The most straightforward way to do this is to structure the data in *parallel arrays*. In this instance, parallel means that the sets of data are stored in separate arrays, but an element of any given index in one array is related to the element(s) at the same index in another array(s). To illustrate this let's look at an example.

Imagine that the phone numbers in the previous example are the numbers of our international offices. If you want to output the phone numbers into an HTML table as you did in the previous example, you probably will want to write them alongside the office locations. To do this you will need to store the office locations in an array as well as the phone numbers. The key to success is making sure that the two arrays are parallel. But what does this mean in practice?

Let's assume that the array where the locations will be stored is called "offices". If the first of our phone numbers is the number of our Amsterdam office, then Amsterdam needs to be written into the table in the element with the same index as the first phone number. For this to happen, "Amsterdam" needs to be stored in the element of the array offices with the index that corresponds to the index of the first phone number. In this case the element index is 0. This means that in the loop when the counter variable i's value is 0 and the first phone number is written, "Amsterdam" will also be written in the same loop and therefore will be in the same table row.

For the same reason if the second number (stored in the element of phoneNos with the index 1) is the number of the Berlin office, then "Berlin" needs to be stored in the array offices with the index 1. Given that the next three telephone numbers are the numbers for the London, New York and Sydney offices respectively, the logical progression is shown in Table 5.1.

TABLE 5.1 Tabulation of offices and phoneNos Arrays

Element Index	Office	Phone Numbers
0	Amsterdam	31 20 305355
1	Berlin	49 30 20670 0
2	London	44 020 4562 2929
3	New York	01 518 463 5622
4	Sydney	02 9663 0551

Let's implement this in a new HTML page. See Listing 5.3.

LISTING 5.3 Creating the Parallel Arrays—offices and phoneNos
INPUT (parallelArrays.htm)

```
<html>
<head>
<title>Office Phone Numbers</title>

</head>
<body>

<h1>Office Phone Numbers</h1>

<table border="1">

<script language="javascript" type="text/javascript">
<!--

var offices     = new Array();
    offices[0] = "Amsterdam";
    offices[1] = "Berlin";
    offices[2] = "London";
    offices[3] = "New York";
    offices[4] = "Sydney";
```

LISTING 5.3   continued

```
var phoneNos    = new Array();
    phoneNos[0] = "31 20 305355";
    phoneNos[1] = "49 30 20670 0";
    phoneNos[2] = "44 020 4562 2929";
    phoneNos[3] = "01 518 463 5622";
    phoneNos[4] = "02 9663 0551";

for (var i=0; i<5; i++) {
  document.write("<tr><td>" + offices[i] + "</td>");
  document.write("<td>" + phoneNos[i] + "</td></tr>");
}

//-->
</script>

</table>

</body>
</html>
```

This script will write out the table and when the document is loaded, you should see the following page in your browser window. See Figure 5.3.

OUTPUT

FIGURE 5.3

International office locations with their telephone numbers.

5

Of course you aren't limited to just two arrays in parallel. You could also have an array for street addresses, an array for e-mail addresses, and so on. It is important to remember that the elements must line up so that the arrays are "parallel."

Okay, now that you know how to create and use arrays, let's find out more about the properties and methods that the Array object makes available to you when working with arrays.

Array Properties

The `Array` object has five properties. These have been listed below:

- The `constructor` property
- The `index` property
- The `input` property
- The `length` property
- The `prototype` property

This chapter will look at only one of the properties of the `Array` object in detail—the `length` property. Although what it does is very simple, it can be an extremely useful tool. Often when you use a `loop` statement to access an array you will use the `length` property. Let's see how it works so that you can understand why it is so useful.

The `length` property simply tells how many elements an array contains. This is demonstrated in Listing 5.4.

LISTING 5.4   Using the `length` Property of the `Array` Object

INPUT   (arrayLength.htm)

```
<html>
<head>
<title>Array Length</title>

<script language="javascript" type="text/javascript">
<!--

var lengthTest    = new Array();
    lengthTest[0] = 0;
    lengthTest[1] = 1;
    lengthTest[2] = 2;
alert(lengthTest.length);

//-->
</script>

</head>
<body>

<h1>Array Length</h1>

</body>
</html>
```

If you were to run this piece of script you would see the following alert box. See Figure 5.4.

OUTPUT

FIGURE 5.4

Using the length
property of the Array
object to display the
length of the array
lengthTest.

ANALYSIS Note that even though the last element in the array has an index of 2, the alert shows the length property has the value 3. This is because the indexing of arrays starts at 0—but there are still three elements. This is a feature that can be confusing initially, so be careful that you don't trip up on that.

The index of the last element of an array is always one less than the value stored in the array's length property. So if you were to use the length property to retrieve the value of the last element, you would have to subtract one from it as shown in the following example:

```
var valueOfLastElement = myArray[myArray.length-1];
```

In the table of operator precedence, the square brackets were at the very top of the table, which means that you can put expressions inside square brackets. The content of the square brackets will evaluate to a single value before the rest of the statement is evaluated. In the example above the expression myArray.length returns the number of elements in the array, and then 1 is taken off so that the result is the index of the last element in the array. Therefore the contents of the last element of the array are assigned to the variable called valueOfLastElement.

When you need to add a new element to the end of an array, you also can make use of the length property. This time, however, let's use the length property unaltered:

```
myArray[myArray.length] = "value for new last element";
```

Again the value of the length property is returned before the rest of the statement is evaluated. The length of the array is one greater than the index of the last element of the array because the first array index is zero. Therefore the index of myArray, which is one past its last element, is assigned the string you see above. This effectively creates a new element at the end of the array. Note also that after the statement has been evaluated the length of the array is increased to reflect the addition of a new element. Therefore you could use this statement in a loop to repeatedly add new elements to the end of an array.

Listing 5.5 shows the length of an array before and after new elements have been added in the manner just discussed.

INPUT **LISTING 5.5**   Using the `length` Property of the `Array` Object to Add Elements to the End of an Array (`lengthUpdated.htm`)

```
<html>
<head>
<title>Length Automatically Updates</title>

<script language="javascript" type="text/javascript">
<!--

var someArray = new Array();
alert(someArray.length);
someArray[0] = "hi";
alert(someArray.length);
someArray[1] = "there";
alert(someArray.length);

//-->
</script>

</head>
<body>

<h1>Length Automatically Updates</h1>

</body>
</html>
```

ANALYSIS   When you load this page you will see three alert boxes in succession. These alert boxes will contain the values 1, 2, and 3 respectively.

Both these examples are good uses of the `length` property, but where the `length` property of the `Array` object can be most helpful is in looping statements. To demonstrate that let's look at another example.

In the two examples earlier with the telephone numbers and office locations, you had to specify in the `for` loop statement exactly how many elements were in the array. If you had used a number that was too large, the loop would have looped too many times, but if you had used a number that was too small not all of the office locations and phone numbers would have been written into the table. Rather than counting the number of elements in the loop you could have used the array's `length` property. Let's see how to create the page again with this modification. See Listing 5.6.

INPUT

LISTING 5.6 Using the `length` Property to Control How Many Times a `for` Loop Loops (`lengthDemo.htm`)

```html
<html>
<head>
<title>Office Phone Numbers</title>

</head>
<body>

<h1>Office Phone Numbers</h1>

<table border="1">

<script language="javascript" type="text/javascript">
<!--

var offices    = new Array();
    offices[0] = "Amsterdam";
    offices[1] = "Berlin";
    offices[2] = "London";
    offices[3] = "New York";
    offices[4] = "Sydney";

var phoneNos    = new Array();
    phoneNos[0] = "31 20 305355";
    phoneNos[1] = "49 30 20670 0";
    phoneNos[2] = "44 020 4562 2929";
    phoneNos[3] = "01 518 463 5622";
    phoneNos[4] = "02 9663 0551";

for (var i=0; i<offices.length; i++) {
  document.write("<tr><td>" + offices[i] + "</td>");
  document.write("<td>" + phoneNos[i] + "</td></tr>");
}

//-->
</script>

</table>

</body>
</html>
```

5

ANALYSIS   In the parentheses of the `for` loop we have told it to keep looping while `i` is less than the `length` property of (number of elements in) the array `offices`. This means that the last loop that will be made is with `i` set to one less than the length of the array. This will always be the index of the last element of an array, which is exactly what we want.

> **Note**
>
> In this example we have specified the `length` property of the array called `offices`, but we could just as easily have used the `phoneNos` array because both have the same length.

For a short simple script like the one above, using the `length` property or writing in the length doesn't really make much difference. Either method is almost as easy as the other. However, for many of our longer or more complex scripts this won't be the case. Often writing the length of an array into loop statements as a number can be inconvenient or may even be impossible, since you can't necessarily know in advance the length of a particular array.

When you have an array that changes regularly and you have hardcoded its length into loop statements as a number, you will need to change these numbers every time you change the array. Tracking down hardcoded lengths in loop statements at various parts of a script can be a real pain—especially in longer more complex scripts. And, of course, if you accidentally miss making one correction or update your script, you will very likely produce all sorts of unexpected and hard to track down errors.

You will also come across occasions when you don't know how many elements an array will contain. This can be because certain processes will alter the length of your arrays by an unknown amount, the arrays are built up from a server-side database, or your site. Regardless of the reason why you can't predict the length of the array, using the `length` property then becomes the practical way to write your code.

> **Tip**
>
> The `length` property should always be used in the condition of the loops that are created to handle arrays. Getting into that habit will save both time and effort in the long run, even if it makes the `for` statement just a little longer.

Having already looked at the `length` property, let's briefly touch on the other properties of the `Array` object, which we will look at in more detail in later chapters.

There are two properties that the `Array` object has that all JavaScript Core objects have in common. These are the `prototype` and `constructor` properties. Both of these properties are intended to enable you to do some advanced scripting, as you will see later in the book. (We will not continue to mention them as we look at each of the other Core objects, but you may wish to be aware that they exist.) Another two properties of the `Array` object, `index` and `input` properties, are specific to the `Array` object and are sometimes generated by *regular expressions*. Regular expressions are a fairly advanced topic that is discussed later in the book.

Array Methods

What the `Array` object lacks in terms of number of properties it more than makes up for with the number of its methods. The methods that belong to JavaScript's `Array` object provide us with powerful tools that make managing arrays and the data they contain much easier. Here is a list of the methods of the `Array` object:

- The `concat()` method
- The `join()` method
- The `pop()` method
- The `push()` method
- The `reverse()` method
- The `slice()` method
- The `shift()` method
- The `sort()` method
- The `splice()` method
- The `toLocaleString()` method
- The `toSource()` method
- The `toString()` method
- The `unshift()` method
- The `valueOf()` method

In this section we will examine most of these methods, but will leave the `concat()`, `slice()`, `sort()`, and `splice()` methods until later in the book. Although those are the most powerful of the `Array` object's methods, they are also the most complicated to use, so for now let's satisfy ourselves with the others.

First, let's look at the first three methods, which return the contents of the array they are applied to as a string. There are occasions when this can be useful, but not often, so we won't spend too much time on them. The other methods that we will look at in this chapter provide a means of organizing and using the data in our arrays, and as such are worthy of careful attention.

The `toString()` Method

When you create an array and pass it by name as an argument to an `alert()` function you see a list of the values in each element separated by commas. For example, as shown in the following:

INPUT
```
var x = new Array(1,2,3);
alert(x);
```

This brings up the alert box seen in Figure 5.5.

OUTPUT

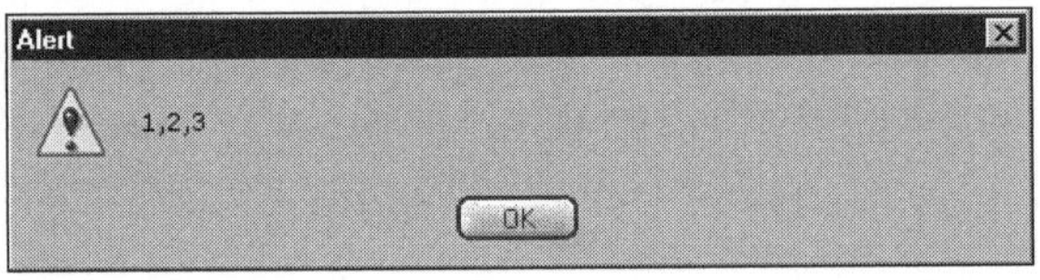

FIGURE 5.5

The content of a new array shown in an alert box.

ANALYSIS As you can see the contents appear as a comma-separated string, but in reality it only exists in this form in the alert box—the array is still an object with all the data in individual elements.

If you want to obtain a string list of the elements of an array as they appear in the alert box, then you need to use the `toString()` method. As a global function that is applied using the dot notation, the `toString()` function is also available to all objects (including the `Array` object) as a method. When used on an array the `toString()` function creates a string from the elements in the array separated by commas—exactly as you saw them in the alert box.

It isn't common to use the `toString()` method, but if, for example, you need to send data you have collected and stored in an array to the server (or another page), then it can make things a lot simpler to send the data as a comma-separated list. Later in the book we will see how to pass data between pages, but for now let's continue with our study of the `Array` object's methods.

The `toLocaleString()` Method

The `toLocaleString()` method has been introduced to JavaScript only recently and is supported by only Internet Explorer 5.5+ and Netscape 6+. It too returns the contents of all the elements of an array strung together as a string, but with a fundamental difference to the `toString()` method. The `toLocaleString()` method returns a string that contains all the numerical elements of the array in local currency format, leaving other data types unchanged, and so creates a single string from all the array's elements modified to local format.

As is the case for the `toString()` method, the `toLocaleString()` method is available as a method of all the JavaScript Core objects. As formatting numbers is more appropriate for discussion in Chapter 7, "Numbers and Math," let's leave a more detailed examination of this method until then. For the moment just note for the future that the `toLocaleString()` method can be applied to arrays of numbers, as well as the numbers we will see it applied to in Chapter 7.

The `join()` Method

The `join()` method is the third method for returning the contents of array elements that are "joined" together as a string. Used just as it is, without a parameter, the `join()` method will behave in exactly the same fashion as the `toString()` method. The `join()` method will simply return a string of the elements of the array that it's applied to separated by commas. But when you pass it a value as a parameter, you can control the separator used.

With the `toString()` method, the items contained within the elements of an array are always returned separated by commas. Sometimes you may wish or even need to separate the elements with some other character (or series of characters). By passing these character(s) to the `join()` method as its sole argument, you can do exactly that. For example:

INPUT

```
var myArr = new Array(1,2,3);
var myStr = myArr.join("---");
alert(myStr);
```

This will bring up the alert box seen in Figure 5.6.

OUTPUT

FIGURE 5.6

Displaying the contents of an array using the `join()` *method.*

5

ANALYSIS As you can see each element has been separated by the three dashes passed to the `join()` method as its argument.

Of course this method can also be used for passing array data to the server or another page, and you may choose it over the `toString()` method if there is a reason for separating the elements with characters other than commas. But, perhaps surprisingly, the `join()` method also comes in very useful when you need to join the elements of an array without a character separator. To do this, simply pass a zero length string as the method's parameter. To do this for the previous example, you would have written it like this:

```
var myStr = myArr.join("");
```

For the moment we won't make much use of this method, but if you need to build up parallel sets of data in small steps, a combination of arrays and the `join()` method is invaluable.

Adding and Removing Elements from an Array

Netscape has had five methods for adding and removing elements from an array since version 4. Two of these methods add and remove elements to and from the beginning of the array, and the other two methods perform the same function at the end of the array. The fifth method is used to add, remove, and edit elements at any point in an array; it is the `splice()` method, which is one of the methods we will look at later in the book.

Caution Unfortunately these methods were not introduced to Internet Explorer until version 5.5. In the future when the version 4 and 5.0 browsers have virtually disappeared, you will be able to make full use of these methods. Note that Internet Explorer 5.0 and under won't recognize them.

Let's look at the first two methods that work at the end of an array. Part of the work done by these two methods can be (almost) as easily achieved by other means, but they also have some helpful features that add to their usefulness.

The `push()` Method

You can make use of the `length` property (as discussed earlier) when you want to add an item to the end of an array. For example, to append a new element to an array called `myArray` you could simply write:

```
myArray[myArray.length] = "data";
```

The value contained in myArray's length property will be one greater than the index of myArray's last element. Therefore when the statement between the square brackets evaluates the string "data" is added to a new last element at the end of the array. After this line of code is executed the length property is automatically updated to reflect the change.

That is fairly concise but you also can use the push() method to achieve the same result. Use the dot notation to apply the method to an array, while supplying the data for the new element as a parameter. If you were to rewrite the previous example to make use of the push() method, it would look like this:

```
myArray.push("data");
```

This is slightly shorter and slightly more readable—especially when the name of the array is quite long. It also can be used to populate an array as shown in the following example:

```
var countArray = new Array();
for (i=0; i<5; i++) {
  countArray.push(i);
}
alert(countArray); // alerts "0,1,2,3,4"
```

However there is a little trick that the push() method has that the above examples don't show. The method also returns the new length of the array it has been applied to, as shown in Listing 5.7:

INPUT

LISTING 5.7 The New Length of an Array Is Returned by the push() Method (lengthReturned.htm)

5

```
<html>
<head>
<title>New Length Returned</title>

<script language="javascript" type="text/javascript">
<!--

var x = new Array(1,2,3);
var newLength = x.push(4);
alert(x);          // alerts 1,2,3,4
alert(newLength);  // alerts 4

//-->
</script>

</head>
<body>
```

LISTING 5.7 continued

```
<h1>New Length Returned</h1>

</body>
</html>
```

ANALYSIS The second line not only assigns the value 4 to the end of the array x, but it also returns the new length of x which has been assigned to the variable newLength.

The pop() Method

The pop() method is similar to the push() method in that it works at the end of an array, but exactly opposite in terms of the action it performs. The pop() method removes the last element from the array it is applied to as you can see in Listing 5.8:

INPUT **LISTING 5.8** Using the pop() Method to Return the Last Element of an Array (lastElement.htm)

```
<html>
<head>
<title>Last Element Returned</title>

<script language="javascript" type="text/javascript">
<!--

var x = new Array("a","b","c","d");
var lastEl = x.pop();
alert(x.length);   // alerts 3
alert(lastEl);     // alerts "d"

//-->
</script>

</head>
<body>

<h1>Last Element Returned</h1>

</body>
</html>
```

ANALYSIS A loop statement also can be used in conjunction with the pop() method to loop through an array, removing all its elements one at a time and performing an action on each one as it is removed.

Let's look at an example that uses a combination of the pop() and push() methods together with a while loop to separate an array of ages into ages belonging to adults and ages belonging to minors. For the purposes of this example, let's assume that a minor is less than 21 years of age. See Listing 5.9.

LISTING 5.9 Using the pop() and push() Methods of the Array Object to **INPUT** Separate Ages (agesSeparated.htm)

```
<html>
<head>
<title>Separating an Array</title>

<script language="javascript" type="text/javascript">
<!--

var ages = new Array(12,57,32,6,21,19);
var adults = new Array();
var minors = new Array();
while (ages.length) {
  var tempAge = ages.pop();
  if (tempAge < 21) minors.push(tempAge);
  else adults.push(tempAge);
}

var msg  = "There are " + adults.length + " adults ";
    msg += "with the ages " + adults.join(", ") + "<br />";
    msg += "There are " + minors.length + " minors ";
    msg += "with the ages " + minors.join(", ");

//-->
</script>

</head>
<body>

<h1>Separating an Array</h1>

<script language="javascript" type="text/javascript">
<!--

document.write("<p>" + msg + "</p>");

//-->
</script>

</body>
</html>
```

5

This will generate an appearance on a page similar to that shown in Figure 5.7.

OUTPUT

FIGURE 5.7

Ages separated and recombined using the pop() *and* push() *methods of the* Array *object.*

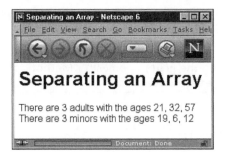

ANALYSIS The first three lines of code create three arrays. The first one (ages) has six numbers in it, representing a group of people's ages, and the other two arrays (called adults and minors) start out empty. Let's remove all the ages one by one from the array ages and move them to one of the other arrays depending on the value of the array elements. In this way the ages of the minors can be separated out from the ages of the adults.

Note that by using the length of the array called ages, you don't even need to use a loop counter or incrementer for your loop. Simply use a while loop to keep removing and sorting elements until the length of the array ages is zero. Once this has happened (when all the elements have been pulled off and sorted), then the loop will stop.

In the statement block of the while loop, first remove the last element from the array called ages and store the value returned in a variable called tempAge. Then use if...else statements to choose to which array to add the age that was removed. The loop continues until all the ages have been assigned to the correct arrays.

After the while loop a message is built up to show the contents of the two arrays: adults and minors. In the first line of this code, you will find the number of adult ages that have been found by using the length property of the adults array. In the next line, the join() method is used to join up these ages to display individual ages separated by a comma and space. After adding a <br /> tag, proceed to do the same with the minors array. In the body of the document, we finally output the separated array in a paragraph.

You may have noticed that the order of the individual ages was reversed by the method used in Listing 5.9. If we had used the reverse() method within the code, to be described later, we could have maintained the ordering of the data.

If we had other arrays that were parallel with the array called ages, such as an array for names or contact details, we could also have separated them as well. We would just have had to create two new arrays for each original one.

The `shift()` and `unshift()` Methods

The names of the methods used to add and remove elements from the front of an array are not quite so vivid as the names `push()` and `pop()`. The `shift()` method is the method that does the same thing to the beginning of an array as the `pop()` method does to the end. It removes and returns the first element of the array to which it is applied. For example, see Listing 5.10.

INPUT

LISTING 5.10   Using the `shift()` Method to Remove the First Element (`firstElement.htm`)

```
<html>
<head>
<title>Removing the first Element</title>

<script language="javascript" type="text/javascript">
<!--

var x = new Array(1,2,3,4);
var firstElement = x.shift();
alert(firstElement);  // alerts 1
alert(x.length);      // alerts 3
alert(x);             // alerts 2,3,4

//-->
</script>

</head>
<body>

<h1>Removing the first Element</h1>

</body>
</html>
```

5

ANALYSIS   There are several things to note about this example. The first alert tells us that the `shift()` method has removed the first element as we said it would, and the second alert shows that the length property of array x has been reduced to 3. But it is the third alert that is really important to note. It shows that the data in the rest of x's elements have all been moved back by 1. If this was not the case, then the first element would have been left empty, and the next time we tried to use the `shift()` method it would simply have returned the value undefined.

The `unshift()` method, as you may have guessed, is the method to add a new piece of data to the beginning of an array. Listing 5.11 shows an example of the `unshift()` method at work.

INPUT **LISTING 5.11**   Using the `unshift()` Method to Add an Element to the
Beginning of an Array (`unshift.htm`)

```html
<html>
<head>
<title>Adding to the Beginning</title>

<script language="javascript" type="text/javascript">
<!--

var x = new Array(1,2,3,4);
var newLength = x.unshift(0);
alert(x.length);   // alerts 5
alert(x);          // alerts 0,1,2,3,4

//-->
</script>

</head>
<body>

<h1>Adding to the Beginning</h1>

</body>
</html>
```

ANALYSIS   As you can see above, it has pushed the number 0 onto the front of the array x
and moved all the other elements back by one. Note that just as the `push()`
method returns the new length of the array, so does the `unshift()` method—but only in
Netscape. For some reason at the time of writing, it is not returned in version 5.5 of
Internet Explorer.

The `shift()` and `unshift()` methods are just an alternative way to add and remove elements to and from an array. Sometimes you may want to add to or remove elements from the end of an array, and sometimes you may want to add to or remove elements from the beginning of an array. The `Array` object provides methods to do both.

If you need to add or remove elements in the middle of an array, you will need to use the `splice()` method. However, it is one of the four methods of the `Array` object that we will leave until later in the book to examine in detail.

Caution   Remember that the `push()`, `pop()`, `shift()`, and `unshift()` methods were only introduced to Internet Explorer at version 5.5. For most of us, this means that we will have to wait some time before we can safely use these methods in a production Web site.

The reverse() Method

As its name suggests, the reverse() method reverses the order of the array elements. Once applied to an array the element that had index 0 will now have the index of the last element in the array. The element that was last will now be first, and all the elements in the middle are moved to their corresponding mirror-image position.

This very fast and efficient means of reverse ordering an array provided by the reverse() method can be very useful. For example if you knew an array was in alphabetical order and wanted to put it in reverse alphabetical order, then you would simply use the reverse() method.

In Listing 5.9 we used the push() and pop() methods to split an array of ages into adults and minors. If we add the reverse() method prior to separating the array in that listing, as shown in Listing 5.12, we would preserve the original ordering of the ages.

INPUT

LISTING 5.12   Using the pop(), push(), and reverse() Methods to Split an Array While Preserving the Order of Elements (orderPreserved.htm)

```
<html>
<head>
<title>Separating an Array</title>

<script language="javascript" type="text/javascript">
<!--

var ages = new Array(12,57,32,6,21,19);
    ages = ages.reverse();   // *** reverse() added ***
var adults = new Array();
var minors = new Array();
while (ages.length) {
  var tempAge = ages.pop();
  if (tempAge < 21) minors.push(tempAge);
  else adults.push(tempAge);
}

var msg  = "There are " + adults.length + " adults ";
    msg += "with the ages " + adults.join(", ") + "<br />";
    msg += "There are " + minors.length + " minors ";
    msg += "with the ages " + minors.join(", ");

//-->
</script>

</head>
<body>
```

5

LISTING 5.12   continued

```
<h1>Separating an Array</h1>

<script language="javascript" type="text/javascript">
<!--

document.write("<p>" + msg + "</p>");

//-->
</script>

</body>
</html>
```

As you can see in Figure 5.8, the ordering of the ages which existed in the ages array has been restored by adding the reverse() method to the code created earlier.

OUTPUT

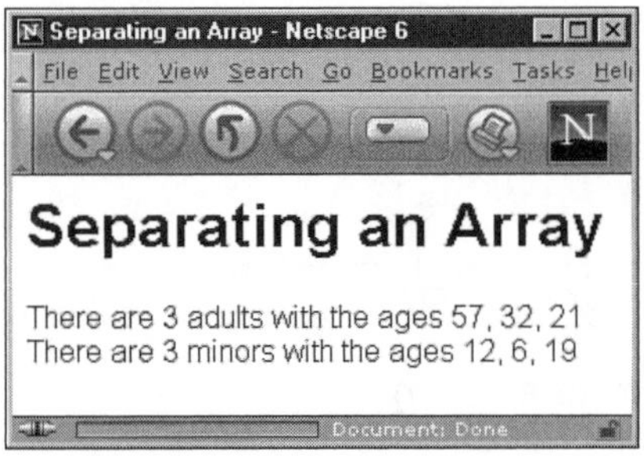

FIGURE 5.8

Using the reverse()
*method to preserve
the ordering of ages
in the new arrays.*

A very useful application of the reverse() method is as a workaround for the lack of support for the shift() and unshift() methods in Internet Explorer 5.0-. The main task of the push() and pop() methods can be easily replicated by using the length attribute to either assign or remove elements from the end of an array. However, the shift() and unshift() methods are not so easily replicated. Unless of course, we use the reverse() method to reverse the array so that we can use the length property to add and remove elements in the same way as we would use it as an alternative to the push() and pop() methods. Then we can reverse the array back to its original order, and it will be as if we had added or removed the elements from the front of the array. For example, assuming we start with an array with the values 2, 3, and 4 in its first, second, and third elements, respectively, and want to insert the values 0 and 1 at the beginning, we might use code similar to that shown in Listing 5.13.

LISTING 5.13 A Technique Using the reverse() Method to Emulate the unshift() Method for Adding Elements to the Beginning of an Array (addElements.htm)

INPUT

```
<html>
<head>
<title>Adding Elements</title>

<script language="javascript" type="text/javascript">
<!--

var x = new Array(2,3,4);
    x.reverse();
    x[x.length] = 1;
    x[x.length] = 0;
    x.reverse();
alert(x);   // alerts 0,1,2,3,4

//-->
</script>

</head>
<body>

<h1>Adding Elements</h1>

</body>
</html>
```

ANALYSIS By doing this you effectively add the elements to the start of the array. This saves you from having to write significantly more complex scripting in order to move all the elements up by one each time you need to insert a new first element.

Caution

When adding more than one element to a reversed array you must add the innermost element first, progressing to what will ultimately be the first element of the array.

You can also use the reverse() method when you want to remove elements from the beginning of an array. This time assume an array starts with a complete list of numbers from 0 to 4 in its corresponding elements and you want to remove the first two elements completely.

5

LISTING 5.14 Using the `reverse()` Method to Emulate the Effect of the `shift()` Method to Remove Elements from the Beginning of an Array

INPUT (`removeElements.htm`)

```
<html>
<head>
<title>Removing Elements</title>

<script language="javascript" type="text/javascript">
<!--

var x = new Array(0,1,2,3,4);
    x.reverse();
var firstElement  = x[x.length-1];
    x.length = x.length-1;
var secondElement = x[x.length-1];
    x.length = x.length-1;
    x.reverse();
alert(firstElement)    // alerts 0;
alert(secondElement)   // alerts 1;
alert(x);              // alerts 2,3,4

//-->
</script>

</head>
<body>

<h1>Removing Elements</h1>

</body>
</html>
```

ANALYSIS This time for each of the two elements we have removed, we have first read their data into a variable (presumably for some sort of processing), and then reduced the length of the array by one to remove that element. Although not as simple as the `shift()` method, by using the `reverse()` method in this way we are saved from the trouble of constructing scripts to shift element data back, element by element, before finally removing the last element of the array.

Let's move on to look at two of the methods listed earlier that you are less likely to use. One of these is the `toSource()` method and the other is the `valueOf()` method.

The `toSource()` Method

When applied to an array the `toSource()` method returns the array's contents as a string in the form that might have been written in the code to create the array in the first place. This is best explained using an example, so take a look at the following piece of code:

```
var x = new Array(1,"b",true);
var y = x.toSource();
alert(y); // alerts [1, "b", true]
```

As you can see the string contained in the variable y looks the same as the literal notation that could have been used to create the array x. Not only have the elements been separated with commas (and optional spaces), but the square brackets are also in place.

The theory is that this string could be turned into code again using the `eval()` function to create an identical copy of the original array. There are times when this could be useful, but unfortunately the `toSource()` method is supported only by Netscape. Unless you know that you will only be scripting for Netscape users, you would be wise not to use the `toSource()` method.

The `valueOf()` Method

The `valueOf()` method is of even less use. In fact, in the context of arrays, it is of no use at all. It exists as a method of the `Array` object simply because the `Array` object inherited it from the object that created it, the `Function` object (remember what we said in the previous chapter about all the Core objects being created from the `Function` object). When used on an array the `valueOf()` method simply returns the array itself—it is the same as if we hadn't included the method at all.

However, that is not to say the `valueOf()` method is useless in the context of other objects! You will see later in the book that it can indeed sometimes be useful. It just means that in the context of arrays the method can be safely ignored.

Associative Arrays

Throughout this chapter we have focused on the benefits of storing data in data containers that we can access using index values instead of names. This is, and will continue to be, our primary way of storing data in arrays. However there is a second method that is available which, surprisingly enough, involves creating array elements using strings rather than index values. For example, after defining the array x, you can create elements like this:

```
var x = new Array();
    x["first"]  = "1st";
    x["second"] = "2nd";
    x["third"]  = "3rd";
```

NEW TERM   This type of array is commonly known as an *associative array*. This is because when elements are created in this way the data they contain is associated with, and can be accessed using, the string in the square brackets.

Associative arrays are not used very often. In past versions of JavaScript, array elements could be created and accessed using both the string they were associated with and an index value. This is no longer the case (at least not for the arrays that we create). However, associative arrays can be used to teach us something more about the nature of objects and how we access them.

The data containers that are created when an element is declared using a string instead of an index value are not included in the indexed elements of the array. They cannot be accessed using an index value, and they do not affect the length property (and so we can't cycle through them using loop statements). The reason for this is that they are not actually elements of the array, they are properties. To demonstrate, try Listing 5.15.

INPUT   **LISTING 5.15**   Creating and Displaying an Associative Array Using Two Notations (notations.htm)

```
<html>
<head>
<title>Mixing Notations</title>

<script language="javascript" type="text/javascript">
<!--

var x = new Array();
    x["first"]  = "1st";
    x["second"] = "2nd";
    x["third"]  = "3rd";

alert(x.first + ", " + x.second + ", " + x.third);

//-->
</script>

</head>
<body>

<h1>Mixing Notations</h1>

</body>
</html>
```

This example will bring up the following alert box, shown in Figure 5.9.

OUTPUT

FIGURE 5.9

Displaying the contents of the associative array in an alert box.

Despite creating the data containers using square brackets and a string, you have been able to access these "elements" (actually properties) by using the dot notation.

What this teaches us is that in fact the dot notation and the notation where we use string values in square brackets are just two different ways of accessing the same thing. Both were marked as "Member" operators in the table of operator precedence in Chapter 2, "Working with Data," and as such both signify that the name/string they operate on respectively are members of the preceding object. All JavaScript objects can be accessed using either method. For example:

```
window["document"]
```

is equivalent to

```
window.document
```

and

```
window.document.body
```

is equivalent to

```
window.document["body"]
```

In fact, we can even write a series of object and property names as strings in square brackets:

```
window["document"]["body"]
```

Try it for yourself by running any of the following lines of code:

```
alert(window["document"])
alert(window.document["body"])
alert(window["document"]["forms"])
```

All of these alert functions will alert you to the fact that you have reached an object.

The only thing you cannot do is begin the first object in your object path in this way. For example:

```
["window"]["document"]
```

5

This will cause an error because you cannot begin a line of code with an opening square bracket in JavaScript. Doing so assumes you are starting a new array using literal notation. The JavaScript interpreter hasn't yet come to the later set of square brackets so it doesn't know it is part of a path name. In the above example, it would start at the left and create a single element array where the first element had the string value `"window"`. When it then came to the second set of square brackets with the string `"document"`, it wouldn't know what to do with them because you can't write two sets of array literals one after another. Hence an error would result.

Clearly, there is no real use for accessing objects, properties, or methods using square brackets containing their names as a string, in open code. But when you pass object names to a function for example, you may pass the object's name as a string rather than as a reference to the object itself. In this case with the name already in a string value, the simplest way to access the object is to insert the function argument that contains the object name into a set of square brackets in the object path. This saves you from the more awkward use of the `eval()` function.

An example of when the square bracket notation must be used was shown in the example in Chapter 4 when we used a `for in` loop to explore an object called `"bike"`. Hopefully you will now be able to understand the syntax we used to return the value of each of bike's properties. Just to make sure that you fully understand what we did earlier, let's go over it. Here is the code again.

```
var props = "";
for (var prop in bike) {
  props += "The bike's " + prop + " is " + bike[prop] + "\n";
}
alert(props);
```

The property name that is given to the variable `prop` during each loop is in the form of a string. Therefore to find out its value you cannot simply write `bike.prop`. You must access the property value by enclosing the variable `prop` in square brackets to show that the string belongs to the object `bike`.

Note that, conversely, indexed elements can be created for any JavaScript object, not just instances of the `Array` object. The difference is that the `Array` object is specifically designed for working with indexed elements. Only with instances of the `Array` object do you get access to its `length` property and a host of useful methods—the most powerful of which we haven't discussed yet. In general, in JavaScript if you want to create a data structure where you can access the data using object and property names, you use the `Object` object; but, if you want to order, sort, and iterate through your data, you use an `Array` object. We will see how to use the `Object` object later in the book.

Storing Objects in Array Elements

Arrays can store references to objects in their elements as well as simple data (literals). Perhaps the best examples of this are the collections belonging to the Document object that we briefly looked at in the previous chapter. These collections are in reality simply arrays containing elements that hold shortcut references to other objects as opposed to data.

There are three ways of using these arrays. To demonstrate, let's assume we want to access a form with the name "myForm" that is the second form on a page. We could access it using any of the following three lines:

```
document.forms[1]
document.forms["myForm"]
document.forms.myForm
```

When we know the order in which an object comes in relative to the other objects in a collection, then we can use an index value to access it (as shown in the first example. Remember that the second element of an array has the index 1!). In addition to this, as long as the object also has a name, then you can also access it using either its name as a string in square brackets (if necessary), or more frequently by referring to it with the dot notation. These two methods of accessing a form are shown in the second and third lines respectively.

An HTML collection is the only object where we are able to automatically access its child objects using their names as well as an index number. Although the forms collection isn't the best example, for some collections it is essential to be able to loop through all its objects as an array. An example of this is the options collection belonging to the forms collection, which we will meet in Chapter 6, "HTML Forms and the String Object."

If it is possible to access an object by name, then that is probably the better of the two methods. Referring to objects by name provides flexibility to reorder your Web pages with ease. If you refer to objects by index in your scripts, then you may need to search through your scripts to change the index numbers used to reference elements when you change the page. But if the references are by name, then you can move things about without worrying about the effects of reordering on your scripts.

Listing 5.16 provides a further example where the links collection is used to add a query string to all links on a page.

5

LISTING 5.16 Modifying the Links Collection (modifyLinks.htm)

```html
<html>
<head>
<title>Link Modifier</title>

</head>
<body>

<h1>Link Modifier</h1>

<p>
<a href="http://www.example.com/">Example</a><br />
<a href="http://www.example.com/">Example</a><br />
<a href="http://www.example.com/">Example</a><br />
<a href="http://www.example.com/">Example</a><br />
<a href="http://www.example.com/">Example</a><br />
<a href="http://www.example.com/">Example</a><br />
</p>

<script language="javascript" type="text/javascript">
<!--

var queryString = "?" + "query string data";
var allLinks = document.links;
for (var i=0; i<allLinks.length; i++) {
  allLinks[i].href = allLinks[i].href + queryString;
}

//-->
</script>

</body>
</html>
```

ANALYSIS In this example, we placed the script block after the contents of the body. This is because if our script tried to change the links on the page before they had arrived in the browser, then it would result in an error.

In the first line of our script, we build up a query string. We have simply concatenated a question mark to another string, but we could have used other processes to build up the query string, such as extracting user data from a cookie so it can be passed to the server depending on which link the user clicks.

In the second line of our code, we assign a reference to the links collection to a variable called allLinks. This saves us from writing document.links in our for loop, helping to keep the code more concise and easier to read.

In the parentheses of the `for` loop, we set the conditions so that it will loop through all the `link` objects in the `links` collection. We then assign the `href` property of each link with the `href` property concatenated to our query string. This has the effect of simply adding the query string to the link. If we hadn't concatenated the URI in the `href` property with the query string to reassign to the `href` property, then the query string would simply overwrite the link.

Summary

In this chapter we have looked at arrays. As we progress through the book their power and usefulness will become increasingly apparent. In Chapter 14, "Advanced Array Management," we will return to the subject of arrays and look at some more advanced topics.

Always look out for ways of using arrays to structure your data so that your scripts can run efficiently. Whenever you have a script that performs a repeated operation on some data, ask yourself if this data might be best organized as an array so a loop statement could be used to make the process easier. This can be much more efficient than hard-coding multiple lines of code. The next chapter will explore the `Form` object and its child objects. To use the `Form` object you will need several of the skills discussed in this chapter for array management.

Workshop

In this workshop we will review what you have learned about arrays in this chapter.

5

Q&A

Q. Is there an easy way to order the data I store in my arrays based on certain criteria, or do we have to write our own scripts to do this?

A. The four methods of the `Array` object that we didn't look at in this chapter are very powerful tools. One especially, the `sort()` method, is designed specifically for the job of rearranging the data stored in an array based on criteria we specify. We will be taking a detailed look in Chapter 14, but if you need the capabilities it provides then feel free to skip to Chapter 14. (You should have learned enough by now to be able to understand the description of how the `sort()` method works.)

Quiz

1. What is the index number of the third element in an array?

2. What are the methods of the `Array` object called that remove an element from the end of an array and add an element to the end of an array?

Quiz Answers

1. The index number of the third element in an array is two. The first element in an array has an index of zero; therefore, the second element has an index of one, and the third element has an index of two.

2. The `pop()` method removes an element from the end of an array. The `push()` method adds an element to the end of an array.

Exercise

Make up some names and create an array called `names` in parallel with the array called `ages` that we separated earlier. Once you have done this add some code to the `for` loop that will separate out the names with the relevant ages. Tip: you will need to create another two arrays perhaps called `minorNames` and `adultNames` that the separated names should be added to. These two arrays should end up in parallel with the arrays `minors` and `adults` respectively.

DAY 6

HTML Forms and the String Object

User interaction with scripts can come in many forms (forgive the pun), but the primary means of collecting input from a visitor to a Web site remains the humble HTML/XHTML form.

Forms provide ready-made HTML/XHTML elements that allow users to interact with a Web page (for example, by entering text, selecting options from select boxes, and ticking checkboxes). So understanding how to manipulate HTML forms using JavaScript is a particularly important subject if you want to efficiently gather information from visitors to your Web site.

Since much of the data collected using HTML forms is in the form of strings, we also will introduce you to techniques that will help you handle strings, which a user may type into a text field or textbox.

This chapter will teach you

- Form properties and methods and how to use some of them
- How to collect data from form elements
- How to process the data you collect

Collecting Data from HTML Forms

First let's briefly look at how to use HTML form elements before going on to look at how JavaScript manipulates the objects associated with those elements.

Tip

> Use HTML/XHTML tables to position form elements on a Web page. Web browsers ignore whitespace so positioning form elements tidily on the page can be a gamble, if you don't use tables or Cascading Style Sheet positioning. In this chapter we will use tables.

Listing 6.1 creates a simple XHTML form that makes use of several form elements. We will discuss their use in a moment.

LISTING 6.1   A Simple Form Using Several XHTML Form Elements

INPUT   (SimpleForm.htm)

```
<!DOCTYPE html
PUBLIC "-//W3C//DTD XHTML 1.0 Transitional//EN"
"http://www.w3.org/TR/xhtml1/DTD/xhtml1-transitional.dtd">
<html>
<head>
<title>XMML.com - Online Survey</title>
</head>
<body>
<form action="http://www.XMML.com" method="POST" name="MyForm">
<table width="600">
<tr><th colspan="3" align="center">XMML.com - Online Survey<br /><br /></th>
</tr>
<tr>
 <td>Your Name:</td>
 <td> </td>
 <td><input type="text" name="YourName"/></td></tr>
<tr>
 <td>Your Gender:</td>
 <td> </td>
```

LISTING 6.1 continued

```
<td>
  <input type="radio" name="Gender" value="Male"/>Male<br />
  <input type="radio" name="Gender" value="Female"/>Female<br />
</td>
</tr>
<tr><td>Which of our consultancy <br />services are you interested in?</td>
<td align="right"> 
</td>
<td>
  <input type="checkbox" name="XML"/> XML<br />
  <input type="checkbox" name="XSLT"/> XSLT<br />
  <input type="checkbox" name="SVG"/> SVG<br />
  <input type="checkbox" name="XSL-FO"/> XSL-FO<br />
  <input type="checkbox" name="XForms"/> XForms<br />
</td>
</tr>
<tr>
<td>Which free gift would you prefer for filling out this survey?</td>
<td> </td>
<td>
  <select name="FreeGift">
  <option value="Choice1">Fresh Air</option>
  <option value="Choice2">A long life</option>
  <option value="Choice3">Contentment</option>
  </select>
</tr>
<tr>
<td>Enter your comments in<br />the text box
</td>
<td> </td>
<td><textarea name="Comments" rows="5" cols="50"/></td>
</tr>
<tr>
<td> </td>
<td> </td>
<td><br /><input type="submit" value="Send Form"/></td>
</tr>
</table>
</form>
</body>
</html>
```

6

Figure 6.1 shows the appearance on screen when Listing 6.1 is displayed in the Netscape 6 browser.

OUTPUT

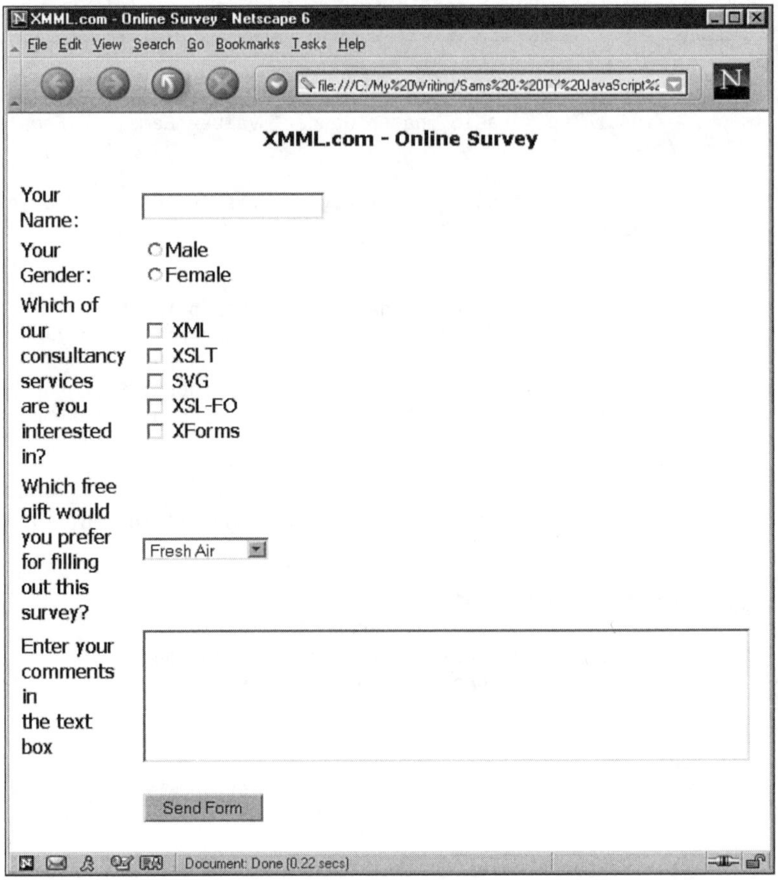

FIGURE 6.1

*An online survey
using an XHTML
form, shown in the
Netscape 6 browser.*

ANALYSIS Most of the elements contained in Listing 6.1 use the `<input/>` element. To create a text field we use the `<input/>` element with the `type` attribute that has a value of `"text"`. To create a radio button we use an `<input/>` element with the `type` attribute that has a value of `"radio"`. In the form we have two radio buttons, only one of which may be selected at a time. Each of the two radio buttons has the same value for the `name` attribute, which is possible because only one of the two is checked. Each radio button has a unique `value` attribute.

To create check boxes, we again use `<input/>` elements that, this time, have a `type` attribute with value of `"checkbox"`. In the form we have five checkbox `<input/>` elements each of which has a different `name` attribute.

The drop-down menu is created using a `<select>` element within which are nested a number of `<option>` elements. Each `<option>` element has a `value` attribute and it is the value of that `value` attribute which is sent to a server for processing. The text that is contained between the start and end tags of the `<option>` element is purely for human information on screen.

Finally, in the data entry part of our form we have a text area, defined by a `<textarea>` element. The `rows` attribute defines the text area as having 5 rows and the `cols` attribute defines it as having 50 columns.

The final part of the form is yet another `<input/>` element. This time it has a `type` attribute with the value of `"submit"`; therefore it is the submit button. So, if we can achieve all this form-related functionality using XHTML alone, the question comes to mind: Why we would want to use JavaScript in forms anyway?

Why Use JavaScript in Forms?

The form created in Listing 6.1 can, if used with HTML alone, create several problems. What happens, for example, if a user leaves blank the name text field? It makes it impossible to sensibly store the data according to user name. The form has no default selection for the radio buttons, so a user could submit the form without having any admitted gender. So we need, somewhere, to ensure that these two vital pieces of data have been entered.

The check boxes (about consultancy services) don't need any boxes to be checked, but we might want to remind users that services are offered.

Checking that the text field has been filled in and that a radio button for gender has been selected could be done on the server-side. A disadvantage of that is that there could be a significant delay, depending on the speed of the user's Internet connection, before an error message is delivered to the user. It makes a lot of sense to check for appropriate filling out of a form on the client side.

Let's move on to the syntax we need to know in order to access a form using JavaScript, and look at its contained elements.

Accessing Form Elements Using JavaScript

In Chapter 5, "An Introduction to Arrays," you saw how the individual forms on a page could be accessed through the shortcut provided by the forms collection. So, if you had a form element with the name attribute set to `"MyForm"` and it was the second form on a Web page, then you would have three options for a syntax to access that form, as shown here:

```
document.forms[1]
document.forms["MyForm"]
document.forms.MyForm
```

Collections provide a convenient shortcut when you need to access certain types of objects. Forms however are exceptional. When you want to access a form you don't need to refer to the particular form through the forms collection—you can simply omit mentioning the collection!

Forms and their elements have been scriptable since the first version of JavaScript was released with Netscape Navigator version 2. At that time, JavaScript was intended only to allow scripting of a limited number of elements, forms being important ones. Also at that time, allowing access to all elements and attributes through a hierarchically structured document object model (DOM) of an HTML document was not available for use. Forms were originally accessible simply by name from the document object. This technique of accessing a form by its name has persisted, in order to ensure backward compatibility; therefore, to access a form that has a given name, you simply would write:

```
document.formName;
```

Of course, for the above syntax to work correctly the form element must have a precisely corresponding name attribute, like so:

```
<form name="formName" ...>
```

Note that forms are the only elements of a Web page that can be accessed in this way. All other elements must be accessed through their collections; or, if not part of a collection, it must be accessed through one of the W3C DOM methods you will learn about in Chapter 8, "The Browser Issue."

In this chapter, we will examine how to access the objects that represent the elements in a form in order to obtain or manipulate the data they contain. Some form elements are relatively straightforward to access and some are more involved, requiring the use of arrays and special properties. But, as you will see, all are scriptable.

Let's look at using JavaScript with all the child objects of a form such as text fields, text areas, radio buttons, and select boxes. First, though, let's look at the form element itself.

Properties of the `<form>` Element

The start tag of a `<form>` element can contain several attributes that identify the form and define its behavior. These attributes are reflected in some of the properties of the form object that JavaScript makes available to us.

The properties that belong to a form naturally include the form's name. If it didn't we wouldn't be able to access it by name using the technique described above. In addition to the name property, we can also access the following properties of the form object:

- acceptCharset
- accessKey
- action
- encoding
- enctype
- length
- method
- tabIndex
- target

If you are familiar with the HTML <form> tag, you may recognize that many of these properties reflect attributes that can be added to the start tag of a <form> element. However take note of the case of the letters used in JavaScript for the property names. In HTML it has been common practice to spell an attribute's tag name using uppercase letters. Now with the arrival of XHTML, it is becoming more common practice to write attribute names using lowercase letters. In JavaScript, you do not have flexibility in how property names should be written. JavaScript property names are case sensitive so it is important to write them correctly within <script> tags. In general, if an attribute name is a single word, then its corresponding JavaScript property name is simply written fully in lowercase letters. But if a property or method name consists of more than one word, then it is written with the first letters of all but the first word capitalized. Therefore, for example, the HTML attribute tabindex is written as tabIndex in JavaScript.

Listing 6.2 illustrates the syntax for accessing and displaying a number of the properties of the Form object for the MyName form shown in Listing 6.1.

INPUT

LISTING 6.2   Using document.write to Display the Values of Properties of a Form Object (SimpleForm02.htm)

```
<!DOCTYPE html
PUBLIC "-//W3C//DTD XHTML 1.0 Transitional//EN"
"http://www.w3.org/TR/xhtml1/DTD/xhtml1-transitional.dtd">
<html>
<head>
<title>XMML.com - Online Survey</title>
</head>
```

LISTING **6.2**   continued

```
<body>
<form action="http://www.XMML.com" method="POST" name="MyForm">
<table width="600">
<tr><th colspan="3" align="center">XMML.com - Online Survey<br /><br /></th>
</tr>
<tr>
 <td>Your Name:</td>
 <td> </td>
 <td><input type="text" name="YourName"/></td></tr>
<tr>
 <td>Your Gender:</td>
 <td> </td>
 <td>
   <input type="radio" name="Gender" value="Male"/>Male<br />
   <input type="radio" name="Gender" value="Female"/>Female<br />
 </td>
</tr>
<tr><td>Which of our consultancy <br />services are you interested in?</td>
 <td align="right"> 
 </td>
 <td>
   <input type="checkbox" name="XML"/> XML<br />
   <input type="checkbox" name="XSLT"/> XSLT<br />
   <input type="checkbox" name="SVG"/> SVG<br />
   <input type="checkbox" name="XSL-FO"/> XSL-FO<br />
   <input type="checkbox" name="XForms"/> XForms<br />
 </td>
</tr>
<tr>
 <td>Which free gift would you prefer for filling out this survey?</td>
 <td> </td>
 <td>
  <select name="FreeGift">
   <option value="Choice1">Fresh Air</option>
   <option value="Choice2">A long life</option>
   <option value="Choice3">Contentment</option>
  </select>
 </td>
</tr>
<tr>
 <td>Enter your comments in<br />the text box
 </td>
 <td> </td>
 <td><textarea name="Comments" rows="5" cols="50"/></td>
</tr>
<tr>
 <td> </td>
 <td> </td>
```

LISTING 6.2   continued

```
<td><br /><input type="submit" value="Send Form"/></td>
</tr>
</table>
</form>
<script type="text/javascript" language="javascript">
<!-- //
document.write("<h3>The properties of the <i>"
 + document.MyForm.name + "</i> form:</h3>");
document.write("<p>The action property has the value: <b>"
 + document.MyForm.action + "</b></p>");
document.write("<p>The method property has the value: <b>"
 + document.MyForm.method + "</b></p>");
document.write("<p>The name property has the value: <b>"
 + document.MyForm.name + "</b></p>");
document.write("<p>The length property has the value: <b>"
 + document.MyForm.length + "</b></p>");
document.write("<p>The enctype property has the value: <b>"
 + document.MyForm.enctype + "</b></p>");
// -->
</script>
</body>
</html>
```

Figure 6.2 shows the new output that has been added to the document displayed in a browser window. In Internet Explorer the value of the enctype property is explicitly shown as "undefined"; whereas in Netscape 6 it is displayed as a blank.

ANALYSIS If you examine the code towards the end of Listing 6.2 you will see that we used document.write to output values of, for example, the action property, which is the representation in the DOM of the action attribute. The value for the enctype property is shown to be undefined because we have not defined a value for it within the <form> element's start tag.

Let's spend a moment clarifying why the length property is displayed as having a value of 11. The length property represents the number of form elements that are *children* of the <form> element. Thus we have one <input> element of type text, two <input> elements of type radio, five <input> elements of type checkbox, one <select> element, one <textarea> element, and one <input> element of type submit. In total, there are 11 elements. The <option> elements nested within the <select> element are not part of the length property since they are not children (although they are descendants) of the <form> element.

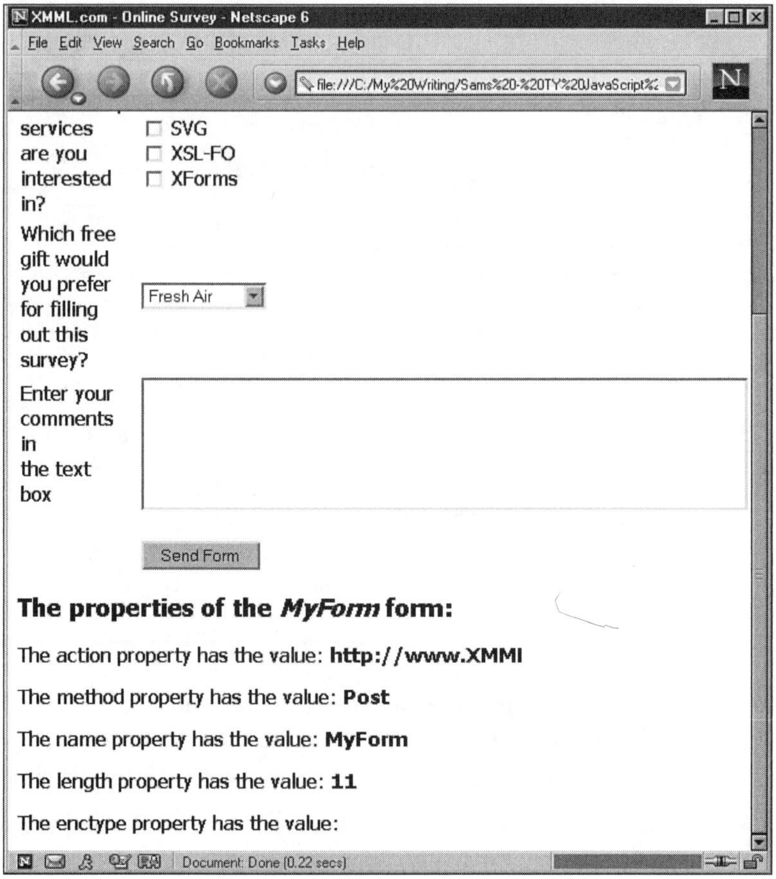

FIGURE 6.2

Values of the form property displayed in the Netscape 6 browser.

Many form attributes can be changed simply by assigning a new value to the corresponding property names; you can change the action attribute of a form based on a choice a user makes. In this way the data entered into a form could be submitted to a different URI for different processes to be carried out. Assuming that this change has been detected (we will see how later), we could change the action property of a form using the following statement:

```
document.formName.action = "http://www.xmml.com/new/page.htm";
```

The same goes for all of the other form attributes that have a corresponding property that belongs to the Form object. The exception is the length property, which is read-only—because it is determined by the number of child elements of the Form object, as we have just discussed.

Methods of the Form Object

Forms have two JavaScript methods that can be applied to them to reflect the standard "submit" and "reset" buttons that can be added to a form using HTML/XHTML input tags. In fact both these methods have the same names as the buttons: submit() and reset(). Note again the case of the letters that make up the names of these methods— JavaScript won't recognize them if you don't spell them using lowercase letters.

Both the reset() and submit() methods are applied to an HTML form by navigating programmatically to the form's object, and then applying them with the dot notation. For example, to submit a form you would write:

```
document.formName.submit();
```

Or, to reset a form using JavaScript's reset() method, you could write:

```
document.formName.reset();
```

If you intend to use the submit() method to submit a form on one of your Web pages, then make sure that it is clear to the user that the form will submit. If the user wasn't expecting the form to be submitted, then it is possible that he will hit the stop button on his browser, which could cause problems on the server side with half-submitted information. The intended use of the submit() method was to allow designers to replace the standard button (which some consider to be ugly), with an image that fits nicely into a site's design.

The reset button should also be used with care. If a visitor to your site has filled out all the information in a (possibly lengthy) form, and it is suddenly wiped because you have made some sort of obscure use of the reset() method, they may not try again. The most obvious use of the reset() method is to create your own reset buttons using images rather than the standard buttons. Alternatively you can change the appearance of the standard buttons using cascading style sheets.

When changing properties in a form you should be aware of a potential problem that could arise if the user chooses to refresh the page. Most JavaScript induced changes are erased during a page refresh; whereas, with the soft refresh caused by simply clicking the browser's refresh button, data entered into the form is not erased. If some information the user had entered were to change the action property of a form and the user then refreshed the page, the action would be changed back to its original value; however, the choice made in the form that should cause the script to change the action property would still exist, but without the action property having been appropriately changed. The form could then end up being submitted to the wrong URI for processing, causing unpredictable and likely undesirable results.

One of the ways around this potential problem would be to create a script that would check for any entries in a form each time the page loaded. It could then act accordingly and make any necessary changes to the form's properties. However, the process of detecting user changes to a form that have persisted through a refresh can be involved and can be as simple or complex as the forms themselves. A much easier way is simply to reset the form entirely.

To make sure our forms are blank every time the page loads, you will need to use an *event handler*. Resetting the forms on a page when the page loads is a fairly simple task, as shown in Listing 6.3.

INPUT   **LISTING 6.3**   Resetting a Form When a Web Page Loads (ResetForm.htm)

```
<!DOCTYPE html
PUBLIC "-//W3C//DTD XHTML 1.0 Transitional//EN"
"http://www.w3.org/TR/xhtml1/DTD/xhtml1-transitional.dtd">
<html>
<head>
<title>Resetting a form on page load</title>
<script type="text/javascript" language="javascript">
<!-- //
function ClearForm(){
document.MyForm.reset();
}
// -->
</script>
</head>
<body onload="ClearForm()">
<table>
<form name="MyForm" action="http://www.XMML.com/" method="Post">
<tr>
 <td width="15%" align="right">First Name: </td>
 <td> <input type="text" name="FirstName"/></td>
</tr>
<tr>
 <td align="right">Last Name: </td>
 <td> <input type="text" name="LastName"/></td>
</tr>
<tr>
 <td align=""right">User Number: </td>
 <td> <input type="text" name="UserNo"/></td>
</tr>
<tr>
 <td> </td>
 <td> <input type="submit" value="Submit Form"/></td>
```

LISTING 6.3 continued

```
</tr>
</table>
</form>
</body>
</html>
```

ANALYSIS On the <body> element notice that there is an onload attribute which has the value of "ClearForm()". When the page loads, the onload event handler is called. The value of the onload attribute specifies that the ClearForm() function is to be called. The only action of the ClearForm() function is to execute the reset() method on the MyForm form.

You may remember from Chapter 4, "JavaScript Is Object-Based," that if you changed the Object Explorer page to explore the properties and child objects of an object other than the navigator object, you would likely see names beginning with the two letters "on". We mentioned at the time that the name for these was "event handlers." The reason for this is that they "handle," or intercept, events that occur due to a user's actions. If there is more than one form in a Web page, we could modify the ClearForm() function to reset all the forms on the page, as shown here:

```
function ClearForm() {
    for (var i=0; i<document.forms.length; i++) {
      document.forms[i].reset();
    }
}
```

An alternate syntax is to omit the onload attribute from the start tag of the <body> element and use onload directly within the <script> element:

```
onload = function() {
    for (var i=0; i<document.forms.length; i++) {
      document.forms[i].reset();
    }
}
```

The loading of a Web page isn't the only event that JavaScript can process. If we use an event handler to capture a click on a button, then we can process that event using a function of our own design. Listing 6.4 shows a very simple form that applies the form object's reset() method when a button is clicked and then outputs an alert box that tells the user that the reset has been carried out.

LISTING 6.4   Using the Form Object's reset() Method to Reset a Form in
Response to User Input (TinyForm.htm)

INPUT

```
<!DOCTYPE html
PUBLIC "-//W3C//DTD XHTML 1.0 Transitional//EN"
"http://www.w3.org/TR/xhtml1/DTD/xhtml1-transitional.dtd">
<html>
<head>
<title>Test for the reset() method</title>
<script type="text/javascript" language="javascript">
<!-- //
function MyReset(){
document.TestForm.reset();
alert("Your form has been reset!");
}
// -->
</script>
</head>
<body>
<form name="TestForm">
<table>
<tr>
 <td width="15%" align="right">Your Name:</td>
 <td ><input type="text" name="Name"/></td>
</tr>
<tr>
 <td align="right">Your Gender:</td>
 <td><input type="text" name="Gender"/></td>
</tr>
<tr>
 <td width="15%"><input type="button" value="Submit"/></td>
 <td><input type="button" value="Reset" onclick="MyReset()"/></td>
</tr>
</form>
</body>
</html>
```

ANALYSIS   Notice in the second <input> element that there is an onclick attribute. The value of the onclick attribute is "MyReset()", in other words the MyReset() function is called. The MyReset() function makes use of the reset() method of the Form object named "TestForm":

```
document.TestForm.reset();
```

Note

Some sources of information state that Netscape 6 does not execute the reset() method. If you run Listing 6.4 in a Netscape 6.0 or later browser, you will see that the form is reset correctly.

Event handlers will be discussed in more detail in Chapter 10, "Events and Events Handling."

The code in Listing 6.4 allows you to create your own submit button. You could have some text that calls the submit() method of a form, as in the listing, but more likely you will want to use an image to achieve a more attractive appearance than the standard gray button.

> **Tip**
>
> If you want to disable a submit or reset button, then you can do so using a function that returns the boolean value false.

Let's move on to look in a little more detail at the HTML/XHTML elements within a form—we will call them "*form elements*"—and how we can manipulate them using JavaScript.

Form Elements

Forms can have, in principle, any number of child elements of several different types. Form elements can be split into three different groups:

- Text-based elements
- Selection-based elements
- Control elements

Text-based elements include textboxes, text areas, hidden inputs, and the file-upload element. Selection-based elements include check boxes, radio buttons, and select boxes. Control elements include buttons, for example.

Note that only certain properties of form elements can be changed. Some are read-only. As a general rule, if the page needs to be restructured in order to implement a change made by a script, then that change is not allowed. For example, the type attribute of the <input> element is read-only. If you were able to change an <input> element's type attribute from "button" to "radio" for example, the page would need to be restructured. Similarly the defaultValue property is also read-only. On the other hand, the name property of any form element is read/write. The page does not need to be redrawn to implement a change that might be made to an element's name, so you can both read and write an element's name property.

> **Caution**
>
> Be careful if you change the name property of a form element. If any of your other code makes use of the original value of the name property before you made a change, then the output of some parts of your code could be unpredictable.

Textual elements do, however, allow their content, and hence appearance, to be changed. This includes not only changes made by a user but also changes made by a script. Therefore we can change the value of a text area to change its content, or even change the value of a button to change the text it shows.

> **Caution**
>
> Netscape Navigator 4 does not resize buttons if you alter the value of the value property of a button object with the intention of relabeling the button. Any text that is longer than the original length that you assign to the value property will simply be truncated if it is too large for the existing button dimensions.

The elements Collection

As well as accessing each element of a form by name, it is possible to access all of them through a collection of the document object. Each form that belongs to the forms collection contains another collection called the elements collection. This collection brings all the elements in the form together so as to make them accessible as an array. As with all the other collections, it doesn't matter how these elements are nested within other HTML elements. If for example a table has been used inside the form to lay out certain elements, the elements collection will skip through the table straight to the elements you need to access.

The elements collection orders the elements of a form in the order in which they were written into the XHTML/HTML that makes up the page. Therefore, you could in theory access the third element of the second form on a page by using this notation, as shown here:

```
document.forms[1].elements[2]
```

However, as with the forms collection, it is recommended that you not use the elements collection as your main means of accessing the elements of your forms. It can be fragile. Suppose you insert an additional <input> element early in a form, then your code for all later form elements will no longer work correctly because they now are in a different position in the elements array.

If you choose to use several forms on the same Web page, you can access the first form and last form. To access the first form on the page use the following:

```
document.forms[0]
```

To access the last form on the page use this syntax:

```
document.forms[document.forms.length-1]
```

To correctly use the syntax for both those techniques you must remember that the first form is numbered from zero.

So far we have accessed forms through the document object and referred to the form by name. But when a script or function is called from the form or an element in the form itself we can use a shortcut. This shortcut is made available through a special JavaScript keyword that refers to the object that the script was called from: the keyword this.

When the keyword this is used in a script contained within a tag, it is that tag's object that it points to. This can save you from navigating through the hierarchy of objects as well as shorten the amount of code you have to write.

Whether you decide to pass a reference to the present object (using this), its form (this.form), or one of its properties (this.property) depends on what you are trying to achieve.

In a script block the this keyword sometimes isn't really the appropriate approach. If you can avoid referring to the window object, then you can also avoid using the keyword this. When used in other locations, the object it refers to is different and so it can be very useful. Listing 6.5 shows a simple example that uses the this object in the value of the onfocus attribute of the <input> element.

INPUT   **LISTING 6.5**   Using the this Object within an onfocus Attribute (This.htm)

```
<html>
<head>
<title>Testing this</title>

</head>
<body>

<h1>Testing this</h1>

<form action="collect.php">
  <input type="text" name="emailAD" size="15"
value="Email Address" onfocus="this.value=''">
  <br /><submit value="Subscribe">
```

6

LISTING 6.5   continued

```
</form>

</body>
</html>
```

ANALYSIS   In the example in Listing 6.5, there is a text box where the information to be entered is indicated by the text it contains: `"Email Address"`. When space is limited this technique can save you from using extra text outside the element explaining what it is for and taking up space. Clearly anyone who wants to send his e-mail address to subscribe has to delete this text from the text box first—unless we do it for the user. And that is exactly what the `onFocus` event handler that has been placed in the `<input>` tag does. It removes the text `"Email Address"` by assigning an empty string to the value of the text box. The neat thing about this is that you can use the keyword `this` instead of a longer reference:

```
document.forms[0].emailAD.value
```

And if you wanted to access the form using its name, as recommended, then you would also have to give the form and text box a name. The `this` keyword bypasses all this however. By using it you are saved from lengthier references that include the document and form name in the object path, as well as sometimes being saved from naming the form concerned. When calling functions using event handlers located in the opening tags of an element this can be very useful.

The `this` keyword can be used to send data more than once. For example you may wish to send an element's name and its value to a function. To do that we would simply write:

```
onclick="myFunc(this.name, this.value)"
```

You can also send references to other elements in a form by using the keyword `this` in conjunction with the `form` property (which references the parent `Form` object) provided by each element to navigate to another element within the form:

```
this.form.otherElement.value
```

The above syntax refers to the parent `Form` object of the `this` object and then finds another form element named `"otherElement"` and finally finds the value of that other form element.

Properties Common to Several Form Elements

All form elements have a `form` property, which contains the identity of the `Form` object within which the form element is contained. You have just seen how it can be used.

Form elements also typically have a `name` property, which corresponds to the `name` attribute on the start tag in the HTML.

When we come to validate data entered into a form, we must be able to access the value entered. We will look in a moment at how that is done, as well as some other issues relevant to individual types of the form element.

The property belonging to text-based form elements that we will make most use of is the `value` property. Using JavaScript we can get and set the text contained in text-based elements using this property, with the exception of one: elements with the type `"file"`. *File upload elements*, as we will refer to them from now on, cannot be set using scripts. If we could then we would be able to upload files from the computer of anyone visiting our site simply by filling in these elements with a likely path to a file. In fact, the element could be hidden so that the user wouldn't even be aware that the file-upload element was on the page. Obviously this could enable serious security breaches and invasions of privacy, hence the restriction.

To access a form element by name, the element must, of course, have a `name` attribute in its start tag. Even if the element is nested inside other elements such as a table, we can still access it as if it was a direct child element of the form. Again this is because forms have been around for a long time and shortcut routes to an object were the original means of accessing elements. Hence we can access a text box by simply writing something similar to the following:

```
document.formName.textboxName
```

However, this is not enough to access the text in the text box. The text box is still a full object, and the text it contains is one of its properties. You may already have guessed that if you can place text in a text box by giving it a `value` attribute in its opening tag that this will be the property name used to access it as well. If you did then you are absolutely correct. To access a text box and assign the text it contains to a variable, you would write a statement like the following one:

```
var myText = document.formName.textboxName.value;
```

The text that is in the text box we have addressed will now also have been assigned to the variable `myText`. Listing 6.6 shows a simple example.

6

INPUT   **LISTING 6.6**   Retrieving Text Using the `value` Property (`ValueProperty.htm`)

```
<html>
<head>
<title>Retrieving Text</title>

<script language="javascript" type="text/javascript">
<!--

function alertText()
{
    var text = document.simpleForm.myText.value;
    alert(text);
}

//-->
</script>

</head>
<body>

<h1>Retrieving Text</h1>

<form name="simpleForm">
  <input type="text" name="myText" size="20" />
  <input type="button" value="Alert Text" onclick="alertText()" />
</form>

</body>
</html>
```

ANALYSIS   The `onclick` attribute that has been added to the start tag of the `<input>` element is of type `button`. The `onclick` attribute is an event handler; however, whereas the `onload` event handler triggers when the page loads, the `onclick` event handler detects when a user clicks on the button. In the listing it calls the function `alertText()` when users click on the button. Note the syntax of the `onclick` event handler, as we will use it often when using buttons to call a function.

Inside XHTML tags we write event handlers completely in lowercase for compliance with the XHTML recommendation. In HTML they are often written with uppercase only. This is not an option for event handler names in JavaScript. Again, JavaScript is case sensitive, and if we assign an event handler using JavaScript we must use correct case letters.

Once the button on the page has been clicked and the function alertText() is called, the first thing that happens is that the function retrieves the text from the text box. It does this through the first statement. In this statement we navigate using the document object to the form called simpleForm, and then to the text box in this form called myText and finally to myText's value property. The value of the value property when found is assigned to the variable called text before the next line when the alert() function is used to bring up an alert box that contains its value for us to see.

> **Caution**
>
> One important point to note about values retrieved from forms is that they have the data type string—even if the characters in the form element concerned were purely numeric. Care must be taken to ensure that the necessary conversions are made if the values are to be used in a process where they won't be converted automatically. We will come back to this point as it arises.

The text Element

This corresponds to an <input> element with the type attribute having a value of "text". Getting access to the value entered into a text element is straightforward since the text element is a child of the form and the text element has a value property.

INPUT Listing 6.7 shows how you can access the value entered into a text field.

LISTING 6.7   Getting the Value Entered into a Text Field (TextValue.htm)

```
<!DOCTYPE html
PUBLIC "-//W3C//DTD XHTML 1.0 Transitional//EN"
"DTD/xhtml1-transitional.dtd">
<html>
<head>
<title>Displaying the value entered in a text field</title>
<script type="text/javascript" language="javascript">
<!-- //
function DisplayValue(){
if(document.MyForm.MyTextField.value!==""){
alert("The value entered was \n" + document.MyForm.MyTextField.value);
}
else{
alert("The text field was empty!\nPlease enter your name.");
}
}
```

6

LISTING 6.7   continued

```
// -->
</script>
</head>
<body>
<form name="MyForm" action="http://www.XMML.com/"
 method="Post" onsubmit="DisplayValue()">
<input type="text" name="MyTextField"/><p>Enter your name</p>
<input type="submit" value="Click to Submit"/>
</form>
</body>
</html>
```

ANALYSIS   Notice on the `<form>` element the `onsubmit` attribute which calls the
`DisplayValue()` function. The `DisplayValue()` function uses the name of the
form and the name of the text field in the value which is alerted. However, if the value in
the text field was the empty string, then a message is displayed, indicating to the user
that they need to enter their name into the text field.

This code only takes us part way to what we want—we can check the value of the `value`
property but that does not prevent the form being submitted. If you run the code then you
will find that even though the data in the text field is invalid the form is still submitted.
We will, later in the chapter, look at how we can prevent that from happening.

First, let's improve on another minor deficiency of the form we just looked at. When the
form loads, try typing your name. What happens? Nothing, because the focus is not on
the text field. So when you type, the text isn't entered into the field. Listing 6.8 uses the
`onload` event to attach focus to the text field, so you can start typing without first moving
your mouse to the text field and clicking there to give it focus.

INPUT   **LISTING 6.8**   Using JavaScript to Attach Focus to a Selected Text Field to
Help Usability (`TextFieldWithFocus.htm`)

```
<!DOCTYPE html
PUBLIC "-//W3C//DTD XHTML 1.0 Transitional//EN"
"DTD/xhtml1-transitional.dtd">
<html>
<head>
<title>Displaying the value entered in a text field</title>
<script type="text/javascript" language="javascript">
<!-- //
onload = function(){
document.MyForm.MyTextField.focus();
}
```

LISTING 6.8   continued

```
function DisplayValue(){
if(document.MyForm.MyTextField.value!==""){
alert("The value entered was \n" + document.MyForm.MyTextField.value);
}
else{
alert("The text field was empty!\nPlease enter your name.");
}
}
// -->
</script>
</head>
<body>
<form name="MyForm" action="http://www.XMML.com/" method="Post"
onsubmit="DisplayValue()">
<input type="text" name="MyTextField"/><p>Enter your name</p>
<input type="submit" value="Click to Submit"/>
</form>
</body>
</html>
```

ANALYSIS   You can see within the `<script>` element the function which is associated with the onload event. You can use the `focus()` method of the `text` property of the form object to attach focus to the desired field. Doing that is more convenient to the user.

The `textarea` Element

Text areas are represented in HTML by the `<textarea>` element, and are intended for the entry of free text. The dimensions of the text area are specified by the values of the `rows` and `cols` attributes. Text areas could be used, for example, to collect customer feedback comments or for detailing delivery instructions for an online purchase.

If you want to access the value of a text area, you can use syntax similar to that which was used for the text field shown earlier. For example, if you have a text area with a name attribute of value `"MyTextArea"` then you can access the value of the text area as follows:

```
document.MyForm.MyTextArea.value
```

In addition to simply gaining access to the value of a text area, you can control whether or not it is accessible to users, depending on what they have done in other parts of the form. In some circumstances, you may want to disable some form elements to ensure that data has been entered elsewhere in the form before allowing the user to enter comments, for example.

6

Listing 6.9 shows an example where users must enter their names into the form before the text area is enabled for them to enter their comments. We will set the text area to read-only until the text field for the user's name has had some text entered into it.

INPUT **LISTING 6.9**   Restricting a User to the Text Field for Their Name until They Enter Some Text (TextAreaReadonly.htm)

```
<!DOCTYPE html
PUBLIC "-//W3C//DTD XHTML 1.0 Transitional//EN"
"DTD/xhtml1-transitional.dtd">
<html>
<head>
<title>Disabling a text area until another field has been completed</title>
<script type="text/javascript" language="javascript">
<!-- //
onload = function(){
document.MyForm.MyTextField.value=""; //
document.MyForm.MyTextField.focus(); // sets focus to MyTextField
document.MyForm.Comments.readOnly = true; // sets text area to read-only
} // end onload

function DisplayValue(){
if(document.MyForm.MyTextField.value!==""){
alert("The value entered was \n" + document.MyForm.MyTextField.value);
}
else{
alert("The text field was empty!\nPlease enter your name.");
}
}// end function DisplayValue()

function ChangeStatus(){
if (document.MyForm.MyTextField.value!==""){
document.MyForm.Comments.readOnly = false;
document.MyForm.Comments.select();
} // end if
else{
document.MyForm.MyTextField.focus();
} //end else
}

function CheckStatus(){
if (document.MyForm.MyTextField.value==""){
alert("First please enter your name");
document.MyForm.MyTextField.focus();
} // end if
else{
document.MyForm.Comments.select();
} // end else
} // end function CheckStatus()
```

LISTING 6.9   continued

```
// -->
</script>
</head>
<body>
<table>
<form name="MyForm" action="http://www.XMML.com/" method="Post"
onsubmit="DisplayValue()">
<tr>
 <td><input type="text" name="MyTextField" onblur="ChangeStatus()"/></td>
 <td>Enter your name</td>
</tr>
<tr>
 <td><textarea name="Comments" rows="6" cols="40"
 onmouseup="CheckStatus()" >Please enter your name first</textarea></td>
 <td>Enter your comments.</td>
</tr>
<tr>
 <td><input type="submit" value="Click to Submit"/></td>
 <td> </td>
</tr>
</table>
</form>
</body>
</html>
```

ANALYSIS   In Listing 6.9, we are really ensuring that the user filled in his name before he did anything else in the form. When the document loads we set focus to the `<input>` element named `"MyTextField"`. If the user tries to tab out of there or clicks on another part of the Web page, then the text field will lose focus—that is, "*blur*." The `<input>` element has an `onblur` attribute which sets the focus back to the text field if no text has been entered; or, if text has been entered, sets the text area to no longer read-only, and puts the focus on the text area. If the user tries to get into the text area (which is read-only) by clicking on it before the user's name has been entered, the `onmouseup` attribute of the `<textarea>` element calls the `CheckStatus()` function and sets focus back to the `MyTextField` text field if no name has been entered.

You may not want to tie down users this tightly, but it can be useful to think about how to control what the user can do using JavaScript.

Historically, text areas used to have text wrap turned off by default. If that was what you wanted then great, but if you didn't then it could be problematic, depending on whether you were scripting for older browsers or not. The reason for this is that different browsers recognized different keywords for turning on text wrap. Because it is not possible to assign an attribute two different values for two different browsers using only

6

HTML, JavaScript became a workaround for detecting which browser was being used. Browser detection is discussed in Chapter 8.

Let's move on to looking at the elements where the user has to make a choice.

Check Boxes

The check box is the easiest choice-based form element to deal with and use. The two main pieces of information you may want to know about a check box are its value and whether it is checked or not. The value assigned to the value attribute of a check box can be obtained or set through the value property of the Checkbox object. The technique is similar to the one we have looked at for text fields and text areas:

```
var valueChecked = document.MyForm.someCheckbox.value
```

Finding out whether a check box is checked or not is also straightforward. Just as the name used for the attribute that causes a check box to start off checked when the page loads is the name "checked", the corresponding property of a Checkbox object is also called checked. The checked property of a Checkbox object can have one of two values. A checkbox is either checked or it isn't, so the checked property can have the value true or false. For example:

```
var chkStatus = document.formName.checkboxName.checked;
```

assigns the value true to the variable chkStatus if the check box being examined is checked, but false if it isn't.

If we have several check boxes in a form it becomes a little cumbersome to write code to check each of them by name. An alternative approach is to loop through the elements array of the form object and check whether or not each element is an <input> element of type checkbox. Listing 6.10 shows this being done in the context of the online survey we saw earlier. Run the code with none, some, or all of the check boxes checked to see the results.

INPUT **LISTING 6.10** Checking and Displaying Whether a Form Element Is a Check Box and Displaying Whether It Is Checked or Not (SimpleFormCheckboxes.htm)

```
<!DOCTYPE html
PUBLIC "-//W3C//DTD XHTML 1.0 Transitional//EN"
"http://www.w3.org/TR/xhtml1/DTD/xhtml1-transitional.dtd">
<html>
<head>
<title>XMML.com - Online Survey</title>
<script type="text/javascript" language="javascript">
<!-- //
function CheckCheckboxes(){
```

LISTING 6.10   continued

```
var elLength = document.MyForm.elements.length;
for (i=0; i<elLength; i++)
{
var type = MyForm.elements[i].type;
if (type=="checkbox" && MyForm.elements[i].checked){
alert("Form element in position " + i + " is of type checkbox and is checked.");
} // end if
else if (type=="checkbox") {alert("Form element in position "
 + i + " is of type checkbox and is not checked.");
} // end else if
else {} // do nothing if not of type checkbox

} // end for
} // end function CheckCheckboxes()
// -->
</script>
</head>
<body>
<form action="http://www.XMML.com" method="POST" name="MyForm">
<table width="600">
<tr><th colspan="3" align="center">XMML.com - Online Survey<br /><br /></th>
</tr>
<tr>
 <td>Your Name:</td>
 <td> </td>
 <td><input type="text" name="YourName"/></td></tr>
<tr>
 <td>Your Gender:</td>
 <td> </td>
 <td>
   <input type="radio" name="Gender" value="Male"/>Male<br />
   <input type="radio" name="Gender" value="Female"/>Female<br />
 </td>
</tr>
<tr><td>Which of our consultancy <br />services are you interested in?</td>
 <td align="right"> 
 </td>
 <td>
   <input type="checkbox" name="XML"/> XML<br />
   <input type="checkbox" name="XSLT"/> XSLT<br />
   <input type="checkbox" name="SVG"/> SVG<br />
   <input type="checkbox" name="XSL-FO"/> XSL-FO<br />
   <input type="checkbox" name="XForms"/> XForms<br />
 </td>
</tr>
<tr>
 <td>Which free gift would you prefer for filling out this survey?</td>
 <td> </td>
 <td>
```

6

LISTING 6.10   continued

```
  <select name="FreeGift">
   <option value="Choice1">Fresh Air</option>
   <option value="Choice2">A long life</option>
   <option value="Choice3">Contentment</option>
  </select>
 </tr>
 <tr>
  <td>Enter your comments in<br />the text box
  </td>
  <td> </td>
  <td><textarea name="Comments" rows="5" cols="50"/></td>
 </tr>
 <tr>
  <td> </td>
  <td> </td>
  <td><br /><input type="submit" value="Send Form"
onclick="CheckCheckboxes()"/></td>
 </tr>
 </table>
 </form>
 </body>
 </html>
```

ANALYSIS   When the "Send Form" button is clicked the `CheckCheckboxes()` function is
called. Within that function we set up a `for` loop to examine each of the element
types in the form's `elements` array. We check whether or not the element in the form's
`elements` array is or is not of type `checkbox`. For each element that is a `checkbox` we
display an alert which states the position of the checkbox in the `elements` array, and
whether it is checked or not. If the member of the elements array is not a check box then
we do nothing, as indicated by the `else` clause towards the end of the
`CheckCheckboxes()` function.

Radio Buttons

Radio buttons are slightly more complicated to deal with than check boxes. However,
with the knowledge you gained from Chapter 5, "An Introduction to Arrays," you already
have the knowledge necessary to work with them.

Tip

> If you want to ensure that a user has consciously checked one of a set of
> radio buttons, then leave them all unchecked when the page loads and then
> verify, before the form is submitted to the server, that a radio button has
> been checked. If no radio button has been checked, then provide a reminder
> for the user that one of the radio buttons provided must be checked.

Radio buttons are, as you perhaps know, grouped together by giving individual radio buttons the same name. Initially this may seem to create a problem if you want access to these elements using JavaScript. After all, if you have several elements in a form with the same name, then you can't access any one of them simply by writing the following:

```
document.formName.radioName
```

If you were to do this how would the JavaScript interpreter know which of the elements with the same name you were referring to? The solution is that JavaScript treats radio button groups as an array. The above line of code would effectively address the array, and to access any of the individual elements you would need to specify an element index. The element that comes first in the HTML that makes up the page is the first element in the array, the element that comes second on the page is second in the array and so on.

Caution

> Remember that the first element in an array is numbered as zero.

The array representing a radio button group has all the properties that you would expect to find in the arrays that you create yourself. For example there is a `length` property for the array that tells you how many entries there are in the array, or in radio button terms, how many radio buttons there are in a radio button group. Each radio button in a group is an object in its own right with its own individual properties. There is no one property that you can examine to discover which radio button in a group of radio buttons is the radio button that has been selected by the user (if any). You will need to examine each button in turn to determine whether it is selected or not. Here the `length` property comes in useful once again. In Listing 6.11 we use the `length` property to allow us to loop through the array of radio button objects to determine which of them has been selected.

INPUT **LISTING 6.11** Detecting Which Radio Button Is Selected (`RadioCheck.htm`)

6

```
<html>
<head>
<title>Checking a Radio Button Group</title>

<script language="javascript" type="text/javascript">
<!--//

function evalGroup()
{
```

LISTING 6.11   continued

```
      var group = document.radioForm.myRadio;
      for (var i=0; i<group.length; i++) {
        if (group[i].checked) break;
      }
      if (i==group.length) return alert("No radio button is checked");
      alert("Radio Button " + (i+1) + " is checked.");
  }

  //-->
  </script>

  </head>
  <body>

  <h1>Checking a Radio Button Group</h1>

  <form name="radioForm">
    Radio Button 1: <input type="radio" name="myRadio" /><br />
    Radio Button 2: <input type="radio" name="myRadio" /><br />
    Radio Button 3: <input type="radio" name="myRadio" /><br />
    Radio Button 4: <input type="radio" name="myRadio" /><br /><br />
    <input type="button" value="Eval Group" onclick="evalGroup()" />
  </form>

  </body>
  </html>
```

ANALYSIS   In this example we have a form consisting of four radio buttons and a button which, when clicked, calls a function. The button has the `onclick` event handler added to call the function `evalGroup()` when clicked. In the first statement of `evalGroup()`, we used a variable called `group` to store a reference to our radio button group. We created a `for` loop that loops through the radio group, but with a difference.

Whereas our loops previously have looped through every element in an array, in this loop we have set it up so that it loops from the start but it will stop looping as soon as it finds a checked element. We can safely do that since only one button of a radio button group can be checked. If we find a radio button that has been checked, then we know that we already have found the only radio button in the radio button group which is checked—and it is pointless to go on and examine the status of the other buttons in the group.

Select Boxes

Select boxes are the trickiest of the form elements to script. A select box contains child elements in the form of `<option>` elements, which isn't the case for any of the other form elements. To add to this complexity, select boxes can take the form of either a drop-down menu where one option can be chosen, or a scroll box where multiple options can be selected. The single choice drop-down menu is the most popular application, so let's concentrate on it.

As is the case for radio button groups, select boxes require array-handling skills. In the case of select boxes however, it is not the select box that is the array. It is the group of options that it contains that are in effect an array. In addition to this, each option is also an object in its own right.

The selectedIndex property tells you which position in the array is occupied by the option object that has been selected.

Now that we know how to find out which option object is the selected option in a select box, we need to discover how to access that option in order to find out its properties, such as its value or the text that it shows in the select box. We do not usually give the options in a select box a name, so initially you may not seem to have any way to refer-ence the array of options. However, JavaScript auto generates another collection for just this purpose—the options collection.

The options collection is just like the other collections we have seen so far. Just as they are generated automatically whenever a document is loaded into the browser, the options collection is automatically generated whenever an options element is present in or written into a form. Whereas collections like the forms collection belong to the docu-ment object, options collections belong to the select box object that they were created for. Therefore to access the third option of a select box you would write the following:

```
document.formName.selectBoxName.options[2]
```

Remember arrays start at 0, so the third element has the index value 2.

The key piece of information to know in order to work with select boxes is that a select object's <option> elements do not have a selected property. This means that you cannot iterate through each option in a select box in turn checking to see if it is selected, as we did for radio button groups. However, happily, the solution is even easier. The select object has a property that tells us which option is selected. This is the selectedIndex property. Therefore to discover which option in a select box is selected you would simply write:

```
document.formName.selectBoxName.selectedIndex
```

Once you are able to access a select box and its options, the two most important proper-ties that you may want to discover are its value property and the text shown by the option in the select box. The value property is just as you have seen before. If you want

6

to discover the value that has been assigned to the second option of a select box, you would simply write:

```
document.formName.selectBoxName.options[2].value
```

As it happens, discovering the text that an option displays in its select box is just as easy. It is contained in a property called the text property. So to access the text for the second option of a select box you would write:

```
document.formName.selectBoxName.options[2].text
```

The following code shows a function that would allow you to output the value and text properties of a selected option object, like so:

```
function getSelected()
{
    var select = document.myForm.dropDown;
    var index = select.selectedIndex;
    var selectedTxt = select.options[index].text;
    var selectedVal = select.options[index].value;
    var msg  = "The " + (index+1) + " option is selected. \n";
        msg += "It is the option " + selectedTxt;
        msg += " and has the value " + selectedVal + ".";
    alert(msg);
}
```

Listing 6.12 shows an example of how to display the selected option of a select object in a form.

INPUT **LISTING 6.12**   Capturing and Displaying the Value of the Selected <option> Element (SelectedOption.htm)

```
<!DOCTYPE html
PUBLIC "-//W3C//DTD XHTML 1.0 Transitional//EN"
"http://www.w3.org/TR/xhtml1/DTD/xhtml1-transitional.dtd">
<html>
<head>
<title>Find the selected option</title>
<script type="text/javascript" language="javascript">
<!-- //
function CheckOption(){
var Selected = document.TestForm.PrizeChosen.selectedIndex;
var SelectedOption = document.TestForm.PrizeChosen.options[Selected].value;
alert("The prize you have chosen is a " + SelectedOption);
} // end function CheckOption()
// -->
</script>
</head>
<body>
<form name="TestForm" action="SomePage.htm" onsubmit="CheckOption()">
```

LISTING **6.12** continued

```
<table>
<tr>
 <td width="15%" align="right">Your Name:</td>
 <td ><input type="text" name="Name"/></td>
</tr>
<tr>
 <td align="right">Your Gender:</td>
 <td><input type="text" name="Gender"/></td>
</tr>
<tr>
 <td width="15%"><select name="PrizeChosen">
  <option value="Ferrari">Red Ferrari</option>
  <option value="Lear Jet">Lear Jet</option>
  <option value="Dream Home">Home to $200,000</option>
 </select>
 </td>
 <td> </td>
</tr>
<tr>
 <td width="15%"><input type="submit" value="Submit the form"/></td>
 <td> </td>
</tr>
</table>
</form>
</body>
</html>
```

Buttons

Buttons can be used to initiate actions in response, for example, to clicking a button. In Listing 6.4 we used an `onclick` attribute on a button to call a function.

Before we go on to look at how you can ensure that only valid data is sent to the server, let's take a step aside to look at some aspects of the String object.

The String Object

In Chapter 1, "Getting the Basics Right," we learned about JavaScript's five data types. At that time we found out that any data in a format that the JavaScript interpreter didn't understand had to be expressed as a string. By storing it in strings, no errors will occur and JavaScript won't attempt to interfere with its structure. It will simply store the characters one after another and leave the choice of processing up to us—and for that of course we will need tools. Fortunately, the String object provides many methods to process the content of strings.

When we write a series of characters surrounded by opening and closing quote marks, we are making use of the String object's literal notation. When the JavaScript interpreter comes across a string literal that contains some characters (or none at all in the case of the empty string) it gives these characters the data type string and stores them. So to store a string in the variable myString we can use a simple JavaScript variable declaration and assignment statement, like so:

```
var myString = "Mary had a little lamb";
```

It is also possible to explicitly create new instances of the String object to store a string:

```
var myString new String("Mary had a little lamb");
```

In modern browsers these two statements are functionally identical. Even the assignment of a string literal to the variable myString allows you to use all the String object's methods or to access its properties.

Listing 6.13 demonstrates that for a String object created using the assignment of a string literal to a variable, the length property of the String object is accessible.

INPUT

LISTING 6.13 Displaying the length Property of a String Object (FirstString.htm)

```
<!DOCTYPE html
PUBLIC "-//W3C//DTD XHTML 1.0 Transitional//EN"
"DTD/xhtml1-transitional.dtd">
<html>
<head>
<title>XHTML 1.0 Transitional Template</title>
<script type="text/javascript" language="javascript">
<!-- //
onload = function(){
 var myString = "Mary had a little lamb";
 document.write("<h3>A first string</h3>");
 document.write(myString + " has a length of " + myString.length + "
characters.");
 }
// -->
</script>
</head>
<body>

</body>
</html>
```

If you run the code in Listing 6.13 you will see that the length of the string literal "Mary had a little lamb" is 22 characters.

You know from earlier chapters how to concatenate strings together using the + or += operators, but in addition to building up strings, you often will need to extract data from them as well.

Listing 6.14 demonstrates both techniques.

LISTING 6.14 Concatenating Strings Using the + or += Operators
(Concatenate.htm)

INPUT

```
<!DOCTYPE html
PUBLIC "-//W3C//DTD XHTML 1.0 Transitional//EN"
"DTD/xhtml1-transitional.dtd">
<html>
<head>
<title>Concatenating Strings</title>
<script type="text/javascript" language="javascript">
<!-- //
onload = function(){
var myString = "Mary had a little lamb";
var mySecondString = "Its fleece was white as snow";
document.write("<h3>Concatenating using a separate variable</h3>");
concatString = myString + "<br />" + mySecondString;
document.write(concatString);
document.write("<br /><br />");
document.write("<h3>Using the <b>+=</b> operator</h3>");
myString += "<br />";
myString += mySecondString;
document.write(myString);
}
// -->
</script>
</head>
<body>

</body>
</html>
```

If you run the code you will see that the visual output is identical when using each technique of concatenation.

String Properties

The String object has only one property that you are likely to make use of on a regular basis. This property is the length property. There are another two properties, which are the constructor and prototype properties that we have mentioned also exist for the Array object. In this instance, let's concentrate on the length property.

6

The String object's length property is similar to the length property that belongs to the Array object. Just as the length property of the Array object tells you how many elements there are in an array, the length property of the String object tells you how many characters exist in a string. This includes spaces and non-alphanumeric characters, for example:

```
var myString = "Ten chars!";
alert(myString.length);  // alerts 10
```

At first sight the length property may seen to be very limited in its usefulness. After all there aren't going to be many occasions when you will want to tell a visitor to your site how many characters make up this or that string. However, the length property is very useful when it comes to string manipulation. Just as the length property of the Array object can be used to help our scripts reliably determine where to find the end of an array, the length property is used to determine where a string ends. For string manipulation this information is often very useful.

String Methods

The String object provides a very large number of methods. Some of these methods will help you when working with your strings—they are listed below. Examples of how to use some of these methods will follow.

- charAt()
- charCodeAt()
- concat()
- fromCharCode()
- indexOf()
- lastIndexOf()
- localCompare()
- match()
- replace()
- search()
- slice()
- split()
- substr()
- substring()
- toLocaleLowerCase()

- toLocaleUpperCase()
- toLowerCase()
- toSource()
- toString()
- toUpperCase()
- valueOf()

The way in which you apply String object methods is very flexible. You probably expect that it is possible to apply the methods to data containers that contain a string value. For example, you can write:

```
var strVal = "My string".valueOf()
```

to assign the value of a string to the variable strVal.

In fact, your applications can be more complex than this. You can apply multiple methods to a string, all on the same line of code, for example:

```
var strUC = "My string".valueOf().toUpperCase();
```

This code takes the value of the string literal, converts it to uppercase, and assigns the uppercase string to the strUC variable.

As usual when multiple operators that are the same or have the same operator precedence are used in an expression, the operands of the member operator (.) are evaluated from left to right. In the example above, the first expression to be evaluated is the string "My string". Once the JavaScript interpreter has parsed this, it then applies the next operand to the right which in this case is the valueOf() method. This method, as we know in the case of literals, simply returns the string itself. Once this result from applying the valueOf() method has been calculated, then the next and final expression is applied to the result using the member operator. As its name implies, this string method converts to uppercase all the characters of the string to which it is applied. Hence the final value that is assigned to the variable strUC is the string "MY STRING".

Let's move on now and look at how to use some of the String object's methods.

Simple Case Transformations with toUpperCase()

When you need to compare strings you can run into the problem that lowercase and uppercase letters have different character codes. If the comparison you want to make is independent of case, then you will need to convert all of the string, or more precisely a variable which holds that value, to a case which is the same as the case of the variable with which it is being compared.

6

Listing 6.15 shows a simple string comparison.

LISTING 6.15 Carrying Out a Case-Insensitive String Comparison Using the `toUpperCase()` Method of the `String` Object (ToUpperCase.htm)

INPUT

```
<!DOCTYPE html
PUBLIC "-//W3C//DTD XHTML 1.0 Transitional//EN"
"DTD/xhtml1-transitional.dtd">
<html>
<head>
<title>String comparisons</title>
<script type="text/javascript" language="javascript">
<!-- //
onload = function(){
var firstString = new String("mary Had A litTle lamb");
var secondString = new String("Mary had a little lamb");
document.write("<h3>Direct comparison of the two strings</h3>");
var comparison = (firstString==secondString);
document.write("Are the strings equal?: " + comparison);
document.write("<h3>Comparison after conversion to upper case</h3>");
var firstUpperString = firstString.toUpperCase();
var secondUpperString = secondString.toUpperCase();
document.write("Are the strings equal?: "
 + (firstUpperString==secondUpperString));
}
// -->
</script>
</head>
<body>

</body>
</html>
```

Extracting String Segments with `charAt()`

The simplest of the methods used to find a sub-string in another string is the `charAt()` method. This method returns a single character taken from a point in another string that you specify. You specify this point by providing an index as a parameter to the `charAt()` method, for example:

```
var str = "My string";
alert(str.charAt(0));   // alerts "M"
```

Just as the elements of an array are numbered starting from 0, so are the characters in a string. Therefore, when you specify the 0th character as the parameter of the `charAt()` method, then it is the first character, the letter "M", that this method returns.

When you know the string's format, then the charAt() method can be the best method for extracting the characters you need.

Searching for Sub-Strings with indexOf()

For other occasions when you do not know the format of the string, then you will need to use other methods of the String object. With these you can look for certain strings without knowing at what point in another string they are located.

The indexOf() method is used to find the position of the first occurrence of a sub-string. See Listing 6.16.

INPUT   **LISTING 6.16**   Using the indexOf() Method (IndexOf.htm)

```
<!DOCTYPE html
PUBLIC "-//W3C//DTD XHTML 1.0 Transitional//EN"
"DTD/xhtml1-transitional.dtd">
<html>
<head>
<title>Using the indexOf() method</title>
<script type="text/javascript" language="javascript">
<!-- //
var myString = "The cat sat on the mat";
var mySubstring = "sat";
var foundAtPosition;
foundAtPosition = myString.indexOf(mySubstring,0);
document.write("<p>The string " + mySubstring +
" was found at position " + foundAtPosition);
// -->
</script>
</head>
<body>

</body>
</html>
```

ANALYSIS   The above code will return the index at which the first (or only) occurrence of the string "sat" occurred. The output of the document.write indicates that sat occurred at position 8, which is correct. It is the position of the first character of the sub-string being searched for that is found using the indexOf() method.

Replacing Sub-Strings with replace()

We can replace sub-strings within a string. This is similar to a search and replace function in a word processor. For example, if you had a description of JavaScript but wanted to be sure that all mentions had the correct case, then you could use the replace()

6

method to replace any incorrectly capitalized versions in the text. Listing 6.17 shows a simple example using the `replace()` method.

INPUT

LISTING 6.17   Using the `replace()` Method of the `String` Object (Replace.htm)

```
<!DOCTYPE html
PUBLIC "-//W3C//DTD XHTML 1.0 Transitional//EN"
"DTD/xhtml1-transitional.dtd">
<html>
<head>
<title>Using the replace() method of the String object</title>
<script type="text/javascript" language="javascript">
<!-- //
var originalString = "George Washington, President of the United States";
var replacedString = "Washington";
var replacementString = "Bush";
var newString = originalString.replace(replacedString, replacementString);
document.write("<h3>" + newString + "</h3>");
// -->
</script>
</head>
<body>

</body>
</html>
```

ANALYSIS   The `replace()` method of the `originalString` `String` object is used to substitute the string `"Bush"`, in the variable `replacementString`, for the string `"Washington"`, in the variable `replacedString`. On screen `document.write()` outputs the string `"George Bush, President of the United States"`.

Concatenating Strings with the `concat()` Method

The `concat()` method will concatenate two strings together. To concatenate two strings you simply apply the method to a string and supply the string that is to be concatenated to the first string as a parameter to the `concat()` method. For example, to concatenate the string `"Hello "` to the word `"there"`, we could use the `concat()` method, as shown here:

```
"Hello ".concat("there");
```

Of course this concatenation could be achieved just as easily using the + operator. In fact concatenating strings using the + operator is actually more concise, as shown by the following:

```
"hello " + "there";
```

Because the + operator is more succinct than the concat() method used with a string literal, the concat() method is not widely used.

Finding Sub-Strings with substr()

In Chapter 4 you learned how to access the hash property of the location object by writing the following:

```
var myHash = location.hash;
```

The problem with this is that it returns the internal document link used preceded by the hash character (#). If you want to find out the name of the internal link then you would need to remove this character from the string that the hash property contains. To do this, use the substr() method of the String object, for example:

```
var myAnchor = location.hash;
myAnchor = myAnchor.substr(1);
```

This will retrieve all the characters after the first character of the hash property's value (that is the character at index zero) is removed, thereby removing the hash character.

In Chapter 2, "Working with Data," we talked about operator precedence and said that when a period character joins two items it means that the righthand one belongs to the left. We also said that when operators have the same precedence, then they are evaluated from left to right. Therefore we can actually write the above code all on one line like this:

```
var myAnchor = location.hash.substr(1);
```

The period and square brackets denote membership of one thing to another and have the highest operator precedence. Therefore the code the period joins will be evaluated first from left to right. The location.hash is evaluated and turns into a string. Only then is the next period applying the sub-string function evaluated because by then the location.hash has evaluated to its string value that is possible.

Even if there was no content to the location object's hash property using the substr() method, starting at the character 1 won't cause an error. It will simply return an empty string.

Having taken a brief look at some of the properties and methods of the String object, let's look at how we can check for the presence of user input and prevent it from being sent to the server while it is incomplete.

6

Checking User Input

So far we have only looked at using HTML forms as a convenient means of letting a user interact with scripts on a page. Another common use is to use JavaScript as an aid to forms when used for their original purpose: collecting input from a user and sending it to the server. In this section we will look at how you can check user input (for completeness) and in Chapter 13, "Regular Expressions Make It Easier," we will look at using regular expressions to check that user input matches the desired input for a field.

When we talk about checking user input, we mean checking it for completeness before the data that a user has entered into a form is sent to the server. The first thing to say about pre-validation using JavaScript is that it should not be used as the only means of checking that the data to be sent is acceptable. Some Internet users use browsers that do not, or cannot, interpret JavaScript. If this is the case, then the form data will be sent to the server without any checks having been performed. If no validation is carried out on the server, then major errors or even security breaches could potentially occur.

The aim of using JavaScript to check user input is to speed up the user's browsing experience. When data is sent to the server there is the risk that, if not filled out properly, the data may have to be returned to the user for corrections. The time taken for the data to be passed through a modem, validated, and returned with instructions to make changes can be considerable and a frustration to the visitors to your site. Using JavaScript to pre-validate a form before it is sent will, for most users (for example, those with browsers that are JavaScript capable), mean almost instantaneous checking of data.

When checking forms there is one event handler that you need to know about. This is the onSubmit event handler. If your validation is to stop the form from submitting if the form is incocompletely filled out, then you need to use this event handler to do that. (We will look in Chapter 13, "Regular Expressions Make It Easier," at how we can ensure that valid information is entered in each part of the form before it is submitted to the server.) More importantly, unlike earlier examples in the chapter, we want to ensure that the form is not submitted to the server until the form is correctly completed.

Listing 6.18 is significantly longer than listings earlier in this chapter. If you take each part one at a time you should find it all understandable. Refer back to Figure 6.1 if you want to remind yourself how the form looks on screen. We will check that three parts of the form are filled in or we will not allow the data to be submitted to the server. The users have to fill in their names, indicate their gender and give information about delivery of the prize, which might be theirs for completing the survey.

LISTING 6.18   Ensuring That the User Has Entered Data Before the Data Is
Sent to the Server (`SimpleFormValidated.htm`)

```
<!DOCTYPE html
PUBLIC "-//W3C//DTD XHTML 1.0 Transitional//EN"
"http://www.w3.org/TR/xhtml1/DTD/xhtml1-transitional.dtd">
<html>
<head>
<title>XMML.com - Online Survey</title>
<script type="text/javascript" language="javascript">
<!-- //

function IsFormValid(){
var IsFormValid = false;
if (document.MyForm.YourName.value!="" && evalRadio()
 && document.MyForm.Comments.value!="")
{
IsFormValid = true;
}
if (IsFormValid==false) DisplayErrors();
return IsFormValid;
} // end IsFormValid() function

function evalRadio()
{
    var group = document.MyForm.Gender;
    for (var i=0; i<group.length; i++) {
      if (group[i].checked) break;
    }
    if (i==group.length) return false;
    else {return true;
          } // end else
} // end evalRadio() function

function DisplayErrors(){
if (document.MyForm.YourName.value=="") alert("Please enter your name");
if (evalRadio()==false)
alert("Please check the radio button\nfor your gender");
if (document.MyForm.Comments.value=="")
alert("Please be sure to tell us the delivery address \nfor your free gift");
} // end DisplayErrors() function;

// -->
</script>
</head>
<body>
<form action="http://www.XMML.com"
 method="POST" name="MyForm" onsubmit="return IsFormValid()">
<table width="600">
<tr><th colspan="3" align="center">XMML.com - Online Survey<br /><br /></th>
```

6

LISTING 6.18   continued

```
 </tr>
 <tr>
 <td>Your Name:</td>
 <td> </td>
 <td><input type="text" name="YourName"/></td></tr>
 <tr>
 <td>Your Gender:</td>
 <td> </td>
 <td>
   <input type="radio" name="Gender" value="Male"/>Male<br />
   <input type="radio" name="Gender" value="Female"/>Female<br />
 </td>
 </tr>
 <tr><td>Which of our consultancy <br />services are you interested in?</td>
 <td align="right"> 
 </td>
 <td>
   <input type="checkbox" name="XML"/> XML<br />
   <input type="checkbox" name="XSLT"/> XSLT<br />
   <input type="checkbox" name="SVG"/> SVG<br />
   <input type="checkbox" name="XSL-FO"/> XSL-FO<br />
   <input type="checkbox" name="XForms"/> XForms<br />
 </td>
 </tr>
 <tr>
 <td>Which free gift would you prefer for filling out this survey?</td>
 <td> </td>
 <td>
  <select name="FreeGift">
  <option value="Choice1">Fresh Air</option>
  <option value="Choice2">A long life</option>
  <option value="Choice3">Contentment</option>
  </select>
 </tr>
 <tr>
 <td>Enter your comments in<br />the text box
 </td>
 <td> </td>
 <td><textarea name="Comments" rows="5" cols="50"/></td>
 </tr>
 <tr>
 <td> </td>
 <td> </td>
 <td><br /><input type="submit" value="Send Form"/></td>
 </tr>
 </table>
 </form>
 </body>
 </html>
```

ANALYSIS The way that JavaScript works revolves around the onsubmit attribute of the
<form> element. When the form is submitted, by clicking the "Send Form" button, the IsFormValid() function is called. The "return IsFormValid()" syntax for the
onsubmit attribute ensures that it is the value ("true" or "false") which is returned
from the IsFormValid() function, which determines whether or not the form is
submitted. If IsFormValid()returns false the form is not submitted.

Within the IsFormValid() function the variable IsFormValid is assigned the value
false. Then the if statement applies three tests all of which have to be true for the
following statement

```
IsFormValid = true;
```

to be executed. If any of the three tests are false, then the DisplayErrors() function is
called. Three if statements within the DisplayErrors() function control which alert
boxes display.

If there are no errors, then the IsFormValid variable is set to "true" and the value
"true" is returned in response to the onsubmit attribute. Then, and only then, can the
form be submitted to a server.

The tests we have applied to the text field, the radio buttons, and the text area are very
simple ones—we have only checked to see that some data has been entered and that none
of the three essential fields has been left blank. In other circumstances, you may want to
check for the length of number (when checking credit cards, for example), whether a
value entered is a valid date, and so forth.

In production forms you may want to carry out more sophisticated checks on data. If you
expect, for example, that a valid date has to be entered for a particular piece of data, then
you would check if it was a valid JavaScript date.

Summary

In this chapter we have introduced you to the use of JavaScript with the Form object and
form elements. You have been shown how to check values entered by the user, to assist
the user by applying focus to a field you want to be filled in first, and how to prevent
data from being sent to the server for processing while it is incomplete.

In addition you have been introduced to some of the properties and methods of the
String object.

6

Workshop

In this workshop we will review what you have learned about forms in this chapter.

Q&A

Q. Do forms have to be embedded in tables to be displayed on screen?

A. No. You can embed forms in an HTML/XHTML Web page without the use of tables. However, using tables makes it possible to line up parts of the form to achieve an attractive presentation. An alternative approach is to use CSS for positioning.

Q. Can I use more than one form on the same HTML/XHTML Web page?

A. Yes, you can. However you will need to think carefully about how data is to be submitted to the server for processing. For instance, you may want to include a submit button only on the second form.

Q. Is it possible to use patterns of characters to search for sub-strings?

A. Yes, JavaScript has a `RegExp` object that allows you to use regular expressions. Regular expressions make it possible to search strings for patterns of characters in addition to searching them for literal sub-strings. In Chapter 13, "Regular Expressions Make It Easier," we will examine how to use regular expressions in JavaScript.

Q. Are password fields on forms totally secure?

A. No. A password field keeps someone from looking over your shoulder seeing on screen the password characters you have typed, but when your password is sent to the server it is not encrypted or disguised in any way.

Quiz

1. List the form elements into which you can type text.
2. How do you create a drop-down menu in a form?

Quiz Answers

1. There are three form elements into which you can type text—the text field, the text area, and a password field. Of course, with the password field you see only an asterisk for each character you type in.
2. The `<select>` element with nested `<option>` elements lets you create a drop-down menu.

Exercises

1. Write a script to check for the substring "man" in the string "A man wrote a manual manually for a manipulative manager".

2. Create a form that asks for a name and credit card information. Write a script that checks that each field has been filled in before the data is sent to the server.

6

DAY 7

Numbers and Math

An essential part of any programming language is the set of tools for working with numbers, and JavaScript has many such tools. If you aren't particularly enthusiastic about the prospect of creating JavaScript applications that are heavily math-oriented then don't worry. The Core JavaScript Number and Math objects provide some powerful mathematical tools to make many of the processes and calculations much easier. As you will see, even when our specific requirements are not covered directly by what JavaScript provides, we can frequently create our own tools with a little bit of ingenuity.

The number of possible JavaScript uses for numbers is enormous. Unless you are particularly interested in math, then you will find that JavaScript provides many mathematical techniques that you may never use. However, in common with all worthwhile programming languages, JavaScript needs to provide powerful and flexible facilities that will allow interested programmers to manipulate numbers.

This chapter will introduce you to some foundational numeric techniques that you can build on if you are interested in this topic. However, we can't look at all the possible numerical techniques for which you could use JavaScript.

This chapter will introduce you to

- The Number object and its properties and methods
- The Math object and its properties and methods
- Examples of carrying out calculations using the Math object

The Number Object

In practice the Number object is seldom used directly by most JavaScript scripters. Usually you only use its methods, which can be very helpful—especially those methods that have been recently introduced in JavaScript 1.5. However, before we examine the Number object's properties and methods, let's quickly take a general look at how numbers are treated in JavaScript.

Numbers in JavaScript

For integers, the numbers that JavaScript outputs seem to be spot on. However for floating-point numbers the situation isn't quite so simple. By default both Internet Explorer and Netscape Navigator will return floating-point numbers rounded to 16 or 17 significant figures. Unfortunately because JavaScript uses the computer's floating-point math (which isn't always accurate to this precision) the results of JavaScript's floating-point calculations are not always entirely accurate. For example, if we divide 10.0 by 3.0 the answer given will be 3.3333333333333335, as running Listing 7.1 will show.

INPUT   **LISTING 7.1**   Exploring the Precision of Numbers (NumberPrecison.htm)

```
<!DOCTYPE html
PUBLIC "-//W3C//DTD XHTML 1.0 Transitional//EN"
"DTD/xhtml1-transitional.dtd">
<html>
<head>
<title>Precision of numbers</title>
<script type="text/javascript" language="javascript">
<!-- //
function Calculate(){
var n = 10.0 / 3.0;
document.write("10.0 divided by 3.0 is " + n);
}
// -->
</script>
</head>
<body onload="Calculate()">

</body>
</html>
```

Most of the time when a piece of arithmetic is expected to return a floating-point number this small glitch at the end of the fractional part isn't too much of a problem. But when numbers should return an integer or are to be output to the screen for a user to see, then small discrepancies can be annoying. If you modify Listing 7.1 so that 0.3 is divided by 0.1, then the answer returned is 2.9999999999999996, which is correct when rounded but may very likely not be what was expected by the user.

Fortunately, for situations such as these, we can remedy this problem to a certain extent as far as the display of numbers is concerned. Listing 7.2 shows how you might handle the situation of dividing 10.0 by 3.0 to a selected number of decimal places.

LISTING 7.2   Controlling the Output Format of Numbers

INPUT   (FormatNumber.htm)

```
<!DOCTYPE html
PUBLIC "-//W3C//DTD XHTML 1.0 Transitional//EN"
"DTD/xhtml1-transitional.dtd">
<html>
<head>
<title>Formatting numbers to a chosen number of decimal places</title>
<script type="text/javascript" language="javascript">
<!-- //
function Calculate(){
var entry;
var first;
var second;
var numPlaces;
alert("Divide a larger number by a smaller number\nto a
chosen number of decimal places\nClick to continue");
entry = prompt("Enter first number: ", "Enter number here");
first = Number(entry);
entry = prompt("Enter second number: ", "Enter number here");
second = Number(entry);
entry = prompt("Enter number of decimal places. ", "Enter number here");
numPlaces = Number(entry);
var n = first / second;
document.write(first + " divided by " + second + " to "
 + numPlaces + " decimal places is " + formatNumber(n,numPlaces));
}

function formatNumber(theNum, numDecPlaces)
{
    var num = new String();
    num = "" + theNum;
    var pos = 0;
    count = 0;
    while (num.substring(pos-1,pos)!== ".") {
     pos += 1 ;
```

7

LISTING 7.2   continued

```
        count += 1;
      } //end while
      while (pos < (count+numDecPlaces)){
      pos +=1;
      } // end while
      return num.substring(0,pos);
}
// -->
</script>
</head>
<body onload="Calculate()">

</body>
</html>
```

ANALYSIS   Let's look at how the code works. On the <body> element there is an onload
attribute which calls the Calculate() function. Within the Calculate() function
we use an alert() box to inform the user what the page will do. We use three prompt()
boxes to gather three numbers chosen by the user. The entry variable is used to hold the
"number" chosen by the user in each prompt() box but, of course, the "number" entered
is actually held as a string. Therefore, in order to use the "numbers" entered for calculation, we must convert each of those strings to a number, using code like this:

```
first = Number(entry);
```

We divide the first number, stored in the first variable, by the second, stored in the
second variable, and store the result of the division in the n variable.

> **Caution**
>
> When you enter a numerical value in a prompt() box the value is held as a
> string. If you attempt to perform calculations then you can expect an error
> since the value on which a calculation is being attempted is a string. To
> avoid such errors you need to convert the numeric-looking string to a
> number using the Number() function.

We used document.write() to output the result of the calculation. Within the
document.write() we called the formatNumber() function passing two parameters—the
result of the calculation in the variable n and the desired number of decimal places in the
variable numPlaces.

We needed to convert the string entries entered into the `prompt()` boxes in the `Calculate()` function to numbers; however, in the `formatNumber()` function, we need to do the opposite and convert the result of the calculation to a string, held in the `num` variable, like so:

```
var num = new String();
num = "" + theNum;
```

The `theNum` variable is the parameter passed into the `formatNumber()` function.

We then used the `substring()` method of the `String` object (to which you were introduced in Chapter 6, "HTML Forms and the `String` Object") to work through the string variable `num` character by character. While we haven't reached the decimal point in that string, we just will carry on looping round a `while` loop, increasing a counter as we go. Once we do reach the decimal point, then we loop again until we have moved the required number of positions through the string variable; then we simply return the `num` string variable to the `document.write()` within the `Calculate()` function. The result of dividing 10.0 by 3.0 to 4 decimal places is shown in Figure 7.1.

OUTPUT

FIGURE 7.1

The result of the output from Listing 7.2 when dividing 10.0 by 3.0 to 4 decimal places.

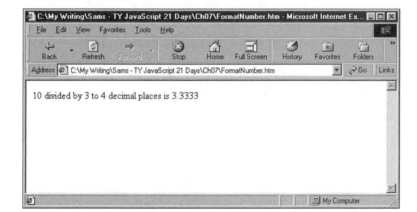

Controlling the format when you expect integer numbers is easier, *if* you are sure that the result will be an integer. Listing 7.3 is an example of how you can round numbers to achieve an integer result.

LISTING 7.3 Using the `round()` Function of the `Math` Object to Output Numbers as Integers (`OutputInteger.htm`)

7

```
<!DOCTYPE html
PUBLIC "-//W3C//DTD XHTML 1.0 Transitional//EN"
"DTD/xhtml1-transitional.dtd">
```

LISTING 7.3   continued

```html
<html>
<head>
<title>Rounding a number to an integer</title>
<script type="text/javascript" language="javascript">
<!-- //
function IntegerCalculate(){
var num1 = 0.3;
var num2 = 0.1;
var result ;
result = num1 / num2;
document.write(num1 + " divided by " + num2 +
" expressed as a whole number is " + Math.round(result));
}
// -->
</script>
</head>
<body onload="IntegerCalculate()">

</body>
</html>
```

ANALYSIS   The round() method of the Math object is used to convert the result variable to an integer number. Of course, you will only want to use the round() method when you either confidently expect the answer to be a whole number or can accept an integer as an adequate approximation of a floating-point value.

It is also worth noting before we go on that JavaScript allows you to enter exponential numbers using the letter "e" (or uppercase "E" if you prefer). As in the following:

```
1e6    //  equivalent to 1,000,000
1E6    //  equivalent to 1,000,000
1e+6   //  equivalent to 1,000,000
1e-6   //  equivalent to 0.000001
```

Notice that when the exponent is to a positive power, then the plus sign does not need to be included. But naturally for a number to a negative exponent, the minus sign must be present.

Note   When using the exponent "E" or "e", the JavaScript interpreter will accept either upper or lower case, one of the few situations in which a JavaScript interpreter will treat upper and lower case the same.

Let's return to the Number object and take a look at its properties.

Properties of the `Number` object

The `Number` object has several built-in properties. As with other objects, they include the `constructor` and `prototype` properties that we will look at later in the book. The other properties are shown below:

- `MAX_VALUE`
- `MIN_VALUE`
- `NaN`
- `NEGATIVE_INFINITY`
- `POSITIVE_INFINITY`

We have already met the `NaN` property earlier in the book. Hopefully you remember that it stands for **Not a Number** and that it is the inevitable result of trying to perform an arithmetic process where one or more of the pieces of data is not numerical.

Listing 7.4 shows how you can test whether or not a user enters a string that is numeric.

INPUT   **LISTING 7.4**   Testing Whether or Not a String Entered Can Be Converted to a Valid Number (`NumberNaN.htm`)

```
<!DOCTYPE html
PUBLIC "-//W3C//DTD XHTML 1.0 Transitional//EN"
"DTD/xhtml1-transitional.dtd">
<html>
<head>
<title>The NaN property of the Number object</title>
<script type="text/javascript" language="javascript">
<!-- //
function Calculate(){
var entry;
var number = new Number();
alert("This page will test whether you enter a
 \nnumber or a non-numeric string.\nClick to continue");
entry = prompt("Enter a number or string: ", "Enter number or string here");
number = Number(entry);
if (isNaN(number)){
document.writeln("<p>You entered: " + entry+ "</p>");
document.write("<p>It was not a number</p>");}
else{
document.writeln("<p>You entered: " + entry + "</p>");
document.write("<p>It was a number.</p>");
} // end else
} // end function Calculate()
// -->
</script>
```

LISTING 7.4   continued

```
</head>
<body onload="Calculate()">

</body>
</html>
```

ANALYSIS   When you load the page the user is presented with an informational `alert()` box. Then, in a `prompt()` box, the user is asked to enter either a number or a string. The `Number()` function is then applied to the string—held in the `entry` variable—that the user had entered. Finally the `isNaN()` function is used to test whether or not a valid number resulted from applying the `Number()` function to the `entry` variable. If no valid number resulted, then the user is shown the string they entered and informed that it was not a number. If, however, the `entry` variable can be converted into a valid number, then the user is reminded of her entry into the `prompt()` box and told that it was a number. Figure 7.2 shows the result when the non-numeric string "abc" was entered into the prompt box.

OUTPUT

FIGURE 7.2

The result of applying the `isNaN()` *function to test a non-numeric value.*

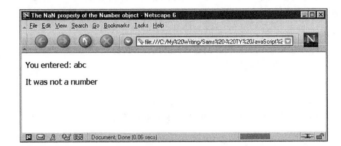

Tip

The `isNaN()` function is the only way to test whether or not a value matches `NaN`. So, if you want to test whether a value is or is not a number remember to use the `isNaN()` function. Do not attempt to test the `NaN` property for equality for example by using `if(x == NaN)`. It doesn't work.

The other properties of the `Number` object reveal key JavaScript values. Note that the name of each property is written completely in uppercase letters. If you remember what we said about naming using uppercase letters in Chapter 2, "Working with Data," you may realize that this shows that they are constants. Therefore we cannot change the values they contain because they are defined by the JavaScript interpreter and/or the environment in which it is operating.

MAX_VALUE and MIN_VALUE

The MAX_VALUE and MIN_VALUE properties contain the value of the absolute maximum and minimum numbers that the JavaScript interpreter will accept before it treats them simply as Infinity or zero respectively. Listing 7.5 displays the maximum and minimum values for you.

LISTING 7.5   Displaying the MAX_VALUE and MIN_VALUE Properties of the Number Object

```
<!DOCTYPE html
PUBLIC "-//W3C//DTD XHTML 1.0 Transitional//EN"
"DTD/xhtml1-transitional.dtd">
<html>
<head>
<title>Displaying Maximum and Minimum Values</title>
<script type="text/javascript" language="javascript">
<!-- //
function ShowLimits(){
var maxAndMin  = "Max Number: " + Number.MAX_VALUE + "\n";
    maxAndMin += "Min Number: " + Number.MIN_VALUE;
alert(maxAndMin);
}
// -->
</script>
</head>
<body onload="ShowLimits()">

</body>
</html>
```

The result you see may vary according to the platform you use. Figure 7.3 shows the alert box as it appears in Netscape 6.

FIGURE 7.3

The maximum and minimum values of the Number object displayed in a Netscape 6 alert box.

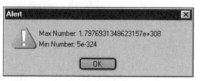

Alert

Max Number: 1.7976931348623157e+308
Min Number: 5e-324

OK

7

You may remember that we also mentioned these values in passing in Chapter 1, "Getting the Basics Right," as exponentials of the number 2. To do this we used these values together with the `toString()` function to turn them into binary form. For example to find the maximum value you could use the following:

```
var x = Number.MAX_VALUE;
    x = x.toString(2);
alert(x);
```

NEGATIVE_INFINITY and POSITIVE_INFINITY

The `NEGATIVE_INFINITY` and `POSITIVE_INFINITY` properties of the `Number` object are also JavaScript constants. There is no real need to use these properties because if you ever need to obtain the values infinity or negative infinity, you can simply write the following:

```
Infinity
```

```
-Infinity
```

rather than navigating to the values through the `Number` object like this:

```
Number.POSITIVE_INFINITY
```

```
Number.NEGATIVE_INFINITY
```

You could also simply divide 1 or -1 by 0 to get the same effect, but it is recommended that you not do so because using the values `Infinity` and `-Infinity` makes your scripts clearer.

Let's move on and look at the methods of the `Number` object.

Methods of the Number Object

The `Number` object's methods are significantly more useful to us than its properties. This is especially so for the methods that were added to the language after the release of ECMAScript Edition 3. The `Number` object's methods are listed below:

- `toExponential()`
- `toFixed()`
- `toLocaleString()`
- `toString()`
- `toPrecision()`
- `valueOf()`

You have already seen the `toString()` function at work in Listing 7.1. Because the `toString()` function is a global function it is available as a method of all Core JavaScript objects—including the `Number` object. When it is used with numbers it simply returns the number converted to the data type `string`.

The `toExponential()`, `toFixed()`, `toLocaleString()`, and `toPrecision()` methods are all new to Internet Explorer 5.5 and Netscape Navigator 6. All of these methods help with number formatting so that the numbers can be displayed in the way that best suits your requirements or the requirements of visitors to your Web sites. First let's look at the `toExponential()` method.

Using the `toExponential()` Method

As mentioned previously, a JavaScript interpreter always converts numbers to their decimal form before it displays them. To force the JavaScript interpreter to display numbers in a base other than base 10, you can use the `toString()` method. The `toString()` method works because it outputs the number as the data type string. Therefore JavaScript ignores the order of the characters and doesn't try to convert them to a decimal value. The same idea (conversion of the data type to string) can be used to help output numbers in other formats that JavaScript wouldn't otherwise allow.

JavaScript will only display numbers between `1000000000000000` (`1e15`) and `0.000001` (`1e-5`) in the standard non-exponential format. Even if you input them in exponential form they are immediately converted to plain numbers. Internet Explorer 5.5+ and Netscape Navigator 6+ allow you to override these rules and display numbers within the range in exponential form. The two methods that provide you with a means to do this are `toExponential()` and `toPrecision()`.

The `toExponential()` method simply displays the numbers it is given in exponential form (as a string). There is nothing special about it other than that. It is applied to a data container using the dot notation, like so:

```
var myNum = 1234;
    myNum = myNum.toExponential();  // returns 1.234e+3
```

The method can also be given an optional parameter to control how many decimal places are returned. This can be especially useful for anyone wanting to display numbers in scientific notation. For example, to display the previous number to 3 decimal places, you would simply write:

```
var myNum = 1234;
    myNum = myNum.toExponential(4);  // returns 1.2340e+3
    myNum = myNum.toExponential(2);  // returns 1.23e+3
```

Listing 7.6 takes a number entered by the user and displays it with from zero to four decimal places.

INPUT   **LISTING 7.6**   Using the `toExponential()` Method to Display a User-Entered
          Number as an Exponential (`toExponential.htm`)

```
<!DOCTYPE html
PUBLIC "-//W3C//DTD XHTML 1.0 Transitional//EN"
"DTD/xhtml1-transitional.dtd">
<html>
<head>
<title>Demonstrating the toExponential() method</title>
<script type="text/javascript" language="javascript">
<!-- //
function CreateExponentials(){
var entry1 ;
entry1 = prompt("Enter a floating point number", "Enter the number here");
number = new Number();
number = Number(entry1);
for (var i=0; i<5; i++){
document.write("<p>The number entered to " + i + " decimal places is "
 + number.toExponential(i) + "</p><br/>");
}
} // end function CreateExponentials()
// -->
</script>
</head>
<body onload="CreateExponentials()">
<p>This listing demonstrates the use of the toExponential() method.</p><br />
</body>
</html>
```

ANALYSIS   On page load the `CreateExponentials()` function is called. A prompt box is
          used to get a floating-point number from the user. Because the `toExponential()`
method belongs to the `Number` object, you convert the string value `entry1` to a numeric
value stored in the `number` variable.

The listing simply loops through a `for` loop displaying the value entered by the user with the number of decimal places indicated by the loop counter variable, `i`, of the `for` loop.

The `toPrecision()` Method

Although you may not have much need to display your numbers in exponential notation you will more than likely want to control their accuracy at some point or another. To do this you have two options. You can either decide on a number of significant figures, or you can decide on a number of decimal points. To choose the accuracy in terms of the number of significant figures, you use the `toPrecision()` method. The method is applied with the dot notation and the number of significant figures is controlled by specifying the number as a parameter of the method. To see this at work, look at the following lines:

```
var myNum = 1234.56;
var to8SF = myNum.toPrecision(8)   // results in 1234.5600
var to6SF = myNum.toPrecision(6)   // results in 1234.56
var to4SF = myNum.toPrecision(4)   // results in 1234
var to2SF = myNum.toPrecision(2)   // results in 1.2e+3
```

Listing 7.7 shows a full example.

INPUT **LISTING 7.7** Using the `toPrecision()` Method to Control Display of a Number (toPrecision.htm)

```
<!DOCTYPE html
PUBLIC "-//W3C//DTD XHTML 1.0 Transitional//EN"
"DTD/xhtml1-transitional.dtd">
<html>
<head>
<title>Demonstrating the toPrecision() method</title>
<script type="text/javascript" language="javascript">
<!-- //
function DisplayPrecision(){
var entry1 ;
entry1 = prompt("Enter a floating point number", "Enter the number here");
number = new Number();
number = Number(entry1);
for (var i=1; i<8; i++){
document.write("<p>The number entered to " + i + " significant figures is "
 + number.toPrecision(i) + "</p><br/>");
}
} // end function DisplayPrecision()
// -->
</script>
</head>
<body onload="DisplayPrecision()">
<p>This listing demonstrates the use of the toPrecision() method.</p><br />
</body>
</html>
```

ANALYSIS Notice that in the above example that we start the `i` variable for the `for` loop at 1, since a value of zero makes no sense for the number of significant figures.

When the number of significant figures specified is greater than the number itself, then the method adds on zeros. When the number of significant figures you specify is greater than the whole part of the number, then the number is returned in the standard form; but

7

when the significant figures specified is smaller than the whole part, it's turned into exponential form.

Effectively it then acts as the `toExponential()` method does when you pass it a number as a parameter. If this isn't what you want, then you can simply apply the `parseFloat()` function to the result. By turning the result into a number then, as long as the value is within the range specified earlier, the number will be displayed in normal form. For example to do this for the last example you could write the following:

```
var myNum = 1234.56;
var to2SF = myNum.toPrecision(2);
var to2SF = parseFloat(to2SF);  // results in 1200
```

Alternatively as a shortcut, you could simply multiply the result by one, although the results of the `toPrecision()` method are in string form. Remember that JavaScript converts the operands of operators to the data type that make most sense for the operation. The only data type that makes sense for multiplication is the type `number` so you could have written it like so:

```
var myNum = 1234.56;
var to2SF = myNum.toPrecision(2) * 1; // results in 1200
```

The `toPrecision()` method may seem to offer a way to force JavaScript to display to a greater accuracy than its standard 16/17 figures. After all, can't we just use the method to specify a number greater than this? Unfortunately, although it can be used to show a greater number of figures, these figures are not accurate. To illustrate this let's use a 20-digit number with figures that iterate from 1 through 0 twice:

```
var myNum = 12345678901234567890;
    myNum = myNum.toPrecision(20);
alert(myNum);
```

Normally this number would be truncated to 17 characters and shown in exponential form. Using the `toPrecision()` method like this in Internet Explorer 5.5 makes the browser display 20 characters. However the characters after the second seven characters are simply replaced by zeros. Netscape Navigator 6 on the other hand is inconsistent with the digits it displays after the 17th digit of a long number. In the case above, it replaces the digits `890` that we might hope for with the digits `168`. The fact is that JavaScript doesn't handle numbers of such length with accuracy.

The `toFixed()` Method

Of the four new methods of the `Number` object, the one you will probably have the most use for is the `toFixed()` method. Rather than returning a value to a fixed number of significant figures as the `toPrecision()` method does, it returns numbers to a fixed number of decimal places.

One aspect of JavaScript that is most frustrating to those who want to use it to deal with money is its handling of numbers. JavaScript will remove any trailing zeros after a decimal point. Therefore if we were to total up the cost of several items using JavaScript, then output it to a Web page without any further processing, we would not know whether it would display correctly. For example, look at the following example of code:

```
var costOfItem1 = 9.10;
var costOfItem2 = 5.60;
var totalCost = costOfItem1 + costOfItem2;  // returns 14.7
```

Clearly, for example, 14.7 would not be acceptable as a currency value for any Web site that might use some sort of JavaScript enhancement to calculate the cost of a visitor's potential shopping cart purchase. There is a workaround for this which you will see shortly, but in the future once post-version 6 browsers become the norm, the toFixed() method should make this redundant. Let's look at some examples:

```
var myNum  = 1234.5678;
var to6DP  = myNum.toFixed(6)    // results in 1234.567800
var to4DP  = myNum.toFixed(4)    // results in 1234.5678
var to2DP  = myNum.toFixed(2)    // results in 1234.56
var to0DP  = myNum.toFixed(0)    // results in 1234
var toN2DP = myNum.toFixed(-2)   // results in 1200
```

As you can see the method does exactly as you would expect. The possible exception to this is the last example where the parameter was set to -2 decimal points. This rounded the number to the hundreds mark. However at the time of writing, this only worked in Netscape Navigator 6.

In the previous example you could display the total cost of the items as currency by writing the following:

```
var costOfItem1 = 9.10;
var costOfItem2 = 5.60;
var totalCost = costOfItem1 + costOfItem2;  // returns 14.7
var totalCost = totalCost.toFixed(2);       // returns 14.70
```

You could if you wanted to then concatenate this with a dollar symbol or a symbol of another currency as appropriate for the Web site.

Note that if the toFixed() method is used with a very large number such as an exponential, the result will still be displayed in standard notation. For example, as that shown here:

```
var myNum = 1e30;
    myNum = myNum.toFixed(3);
alert(myNum);   // alerts 1000000000000000000000000000000.000
```

There are occasions when this could be useful. For example if you don't want to output a large number in exponential form, you could use this method with the parameter set to zero.

The `toLocaleString()` Method

Although the `toFixed()` method can be used for formatting numbers as currency, it is the `toLocaleString()` method that is specifically intended for this job. It uses the system language of the computer it is running on to format a number to the currency notation of that language.

Let's look at an example that illustrates this. Listing 7.8 will allow a user to enter a floating-point number that is displayed according to the browser settings.

INPUT **LISTING 7.8**   Using the `toLocaleString()` Method to Demonstrate the Current Browser Language Settings (`toLocaleString.htm`)

```
<!DOCTYPE html
PUBLIC "-//W3C//DTD XHTML 1.0 Transitional//EN"
"DTD/xhtml1-transitional.dtd">
<html>
<head>
<title>Demonstrating the toLocaleString() method</title>
<script type="text/javascript" language="javascript">
<!-- //
function DisplayLocale(){
var entry1 ;
entry1 = prompt("Enter a floating point number", "Enter the number here");
number = new Number();
number = Number(entry1);
document.write("<p>The number entered by the user expressed for the locale is "
 + number.toLocaleString() + "</p><br/>");
} // end function DisplayLocale()
// -->
</script>
</head>
<body onload="DisplayLocale()">
<p>This listing demonstrates the use of the toPrecision() method.</p><br />
</body>
</html>
```

Again, remember that the `toLocaleString()` method belongs to the `Number` object and that a prompt box accepts a string value.

In the United States or in the United Kingdom, Listing 7.8 will result in the display shown in Figure 7.4 when the number 1234.56 is entered by a user.

OUTPUT

FIGURE 7.4

Display using
`toLocaleString()` *as
it would appear in
the United States or
United Kingdom.*

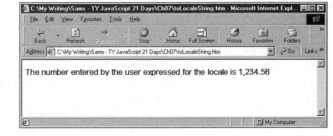

ANALYSIS As you can see, it removes the extraneous digits after the decimal point and
inserts commas between each triplet of the whole part of the number.

However, other countries don't format numbers in this way. So if the system's language
setting is German, for example, then the listing will format it differently, as shown in
Figure 7.5.

Tip To alter the system language settings in Windows 98, for example, choose
Start, Control Panel, Regional Settings. On the Regional Settings tab choose,
for example, German (Standard).

OUTPUT

FIGURE 7.5

Display using
`toLocaleString()` *as
it appears when the
browser language is
set to German in
Internet Explorer.*

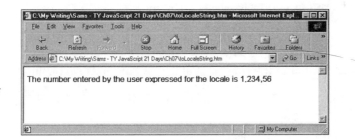

ANALYSIS This time it has used a comma as the decimal point and periods to separate each
triplet, as is the standard German numerical notation.

Caution At the time of writing although the `toLocaleString()` method was recognized by Netscape 6, it did not seem to have any effect on the numbers to
which it was applied.

7

Many European languages use a format similar to that displayed in Figure 7.5 for the German language.

Remember from the previous chapter that we stated that the `toLocaleString()` method is also applicable to arrays. If you have gathered monetary data and stored it in a string, you do not need to apply the `toLocaleString()` method to each element of the array in turn. You simply apply it to the array as a whole.

> **Caution**
>
> It is important to remember that the `toExponential()`, `toFixed()`, `toLocaleString()`, and `toPrecision()` methods all return their results as strings. If the number is then to be used in an addition operation, you must convert it to the data type `number`; otherwise the + operator will concatenate strings, not perform an addition calculation.

The `valueOf()` method

The `valueOf()` method of a `Number` object returns the value of a `Number` object as a number datatype. If JavaScript had been created from the start as a fully object-oriented technology you might well have expected a `Number` object to possess a `value` property. The fact that it doesn't is a reflection of the time in JavaScript's history when it was much less object-oriented than JavaScript 1.5.

Listing 7.9 shows an example using the `Number` object's `valueOf()` method.

LISTING 7.9 Finding the Numeric Value of a `Number` Object Using the `valueOf()` Method (`valueOf.htm`)

```
<!DOCTYPE html
PUBLIC "-//W3C//DTD XHTML 1.0 Transitional//EN"
"DTD/xhtml1-transitional.dtd">
<html>
<head>
<title>Demonstrating the valueOf() method</title>
<script type="text/javascript" language="javascript">
<!-- //
function DisplayValue(){
var entry1 ;
entry1 = prompt("Enter a floating point number", "Enter the number here");
var number = new Number();
number = Number(entry1);
if (isNaN(number)){
document.write("<p>You did not enter a valid number.<br />
 Hit your browser's Refresh button to try again.</p>");
}
```

LISTING 7.9   continued

```
else{
document.write("<p>The value of the number entered is "
 + number.valueOf() + "</p>");
} // end else
} // end function DisplayValue()
// -->
</script>
</head>
<body onload="DisplayValue()">
<p>This listing demonstrates the use of the valueOf() method.</p><br />
</body>
</html>
```

The processing of an entered number seems to do very little, but as was the case in some examples earlier in this chapter, there is quite a bit of type casting going on. The string entered in the prompt box is assigned to the Number object in the variable number. Before using the document.write() method we use the isNaN() function to output an error message; if no valid number was entered and, if a valid number was entered into the prompt box, then we output the result returned by the valueOf() method of the Number object.

Having looked at the properties and methods of the Number object, let's move on and learn a little about the Math object.

The Math Object

You have already seen, and are hopefully now comfortable with, a lot of the mathematical operators that JavaScript provides. For much of the time those operators are perfectly adequate for the arithmetical processes that need to be carried out. But whenever more than the most basic of mathematical operations is needed, then we need something more specific or more powerful.

JavaScript has its own Math object. The Math object provides some powerful tools and useful mathematical constants, which we can use in any mathematical operations.

Predefined Properties

The Math object's properties are all constants so as you would expect they are read-only and can't be changed. In line with traditional constant notation in JavaScript, the names of the properties are written completely in uppercase letters. Be careful to remember this, as writing the properties with one or more lowercase letters is a common mistake. See Table 7.1.

TABLE 7.1   The Mathematical Constants Provided in the Math Object's Properties

Property	Value	Description
E	2.718281828459045	Euler's constant
LN2	0.6931471805599453	Natural log of 2
LN10	2.302585092994046	Natural log of 10
LOG2E	1.4426950408889634	Log to base 2 of E
LOG10E	0.4342944819032518	Log to base 10 of E
PI	3.141592653589793	π
SQRT1_2	0.7071067811865476	Square root of 0.5
SQRT2	1.4142135623730951	Square root of 2

INPUT   **LISTING 7.10**   The Properties of the Math Object (MathProperties.htm)

```
<!DOCTYPE html
PUBLIC "-//W3C//DTD XHTML 1.0 Transitional//EN"
"DTD/xhtml1-transitional.dtd">
<html>
<head>
<title>The Properties of the Math object</title>
<script type="text/javascript" language="javascript">
<!-- //
function DisplayMath(){
document.write("<br/><p>The value of Euler's constant <i>E</i> is: "
 + Math.E + "</p>");
document.write("<br/><p>The value of the natural Logarithm of 2 is: "
 + Math.LN2 + "</p>");
document.write("<br/><p>The value of the natural Logarithm of 10 is: "
 + Math.LN10 + "</p>");
document.write("<br/><p>The value of the Logarithm to base 2 of E is: "
 + Math.LOG2E + "</p>");
document.write("<br/><p>The value of the Logarithm to base 10 of E is: "
 + Math.LOG10E + "</p>");
document.write("<br/><p>The value of the constant PI is: "
 + Math.PI + "</p>");
document.write("<br/><p>The value of the square root of 1/2 is: "
 + Math.SQRT1_2 + "</p>");
document.write("<br/><p>The value of the square root of 2 is: "
 + Math.SQRT2 + "</p>");
} // end function DisplayMath()
// -->
</script>
</head>
<body onload="DisplayMath()">

</body>
</html>
```

As with other numbers, the values held by the Math object's properties are accurate to approximately 16 significant figures.

When using these properties remember that they must be referred to as properties of the Math object. Also take care to remember that the Math object starts with an uppercase "M". If you only use the Math object occasionally, then both of these important details are easy to forget. Listing 7.11 shows an example of how to use the Math.PI property in calculating the area and circumference of a circle.

INPUT

LISTING 7.11 Using Math.PI to Calculate the Area and Circumference of a Circle (FindArea.htm)

```
<!DOCTYPE html
PUBLIC "-//W3C//DTD XHTML 1.0 Transitional//EN"
"DTD/xhtml1-transitional.dtd">
<html>
<head>
<title>Find the area and circumference of a circle</title>
<script type="text/javascript" language="javascript">
<!-- //
function FindArea(){
var entry1 ;
entry1 = prompt("Enter the radius of a circle", "Enter the number here");
var number = new Number();
number = Number(entry1);
if (isNaN(number)){
document.write("<p>You did not enter a valid number.<br />
 Hit your browser's Refresh button to try again.</p>");
}
else{
document.write("<p>You entered a radius of " + number + "</p>");
document.write("<p>The area of the circle is "
 + (number * number * Math.PI) + "</p>");
document.write("<p>The circumference of the circle is "
 + (2 * number * Math.PI) + "</p>");
} // end else
} // end function FindArea()
// -->
</script>
</head>
<body onload="FindArea()">

</body>
</html>
```

7

We ask the user to input a chosen radius for the circle and, if a valid number has been entered, we calculate the area and circumference of the circle—each calculation uses `Math.PI`, as well as the `document.write()` method to output the results to screen.

Let's move on to look at the methods of the `Math` object.

Methods of the `Math` Object

No matter what you are using JavaScript for it is unlikely, unless you want to use it for ambitious mathematics, that you will find it lacking in terms of mathematical functions. The `Math` object has a large number of methods that cover many eventualities. See Table 7.2.

TABLE 7.2   The Methods of the JavaScript `Math` Object

Method	Description
`abs()`	Returns the absolute (positive) value of a number
`acos()`	Returns the arc cosine of a value
`asin()`	Returns the arc sine of a value
`atan()`	Returns the arc tangent of a value
`atan2()`	Returns the angle of two polar coordinates
`ceil()`	Rounds up a fractional number to the next integer
`cos()`	Returns the cosine of an angle
`exp()`	Returns Euler's constant raised to the power of a number
`floor()`	Rounds down a fractional number to the next integer
`log()`	Returns the natural logarithm of a number
`max()`	Returns the maximum number from a comma separated list
`min()`	Returns the minimum number from a comma separated list
`pow()`	Returns one number raised to the power of another
`random()`	Generates a random number between 0 and 1
`round()`	Rounds a number to the nearest integer (rounding .5 up)
`sin()`	Returns the sine of an angle
`sqrt()`	Returns the square root of a number
`tan()`	Returns the tangent of an angle

> **Caution**
>
> Remember that the properties of the Math object are expressed only in uppercase characters and the methods of the Math object are expressed in lowercase characters. Mixing the case of a property or method name can cause obscure errors, particularly in lengthy calculations.

Many of these methods provide trigonometric functions. Maybe you already know that you will have a use for them, but if you don't then don't ignore them. They can be useful for all sorts of things such as creating some special dynamic HMTL effects. In the remainder of the chapter, we will look at some, but not all, of the Math object's methods.

Finding Absolute Values Using the abs() Method

The simplest of the Math object's methods is probably the abs() method. It finds the absolute value of the number it is applied to. The absolute value of a number is the difference from zero, and it is always expressed as a positive number, whether the original number was positive or negative. For example, as shown in the following:

```
Math.abs( 1)  // returns 1
Math.abs(-1)  // returns 1
```

Hopefully, from this example it isn't too difficult to see that the absolute value of a number was the positive magnitude of that number.

Finding Square Roots Using the sqrt() Method

The sqrt() method is another method belonging to the Math object, and it returns the square root of its argument. When we want to find the square root of a number we simply pass it to this method as its sole argument. The value it returns is the root of the number we send it:

```
Math.sqrt(4)   // returns 2
Math.sqrt(9)   // returns 3
Math.sqrt(16)  // returns 4
Math.sqrt(25)  // returns 5
```

The ceil(), floor(), and round() Methods

JavaScript provides three methods you can use for rounding numbers. The ceil() method is for rounding up, the floor() is for rounding down, and the round() method is for rounding off.

The ceil() method is the means of rounding up numbers to the nearest integer. In order to use it, you need to address it through the Math object and send it the number you want to round up as a parameter. Here are some examples:

```
Math.ceil( 1.0001)  // returns  2
Math.ceil( 1.9999)  // returns  2
Math.ceil(-1.0001)  // returns -1
Math.ceil(-1.9999)  // returns -1
```

If you want to round down a number, then you need to use the `floor()` method. It is used in exactly the same way as the `ceil()` method—a single number is provided as the argument of the method. Here are some examples:

```
Math.floor( 1.0001)  // returns  1
Math.floor( 1.9999)  // returns  1
Math.floor(-1.0001)  // returns -2
Math.floor(-1.9999)  // returns -2
```

Of course sometimes you will need to round up numbers if their fractional part is greater than a half, but if it is less, then you will want to round it down. This is where the `round()` method comes in. When you round off numbers in this way a choice needs to be made about which side a number with a fractional part of exactly one half will be rounded. In the case of JavaScript, the choice was made that it should be rounded up. To demonstrate the use of the `round()` method, here are some more examples:

```
Math.round(1.0001)  // returns 1
Math.round(1.4449)  // returns 1
Math.round(1.5000)  // returns 2
Math.round(1.5001)  // returns 2
Math.round(1.9999)  // returns 2
```

Note that when you pass a data container such as a variable as the parameter to one of the three rounding methods the data container's original value is not changed. Therefore if you want to use the rounded number at some point later in a script, you will need to store the result.

Finding Maximum and Minimum Values Using the `max()` and `min()` Methods

To find the maximum or minimum number in a series of numbers, we could of course write a script—perhaps as a function to make reuse easier. This would likely involve storing the numbers in arrays and string comparisons. As you might imagine, it could all get a bit messy. Thankfully we don't need to script that ourselves because the `Math` object provides a couple of methods.

The `max()` and `min()` methods are fairly self-explanatory in what they do. Listing 7.12 shows the `max()` and `min()` methods in use.

INPUT

LISTING 7.12 Finding the Smallest and Largest Numbers Among Three Values (`FindMaxAndMin.htm`)

```html
<!DOCTYPE html
PUBLIC "-//W3C//DTD XHTML 1.0 Transitional//EN"
"DTD/xhtml1-transitional.dtd">
<html>
<head>
<title>Finding the maximum and minimum number</title>
<script type="text/javascript" language="javascript">
<!-- //
function SetFocus(){
document.SimpleForm.FirstInput.focus();
} // end function SetFocus()

function FindMaxAndMin(){
var num1 = document.SimpleForm.FirstInput.value;
var num2 = document.SimpleForm.SecondInput.value;
var num3 = document.SimpleForm.ThirdInput.value;
if (isNaN(num1) || isNaN(num2) || isNaN(num3)){
alert("You made an invalid entry. Please start again.");
document.SimpleForm.reset();
SetFocus();
} // end if
else { // all entries are valid numbers
var MaxNum = Math.max(num1,num2,num3);
var MinNum = Math.min(num1,num2,num3);
var alertString = "You entered " + num1 + ", " + num2 + " and " +num3;
alertString += "\nThe largest number is " + MaxNum;
alertString += "\nThe smallest number is " + MinNum;
alert(alertString);
document.SimpleForm.reset();
SetFocus();
} // end else
} // end function FindMaxAndMin()

// -->
</script>
</head>
<body onload="SetFocus()">
<form name="SimpleForm">
<table>
<tr>
 <td width="25%" align="right">Enter first number:</td>
 <td><input name="FirstInput" type="text"></td>
</tr>
<tr>
 <td width="25%" align="right">Enter second number:</td>
 <td><input name="SecondInput" type="text"></td>
</tr>
```

LISTING 7.12   continued

```
<tr>
 <td width="25%" align="right">Enter third number:</td>
 <td><input name="ThirdInput" type="text"></td>
</tr>
<tr>
 <td width="25%" align="right"> </td>
 <td><button type="Button" onclick="FindMaxAndMin()">
Click to calculate</button></td>
</tr>
</table>
</form>
</body>
</html>
```

ANALYSIS   In the example in Listing 7.12, we used an XHTML form to collect three numbers which are to be processed to find the maximum and minimum of the three
values.

The page opens with the focus set on the first <input> element in the form, by means of
an onload attribute on the <body> element which calls the SetFocus() function. The user
enters three values, one in each of the <input> elements. Each of the values entered is
assigned to three variables—num1, num2, and num3. If even one of the three variables is
not a number, which we test by means of the isNaN() function, then an error message is
output, the form is reset, and the focus is again placed on the first <input> element in the
form.

If three valid numbers are entered then a string, held in the alertString variable, is displayed using an alert box. The three numbers entered are listed in the order in which they
were entered and the maximum and minimum values of the three numbers are displayed.
Once the user has acknowledged the alert box then the user can enter three more
numbers.

Note   The text you want to add to the <button> element must be placed between
the <button> start tag and a </button> end tag. If you try to use a
<button/> tag with attributes, then you will have only a tiny button with no
text displayed on screen.

Creating Random Numbers Using the `random()` Method

Possibly the most fun method we have belonging to any JavaScript object is the `Math` object's `random()` method, although it can be put to serious practical uses too. The `random()` method generates a random number between 0 and 1. So, if we wanted to create random numbers greater than 1, we would generate a random number between 0 and 1 and multiply by an appropriate number to achieve the correct range of random numbers.

Listing 7.13 provides a page where the user can choose a maximum number and one or more random numbers, up to the chosen maximum, will be generated.

INPUT

LISTING 7.13 Generating Random Numbers up to a User Selected Maximum (RandomNumbers.htm)

```
<!DOCTYPE html
PUBLIC "-//W3C//DTD XHTML 1.0 Transitional//EN"
"DTD/xhtml1-transitional.dtd">
<html>
<head>
<title>Generating random numbers</title>
<script type="text/javascript" language="javascript">
<!-- //
var MaxNum = 0;
var ToDisplay;

function SetFocus(){
document.SimpleForm.FirstInput.focus();
} // end function SetFocus()

function SubmitMax(){
var num1 = document.SimpleForm.FirstInput.value;
if (isNaN(num1)){
alert("You made an invalid entry. Please start again.");
document.SimpleForm.reset();
SetFocus();
} // end if
else { // entry is a valid number
MaxNum = document.SimpleForm.FirstInput.value;
} // end else
} // end function SubmitMax()

function GenerateRandom(){
if (MaxNum!==0){
ToDisplay = (MaxNum * Math.random());
ToDisplay = formatNumber(ToDisplay, 0);
alert("Random number up to " + MaxNum + " is " + ToDisplay);
document.SimpleForm.reset();
SetFocus();
```

7

LISTING 7.13   continued

```
} // end if
} // end function SubmitMax()

function ClearAndSet(){
document.SimpleForm.reset();
SetFocus();
MaxNum = 0;
}

function formatNumber(theNum, numDecPlaces)
{
    var num = new String();
    num = "" + theNum;
    var pos = 0;
    count = 0;
    while (num.substring(pos-1,pos)!== ".") {
     pos += 1 ;
     count += 1;
    }
    while (pos < (count+numDecPlaces)){
    pos +=1;
    } // end while
    return num.substring(0,pos);
}

// -->
</script>
</head>
<body onload="SetFocus()">
<h3>Generate random numbers up to a chosen maximum.</h3>
<form name="SimpleForm">
<table>
<tr>
 <td width="30%" align="right">Enter maximum number:</td>
 <td><input name="FirstInput" type="text"></td>
</tr>
<tr>
 <td width="25%" align="right"> </td>
 <td><button type="Button" onclick="SubmitMax()">
Submit max. number</button></td>
</tr>
<tr>
 <td width="25%" align="right"> </td>
 <td> </td>
</tr>
<tr>
 <td width="25%" align="right"><button type="Button"
 onclick="ClearAndSet()">Clear and Start again</button></td>
 <td><button type="Button" onclick="GenerateRandom()">
```

LISTING 7.13   continued

```
Click to calculate random number</button></td>
</tr>
</table>
</form>
</body>
</html>
```

ANALYSIS   The listing is longer than many of the others that you have seen, so let's take it one step at a time.

The onload attribute on the <body> element calls the SetFocus() function to set focus on the <input> element named "FirstInput". In addition, the variable MaxNum is set to zero.

When the user enters a number and then clicks on the button labeled "Submit max. number", the SubmitMax() function is called and the chosen maximum number is stored in the variable MaxNum.

Clicking on the button labeled "Click to calculate random number" calls the GenerateRandom() function which, using an if statement to control what happens, generates and displays a random number only if the MaxNum variable is not equal to zero. During the process of displaying the generated random number the GenerateRandom() function calls the formatNumber() function that you saw in Listing 7.1. On this occasion we set the number of decimal places to zero so that an integer number is displayed. If you want to generate random numbers which allow numbers beyond the decimal point, then adjust the second argument of the call to the formatNumber() function. The user can generate multiple random numbers up to the chosen maximum, until such time as a new maximum number is passed to the SubmitMax() function or the form is cleared by clicking the button labeled "Clear and Start again".

The button labeled "Clear and Start again" resets the form and returns focus to the <input> element. In addition, the MaxNum variable is set to zero. Thus, if the button labeled "Click to calculate number" is clicked after the form has been cleared, then it does nothing until a new maximum number has been entered by the user, and the button labeled "Submit max. number" has been clicked.

The exp() and pow() Methods

The Math object has two methods for raising numbers to a power. The first is specific and is provided as a shortcut to a common mathematical process. This method is the exp() method. It returns Euler's constant raised to the power of the numeric parameter it is given. For example, as shown here:

```
// Euler's constant, e = 2.718281828459045
Math.exp(1)    // returns 2.718281828459045
Math.exp(2)    // returns 7.38905609893065
Math.exp(3)    // returns 20.085536923187668
```

In the first example, e is raised to the power of one, which of course simply is the value of e itself. In the second example, e is raised to the power of 2 (e squared), and in the third and final example, e is raised to the power of 3 (e cubed).

This may be a handy shortcut for some advanced math, but we also have a more general method for raising other numbers to powers that we specify. To do this we use the pow() method. With the pow() method, you must specify two parameters. The first is the number that you want to raise, and the second is the number that you want to raise it by. Here are some examples just to make sure that is clear:

```
Math.pow(2,2)  // returns  4
Math.pow(2,3)  // returns  8
Math.pow(2,4)  // returns 16
Math.pow(2,5)  // returns 32
```

The first line is 2 raised to the power of 2 (2 squared), the second line is 2 raised to the power of 3 (2 cubed), and the third and fourth lines are 2 raised to the power of 4 and 5 respectively. These numbers can of course be any values you want to use. This includes raising numbers to negative powers (which is the same as 1 over the number raised to the same positive power). The following shows you some examples:

```
Math.pow(2,-2)  // returns 0.25     (1/Math.pow(2,2))
Math.pow(2,-3)  // returns 0.125    (1/Math.pow(2,3))
Math.pow(2,-4)  // returns 0.0625   (1/Math.pow(2,4))
Math.pow(2,-5)  // returns 0.03125  (1/Math.pow(2,4))
```

Creating Your Own Math Functions

Although the Math object has many methods, if you use math extensively in your scripts you will probably run across situations where you need a function that isn't present as a method of the Math object. If this happens we would encourage you to think about how you could use the methods that the Math object does have to create your own functions. We have included three functions that you may find useful. If you don't foresee yourself using a lot of math on your Web site, feel free to skip these examples and come back to them at a later time, if you find you need them after all.

Finding the Factorial of a Number

The factorial of a number can be calculated using the ability of functions to recurse (call themselves repeatedly), as shown here:

```
function factorialOf(theNum)
{
    if (theNum > 0)
        return theNum * factorialOf(theNum-1);
    else return 1
}
```

Let's follow the flow through the `factorialOf()` function. If the number that is the function's argument is 0 then the number 1 is returned.

If the `theNum` argument is greater than zero, then the fourth line of the `factorialOf()` function calls itself but with an argument one less than the `theNum` argument. This process is called recursion.

Let's look at what happens if the argument passed to the `factorialOf()` function is 3. The number to be returned is 3 multiplied by `factorialOf(2)`, which returns 2 and calls the `factorialOf(1)`, which returns 1 and calls `factorialOf(0)`, which returns 1. Thus `factorialOf(0)` returns 1, which is multiplied by the value returned by `factorialOf(1)`, which is 1, which in turn is multiplied by the value returned by `factorialOf(2)`, which in turn is multiplied by the number within `factorialOf(3)`. Thus we have the following:

```
1 * 1 * 2 * 3
```

So the expression `factorialOf(3)` returns the value of 6.

When using recursion you need to be sure that there is some situation where recursive calls stop being made. In this example, when the argument reaches zero the value returned is 1 and no further recursive function calls are made.

Finding the nth Root

Another function that may come in useful is being able to find roots of a number other than the square root. Before we try to write a function to do this, let's consider how we might do it with math notation. To demonstrate, consider the following expression that contains three numbers x, y, and z:

```
x = y ^ z
```

In this example, let's assume that we know the values of x and z, and we need to find the value of y. If we were using a calculator, we would find the zth root of x. But how would we do it if our calculator only had a square root button (as JavaScript does)? Well we could cancel off the power of z from the righthand side by raising it to one over z. However, if we do that then we also have to raise the lefthand side to one over z, as shown here:

```
x ^ (1/z) = y ^ z ^ (1/z)
```

7

On the righthand side the z ^ (1/z) reduces to 1 and we are simply left with y. We now have a formula for finding y, which if we swap the sides is as follows:

```
y = x ^ (1/z)
```

Therefore the zth root of x is the same as raising x to the power of one over z. There is a method belonging to the Math object which can do this, as shown here:

```
function nthRootOf(theNum, theRoot)
{
    return Math.pow(theNum, 1/theRoot)
}
```

Later in the book you will see how you can add this function to the Math object as one of its methods.

Log to Base N

The proof for the following function will not be included, but we have included the function as you may find it useful at some point. The Math object has a method that finds the natural log (log to base e) of the number you pass to it as a parameter. Unfortunately it does not include a method for the other common log function which is log to base 10. This is quite easily solved.

To find the log of a number to any base, you simply need one log function. It doesn't matter which base it is for. We already have the method for the natural log, which will do nicely. As long as we use the same log function, if we divide the log of one number by the log of another number, the result is the same as if we had taken the log of the first number to the base of the second. Therefore if we were to use JavaScript to find the log to base 10 of x, we would simply write the following:

```
Math.log(x) / Math.log(10)
```

We could of course incorporate this into a function, given a suitable name such as "log10()". However we can make it even more general and create a function that will find the log of any number to any base. To do this, you could write something like the following:

```
function logN(theBase, theNum)
{
    return Math.log(theNum) / Math.log(theBase);
}
```

There are many, many more things you can do with JavaScript from a mathematical point of view. We hope you are starting to feel comfortable with the ways these objects and their methods and properties can be used in Web pages where calculations are needed.

Summary

In this chapter we have gone beyond simple arithmetic operators and introduced you to the use of the JavaScript `Number` and `Math` objects for numerical calculations. We also looked at the properties and methods of the `Number` object and created some examples that used the `Number` object.

In addition you have been introduced to the properties and methods of the `Math` object which can be very useful in a variety of situations where mathematical calculations are needed.

Workshop

In this workshop we will review some of the new material that you have learned about the `Number` and `Math` objects in this chapter.

Q&A

Q. True or False. The `Number` object has a NaN property which you can use to test whether or not a value is a number.

A. False. You need to use the `isNaN()` function to test whether or not a value is a number.

Q. What property of the `Math` object would you use when calculating the area of a circle?

A. The Math.PI property is used in the calculation of the area of a circle. The area of a circle is PI times the radius squared.

Quiz

1. The `Number` object has a value property. True or False?

2. Which methods of the `Math` object allow you to find the largest and smallest of a set of numbers?

3. Which property of the `Math` object is used in the calculation of the area of a circle?

4. How can you create random numbers using the `Math` object?

Quiz Answers

1. False. To access the numeric value of a `Number` object, you use the `valueOf()` method.

2. To find the largest and smallest of a set of numbers, you would use `Math.max()` and `Math.min()`.

3. The PI property of the Math object is used to calculate the area of a circle. The area of a circle is the radius squared multiplied by Math.PI.

4. The Math object has a random() method which finds random numbers between 0 and 1. To create larger random numbers you would need to multiply the number generated by the random() method by the maximum limit within that which you want to generate a random number.

Exercises

1. Look at Listing 7.1 and adapt it so that instead of using prompt boxes, the numbers are entered using an XHTML form.

2. Create a Web page that uses the JavaScript function that you were shown to raise a number to its nth power.

WEEK 2

Let's Take It Further

DAY 8

The Browser Issue

JavaScript runs on almost all of the current versions of Web browsers available today, including specifically Microsoft Internet Explorer and Netscape Navigator. Unfortunately, each browser that allows for JavaScript scripting does not support the same JavaScript features. In fact, the versions of JavaScript supported by the different browsers varies from browser to browser. This chapter looks at the differences in the various versions of JavaScript supported by browsers—specifically the differences between Internet Explorer and Netscape Navigator. We also will discuss how to design your JavaScript code for cross-browser compatibility.

Finally, we will look at the W3C DOM developed by the World Wide Web Consortium as a common document object model and how you can use it for accessing specific elements of the Web page. This chapter will teach you:

- The differences between JavaScript versions supported by different browsers
- Cross-browser compatible scripting
- About the W3C DOM

Different Browsers, Different JavaScript

As we have previously discussed, JavaScript differs from most other programming languages in that it is a scripting language, not a compiled language. Languages, such as C++ and Java, are used to create program code that is compiled allowing it to run on virtually any machine. Typically, the operating system where the code will run (such as Microsoft Windows or the Macintosh OS) is the developer's only consideration when distributing the compiled code.

A scripting language, on the other hand, relies on the browser to interpret the scripted code on the Web page. In other words, each line of JavaScript code is interpreted at runtime by the browser that accesses the page containing the code. Because of this factor, it is obvious that JavaScript code can only run on a browser that supports JavaScript. The most popular browsers today, Netscape Navigator and Internet Explorer both provide strong support for JavaScript, but unfortunately the JavaScript features supported by these browsers varies.

JavaScript History

JavaScript originally got its start as a scripting language for Netscape Navigator. Netscape originally recognized the need for a scripting language to do the following: allow Web server administrators to manage the Web server and connect its pages to other services, provide Web page authors the ability to create scripts to run on a Web page and perform tasks such as verifying a value typed into a field, and create an interface for communicating with Java applets placed on an HTML page. This scripting language was originally called "LiveScript."

Before the release of Navigator 2, Netscape and Sun formed an agreement to call the new scripting language JavaScript. JavaScript was then introduced by Netscape as part of Netscape Navigator 2. When Navigator 3 was released, it included an updated version of JavaScript, JavaScript 1.1.

At the same time Netscape was releasing Navigator 3, Microsoft released Internet Explorer 3 with its own version of JavaScript named JScript. Because the Java name was trademarked by Sun, Microsoft chose to call it JScript to avoid the need to license the name from Sun. Although JScript was intended to parallel the capabilities of the JavaScript 1.1 available with Navigator 3, its functionality more closely resembled that which was available in the original version of JavaScript released with Navigator 2.

Finally, with the release of Navigator 4 and Internet Explorer 4, JavaScript and JScript essentially mirrored core functionalities. Although Microsoft continued to call its version JScript, Internet Explorer `script` tags recognized both JScript and JavaScript, allowing

8

for both types of scripting. Of course, that was not true of Netscape Navigator, which only recognizes JavaScript `script` tags.

In an effort to create a more standardized core language, the European Computer Manufacturers Association (ECMA) met with Microsoft, Netscape, and other organizations with JavaScript interests. Formal language specifications were published as standards for the language. Because of the licensing issues with the name JavaScript, the new language was named ECMAScript.

Currently the ECMA maintains the standards for the core language. The core language typically maintains the most compatible features consistent between Netscape Navigator and Microsoft Internet Explorer. Therefore, you can generally feel confident that everything within the ECMA standard will work on the current browser versions for both Navigator and Internet Explorer, but may not be backward compatible to previous browser versions, or any of the many other browsers available.

Unfortunately the ECMA standard does not include specifications for all the fun and exciting features you find on various Web sites that you visit today. Most of these extended features are built in to the browsers by Microsoft and Netscape. In order to take advantage of these features, you potentially limit the capability of your audience to view your site in all its glory. One good example of this would be when Navigator 3 provided additional capability with the Browser object that allowed Web developers to create rollover button effects like those which you see on most current sites today. Microsoft was slower to add this type of feature. So Internet Explorer users did not see the rollover effects when visiting sites that had incorporated that feature. Of course this functionality was later added to Internet Explorer. As you can probably deduce, the total functionality available is based not only on the version of JavaScript supported by the browser but also the browser version and its browser object model.

> **Note** You can refer to Appendix E, "A Short History of JavaScript," for a more detailed history.

ECMA Standards

As mentioned earlier, the ECMA maintains the standards for the core JavaScript language, called ECMAScript because of licensing issues with Sun. Both Netscape Navigator and Microsoft Internet Explorer maintain that they are ECMA-compliant, meaning that they include all of the core language features as outlined by the ECMA standard. The ECMA standards body maintains a document called ECMA-262, which contains all core ECMAScript language standards. You can find the latest version of this document at `http://www.emca.ch`.

It is important to recognize that the ECMA provides only core language standards. It is important to be familiar with some of these standards so that you can determine more quickly if the JavaScript functionality you want to add will be supported by all current browsers. For example, EMCAScript Edition 3 specifies the following core components:

- Types—There are nine different types that can be used in expressions: Undefined, Null, Boolean, String, Number, Object, Reference, List, and Completion.

- Objects—There are 11 different object types that are part of the core language standard: Global, Object, Function, Array, String, Boolean, Number, Math, Date, RegExp, and Error objects. As you work with different browsers, you will find that each browser has its own set of objects for accessing the components of the browser window.

- Keywords—The following words are used as keywords: break, case, catch, continue, default, delete, do, else, finally, for, function, if, in, instanceof, new, return, switch, this, throw, try, typeof, var, void, while, with.

- Reserved Words—These words have been reserved for future use within JavaScript and therefore should be avoided within your scripts: abstract, boolean, byte, char, class, const, debugger, double, enum, export, extends, final, float, goto, implements, import, int, interface, long, native, package, private, protected, public, short, static, super, synchronized, throws, transient, volatile.

Cross-Browser Compatible Scripting

Because your Web site has the potential to be accessed by multiple browsers, your best bet is to create cross-browser compatible code. What does this mean? Essentially, if your code is cross-browser compatible it should execute reliably on all browsers. On the surface this sounds like a fairly straightforward statement. The problem comes in deciding what you want to use for your standard, for example, browser version, language, or platform.

As previously mentioned, the ECMA standard creates a standard for core JavaScript code that will execute reliably on the latest versions of Netscape Navigator and Microsoft Internet Explorer. Since these browsers are the most widely used, it is feasible to assume that the majority of the visitors that will be visiting will be using one of these browsers. However, it also is highly probable that they may not be running the latest version of either browser.

Although it is assumed that visitors will have either Navigator or Internet Explorer, this may not necessarily be the case. Especially with the surge of new mobile devices, it is highly likely that many visitors will have browser interfaces that do not support scripting.

Because this book focuses on JavaScript 1.5, most of the examples in the book are designed to work on browsers that support that version. If you want to code for earlier browsers you can refer to Appendix A, "New Features in JavaScript 1.5," for the list of new features that were added to JavaScript 1.5. Table 8.1 identifies each of the JavaScript versions and the corresponding browsers that supported them.

TABLE 8.1 JavaScript Version Support

JavaScript Version	Browser Support
JavaScript 1.1	Netscape 3.01
JavaScript 1.2	Netscape 4.05, Internet Explorer 4.01
JavaScript 1.3	Netscape 4.61, Internet Explorer 5.0
JavaScript 1.4	Mozilla 5.0, Alpha Pre-Release
JavaScript 1.5	Netscape 6, Internet Explorer 5.5

As you can see from the table, JavaScript 1.5 features were supported beginning with Netscape Navigator 6 and Internet Explorer 5.5. Let's look at ways to identify browsers that don't support this version of JavaScript, and how to design your code to avoid these problems.

Browsers That Don't Support JavaScript

Although users can download the latest browser for free from the appropriate site, the chance of being visited by browsers that don't support JavaScript would appear to be very limited. After all, JavaScript has been supported by Microsoft and Netscape since around 1996. But, as Internet access becomes available on more different devices, such as palm-sized devices and cell phones, it is quite common for sites to be accessed by browsers that do not support JavaScript. These types of browsers run on devices with limited resources, so more demanding features, such as JavaScript support, are not available on most of these devices.

Because of the growing potential of your site being accessed by a device that does not support JavaScript, you will want to design your site so that it avoids any of these potential errors.

Most older browsers ignore HTML tags that they do not recognize, therefore, when they encounter a <script> tag they typically ignore that tag. But because JavaScript code is not placed within brackets <> those lines of code will be placed on the Web page as text. Because of this situation, we need to use the HTML comment markers around the JavaScript code. By doing this, the non-JavaScript supporting browsers will ignore your

JavaScript code, but the browsers that support JavaScript will ignore the comment markers and execute the JavaScript code. You place the comment markers in your JavaScript code as follows:

```
<script language="JavaScript" type = "text/javascript">
<!--
  window.alert("JavaScript code goes here.");
//..>
</script>
```

Notice the `<!--` tag marks at the beginning of the JavaScript code and the `//..>` tag marks the end of the script. The browsers that do not support scripting will ignore all code between those tags. Of course, they will also ignore the HTML `</script>` tag that signals the end of the JavaScript code.

> **Caution**
>
> Be aware there are some older America Online browsers that do not ignore the code placed within the HTML comment lines. If a user visits your page using one of these old browsers, your JavaScript code will appear on the Web page. Fortunately, these browsers are very outdated and rarely used at this time.

Keep in mind, the HTML comment markers do not hide your JavaScript code. They only tell the browser to ignore the code during processing. As you are probably well aware, most browsers allow for the source code of a page being visited to be viewed by the visitor. This will include any JavaScript code that you have embedded within your page.

Browsers with JavaScript Support Turned Off

Even though a browser supports JavaScript, there is still the possibility that the JavaScript support may be disabled for that particular browser. Nearly all browsers that support JavaScript provide the option of disabling JavaScript. Although browsers default to allowing JavaScript, many IS departments choose to disable Java and JavaScript support to eliminate any potential security violations. Even if the browser is set to support JavaScript, the corporate Firewall may attempt to filter out JavaScript lines from the incoming HTML code. It is quite simple to disable the support of JavaScript from a browser as shown in Figure 8.1, which illustrates the Netscape Navigator Preferences window.

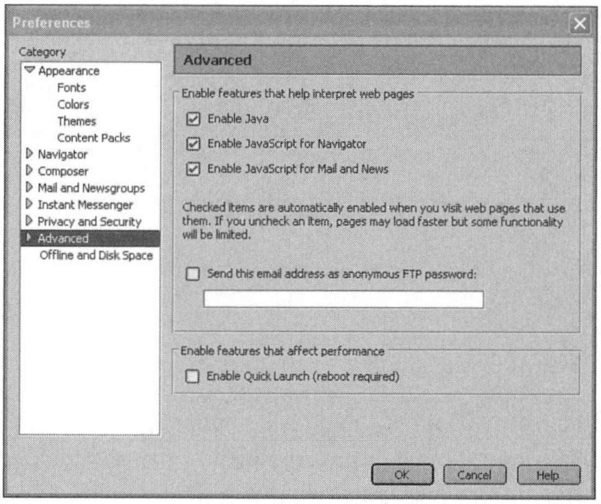

FIGURE 8.1

*Netscape allows
each user to specify
whether to allow
JavaScript code to
execute.*

To allow for the potential that the scripting support for the browser has been disabled, each of the browsers that support JavaScript provides an additional set of HTML tags— <noscript> and </noscript>. Each browser will execute the code within these tags if the JavaScript support is disabled for the browser. Listing 8.1 illustrates code you can use to notify the user that the JavaScript support has been disabled for his browser.

INPUT   **LISTING 8.1**   Catching Browsers with JavaScript Disabled (JSDisabled.htm)

```
<head>
<script language="JavaScript" type = "text/javascript">
<!--
window.alert("JavaScript is enabled on this browser.");
//..>
</script>
<title>Check to See if Scripting is Enabled</title>
<noscript>
<b>Your browser has JavaScript disabled.</b>
</noscript>
</head>
<body>
</body>
</html>
```

As you can see in Figure 8.2, if the browser does not have JavaScript support enabled, the code within the <noscript> </noscript> tags will execute. Remember, you cannot place any script within those tags because the browser will not know how to execute it. Therefore, you can only use HTML tags within the tags.

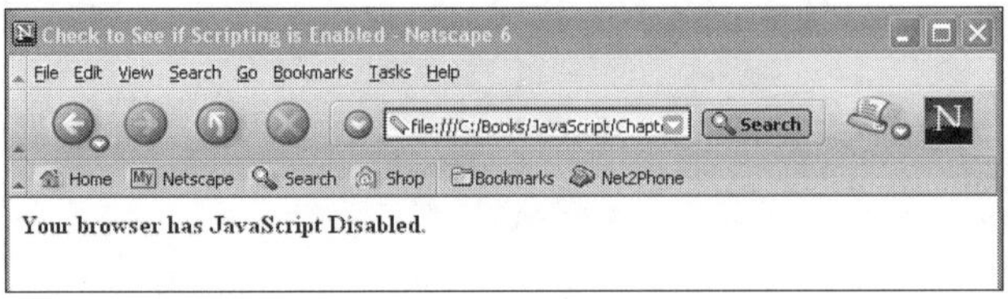

FIGURE 8.2

When your page displays on a browser with JavaScript disabled, the HTML code within the <noscript> *tags executes.*

> Check to See if Scripting is Enabled - Netscape 6
> File Edit View Search Go Bookmarks Tasks Help
> file:///C:/Books/JavaScript/Chapt   Search   N
> Home   My Netscape   Search   Shop   Bookmarks   Net2Phone
>
> Your browser has JavaScript Disabled.

Keep in mind that you will want to add the <noscript> tags after each location where you have <script> tags. This instructs the browser as to the code to run if the JavaScript support is disabled.

Determining Browser Information

Another way to create cross-browser code is to determine the browser type and version for the user that is visiting you. You can get browser-specific information from the Navigator object. The Navigator object was originally added by Netscape to Navigator 2.0, but other browsers soon followed suit. It has become a standard for all browsers that support JavaScript, making it another good method to use when determining whether your code will run on a user's browser.

Although the Navigator object does appear on browsers that support JavaScript, it is not a JavaScript object. Also, it is not part of the DOM (Document Object Model) that we will be discussing later in this chapter. In fact, the Navigator object sits alone with the sole purpose of gathering browser-specific information that can be accessed with its properties. You can access a property of the object by typing the following:

```
navigator.propertyname
```

There are several different properties available for the Navigator object, as shown in Table 8.2. Although this object was originally implemented by other browsers to be consistent with Netscape, there are properties supported only by Internet Explorer, and others that only Netscape supports. Therefore, to avoid potential issues, the table identifies the browsers that support each property.

TABLE 8.2   Navigator Properties

Property	Browser	Description
appCodeName	both	Returns the internal code name of the browser. Both Navigator and Internet Explorer return a value of Mozilla.
appMinorVersion	IE 4.0+	Specifies the minor version number of the browser. Minor version number changes occur due to patches or service-pack updates.
appName	both	Returns the official name of the browser.
appVersion	both	Returns the version number of the browser.
browserLanguage	IE 4.0+	Identifies the language supported by the browser.
cookieEnabled	both	Returns a Boolean value of True if the browser is set to allow cookies, or False if cookies are not allowed.
cpuClass	IE 4.0+	Specifies the type of CPU being used by the computer where the browser is running.
language	Netscape 4.0+	Identifies the language supported by the browser.
online	IE 4.0+	Returns a value of True if the browser is in online mode. Otherwise, a value of False is returned.
platform	both	Specifies the platform (operating system) on which the browser is running.
securityPolicy	Netscape 4.7+	Specifies the encryption policy specified on the computer.
systemLanguage	I.E. 4.0+	Identifies the default language supported by the user's operating system.
userAgent	both	Returns a string containing the following property values: appCodeName, appName, appVersion, language, and platform.
userLanguage	I.E. 4.0+	Names the language the user has specified on their system.
vendor	Netscape 6.0+	Returns the name of the company that makes the browser.

As you can see there are several different properties supported by the Navigator object, depending on which browser you are using. You will probably find additional properties of the Navigator object available only on specific browsers. Typically when using the Navigator object to determine browser-specific information you are going to want to select properties supported by all browsers, such as appName and appVersion.

Probably the easiest method for determining which browser a user has is to use the appName property as illustrated in Listing 8.2.

INPUT   **LISTING 8.2**   Checking Browser Name (NameBrowser.htm)

```
<html>
<head>
<script language="JavaScript" type = "text/javascript">
<!--
if (navigator.appName == "Microsoft Internet Explorer")
{
 alert("Your browser is Microsoft Internet Explorer.");
}
else if (navigator.appName == "Netscape")
{
 alert("Your browser is Netscape Navigator.");
}
else
{
 alert("You are not using Netscape Navigator or Internet Explorer.");
}
//..>
</script>
<title>Find Browser Name</title>
</head>
<body>
</body>
</html>
```

The code in Listing 8.2 displays an alert window with a message indicating the browser name, as shown in Figure 8.3. You will notice that I added an else statement to accommodate any other browsers that were not Netscape Navigator or Internet Explorer.

OUTPUT

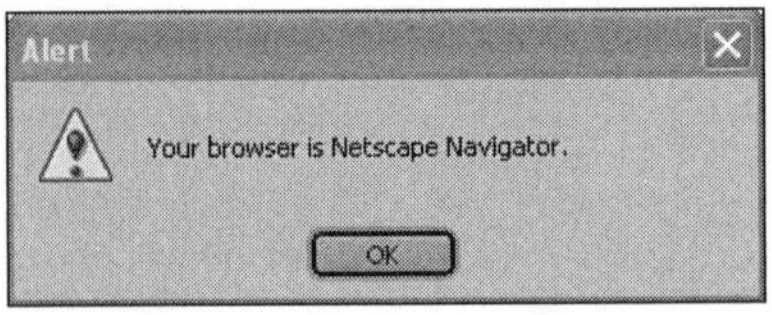

FIGURE 8.3

The appName *property returns the name of the browser that is viewing your Web page.*

ANALYSIS The final `else` statement may initially appear to handle all issues, but it doesn't. Some browsers, specifically Opera, have the ability to customize your browser identification. By changing this setting in the preferences, an Opera browser can appear to be Netscape Navigator or Internet Explorer. Although this setting was added to the browser to ensure access to sites that are coded for a specific browser type, it defeats your purpose for checking.

Fortunately there is another property that you can use to get this same information, the `userAgent` property. Since this property returns more than the browser name, you have to look in the string to determine what value was returned for the `appName` value property.

When you use the `userAgent` property it returns a string that contains information about the user's browser. The browser and operating system that are being used to access your site determines which property values are actually returned by the `userAgent` property. Nearly always the following properties are returned in the string: `appCodeName`, `appVersion`, `appName`, and `platform`. For example, Figure 8.4 illustrates the string returned by Internet Explorer 6.0 running on Windows XP.

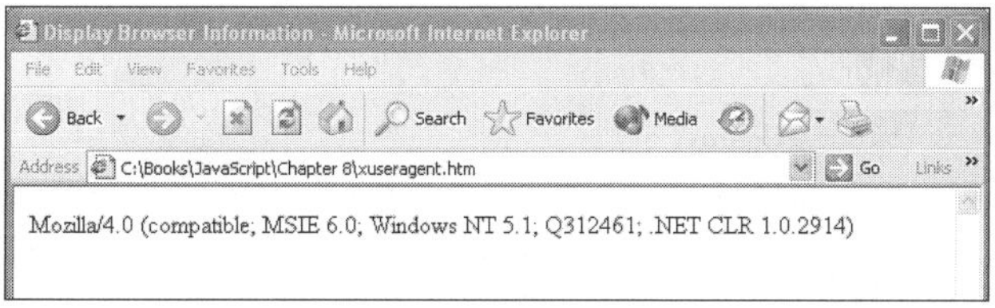

FIGURE 8.4

The actual string returned by the userAgent *property varies slightly based upon the user's browser and operating system.*

As you can see in Figure 8.4, the string returned by the `userAgent` property is fairly lengthy. To determine if a specific browser name is in the string, you will need to search the string. One good method to use is the `indexOf()` string method, which will determine if one string contains another string.

Note

The `indexOf()` method allows you to compare the two strings, and it returns an integer value indicating the location where the second string is located within the first string. If the string is not found, the method returns a value of -1.

By combining the indexOf() method with if statements, you can determine which browser is visiting your site, as shown in Listing 8.3.

INPUT   LISTING 8.3   Using the userAgent Property (UserAgent.htm)

```html
<html>
<head>
<script language="JavaScript" type = "text/javascript">
<!--
var bname = "browser";
if (navigator.userAgent.indexOf("MSIE") != -1)
{
 bname = "Internet Explorer";
}
else if (navigator.userAgent.indexOf("Opera") != -1)
{
 bname = "Opera";
}
else if ((navigator.appName.indexOf("Netscape") != -1) ||
parseFloat(navigator.appVersion >= 3.0))
{
 bname = "Netscape Navigator";
}
else
{
 bname = "Unknown Browser";
}
document.write("Your browser is: " + bname);
//..>
</script>
<title>Display Browser Information</title>
</head>
<body>
</body>
</html>
```

ANALYSIS   You will notice that we still had to use a different property combination to check for Netscape. When working with the userAgent property, the application name (Netscape) is not part of the userAgent string for Netscape Navigator versions prior to 6.0. Therefore, you cannot just use the userAgent property to check for "Netscape" if you want to detect Netscape versions prior to 6.0. Figure 8.5 shows how the code detects the browser name.

OUTPUT

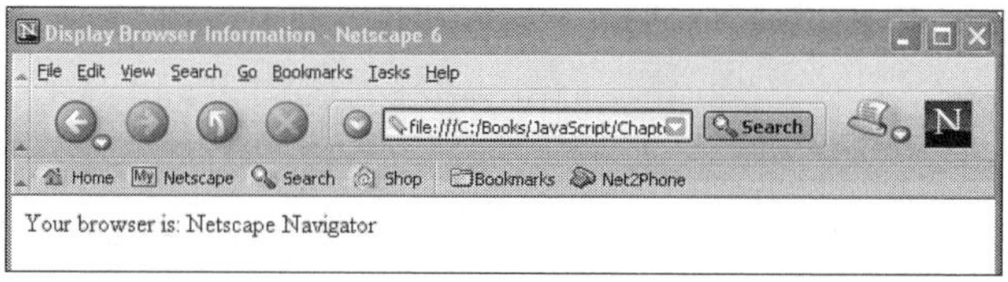

FIGURE 8.5

The userAgent *property provides another method for determining the actual browser type.*

Of course, instead of concentrating on the browser name, you may be more interested in looking at the browser version to determine if your JavaScript code will execute properly. You can check the browser application version using the appVersion property. If you remember from Table 8.1, JavaScript support was added to Netscape Navigator version 3.0 and to Internet Explorer 4.01. Therefore, by making sure the browser version is greater than 3.0 for Netscape and 4.01 for Internet Explorer, you are assured that JavaScript is supported by those browsers. We did this type of check when looking for Netscape in the preceding Listing 8.3 above.

Determining Browser Support for Specific Objects

Another method for creating cross-browser scripting is to use specific object support to determine whether or not your code will execute on the specific browser. So what exactly does that mean? Even though Netscape Navigator and Internet Explorer both have objects for the various elements of the browser window, not all of the objects are supported by both browsers. Also, remember that even objects (such as the Document object), which both browsers support, do not always have the same properties on both browsers. Therefore, by checking for specific object property values you are able to ensure that your browser supports your JavaScript code.

For example, both Netscape and Internet Explorer have an Event object that tracks information about each event. Although they both support the same object, they do not support the same properties. In fact, Netscape Navigator supported different properties for the object with versions 4 and 5 than with version 6. Therefore, in order to use this object without errors on the other browsers, you need to create code to check for browser support. One good way to do this is to use the Document object. This is a common method used to distinguish between Internet Explorer, Navigator 6, and Navigator 4. To do so you can use if statements to determine which document object property is supported, as shown in the following code:

```
if (document.all)
//Checks for IE 4.0 or later
{
```

```
    document.form1.text2.value = String.fromCharCode(event.keyCode);
}
else if (document.getElementById)
//checks for Netscape 6 or later
{
    document.form1.text2.value = String.fromCharCode(key_event.which);
}
else if (document.layers)
//Checks for Netscape 4
{
    document.form1.text2.value = String.fromCharCode(key_event.which);
}
}
```

You will notice that although each one of the `assign` statements are assigning the key pressed to the object, a different property is being used for each.

> **Note**
>
> You can find out more about the `Event` object in Chapter 10, "Events and Event Handling."

The W3C DOM

In Chapter 4 we looked at how JavaScript is object-based allowing you to access various elements of the browser by changing the properties of a particular object. The objects or elements of the browser are all part of the Document Object Model (DOM). Initially both Microsoft Internet Explorer and Netscape Navigator developed their own independent DOMs, making object scripting reliant on one specific browser. To help standardize the object models to allow developers to create object-oriented scripting for multiple browsers, the World Wide Web Consortium (W3C) developed a `Document` object specification commonly referred to as the W3C DOM.

The DOM describes the relationship of all objects on the HTML page. The relationship resembles a tree-like structure. Each object within the DOM is referred to as a node. The first element on the tree is the `Document` object, and the tree structure branches out from there. For example, the <HTML> tag is a node of the document, and the <Title> and <Body> tags are child nodes of the <HTML> tag. Of course you are aware that the `Document` object does not appear in the actual HTML code listing. The `Document` object is always loaded with the page as the first element for the page.

Again every element of the page is a *node*, including text which is referred to as a `Text` node. A node that contains other nodes, including text, is referred to as a *parent node*. A node contained within another node is a *child node*. Therefore each line of code you specify creates nodes. For example, the following HTML code creates two different nodes:

```
<p>Paragraph Text</p>
```

The code creates a p element and a text node containing "Paragraph Text." Since the text node is inside of our element p node, it is considered to be a child node. To better understand the node concept of the W3C DOM let's look at the following code:

```
<html>
<head>
<title>Header Text</title>
</head>
<body>
<p><i>Body Text</i></p>
<div>
<a href ="link.htm">link text</a>
<img src = "test.gif">
</div>
</body>
</html>
```

If you look at this code closely, you will see that the HTML tags enclose the entire document code. The html node is a child of the Document node. In fact, the HTML node is the only child of the Document node. The Head and Body nodes are child nodes of the html node, as illustrated in Figure 8.6.

FIGURE 8.6

The W3C DOM treats each element of the HTML document as a separate node, creating a tree-like structure.

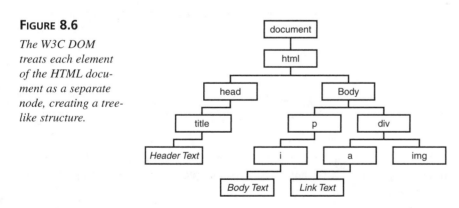

Another thing to notice with the representation in Figure 8.6 is that the DOM also tracks sibling relationships. For example, the img and a nodes are siblings because they belong to the same parent node (div).

Okay, I am sure that all sounds good, but you are probably wondering what nodes really have to do with creating Web pages. After all, you have been able to do a lot of coding up to now without dealing with different node issues. But like I mentioned at the beginning of this section, the DOM is designed to enable you to have a more dynamic page by interacting with elements of the browser page. The DOM nodes provide a method for accessing and modifying various objects on the page.

Accessing Nodes

Once you understand the concept of a node as specified by the W3C DOM, we can look at how to access specific nodes or elements of the page.

As we mentioned earlier, each node has a child node. For example, html is a child node of the Document node. The child nodes for a node are accessed in an array-like fashion using the childNodes collection. For example, to access the html node from the Document node you would type the following:

```
document.childNodes[0]
```

Notice that we use 0 to access the html node. This is because the values within a collection start at 0. As a result, you can expand the reference to access the first child of the html node by typing:

```
document.childNodes[0].childNodes[0]
```

This line would access the Head node of the document. There are two additional shortcut properties you can use to access the first and last child nodes. For example, to access the first child node for the Document object you can type:

```
document.firstChild
```

Again, this code accesses the html node because that is the only child of the Document object. You can also use the lastChild property to get the last child node for a parent node.

In much the same fashion that we stepped down through the tree, you can also back up and determine the parent node for any node. For example, assume we have assigned the Title node value to the titlenode variable as follows:

```
titlenode = document.childNodes[0].childnodes[0]
```

Later we can return the parent to the Title node by typing the following:

```
titlenode.parentNode
```

It doesn't take long to realize that references to nodes within a document can get quite long as you step through the different levels. To solve this issue, the DOM provides methods for specification based on the element identification or the HTML tag name.

Accessing an Element by ID

Rather than traversing the nodes to find the element that you want to access, you also can access an element using the Id attribute assigned to the HTML element. To do this you use the getElementById method. For example in Listing 8.4, we illustrate how this method can be used to return the value of a text input field on a form.

LISTING 8.4 Using the getElementById() method
INPUT (GetElementByIDMethod.htm)

```html
<html>
<head>
<title>New Page 1</title>
<script language="JavaScript" type = "text/javascript">
<!--
function Test()
{
alert(document.getElementById("testinput").value);
}
//..>
</script>
</head>
<body>
<form name="textfield">
   <input type="text" name="T1" size="20" id="testinput">
    <input type="button" value="Click Here" name="B1" onclick="Test()"></p>
</form>
</body>
</html>
```

ANALYSIS Notice that we are referencing the text input field with the code:

```
document.getElementById("testinput").value
```

This method makes accessing the value of the form field much easier than traversing the tree of document nodes as illustrated earlier.

> **Note**
>
> Because the `getElementById()` is a method that is specific to the W3C DOM it is frequently used to verify a browser's W3C compliance, as illustrated with the following code:
>
> ```
> if (document.getElementById)
> {
>  document.write("Browser is DOM compliant");
> }
> ```
>
> You can use this type of compliance check to identify Internet Explorer 5 and later or Netscape 6 and later which are both W3C DOM compliant.

Accessing Elements by Tag Name

Another method you can use to quickly access individual elements of a page is to access the elements with the same tag name. For example, you could access all p tags, or all a tags. This can be accomplished using the `getElementByTagName` method. When you use this method it returns a collection of all elements with the specified tag name. For example, if you have the following code:

```
<p>Paragraph 1</p>
<p>Paragraph 2</p>
<p>Paragraph 3</p>
```

You can access the first p tag by typing `document.getElementsByTagName("p")[0]`. Keep in mind, this method is only referencing the actual tag name and not a value specified with the Name attribute for an HTML element.

> **Note**
>
> Of course accessing the nodes of your HTML document is only a small portion of what can be accomplished with the W3C DOM. Working with DHTML you can perform more powerful options such as changing the attributes of a tag, adding an attribute to a tag, or even removing tags. You can even change styles of text. We look at these options in more depth in Chapter 11 where we discuss DHTML.

Summary

In this chapter we have looked at a lot of different aspects of JavaScript and the browsers where your code runs. We explored the fact that different browsers support different versions of JavaScript, making it a challenge to determine what JavaScript features to use when developing your Web page.

8

We briefly looked at the history of JavaScript and how it has evolved. We discussed that the ECMAScript Standard maintains the standards for the JavaScript supported by all browsers. Although this is the standard, each browser provides additional JavaScript features.

Next we looked at how to determine if a browser supported JavaScript, and if the JavaScript code was active. We looked at how the browser information can be determined using the `Navigator` object. Using the properties associated with the `Navigator` object you can determine which browser a user has when he connects to your site and execute specific code based upon that browser's settings. We also looked at how you can also use properties of the `Document` object to determine which code to run.

Finally, we began looking at the W3C DOM and how it provides a standard Document Object Model for each browser. Using the DOM you can access each element of your Web page as a node. This foundation on the DOM sets the stage for the DOM work we will do in Chapter 11 when we work with DHTML.

Workshop

In the workshop today we will use the questions to review what you have learned in this chapter about cross-browser compatibility issues and working with the W3C DOM.

Q&A

Q. How do I handle code for each specific browser?

A. As we have discussed, different browsers and browser versions support different JavaScript features. This means that creating code to run for each scenario can become quite complex if it is all maintained on one page. A common method is to call a separate page for each browser. For example, load one page for Netscape and another for Internet Explorer.

Q. What do I do about browsers other than Netscape Navigator and Internet Explorer?

A. There have been an abundance of different browsers that have surfaced over the years, and more will continue to come out. In this chapter we concentrated on the two most commonly used browsers: Netscape Navigator and Microsoft Internet Explorer. You should make a point to support the most widely used browsers in your script. Another browser that has gained popularity that you may want to support is Opera. This browser also supports JavaScript. You can find more information about this browser at `www.opera.com`.

Q. **Can I design my Web page to capture more specific information about the user, such as name or e-mail address?**

A. No, the `Navigator` object that we discussed in this chapter is only able to provide information about the user's browser and operating system. The only way to get any more specific information about a user is to use a signed script. We'll look at the use of signed scripts in Chapter 17, "Privacy and Security."

Quiz

1. What is the ECMAScript Standard?

2. How do you ensure your script is ignored on browsers that don't support JavaScript?

3. What tags do you use for browsers with JavaScript disabled?

4. What object can you use to gather information about the user's browser?

Quiz Answers

1. The ECMAScript Standard specifies the JavaScript standards that should be supported by all browsers. Because the ECMAScript Standard is typically behind the times based upon the features of the new browser versions, browsers typically provide additional features that are not part of the ECMAScript Standard. Because these new features are not part of the standard, you need to exercise caution when using them to ensure that they will run properly on all browsers.

2. When placing JavaScript on your Web page you need to place the HTML comment tags <!-- and //..> within the <script> tags to mark the block of code to be treated as comments by non- JavaScript supported browsers. When a browser that does not support JavaScript encounters the <script> tags, it recognizes they are HTML tags it does not support, so they are ignored. The actual code must be placed within the comment tags so that the browser does not write the code to the page as text.

3. Any browser that supports JavaScript includes the <noscript> tags to be used to specify the code that should execute if the JavaScript option is disabled. Remember, you want the code placed within these <noscript> tags to be HTML only. Since the JavaScript has been disabled the only type of code that will execute is HTML.

4. The `Navigator` object is available with all current browsers. This object maintains information about the current browser. You can use the properties associated with this object to return specific information about the object. For example, the `appName` property returns the name of the current browser.

Exercises

1. Use the `Navigator.appVersion` property to determine if the browser supports JavaScript. For a list of browser versions that support JavaScript, refer to Table 8.1. Also, include the code to run, if the JavaScript support is not active.

2. Create a W3C-DOM page that only executes on Web pages that are DOM-compliant. Use the nodes to access the value which is typed in the second form field and displayed in an Alert window.

8

DAY 9

Date and Time Manipulation

As you are aware, dates and times are a key part of each of our lives. In fact, our lives revolve around specific times that indicate the occurance of events. This holds true when dealing with Internet information as well. Typically everything has a date and time correlation—whether it is the date when a particular item is on sale, hours of operation for a business, or even just displaying current date and time information on your Web page.

This chapter will look at working with dates and time within JavaScript; and, more specifically, how to work with the Date object. This JavaScript object is responsible for maintaining not only the date information but also the corresponding time information.

This chapter will teach you

- What the Date object is
- How to format dates
- How to format times
- How to convert date and time formats

JavaScript and Dates

On the surface the concept of working with dates and times seems very straightforward. After all, we all learned in grade school how to interpret 4:30 p.m. But the difficulty with dates in JavaScript comes from understanding how JavaScript calculates dates.

JavaScript stores all dates as numeric values. The date value is actually the number of milliseconds that have passed since 12:00 a.m., January 1, 1970. In other words, all dates and times since that date are stored as a numeric value, where 10 represents 10 milliseconds after midnight on January 1, 1970. Any dates and times prior to that date are represented as negative values, counting backwards from that date and time.

Because JavaScript stores all dates and times as numeric values, calculations to compare dates are quite simple because you are basically just comparing two numeric values. For example, if you want to determine the amount of time that has elapsed between two dates, you are actually performing a simple mathematical calculation by subtracting one date from the other date.

When JavaScript executes it always pulls the date and time information from the user's computer. Therefore, the date and time information is only as accurate as the settings on an individual's computer.

Although JavaScript displays times based on the user's current computer settings, it actually stores and manipulates all dates based on Greenwich Mean Time (GMT). If you are not familiar with GMT, it is the time zone from which all other times zones are calculated. This time zone, which is situated over Greenwich, England, gets its name from its location. So, for example, Central time is six hours behind GMT.

Actually JavaScript's treatment of the dates is handled basically in the same fashion as your computer. Your personal computer's clock settings are based on GMT. Typically when you install an operating system, such as MS Windows, on your computer, you are requested to specify the time zone where you live. For example, if you are in the Central time zone your machine knows that it has to use the offset from GMT to calculate your local time frame, in this case, six hours behind GMT. If you happen to live in an area that recognizes daylight savings time, your machine also maintains a separate offset that it uses during that time of the year.

Therefore, when you request the date and time from your computer, JavaScript is capturing the time from the personal computer's system clock. The date values are converted from the user's current date and time. Again, this all assumes that the system clock is correct.

Each browser stores all date and time information in a single `Date` object that you can access from your JavaScript code. In order to access any date or time, you have to access a specific `Date` object, as covered in the next section.

The `Date` Object

In order to work with dates and times in JavaScript, you must use the `Date` object. Although the `Date` object is one of the JavaScript Core objects, there is an instance of the object created for each browser window (that recognizes JavaScript), or frame. The `Date` object always represents one specific instance of time, such as April 2, 2001, 4:15 p.m. You can specify a range of time with the `Date` object.

Typically when working in JavaScript, you are going to use the `Date` object to grab the current date and time from the user's system settings. Therefore, the date information that is captured is only as accurate as the system clock. Therefore, avoid relying on specific date and time information within your program. For example, if you plan to launch a special greeting on a certain date, if the system clock on the user's computer is not properly set your greeting may never display.

To capture the date and time information, you typically assign the `Date` object value to a variable. Once you do this, you can make desired modifications to the date information, such as changing the formatting.

```
var currentdate = new Date();
```

Each time JavaScript encounters the `new Date()` statement, it assigns the current date and time information to the corresponding variable. Again, be aware that the date information is captured at the point in your code where JavaScript encounters the statement. If, for example, the date was captured at the beginning of your code, but your code took two minutes to execute, the variable would still contain the time information from when the date and time was captured with the `Date` object.

Don't get confused with the name of the object. Even though the object is called `Date`, as we have previously discussed, the object is used to capture both the date and time information. Therefore, even if you only want to know the current date, the object still will contain the time information, to the exact millisecond from when the `Date` object was created. The way the date information displays on your page is ultimately governed by the default date formatting of the browser. To display the actual system date information, you would create a script similar to the code in Listing 9.1.

LISTING 9.1   Displaying the Current Date (specifydate.htm)

```
<script language="JavaScript" type = "text/javascript">
<!--
current_date = new Date();
document.write(current_date);
//..>
</script>
```

ANALYSIS   This code captures the current system date and formats it differently based on the selected browser, as illustrated in Figure 9.1. For example, Netscape 6 displays the Date object as:

```
Mon Nov 05 22:56:58 GMT-0600 (Central Standard Time) 2001
```

This formatting will vary if you view the code on a Netscape browser running on a Macintosh computer. If you display the same JavaScript code using Microsoft Internet Explorer 6.0, you would get the following:

```
Mon Nov 5 22:59:49 CST 2001
```

OUTPUT

FIGURE 9.1

The Date *object is formatted differently depending upon the browser and the operating system.*

In this code, you will notice that we are using the keyword new before the Date object. When you use the new keyword in your code, you are instructing JavaScript to create a new Date object that you can then work with. When a Date object is created, it will always evaluate to an object data type and not a string or numeric value.

Creating a Specific Date Object

There also will be instances when you may want to ensure that you are working with a specific date. Instead of capturing the date from the user's computer system, you can create a Date object to contain a specific date value. For example, if you want to perform calculations based on the number of days between today and Christmas, you could create a Date object that contains the date for Christmas as follows:

```
Var Christmas = new Date("December, 25 2002");
```

You can specify a date or time value for the Date object using any combination of the Date object arguments as outlined in Table 9.1. For example, when we specified the date for Christmas 2002, we actually passed the date value in the format of the month, day, year. In other words we used the arguments Month, dd, yyyy.

TABLE 9.1 Date Object Arguments

Argument	Description
dd	The day of the month specified with an integer value between 1 and 31
hh	The hour of the day specified with an integer value between 0 (representing midnight) and 23 (11:00 PM)
mm	The minute of the hour specified with an integer value between 0 and 59
Month	The full name of the month from "January" to "December"
mth	The month of the year specified as an integer value between 0 and 11 where 0 represents January and 11 represents December
ms	The millisecond portion of the time specified as an integer value between 0 and 999
ss	The second portion of the time specified as an integer value between 0 and 59
yyyy	A four-digit integer representing the year
yy	A two-digit integer between 00 and 99 representing the year

You can use any combination of these arguments to specify a date value for the Date object. For example, you could use the following argument combination to specify the date and time:

```
var date_time = new Date(yyyy, mth, dd, hh, mm, ss);
```

You can create the actual date using this date and time format as illustrated:

```
Var date_time = new Date(2001, 11, 05, 13, 15, 45);
```

This date would be evaluated and then would display in an Internet Explorer browser window as:

```
Mon Nov 5 13:15:45 CST 2001
```

As you can see, no matter what format you use to pass the date to the Date object, the same information is always created for the object. If you simply write the contents of the Date object to the page, as demonstrated with Listing 9.1, the date information always displays the same based upon the settings of the particular browser.

Obviously, you are not always going to be content to have that type of date output. Fortunately, the Date object includes several different methods that you can use to customize date and time output. For information about customizing the output from the Date object refer to the next two sections.

Date Formatting

As discussed earlier in this chapter, when you use the document.write statement to write the contents of the Date object to the browser window you get the date information formatted based on the default settings for each browser and operating system. For example, not only does Netscape Navigator display the date differently than Microsoft Internet Explorer, but the date information is also displayed differently on a Macintosh computer than a Microsoft Windows machine. That being the case, you are typically going to want to have more control over the actual display of the date information on the browser window. This can be accomplished by using the various methods available with the Date object for formatting the date portion.

JavaScript provides methods for accessing each element of a date within a Date object and returning that particular value. For example, to return the month portion of a date you would use the getMonth() method. Listing 9.2 illustrates how to use the getMonth() method to return the numeric value that represents the current month.

INPUT **LISTING 9.2** Returning the Current Month (formatdate.htm)

```
<html>
<head>
<title>Current Month</title>
</head>
<body>
<script language="JavaScript" type="text/javascript">
<!--

var current_date = new Date();

month_value = current_date.getMonth();

document.write("Current Month is " + month_value);

//-->
</script>
</body>
</html>
```

ANALYSIS The code in Listing 9.2 captures the current system date and then uses the getMonth() method to determine the current month portion of the date. The method returns a numeric value between 1 and 12 that represents the month of the year, as illustrated in Figure 9.2.

FIGURE 9.2

The getMonth() *method of the* Date *object returns a numeric value representing the month of the year.*

9

Caution Be mindful of the fact that JavaScript counts the months in the year starting with 0. Therefore, January is actually 0 and December is 11. Make sure you remember this when you are converting dates.

The Date object includes a specific method for each element of the date, as shown in Table 9.2.

TABLE 9.2 Methods for Getting Date Values

Method	Description
getFullYear()	Gets the year portion of the date as a four-digit number, such as 1998 or 2001
getYear()	Gets the year portion of the date as either a two or four-digit year depending on the browser used. Internet Explorer always returns a four-digit year. Netscape 4 and later subtracts 1900 from the date and returns the result. Earlier versions of Netscape truncate and return a two-digit year.
getMonth()	Gets the month of the year in the range of 0 to 11, where January is represented by 0 and December is 11
getDate()	Gets the numeric equivalent of the day of the month in the range of 1 to 31
getDay()	Gets the numeric equivalent of the day of the week in the range of 0 to 6 Sunday is 0 and Saturday is 6

Be very careful about using the getYear() function. In fact, it is probably going to end up causing you more grief than anything. As mentioned in the table, when Netscape Navigator versions 4 or later see the getYear() method, the browser returns a year value by subtracting 1900 from the current year value. As you can imagine, this concept worked pretty well before the new millennium. For example, if the year is 1997 and you subtract 1900 you get a two-digit year of 97. But this type of date conversion no longer works. When you subtract 1900 from 2001 you get a value of 101. This being said, I would recommend just using the getFullYear() to return the year portion of any date.

Another thing to keep in mind is the numeric range used to represent the months of the year and days of the week. Most of us are used to the concept of 12 months in a year and seven days in a week. That being said, the first month of the year is January and the last month is December. JavaScript uses a different numbering pattern in that both of these ranges start with the number zero, making the first value actually 0 instead of 1. If you want to return the actual name of the month or day you need to create code to convert the numeric value, as discussed in the following section.

Converting the Numeric Day and Month Values

More than likely when capturing the day of the week or even the month of the year you are going to want to display the text equivalent of the numeric value returned. As you noticed in Figure 9.1, each browser converts the Date object to display the text equivalent of the day of the week and the month of the year by default. Unfortunately if you decide to create your own date layout there are not any methods for the Date object to display the text equivalent of either the day of the week or the month value. Therefore, in order to display these values you must create your own JavaScript code to convert the numeric value returned by the getMonth() method and the getDay() method.

Of course, as with anything you code, there are multiple ways that you can code the conversion from a numeric value to a text value. The most common methods would be to use an array of values as we discussed in Chapter 5, "An Introduction to Arrays." Listing 9.3 illustrates how to use an array to convert the numeric value returned by the getDay() method to an actual day of the week.

INPUT   **LISTING 9.3**   Converting the Day of the Week (convertday.htm)

```
<html>
<head>
<title>Convert Day of the Week</title>
</head>
<body>
<script language="JavaScript" type="text/javascript">
<!--

var weekdays = new Array(7);
weekdays[0] = "Sunday";
weekdays[1] = "Monday";
weekdays[2] = "Tuesday";
weekdays[3] = "Wednesday";
weekdays[4] = "Thursday";
weekdays[5] = "Friday";
```

LISTING 9.3   continued

```
weekdays[6] = "Saturday";

var current_date = new Date();

weekday_value = current_date.getDay();

document.write("Today is " + weekdays[weekday_value]);

//-->
</script>
</body>
</html>
```

9

ANALYSIS   This code takes the numeric value that is returned by the getDate() method and uses it as the index value for the weekdays array. Since the weekdays array contains 7 values from 0 to 6 the index values for the array elements match the numeric values returned by the getDate() method. For example, if today is Tuesday, the getDate() method returns a value of 2 and assigns that value to the weekday_value variable. The weekday_value variable is used as an index value to access the array. Since the element of the array with an index value of 2 is Tuesday, the JavaScript code displays that value on the page, as illustrated in Figure 9.3.

OUTPUT

FIGURE 9.3

You can create your own JavaScript code to convert the numeric value returned by getDate() *to a day name.*

Of course you can create the same type of code to convert the numeric value returned by the getMonth() method into the name of the month. Again, keep in mind the fact that the getMonth() method returns a numeric value between 0 and 11 representing the month. Therefore, you need to make sure you design your code so that 0 represents January and 11 represents December, so that you will get the correct conversion of the numeric value returned by the method.

Combining Date Values

Up until now we have seen how easy it is to use methods for getting the elements of the Date object and to return a portion of the date, such as the day of the week, or even the current year. Obviously the main reason for manipulating the contents of the Date object would be to format the date value to match your own requirements for the date output. For example, you may want the ability to display the date in the format "month day, year," or November 6, 2001. In order to display the date in this fashion you cannot just dump the contents of the Date object, as shown with Figure 9.1. However, making the date appear as you want is still quite simple. It simply requires using the concatenation operator (+) to join together the date elements you want to create your string.

As you are aware, when you concatenate values together you are essentially creating one string of values from the original string. If you want to display the current date in the format mentioned above with the month followed by the day and year values, you need to concatenate those values together as illustrated in Listing 9.4.

INPUT   **LISTING 9.4**   Combining Date Method Values (combinedate.htm)

```
<html>
<head>
<title>Combine Date Values</title>
</head>
<body>
<script language="JavaScript" type="text/javascript">
<!--

var months = new Array(12);
months[0] = "January";
months[1] = "February";
months[2] = "March";
months[3] = "April";
months[4] = "May";
months[5] = "June";
months[6] = "July";
months[7] = "August";
months[8] = "September";
months[9] = "October";
months[10] = "November";
months[11] = "December";

var current_date = new Date();
month_value = current_date.getMonth();
day_value = current_date.getDate();
year_value = current_date.getFullYear();
```

LISTING 9.4 continued

```
document.write("The current date is " + months[month_value] + " " +
day_value + ", " + year_value);

//-->
</script>
</body>
</html>
```

9

ANALYSIS Notice with this code we use the array method that we discussed in the previous section to determine the month name that should be displayed as the current month name. When concatenating values together, remember you need to manually insert any spacing that you want in your string. Figure 9.4 shows the result of the code in Listing 9.4.

OUTPUT

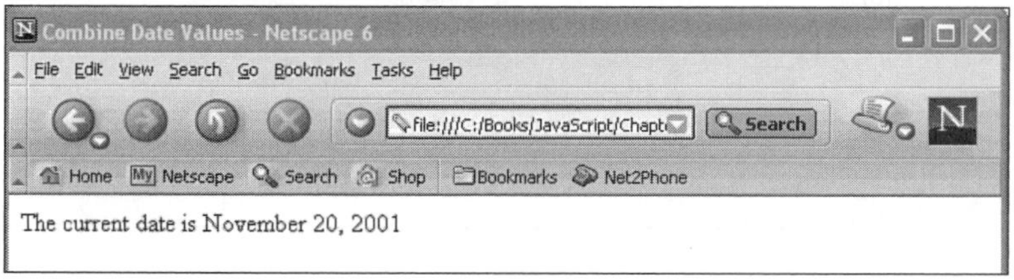

FIGURE 9.4

Create the desired formatting for your date by combining the values returned by the date methods.

The current date is November 20, 2001

As you can probably imagine, there are an infinite number of ways you can express a date, especially once you have retrieved the elements of the date that you need to display. In addition to working with the basic date portions of the Date object, don't forget, the object also houses the time information for when the date is captured. You can combine any of the time information with your date statement for even more ways to customize your date statement. Let's look at time values of the Date object in the next section.

Time Formatting

It seems quite odd to be looking in the Date object for time information, but that is where you will find it when working in JavaScript. As you remember from our discussion earlier in this chapter, JavaScript stores the information in the Date object as a millisecond value. In other words, the value of the Date object is a long number indicating the total number of milliseconds that passed between January 1, 1970 and the time when the Date object was created. So you see, although the object is called Date, it actually indicates a time value by specifying the amount of time since that date.

Just like the date elements, you can also retrieve the individual elements of time from the Date object by using the associated methods. For example, you can use the getHours() to return the number of hours in the time portion of the Date object, as shown in Listing 9.5.

INPUT   **LISTING 9.5**   Returning the Current Hour (ReturnHour.htm)

```
<html>
<head>
<title>Current Hour</title>
</head>
<body>
<script language="JavaScript" type="text/javascript">
<!--

var current_date = new Date();
hour_value = current_date.getHours();
document.write("The current hour is " + hour_value);

//-->
</script>
</body>
</html>
```

ANALYSIS   The code in Listing 9.5 returns an integer value that represents the hour portion of the time. You will probably quickly notice that there are no AM or PM times. The value returned by the getHours() method is in a 24-hour clock format or what is commonly referred to as military time, as shown in Figure 9.5.

OUTPUT

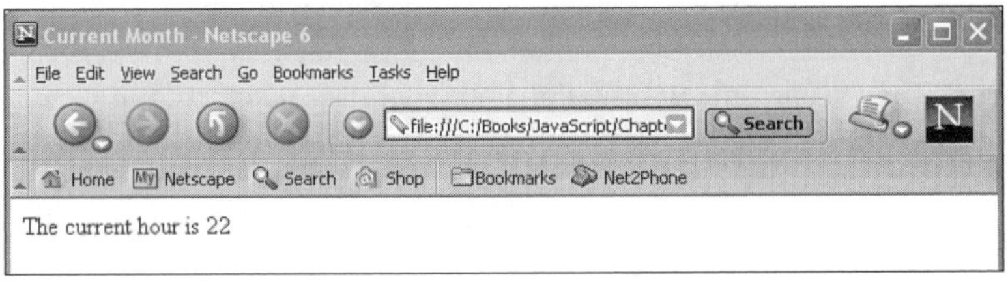

FIGURE 9.5

Use of the
getHours() *method*
returns an integer
value based on a
24-hour clock.

The current hour is 22

Obviously there are other methods that you can use to return the other portions of the time. Table 9.3 lists the different methods that you can use with the Date object to return the time portions.

TABLE 9.3 Methods for Getting Time Values

Method	Description
getHours()	Gets the number of hours in the time. The method returns a value between 0 and 23, where 0 represents midnight and 23 represents 11:00 PM.
getMinutes()	Gets the number of minutes in the hour. The value returned is in the range of 0 to 59.
getSeconds()	Gets the number of seconds in the minute. The value returned is in the range of 0 to 59.
getMilliseconds()	Gets the number of milliseconds in the second. The value returned is in the range of 0 to 999.
getTime()	Returns a numeric value representing the total number of milliseconds since January 1, 1970 GMT.

The getTime() method basically just returns the numeric value that JavaScript stores for the Date object. For example, if you create a Date object for the date 12/24/2001 the getTime() method returns a millisecond value of 1009173600000. This value is the same as the value that JavaScript uses to store the date.

The time values returned from the Date methods can be combined with the same method used to create a custom date. For example, you can display an hour and minute combination by combining the values returned by the getHours() method with the getMinutes() method value.

```
var current_date = new Date();
hour_value = current_date.getHours();
minute_value = current_date.getMinutes();

document.write("The time is " + hour_value + ":" + minute_value);
```

Make sure that when you combine the time values you insert the colon (:), or whatever symbol you want to use to differentiate between an hour, minute, or second value. Of course all of these times will be based upon a 24-hour clock, so if it is 8:30 PM, the time displays as 20:30. The only way to remedy this is to manually convert the time value before displaying it.

Converting to an AM/PM Time Frame

Depending upon where you live and how you were taught to tell time, you probably will not be content to get a 24-hour clock format for the time. Even if you like stating it as 1900 hours, visitors to your site most likely would prefer seeing the time displayed in the more traditional fashion of 7:00 PM. That being said, JavaScript obviously does not provide a default solution for doing this. If you want to display the AM and PM times, you need to manually code a method to convert the value returned by the getHours() method to the desired format.

If you are familiar with the 24-hour clock concept, you know that the hours start counting at midnight with 0. Noon is considered to be 12:00 which is followed by 13:00 (commonly referred to as 1:00 PM). With a 24-hour clock, each hour gets progressively higher until 23:00, or 11:00 PM. Of course, at midnight the counting starts over.

Listing 9.6 illustrates a simple method to taking the current time and converting it to display in the AM/PM format.

INPUT   **LISTING 9.6**   Returning the Current Hour (ConvertTime.htm)

```
<html>
<head>
<title>Convert Time</title>
</head>
<body>
<script language="JavaScript" type="text/javascript">
<!--

var current_date = new Date();
var hour_value = current_date.getHours();
var minute_value = current_date.getMinutes();
var second_value = current_date.getSeconds();
var AMorPM = "AM";

if (hour_value > 12)
{
  hour_value -= 12;
  AMorPM = "PM";
}

document.write("The current time is " + hour_value + ":" + minute_value +
":" + second_value + " " + AMorPM);

//-->
</script>
</body>
</html>
```

ANALYSIS   The code in Listing 9.6 takes the numeric value returned by the getHours() method and subtracts 12 from it, if the value is larger than 12 and sets the AMorPM variable to PM. For example, if the time is 17:30 the code converts it to 5:30 PM, as illustrated in Figure 9.6.

OUTPUT

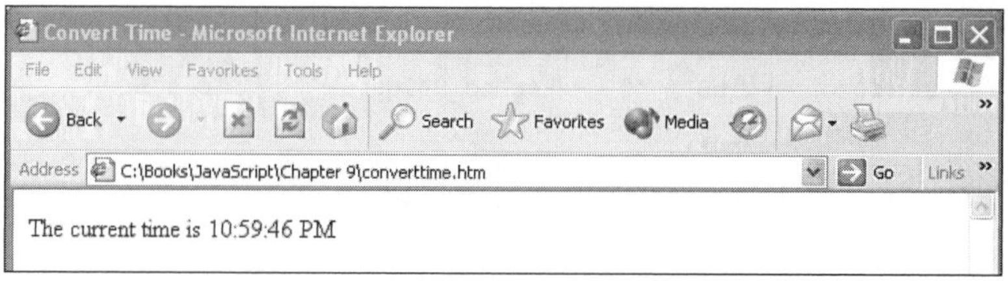

FIGURE 9.6

You can create custom JavaScript code to convert from 24-hour clock to AM/PM times.

9

This code works well for displaying the current time information on the browser page. But there is one small issue. Since the values that are returned are all integer values it only displays single digits for values less that 10. This can make a time like 10:05 look a little odd when it displays as 10:5. To fix this problem, you can add additional `if` statements that look at the value returned by the `getMinutes()` and `getSeconds()` methods, and adds a zero to the front if the value is less than 10, as shown in Listing 9.7.

INPUT **LISTING 9.7** Adjusting Time Values under 10 (`AdjustTime.htm`)

```
<html>
<head>
<title>Convert Time</title>
</head>
<body>
<script language="JavaScript" type="text/javascript">
<!--

var current_date = new Date();
var hour_value = current_date.getHours();
var minute_value = current_date.getMinutes();
var second_value = current_date.getSeconds();
var AMorPM = "AM";

if (hour_value > 12)
{
  hour_value -= 12;
  AMorPM = "PM";
}

if (hour_value == 0)
   {
   hour_value = 12;
   AMorPM = "AM";
}

if (second_value < 10)
{
```

Listing 9.7   continued

```
  second_value = "0" + second_value;
}

if (minute_value < 10)
{
  minute_value = "0" + minute_value;
}

document.write("The current time is " + hour_value + ":" +
minute_value + ":" + second_value + " " + AMorPM);

//-->
</script>
</body>
</html>
```

ANALYSIS If you look at the code in Listing 9.7, you will see that the `if` statements check the value of the `second_value` and `minute_value` variables. If either of the variables contains a value less than `10`, a value of zero is placed in front of that value. Therefore, your times will all display in the format HH:MM:SS.

Working with Time Zones

As we have already talked about, each computer system maintains the time zone information in relation to GMT. Of course, the time zone setting is only accurate if the user has properly set it. You may find the need to capture the user's time zone in order to perform different time calculations, such as determining the amount of time before a specific event transpires.

In order to do this you can use the `getTimezoneOffset()` method of the `Date` object to determine the number of minutes between the current time zone and GMT. Listing 9.8 illustrates how to use the `getTimezoneOffset()` method to determine the number of minutes from GMT for the user's machine.

INPUT   **Listing 9.8**   Determining Time Difference from GMT (gettimezone.htm)

```
<html>
<head>
<title>Determine Time Zone</title>
</head>
<body>
<script language="JavaScript" type="text/javascript">
<!--
```

LISTING 9.8 continued

```
var current_date = new Date();
var current_timezone = current_date.getTimezoneOffset();

document.write("Your time zone is " + current_timezone + " minutes from GMT");

//-->
</script>
</body>
</html>
```

ANALYSIS Again this code is quite simple, but it illustrates how easy it is to determine the user's time zone, as shown in Figure 9.7. If you want to have an event transpire at a specific time based on your time zone, you can use the `getTimezoneOffset()` method to determine the user's time zone offset, and then use the offset for your time zone to make the comparisons.

OUTPUT

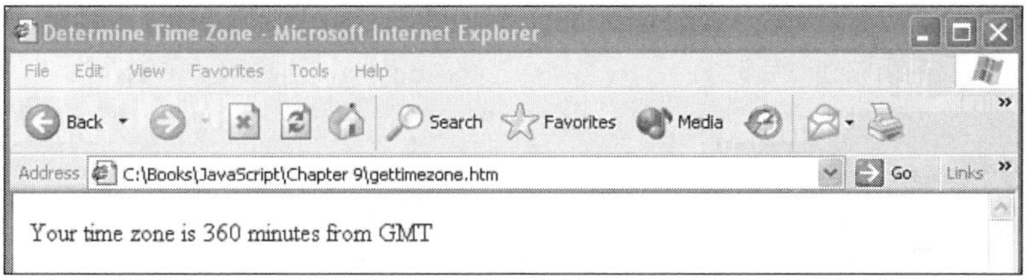

FIGURE 9.7

You can determine the actual difference in time between your location and the user by working with the time zone offset value.

Your time zone is 360 minutes from GMT

Converting Date and Time Formats

So far in this chapter we have talked about the process of retrieving a date or a portion of a date value from a particular `Date` object. Of course, retrieving the date and time information is not the only process that you can or will want to do. Sooner or later you will want to modify the contents of a `Date` object based on particular date calculations, such as calculating a shipping date 30 days away, or determining a final payment date. Whatever the reason, there are many options for working with the date information to achieve the desired results.

Typically the best method of changing a date is to create an initial `Date` object and then perform the desired calculations on the date. Once you have the new date, you can make the appropriate modifications to the `Date` object by using the `Date` object method for changing the object. These methods, shown in Table 9.4, allow you to change all portions of the Date object, including the time elements.

TABLE 9.4 Methods for Setting Date Object

Method	Description
setDate(dd)	Accepts an integer value between 1 and 31 to specify the actual day of the month
setFullYear(yyyy)	Accepts a four-digit number that specifies the year, such as 1998 or 2002
setHours(hh)	Accepts an integer value between 0 and 23 specifying the hour
setMilliseconds(ms)	Accepts an integer value between 0 and 999 specifying the number of milliseconds
setMinutes(mm)	Accepts an integer value between 0 and 59 specifying the number of minutes
setMonth(mth)	Accepts an integer value between 0 (January) and 11 (December) specifying the month number
setSeconds(ss)	Accepts an integer value between 0 and 59 specifying the number of seconds
setTime(ms)	Sets the time by passing a number representing the number of milliseconds that have passed since January 1, 1970 GMT
setYear(yy)	Accepts a two-digit or four-digit number that specifies the year

Note

If you use the setYear() method, you should always specify a four-digit year to avoid any confusion with the actual date. The two-digit date only works for dates between 1900 and 1999. If you type a 01 for 2001, JavaScript assumes you are referring to the date 1901 and treats it as such. By always typing a four-digit date you avoid any potential problems.

As you have noticed, all of the methods in Table 9.4 require an argument containing the value to be passed to the Date object. You should recognize these arguments as the same arguments that we looked at in Table 9.1. For example, to change the day of the month you need to use the setDate() method with the dd argument. For example, you can change the year of the Date object by assigning a new year with the setYear() method as illustrated in the following lines of code that retrieve the new year from the user and assign it to the Date object.

```
var user_date = new Date();

var new_year = prompt("Enter Year");

user_date.setYear(new_year);
```

As you can see it is fairly easy to modify the value of a Date object at any time simply by using the methods outlined in Table 9.4. The modifications to the date can either come from user input, as shown in the lines of code above, or by calculations performed on the date information. For example, you may want to add 45 days to a date. Of course the types of calculations that can be performed on a date are unlimited, as we will discuss in the following section.

Date Calculations

So far in this chapter we have looked at creating the Date object, retrieving information from the Date object, and modifying the value of the Date object. Quite often you will want to perform some type of calculation on the date values before writing the results to the Date object.

Since the Date object stores the entire date and time information as a numeric value it makes the value quite easy to work with. The complexity comes with the fact that the numeric value is stored in milliseconds. Therefore, in order to calculate the amount of time between dates you need to convert the numeric value accordingly. For example, there are 1000 milliseconds in just one second. Table 9.5 illustrates the conversion rates for each element of the Date object.

TABLE 9.5 Converting Date Values

Date Value	Conversion
Second	1000 milliseconds
Minute	60 * 1000 = 60,000 milliseconds
Hour	60 * 60 * 1000 = 3,600,000 milliseconds
Day	24 * 60 * 60 * 1000 = 86,400,000 milliseconds
Week	7 * 24 * 60 * 60 * 1000 = 604,800,000
Month	(days in month) * 7 * 24 * 60 * 1000
year	365 * 24 * 60 * 60 * 1000 = 31,536,000,000 milliseconds

As show in Table 9.5, it doesn't take much to create some very large Date values. In fact, each year that passes is equal to 31,536,000,000 milliseconds.

You will want to keep these conversions in mind as you start manipulating different date values to ensure you return the appropriate results. For example, Listing 9.9 illustrates how you can prompt the user for a future date and determine the number of years, months, and days between the current date and the future date.

INPUT   **LISTING 9.9**   Comparing Dates (`setdate.htm`)

```
<html>
<head>
<title>Find Time Until Future Date</title>
</head>
<body>
<script language="JavaScript" type="text/javascript">
<!--

var user_date = prompt("Enter a future date: ")

var user_date = Date.parse(user_date);
var today_date = new Date();
var diff_date =  user_date - today_date;
var num_years = diff_date/31536000000;
var num_months = (diff_date % 31536000000)/2628000000;
var num_days = ((diff_date % 31536000000) % 2628000000)/86400000;

document.write("Number of years: " + Math.floor(num_years) + "<br>");
document.write("Number of months: " + Math.floor(num_months) + "<br>");
document.write("Number of days: " + Math.floor(num_days) + "<br>");
//-->
</script>
</body>
</html>
```

ANALYSIS   Notice how in Listing 9.9 we had to take the total date value and divide it by the total number of milliseconds in a year to determine how many years were between the current date and the specified future date. Next we take the remainder of the year calculation and determine the number of months, and then the number of days. The code displays the total amount of time between the current date and the future date broken into the number of years, months, and days between the dates, as shown in Figure 9.8.

You should pay close attention to the fact that the code in Listing 9.9 accepts a date value entered by the user and then uses the `parse()` method to convert the date value to a `Date` object. The `parse()` method definitely comes in handy when you want to receive a date from a user. By using this method you can take any date string and convert it into a `Date` object. The following section talks more about this method.

FIGURE 9.8

You can perform calculations to determine the specific amount of time between two dates.

Converting Between Strings and Dates

Obviously when you prompt a user for a date you are going to get some form of a date string. For example, a user could enter the date for Thanksgiving 2001 as 11/22/2001, November 22, 2001, or even Nov. 22, 2001. Of course you could always ask for each individual portion of the date, such as the year, month, and day and then piece the date together using the set methods discussed in Table 9.4, but that is cumbersome. The easier method is to accept the date string and then convert the string into a Date object. This can be accomplished by using the parse() method.

The parse() method accepts any valid date string and converts it into a standard Date object. We used this method in Listing 9.9 when we converted the string entered by the user. We needed to convert the date value to a Date object so that we could calculate the difference between that date and the current date, or the number of milliseconds between the two dates.

Summary

In this chapter we looked at the JavaScript Date object, and how dates and times are stored as a millisecond value. The value is calculated as the number of milliseconds since January 1, 1970. Because JavaScript stores date and time information in one object, you can extract the elements of the object that you need to perform the desired calculations by using any of the different get methods available with the Date object.

You can also modify the contents of a Date object using the various set methods. For example, you may want to change the date to reflect a date 30 days in the future. You can do this by using the setDate() method.

Finally, we explored how the millisecond values can be manipulated to perform desired calculations, such as determining the amount of time between two dates. Because there are 1000 milliseconds within just one second, the size of the number stored by a Date object is typically quite large.

Workshop

In the workshop today we will look at some Q&A issues related to working with the Date object and we will use the questions and exercises to review what you have learned in this chapter about the Date object.

Q&A

Q. When do I need to use the new keyword with the Date object?

A. The new keyword always precedes the Date object. The object is declared in the form: var objectname = new Date().

Q. Why does my 02 appear as 1902, instead or 2002, in the browser window?

A. Most browsers assume that a two-digit date represents a date between 1900 and 1999. If a value of 01 is specified for a date, it will be interpreted as 1901. You need to specify a four-digit year value to avoid year conversion errors.

Q. When I convert 24-hour clock times to AM and PM I get 00 for times between midnight and 1:00 AM, how do I fix that?

A. When working with a 24-hour clock, times between midnight and 1:00 AM are displayed with the hour as 00. Therefore, 12:15 AM will actually appear as 00:15. In order to make this more readable, you need to convert the hour value to 00. You can do this with the following code:

```
if (hour_value == 0)
    {
    hour_value = 12;
    AMorPM = "AM";
}
```

Quiz

1. What is the basic unit used for storing date and time values with the Date object?

2. What is the range of integer values used to represent the months of the year?

3. Why worry about custom formatting a date before displaying it on the browser window?

4. What is a 24-hour clock format and how would you convert it to AM/PM?

Quiz Answers

1. All date and time information is stored in milliseconds.

2. The 12 months of the year are specified from 0, representing January, to 11 for December.

3. Each browser displays the Date object using a different format. Typically you want your date and time information to display consistently on all browsers. In order to do so, you need to custom format the date output using the set methods for the Date object.

4. When you request an hour from a Date object it returns the value based upon a 24-hour clock. The 24-hour clock starts counting with 0 at midnight and 11:00 PM returns as 23. In order to convert to an AM/PM time you can subtract 12 from all times that are 13 and over, and specify PM for those times.

Exercises

1. Create an HTML page to count down the number of days until a special event, such as Christmas, or a special vacation.

2. Create an HTML page to determine how old an individual is based on his birthdate.

9

DAY 10

Events and Event Handling

Whenever anything occurs within a browser window an event is created. An event can be as simple as a mouse cursor moving across the screen or it can be a result of opening a new page.

In this chapter we will look at the different types of events that can occur within the browser window and how you can monitor these events to determine when your code should perform certain actions. We also will look at performing the most popular type of event handling these days—the creation of image rollovers.

This chapter will teach you:

- What an event is
- Types of events
- How to handle events
- How to create mouse-over effects

Understanding Events

Whenever anything happens, your JavaScript code changes the value of an object; or, for example, even when an error occurs, an event takes place. For instance, if the user clicks a button on a page, a Click event occurs for that button. If your code updates the value of a form field, a Change event occurs. By interacting with the HTML code on the page, you have the ability to capture the events that occur in the browser window and perform different actions based upon the specific events.

Probably the most commonly captured event is the Click event. This event occurs whenever a single mouse click occurs on the browser window. Of course, you may not care about all mouse clicks, but if the user clicks on a Submit button at the bottom of the form you definitely want to be aware of that event. As a conscientious programmer you want to capture the Click event from a Submit button to verify the data entered on the form. This ensures the values are within the appropriate ranges before the information is submitted to the server. For example, if a form field must contain a value between 1 and 10, you can verify the contents of the field and display a message for the user to correct the value if it is incorrect.

NEW TERM When you create JavaScript code to capture an event you are writing what is commonly referred to as an *event handler*. The event handler specifies what actions you want to perform when the particular event occurs on the page. An event handler typically consists of two pieces as described in the following section.

Creating an Event Handler

Events can occur all day long on your HTML pages, but if you do not create code to capture and handle the events, the events are meaningless. For example, you can place a button on a form, but if you do not create the code to recognize the fact that the button has been depressed, the vistor to your site can press the button, but there will be no response. The coding that is done to handle the event is the event handler.

Although an HTML object typically triggers an event, HTML cannot handle an event on its own. In order to respond to an event you must use some other language, such as JavaScript. What we are going to do is create event handlers that respond when specific properties are set by HTML objects. For example, the following HTML tag includes an onClick event handler to capture the clicking of the button by the user.

```
<input type="button" value="Push Button" name="Button1"

 onclick="window.alert('Button Pressed');">
```

There are basically three types of event handlers that you can create. Each type requires the capture of an HTML object property, as outlined in Table 10.1.

TABLE 10.1 Types of Event Handlers

Type	Description
Statement Event Handler	As shown in the sample code above, the HTML tag property value is assigned a JavaScript statement that executes when the event occurs.
Function Event Handler	The HTML tag property is set to call a specific JavaScript function when the corresponding event occurs such as, `onclick="Button_Clicked();"`
JavaScript Capture Events	Used to create generic JavaScript code that executes each time a specific event occurs, such as loading a particular page.

Each of these event handling methods is discussed in detail in the following sections.

Handling an Event with a JavaScript Statement

When you want to perform a simple action, such as display a message, when an event occurs you can place the entire event handler within the tag of the HTML object. For example, the following code displays an alert message box when the `onclick` property is triggered for the Input button.

```
<input type="button" value="Push Button" name="Button1"

 onclick="window.alert('Button Pressed');">
```

You add the event handler to your HTML code as part of the particular object's tag. Each event handler must be made up of two specific elements: the event handler attribute and the value of the attribute. In the above sample code, the event handler is `onclick` and the value of the attribute is `window.alert('Button Pressed');` as soon as the button is pressed, the alert message displays in the browser window, as shown in Figure 10.1.

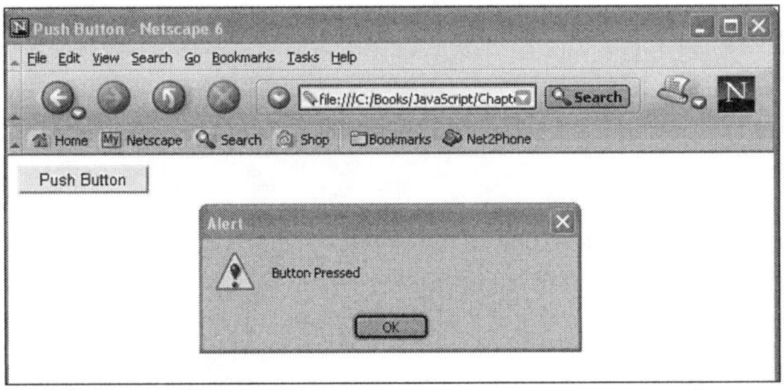

FIGURE 10.1

When the specified event is triggered the corresponding JavaScript code executes.

Be sure to notice that the JavaScript code that executes for the event is placed in double quotes within the HTML tag. HTML does not know how to decipher the JavaScript code. By placing the code in quotes, it is ignored by HTML and executes as JavaScript code.

> **Tip**
>
> Remember when you need to put quotes around values that are already within quotes you need to differentiate between the two types of quotes by alternating between double and single quotes. For example, in the event handler code `onClick="window.alert('Button Pressed');"` the double quotes are used to specify the event handler code and the single quotes are used to indicate the text to display on the alert box. You can use the quotes in any order, either double and then single or vice versa as long as you make sure they match up correctly.

You can use this type of event handling when you only have one JavaScript statement to execute. If you have multiple statements, it is better to call a JavaScript function, described in the following section.

Handling Events with JavaScript Function Calls

So far we have looked at launching a JavaScript command directly from an HTML object tag. When you have more than one JavaScript statement to launch, it makes more sense to call a JavaScript function from the HTML object tag. In other words, you still use the HTML object property to determine when the event has occurred by setting the value of the property to call a JavaScript function, as shown in Listing 10.1.

INPUT **LISTING 10.1** Calling a JavaScript Function for an Event (`eventscript.htm`)

```
<html>
<head>
<script language="JavaScript" type = "text/javascript">
<!--
function CheckValue()
{
if ((document.golf.balls.value >= 1) && (document.golf.balls.value <= 10))
{
   var total_amount = document.golf.balls.value * 25;
   window.alert("Total Cost is: " + "$" + total_amount);
}
else
  window.alert("Type a value between 1 and 10");
}
```

LISTING 10.1 continued

```
//..>
</script>
<title>Golf Balls</title>
</head>
<body>
<form name="golf" method="POST" >
  <font size="4">Golf Balls</font><br>
  $25.00/dzn.    Quantity <input type="text" name="balls"
 size="5">   
  <input type="button" value="Order" name="Order" OnClick="CheckValue()"></p>
</form>
</body>
</html>
```

10

In Listing 10.1, the onClick property triggers the CheckValue function if the Order button is pressed. The CheckValue function verifies that the value specified in the Quantity text box is within the appropriate range and then displays the total cost, as illustrated in Figure 10.2.

OUTPUT

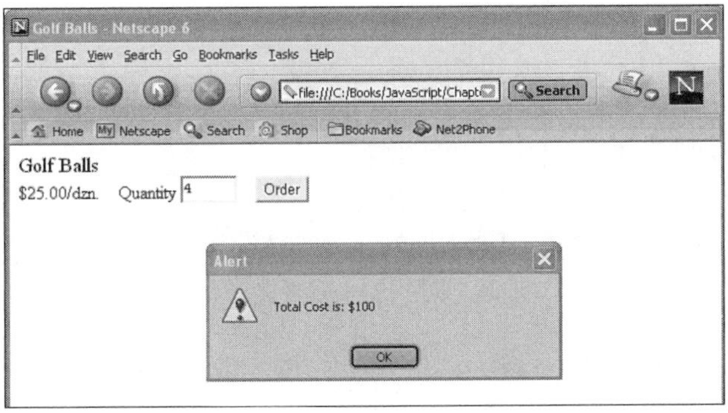

FIGURE 10.2

By capturing the events with a form you can verify that the form contains the appropriate values before submitting the form information to the server.

Button events are very commonly used to validate values on a form, as shown in Listing 10.1. The form validation can be done with either an onClick event, or an onSubmit event triggered from a Submit button being pressed on a form.

There are some objects though that do not have HTML tags. Events triggered by these objects require a different type of event handling, as outlined in the following section.

Capturing Events Directly Within JavaScript

The final method for capturing object events is to create JavaScript code that watches for a particular event to occur. This type of coding works best for objects (such as the Document object) that do not have HTML tags, although you can use this method for any event. Keep in mind this method captures all occurrences of the specified event for the object.

In order to use this type of method, you need to specify the event handler code statement within your JavaScript code. The event handler is coded as follows:

```
objectname.eventname = eventhandler
```

The `objectname` value is the name of the object for which you want to capture events. If you want to capture all events of a type that occur on the entire page, you will want to specify the `Document` object.

When you specify the `eventname` value you must place the word on in front of the event and the entire name must be all lowercase. For example, to track the `Load` event, you would type `onload`.

The event hander is simply a call to a JavaScript function to handle the event. This resembles the function calls we made in the previous section. The only major difference is that you do not place the parentheses after the function name. It also means that you cannot pass data values into the function. The event handler is coded as follows:

```
Window.onresize = DisplayMsg;
```

The code in Listing 10.2 illustrates how to create an event handler for any events of a specified type. For example, the sample code watches for the browser window to be resized, and then displays a message.

INPUT   **LISTING 10.2**   Capturing Events Within JavaScript (`resizescript.htm`)

```
<html>
<head>
<script language="JavaScript" type = "text/javascript">
<!--

window.onresize = DisplayMsg;

function DisplayMsg()
{
window.alert("You just resized the window.");
}

//..>
</script>
<title>Window Resizing</title>
</head>
<body>
</body>
</html>
```

With the code in Listing 10.2, the `DisplayMsg` function launches each time the browser window is resized, and then displays a message indicating what occurred, as shown in Figure 10.3. Notice that we are monitoring the `Window` object for the event to occur. We will discuss more about which objects trigger the events you want to monitor later in this chapter.

OUTPUT

FIGURE 10.3

The resize event handler is triggered within your JavaScript code each time that type of event occurs.

10

Types of Events

As we have already seen so far, there are several different types of events for which you can create event handlers. All of the events available in JavaScript mirror the HTML events. Although JavaScript does not allow you to script for all events that may occur on the page, you will see in Table 10.2 that you can capture pretty much all the events you need to make your code run effectively.

One thing you are going to notice with events is that each object triggers a series of events, although the same events can be triggered by multiple objects. For example, the Click event is triggered by several different objects including the `Document`, `BUTTON`, `RadioButton`, and `TABLE` objects.

You create an event handler for each of the events that JavaScript supports by using the keyword on before the name of the event, as illustrated in Table 10.2.

TABLE 10.2 JavaScript Events

Event	Event Handler	Description
Abort	onabort	Occurs when loading of a page or image is canceled
Blur	onblur	Occurs when the focus moves to a different object
Change	onchange	Occurs when a field on a form is modified
Click	onclick	Occurs when an object is clicked with the mouse
DblClick	ondblclick	Occurs when an object is double-clicked with the mouse

TABLE 10.2 continued

Event	Event Handler	Description
Error	onerror	Occurs when an error occurs on the page. (We are not going to deal with the Error object in this chapter. Error handling is covered extensively in Chapter 15.)
Focus	onfocus	Occurs when an object receives focus
KeyDown	onkeydown	Occurs when a key is pressed on the keyboard
KeyPress	onkeypress	Occurs when a key is pressed and then released on the keyboard
KeyUp	onkeyup	Occurs when a pressed key is released on the keyboard
Load	onload	Occurs when a page or image loads
MouseDown	onmousedown	Occurs when a mouse button is pressed
MouseMove	onmousemove	Occurs when the mouse pointer is moved
MouseOut	onmouseout	Occurs when the mouse pointer moves off of an object
MouseOver	onmouseover	Occurs when the mouse pointer moves over an object
MouseUp	onmouseup	Occurs when a pressed mouse button is released
Move	onmove	Occurs when the browser window is moved
Reset	onreset	Occurs when the Reset button is pressed on a form
Resize	onresize	Occurs when the browser window is resized
Select	onselect	Occurs when text is highlighted on the page
Submit	onsubmit	Occurs when the Submit button is pressed on the form
Unload	onunload	Occurs when the page unloads

Note

The events listed in Table 10.2 reflect those that are available and supported by both JavaScript and JScript, ensuring that they are valid in both Internet Explorer and Netscape Navigator. You will find that there are additional event handlers that you can use that are only supported by one of the two languages, such as onCut, which is an Internet Explorer-only event handler. If you are creating code specific to one browser type, you can use the additional events supported by that browser. Refer to Chapter 8, "The Browser Issue," for more information on browser compatibility issues.

How to Handle Events

Earlier in the chapter we looked at the different methods you can use for creating event handler code. If you remember we looked at how the event handler can be handled as either part of the HTML `object` tag or as a separate JavaScript function. Of course the type of event handler you use will vary based on the type of event you are handling.

We now need to look at handling specific event types in more detail and the corresponding objects that trigger each event.

Monitoring Form Changes

As we discussed previously, events are very useful when working with forms. By capturing events related to the form, you can determine when the user changes a field or presses a button.

In Listing 10.1 we used the `Click` event to determine when a button had been pressed. If you remember, after the button was pressed we checked the value of the text box to ensure that it contained a valid value. This same process can be accomplished by monitoring a `Submit` event triggered by a Submit button. We will talk more about using the `Click` event as we deal with mouse actions later in the chapter.

Of course the use of the Click or Submit event requires waiting for the user to press a button before any type of validation can be performed on the values in the form fields. This can become onerous if you have a long form. A better method would be to be able to validate the values in a form field each time the field changes. This type of event handling can be accomplished using the `Change` event.

You can use the `Change` event with the form fields that accept values including text boxes, check boxes, and radio buttons. Each time the value of one of these fields changes the `Change` event is triggered. You can create code to validate the specified form field value, as shown in Listing 10.3.

INPUT **LISTING 10.3** Capturing Change Events (`changeevent.htm`)

```
<html>
<head>
<script language="JavaScript" type = "text/javascript">
<!--

function CheckValue(field_change)
{
switch(field_change.name)
{
```

LISTING 10.3   continued

```
case "balls" :
if ((field_change.value <= 0) || (field_change.value >= 10))
{
  window.alert("Type a value between 1 and 10");
}
break;
case "tees":
if ((field_change.value <= 0) || (field_change.value >= 20))
{
  window.alert("Type a value between 1 and 20");
}
break;
case "gloves":
if ((field_change.value <= 0) || (field_change.value >= 5))
{
  window.alert("Type a value between 1 and 5");
}
break;
}
}
//..>
</script>

<title>Golf Balls</title>
</head>

<body>

<form name="golf" method="POST" >
  <font size="4">Golf Balls</font><br>$25.00/dozen     
 Quantity    <input type="text" name="balls"  size="5"
 onchange="CheckValue(this)">     <p>
<font size="4">Golf Tees</font><br>$1.00/hundred    Quantity
  <input type="text" name="tees"  size="5" onchange="CheckValue(this)"></p>
  <p>Golf Glove<br>$15.00/each       
Quantity

  <input type="text" name="gloves"  size="5" onchange="CheckValue(this)"></p>
  <p> </p>
  <p>            
     <input type="button" value="Order" name="Order" ></p>
  </p>
</form>
</body>
</html>
```

ANALYSIS The code in Listing 10.3 monitors the three different text fields to determine when the value changes. If the value changes the Change event is triggered and the CheckValue function determines if the value specified in the text box falls within the range of acceptable values.

Notice that we are calling the same function for the Change event on each text box. The CheckValue function determines which text box was modified and executes the appropriate code. In order to know which text box has been modified, we are using the this keyword to pass the reference to the object to the function. Once the reference is passed to the CheckValue function the name value of the text box object is checked to determine which text box was altered. We then use the Switch statement to determine which statements to execute based on the text box that was modified. Once the appropriate code executes, an alert message displays if the value of the text box is not within the appropriate range, as illustrated in Figure 10.4.

FIGURE 10.4

You can use the Change *event to monitor changes to specific form fields.*

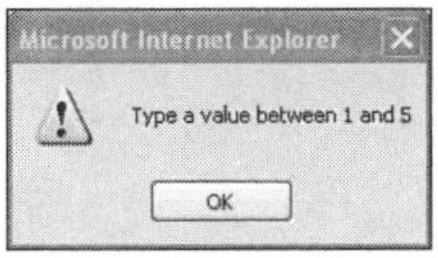

Note We discussed forms in Chapter 6, "HTML Forms and the String Object." For more information on form fields refer to that chapter.

Using the `this` Keyword with Event Handlers

When creating event handlers you will need to know which object triggered a specific event. Since multiple objects can trigger the same event, you need a means of capturing that information. This can be accomplished using the this keyword, as we did in Listing 10.3.

The this keyword allows you to pass a reference to an object as an argument for a function. For example, in Listing 10.3 we have the following code for each text box:

```
onchange=CheckValue(this)
```

When the Change event is triggered for a particular text box the CheckValue function is called and it receives a reference to the actual object that triggered the Change event. You then can access properties of the object. For example, we are using the Name property to determine which object was triggered.

Working with Keyboard Events

When dealing with user input you may want to monitor what keys are pressed on the keyboard. Each time you press a key on the keyboard there are actually a sequence of three different events that are triggered. When you press down the key, a KeyDown event is triggered; as the key is released, a KeyUp event triggers; and finally, after you have pressed a key a KeyPress event triggers. These events occur for every key that is pressed.

You can use these three keyboard events for monitoring input in a specific Form object, such as a text box, or any other location on the Document object. For example, Listing 10.4 monitors any key presses that occur on the Web page and then displays a message indicating that a key was pressed.

INPUT   **LISTING 10.4**   Capturing Keyboard Events (keypress.htm)

```
<html>
<head>
<script language="JavaScript" type = "text/javascript">
<!--

document.onkeypress = DisplayMsg;

function DisplayMsg()
{
window.alert("You just pressed a key.");
}

//..>
</script>
<title>Keyboard Event</title>
</head>
<body>
</body>
</html>
```

ANALYSIS   If you look closely at the code in Listing 10.4, you will notice that the alert message displays for every key that is pressed. If you are only concerned with the keyboard events within a specific form field, you again can monitor only that specific object for keyboard events.

Note   Keep in mind that you can rely only on receiving these events when keys with values on the ASCII table are pressed. This includes all alphanumeric keys, the Enter key, and the spacebar. Typically you will not receive events from pressing function keys, arrow keys, or any other navigational key.

Of course, just knowing a key has been pressed may not be adequate. It also comes in handy to know which key was actually pressed. In order to do that we need to use the Event object so that we can get more information about the event that transpired.

Using the Event Object

Both the Netscape and Internet Explorer object models provide an Event object which stores information about the current event. JavaScript can access this object at anytime in order to gather more information about an event. Since it is an object, we can access any of the properties associated with the object to get more information about the event—that's the cool part of the deal.

Unfortunately Microsoft and Netscape do not support the same properties for this object. Because of this fact, in order for our script to work on both browsers we must create browser-specific code for each browser, as shown in Listing 10.5.

10

> **Note**
>
> For specific information about creating cross-browser code refer to Chapter 8.

INPUT   **LISTING 10.5**   Determining Which Key Was Pressed (capture keypress.htm)

```
<html>
<head>
<script language="JavaScript" type = "text/javascript">
<!--

document.onkeypress = DisplayMsg;

function DisplayMsg(key_event)
{
if (document.all)
//Checks for IE 4.0 or later
{
  document.form1.text2.value = String.fromCharCode(event.keyCode);
}
else if (document.getElementById)
//checks for Netscape 6 or later
{
  document.form1.text2.value = String.fromCharCode(key_event.which);
}
else if (document.layers)
//Checks for Netscape 4
{
  document.form1.text2.value = String.fromCharCode(key_event.which);
```

LISTING 10.5   continued

```
      }
    }
  //..>
  </script>
  <title>Capture Key Pressed</title>
  </head>
  <body>
  <form name="form1">
  <b>Type value in field:         
        
    See what you typed:</b><br>
  <input type = "text" name = "text1" onkeypress="DisplayMsg(event)" size="20">
       
  <input type = "text" name = "text2" onkeypress="DisplayMsg(event)" size="20">
  </form>
  </body>
  </html>
```

The code in Listing 10.5 captures the value typed in the first text box and displays it in the second text box, as shown in Figure 10.5.

OUTPUT

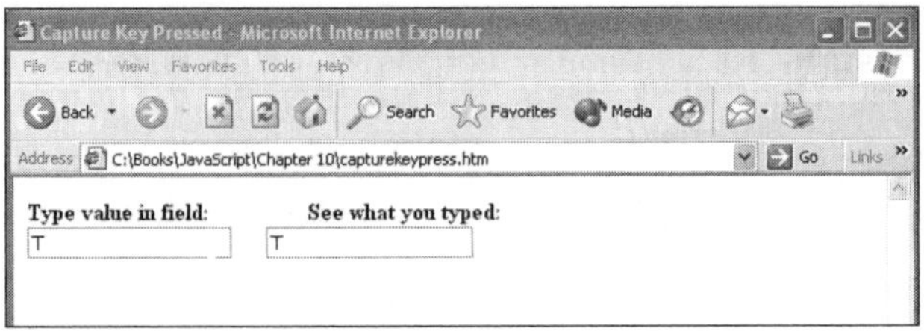

FIGURE 10.5

Use the Event *object to capture the actual keys pressed on the keyboard.*

Again keep in mind that in order to work with the Event object you need to design your code so that it is browser specific. For example, in Listing 10.5 we used the Document object with an if statement to determine which browser type was being used. If you attempt to access an Event property on a browser that does not support that property, your code will be ignored.

Monitoring an Object's Focus

Another type of event that we can monitor is to determine when an object has focus. An object has focus when it is selected. For example, if you have a text box on a form, it has focus when it is selected to receive keyboard input.

The Focus event is triggered whenever a window, frame, or form object gains focus. When the specific object is selected, it has focus.

The Blur event, on the other hand, is triggered when focus is removed from an object. This event is triggered by the same objects as the Focus event. The Blur event works well for checking a form field that a user has just left and verifying the values.

Listing 10.6 illustrates how to use the Focus event to determine when an object receives focus and displays a message in the status bar.

INPUT   **LISTING 10.6**   Monitoring for an Event to Have Focus (focusevent.htm)

```
<html>
<head>
<script language="JavaScript" type = "text/javascript">
<!--

function DisplayMsg(NumVal)
{
if (NumVal == 1)
{
 status = "Type your name in the field" ;
}
if (NumVal == 2)
{
  status = "Type your phone number in the field"
}
}
//..>
</script>
<title>Keyboard Event</title>
</head>
<body>
<form name="form1">
<b>Name:</b>  <input type = "text" name = "text1"
 onfocus="DisplayMsg (1)" size="20"><p>
<b>Phone:</b>  <input type = "text" name = "text2"
 onfocus = "DisplayMsg(2)" size="20"></p>
</form>
</body>
</html>
```

ANALYSIS   In Listing 10.6, the onFocus event handler is triggered whenever the field is selected, as shown in Figure 10.6. You can also monitor when an object loses focus by using the onBlur event. Keep in mind that if you use both the onFocus and onBlur event handlers for fields on a form, as you tab through fields the onBlur event fires as you leave a text box and the onFocus fires for the next text box.

10

OUTPUT

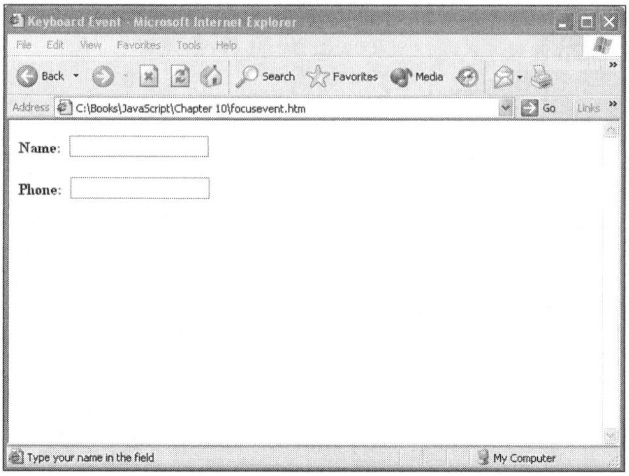

FIGURE 10.6

You can use the Focus *event to monitor the selection of fields on a form.*

Monitoring Window and Document Events

JavaScript allows you to monitor events that occur relative to an actual window and the corresponding document. For example, whenever a new document loads a Load event is triggered. You can use the onLoad event handler to specify code that you want to run after the page loads. For example, the following line of code would display an alert box with a welcome message:

```
<body onload=alert("Welcome to my site.")>
```

This alert box loads as soon as the page is loaded. In this case, the onLoad event handler was added to the Body tag, but it can be used to monitor the loading of any object.

By the same token, you can use the Unload event to specify code to execute before unloading a particular page. If you use this code it executes as soon as the user switches to another Web page.

Another useful Window event to monitor is the Resize event. This event is triggered whenever the browser window is resized. If you remember, we used this event in Listing 10.2. In that code we displayed a message each time the browser window was resized. You can also use the Move event in much the same fashion if you want to monitor when the browser window is moved.

Capturing Mouse Actions

The mouse is probably the most-used device for interacting with a Web page. Because of that fact, there are several different events that are triggered because of mouse actions. In fact, some mouse actions actually trigger multiple events. For example, when you click on a button with the mouse not only does the Click event trigger, but also the MouseDown and MouseUp events. In fact the events are actually triggered in the following order: MouseDown, MouseUp, and then Click.

Of course clicking the mouse is not the only action you can perform. In fact the browser actually keeps track of the mouse cursor location and triggers a MouseMove event with each mouse movement. As the mouse moves across an object, a MouseOver event is triggered. When you move the mouse off of the object, a MouseOff event is triggered.

Intercepting Mouse Clicks

Probably the most commonly used event handler for the mouse is the onClick event handler. As I mentioned, this event handler indicates that the mouse has been clicked on a particular object. By adding the onClick event handler to the HTML object tag, you can customize how the Web page responds to a mouse click on a particular object. For example, the onClick event handler in the following code is triggered when the button is clicked.

```
<input type="button" value="Push Button" name="Button1"

 onclick="window.alert ('Button Pressed');">
```

Besides monitoring form fields for mouse clicks, you also may want to capture the Click event for a link. For example, you may want to display a message before opening a link clicked on your Web page, as illustrated in the code in Listing 10.7.

INPUT   **LISTING 10.7**   Verifying Before Opening a Link (clicklink.htm)

```
<html>
<head>
<script Language="Javascript" type = "text/javascript">
<!--
var newurl
function CheckRequest(newurl)
{
 if (confirm("Do you want to visit " + newurl + " site."))
{
  return true
}
 else
{
 return false
}
 }

//-->
</script>
```

10

LISTING **10.7**   continued

```
<title>Capturing Links</title>
</head>
 <P><A href="http://www.microsoft.com" onclick = "return
 CheckRequest('Microsoft')">Microsoft</A></P>
 <P><A href="http://www.netscape.com" onclick = "return
 CheckRequest('Netscape')">Netscape</A></P>
</body>
</html>
```

ANALYSIS   As you can see in Listing 10.7, using the `onClick` event within a `link` object allows you to specify code that should execute before displaying the corresponding link. The code I used for the event handler may look slightly different from other examples that we have used. In this example, we have added the `return` keyword before the JavaScript function call. By doing this you can use the `Confirm` method to verify that the user wants to view the Web site before switching to that link. The `Confirm` method displays a dialog box, as shown in Figure 10.7. The method returns a value of `True` if the user selects the OK button; otherwise, the value of `False` is returned if the Cancel button is selected and the new link does not display.

OUTPUT

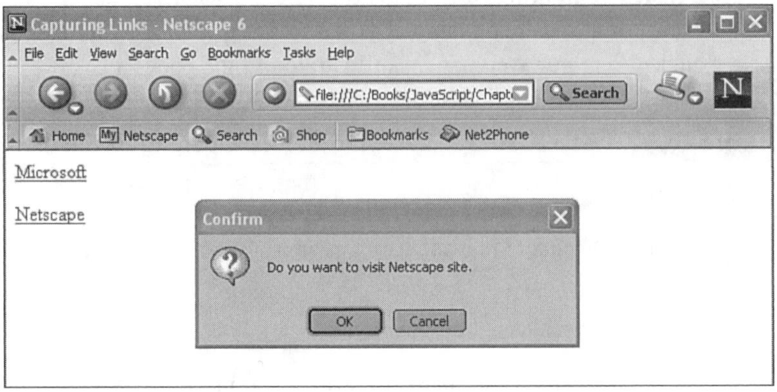

FIGURE 10.7

By capturing the `Click` *event for a link, you can customize how the link displays.*

Of course the `DblClick` event can be captured using the same type of coding. If you want to capture a double click of the mouse instead of the single click, you will need to use the `DblClick` event handler. Keep in mind that you will want to be careful capturing both the `Click` and `DblClick` events for the same object. Of course the `Click` object is always going to be triggered when the first mouse click occurs, and then the `DblClick` event triggers after the second mouse click. Therefore, it can be difficult to distinguish whether a click or double click occurred.

In addition to the actual clicking of the mouse, you can also capture the events of pressing and releasing the mouse using the MouseDown and MouseUp events. These two events are actually triggered before the Click event.

Creating Mouse-Over Effects

One of the most commonly used visual effects on current Web sites is the changing of menu items, or other items on a Web page, as the mouse cursor drags across the items. This may appear to be indicative of the use of cool graphics, but it is actually accomplished by simply using mouseover effects that are triggered by the MouseOver and MouseOut events. This process of changing images based upon the movement of the mouse is commonly referred to as mouse-over effects or hovering.

When you add mouse-over effects to your Web page you are basically capturing the mouse movement across a particular image or link. If the mouse moves over the object, a MouseOver event triggers. When the event triggers you simply swap the image. When the user moves the mouse off of the object, you swap the image back to the original image. This type of event capturing and image changing gives the appearance of a much more dynamic Web page.

10

In Listing 10.8, we create a Web page that changes the menu-button images when the mouse moves across the image. The images change again if when the mouse clicks on a button image to give the impression of a pressed button.

INPUT   **LISTING 10.8**   Creating Mouse-Over Effects (mouseaction.htm)

```
<html>
<head>
<title>Mouse Over Buttons</title>
<script language="JavaScript" type="text/javascript">
<!--
{
if (document.images)
  button1on = new Image();
  button1on.src = "about-pressed.gif";
  button2on = new Image();
  button2on.src = "product-pressed.gif";
  button3on = new Image();
  button3on.src = "service-pressed.gif";
  button4on = new Image();
  button4on.src = "contact-pressed.gif";

  button1 = new Image();
  button1.src = "about-unselected.gif";
  button2 = new Image();
  button2.src = "product-unselected.gif";
```

LISTING 10.8   continued

```
     button3 = new Image();
     button3.src = "service-unselected.gif";
     button4 = new Image();
     button4.src = "contact-unselected.gif";

     button1up = new Image();
     button1up.src = "about-highlighted.gif";
     button2up = new Image();
     button2up.src = "product-highlighted.gif";
     button3up = new Image();
     button3up.src = "service-highlighted.gif";
     button4up = new Image();
     button4up.src = "contact-highlighted.gif";
   }

   function Down(buttonname)
    {
     if (document.images)
      {
       document[buttonname].src = eval(buttonname + "on.src");
      }
    }

   function Off(buttonname)
    {
     if (document.images)
      {
       document[buttonname].src = eval(buttonname + ".src");
      }
    }

   function Over(buttonname)
    {
     if (document.images)
      {
       document[buttonname].src = eval(buttonname + "up.src");
      }
    }
   // -->
   </script>
   </head>
   <body>

   <table width=118 border=0 cellpadding=0 cellspacing=0>
   <tr>
   <td width=1><a href="javascript:void(0)" onmouseover="Over('button1')"
    onmouseout="Off('button1')" onclick="Down('button1')">
   <img name="button1" src="about-unselected.gif" alt="About Us" border=0
    width="119" height="31"></a></td>
```

LISTING 10.8   continued

```
</tr>
<tr>
<td width=1><a href="javascript:void(0)" onmouseover="Over('button2')"
 onmouseout="Off('button2')" onclick="Down('button2')">
<img name="button2" src="product-unselected.gif" alt="Products"
 border=0 width="119" height="31"></a></td>
</tr>
<tr>
<td width=1><a href="javascript:void(0)" onmouseover="Over('button3')"
 onmouseout="Off('button3')" onclick="Down('button3')">
<img name="button3" src="service-unselected.gif" alt="Services"
 border=0 width="119" height="31"></a></td>
</tr>
<tr>
<td width=1><a href="javascript:void(0)" onmouseover="Over('button4')"
 onmouseout="Off('button4')" onclick="Down('button4')">
<img name="button4" src="contact-unselected.gif" alt="Contact Us"
 border=0 width="119" height="31"></a></td>
</tr>
</table>
</body>
</html>
```

As shown in Figure 10.8, the code in Listing 10.8 creates a menu that contains four button options. When the mouse cursor drags across a button image, the button appears highlighted to indicate the mouse's position. If the mouse clicks on a button image, the button image changes to an image that gives the impression of a pressed button.

OUTPUT

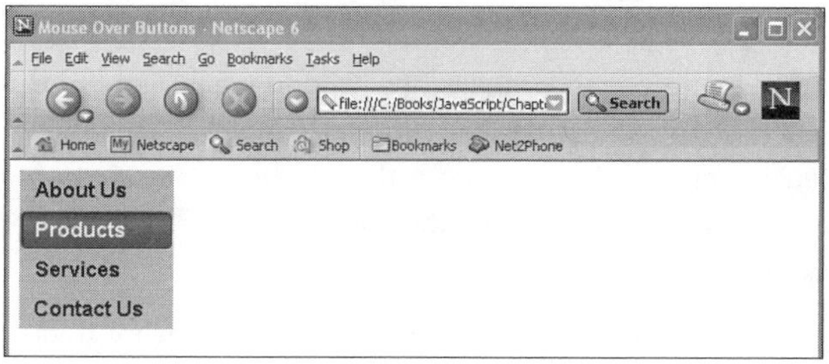

FIGURE 10.8

Mouse-over effects allow you to create the illusion of actual buttons on your Web page.

ANALYSIS   You will notice that the HTML code contains a table with four links as menu items. Initially an image that represents our unselected button displays for each link.

10

Tip

You will notice that instead of assigning another page to each link, I used the statement `javascript:void(0)`. This statement essentially disables the link so it remains on the same page. This statement works well anytime you need to disable a link that you do not want a user to visit.

Also, in order for each button image to be changed when the user drags the mouse over, or clicks on the image, you need to make sure each image is named. This is done by using the `name` property. The `OnClick`, `OnMouseOver`, and `OnMouseOff` event handlers are used to specify the actions to perform when the corresponding events take place. Each event handler calls the corresponding JavaScript function by passing the name of the image that was selected.

Now let's look at the JavaScript code at the top. The first thing you want to do when creating this type of code is preload all of the graphics into `Image` objects. As you create the individual `Image` objects, you will assign the path of the graphic to the `src` property for each object.

Note

You will notice that we used an `if` statement before creating the `Image` objects. The `if` statement is designed to verify that the browser your code is running in actually supports the `Image` object. When `if (document.images)` returns a value of `True` the browser supports the `Image` object and your JavaScript code executes. If the statement returns a value of `False`, the code is ignored.

After preloading all of the images, we need to create functions to handle the mouse movements. The `Over()` function executes whenever the `MouseOver` event triggers, and the `OnMouseOver` event handler calls the function. The `Off()` function executes when the `MouseOut` event triggers. Finally, the `Down()` function executes when the `Click` event triggers.

You can expand on this basic version of the mouse-over effects as you implement it into your Web page. If you want to give the appearance of the button remaining pressed as you switch to another page, you would change the HTML code for the button to ignore the `MouseOver` and `MouseOff` events. For example, if you were displaying the Products page, the link on that page would be modified to display as follows:

```
<tr>
<td width=1><a href="javascript:void(0)" onclick="Down('button2')">
<img name="button2" src="product-unselected.gif" alt="Products"
 border=0 width="119" height="31"></a></td>
</tr>
```

You will notice that I removed the OnMouseOver and OnMouseOut event handlers from the code. By not capturing those events for this button, the button image appears the same until you select the next link.

Another thing to keep in mind, if you are switching between pages, is that it is not always necessary to add the onClick event to the HTML tag. Because as soon as the Click event occurs the link will load the new page. You can simply load the new page with the button selected image.

> **Tip**
>
> There are many ways that you can make the image-over effects work on your Web page. Another common feature is to have another image modified as part of the mouse event. To change another image, you would simply identify the image to be changed as part of your JavaScript functions.

Summary

This chapter explored how JavaScript intercepts various browser events and allows you to execute code based upon the event being triggered. By capturing events, you are able to add a more dynamic feel to your Web site because you are performing specific actions based on the occurrence of the specific events.

Each event is captured using a corresponding event handler. Typically the event handler is specified as part of the tag for the HTML object. Although we looked at the fact that some HTML objects do not have corresponding tags, you will need to create specific JavaScript code to capture those events.

You can monitor keyboard, mouse, error, window, and document events and perform actions when any of those events are triggered. Probably the most commonly monitored mouse event is the Click event. This event can be captured using the onClick event handler. This event is typically used to monitor the clicking of a link or form button.

Keep in mind that event handling is the basis for Dynamic HTML (DHTML), which we will discuss in detail in Chapter 11, "Dynamic HTML."

Workshop

In the workshop today we will use the questions to review what you have learned in this chapter about working with events in JavaScript.

Q&A

Q. Should I validate form fields as the user types values or after the form is submitted?

A. This is really a personal preference. If you have a large form with several fields, you may want to validate individual fields to be able to easily indicate to the user which fields are not valid. The downside to doing so is that the user may already intend to change form field values before submitting the form, and your messages on each field may only be an aggravation. Ideally you only validate the form fields after the form is submitted, but design your messages to properly inform the user of the fields that need to be modified.

Q. When I use both the `Change` and `Blur` events they appear to fire simultaneously. Is that correct?

A. The `Change` event always fires immediately after the `Blur` event. Therefore it makes more sense to only use one of the events as your event handler. Typically the `Change` event is more reliable and is the preferred event handler for monitoring changes to a form field.

Q. How do I capture events that are triggered by objects that do not have corresponding HTML tags?

A. Some objects do not have HTML object tags, such as the `Document` object. In order to capture these events you need to create JavaScript code that monitors these events directly. This code is created as follows:

```
objectname.eventname = eventhandler
```

Quiz

1. What is the best method for verifying input on a form before it is submitted?
2. What is another event to monitor to determine when a field changes?
3. How do you pass a reference to the object with the event hander JavaScript function call?
4. What is the `Event` object?

Quiz Answers

1. You can use the `onSubmit` event handler to call a JavaScript function to verify the values in the fields on the form. For example, if you require a number within a specific range of values you can check the field to ensure that it contains the appropriate values.

2. The `Change` event is triggered whenever a field on a form is modified. You can use the `onChange` event handler to monitor the field and launch the appropriate code to validate the value typed in the field.

3. By using the `this` keyword as the argument for your JavaScript function call you can pass a reference to the object back to your JavaScript function. Once you have passed the object reference into your function, you can use the properties of the object to reference it. For example, the `Name` property can be used to reference the object name.

4. The `Event` object stores detailed information about the most recent event. Although the object is supported by both Netscape and Microsoft, they each support different object properties.

Exercises

1. Create a Web page that uses the `Focus` event to display a status bar message describing what should be typed when a text box is selected.

2. Create a Web site that uses the mouse-over effects for the menus. Keep in mind you want the newly displayed pages to display the selection on the menu. Therefore, you want the selected menu option to be displayed on the new page.

10

DAY 11

Dynamic HTML

Dynamic HTML, or DHTML as it is commonly called, has become widely recognized as a method for adding dynamic effects to your Web page. With DHTML you can access and modify the attributes of nearly every HTML element.

This chapter will look at the elements that make up DHTML and you will learn how to combine these elements to create dynamic visual effects on your Web page.

This chapter will teach you

- What DHTML is
- How to use Cascading Style Sheets
- How to work with layers
- How to change element attributes
- How to move things

What is DHTML?

In the last few chapters, you have looked at different methods for creating "dynamic" effects on your Web page. For example, in Chapter 10, "Events and Events Handling," you found out how to capture events that happened on the Web page, and how to perform actions as a result of an event. Even though we learned to do some pretty cool stuff such as creating mouse-over effects with a movement of the mouse, everything we have done has really just added a little life to an otherwise static Web page. So what options are there? After all, HTML is a just a glorified version of a printed page, right? Well actually there is another option to look at—Dynamic HTML.

DHTML is a method for gaining control in order to create a dynamic Web page with the ability to modify content, layout, and design after the page has loaded. In the ideal sense, DHTML gives you total control over everything on the Web page, not only before it loads but even after it loads. Of course, keep in mind I said "ideal sense"; part of our goal in this chapter is to provide a realistic view of what can be accomplished in today's browsers with DHTML.

Okay, before you think you have to learn some other language now, let me tell you what DHTML really is. DHTML is simply a combination of HTML 4.0 (or later), Cascading Style Sheets, JavaScript, and W3C DOM to produce a "dynamic" Web page. So really the only thing that we haven't discussed so far in this book is Cascading Style Sheets, which we will talk about in the next section.

The main thing to keep in mind is that DHTML standards are only well supported by Netscape 6 or higher and Internet Explorer 5 and higher. (Other browsers support these standards too, but we are concentrating on the two main browsers.) The prior versions of these browsers, particularly the 4.0 versions, supported forms of DHTML but the support was really proprietary to each browser, making it a bigger challenge to create cross-browser compatible code. Of course, since these browser versions are still in existence today, you need to allow for them in your coding, and we will touch on some of the issues of the earlier browser versions throughout this chapter.

Because Cascading Style Sheets (CSS) play such an important role in the development of DHTML pages, we will focus a great deal of attention on CSS styles and the creation of rules. We will also focus on the various properties that you can set. Although these properties are set as CSS rules, they can also be modified through DHTML.

Using Cascading Style Sheets

As you are probably quite aware, styles allow you to specify how a particular block of text appears on a page. Since an HTML page is really just another way to display a written document, at least that was the original purpose for HTML, most of the HTML tags available allow you to modify the look of your HTML page. For example, applying any of these styles changes how your text appears: <h1>, <h2>, <h3>, <p>, <b>, <i>, <u>. Of course the list of HTML tags that affect the look of your page is really rather extensive. Therefore, your first thought might be to wonder why you would even want to bother with any other type of styles. But let's stop and think about things for a bit. Have you ever noticed that when you apply an HTML tag to your page that the appearance can be quite different between one browser and another? Have you ever wanted to not only make the text bold, but also change the color or font? Yes, HTML with the help of individual browsers does provide some limited support for customizing styles. However, in order to create style effects that appear consistently on all browsers requires that you apply Cascading Style Sheets.

As mentioned earlier, Microsoft, Netscape, and other browsers started recognizing the fact that users wanted more control over the actual presentation of their documents. Therefore, each browser started adding methods for customizing individual HTML tags. Luckily, the World Wide Web Consortium (W3C) quickly realized the need for this type of document control and developed the Cascading Style Sheet standard (CSS). CSS provides new features that you can use with a standard HTML document to control the actual style and appearance. For example, you can use code similar to the following to change the color of the Level 1 Header:

```
<h1 style="color: red">Document Header 1</h1>
```

As you can hopefully begin to see, by applying CSS styles you are able to have more control over how your page appears on each browser. No longer are you bound to the individual browser's interpretation of the particular HTML tag; you can actually customize each tag.

As you can see, CSS styles can be added directly to the HTML tag by combining it with the style tag. Although this is quite handy for tags that appear only once on a page, for HTML tags that repeat, such as <p> or <b>, you also have the ability to specify the style definitions in a central location either at the top of the HTML page or in another document. We are going to discuss these three methods of style placement within this section. But first, let's look at how to specify your styles.

Defining Styles

First off, in order to define any styles you must use the <style> tag within your HTML document. This tag identifies the custom styles that you want to use within the page. The style tag includes the Type attribute that indicates the type of styles being defined, in this case CSS:

```
<style type ="text/CSS">
```

As with most other HTML tags, the `<style>` tag has a closing `</style>` tag that marks the end of the custom styles. Between the open and closing `style` tags, you specify the rules to apply to each HTML tag. Creating rules will be discussed in the next section.

As mentioned earlier, you can place the styles either at the top (in the head section) of your HTML page, or in a separate document. If you only want to apply this set of rules to one particular page, it is just as easy to place the styles at the top of your HTML page. To do so, your HTML code would look something like the following:

INPUT

```
<html>
<head>
<style type="text/css">
h1 {color: red;
    text-align: center;
    font-family: arial}
p {color: blue;
   font-family: times;
   font-size: 120%}
</style>
</head>
<body>
<h1>Heading 1</h1>
<p>This is the first paragraph</p>
<p>This is the second paragraph</p>
</body>
</html>
```

By placing these styles at the top of the page, each time a particular HTML tag is used the corresponding CSS style rule is applied to the tag. For example, the code above causes the `<p>` tags to create text that is blue and 20% larger than normal, as shown in Figure 11.1.

OUTPUT

FIGURE 11.1

By using CSS styles consistent formatting can be applied throughout an HTML page.

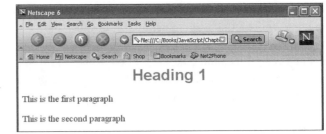

The cool thing about the use of the styles is the fact that you don't have to remember that you want all paragraph text to be blue or bold; the style is automatically applied to that HTML tag. Of course for tags that occur only once on the page, you can still place the style code within the tag, as we did earlier with the <h1> tag. In fact you can do this for all tags if you want, but that would defeat the purpose of the style sheet.

```
<h1 style="color: red">Document Header 1</h1>
```

Of course placing the styles at the top of the page works well for an individual page, but what if you want to apply the styles to an entire Web site? It can be a nuisance to remember to add all your styles to the top of each page. Luckily, this process has a much simpler solution: simply create a separate style sheet that you can call from each page.

NEW TERM Creating a separate style sheet (called an *external style sheet*) is similar to adding the style sheet to the top of the page. You can create the external style sheet in any text editor. There are basically two rules you must follow:

- The style sheet file must have a .css file extension, such as styles.css.

- The external style sheet must not contain any HTML tags. The file simply contains your rules (style definitions) as shown in Listing 11.1.

INPUT   **LISTING 11.1**   The Contents of an External Style Sheet (styles.css)

```
h1 {color: red;
    text-align: center;
    font-family: arial}
h2 {color: green;
    text-align: right;
    font-family: arial}
p {color: blue;
   font-family: times;
   font-size: 120%}
```

You call your style sheet from any HTML page using the <link> tag. Just like with the internal style sheet, you need to place the <link> tag within the head section of your HTML tag. The <link> tag requires three different attributes: rel, type, and href, as shown in Listing 11.2, which calls the style sheet created with Listing 11.1.

INPUT   **LISTING 11.2**   Calling External Style Sheet (externalstyle.htm)

```
<html>
<head>
<link rel="stylesheet" type="text/css"
href="styles.css" />
</head>
<body>
<h1>This is header 1</h1>
<h2>This is header 2</h2>
```

11

LISTING 11.2   continued

```
<p>This is the first paragraph</p>
<p>This is the second paragraph</p>
</body>
</html>
```

When the HTML document loads it opens the associated .css file and applies those styles to the page to produce the appropriate results, as illustrated in Figure 11.2.

FIGURE 11.2

An external style sheet specifies the styles to apply to the HTML document that calls it.

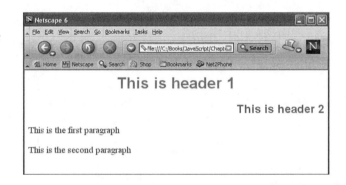

Again, when you use the <link> tag you need to make sure you also use the appropriate attributes. These attributes, listed in Table 11.1, specify the .css file to load.

TABLE 11.1   Link Tag Attributes for Loading a CSS File

Attribute	Description
href	Specifies the location (URL) of the document to link to the current HTML document
rel	Indicates the relationship between the current HTML document and the document that is being linked by the href attribute
Type	Indicates the type of the file being linked by the href attribute

Note

You can actually have multiple CSS files linked to a single HTML document, or even an internal CSS style definition that links to an external CSS file. The confusion comes when the same HTML tag has multiple rules defined. Fortunately, there is a predefined order that the browser uses when determining which rule to apply. Rules have the following order of precedence:

- Inline style (within the HTML tag)
- Internal Style Sheet (within the Head section)

- External Style Sheet (.css file)
- Browser default

This means that if the tag has a style definition that definition takes precedence over any other style definitions that may be available for that tag.

You have total freedom to decide where you want to place your style rules. In fact, it is quite common to use a combination of an external style sheet, an internal style sheet, and inline styles within one HTML page.

Of course, now that we have looked at where to place the style definitions, we need to discuss what can actually be defined, as outlined in the next section.

Creating CSS Rules

Each style definition within the style sheet is called a rule. Essentially a rule consists of three parts: HTML element (called a *selector*), and a *declaration* consisting of a property, and value. The rule is created by specifying the HTML element, and then specifying the property and property value in curly brackets as shown:

```
h1 {color: red}
```

This definition specifies that the <h1> heading level should be red. One thing to keep in mind, only the portions of the elements' style that you specify within your CSS style sheet are modified. In other words, if the default font for the HTML element is Times Roman and you do not specify a different font, the font value of the browser is used.

You can also specify the values of multiple properties for each HTML element by placing a semicolon after each declaration within the brackets:

```
h1 {color: red;
    font-family: arial;
    text-align: center}
```

Notice three different properties were specified for the h1 heading level. By the same token, you can also apply the same property values to multiple HTML elements using the same rule:

```
h1, h2, h3  {color: red;
    font-family: arial;
    text-align: center}
```

Essentially you can define properties of any HTML element within the style sheet. As you can see, the use of CSS is very valuable when creating a consistent look and feel for your Web site. You can change the alignment, background, colors, fonts, margins, padding, and list properties for each HTML element.

11

> **Note**
>
> Below you will find several tables with the properties you can use with your Cascading Style Sheets. Unfortunately in one chapter it is not possible to thoroughly discuss each property and its corresponding values, but these tables allow you to see the versatility you have in defining your rules.

Controlling the Background Properties

You can use the various background properties to control the background appearance for a particular HTML element. For example, the following code would change the background color of the HTML page to red:

```
body {background-color: red}
```

Besides changing the color, you can specify background images as well as the location of the background image. The properties you can set are outlined in Table 11.2.

TABLE 11.2 CSS Background Properties

Property	Values
background-attachment	scroll Image scrolls with the rest of the page. fixed Image remains in fixed location as page scrolls.
background-color	Can be a color name, RGB value, or Hex value representing the color. See Appendix B for color codes. Also, use transparent for a transparent background.
background-image	No background image. Can be the URL of the image to display for the background.
background-position	One of these values: top left, top center, top right, center left, center center, center right, bottom right, bottom center, bottom left. Also, can use x% and y% to specify horizontal and vertical positioning. Or x-pos and y-pos to specify positioning in any CSS units, such as 10px 20px.
background-repeat	repeat Repeats image vertically and horizontally. repeat-x Repeats image horizontally. repeat-y Repeats image vertically. no-repeat Does not repeat image.

> **Note**
>
> CSS allows you to use several different units of measurement when you specify values for various properties. The only catch is that you must specify the unit identifier after the numeric value, such as 10px represents 10 pixels. Table 11.3 lists the different units of measurement.

TABLE 11.3 CSS Units of Measurement

Unit	Description
%	Specific percentage
in	Inch
cm	Centimeter
mm	Millimeter
em	Font size of the current element
ex	The x-height of the font—normally about half the font size
pt	Point (1pt = 1/72 inch)
pc	Pica (1pc = 12pt)
px	Pixels – (1px = 1 dot on the screen)

Adjusting Borders

You can use the border properties to control the style, color, and width of a particular HTML element. The properties you can set are outlined in Table 11.4.

TABLE 11.4 CSS Border Properties

Property	Values
border-bottom	Sets properties for the bottom border by setting border-bottom color, border-bottom style, and border-bottom width.
border-color	Up to four values specifying top, right, bottom, and left borders. Can be a color name, RGB value, or Hex value representing the color. See Appendix B for color codes.
border-left	Sets properties for the left border by setting border-left color, border-left style, and border-left width.
border-right	Sets properties for the right border by setting border-right color, border-right style, and border-right width.
border-style	Up to four values specifying top, right, bottom, and left borders. Use the following values: none, hidden, dotted, dashed, solid, double, groove, ridge, inset, outset.
border-top	Sets properties for the top border by setting border-top color, border-top style, and border-top width.
border-width	Up to four values specifying the top, right, bottom, and left borders. Possible values: thin, medium, thick, or a CSS unit that indicates thickness of the border.

11

Specify the Classification Properties

You can use the classification properties to control the appearance of an HTML element, its location in respect to another HTML element, and the visibility of the HTML element. Table 11.5 outlines these properties for setting the classification of an element.

TABLE 11.5 CSS Classification Properties

Property	Values
clear	Indicates sides where floating elements are not allowed: left, right, both, or none
cursor	URL of cursor to display, or one of the following: auto, crosshair, default, pointer, move, e-resize, ne-resize, nw-resize, n-resize, se-resize, s-resize, w-resize, text, wait, help, or hand
display	Value indicating how element displays: none, inline, block, list-item, run-in, compact, marker, table, inline-table, table-row-group, table-header-group, table-footer-group, table-row, table-column-group, table-cell, or table-caption
float	Where an image or text appears on the element: left, right, none
visibility	Visibility value: visible, hidden, collapse

Specifying the Dimension Properties

You can use the dimension properties to control the width and height of a particular image. You can also use these properties to specify the distance between lines of text. For example, the following rule sets the height and width of an <img> tag:

```
img { height: 100px;
      width: 100px }
```

Table 11.6 outlines the dimension properties you can use.

TABLE 11.6 CSS Dimension Properties

Property	Values
height	auto Browser uses actual image height. You can specify a numeric value in px, cm, or another CSS unit. You can also specify a percentage of the block containing the image.
line-height	normal Browser sets the height. Use a number, such as 2, that is multiplied by font size to set distance. Specify a CSS unit, such as 10px. You can also specify a percentage of the current font size.
width	auto Browser uses actual image width. You can specify a numeric value in px, cm, or another CSS unit. You can also specify a percentage of the block containing the image.

Changing the Font Properties

Probably one of the most obvious reasons for having style sheets is to have the ability to adjust the font properties for an HTML element. For example, you may want to make sure that the text is always displayed in a particular font, or that the headings are bold and underlined. Table 11.7 outlines the various font properties that you can set in the Cascading Style Sheet.

Caution

Keep in mind, if a browser does not support a font you specify, the browser's default font is used. Therefore, try to use common fonts that most people have on their systems to ensure your page displays as intended.

TABLE 11.7 CSS Font Properties

Property	Values
font-family	List of font names to use for the HTML element. By providing multiple fonts, the browser has another font to use if the first font is not available. Separate the list with commas.
font-size	Specify a fixed size in pixels, such as 10px, or a percentage of the parent element. Use smaller or larger to adjust the size based on the parent element. You can also use: xx-small, x-small, small, medium, large, x-large, and xx-large.
font-style	normal Displays normal font. italic Displays an italic font. oblique Displays an oblique font.
font-variant	normal Displays normal font. small-caps Displays text with smallcaps.
font-weight	normal Displays normal characters. bold Displays thick characters. bolder Displays thicker characters. lighter Displays lighter characters. 100 – 900 Numeric value defining thin to thick. 400 equals normal and 700 equals bold.

11

Setting List Properties

You can customize the way your lists display using the different list style properties outlined in Table 11.8.

TABLE 11.8   CSS List Style Properties

Property	Values
list-style-image	Specifies the URL of the image to use as the list marker. If you do not want an image, specify the value none.
list-style-position	inside Indents the marker and the list. outside Keeps the marker and the text on the left.
list-style-type	One of these values to specify list marker type: none, disc, circle, square, decimal, decimal-leading-zero, lower-roman, upper-roman, lower-alpha, upper-alpha, lower-latin, upper-latin, hebrew, armenian, georgian, cjk-ideographic, hiragana, katakana, hiragana-iroha, and katakana-iroha.

Setting the Spacing

You can use the Margin properties to set the spacing around HTML elements. Whereas, the Padding properties specify the spacing between the border of the HTML element and the content, like the padding for a table. Table 11.9 shows these properties.

TABLE 11.9   CSS Margin and Padding Properties

Property	Values
padding-bottom	Sets the bottom padding as a CSS unit or a percentage of the element width.
padding-left	Sets the left padding as a CSS unit or a percentage of the element width.
padding-right	Sets the right padding as a CSS unit or a percentage of the element width.
padding-top	Sets the top padding as a CSS unit or a percentage of the element width.
margin-bottom	auto Browser sets bottom margin. Specify a fixed bottom margin or a percentage of total height of document.
margin-left	auto Browser sets left margin. Specify a fixed left margin or a percentage of a total width of document.
margin-right	auto Browser sets right margin. Specify a fixed right margin or a percentage of total width of document.
margin-top	auto Browser sets top margin. Specify a fixed top margin or a percentage of total height of document.

Customize Text Properties

You can use the various text properties to control the actual appearance of the text. Table 11.10 shows the various possibilities, such as changing the text color, adjusting the alignment of the text, and even specifying the indentation.

TABLE 11.10   CSS Text Properties

Property	Values
color	Can be a color name, RGB value, or Hex value representing the color. See Appendix B for color codes.
letter-spacing	normal Applies normal spacing based on font settings. Specifies a CSS unit, such as 2px, to indicate spacing between characters.
text-align	Specifies alignment value: left, right, center, or justify.
text-decoration	Specifies text decoration: none, underline, overline, line-through, or blink.
text-indent	Specifies a CSS unit or percentage to indent the text.
text-transform	Specifies how to transform text: none, capitalize, uppercase, or lowercase.
white-space	normal Ignores white space in element. pre Preserves white space in element. nowrap Text in element does not wrap.

11

Creating Classes

CSS styles allow you to take rules a step further by creating class rules for an HTML element. A class is essentially just a subset of a particular element. For example, a common HTML element is the <a> tag used to create links within your page. You are probably used to the fact that browsers typically show the text in different colors depending upon whether the user has visited that link recently. However, with CSS you can actually specify the colors and any other attributes that you want applied to each stage of the <a> tag. For example, the following code assigns a different color to the active (selected), visited, link (unvisited), and hover (with mouse) states of the link.

```
a:active {color:blue}
a:visted {color:red}
a:link {color:green}
a:hover {color:yellow}
```

By applying these classes to your HTML document the links change colors based on their current state.

You can create your own classes for HTML elements in much the same fashion. For example, you may want to apply different formatting to the first paragraph of each page. To do this you would first create the paragraph style in your Cascading Style Sheet and then you would call that style as part of the <p> tag, as illustrated in Listing 11.3.

INPUT   **LISTING 11.3**   Using CSS Classes (`subclass.htm`)

```
<html>
<head>
<style type="text/css">
h1 {color: red;
    text-align:center}
p {font-family: arial}
p.paragraph1 {color:blue;
              font-weight:bold}
</style>
</head>
<body>
<h1>Creating Custom Classes</h1>
<p class="paragraph1">This is the first paragraph</p>
<p>This is the second paragraph</p>
</body>
</html>
```

Note that to create the class rule, you type the name of the HTML element followed by a period and the name of the class. Within your HTML document, you specify the class rule by typing the HTML tag followed by `class=` and the name of the class. As you will notice in Figure 11.3, the class element receives both the styles for the <p> element and `<p class="paragraph1">`.

Tip

> You can also define a class rule that can be assigned to any element. This is useful when you have styles that you want to apply to multiple elements. To do so, simply type a period followed by the class name. For example, `bold-text {font-weight:bold}` creates a class that can now be applied to multiple HTML elements. You call this class using the same method as above, but by typing `class="classname"`.

CSS does provide a couple of built-in psuedo-classes that you can use with the <p> tag. The first-line psuedo-class allows you to specify a rule for the first line of a paragraph. You can use the first-letter psuedo-class to define a rule for the first letter of the paragraph. To create the rules for these psuedo-classes you use the same approach as above by typing the psuedo-class rule in the style sheet section, only you place a colon, not a period, between the element and the psuedo-class.

```
P:first-line {color:blue}
P:first-letter{font-size:150%}
```

FIGURE 11.3

By creating CSS class rules you can create custom definitions that you can apply to specific HTML elements.

Creating Custom Classes

This is the first paragraph

This is the second paragraph

Unlike the custom classes that you create, when your HTML document loads, the rules defined for these styles are automatically applied to each <p> paragraph.

Working with Layers

Netscape originally added the concept of "layers" to Netscape 4.0 to provide the ability to define a portion of the page that could be positioned, moved, or even hidden on the screen using DHTML. In order to accomplish this, each layer's elements where placed within the <layer> tags. Although this was a great concept, it was proprietary, making it only supported by Netscape Navigator 4+ browsers, although they are not supported by Netscape Navigator 6.

Fortunately the CSS specification also included a positioning specification that could be used with all HTML elements. To replace the proprietary <layer> element, you can use the <div> element that is supported by all browsers that support HTML 3.0 or higher. Just like the layering concept, the <div> element defines a group or section of the page. By combining the CSS positioning properties with the <div> element you can create the layering effects first introduced by Netscape.

There are several different CSS positioning properties that you can use to specify the position and shape of the HTML element. The properties are outlined in Table 11.11.

11

TABLE 11.11   CSS Positioning Properties

Property	Values
bottom	auto Browser calculates bottom position of element. Specifies a CSS unit, such as 100px, or a percentage, for position from the bottom of a parent block.
clip	auto Browser sets the clipped size. Specifies the size as rect (top, right, bottom, left). For example, rect(10px, 5px, 10px, 4px).
left	auto Browser calculates left position of element. Specifies a CSS unit, such as 100px, or a percentage, for position from the left of a parent block.
overflow	auto Displays entire element outside specified size. hidden Content clipped to fit. scroll Content clipped to fit and scrollbar adds to view rest of element. auto Browser displays scrollbar if content is clipped.
position	static Items are laid out in normal HTML fashion and cannot be moved. absolute Item is positioned based upon specified coordinates. relative Item is positioned based upon an offset from the static location where HTML would have placed the item.
right	auto Browser calculates right position of element. Specifies a CSS unit, such as 100px, or a percentage, for position from the right of a parent block.
top	auto Browser calculates top position of element. Specifies a CSS unit, such as 100px, or a percentage, for position from the top of a parent block.
vertical-align	Value specifying vertical alignment: baseline, sub, super, top, text-top, middle, bottom, text-bottom. You can also specify a CSS unit, such as 100px, or percentage, indicating vertical alignment.

Probably the most used positioning property is the Position property. By using the absolute and relative positioning values you can specify exactly where on the page you want the particular layer to be placed. For example, the code in Listing 11.4 illustrates how to define the absolute positioning for a "layer."

INPUT   **LISTING 11.4**   Specifying the Positioning of a Layer (PositionLayer.htm)

```
<html>
<head>
<style type="text/css">
```

LISTING 11.4 continued

```
div.layer1 {position:absolute;
            left:75px;
            top:75px;
            color:red}
div.layer2 {position:absolute;
            right:75px;
            bottom:75px;
            font-family: arial;
            color:blue;
            font-weight:bold}
</style>
</head>
<body>
<div class="layer1">
<h1>Positioning Layers</h1>
<p>This is the first layer1 paragraph</p>
<p>This is the second layer1 paragraph</p>
</div>
<div class="layer2">
<p>This is the first layer2 paragraph</p>
<p>This is the second layer2 paragraph</p>
</div>
</body>
</html>
```

11

ANALYSIS Notice the fact that not only did we use the positioning properties with the <div> element but also some of the other CSS properties for specifying the appearance of the text within each layer. By using absolute positioning, each layer is placed on the screen at the specified position. HTML does not care how the positioning affects another layer. In fact, depending upon how the browser window is sized, the layers may even overlay, as shown in Figure 11.4.

OUTPUT

FIGURE 11.4

Use the <div> HTML element to create layers on your page.

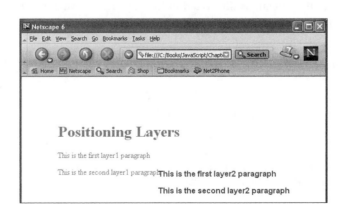

Note

Keep in mind, HTML allows you to nest <div> layers. This means you can place one or more layers inside another layer. When you do this, the rules of the parent layer are applied to all child layers. But if any of the properties are changed within the child layer rules, those new property values are applied to the child only.

Now that you have seen how to create layering effects within your HTML document, let's look at how to change those properties within your JavaScript code to create a more "dynamic" page.

Changing Attributes of an HTML Element

Now that we have discussed CSS and how layers can be used to apply CSS rules to multiple elements, we are ready to look at the process of changing the value of a property. In order to do this effectively, we need to use the W3C DOM that we talked about in Chapter 8, "The Browser Issue."

If you remember our discussion in Chapter 8, we looked at how the DOM specifies the elements of the HTML document in a tree-like structure with the Document object being the base of the tree and all other elements of the page are child nodes of the Document object node. We also discussed that the easiest method for accessing a particular element is to use the getElementById() method. This method allows you to access any HTML element based on the ID attribute.

Of course accessing a property of an HTML element is only half of what you can accomplish with the W3C DOM; you can also change the property in much the same fashion. In fact, you may not realize that you can even change text after it has been written to the screen, as illustrated in Listing 11.5 where the text for a paragraph changes when the button is clicked.

INPUT   **LISTING 11.5**   Changing Window Text (ChangeText.htm)

```
<html>
<head>
<script language="JavaScript" type = "text/javascript">
<!--
function ChangeText()
{
var curtextval = document.getElementById("ptext");
curtextval.innerHTML = "New Paragraph 1"
}
```

LISTING 11.5   continued

```
//..>
</script>
</head>
<body>
<form>
<p id="ptext">This is the first paragraph</p>
<p>This is the second paragraph</p>
  <input type="button" value="Click to Change Text" onclick="ChangeText()"></p>
</form>
</body>
</html>
```

As you can see, it requires very little coding to create dynamic effects that change the context of the window after it has been loaded. As you can see in Figure 11.5, the text in the first paragraph changes as soon as the button is clicked.

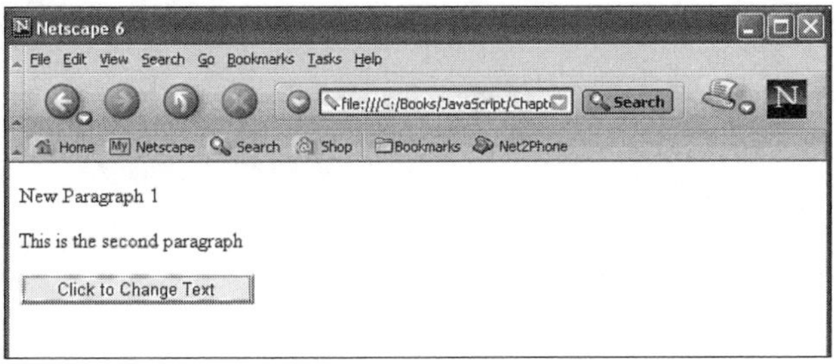

FIGURE 11.5

With the use of the DOM, you can change the characteristics of HTML elements at any time.

11

You may have occasions when the attribute that you want to add to an HTML tag does not currently exist for that tag. If that is the case, you will need to use the setAttribute() method. This method requires two parameters: the name of the attribute to add and the value of the attribute. A good use of this method would be to specify that a link open in another window by adding the target attribute.

```
selectedlink.setAttribute("target", "_blank")
```

On the other hand, you may want to remove an attribute from an element. This can be accomplished by using the removeAttribute() method. This method simply requires the name of the attribute to be removed.

```
selectedlink.removeAttribute("target")
```

Listing 11.6 illustrates how to combine changing attribute values by setting and removing attributes.

INPUT   **LISTING 11.6**   Changing URL Text (ChangeAttribute.htm)

```html
<html>
<head>
<script language="JavaScript" type = "text/javascript">
<!--
function ChangeLink()
{
var newlink = document.getElementById("urltext");
var curlink = document.getElementById("oldurl");
curlink.href = ("http://" + newlink.value);
curlink.innerHTML = newlink.value;
}
function NewWindow(prefval)
{
var curlink = document.getElementById("oldurl");
if (prefval == 1)
{
curlink.setAttribute("target", "_blank");
}
else if (prefval == 2)
{
curlink.removeAttribute("target");
}
}
//..>
</script>
</head>
<body>
<form>
<a id="oldurl" href="http://www.microsoft.com">www.microsoft.com</a>
<p><input type="radio" value="V1" name="R1"
onClick="NewWindow(1)">Open in New Window</p>
<p><input type="radio" name="R1" checked value="V2"
onClick="NewWindow(2)">Open in Same Window</p>
  <input type="text" id="urltext" size="20"> 
  <input type="button" value="Change Link" name="B3" onClick="ChangeLink()"></p>
</form>
</body>
</html>
```

As you can see in Figure 11.6, the code in Listing 11.6 allows you to change not only the URL that displays when the user clicks the link, but also the text describing the URL to match the new URL name. The setAttribute() and removeAttribute() methods are used to specify whether or not the link opens in a new window.

OUTPUT

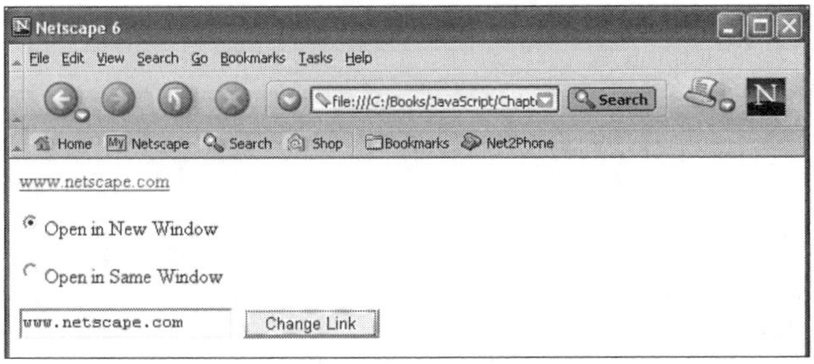

FIGURE 11.6

Changing the attributes of HTML elements allows you to create dynamic effects on the page based upon user selections.

Keep in mind, you can use any of the property values we discussed with Cascading Style Sheets to change the attributes of an HTML element. Of course changing the attributes of HTML elements is quite a cool effect, but there are even more effects that can be created using DHTML, as outlined in the following section.

Moving Things

Now that we have established a basis for DHTML the list is quite long of the effects you can create on your HTML page. Effects such as animating images, scrolling text, keeping portions of your page visible when the user scrolls, and even creating drop-down menus can all be accomplished through DHTML. In the remaining portion of this chapter, let's look at how to go about moving things dynamically on the screen.

One of the most common reasons people decide to use DHTML is to add some type of animation to their pages. Using DHTML you can animate an element of the page whether it is text or an image. For example, in Listing 11.7 we scroll the text within the `<div>` layer across the screen.

INPUT **LISTING 11.7**   Animating Text (`animatetext.htm`)

```
<html>
<head>
<style>
div { position:relative;
      color:red}
</style>
<title>Animating Text</title>
<script language="JavaScript" type = "text/javascript">
var pos1=0;
function next() {
pos1 += 5;
```

LISTING 11.7   continued

```
if (pos1 > 640) pos1 = 0;
document.getElementById("movetext").style.left = pos1;
window.setTimeout("next();",30);
}
 </script>
 </head>
 <body onLoad="next();">
<div id="movetext">
<b>DHTML provides the ability to animate any <br>
HTML elements on your browser window.</b>
 </div>
 </body>
 </html>
```

ANALYSIS   This script moves the text across the screen from left to right, as shown in Figure 11.7. When the position of the text is beyond 640, the position changes back to 0 so that it appears to wrap around the screen. Keep in mind, 640 is used as the maximum position value because the browser window was sized to 640x480. To run this script on a larger browser, you can adjust that value.

OUTPUT

FIGURE 11.7

Creating animations of images and text is one of the popular uses of DHTML.

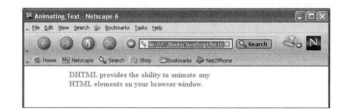

You can reverse the scroll direction from right to left by changing the script as follows:

```
<script language="JavaScript" type = "text/javascript">
var pos1=640;
function next() {
pos1 -= 5;
if (pos1 < 0) pos1 = 640;
document.getElementById("movetext").style.left = pos1;
window.setTimeout("next();",30);
}
 </script>
```

Notice that now the position is checked to see if it is less than zero; if so, set the position of the text back to the right side of the browser.

The types of animations available with DHTML are limitless when you use the CSS Positioning properties covered in Table 11.11.

Another very common use, and probably more useful, of DHTML is to create menus. With DHTML there are many different types of menu systems you can create.

In Chapter 10, "Events and Events Handling," we looked at creating a mouse-over menu where the buttons changed based on the location of the mouse cursor. If you remember, this menu-creation option required the use of three different graphic buttons for each menu option to give the appearance of the button changing. In Listing 11.8 we create a similar menu, but this time it is created with DHTML. By using DHTML we are able to change the contents of the table cells based on the mouse location.

INPUT   **LISTING 11.8**   Dynamic Menus (`dynamicmenu.htm`)

```
<html>
<head>
<style type="text/css">
td.menu {font-family:Arial;
        font-weight:bold;
        background-color:blue;
        cursor:hand}
a{
text-decoration:none;
color:black;
}
</style>
<script language="javascript" type = "text/javascript">
<!--
function selectlink(sellink,linkdesc){
sellink.style.background='yellow';
if (document.getElementById)
  document.getElementById("selectdesc").innerHTML=linkdesc;
else
  selectdesc.innerHTML=html;
}
function leavelink(sellink){
sellink.style.background='blue';
if (document.getElementById)
  document.getElementById("selectdesc").innerHTML=' ';
else
  selectdesc.innerHTML=' ';
}
//-->
</script>
</head>
<body>
<table bgcolor="black" border="1" bordercolor="white" cellpadding="2"
```

11

LISTING 11.8   continued

```
cellspacing="0">
<tr>
<td class="menu" bordercolor="black" id="choice1"
  onmouseover="selectlink(this,'Developers of Internet Explorer')"
onmouseout="leavelink(this)"">
  <a href="http://www.microsoft.com">Microsoft</a></td></tr>
<td class="menu" bordercolor="black" id="choice2"
  onmouseover="selectlink(this,'Developers of Netscape Navigator')"
onmouseout="leavelink(this)">
  <a href="http://www.netscape.com">Netscape</a></td></tr>
<td class="menu" bordercolor="black" id="choice3"
  onmouseover="selectlink(this,'Responsible for the W3C DOM')"
onmouseout="leavelink(this)">
  <a href="http://www.w3.org/">W3C</a></td></tr>
<td class="menu" bordercolor="black" id="choice4"
  onmouseover="selectlink(this,'Publisher of Computer Books')"
onmouseout="leavelink(this)">
  <a href="http://www.samspublishing.com">Sams Publishing</a></td></tr>
<tr>
<td bordercolor="black" bgcolor="white" height="18">
<font id="selectdesc" size="2"></font></td></tr>
</table>
</body>
</html>
```

If you run the code in Listing 11.8, you will see that we added an additional feature to this menu. When the user drags the cursor across a menu option, a description of the menu option displays in the last table cell, as shown in Figure 11.8.

OUTPUT

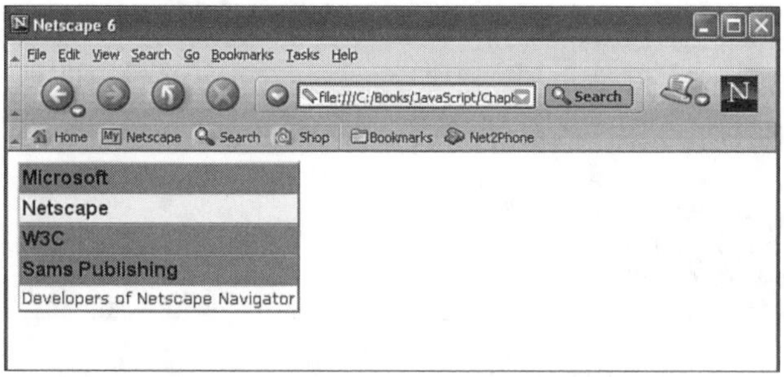

FIGURE 11.8

You can create some dynamic menus using DHTML.

Summary

In this chapter, you first learned that DHTML is actually comprised of four different components: CSS, HTML 4.0 (or later), JavaScript, and the W3C DOM. Cascading Style

Sheets (CSS) provide a means for creating style rules that can be applied to an entire document, or for that matter an entire site. You can create rules for any HTML element. You can also create rules for sub-class elements, which are simply a sub-class of a particular element. CSS provides several different types of properties that you can apply to your HTML elements. For example, to set a particular element to be underlined you set the text-decoration property value to underline. You can place CSS rules in three different locations. They can be part of the HTML tag, listed at the top of the HTML page in the Head section, or exist in an external style sheet.

Netscape introduced the concept of layers as an addition to DHTML to provide a means for applying dynamic effects to portions of a page. Unfortunately layers are specific only to Netscape 4+, but the same effect can be accomplished on a cross-browser basis using the <div> element.

Finally, we looked at how to combine the elements of DHTML to create dynamic effects on your page such as changing the values of static text on the page, animating elements, and even creation of dynamic menus.

Workshop

In the workshop today we will use the Q&A to look at other issues you may face with DHTML, and we'll use the questions and exercises to review what you have learned in this chapter about working with DHTML.

Q&A

Q. How do I avoid conflicts between styles within the document and those in an external style sheet?

A. Keep in mind, the styles applied as part of the HTML tag will always supercede any other styles related to that same element. The best practice is to create your general styles and store them in the external style sheet to be applied to all pages. Then if you have special situations where you want to change a style, make that change at the tag level.

Q. Why should I bother to create Cascading Style Sheets?

A. By creating styles you can specify how a particular HTML element should appear on the page. For example, you may want your heading levels to be a specific font style and size. You create specific rules that define the styles to apply to each element.

Q. How do I apply the layer effect of Netscape 4+ in cross-browser code?

A. Layers were first introduced by Netscape as a means to group portions of the page together. You can apply layering effects to all browsers using the `<div>` tag. With the use of layering you can set the location of each layer independently.

Quiz

1. What advantage is gained by creating a separate CSS file for your style rules?
2. What is the precedence order for applying CSS styles?
3. How do you change the text in a paragraph using DHTML?

Quiz Answers

1. You actually have the ability to place your CSS rules in three different locations. You can add the style information directly to the HTML tag by using the style attribute as part of the tag. For styles that appear frequently within the page you can create a CSS-style page within the Head section of the HTML page. If you want the styles applied to multiple pages on your site, you can create a `.css` file containing the rules that can be called by each page.

2. With CSS you have the potential of having multiple styles for the same HTML element. If rules exist for the same property of the HTML element, the rules are applied using the following order: inline style (with HTML tag), internal style sheet, external style sheet, and finally the browser default. In other words, if the rule exists in the inline style, that is the rule that is applied for that property—regardless of what the rule in the internal style sheet states.

3. In order to modify the value of a specific HTML element you must access the element by its ID attribute. Therefore, for each HTML element that you want to be dynamic, you must add an ID attribute to the corresponding HTML tag. You can access the HTML element using the `getElementById` method.

Exercises

1. Create a Web page that scrolls text or images vertically on the page.
2. Create a Web site that has a dynamic menu that displays across the top of the page. Try adding a description of the menu link to the status bar.

DAY 12

Windows and Frames

The Window object is the top-most, or main, object in each browser. Consequently, all other objects are child objects of the Window object. In this chapter, we will look at the Window object and how it compares to the Frame object. We will see that frames are nothing more than a method for displaying multiple windows within one browser window; however, each frame is independent.

We will also look at several aspects of the Window object, and how they can be accessed from JavaScript. These elements are the Location object, the History object, and the Window object methods for displaying popups. We will also look at how to make changes to the status line of your window.

This chapter will teach you

- What windows and frames are
- How to determine window location
- How to work with the window history
- How to work with the status line
- How to use the Screen object

- How to work with frames
- How to work with popups

What Are Windows and Frames?

You are used to hearing the word "window." After all, the word appears in the name of every Microsoft operating system. If you remember our discussion of objects in Chapter 4, "JavaScript Is Object-Based," you know that with JavaScript the Window object represents the browser window. In other words, it is the main object and all other objects are children of the Window object. The Window object contains three different objects—the Document object (discussed in Chapter 11, "Dynamic HTML," which contains all other page elements), the Location object, and the History object (each of which will be discussed in this chapter).

A frame, on the other hand, is very similar to a window. In fact, it is essentially a separate window in your browser window. By using frames you can have multiple pages open simultaneously within your browser window. Each frame functions independently of the other frames on the page. Therefore, because each frame contains all the properties of a window, each frame is considered to be a Window object. Figure 12.1 illustrates how two frames can display within one browser window.

FIGURE 12.1

Frames are often used to display multiple documents on one page.

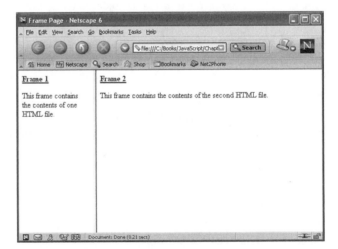

We will delve into frames in more detail later in this chapter. First let's look at windows in a little more detail.

Because JavaScript treats each frame as a separate window, you will see later that dealing with multiple windows and frames can get a little confusing. In order to keep track of each window and frame, you need to have a method of differentiating between them. The best method for doing so is to assign a window to a variable. That way, you can reference the appropriate window or frame based on its variable name.

```
first_window = window
```

Once you have assigned the window to the variable, you can reference the window from any location. By doing so you can make modifications to its properties.

Window Properties and Methods

Chapter 4 discussed the method of referencing properties and methods for an object. Just like all other objects, the `Window` object has its own properties and methods that you can use. Chapter 4 also discussed the fact that the standard notation for referencing an object's property or method is to specify the object name, a period, and the property name or method, as shown below:

```
window.close()
```

With JavaScript, the `Window` object is the default object. This means that if JavaScript encounters a property of a method that does not have an object specified, it automatically assumes that the property or method belongs to the `Window` object. Therefore, you can also specify a property or method without the object reference, shown as follows:

```
alert("Hi")
```

Also mentioned earlier was the fact that you could use a variable to reference a specific `Window` object, which is ideal when referencing another window or frame (as we will talk about later). However, JavaScript also provides a handy `self` property that you can use to ensure that the property and method calls are associated with the current window. To use this property, you simply type it, followed by the property or method you want to use, as shown below:

```
self.close()
```

The list of properties and methods that are associated with the `Window` object is quite extensive. Of course, as with other JavaScript objects, some methods and properties are browser-dependent and should probably be avoided when creating cross-browser code.

Probably the most common events you will use with the `Window` object are `open()` and `close()`. These methods allow you to open (create) new windows and close open windows.

12

Opening a Window

If you have done much work with HTML you know that opening a new window is a fairly simple task that you can accomplish by simply setting the `target` attribute of the <a href> HTML tag.

```
<a href="http://www.samspublishing.com" target="_blank">Sams Publishing</a>
```

With the above statement, the specified Web site is opened in a new window because we specified a value of _blank for the `target` attribute. In fact, with the `target` attribute you actually have the option of specifying which window receives the new document, as outlined in Table 12.1.

TABLE 12.1 Target Attributes for Opening a Window

Attribute	Description
_blank	Opens the specified Web page within a new window
_parent	Opens the specified Web page within the parent frame
_self	Opens the specified Web page within the current window or frame
_top	Opens the specified Web page within the current window, eliminating the existing frames

Another thing to be aware of is the fact you can also use the `target` attribute to not only load the Web page in a new window but also to assign a name to the window. By doing so, you are able to assign new Web pages to that same window using the same value for the `target` attribute. See example shown below:

```
<a href="http://www.samspublishing.com" target="sams">Sams Publishing</a>
```

Of course I am sure by now you are thinking this is all good HTML information, but what does it really have to do with JavaScript? I gave you these HTML basics and a foundation for what you can accomplish with the `open()` method of the `Window` object. Essentially you can use the `open()` method within your JavaScript code to open an HTML page in much the same fashion as using the <a href> tag. Actually, in practice, you have even more capability with this method than you do in HTML.

In order to use the `open()` method, there are basically two values you must specify: the URL of the file to open and the name of the window to open. For example, to open the Sams Publishing site, you would type the following:

```
window.open("http://www.samspublishing.com", "Sams");
```

When you call the open() method it actually returns a reference to the new window, so if you assign the open() method return value in a variable, you can reference the window later using the variable.

```
winvar = window.open("http://www.samspublishing.com", "Sams");
```

Besides specifying the window name, you can also specify the size and position of the browser window when it opens. By default, the new window opens as the same size as the default browser window. You can use the attributes in Table 12.2 to change the size and location of the new window.

TABLE 12.2 Positioning Attributes for the open() Method

Attribute	Description
height	Indicates the height of the new window in pixels
width	Indicates the width of the new window in pixels
left	The number of pixels from the left edge of the screen to the left edge of the window
top	The number of pixels from the top edge of the screen to the top edge of the window

For example, you can create a new window that is 300 pixels wide and 300 pixels high by typing the following:

```
winvar = window.open("http://www.samspublishing.com", "Sams", "height = 300,
width = 300");
```

NEW TERM You can also specify information about the appearance of the window, such as whether there are toolbars, scrollbars, and so forth displayed for the new window. These window features are commonly referred to as the *window chrome*. Table 12.3 lists the window chrome features that you can specify for the window.

TABLE 12.3 Window Chrome Features with the open() Method

Feature	Description
directories	Displays the Links bar in Internet Explorer, the Personal toolbar in Netscape 4.0 or later, or the Directory buttons in Netscape 2 and 3
location	Displays the Address box in Internet Explorer, or the Location box in Netscape (This feature only displays if the toolbar is also displayed.)
menubar	Displays the Menu bar
resizable	Indicates that the user can resize the window

12

TABLE 12.3   continued

Feature	Description
scrollbars	Displays vertical and horizontal scrollbars, if needed
status	Displays the status bar
toolbar	Displays the toolbar

By using these window chrome features you can easily customize how a particular window displays. For example, if you pop up a page in a separate window, you may want to eliminate the navigational ability within that window by removing the Address box. The code in Listing 12.1 illustrates how to customize the appearance of the window by allowing the user to select the desired window chrome features.

INPUT   **LISTING 12.1**   Opening a Custom Window (openwindow.htm)

```
<html>
<head>
<title>Open Window</title>
<script language="JavaScript" type =" text/javascript">
<!--
function ChangeLink(currentform)
{
var window_feature = "";

for (var cb=0; cb<currentform.length - 1; cb++) {
if (currentform[cb].checked)
{
 currentform[cb].value = 1;
}
else
{
 currentform[cb].value = 0;
}
 window_feature = (window_feature + "," + currentform[cb].name + "="
➥+ currentform[cb].value);
}
window.open("http://www.samspublishing.com", "_blank", window_feature);
}
//..>
</script>
</head>
<body>
<form name="form1">
➜><input type="checkbox" name="directories" value="0">Directories Option</p>
  <p><input type="checkbox" name="location" value="0">Location Option</p>
```

LISTING 12.1 continued

```
    <p><input type="checkbox" name="menubar" value="0">Menu Bar</p>
    <p><input type="checkbox" name="resized" value="0">Allow Window to
be Resized</p>
    <p><input type="checkbox" name="scrollbars" value="0">Scrollbars</p>
    <p><input type="checkbox" name="status" value="0">Status Bar</p>
    <p><input type="checkbox" name="toolbar" value="0">Toolbar</p>
    <p><input type="button" value="Create Window" name="CreateWin"
onClick="ChangeLink(this.form)"></p>
</form>
</body>
</html>
```

ANALYSIS If you notice we use a `for` loop to cycle through the checkboxes on the form and to build the `window_feature` string, indicating the window options to display. Since there are actually eight options on the form, seven checkboxes and one button, we subtracted one from the `length` property value to ignore that form field. The user selects the checkboxes corresponding to the desired window properties, as shown in Figure 12.2. When the button is clicked the new window opens as specified.

OUTPUT

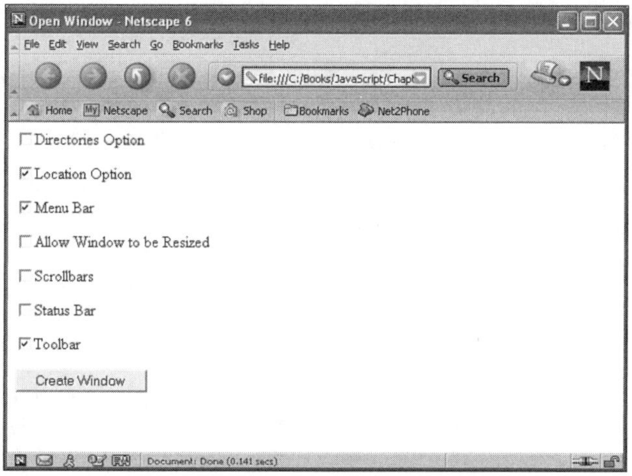

FIGURE 12.2

Use the Window Chrome features to customize the look of the window you want to open.

12

Closing a Window

Of course if you can open a window, you also need the ability to close a window. You can close a window from JavaScript using the `close()` method. To close the current window, you would use the following code:

```
window.close()
```

When your command executes, the current browser window will close. Typically though, you are going to want to close yet another window with this command. In order to do this, the window you want to close needs to be referenced. The easiest method is to assign the statement that opens the window to a variable. As mentioned in the previous section, this gives the variable a reference to the specified window thereby allowing you to reference the window at any point to close it, as shown below:

```
ourwindow = window.open("http://www.microsoft.com/");
ourwindow.close();
```

You should be aware that JavaScript has a `closed` property for each `Window` object. When a window closes, the `closed` property is set to `True`. If the window is still open, the `closed` property is set to `False`. You can use this property to determine whether or not you need to close a window. You should also be aware that the property returns a `null` value if the window was never opened.

Determining Window Location

In terms of JavaScript and the `Window` object, location simply specifies the URL, or location of the Web page that displays in the window. There are two methods to work with the window location:

- Use the `Location` property of the `Window` object. For example, to set the location of a window called mywindow you type the following: `mywindow.location = "http://www.netscape.com";`

- Use the `Location` object to set or return the URL information using the `Location` object properties discussed in Table 12.4. For example, you would type the following to set the window location using the `Location` object:
  `mywindow.location.href = "http://www.netscape.com";`

> **Note**
>
> It may seem a little odd that there is a `Location` property for the `Window` object and a `Location` object. This is not at all unusual. In fact the `Location` property of the `Window` object actually loads the `Location` object with the specified URL. Essentially, each child object of an object is actually a property of the same object.

As we just specified, the `Location` object represents the actual URL for the page. Although the `Location` object only contains a URL, it does have several properties you can use to examine parts of the URL, as outlined in Table 12.4.

TABLE 12.4 Location Object Properties

Property	Description
hash	The name of the anchor specified in the URL address. The anchor value is the portion of the address that follows the hash sign (#). Anchors are typically set to jump to a specific location on a page, such as #top.
host	The host name and the port used to communicate with the server
hostname	The host name of the server
href	The entire URL address
pathname	The directory path and filename of the document
port	The port used by the browser to communicate with the server
protocol	The protocol used for communication between the browser and the server (Common protocols are http and ftp.)
search	The portion of the URL that contains the search string. This is the value that follows a ? in the URL

So, you can change the URL displayed by an open window by either using the window.location property or the Location.href property. Actually, when you do use Window.location to change the URL, JavaScript is actually just changing the href property of the corresponding Location object. For example, the code in Listing 12.2 illustrates how to change the URL displayed in one frame to the value specified by the user in the other frame. Keep in mind working with frames will be discussed in more detail later in this chapter.

INPUT **LISTING 12.2**   Changing the Window URL (changelocation.htm)

```
<html>
<head>
<script language="JavaScript" type = "text/javascript">
<!--
function changeLocation()
{
parent.frames[1].location = document.form1.NewURL.value;
}
//..>
</script>
</head>
<body>
<title>Specify URL</title>
</head>
<body>
```

12

LISTING 12.2   continued

```
<form name="form1">
   <input type="text" name="NewURL" size="50">
   <input type="button" value="Change URL" name="URLButton"
onclick = "changeLocation()"></p>
</form>
</body>
</html>
```

ANALYSIS   You will notice that we use the href property of the Location object to set the
URL for the second frame, as shown in Figure 12.3. Keep in mind, the href
property is the default property for the Location object. Therefore, it is not necessary to
specify the property name. In fact, if you omit it, JavaScript automatically applies the
changes to that property.

OUTPUT

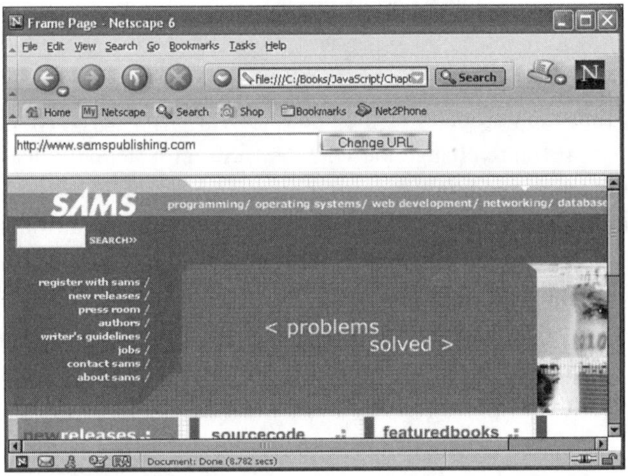

FIGURE 12.3

The Location *object
maintains the URL
information for the
window.*

The Location object also has three methods that you can use: the assign() method, the
reload() method, and the replace() method. Each method is fairly easy to use.

Remember there are two methods that you can use to assign a URL. You can either use
the Location property of the Window object or set the href property of the Location
object. Whichever method you decide to use, JavaScript uses the assign() method to
assign the new URL to the browser window. You can also use this method, if desired, but
it is not necessary. To use it, you simply specify the new URL, as follows:

```
location.assign("http://www.netscape.com");
```

You can use the `reload()` method to reload the current page in the browser. This is basically the same as selecting the Refresh or Reload option within the browser. The only difference is that you can specify whether the page reloads from the browser cache or from the server using the optional Source attribute, as follows:

```
location.reload
```

By default, the `reload()` method simply reloads the specified page from the browser cache. This means that the page loads much faster; it also means that any changes to the page will not be reflected when it is reloaded. If you want to force the page to reload from the server, you need to specify a value of `True` for the Source attribute, as shown below:

```
location.reload(true)
```

By reloading the page from the server, you are ensured that the visitor will see the most current version of the page.

The other method available with the `Location` object is the `replace()` method. This method allows you to change the page that displays when the user clicks the Back button. This may sound like an odd behavior, but have you ever visited a Web site where the page did not load properly when you clicked the Back button on the browser? When the Back button is clicked you can choose whether to display a customized page or the default page displays by using the following code:

```
location.replace(www.microsoft.com/default.htm);
```

When you use this method, the page you specify replaces the current page in the history list—that is, when the Back button is pressed, this is the page that will display. We are going to talk more about the window history in the next section.

12

Working with Window History

As you are probably aware, the browser window maintains a history of the pages that have been viewed during the current session. This information is stored in the `History` object. From the browser window you can scroll back and forth through the history list using the Back and Forward buttons.

In the previous section, we looked at how you can modify the page that displays when the Back button is clicked. In addition, you can also use the methods associated with the `History` object to move through the history list. There are three different methods that you can use with the `History` object, as outlined in Table 12.5.

TABLE 12.5   History Object Methods

Method	Description
back()	Moves back through the history list from the current position. Simulates the Back button on the browser.
forward()	Moves forward through the history list from the current position. Simulates the Forward button on the browser.
go()	Moves forward or backward within the history list. A negative number moves backward through the list the specified number of pages and a positive number moves forward. If you specify a value of zero, the current page refreshes.

Keep in mind that if the history does not exist in the direction you specify with these methods, the browser remains on the current page.

As you can see from Table 12.5, the go() method provides the most flexibility by allowing you to jump to any page within the history list. For example, you can create your own back link to move back two pages in the history list, as follows:

```
<a href="javascript:void(0)" onclick="history.go(-2)">Return to Main Page</a>
```

Again, this code causes the browser to display the page that displayed two pages prior to the current page. This allows you to customize how the user moves through the history. By the same token, you may want the movement within the list to display a specific page, which can be accomplished by specifying a URL. For example, the following code would jump to the default page for Microsoft:

```
<a href="javascript:void(0)" onclick="history.go(http://www.microsoft.com)>
 Return to Home Page</a>
```

You need to keep in mind that if you specify a URL for the go() method, the URL must be within the history list or the browser will remain on the current page.

> **Note**   Be aware that you cannot access URLs that are listed in the history list. You can simply scroll through the list by going back and forward.

Working with the Status Line

Earlier in this chapter, when the window chrome features were introduced that can be specified for the Window object, we looked at how to specify whether or not the status bar would display at the bottom of the window. The status bar normally contains messages related to the page being viewed. For example, the status bar displays the URL when you drag your mouse cursor across a link. You also can place custom messages in the status bar by using the Status property of the Window object.

To put a message in the status bar, you simply set the value of the status property equal to the message you want to display, as follows:

```
status ="Welcome to our Web Site";
```

Notice that although the property is associated with the Window object, as we discussed at the beginning of the chapter, it is not necessary to use the Window object reference with the properties because JavaScript automatically assumes that the property belongs to the Window object.

Keep in mind, the message will display on the status bar until a new message is assigned to the status bar, either by you or the browser. With that in mind, look at the code in Listing 12.3, which displays information about links in the status bar when the mouse cursor drags across the link.

INPUT   **LISTING 12.3**   Changing the Status Bar Message (statusmsg.htm)

```
<html>
<head>
<script language="JavaScript" type = "text/javascript">
<!--
function StatusMsg(LinkURL, LinkDesc)
{
if (LinkURL == "")
{
 status = " "
}
else
{
status = ("Visit " + LinkDesc + " at " + LinkURL)
}
return true
}
//..>
</script>
</head>
<body>
<title>Change Status Message</title>
</head>
<body>
<p><a href = "http://www.microsoft.com"
   onmouseover = "return StatusMsg(this.href, 'Microsoft')"
   onmouseout = "return StatusMsg('','')">Microsoft</a></p>
```

12

LISTING 12.3   continued

```
<p><a href = "http://www.netscape.com"
   onmouseover = "return StatusMsg(this.href, 'Netscape')"
   onmouseout = "return StatusMsg('','')">Netscape</a></p>
<p><a href = "http://www.samspublishing.com"
   onmouseover = "return StatusMsg(this.href, 'Sams Publishing')"
   onmouseout = "return StatusMsg('','')">Sams</a></p>
</body>
</html>
```

ANALYSIS   If you look at the code in Listing 12.3, you will notice that at the end of the
StatusMsg function there is a `return true` statement. When using the status
property with the `onMouseOver` event, you must use the return statement in order for your
JavaScript to function properly. Although it is rare to use the return statement with your
JavaScript code, in this instance it is necessary. When the user drags the cursor across a
link the message in the status bar changes to describe where the link goes, as shown in
Figure 12.4.

OUTPUT

FIGURE 12.4

*You can change the
status bar message
using the* status
property.

The code to change the status bar message is typically quite short and, therefore, it is
typically included in only the `<a href>` tag. Doing so eliminates the need to create a
separate JavaScript function. Although, if you do, you need to make sure you include
both the code to set the status bar message and the `return true` statement discussed
above. To do so, you need to separate each statement with a semicolon as illustrated in
this code:

```
<a href = "http://www.netscape.com" onmouseover = "window.status =
'Visit Netscape at: ' + this.href ; return true">
```

When you open most pages the status bar is typically empty. This is because the default status bar message is blank. You can customize the default message that displays when other messages are not displayed by using the `defaultstatus` property. You set this property in the same fashion that the `status` property was set earlier:

```
defaultstatus = "Welcome to this JavaScript site";
```

When you have the `defaultStatus` property specified in your code, the text specified for the property displays anytime another message is not displayed on the status bar. If another message displays, as soon as that message finishes, the default message displays again.

Using the Screen Object

In addition to the browser that the visitor to your site is using, the other issue to keep in mind is the screen resolution. Although most developers have learned to run high resolutions to provide more screen space, many visitors run much lower resolutions. So the main issue becomes determining at what screen size to code your page. If you go with the lowest common denominator, 640 x 480, everyone can view the site; however, you are greatly limited to the amount of stuff that you can place on the screen, and visitors with higher resolutions will see a lot of white space on the right side of the browser window. Luckily, there is a way to get the resolution information and adjust your code as desired.

Note Keep in mind that creating a site that looks good at a higher resolution does not keep a lower resolution browser from visiting your site. It simply means that those visitors will not see as much on the page without scrolling.

12

In order to get the resolution information for the visitor's screen, you need to access the properties of the `Screen` object. All of these properties, listed in Table 12.6, are read-only and therefore you cannot change the properties; however, you can adjust your own HTML page code to fit within the parameters.

TABLE 12.6 Screen Object Properties

Property	Description
availHeight	Indicates the maximum height of the viewing monitor in pixels
availWidth	Indicates the maximum width of the viewing monitor in pixels
colorDepth	Indicates the bits per pixel

TABLE 12.6 continued

Property	Description
height	The actual height of the monitor in pixels
width	The actual width of the monitor in pixels

The availHeight and availWidth measurements indicate the maximum size of the browser window. As you are aware, on most operating systems there are other elements that require part of the screen space, such as the toolbar on a Microsoft Windows operating system.

For example, with the use of these properties you can create JavaScript code that automatically resizes the browser window to fill the screen, as follows:

```
Window.moveTo(0,0);
Window.resizeTo(screen.availWidth, screen.availWidth);
```

Notice the resizeTo() method was used to change the size of the current browser window. We also used the moveTo() method because we wanted to move the browser window to the upper-lefthand corner of the screen before resizing it. That way, the window will appear to cover all available space.

You can of course create code for different resolutions, and then the appropriate code based upon the screen settings. For example, you can use if statements to check screen resolution and then execute appropriate code, as shown in Listing 12.4.

INPUT **LISTING 12.4** Checking Screen Resolution (checkresolution.htm)

```
<html>
<head>
<script language="JavaScript" type = "text/javascript">
<!--
if (screen.width == 640)
  {
   alert("Resolution is 640 by 480");
  }
else if(screen.width == 800)
    {
     alert("Resolution is 800 by 600");
    }
else if (screen.width == 1024)
    {
     alert("Resolution is 1024 by 768");
    }
else if (screen.width > 1024)
  {
```

LISTING 12.4 continued

```
    alert("Resolution is greater than 1024 by 768");
  }
//..>
</script>
</head>
<body>
</body>
</html>
```

Notice in Figure 12.5 that we display a different message depending upon the screen resolution. Remember, although 640 x 480 is considered to be the lowest resolution, there are probably going to be even higher resolution monitors developed which you may need to bear in mind as you write your code.

OUTPUT

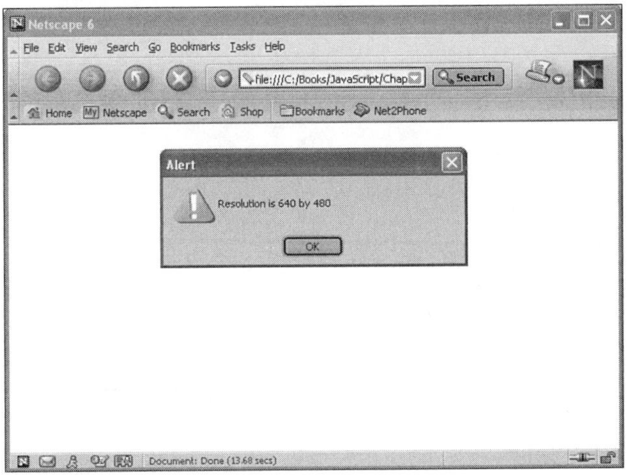

FIGURE 12.5

You can use the Screen *object's properties to determine the resolution of the visitor's monitor.*

12

As you can see, there are multiple methods you can use to set up your code to best utilize the visitor's screen size. Again, this type of coding does not affect the ability of your JavaScript code to run, but it does affect how it appears on the screen.

Working with Frames

Since you are learning JavaScript, you probably have heard of frames—especially if you have done much work with HTML. Frames provide the ability to create the appearance of multiple windows in one browser window. In other words, by using frames you are able to display multiple pages in one browser window each within its own frame, and

each frame is totally independent of the other frames in the browser
window. The user of frames is illustrated in Figure 12.1, shown earlier in this chapter.

Although frames were incredibly popular three or four years ago, they have lost their
popularity among many Web developers and users. There are different reasons for this, in
particular the difficulty of printing an entire Web page. Even so, they are still a great way
to layout a Web page and maintain navigation buttons and other pertinent information in
the same location on screen. For example, if you want a column of buttons displayed on
the left side of the window that will remain there no matter what direction the user
scrolls, frames are the only method to accomplish this.

Before looking at how you can manipulate the contents of frames using JavaScript, let's
review some basic frame technology to clarify our discussion.

In order to use frames you must first have an HTML page that defines the frame layout
using the `<frameset>` tag. The `<frameset>` tag describes how the frames are laid out on
the page, as shown in Listing 12.5.

INPUT   **LISTING 12.5**   Defining the Frame Layout (`framepage.htm`)

```
<html>
<head>
<title>Frame Page</title>
</head>
<frameset cols="25%,75%">
  <frame src="frame1.htm" name="frame1">
  <frame src="frame2.htm" name="frame2">
</frameset>
</html>
```

ANALYSIS   Each frameset defines the layout using multiple rows or columns. For example,
in Listing 12.5 there are two columns and the first column takes up 25% of the
browser window, while the second column takes the remaining 75%. You can also define
the size of the row or column as an exact pixel size, or you can use * to let the browser
set its size.

Note   The layout of the frameset can become very complex in that you can create
nested framesets. For example, you can create a frameset with two columns
and then break one column into three rows.

Each frameset contains at least one <frame> tag that defines the contents of the frame. The frame always has a src attribute that specifies the URL of the page to display in the particular frame. There are also some other attributes that you can use when defining the frame, as outlined in Table 12.7. Later in this section we will discuss how you can also change the values of these attributes using JavaScript.

TABLE 12.7   Frame Attributes

Property	Description
frameborder	Specifies whether or not a border displays for the frame. A value of 1 displays the frame and 0 hides the frame.
marginheight	Indicates the pixel size of vertical margins within the frame.
marginwidth	Indicates the pixel size of the horizontal margins within the frame.
name	Indicates the name of the frame. This is needed so you can reference the frame within your JavaScript code.
noresize	A value of true allows the user to resize the frame; whereas, specify false if the frame should not be resized.
scrolling	Specifies whether scrolling is allowed in the frame. Specify a value of yes to allow scrolling; specify no, if scrolling should not be allowed, or auto to let the browser determine if scrolling is needed.
src	Indicates the URL of the file to display in the frame.

Note

> If you look at the frameset and frames in a slightly different approach, you will see that the frameset is the parent window and each frame is a child window. Keep this in mind when we discuss referencing different frames.

12

Unfortunately there are still instances where the user may have a browser that does not support frames. This is very possible with the many new mobile devices coming to market. If so, you need to have a way to catch and redirect those users to other code. This can be accomplished using the <noframes></noframes> tag pair. You add the <noframes> tag to your frameset definition so that the browser knows what command to execute if frames are not supported.

```
<frameset cols="25%,75%">
  <frame src="frame1.htm" name="frame1">
  <frame src="frame2.htm" name="frame2">
  <noframes>Your browser does not support frames</noframes>
</frameset>
```

Finally, let's discuss one more frame element—the inline frame, which is indicated by the `<iframe>` tag.

INPUT

```
<iframe src = "http://www.microsoft.com"></iframe>
```

The inline frame is used to place a frame on an HTML page, as shown in Figure 12.6, which shows a single inline frame placed on an HTML page.

OUTPUT

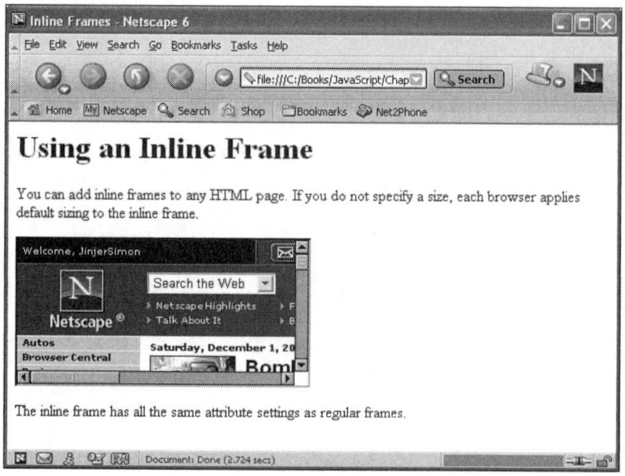

FIGURE 12.6

You can use inline frames on HTML pages where you want to insert the contents of a single page.

Keep in mind that you can use all of the attributes listed in Table 12.7 to customize the look of your inline frame.

Now that we have covered the basics of working with frames, let's look at the process of working with frames in JavaScript. As discussed at the beginning of this chapter, frames are essentially just windows and therefore you are going to see a lot of the same processes that were discussed early on in this chapter.

As mentioned earlier, just like the other elements of the HTML page, frames have a tree-like hierarchy. But, because frames are essentially just windows, when you use frames the frameset is the parent window and each frame it references is a child window. Actually, the parent window, or frameset, has a Frames property that contains an array of the child frames. By using the frames array, you can reference each frame in the order in which it is listed in the frameset with the first frame referenced as frame[0]. This being the case, you can reference a frame using either the frame name or the frames array. For example, look at the following frameset code:

```
<frameset cols="25%,75%">
  <frame src="frame1.htm" name="frame1">
  <frame src="frame2.htm" name="frame2">
  <noframes>Your browser does not support frames</noframes>
</frameset>
```

From the frameset page, you would reference the first frame as either `frame1` or `frame[0]`. From the child frame you can reference the parent window, or frameset, simply as `parent`. Probably the bigger issue becomes the ability to reference another child frame from the current child frame. In order to do this you will need to reference the parent window. So, with our sample code `frame1`, you can reference `frame2` by one of the following two methods:

```
parent.frame2
```

```
parent.frames[1]
```

There are a couple of properties that you should keep in mind when dealing with frame references. The `self` property allows you to reference the current frame. For example, you can type `self.parent` to refer to the `parent` frame; or as was mentioned earlier, simply `parent`. In most cases, the `self` property is not needed, but using it helps clarify your point of reference.

Another property that you need to keep in mind is the `top` property. This property refers to the top window object in the browser. This property comes in handy when you have nested loops because it allows you to back up to the top window and then specify your reference.

Keep this hierarchical structure in mind as we look at changing properties of different frames in the rest of this section.

Referencing Frame Locations

As already discussed, you specify the location or URL of the page in order to display in a frame part of the frameset definition in HTML.

```
<frame src="frame1.htm" name="frame1">
```

The HTML definition of the frame contents works well for initially loading the window. Typically, however, you will want to update your Web pages dynamically by changing the content of one or more frames within your JavaScript code. As with all window objects, the URL information for each frame is stored in the `Location` object. Therefore, to change the contents of the current frame, you would specify the following:

```
location = URL
```

12

URL is the address of the page to display in the current frame. For example, to display another file on the same Web server, you would simply specify the filename, as follows:

```
location = "menu2.htm"
```

Although when dealing with frames, you typically will want to change the contents of another frame. For example, you may have a list of sites in one frame and when you click on a link the contents of the second frame change. If the frame containing the menu is the first frame, a change to the URL displayed in the second frame would be accomplished by typing the following:

```
parent.frame[1].location = "http://www.netscape.com"
```

Of course, if you know the name of the frame, you can also write this statement as follows, which uses frame2 as the second frame name:

```
parent.frame2.location = "http://www.netscape.com"
```

As seen earlier, when you only have one line of JavaScript code to execute, you can also add the code to the corresponding HTML tag. For example, you can specify the following code to change the contents of the second frame:

```
<a href="javascript:void(0)" onclick="parent.frame[1].location =
"http://www.netscape.com">Netscape</a>
```

As you can see, you can change the contents of a frame fairly simply, as long as you understand the tree-structure that JavaScript follows to locate each frame. When you use this structure, you can change one frame or multiple frames simultaneously, as shown in Listing 12.6.

INPUT   **LISTING 12.6**   Changing Multiple Frames (ChangeFrame1.htm)

```
<html>
<head>
<script language="JavaScript" type = "text/javascript">
<!--
function changeLocation()
{
top.frame2.location.href = document.form1.NewURL1.value;
top.frame3.location.href = document.form1.NewURL2.value;
}
//..>
</script>
</head>
<body>
<title>Specify URL</title>
</head>
<body>
```

LISTING 12.6   continued

```
<form name="form1">
    Left Frame: <input type="text" name="NewURL1" size="40"><br>
    Right Frame: <input type="text" name="NewURL2" size="40">
<input type="button" value="Change URLs" name="URLButton"
onclick = "changeLocation()"></p>
</form>
</body>
</html>
```

As with any frames, you must have a frameset page. For the code in Listing 12.6, we have a frameset page made up of two nested framesets, as shown in Listing 12.7.

INPUT   LISTING 12.7   Nested Frames (Changeframesmain.htm)

```
<html>
<head>
<title>Changing Frames</title>
</head>
<frameset rows="20%,80%">
  <frame src="changeframe1.htm" name="frame1">
  <frameset cols = "50%,50%">
    <frame src="changeframe2.htm" name="frame2">
    <frame src="changeframe3.htm" name="frame3">
 </frameset>
</frameset>
</html>
```

Because the frames are nested, we refer to the frames with URL locations we want to change by starting with the top property to reference the very top window. The bottom two frames are updated to reflect the specified URLs, as shown in Figure 12.7.

You can change the URL displayed in multiple frames simultaneously. As you can see, it is fairly easy to change the URL of the page displayed in each frame. You just need to be careful that you reference the frame correctly. One potential problem when referencing frames is the fact that another site can load your site within its own frames. To avoid any potential reference problems, you can create code that breaks your site out of another site's frames, as described in the next section.

12

FIGURE 12.7

Breaking Out of Frames

One common feature of many sites is to open another URL within existing frames. This process keeps the visitor on your site with a frame displaying the other URL. This is similar to what we did in Figure 12.7, where we displayed two different sites, Netscape and Microsoft, on the same page simultaneously, while the top frame displayed content from our own site.

Although this is a cool feature, especially for the main site, it can become quite cumbersome, especially when you have more frames inside of those frames. Also, it can become a nuisance for your own JavaScript code to run within the frame of another site, because now when you reference the top frame, you are actually referencing a frame on another site.

To eliminate any potential issues, you can add code to your site to break out of frames from the site that called your page. This code is fairly simple, and you can use it whether or not you are using frames on your site. In fact, by doing so, you can ensure that your site never appears as a frame in another site.

To break out of frames from another site, you simply need to add the following code to the pages on your site.

```
if (top != self)
{
 top.location = self.location;
}
```

Of course, this statement also will break up frames on your own site. Therefore, if you are using frames on your own site, you will need to modify the code slightly to ensure that your main frame page becomes the top page, as outlined in the next section.

Forcing Frames

Once you set up frames for your Web site, you will want to ensure that the frames always load when people visit your site. This typically isn't an issue when they access your default page, but if they access your site using a link from a search page, it is possible that they will access a non-frameset page. To ensure that they see the frames, you can add code to the top of the page to ensure that the frames display.

```
if (top == self)
{
 top.location = "default.htm";
}
```

The above code works great for ensuring that the visitor sees the main page of your Web site. More than likely though, they will lose the link to the page where they entered your site and now will be forced to relocate it. So, in an ideal world, you would design your code to open the frames and display the page that was specified when your site was accessed in the appropriate frame. Of course, this takes a little more complex coding, but once you place this code on each page your site maintains a consistent look and feel. For example, Listing 12.8 illustrates the type of code you would place in each frame page to call the main frameset page.

INPUT   **LISTING 12.8**   Forcing Frames (`loadframepage.htm`)

12

```
<html>
<head>
<script language="JavaScript" type = "text/javascript">
<!--
if (top==self)
{
    var main_frame = "mainframepage.htm";
    var cur_url = self.location.href;
    var setframes = main_frame + "?" + cur_url;
    location.href = setframes;
}
//-->
</script>
</head>
<body>
<h1>Frame Page</h1>
This page loads within Main Frame page.
</body>
</html>
```

Notice that we created a search string to pass the URL of the current page into the main frameset page. When the frameset page, illustrated in Listing 12.9, receives the search string it places the specified URL in the appropriate frame.

INPUT   **LISTING 12.9**   Main Frame Page (`mainframepage.htm`)

```
<html>
<head>
<script language="JavaScript" type = "text/javascript">
<!--
var frame_URL;
if (location.search)
{
    frame_URL = location.search.substring(1);
}
else {
    frame_URL = "changeframe2.htm";
}
{
 document.write("<frameset rows = '20%, 80%'>")
 document.write("  <frame src='frame1.htm'>")
 document.write("<frame src='" + frame_URL + "'>")
 document.write("  </frameset>")
}
//..>
</script>
</head>
<body>
</body>
</html>
```

ANALYSIS   The code on this page is designed so that the page can be accessed directly or from another page. In other words, if the page is not called from one of the pages on your site, a search string is not passed and the default page is opened in the second frame. Otherwise, the URL of the page that called the main frame page is opened in the second frame.

Now we should consider combining the code to break out of another site's frames and to force the frames thereby ensuring that the visitor gets the ideal visit. You can do this by adding the code we looked at in the previous section to the top of your frameset page.

This type of frame coding can get rather complex, especially if you start coding for nested frames. But once you master this type of coding you can ensure not only that frames display but also that you don't get trapped in someone else's frames.

Working with Popups

Earlier in this chapter we looked at how you can create windows that are specific sizes and control which window chrome displays on the window. This works well for loading a new page of information and maintaining the current browser open window. In fact, popup windows are commonly used on Web sites for displaying advertisement-type messages. You can create these types of popup windows fairly easily. For example, the code in Listing 12.10 creates a popup window that displays the text "Good Morning!"

INPUT   **LISTING 12.10**   Creating Popup Windows (popupwindow.htm)

```
<html>
<head>
<script language="JavaScript" type = "text/javascript">
<!--
function GreetingWin()
{
 DisplayGreeting = window.open("", "_blank", "toolbar=no, status=no,
width=200,height=200");
 greeting = "<b>Good Morning!</b>"
 DisplayGreeting.document.write(greeting);
}
//-->
</script>
</head>
<body>
<input type="button" value="Click Button" onclick="GreetingWin()">
</body>
</html>
```

12

As you can see in Figure 12.8, the code in Listing 12.10 creates a window that appears to popup as soon as the button is clicked on the page. You can also have windows that popup when a page loads, or when any other event occurs. Actually, the Window object provides three other built-in popup windows that you can use as needed for different situations. Each of these methods is easy to use, and also provides the ability to gather input from the user. In fact, we have already used the alert() method in several examples in the last few chapters to display popup messages. These three methods are outlined in Table 12.8.

FIGURE 12.8

You can create windows that appear to popup when a particular event occurs.

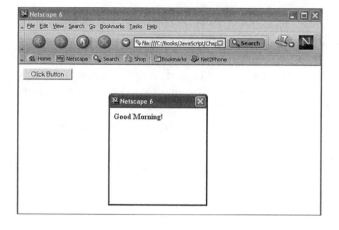

TABLE 12.8   Window Methods for Creating Popups

Method	Description
alert	Displays a message to the user in a popup window. The window contains one OK button, which can be used to close the window.
confirm	Displays a message in a popup window with a Yes and a No button. You can get the user's input and use it to determine which tasks to perform.
prompt	Displays a message in a popup window with a text field where the user can type a response. The popup window also includes an OK and a Cancel button.

To illustrate the difference between these three different popup windows, you can view the code in Listing 12.11, which uses the prompt() method to request the user's name, the confirm() method to verify, and then the alert()method to display a message.

INPUT   **LISTING 12.11**   Using Window Object Popup Methods (popupmethods.htm)

```
<html>
<head>
<script language="JavaScript" type = "text/javascript">
<!--
var username = prompt("Type your name:", "");

if (confirm("Your name is: " + username + ". Is that correct?") == true )
{
  alert("Hello " + username);
}
else
{
```

LISTING 12.11   continued

```
 alert("Hi");
}
//-->
</script>
</head>
</html>
```

ANALYSIS   As you can see, each of the three methods displays a different type of popup
window. We used an `if` statement to determine how to respond based on the button selected in the confirm popup, shown in Figure 12.9. If the user selects the OK button, then the alert method displays `"Hello"` and his name; otherwise the alert method
simply displays the message `"Hi"`.

OUTPUT

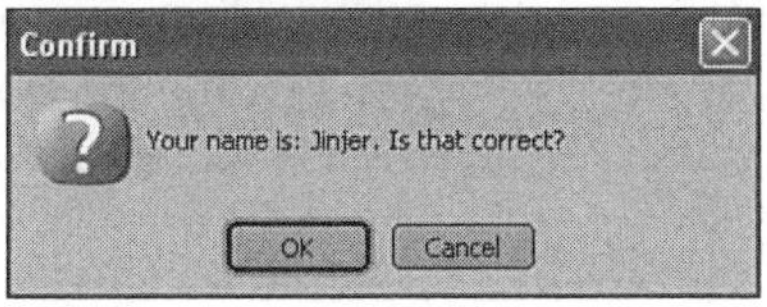

FIGURE 12.9

You can use the
`alert()`, `confirm()`,
and `prompt()` *meth-
ods as popups to
display and gather
values from the user.*

Summary

We have looked at many different elements of the `Window` and `Frame` objects in this
chapter. We found out that in reality a frame is just another window; unlike the original
concept we discussed where the `Window` object is the main object in the browser, and
all other objects are children. When you are using frames you have multiple `Window`
objects. Your main frameset window is the parent window and all other frames are child
windows.

We discussed how properties and methods can be applied to the current window or frame
by simply using the property or method without an object reference.

We looked at objects associated with the `Window` object, such as the `Location` object that
stores the URL information for the currently displayed page and the `History` object that
maintains a list of the pages viewed during the current session.

We looked at how the Screen object properties can be accessed to determine the resolution settings for the user's browser. We also showed how you can customize the messages that display on the status bar for the window.

Workshop

In the workshop today, we will use the questions and exercises to review what you have learned in this chapter about working with windows and frames.

Q&A

Q. Why should I use the Location object?

A. Every Window object has a corresponding Location object. This object maintains the URL or location information for the information displayed on the browser window. By changing the properties of the Location object, you can change the URL of the page that is being displayed. You can also use the methods associated with this object to reload the content displayed in the browser window.

Q. Do I really need to know what the user's resolution is?

A. The Screen object provides information about the resolution of the user's monitor. By determining the resolution used by the user you can execute resolution specific code so that your page displays optimized for that specific resolution. This means by knowing this information you can make sure you don't try to display something larger than the user's resolution settings. For example, if you have several frames on your page you need to make sure they can all display within the user's resolution settings.

Q. How do I access different frames on the page?

A. The frames property creates a frames array that stores references to each frame. The frames references are added to the array in the order in which they are listed in the frameset. You can reference a particular frame using the corresponding reference in the array. For example, to reference the first frame on the page you would use frame[0].

Quiz

1. How do you set the default status bar message that displays when no other messages are displayed on the status bar?

2. If you have the following frameset code, how would you reference and change the location for frame2 to display the page changeframe4.htm by making the call from the page displayed in frame1?

```
<html>
<head>
<title>Changing Frames</title>
</head>
<frameset rows="20%,80%">
  <frame src="changeframe1.htm" name="frame1">
      <frame src="changeframe2.htm" name="frame2">
      <frame src="changeframe3.htm" name="frame3">
</frameset>
</html>
```

3. What are the differences generated by the following popup methods: `alert()`, `confirm()`, and `prompt()`?

Quiz Answers

1. You can customize the default status bar message using the `defaultStatus` property. By setting this property, your default message displays on the status bar whenever there is not another message that needs to display in that location. You set the default status message by simply assigning the text value to the property: `defaultStatus = "text message"`.

2. To change the URL displayed by `frame2`, you need to reference the parent or top frame and then call the frame. You can either reference the frame by its name or by using the `Frames` array. Either one of these answers is correct.

   `parent.frame2.location = "changeframe4.htm"`

   `parent.frames[1].location = "changeframe4.htm"`

3. The `alert()` method simply allows you to create a popup window that displays a message to the user. This method does not expect any response from the user. The `confirm()` method creates a popup window and expects the user to provide a confirmation by selecting the appropriate button. The `prompt()` method displays a popup window containing a textbox where the user can type a value to return to your code.

Exercises

1. Create a Web page that requests the user's name, and then displays a custom greeting on the status bar.

2. Create a Web page with at least two frames. One frame should be a navigation menu that lists available pages on your Web site. When the user clicks a page, the corresponding page displays in the second frame. Be sure to add code for browsers that don't support frames.

12

DAY **13**

Regular Expressions Make It Easier

We looked at string manipulation and some simple validation of user input briefly in Chapter 6, "HTML Forms and the `String` Object," using some of the `String` object's methods. At that time we mentioned that the processing we could achieve could be very much enhanced by the use of regular expressions. This was not an overstatement. Regular expressions, properly used, are a very powerful tool for the manipulation of strings and for precise validation of form, and other, data. In this chapter, we will discover some of the important tasks regular expressions can perform and just how much work regular expressions can save you when programming in JavaScript.

This chapter will teach you

- Why regular expressions are useful
- What regular expressions are
- How regular expressions are created
- Several ways of using regular expressions

Why Regular Expressions Are Useful

There are many times when you might benefit from using regular expressions. However, if you were unaware of their existence, or unaware of how to use them, you could spend a lot of time creating a custom piece of programming to achieve an end that an appropriate regular expression could achieve much more quickly and much more easily.

Let's think about some real-world Web programming situations where you might find a regular expression useful. Suppose you have an e-commerce site where you want a customer to enter a credit card number, and you want to check if the credit card number is valid before you send it and the other form data to the server. One common structure for a credit card number is four groups of numerical digits, each of the four-digit groups with a space between each group. So, if you chose to have the user input in that format, the credit card number might look like the following:

```
1234 5678 9012 3456
```

If you wanted to conduct client-side validation of a credit card number how could you go about it? Your first thought might be to treat the credit card number as a large integer, but integers don't allow spaces between the numerical digits. Perhaps you might think of treating the credit card number as a string. If you treated it as a string how, with the JavaScript you have seen so far, would you be able to check the structure of the string? In theory you might be able to create a new function that checks each group of digits and whether or not they are in the range 0 to 9. To achieve that you would need many nested if and else statements. The logic would be fairly complex, and you would need to conduct extensive testing on your new code to make sure that you had allowed for all possible permutations of how a customer might enter a card number incorrectly.

Perhaps, after a lot of effort, you may have created a script which will correctly process credit card numbers that consist of four groups of four digits separated by space characters. Quite possibly soon after you think you have finished that task and the site goes online customer complaints flood in because some customers want to enter their credit card number as 16 consecutive digits without any spaces. And, perhaps you succeed in writing yet more if and else statements to enable the script to handle both possibilities. However, just when you are feeling proud of your achievements a manager comes along and tells you that not all credit cards are 16 digits and that you also need to allow for credit card numbers of different lengths. What do you do? Your code is getting pretty complex already. Oh, and remember to add in debit cards, which have yet another set of number constraints. At that stage, you could be forgiven for regretting the day you got involved with JavaScript Web programming at all.

Or suppose, for some confidential employment site, you need to collect personal identifiers such as a United States social security number (SSN) or a United Kingdom SSN, since your company has offices in both countries. How do you handle that? An American SSN is wholly numerical, while a UK SSN starts with two letters, has six numeric digits (usually in three groups of two), and a final letter. Adding code to check for one or both of those to the code you have created to accept credit card details is an intimidating task, particularly if you are not yet fully up to speed with JavaScript.

Regular expressions are designed to solve programming problems exactly like this. What regular expressions do is transfer part of the burden of processing text structures (similar to the ones we have just considered) from you (the JavaScript programmer) to a regular expressions processor within the JavaScript interpreter. When you use regular expressions the burden of writing the JavaScript code, and working out the logic it represents, is lifted from you. All you need to do is be capable of expressing exactly what *patterns* of string you designate as allowable. The JavaScript interpreter takes care of the *how* of making sure that the designated pattern is allowed and all undesirable patterns are disallowed.

Not surprisingly, a JavaScript interpreter must be given a very precise description of which patterns, or regular expressions, you want it to accept. So, let's move on and consider what a regular expression is and how you can express the idea of a string pattern using JavaScript.

What Is a Regular Expression?

A regular expression, if it were expressed in plain English, is a description of a pattern of characters in a string. If we tried to describe what we wanted for the credit card example, we might say: "We want a pattern of four numeric digits, followed by an optional space character, followed by four numeric digits, followed by an optional space character, followed by four numeric digits, followed by an optional space character, which is then followed by four numeric digits." As you can see it takes many words and quite a bit of space to express what we want.

A regular expression does the same thing. It is simply a collection of special characters which represent a pattern. A regular expression is much more compact than saying the same thing in English. Saving space is, in one sense, a good thing; but saving space involves using symbols, which can get in the way of understanding until you become thoroughly familiar with them. So we will look first at very simple regular expressions, and then build up to more complex (and more useful) regular expressions.

13

The pattern in a regular expression can be used to search a string for anything that matches the regular expression. The search could be for something very simple such as a certain name or number but simple tasks like that also could be done using the `indexOf()` method of the `String` object. The real power of regular expressions is the way they allow you to match something that is a pattern of characters rather than a literal sequence of characters.

For example, we can use methods of the `String` object to look for literal strings such as `"ABC"`. But the `String` object's methods don't allow us to carry out tasks such as "Search for three uppercase characters among A, B and C" which is a pattern that a regular expression could deal with easily.

Many scripters when they look at regular expressions for the first time find them very intimidating. This is probably because regular expressions look for a pattern, which is something that many scripters haven't had to program for in their previous experience. So the syntax is very unfamiliar. Regular expressions can, at first glance, appear to be an impenetrable mish-mash of seemingly random characters.

Although we can't deny that the more advanced uses of regular expressions can be pretty complex, simpler regular expressions are fairly easy to understand and write once you grasp the basics of the syntax. We are going to take them one step at a time. Hopefully, you will gradually pick up exactly how they work.

Let's look at what is arguably the simplest type of regular expressions—matching a sequence of literal characters.

Matching a Literal Character Sequence

As well as matching more abstract or complex patterns, JavaScript regular expressions also allow us to match single literal characters or sequences of literal characters.

For example, if you wanted to assign a JavaScript regular expression that matches the single literal alphabetic character "a" to the variable `myRegExp`, you could write this:

```
var myRegExp = /a/ ;
```

This syntax is similar to the assignment of a string to a variable:

```
var myString = "a" ;
```

When assigning a string, you use an opening quote mark, then the string, and then a closing quote mark. When you use a regular expression, you use an opening forward slash, /, followed by the pattern (in the example just shown, a single literal character), followed by a closing forward slash. All the text, or regular expression syntax (which we will look at soon), between the opening / and the closing / defines the pattern that the regular expression matches.

Listing 13.1 shows a simple use of a simple regular expression in a character-guessing task.

LISTING 13.1 The Regular Expression Matches a Single Lowercase "a" Only

INPUT (SingleCharGuess.htm)

```
<!DOCTYPE html
PUBLIC "-//W3C//DTD XHTML 1.0 Transitional//EN"
"DTD/xhtml1-transitional.dtd">
<html>
<head>
<title>Matching a single literal character</title>
<script type="text/javascript" language="javascript">
<!-- //
function IsMatchingChar(str){
var myRegExp = /a/ ;
return myRegExp.test(str)
} // end function IsMatchingChar()

function TestGuess(){
var guess = prompt("Enter a lower case character here and see if it matches",
 "It must be a lower case character");
if (IsMatchingChar(guess)){
alert("You guessed correctly. The correct answer was " + guess);
} // end if
else{
alert("Sorry " + guess + " doesn't match");
} // end else
}
// -->
</script>
</head>
<body>
<h3>This page allows you to guess a single literal lower case character</h3>
<form>
<button type="Button" onclick="TestGuess()">Click here to guess</button>
</form>
</body>
</html>
```

13

ANALYSIS In Listing 13.1 the user is invited, via a prompt box, to enter a single character to see whether it matches the character chosen by the program, in this example the single lowercase character "a".

The default behavior of a regular expression is that the pattern is case sensitive. Thus if you run Listing 13.1 you will find that you can enter the single lowercase character "a" and receive the message that you guessed the correct character. However, if you enter the uppercase character "A", you will receive a message that you guessed incorrectly, just as you would if you had entered a "b", a "c", or some other character that does not match the pattern /a/.

We can use longer literal strings using the same syntax. Thus, we could use the following in a Web page that asked the user to guess the FBI's most wanted man:

```
var mostWanted = /Osama Bin Laden/ ;
```

However, we also might want to allow for people to make a guess using the string, "Osama bin Laden" (lowercase for the initial letter of "bin", since the default behavior is that the pattern is case sensitive. We specify alternate literal strings of characters like this:

```
var mostWanted = /Osama Bin Laden|Osama bin Laden/ ;
```

The pipe character, "|", allows you to specify two or more options for a literal string that matches the regular expression.

Listing 13.2 shows how you can test for a long string of the type just shown and accept two possible literal strings as correct matches.

LISTING 13.2   Matching on More Than One Allowed Literal String (MostWanted.htm)

INPUT

```
<!DOCTYPE html
PUBLIC "-//W3C//DTD XHTML 1.0 Transitional//EN"
"DTD/xhtml1-transitional.dtd">
<html>
<head>
<title>FBI Most Wanted Person</title>
<script type="text/javascript" language="javascript">
<!-- //
function IsMatchingPerson(str){
var myRegExp = /Osama Bin Laden|Osama bin Laden/ ;
return myRegExp.test(str)
} // end function IsMatchingPerson()

function TestGuess(){
var guess = prompt("Enter a name here and see if it matches",
"It must be a full name");
if (IsMatchingPerson(guess)){
alert("You guessed correctly. " + guess + " was a correct answer");
```

LISTING 13.2   continued

```
} // end if
else{
alert("Sorry " + guess + " doesn't match");
} // end else
} // end function IsMatchingPerson()
// -->
</script>
</head>
<body>
<h3>This page allows you to guess the FBI's
most wanted person in Quarter 4 2001</h3>
<form>
<button type="Button" onclick="TestGuess()">Click here to guess</button>
</form>
</body>
</html>
```

ANALYSIS   If you run Listing 13.2 you will find that there are two, and only two, ways you can guess correctly. One correct string is `"Osama Bin Laden"` and the other is `"Osama bin Laden"`. If you try to enter a first name only, you will be told that there is no match, or if you try the alternate spelling "Usama Bin Laden" that won't match either.

Be careful that you don't leave a space character after the pipe character within the variable assignment:

```
var myRegExp = /Osama Bin Laden| Osama bin Laden/ ;
```

Adding an extraneous space character means that the JavaScript interpreter will only match the second string if it begins with a literal space character. Thus, when you provide multiple options using the literal syntax you must avoid space characters around the pipe character (unless, of course, you really want space characters to be there). This means that a list of many options can be quite difficult to read, for example:

```
var myRegExp = /Option1|Option2|Option3|Option4|Option5/ ;
```

13

Caution   JavaScript regular expressions behave a little differently from patterns in W3C XML Schema, for example. If you enter a space character at the beginning of the text in the prompt box, then a match will be declared. In a W3C XML Schema pattern that would not be a match because a space character does not match an initial uppercase "O". JavaScript appears to strip whitespace at the beginning of a literal string.

Some Simple Patterns

Let's move on to look at some simple patterns using regular expressions. First let's look at the simple case where we want to offer a choice of an uppercase or lowercase character.

Single Literal Character Choices

As you saw a moment ago, you could do this using the pipe character. So, to define a pattern for uppercase or lowercase "A" or "a" you could use the following code:

```
var myRegExp = /a|A/ ;
```

For the following example, let's use an alternate syntax to express the same choice:

```
var myRegExp = /[aA]/;
```

The square brackets express a choice of characters. In Listing 13.3, we use that syntax to allow the choice between an uppercase "A" and a lowercase "a". In a moment we will come to the advantages of the square bracket syntax.

INPUT　　**LISTING 13.3**　Allowing the Choice of Case in the Guess of a Single Character (`SingleCharGuess2.htm`)

```
<!DOCTYPE html
PUBLIC "-//W3C//DTD XHTML 1.0 Transitional//EN"
"DTD/xhtml1-transitional.dtd">
<html>
<head>
<title>Matching a single literal character</title>
<script type="text/javascript" language="javascript">
<!-- //
function IsMatchingChar(str){
var myRegExp = /[aA]/ ;
return myRegExp.test(str)
} // end function IsMatchingChar()

function TestGuess(){
var guess = prompt("Enter a character here and see if it matches",
"It can be either a lower or upper case character");
if (IsMatchingChar(guess)){
alert("You guessed correctly. The correct answer was " + guess);
} // end if
else{
alert("Sorry " + guess + " doesn't match");
} // end else
}
```

LISTING 13.3   continued

```
// -->
</script>
</head>
<body>
<h3>This page allows you to guess a single
 literal character of either case</h3>
<form>
<button type="Button" onclick="TestGuess()">Click here to guess</button>
</form>
</body>
</html>
```

ANALYSIS If you enter an "a" or "A" you will get a message indicating you successfully chose the correct matching character. If you choose other single characters, you will receive a message indicating that you made an incorrect guess.

If you tried to enter a multi-character string beginning with the correct character, then you will get a message (erroneously) indicating that you made a correct choice. Why is that? The reason behind the apparently incorrect behavior is that length of a string is an independent characteristic from the pattern. In other words, a pattern seeks a match for itself but also accepts longer matches which begin with the stated pattern. So, if you want to match a pattern and a length at the same time, you would need to test for the string length as well as whether it matches the regular expression. In the next example, we will add that length "error" trapping routine.

First let's look at how we can use the square brackets syntax in more complex examples.

Suppose you wanted to ensure that the identifier for a machinery part started with an alphabetic character. How could you do that? You could use the pipe character and add a total of 52 choices (assuming that all alphabetic characters were valid). The square bracket syntax allows a much more compact way of expressing those multiple choices. For example, you could write the following:

```
var myRegExp = /[a-zA-Z]/ ;
```

What that means is that any character starting with lowercase "a" through lowercase "z" (expressed by the characters a-z in the pattern) or starting at uppercase "A" through uppercase "Z" (expressed by the characters A-Z in the pattern) would be acceptable. In Listing 13.4, we will allow this to be tested, as well as testing for the desired length (in this case one character).

13

LISTING 13.4   Allowing Any Alphabetic Character in a String of One-
Character Length (AlphabeticOne.htm)

```
<!DOCTYPE html
PUBLIC "-//W3C//DTD XHTML 1.0 Transitional//EN"
"DTD/xhtml1-transitional.dtd">
<html>
<head>
<title>Matching a single literal character</title>
<script type="text/javascript" language="javascript">
<!-- //
function IsMatchingChar(str){
var myRegExp = /[aA]/ ;
return myRegExp.test(str)
} // end function IsMatchingChar()

function TestGuess(){
var guess = prompt("Enter a character here and see if it matches",
"It can be either a lower or upper case character");
if (IsMatchingChar(guess) && (guess.length==1)){
alert("You guessed correctly. The correct answer was " + guess);
} // end if
else if (guess.length!==1){
alert("Sorry you entered a character string of the wrong length");
}
else {
alert("Sorry " + guess + " doesn't match");
} // end else
}
// -->
</script>
</head>
<body>
<h3>This page allows you to guess a single
 literal character of either case</h3>
<form>
<button type="Button" onclick="TestGuess()">Click here to guess</button>
</form>
</body>
</html>
```

ANALYSIS   Notice the if, else if and else statements in the TestGuess() function. If the
text entered via the prompt box matches the pattern in the myRegExp variable and
is the correct length (one character), then a message is displayed indicating success. If
the length is incorrect, then that is indicated, no matter what the first character may be. If
you were using the pattern to test whether a string contained rather than consisted of the
pattern, then you would omit that part of the code. If the length is correct and the chosen
character is incorrect, then that is indicated.

We can use the same technique to allow the two options for the spelling of the name "Osama Bin Laden". A suitable regular expression is /Osama [Bb]in Laden/.

Choices Using Sequences of Literal Characters

Now let's take this one step further. Suppose we had a catalog of parts that used an uppercase alphabetic character as the first character and a single numeric character as the second character. If we used the pipe syntax, we would need 260 choices explicitly expressed. However, by using the square bracket syntax we need only write the following:

```
var myRegExp = /[A-Z][0-9]/
```

The syntax [A-Z] indicates that the first character is an uppercase character between A and Z. The syntax [0-9] indicates that any numeric character from 0 to 9 inclusive is acceptable as the second character. You can try this out in Listing 13.5. Remember that we now are accepting a two-character parts code such as A4, C9, or W3.

> **Note**
>
> When we group possible characters using syntax such as [A-Z] we are creating a new *character class*. In JavaScript character classes are not named. However, it is reasonable, for example, to refer to [A-Z] as the uppercase alphabetic character class or to refer to [0-9] as the numeric digits character class.

INPUT

LISTING 13.5 Combining Simple Character Classes in a Regular Expression Pattern (PartsCode.htm)

```
<!DOCTYPE html
PUBLIC "-//W3C//DTD XHTML 1.0 Transitional//EN"
"DTD/xhtml1-transitional.dtd">
<html>
<head>
<title>Matching a sequence of literal characters</title>
<script type="text/javascript" language="javascript">
<!-- //
function IsMatchingCode(str){
var myRegExp = /[A-Z][0-9]/ ;
return myRegExp.test(str)
} // end function IsMatchingCode()

function TestGuess(){
var guess = prompt("Enter a two character parts code here",
"Enter an upper case character followed by a number");
if (IsMatchingCode(guess) && (guess.length==2)){
```

13

LISTING 13.5   continued

```
alert("You chose a valid parts code: " + guess);
} // end if
else if (guess.length!==2){
alert("Sorry parts codes must be two characters long. Try again.");
}
else {
alert("Sorry " + guess + " doesn't match a valid parts code.");
} // end else
}
// -->
</script>
</head>
<body>
<h3>This page allows you to choose a two character parts code</h3>
<form>
<button type="Button" onclick="TestGuess()">Click here to guess</button>
</form>
</body>
</html>
```

ANALYSIS   In order to elicit the message that a string entered was correct the string must be exactly two characters in length, and it must have an uppercase alphabetic character as its first character and a numeric character as its second character.

We could use a similar approach if we wanted only characters A to M inclusive as the first character. In which case, we would define a new character class that contains only the uppercase alphabetic characters from A to M inclusive. The following code would express that:

```
var myRegExp = /[A-M][0-9]/ ;
```

Patterns That Use Numbered Occurrences of Classes

Let's move on and make it just a little more complex. Suppose we have a parts catalog that has a structure of two uppercase alphabetic characters, a dash, and three numeric characters. We can express that using the following syntax:

```
var myRegExp = /[A-Z]{2}-[0-9]{3}/ ;
```

The syntax [A-Z] indicates, as before, a choice from a character class of uppercase alphabetic characters. The syntax {2} indicates that we have a sequence of exactly two such uppercase alphabetic characters at the beginning of the pattern. The single "-" character indicates a literal dash. The syntax [0-9] indicates a choice from the numeric characters 0 to 9 inclusive, and the {3} indicates that we have exactly three such numeric characters.

In Listing 13.6 you can test this six-character code.

LISTING 13.6   A Pattern Combining Numbers of Characters from Defined
INPUT   Character Classes (`SixCharCode.htm`)

```
<!DOCTYPE html
PUBLIC "-//W3C//DTD XHTML 1.0 Transitional//EN"
"DTD/xhtml1-transitional.dtd">
<html>
<head>
<title>Matching sequences of more than one literal character</title>
<script type="text/javascript" language="javascript">
<!-- //
function IsMatchingCode(str){
var myRegExp = /[A-Z]{2}-[0-9]{3}/ ;
return myRegExp.test(str)
} // end function IsMatchingCode()

function TestGuess(){
var guess = prompt("Enter a six character parts code here",
"The format is two upper case letters, a dash and three numbers.");
if (IsMatchingCode(guess) && (guess.length==6)){
alert("You chose a valid parts code: " + guess);
} // end if
else if (guess.length!==6){
alert("Sorry parts codes must be six characters long. Try again.");
}
else {
alert("Sorry " + guess + " doesn't match a valid parts code.");
} // end else
}
// -->
</script>
</head>
<body>
<h3>This page allows you to choose a six character parts code</h3>
<form>
<button type="Button" onclick="TestGuess()">Click here to guess</button>
</form>
</body>
</html>
```

13

ANALYSIS   This technique of using numbers of characters from defined character classes
begins to open up solutions to some of the problems that were discussed earlier
in this chapter.

Let's look again at the 16-digit credit card number problem. The digits we use are all in
the character class represented by [0-9]. We saw from Listing 13.6 that we can mix

sequences of characters with literal characters. So we want to express a character class of numeric characters (of which there should be four) followed by a single space character, followed by four numeric digits, followed by a single space, followed by four numeric digits, followed by a single space, which is then followed by four numeric digits. Using a regular expression we can express that as follows:

```
var myRegExp = /[0-9]{4} [0-9]{4} [0-9]{4} [0-9]{4}/ ;
```

The syntax `[0-9]{4}` expresses the character class of numeric digits. The second part of the sub-expression, `{4}`, indicates that we use four successive characters from the numeric digits character class.

If we want to use that pattern to test a credit card number, then we must remember to check that the length is 19 characters long exactly. So Listing 13.7 will allow us to get part way to solving the credit card validation problem that we discussed earlier.

INPUT   **LISTING 13.7**   Validating a 16-Digit Credit Card Number Separated by Single Space Characters (`CreditCard01.htm`)

```
<!DOCTYPE html
PUBLIC "-//W3C//DTD XHTML 1.0 Transitional//EN"
"DTD/xhtml1-transitional.dtd">
<html>
<head>
<title>Matching a 16 digit credit card number
 separated by a single space</title>
<script type="text/javascript" language="javascript">
<!-- //
function IsMatchingCard(str){
var myRegExp =  /[0-9]{4} [0-9]{4} [0-9]{4} [0-9]{4}/;
return myRegExp.test(str)
} // end function IsMatchingCard()

function TestGuess(){
var cardNo = prompt("Enter a credit card number here",
"The format is 4 numbers, a space,
 4 numbers, a space, 4 numbers, a space, 4 numbers");
if (IsMatchingCard(cardNo) && (cardNo.length==19)){
alert("You entered a valid credit card number: " + cardNo);
} // end if
else if (cardNo.length!==19){
alert("Sorry you entered a credit card
 number of the wrong length. Try again.");
}
else {
alert("Sorry " + cardNo + " isn't a valid credit card number.");
} // end else
}
```

LISTING **13.7** continued

```
// -->
</script>
</head>
<body>
<h3>This page allows you to enter and check a 16 digit credit card number</h3>
<form>
<button type="Button" onclick="TestGuess()">
Click here to enter card number</button>
</form>
</body>
</html>
```

You also can use a similar technique to handle zip codes. To test for a standard zip code you could use the following syntax:

```
var myRegExp = /[0-9]{5}/ ;
```

The pattern indicates that five numeric digits make up the pattern.

If we want to accept zip codes only in the extended zip code format, we can use the following pattern:

```
var myRegExp = /[0-9]{5}-[0-9]{4}/ ;
```

The pattern indicates that there are five numeric digits, followed by a single literal dash followed by four numeric digits.

To accept both standard and extended zip codes, we would use the pipe character we used earlier, as shown here:

```
var myRegExp = /[0-9]{5}-[0-9]{4}|[0-9]{5}/ ;
```

Similarly, we can also now solve the United States SSN problem. In that case, we have three digits followed by a dash followed by two digits followed by a dash followed by four digits. So the following code would meet our need:

```
var myRegExp = /[0-9]{3}-[0-9]{2}-[0-9]{4}/ ;
```

If we want to be able to accept the format using dashes as well as accept the format simply using a sequence of digits we could use the following syntax, with the pipe character separating the two acceptable formats:

```
var myRegExp = /[0-9]{3}-[0-9]{2}-[0-9]{4}|[0-9]{9}/ ;
```

Not all the problems we might want to solve use a fixed numbers of characters chosen from particular sequences of characters. So let's move on to examine how we can use

13

(within a pattern) variable numbers of characters which are chosen from defined character classes that don't necessarily use sequences of characters.

Patterns Using Variable Numbers of Occurrences

We have made much progress in solving the problems discussed earlier. By adding syntax to allow for variable numbers of characters, we can add yet more power and flexibility to our growing repertoire of regular expressions.

As a next step, let's look at how we can allow for a user entering a credit card number to accidentally or deliberately omit one or more spaces. In Listing 13.7, omitting any spaces would result in a message that the credit card number entered was not valid. We need a syntax that allows for zero or one space character between the groups of four numeric digits.

The following syntax allows the user to omit one or more of the space characters:

```
var myRegExp =  /[0-9]{4} {0,1}[0-9]{4} {0,1}[0-9]{4} {0,1}[0-9]{4}/;
```

The only difference in this code from that used in Listing 13.7 is that rather than having a single space character with the unexpressed default count of 1, we use the curly brackets syntax in a new way, {0,1}, to indicate that the literal space character may occur a minimum of zero times and a maximum of one time.

Since we are now allowing the user to possibly omit spaces, we cannot continue to use a simple fixed length for the credit card number string. The shortest possible length is 16 characters (when all spaces are omitted), and the maximum length is 19 characters (when all single space characters are present).

Listing 13.8 will show you how to implement this new flexibility on the regular expression pattern and length. It will still report an error when a user enters an alphabetic character, or if a user inserts a space anywhere but between the allowed four numeric characters from the defined character class.

LISTING 13.8   Allowing Variable Whitespace in a Credit Card Number
INPUT   (CreditCard02.htm)

```
<!DOCTYPE html
PUBLIC "-//W3C//DTD XHTML 1.0 Transitional//EN"
"DTD/xhtml1-transitional.dtd">
<html>
<head>
<title>Matching a 16 digit credit card number
 with variable number of space characters</title>
<script type="text/javascript" language="javascript">
```

LISTING 13.8 continued

```
<!-- //
function IsMatchingCard(str){
var myRegExp = /[0-9]{4} {0,1}[0-9]{4} {0,1}[0-9]{4} {0,1}[0-9]{4}/;
return myRegExp.test(str)
} // end function IsMatchingCard()

function TestGuess(){
var cardNo = prompt("Enter a credit card number here",
"The format is 4 numbers, a space, 4 numbers,
 a space, 4 numbers, a space, 4 numbers");
var validLength = ((cardNo.length>=16) && (cardNo.length<=19));
if (IsMatchingCard(cardNo) && (validLength)){
alert("You entered a valid credit card number: " + cardNo);
} // end if
else if (!validLength){
alert("Sorry you entered a credit card number
 of the wrong length. Try again.");
}
else {
alert("Sorry " + cardNo + " isn't a valid credit card number.");
} // end else
}
// -->
</script>
</head>
<body>
<h3>This page allows you to enter and check a 16 digit credit card number</h3>
<form>
<button type="Button" onclick="TestGuess()">Click here to enter card
number</button>
</form>
</body>
</html>
```

ANALYSIS If you run Listing 13.8 and check the various possibilities that we have allowed the user, you will find that we have permitted any combination of zero or one space characters at the appropriate places. In addition, perhaps surprisingly, you will find that the user can now enter a leading space character and be told that the number is valid if one or more of the later space characters are omitted.

We can also apply the variable frequency technique to situations where we may need to allow variable occurrences of a character class. Suppose we have a parts catalog where the parts numbers can be of the forms A12 or AB12. We can express that using the following code:

```
var myRegExp = /[A-M]{1,2}[0-9]{2}/ ;
```

13

The sub-expression [A-M] defines a character class and its permitted occurrences as {1,2}. Expressed in plain English, uppercase alphabetic characters from "A" to "M" inclusive, which may occur once or twice, are allowed.

Another time when you might want to use a pattern is where you want to allow variable length occurrences of a character class to check whether an e-mail address entered by a user is or is not valid.

Let's pause and think how an e-mail address is made up. First let's look at the simple form structure of an e-mail address:

```
consultancy@xmml.com
```

There is a sequence of alphabetic characters followed by a literal "@" character followed by alphabetic characters representing the domain name, followed by a period, which is then followed by a sequence of characters representing such entities as "com", "net," and so on.

We need to remember that numeric characters are also allowed in the part that is to the left of the @ sign and in the domain name. Additionally, in the domain name, a hyphen character is allowed. However, remember that the underscore character is not allowed in a domain name.

There is an additional issue about whether we allow and test the pattern for upper- and lowercase characters or only lowercase characters. The solution shown here uses only lowercase alphabetic characters. In parallel with that in the listing that follows, we will use a method of the String object to convert the e-mail address to lowercase characters before testing the pattern.

Finally, how many characters should to be allowed? The maximum number of characters permitted for a domain name is 65, as shown here:

```
var myRegExp = /[a-z0-9-]{1,30}@[a-z0-9-]{1,65}.[a-z]{3}/ ;
```

Listing 13.9 is an example of the e-mail checking routine in place. We need to check for a minimum length since an e-mail address such as j@j.net is the shortest allowed by the regular expression pattern. Thus, we define the validLength variable as being greater than or equal to 6 characters in length.

INPUT **LISTING 13.9** Checking an E-Mail Address, Version 1 (CheckEmail01.htm)

```
<!DOCTYPE html
PUBLIC "-//W3C//DTD XHTML 1.0 Transitional//EN"
"DTD/xhtml1-transitional.dtd">
<html>
```

Listing 13.9   continued

```
<head>
<title>Checking an email address - Version 01</title>
<script type="text/javascript" language="javascript">
<!-- //
function IsMatchingAddress(str){
var myRegExp = /[a-z0-9-]{1,30}@[a-z0-9-]{1,65}.[a-z]{3}/ ;
return myRegExp.test(str)
} // end function IsMatchingAddress()

function TestGuess(){
var EmailAddr = new String();
entry = prompt("Enter an email address here",
"Please type it carefully");
EmailAddr = entry;
EmailAddr = EmailAddr.toLowerCase();
var validLength = (EmailAddr.length>=6);
if (IsMatchingAddress(EmailAddr) && (validLength)){
alert("You entered a valid email address: " + EmailAddr);
} // end if
else if (!validLength){
alert(EmailAddr.length);
alert("Sorry you entered an email address of the wrong length. Try again.");
}
else {
alert("Sorry " + EmailAddr + " isn't a valid email address.");
} // end else
}
// -->
</script>
</head>
<body>
<h3>This page allows you to enter and check
 an email address such as consultancy@xmml.com</h3>
<form>
<button type="Button" onclick="TestGuess()">
Click here to enter email address</button>
</form>
</body>
</html>
```

13

ANALYSIS   The code in Listing 13.9 will pick up many possible errors in an e-mail address. It will, for example, limit domain names to alphabetic characters, numeric characters, and a dash (hyphen) in accordance with the domain-naming conventions.

However, it has limitations in a number of respects. As currently written, it will incorrecetly indicate an error for the valid (but fictional) e-mail address of john.doe@samspublishing.com.

It will also accept as its final three characters, any three alphabetic characters. So `sleazy@dubious.xxx` would wrongly be accepted as a valid e-mail address. With the advent of domains such as `.info` a pattern of three alphabetic characters is no longer comprehensive, even for top-level domains. In addition, country-level domains that may be used in an e-mail address would wrongly be rejected as invalid.

If you want to be sure that no valid e-mail addresses are incorrectly rejected, then you could opt for the simple but safe solution, which basically checks for an "@" character and allows almost anything else, like so:

```
var myRegExp = /[a-z0-9-.]{1,40}@[a-z0-9-.]{4,70}/
```

This regular expression allows alphanumeric characters plus a dash and a period in any sequence from one to 40 characters in length. This is followed by an "@" character, which in turn is followed by a minimum of 4 characters (for possible country-level domains such as a `.tv`) up to 70 characters in length to allow for 65-character domain names followed by a period, followed by four character domains such as ".info".

Alternatively, we can attempt to list the current (for the moment) global top-level domains, `com`, `net`, `org`, `info`, and `biz`, and add further options to cover country-level domains too. The following regular expression lists, within parentheses, the global top-level domains just mentioned, separated by the pipe character, offers additional options:

```
var myRegExp = /[a-z0-9-.]{1,30}@[a-z0-9-]{1,65}
.(com|net|org|info|biz|([a-z]{2,3}.[a-z]{2}))/ ;
```

The following would match the regular expression:

```
Andrew.Watt@XMML.com // matches literal "com"
```

```
Andrew.Watt@XMML.co.uk // matches [a-z]{2,3}.[a-z]{2}
```

```
Andrew.Watt@XMML.org.uk // matches [a-z]{2,3}.[a-z]{2}
```

```
Andrew.Watt@XMML.net // matches literal "net"
```

Listing 13.10 uses the more precise test for an e-mail address to allow you to explore this issue further.

INPUT   **LISTING 13.10**   Checking E-Mail Addresses, Version 2.htm)

```
<!DOCTYPE html
PUBLIC "-//W3C//DTD XHTML 1.0 Transitional//EN"
"DTD/xhtml1-transitional.dtd">
<html>
<head>
<title>Checking an email address - Version 02</title>
<script type="text/javascript" language="javascript">
<!-- //
```

LISTING 13.10   continued

```
function IsMatchingAddress(str){
var myRegExp = /[a-z0-9-.]{1,30}@[a-z0-9-]{1,65}.(com|net|org|info|biz|([a-
z]{2,3}.[a-z]{2}))/ ;
return myRegExp.test(str)
} // end function IsMatchingAddress()

function TestGuess(){
var EmailAddr = new String();
entry = prompt("Enter an email address here",
"Please type it carefully");
EmailAddr = entry;
EmailAddr = EmailAddr.toLowerCase();
var validLength = (EmailAddr.length>=6);
if (IsMatchingAddress(EmailAddr) && (validLength)){
alert("You entered a valid email address: " + EmailAddr);
} // end if
else if (!validLength){
alert(EmailAddr.length);
alert("Sorry you entered an email address of the wrong length. Try again.");
}
else {
alert("Sorry " + EmailAddr + " isn't a valid email address.");
} // end else
}
// -->
</script>
</head>
<body>
<h3>This page allows you to enter and check an email address
 such as consultancy@xmml.com,</h3>
<h3>consultancy@xmml.co.uk or consultancy@xmml.org.uk</h3>
<form>
<button type="Button" onclick="TestGuess()">
Click here to enter email address</button>
</form>
</body>
</html>
```

13

Tip

The listings given for checking e-mail addresses only check to determine whether the structure of the string entered corresponds to an e-mail address. To ensure that spelling or typing errors such as, `conslutancy@xmml.com`, are caught, consider asking the user to enter an e-mail address twice. Also think about building in a further check, by sending a message to the e-mail address asking for confirmation, so that a malicious visitor to your site doesn't cause problems for the genuine owner of an e-mail address.

Now that you have an understanding of regular expressions up to this point, let's take a step to one side and look a little more formally at regular expressions.

Regular Expressions Overview

The RegExp object is a Core JavaScript object. There is one RegExp object per Window object.

Regular expressions were introduced to JavaScript in the version 4 browsers—that is, with JavaScript 1.2. If a significant percentage of the visitors to your site use pre-version 4 browsers, you will need to avoid using regular expressions at all in your JavaScript code, or use them only within a suitable routine to provide conditional processing—depending on whether or not a user's browser supported regular expressions. Although the scenario of pre-version 4 browser use is becoming less and less important, you would likely need to apply regular expressions or some equivalent string-validation on the server side, thereby slowing down validation of user entered text.

Defining Regular Expressions

As for all the other Core JavaScript objects that we have met, regular expressions can be created in one of two ways. You can use either literal notation (as we have done up to this point) or the RegExp object as a constructor function. Both of these methods create a full object, but there are some differences between them.

Creating a Regular Expression Using Literals

The way we have constructed a regular expression thus far in this chapter is to use literal notation.

When creating a regular expression literal we have to mark it out just as we marked out a string literal by surrounding it with quote marks. In the case of regular expression literals, we use a different character to mark out our literals. We use the forward slash character to indicate the start of the regular expression and to mark its end. Here is an example:

```
var myRegExp = /Sams/;
```

As you can see, this is fairly simple. We have created a new regular expression object (using literal notation) and assigned it to the variable myRegExp. This regular expression will match the string "Sams" in any string it is applied to. Of course this isn't any different than what we could achieve by using the indexOf() method of the String object and giving it the parameter "Sams".

As you have seen, the real power of regular expressions is in matching patterns as opposed to exact strings.

In order to match certain characters, you need to have a means of representing these characters. For example, you may need to know whether a string contains at least one number, but not be concerned as to which number it is. You could achieve this by doing 10 searches for each numerical digit using the String object's indexOf() method, but this is very inefficient when you could just do it in one search using regular expressions. To match certain characters you need to use special characters. These special characters are simply normal characters that have been escaped using a backslash. For example \d is the special character that matches any of the 10 numeric digits, 0 to 9 inclusive. Therefore to create a regular expression that could be used to search for a numerical digit you would write the following:

```
var myRegExp = /\d/;
```

Alternatively, you can use the syntax you saw earlier:

```
var myRegExp = /[0-9]/ ;
```

As you can see when you use an escaped character, this is beginning to show signs of the possibility of regular expression becoming very cryptic. The nature of having characters that represent a group of characters will inevitably mean that regular expressions will not be immediately readable.

After we look at creating a regular expression using a constructor function, we will move on and take a more detailed look at the special characters available to us when using regular expressions in JavaScript.

Creating Regular Expressions Using a Constructor

The other option that we can use to create a new regular expression is shown here as follows:

```
var myRegExp = new RegExp("[0-9]");
```

You may have noticed that instead of using a pair of forward slashes as delimiters (as we did when using literal notation), we used a pair of quote marks when using the RegExp() constructor. You might well suggest that what we have, delimited by quote marks, is a string. If so, you would be correct.

13

Note

Remember that the delimiter is / for literal regular expression syntax, and that the constructor syntax uses the " character as the delimiter.

When we use the `RegExp()` constructor we are actually storing a string, rather than a regular expression. This means that when we want to use that string as a regular expression then the JavaScript interpreter has to convert the content of the string to a regular expression. This form, which is already in place when we used the literal notation, allows the use of the regular expression by the JavaScript interpreter. The time to compile the string to the internal format for the regular expression is not long, but will make a slightly less efficient computation.

However, using the `RegExp()` constructor allows you to more easily create or define a new regular expression from a string variable. You can use the `RegExp()` constructor, for example, to create a test bed to check how well you have grasped regular expression syntax.

Listing 13.11 shows a simple test bed that allows you to easily create and test regular expression patterns. Notice that it is a pattern without the / delimiters which is needed.

INPUT

LISTING 13.11   Creating and Testing Regular Expressions (RegExpTester.htm)

```
<!DOCTYPE html
PUBLIC "-//W3C//DTD XHTML 1.0 Transitional//EN"
"DTD/xhtml1-transitional.dtd">
<html>
<head>
<title>Regular Expression Tester</title>
<script type="text/javascript" language="javascript">
<!-- //
var myRegExp = "";

function SetFocus(){
document.SimpleForm.FirstInput.focus();
} // end function SetFocus()

function SubmitPattern(){
var pattern = document.SimpleForm.FirstInput.value;
if (pattern.length==0){
alert("You made an invalid entry. Please start again.");
document.SimpleForm.reset();
SetFocus();
} // end if
else { // pattern is at least one character long
myRegExp = new RegExp(pattern);
alert("Current pattern is " + myRegExp);
} // end else
} // end function SubmitPattern()
```

LISTING 13.11   continued

```
function TestString(){
testString = document.SimpleForm.TestInput.value;
if (IsMatchingString(testString)){
alert("The test string: " +testString +
"\nmatched the current pattern: " + myRegExp);
} // end if
else{
alert("The test string: " +testString +
"\ndid not match the current pattern: " + myRegExp);
} // end else
} // end function TestString()

function ClearAndSet(){
document.SimpleForm.reset();
SetFocus();
MaxNum = 0;
}

function IsMatchingString(str){
return myRegExp.test(str)
} // end function IsMatchingString()
// -->
</script>
</head>
<body onload="SetFocus()">
<h3>This page allows you to create and test regular expression patterns</h3>
<h3><b>Be careful! - There is no logic to test string length.</b></h3>
<form name="SimpleForm">
<table>
<tr>
 <td width="30%" align="right">Enter a pattern:</td>
 <td><input name="FirstInput" type="text"></td>
</tr>
<tr>
 <td width="25%" align="right"> </td>
 <td><button type="Button" onclick="SubmitPattern()">
Submit new pattern</button>
</td>
</tr>
<tr>
 <td width="30%" align="right">Enter a string to match the pattern:</td>
 <td><input name="TestInput" type="text"></td>
</tr>
<tr>
 <td width="25%" align="right"><button type="Button" onclick="ClearAndSet()">
Clear and Start again</button></td>
 <td><button type="Button" onclick="TestString()">
Click to test the string you entered</button></td>
</tr>
```

13

LISTING 13.11 continued

```
</table>
</form>
</body>
</html>
```

ANALYSIS This page allowed you to enter a regular expression pattern as a string. When the "Submit new pattern" button is clicked an alert box shows the user the pattern that has been created and which is available for testing. The user then has the option of entering test strings in the second input box and submitting them for testing against the regular expression when the "Click to test the string you entered" button is clicked.

> **Note**
>
> When using Listing 13.11 to test regular expression patterns you need to be aware that the special characters (described in the next section) need to be entered double escaped. Thus, for example, to achieve "\b" in the regular expression created from the string, you would enter "\\b" in the form text field.

Special Characters

There are certain characters that we can't simply write into our regular expressions in order to find a match for them. These characters are the regular expression special characters. And, because they have special meaning, simply writing them in as characters and expecting a match will produce unexpected results or an error.

For example, we can't just place a forward slash into a regular expression literal and expect a match on the forward slash character. The forward slash denotes the beginning and end of a regular expression. So if we want to find a match for the string "Dear Sir/Madam" we could not just write the following:

```
var myRegExp = /Dear Sir/Madam/;
```

JavaScript would get to the forward slash after "Sir" and think that the forward slash indicated the end of the regular expression. When the JavaScript interpreter processed the rest of the line and found the string "Madam", it would attempt to process it as a piece of JavaScript syntax and an error would result.

The correct syntax is to use a literal forward slash character within a regular expression to precede the forward slash, which is intended to be interpreted as a literal, with a backslash, like so:

```
var myRegExp = /Dear Sir\/Madam/;
```

There are several other special characters used in regular expressions that we can't just write into a regular expression. These include the following:

```
\ ^ $ * + ? . ( ) { } [ ] |
```

All these characters have special meaning when used within regular expressions and will not be literally matched. You have seen, for example, how the curly braces are used to enclose the number of permitted occurrences of a character literal or a character class. If you want to actually match special characters literally, then you will need to remove their special meaning. You can do this by using another special character, the backslash character, to escape them. As you will see, the backslash character is a very important character in regular expressions. To create a regular expression that matches the string "Enter (Yes/No)" you would write the following:

```
var myRegExp = /Enter \(Yes\/No\)/;
```

By using the backslash character to escape the forward slash in the string "Yes/No", you remove the forward slash's special meaning and so the JavaScript interpreter knows the forward slash is part of the pattern and not the end of the regular expression. The backslash itself isn't part of the string to be matched. It only has influence on the character that follows it, as in the example above, to remove special meaning. Similarly the backslash which precedes the opening parenthesis, "(", and the closing parenthesis, ")", indicate that the character is to be interpreted literally, rather than used to group a sub-expression within a regular expression.

The backslash can be used in the same way with all the other special characters in the list shown earlier. If you want to match them literally as opposed to using them with their special meaning, then you would need to escape them with the backslash character.

One thing that may be confusing about matching characters that have special meaning is in matching the backslash itself. In the above examples, we have used the special meaning of the backslash character to remove the special meaning of other special characters. But how do we remove the special meaning from the backslash character itself? You simply use another backslash character. So if you (for some unknown reason) wanted to match the string

```
c:\My Writing\TY JavaScript
```

then you could create a regular expression like this:

```
var myRegExp = /c:\\My Writing\\TY JavaScript/;
```

Each time you see \\ within the regular expression indicates a literal backslash character.

13

Earlier in the chapter you learned about special characters such as the curly braces. Shortly, we will examine what the other special characters are used for, but for now let's look more closely at how to use the backslash character.

The backslash character is key to working with regular expressions. Not only does it remove special meaning from special characters so you can actually include them in the pattern to be matched, but it also adds special meaning to non-special characters. At first this may seem confusing, but you have already seen an example of this behavior in use. We mentioned previously that you can match any of the 10 numerical digits by using the following regular expression:

```
var myRegExp = /\d/;
```

If the regular expression had simply been,

```
var myRegExp = /d/;
```

then it would have matched the character "d". But by escaping the d we give it special meaning. In this case the escaped "d" now represents any digit from 0 through 9.

Table 13.1 shows a list of the special characters, including those that will be of most use to you that can be created by escaping a letter.

TABLE 13.1   The Special Characters in JavaScript Regular Expressions

Escaped Character	Character(s) Matched
^	Beginning of input
$	End of input
.	Any character but the new line character (\n)
\b	Any word boundary character
\B	Any character that is not a word boundary character
\d	Any numeric digit character
\D	Any character that is not a numeric digit character
\n	A new line (line feed) character
\r	A carriage return character
\s	Any whitespace character
\S	Any character that is not a whitespace character
\t	A tab character
\w	Any alphanumeric character (includes the underscore character)
\W	Any character that is not an alphanumeric character (excludes the underscore character)

Notice that \n matches the new line character. You have used this syntax in connection with alert boxes in earlier chapters.

Most of the special characters are created by escaping a letter that gives some indication as to which character(s) it will match. For example, \s is used for the special character that matches whitespace. Hopefully this will help to make it easier to remember which letter should be escaped to create the special character you need.

You may have noticed another implicit rule in the letters used to create special characters. If the letter is lowercase, then it matches the characters indicated by the escaped character, but if it is uppercase then it matches any characters except the characters indicated by the letter. Again this should make it slightly easier to remember which letter is used to create which special character.

Some characters matched by some of the special characters, or the differences between some special characters, may not be immediately apparent. So let's clarify their meanings.

Whitespace Versus Word Boundary

The distinction between the word boundary special character \b and the whitespace special character \s is one of those that may initially be unclear. However the key difference between the two can be made clear through an example.

For example, you may want to check for a word in a string, such as "man"—a sub-string, but an actual individual word, "man"; but not to include words such as "manly" or "manual". This means that if you were looking for "fun" you wouldn't want a match if the word "funny" was in the string. To do this you need to wrap special characters around the word "man" or "fun" to indicate that you are looking for the exact word and not just the pattern "man" or "fun". The following code does this by making use of the whitespace special character:

```
var sentence = "What fun regular expressions are.";
var myWord = /\sfun\s/;
var wordFound = myWord.test(sentence);
alert(wordFound);
```

13

In the example above the regular expression will match any string that starts with a whitespace character followed by the letters "f", "u" and "n", and then another whitespace character. Because that string is indeed within the string contained in the variable called sentence the test will return true. But there are situations when using whitespace to mark out a word will fail to return the correct result. Let's change the string slightly and see what happens:

```
var sentence = "What 'fun' regular expressions are.";
var myWord = /\sfun\s/;
var wordFound = myWord.test(sentence);
alert(wordFound);
```

This time the test returns the value `false`. Although the word "fun" is in the string, because we specified that a match would be surrounded by whitespace characters, the regular expression didn't match it. The apostrophe (or single quote) is not a whitespace character. The solution is to use the regular-expression tool specifically designed for the job—*the word-boundary special character*. The word-boundary character will match all whitespace characters but in addition to this it will match punctuation marks such as commas, full stops, quotation marks, or any other characters that can come before or after a word in written English. By replacing the whitespace special characters with word-boundary special characters in the example above, we will obtain the result we were looking for:

```
var sentence = "What 'fun' regular expressions are.";
var myWord = /\bfun\b/;
var wordFound = myWord.test(sentence);
alert(wordFound);
```

The above code would return `true`, since the regular expression recognizes the word boundary expressed by the apostrophe (single quote) characters that delimit "fun".

Of course, at times the whitespace special character will be what you are looking for. But you should be careful that it is specifically whitespace that you want to match. If searching for a word, then the word-boundary character is the one to use if you don't want to miss words that are contained, for example, in quote marks.

Matching Any Alphanumeric Character

The alphanumeric special character, \w, will match both uppercase and lowercase letters as well as numbers and the underscore character. Conversely, the special character \W will match any character except an alphabetical character or numerical character.

Quantifiers

The special characters in the previous section simply match one character. We could get around this by writing multiple character classes, but as you saw in earlier examples, we can use syntax such as curly braces, {1,2} for example, to indicate the lower and upper permitted cardinality.

However, in regular expressions certain common occurrences have a more abbreviated syntax. If a character is optional, you can indicate that situation using the ? cardinality operator. So if you have part numbers that are of the form of two uppercase alphabetic characters, two numeric digits, and an optional alphabetic character, you can express that using the following code:

```
var myRegExp = /[A-Z]{2}\d[A-Z]?/
```

Notice that following the second character class [A-Z], we used the ? character to indicate that that final character is optional—that is, it may occur 0 or 1 times. Alternatively, but slightly less compactly, we could have expressed the same pattern using the curly brace syntax, like so:

```
var myRegExp = /[A-Z]{2}\d[A-Z]{0,1}/
```

If we wanted to express the idea that the final character was necessary but could occur multiple times, then we would use the + character:

```
var myRegExp = /[A-Z]{2}\d[A-Z]+/
```

An alternate way of expressing that idea using curly braces is shown here:

```
var myRegExp = /[A-Z]{2}\d[A-Z]{1,}/
```

The syntax {1,} indicates that the minimum occurrence is one time but that the upper limit for occurrence is undefined—that is, the character class must occur at least once but is permitted to occur an unlimited number of times.

Similarly if we wanted to indicate the final character is optional but it is also permitted to occur an unlimited number of times, then we would use the * character:

```
var myRegExp = /[A-Z]{2}\d[A-Z]*/
```

The equivalent meaning expressed using the curly braces syntax is shown here:

```
var myRegExp = /[A-Z]{2}\d[A-Z]{0,}/
```

In other words the minimum permitted occurrence is zero times and the maximum is unbounded.

The cardinality syntax in regular expressions is summarized in Table 13.2.

13

TABLE 13.2 Cardinality Syntax in JavaScript Regular Expressions

Quantifier	Matched Preceding Character
*	Zero or more times
?	Zero or one times
+	One or more times
{n}	Exactly n times
{n,}	n or more times
{n,m}	Between n and m times (inclusive)

The Methods of the `RegExp` Object

Like many other JavaScript objects, the `RegExp` object has several methods. The methods of the `RegExp` object are listed here:

- `compile()`
- `exec()`
- `test()`
- `toString()`
- `valueOf()`
- `watch()`
- `unwatch()`

The simplest of the methods used to search for a string is the `test()` method, which tests for a string or substring which matches the regular expression pattern. It will return `true` if it finds a substring that matches the pattern described by the regular expression used, or `false` if it doesn't.

Regular expression methods are applied to the regular expression containing the pattern you wish to test for, passing the string to be examined as a parameter. For example, to test for numbers in a string called `myAge` you might use the following lines of code:

```
var myAge = "I am 21 years old";
var digits = /\d/;
var digitsPresent = digits.test(myAge);
alert("There are " + (digitsPresent? "": "no") + " digits.");
```

In this example the value returned is `true`. The regular expression finds the number 2 in "21" and stops there to return `true`.

Using the `exec()` Method

The `exec()` method provides more information about a match found in a string. It provides this information in the form of an `Array` object that it returns when evaluated. Therefore to capture this information you need to use the `exec()` method to the right of an assignment operator and assign the returned array to a variable, like so:

```
var results = RegExp.exec(str);
```

As well as having data filled out in some of its elements, the array that is returned has two properties that are of interest to us. These are the `index` and `input` properties. The `input` property is simply the string that was sent to the `exec()` method as its parameter to search through. The `index` property, on the other hand, contains a number that is the index of the first character of the match in the input.

The element that is of most interest to us is the first element of the array. It contains the substring that the exec() method found that matched the pattern in the regular expression it was applied to. For example, as shown in the following text:

```
var caps = /[A-Z]/;
var str = "a sentence With some Capital letters"
var result = caps.exec(str);
alert(result[0]);  // alerts "W"
```

The contents of the first element of the array that was returned from the exec() method was the string it matched. In this case that was simply the uppercase letter W. The contents of this first element are identical to the lastMatch property of the core RegExp object. The benefit of this is that, as long as we don't intentionally overwrite the contents of the variable result, the array will maintain the results of an individual search that returned a match even after doing multiple searches using regular expressions. However each new search will assign new values to the RegExp object's properties.

The other elements of the array that are returned are also copies of the values assigned to the array.

If no match is found using the exec() method, then the value null is returned in place of an array. This enables you to test whether or not you should attempt to carry out any processing on possible results that may have been returned.

Using the test() Method

The RegExp object's test() method's main function is to check for a match in a string.

Each time the test() method finds a match it sets the lastIndex property of the regular expression used to the string index of the last character in the match. The lastIndex property tells the test() method from where to start checking. When using the test() method repeatedly on the same string, this allows a later test of the regular expression to start where the previous one left off.

13

Caution   Always set the lastIndex property of a regular expression to 0 after each test if it is not going to be used again on the same string. If the lastIndex property is not set to zero, then a search for a match may start at an unpredictable place part way through a string.

The Properties of the `RegExp` Object

The `RegExp` object has the following properties that are listed here. Only some of these will be discussed.

- `$1-$9`
- `$*, $&, $_, $+`
- `constructor`
- `global`
- `ignoreCase`
- `input`
- `lastIndex`
- `lastMatch`
- `lastParen`
- `leftContext`
- `multiline`
- `prototype`
- `rightContext`
- `source`

Scoping a Regular Expression Using the `global` Property

The `global` property specifies whether or not a search should be made for all possible matches of a pattern. The `global` property can be set or tested directly. Alternatively the literal regular expression syntax allows a succinct way to express it, by adding a single character "g" after the closing forward slash of a regular expression, like so:

```
var myString = "My man created a manual manually";
var myRegExp = /man/ ;
```

It will search for the pattern man and stop when the first occurrence is found. However, by either setting the `global` property explicitly or adding a g flag to the literal syntax the full string is searched, rather than stopping after finding the first match.

```
var myString = "My man created a manual manually";
var myRegExp = /man/g ;
```

Making a Regular Expression Case Insensitive Using the `ignoreCase` Property

The `ignoreCase` property can be set explicitly, as it is here:

```
var myRegExp = new RegExp();
myRegExp.ignoreCase = true;
myRegExp.test("i doN't CAre what case is");
```

The same effect can be achieved using the literal regular expression syntax using the `i` flag, following the closing forward slash of the literal syntax:

```
var myRegExp = /i doN't CAre what case is/i ;
```

There is much more to regular expressions than we have been able to introduce you to in this chapter. We hope that you have been able to see how powerful regular expressions can be and will want to explore further the power they provide.

Summary

In this chapter, we looked at some practical problems of string validation that you might encounter in a production Web site. We also explored step-by-step how regular expressions provide the techniques to allow you to validate the structure of strings entered to represent textual or numerical data.

If you are able to express in plain English the pattern you want to represent, then you have already learned many of the parts of regular expression syntax that represent them and allow you to apply powerful validation techniques in your own Web sites.

Workshop

In this workshop we will review what you have learned about regular expressions in this chapter.

13

Q&A

Q. If some data is entered and tested using a regular expression, can I be sure that the data can be processed further?

A. No, you cannot be certain about that. For example, if a currency amount is entered a regular expression can check if it is a valid structure but that doesn't mean you can use the string (which represents a number) in numerical calculations. You may need to use the `Number()` method to ensure that the value is used as a number.

Q. If I use the correct regular expression when validating data, do I, or a colleague, need to carry out validation on the server side?

A. Someone still needs to make checks on the server side. For example, when validating a form with user contact information, indicate to the users that they will receive an e-mail requesting confirmation in a few minutes, and if they don't receive it then they should re-enter their contact details. Additionally, you may need to restructure data before storing it in a database. If you have a field for a U.S. SSN and allow entry to be in the formats 123-4567-89 or 123456789 then you will need to convert entries to a single format if you want to achieve efficient sorts or searches within the data.

Quiz

1. What flag do you use to indicate that a regular expression pattern is case insensitive?

2. Which special character do you use in a regular expression pattern to represent numeric digits?

3. Give two ways in which you can indicate that a character is optional, but if it occurs it can occur only once.

4. What character indicates that a character or character class must be present, but can occur more than once?

Quiz Answers

1. Adding an i after the closing forward slash indicates the pattern is to be applied case insensitive.

2. You can use the \d special character to indicate numeric digits. Alternatively you can use the [0-9] character class.

3. The ? cardinality character indicates that a character is optional but, if it occurs, it can occur only once. We can also indicate the same by writing the following: {0,1}.

4. The + character indicates that a character or character class occurs one or more times.

Exercises

1. Adapt the Regular Expression Tester (RegExpTester.htm) to allow a string length to be entered and to add the length to the testing of test strings which the user has entered.

2. Create a program, using regular expression patterns, to test a United Kingdom Social Security Number, which takes the form "AB 12 34 56 C." The first two characters and the final character may be any uppercase alphabetic characters.

3. Create a program to test whether a string entered is a valid U.S. telephone number. Remember that the opening and closing parentheses have a special purpose in regular expressions.

13

DAY 14

Advanced Array Management

In Chapter 5, "An Introduction to Arrays," you were introduced to JavaScript arrays and some of the ways in which you can use them. In this chapter, we will build on what you learned earlier, examine more fully the methods of the Array object, and go on to look at how you can use arrays to represent multidimensional data structures.

This chapter will teach you

- How to use more of the Array object's methods
- How to simulate a multidimensional array

The Array Object's Methods

In Chapter 5 we looked at several of the Array object's methods, but didn't look at all of them. In this chapter we will complete our study of those methods, enabling us to access the full power of arrays for storing and managing our data.

Here is a list of the methods of the `Array` object:

- `concat()`
- `join()`
- `pop()`
- `push()`
- `reverse()`
- `slice()`
- `shift()`
- `sort()`
- `splice()`
- `toLocaleString()`
- `toSource()`
- `toString()`
- `unshift()`
- `valueOf()`

In Chapter 5, we looked at all of the methods except the `concat()`, `slice()`, `sort()`, and `splice()` methods. However these are the `Array` object's most powerful methods. We need to understand how to use them to unleash the potential of JavaScript for structuring and manipulating our data using arrays.

The `concat()` Method

The `concat()` method enables you to add one array to the end of another array to create a third and longer array. The name of the `concat()` method comes from the term concatenation, which you may remember from our discussion of the plus sign acting as the concatenation operator for adding one string to the end of another. Although the `concat()` method isn't quite as simple to use as the concatenation operator, it's still relatively easy. The `concat()` method is applied to an array using the dot notation, and the name of the array to be concatenated to it is written into the parentheses as a parameter.

Listing 14.1 shows a simple example of how to use the `concat()` method to combine two arrays.

LISTING 14.1   Using the `concat()` Method to Combine Two Arrays

INPUT   (ConcatArrays01.htm)

```
<!DOCTYPE html
PUBLIC "-//W3C//DTD XHTML 1.0 Transitional//EN"
"DTD/xhtml1-transitional.dtd">
<html>
<head>
<title>Using concat() method to combine two arrays</title>
<script type="text/javascript" language="javascript">
<!-- //
function ConcatArrays(){
var firstArray  = new Array(1,2,3);
var secondArray = new Array(4,5,6);
var combinedArray = firstArray.concat(secondArray);
var fa = firstArray.join(", ");
var sa = secondArray.join(", ");
var ca = combinedArray.join(", ");
document.write("<p>The first array contains: <b>" + fa + " </b></p>");
document.write("The second array contains: <b>" + sa + " </b></p>");
document.write("The combined array contains: <b>" + ca + " </b></p>");
document.write("The combined array length is: <b>" + combinedArray.length + "
</b></p>");
}
// -->
</script>
</head>
<body onload="ConcatArrays()">

</body>
</html>
```

ANALYSIS   The secondArray elements have been added to the end of the firstArray elements to create the new array called combinedArray. Note that the process of concatenating two arrays creates a new array. The original two arrays from which it was made are unaffected. They both remain intact and separate. We have used the join() method of the Array object to display the elements of the first, second, and combined arrays. You may remember that the join() method allows you to display the elements of an array with a separator of your choosing.

Figure 14.1 shows the output from Listing 14.1. Notice particularly the content of the combined array and the sequence of elements.

14

OUTPUT

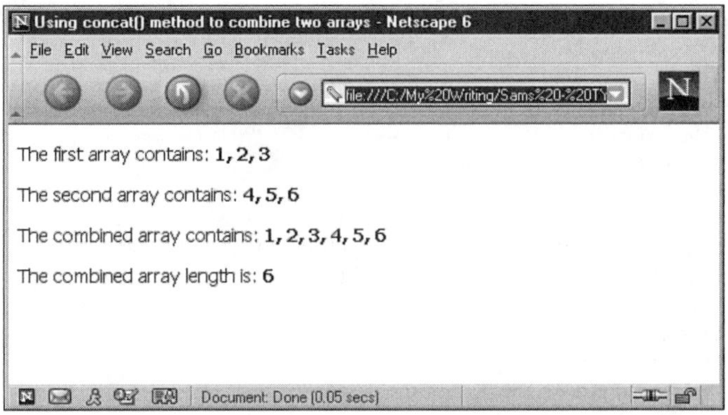

FIGURE 14.1

The output after concatenating the secondArray *to the* firstArray.

```
The first array contains: 1, 2, 3

The second array contains: 4, 5, 6

The combined array contains: 1, 2, 3, 4, 5, 6

The combined array length is: 6
```

When concatenating two arrays it is essential to make sure that you understand the order of elements in the new array. Listing 14.2 shows how you can concatenate firstArray to secondArray. In that situation, as you can see in Figure 14.2, the ordering of elements in the combined array is different. If you had assumed the ordering which resulted from Listing 14.1 but used the approach in Listing 14.2, you likely would have unexpected results when you processed one or more array elements.

INPUT

LISTING 14.2   The concat() Method Used in the Opposite Order (ConcatArrays02.htm)

```
<!DOCTYPE html
PUBLIC "-//W3C//DTD XHTML 1.0 Transitional//EN"
"DTD/xhtml1-transitional.dtd">
<html>
<head>
<title>Using concat() method to combine two arrays</title>
<script type="text/javascript" language="javascript">
<!-- //
function ConcatArrays(){
var firstArray  = new Array(1,2,3);
var secondArray = new Array(4,5,6);
var combinedArray = secondArray.concat(firstArray);
var fa = firstArray.join(", ");
var sa = secondArray.join(", ");
var ca = combinedArray.join(", ");
document.write("<p>The first array contains: <b>" + fa + " </b></p>");
document.write("The second array contains: <b>" + sa + " </b></p>");
document.write("The combined array contains: <b>" + ca + " </b></p>");
document.write("The combined array length is: <b>"
 + combinedArray.length + " </b></p>");
}
```

LISTING 14.2   continued

```
// -->
</script>
</head>
<body onload="ConcatArrays()">

</body>
</html>
```

OUTPUT

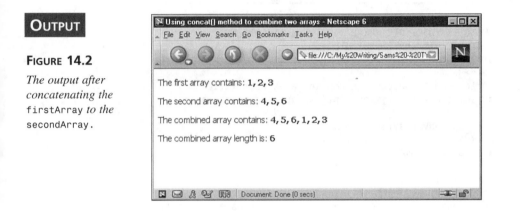

FIGURE 14.2

The output after concatenating the `firstArray` *to the* `secondArray`.

Making Copies of an Array

At this point let's go back and consider the difference between a variable name actually containing an array (which it doesn't) and containing a reference to an array (which it does).

We mentioned in Chapter 5 that arrays don't actually have their own names. They are only accessed by data containers (usually a variable), which hold a reference to the array. The significance of this may not be immediately obvious. You can use the variable name just as if it was the name of the array. However, if you try to create a copy of an array and don't understand this topic, then you can run into some difficulties, which can waste a lot of time. Before you consider making copies of arrays, let's first review how we make a copy of a variable.

There is a major difference between the way you create a copy of a variable and the way you create a copy of an array. For variables it is very simple: You simply declare a variable name for the copy and assign the value of the original to the new variable as shown below:

```
var myVar  = "some value";
var myCopy = myVar;
```

14

In this way, you can perform any number of operations on the original variable `myVar` and then, if needed, revert back to its original value as stored in the variable `myCopy`. Unfortunately when you need to create a copy of an array things are not quite so simple. Let's look at an example (Listing 14.3) to see what would happen if we were to attempt it in the same way that we copied the variable `myVar`.

LISTING 14.3   The Seemingly Successful Copying of an Array
INPUT   (CopyArray01.htm)

```
<!DOCTYPE html
PUBLIC "-//W3C//DTD XHTML 1.0 Transitional//EN"
"DTD/xhtml1-transitional.dtd">
<html>
<head>
<title>Seeming success in copying an array</title>
<script type="text/javascript" language="javascript">
<!-- //
function CopyArray(){
var myArray = new Array(1,2,3);
var myCopy  = myArray;
var ma = myArray.join(", ");
var mc = myCopy.join(", ");
document.write("<p>The original array
 <u><code>myArray</code></u> contains: " + ma + " </p>");
document.write("<p>The copied array
 <u><code>myCopy</code></u> contains: " + mc + " </p>");
}
// -->
</script>
</head>
<body onload="CopyArray()">

</body>
</html>
```

Figure 14.3 shows the result of the (seeming) array copy.

Our attempt at copying an array seems to have worked. However, let's make some changes to the original array `myArray`, and then see if we can revert to its original values using the copy of the array, `myCopy`. You can test this with Listing 14.4.

Figure 14.3

The seemingly successful result of an array copy.

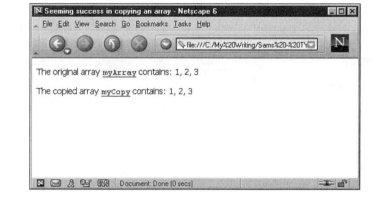

Listing 14.4 Copying an Array and Then Changing the Original (CopyArray02.htm)

```
<!DOCTYPE html
PUBLIC "-//W3C//DTD XHTML 1.0 Transitional//EN"
"DTD/xhtml1-transitional.dtd">
<html>
<head>
<title>Seeming success in copying an array</title>
<script type="text/javascript" language="javascript">
<!-- //
function CopyArray(){
var myArray = new Array(1,2,3);
var myCopy  = myArray;
    myArray[0] = 10;
    myArray[1] = 20;
    myArray[2] = 30;
var ma = myArray.join(", ");
var mc = myCopy.join(", ");
document.write("<p>The original array
 <u><code>myArray</code></u> contains: " + ma + " </p>");
document.write("<p>The copied array
 <u><code>myCopy</code></u> contains: " + mc + " </p>");
}
// -->
</script>
</head>
<body onload="CopyArray()">

</body>
</html>
```

14

If you run Listing 14.4, you will see the result shown in Figure 14.4. Both the original array and the copy of that array return the same values for the array elements.

OUTPUT

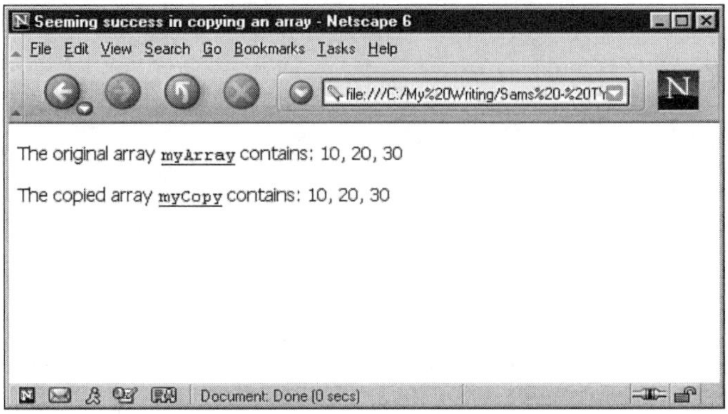

FIGURE 14.4

Copying and changing an array changes its copy too.

ANALYSIS The changes we made to the original array myArray also seem to have affected the copy myCopy! At first sight that may seem bizarre, and it can cause a great deal of frustration if you don't know what's going on. The reason that the changes we made to the original array myArray were also reflected in the copy myCopy, is that myCopy wasn't actually a copy of the array at all. To understand this we need to come back to the topic of references.

The variable myArray contained a reference to a part of the computer's memory where the array originally created was stored. The consequence of this is that when we tried to copy the array we had created to a new variable called myCopy, myCopy was really just a copy of the reference that the variable myArray contained. This means the variable myCopy ended up pointing to exactly the same array as the variable myArray. They never were two distinct arrays—there was only one array but two separate references pointing to the same array.

Whenever we create our own objects the names we give them are always variables, and as such they only contain references to the objects we create. These references are internal and we don't get to see them, but they are real nonetheless. We can only create true copies of actual pieces of data, so normally when we want to create a copy of an object, we need to copy each property individually. Thankfully when it comes to arrays this is not the case. We can use the concat() method to save time and effort.

In the previous examples of using the concat() method, the method was used to concatenate one array with another. The two arrays it was applied to were left intact and separate. The new array had to be assigned to a new variable name. To achieve this the concat() method internally copied each piece of data contained in the elements of the original arrays to build up a new array. This built-in copying feature can be used to our advantage and save us from writing the code to do it. To do this, we simply need to concatenate the array to be copied with an empty array. Listing 14.5 shows how we would modify the previous example to do this.

LISTING 14.5   Using the concat() Method of the Array Object to Create a
INPUT   True Copy (CopyArray03.htm)

```
<!DOCTYPE html
PUBLIC "-//W3C//DTD XHTML 1.0 Transitional//EN"
"DTD/xhtml1-transitional.dtd">
<html>
<head>
<title>Actual success in copying an array using concat()</title>
<script type="text/javascript" language="javascript">
<!-- //
function CopyArray(){
var myArray = new Array(1,2,3);
var emptyArray = new Array();
var myCopy  = myArray.concat(emptyArray);
    myArray[0] = 10;
    myArray[1] = 20;
    myArray[2] = 30;
var ma = myArray.join(", ");
var mc = myCopy.join(", ");
document.write("<p>The original array
 <u><code>myArray</code></u> contains: " + ma + " </p>");
document.write("<p>The copied array
 <u><code>myCopy</code></u> contains: " + mc + " </p>");
}
// -->
</script>
</head>
<body onload="CopyArray()">

</body>
</html>
```

When we run the code in Listing 14.5 we see that we have successfully copied the array, as you can see in Figure 14.5.

14

FIGURE 14.5

A successful array
copied using the
concat() *method.*

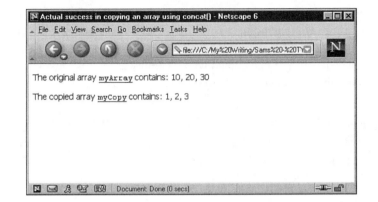

The original array myArray contains: 10, 20, 30

The copied array myCopy contains: 1, 2, 3

INPUT The variable myCopy has the original values of the array myArray. We have suc-
ceeded in making a true copy that we can refer back to or use as a backup—even
if we have modified the original. If we use the literal notation to create the array, we can
actually shorten this as shown below:

```
var myArray = new Array(1,2,3);
var emptyArray = [];
var myCopy   = myArray.concat(emptyArray);
    myArray[0] = 10;
    myArray[1] = 20;
    myArray[2] = 30;
```

Or we can even place the array literal in the parentheses of the concat() method to make
it even shorter:

```
var myArray = new Array(1,2,3);
var myCopy   = myArray.concat([]);
    myArray[0] = 10;
    myArray[1] = 20;
    myArray[2] = 30;
```

The only time this does not work is when one or more elements of the array being copied
is a reference to another array (or other object). In this case, once again, it will be the
references and not the object that will be copied. Any changes to this object will be
reflected in both arrays. For the moment this is unlikely to be an issue for you as you are
unlikely, initially at least, to store objects in your array elements. However, if you do
start to use the multidimensional arrays that we will see later in this chapter, you may
need to bear this in mind.

The `slice()` Method

Whenever we need to work with a limited number of consecutive elements contained within an array it is often useful to create a new array out of these elements. To create this array, we could use a loop statement to loop through the elements between two index values and copy each element to a new array, but we are saved the trouble of such custom programming by the `slice()` method of the `Array` object, which makes the task a simple one-line affair.

The `slice()` method requires two parameters. With the first one we specify the start index of the section of the array that we want to copy; and with the second one, we specify the first index *after* the section to be copied. All the elements between these two indexes are copied into a new array. For example, assume we have an array of names that are ordered alphabetically and that we have found the indexes of the first and last elements with contents that begin with "B" (we can do both these things, as we will see later). To extract the names beginning with B, we could use the `slice()` method, as shown in Listing 14.6.

INPUT

LISTING 14.6 Using the `slice()` Method to Create an Array with Selected Content (`SliceArray01.htm`)

```
<!DOCTYPE html
PUBLIC "-//W3C//DTD XHTML 1.0 Transitional//EN"
"DTD/xhtml1-transitional.dtd">
<html>
<head>
<title>Using the slice() method of the Array object</title>
<script type="text/javascript" language="javascript">
<!-- //
function BNameArray(){
var allNames = new Array("Allan", "Bart", "Ben", "Bob", "Colin");

// Process to find first and last indexes of "B's" done here

var firstB = 1;
var firstNonB  = 4;
var bNames = allNames.slice(firstB, firstNonB);
var an = allNames.join(", ");
var bn = bNames.join(", ");

document.write("<p>The original array
  <u><code>allNames</code></u> contains: " + an + " </p>");
document.write("<p>The array created using slice(),
  <u><code>bNames</code></u>, contains: " + bn + " </p>");
}
```

14

LISTING **14.6** continued

```
// -->
</script>
</head>
<body onload="BNameArray()">

</body>
</html>
```

Running Listing 14.6 will produce an appearance like that shown in Figure 14.6.

OUTPUT

FIGURE 14.6

Using the slice() *method to create a new array derived from an existing array.*

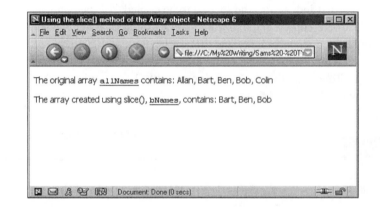

ANALYSIS The slice method has copied elements 1 through 3 and built up a new array, which we have assigned to the variable bNames. Note the values of the two indexes we had to specify to do this. The first index was the index of the first "B", but the second index was the one after the index of the last element containing a name beginning with B. The index of Bob is 3, but we had to specify 4. This is a rule that is important to remember, as it is the same for all the other array methods to which we need to give index values.

The slice() method can only be used to select a continuous segment of an existing array. If you want to create a new array which uses more than one segment of an existing array, then you would need to concatenate the arrays created using the slice() method with the concat() method.

The splice() Method

As you can imagine (from Chapter 5), the four methods for removing and adding elements from the start and end of an array are often very useful, but we may need to do something slightly more sophisticated. We may want to remove or insert elements located part way through an array. The `splice()` method enables us to do this and more. Not only can we use it for the removal and insertion of elements, but it is also our means of replacing/editing multiple elements with one line of code.

When we want to delete elements from an array we can use the `delete` statement. It is applied to one element at a time, and removes any data that is contained within that element. For example, if we subsequently try to use that element, it will have the value `undefined`—just as it would have if it never had been assigned a value:

```
var x = new Array("a", "b", "c", "d");
delete x[1];

alert(x[1]);      // alerts undefined
alert(x.length);  // alerts 4
alert(x);         // alerts "a,,c,d"
```

Note that the data contained in element 1 has been removed—that is, the value of element 1 has been set to a value of `undefined`. The length property of the `Array` object still has the value of 4, and the data in the last two elements have not been moved into earlier elements.

If all you want to do is remove the data contained in a specific element, then the `delete` statement is the correct syntax. However sometimes when we remove an element from an array, we will want the elements that follow it to be moved back by one (assuming we deleted a single array element), thereby filling the place of the removed element and reducing the array's length. In the example above, we might want "c" to move back to x[1], and "d" to move back to x[2], and of course the length property to be reduced by one to reflect these changes. However, the `delete` method was not designed to achieve this. It simply removes the data from the element to which it is applied.

To carry out a more sophisticated removal of elements with the desired backshift of any following elements, we need to use the `splice()` method. In its simplest form the `splice()` method simply deletes one or more elements from inside an array, but unlike the `delete` method, it moves all the proceeding elements back one or more places. To achieve this we must specify 2 parameters with the `splice()` method. The first parameter is the index of the first element we want to remove, and the second parameter is the number of subsequent elements we want to remove. To demonstrate let's look at the previous example modified to provide a more complete removal of the second element, as shown in Listing 14.7.

14

LISTING 14.7   Using the `splice()` Method of the Array Object
(SpliceArray01.htm)

```
<!DOCTYPE html
PUBLIC "-//W3C//DTD XHTML 1.0 Transitional//EN"
"DTD/xhtml1-transitional.dtd">
<html>
<head>
<title>Using the splice() method of the Array object</title>
<script type="text/javascript" language="javascript">
<!-- //
function SpliceArray(){
var x = new Array("a", "b", "c", "d");
var xj = x.join(", ");
document.write("<p>The original array
 <u><code>x</code></u> contains: " + xj + " </p>");
document.write("<p>The length of the original array
 <u><code>x</code></u> is: " + x.length + " </p>");
var y = x.splice(1,1);
var yj = y.join(", ");
document.write("<p>The array <u><code>y</code></u>
 after using splice() contains: " + yj + " </p>");
document.write("<p>The length of the array <u><code>y</code></u>
 after splice() is: " + y.length + " </p>");
var xj = x.join(", ");
document.write("<p>The original array <u><code>x</code></u>
 now contains: " + xj + " </p>");
document.write("<p>The length of the original array
 <u><code>x</code></u> is now: " + x.length + " </p>");
}
// -->
</script>
</head>
<body onload="SpliceArray()">

</body>
</html>
```

Figure 14.7 shows the output when you run Listing 14.7.

OUTPUT

FIGURE 14.7

The array x before and after using the splice() *method.*

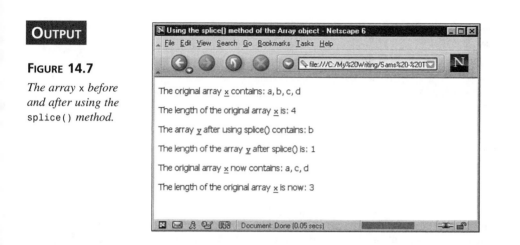

As we can see, not only has the original data contained in the second element been removed, but the values c and d have been moved up to occupy elements 1 and 2, and the length property has changed to 3. Notice also that when the splice() method deleted the second element from the array x it returned it so that it was assigned to the variable y. Although this example doesn't show it, the element isn't just returned as a piece of data, but rather as a single element array object.

If we wanted to remove more elements from the array, we would just have to specify a higher number as the second parameter. For example if we want to remove the second and third elements, we would write:

```
y = x.splice(1,2);
```

The 2 indicates that we want to remove 2 elements, and the 1 specifies that the removal should start at element 1. As before, the removed elements would be returned by the method, this time as a two-element array.

As well as using the splice() method to delete elements, we can also use it to insert new elements without removing any of the existing ones. To do this we need to specify an insertion point and the data to insert. When doing this, the first parameter of the sort() method specifies the insertion point and the second parameter must be set to zero. When the second parameter is set to zero, then the number of array elements to be deleted is zero. We will see the effect of a nonzero second parameter shortly. All the data we want to insert must then be included as extra parameters. Let's say this time that array x is created with only two elements with the values a and d respectively. If we then want to insert the values b and c between these elements, then we could use code such as that found in Listing 14.8.

14

INPUT **LISTING 14.8** Using the `splice()` Method to Insert Array Elements (`SpliceArray02.htm`)

```
<!DOCTYPE html
PUBLIC "-//W3C//DTD XHTML 1.0 Transitional//EN"
"DTD/xhtml1-transitional.dtd">
<html>
<head>
<title>Using the splice() method to insert elements</title>
<script type="text/javascript" language="javascript">
<!-- //
function SpliceArray(){
var x = new Array("a","d", "e", "f");
var xj = x.join(", ");
document.write("<p>The original array
 <u><code>x</code></u> contains: " + xj + " </p>");
document.write("<p>The length of the original array
 <u><code>x</code></u> is: " + x.length + " </p>");
x.splice(1, 0, "b", "c");
var xj = x.join(", ");
document.write("<p>The original array <u><code>x</code></u>
 now contains: " + xj + " </p>");
document.write("<p>The length of the original array
 <u><code>x</code></u> is now: " + x.length + " </p>");
}
// -->
</script>
</head>
<body onload="SpliceArray()">

</body>
</html>
```

Figure 14.8.shows the result from running the code in Listing 14.8.

OUTPUT

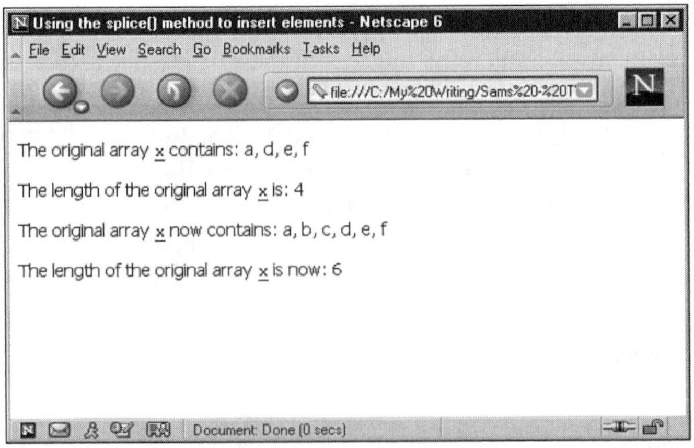

FIGURE 14.8

Inserting elements into an array using the `splice()` *method.*

The original array x contains: a, d, e, f

The length of the original array x is: 4

The original array x now contains: a, b, c, d, e, f

The length of the original array x is now: 6

ANALYSIS As you can see, the second element containing the value d has moved up to make space for the new elements b and c, and the length property has changed to reflect the addition of the new elements to the array. When applied to x the splice() method has returned an Array object.

By varying the second parameter, we can do everything from a pure delete through to an exact replace to a partial or pure insertion. If we specify a number of array elements to be removed using the second parameter, then they are removed; but at the same time, we can also specify elements to insert. The number of elements deleted need not necessarily be the same as the number of new elements inserted. However, if this happens to be the case, then the result is that the elements are effectively replaced.

The final use of the splice() method is, in a sense, a combination of the two uses just discussed. We can use it to replace elements within an array. Listing 14.9 shows you how.

INPUT **LISTING 14.9** Using the splice() Method to Replace Elements Within an Array (SpliceArray03.htm)

```
<!DOCTYPE html
PUBLIC "-//W3C//DTD XHTML 1.0 Transitional//EN"
"DTD/xhtml1-transitional.dtd">
<html>
<head>
<title>Using the splice() method to replace elements</title>
<script type="text/javascript" language="javascript">
<!-- //
function SpliceArray(){
var x = new Array("a","b", "c", "d");
var xj = x.join(", ");
document.write("<p>The original array
 <u><code>x</code></u> contains: " + xj + " </p>");
document.write("<p>The length of the original array
 <u><code>x</code></u> is: " + x.length + " </p>");
x.splice(1, 2, "B", "C");
var xj = x.join(", ");
document.write("<p>The original array <u><code>x</code></u>
 now contains: " + xj + " </p>");
document.write("<p>The length of the original array
 <u><code>x</code></u> is now: " + x.length + " </p>");
}
// -->
</script>
</head>
<body onload="SpliceArray()">

</body>
</html>
```

14

The result of running Listing 14.9 is shown in Figure 14.9.

OUTPUT

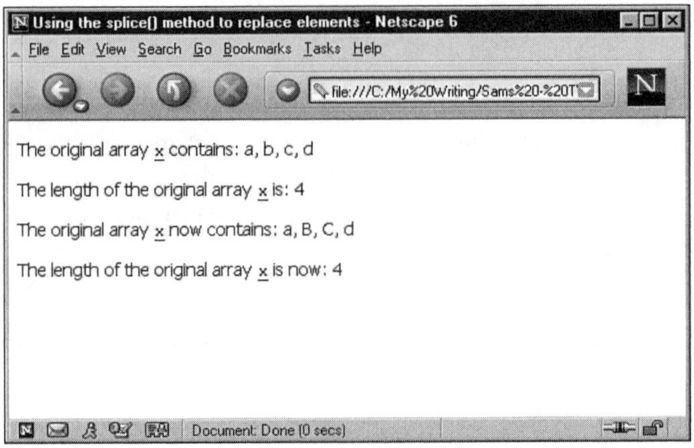

FIGURE 14.9

Using the splice()
*method to remove
and insert array ele-
ments with the over-
all effect of replacing
two elements.*

N Using the splice() method to replace elements - Netscape 6

File Edit View Search Go Bookmarks Tasks Help

file:///C:/My%20Writing/Sams%20-%20T

The original array x contains: a, b, c, d

The length of the original array x is: 4

The original array x now contains: a, B, C, d

The length of the original array x is now: 4

Document: Done (0 secs)

ANALYSIS   In this example, the first parameter of the splice() method is the number 1 and the second is the number 2. Therefore we have specified that starting at the element with index 1 two elements should be deleted. At the same time, we have also supplied two additional pieces of data to be inserted, and the insertion point for this data is also the element with the index of 1. The result is that the values b and c are removed from the second and third elements, and the values B and C are inserted at the same point. The overall effect is that the second and third elements are overwritten with the values B and C, as we can see in Figure 14.9. Note that if we had assigned to a variable y, as we did in Listing 14.7, the elements that were deleted would be returned from the splice method and stored in the variable y, as we have seen previously.

Normally we will want to do a delete, a replace, or an insert but, as we said earlier, it isn't necessary that the number of elements removed be the same as the number of elements inserted. We can specify more or less of either to get a mixture of the two effects. The number of elements we specify for deletion will first be deleted, but then the number of elements we specify for insertion will be inserted at the same point. However, if you do use the splice() method in such a way, make very sure that you know the effects on the length property and the positioning of individual elements if you will need to access them later in your code.

The sort() Method

The sort() method is one of the most powerful of the Array object's methods. When applied to an array in its most simple form, it rearranges the data stored in the elements of the array so that the data is ordered lexicographically. Listing 14.10 shows an example of the sort() method at work.

INPUT **LISTING 14.10** Using the `sort()` Method to Order a Number of Strings in an Array (`SortString01.htm`)

```
<!DOCTYPE html
PUBLIC "-//W3C//DTD XHTML 1.0 Transitional//EN"
"DTD/xhtml1-transitional.dtd">
<html>
<head>
<title>Using the sort() method</title>
<script type="text/javascript" language="javascript">
<!-- //
function SortElements(){
var colors = new Array("red","blue","green");
    colors.sort();
var cj = colors.join(", ");
alert("The sorted array contains: " + cj);
}
// -->
</script>
</head>
<body onload="SortElements()">

</body>
</html>
```

Running Listing 14.10 will bring up the alert box shown in Figure 14.10.

OUTPUT

FIGURE 14.10

The result of an array of sorted strings.

ANALYSIS As you can see the elements of the array have been ordered as we would order them if we were to put them into alphabetical order. However, this is slightly misleading. The order in which the elements are ordered is based on the order that characters appear in the Unicode standard. Let's look at another example to demonstrate the difference between alphabetical ordering and lexicographical ordering based on the order of the Unicode characters. This time we will include a mixture of words starting with uppercase and lowercase letters. See Listing 14.11.

14

INPUT

LISTING 14.11   The Effect of Case on Ordering by Using the `sort()` Method
(`SortString02.htm`)

```
<!DOCTYPE html
PUBLIC "-//W3C//DTD XHTML 1.0 Transitional//EN"
"DTD/xhtml1-transitional.dtd">
<html>
<head>
<title>Using the sort() method</title>
<script type="text/javascript" language="javascript">
<!-- //
function SortElements() {
var colors = new Array("red","Red","blue","Blue","green","Green");
    colors.sort();
var cj = colors.join(", ");
alert("The sorted array contains: " + cj);
}
// -->
</script>
</head>
<body onload="SortElements()">

</body>
</html>
```

The alert box displayed by Listing 14.11 is shown in Figure 14.11.

OUTPUT

FIGURE 14.11

When using the
`sort()` *method*
uppercase comes
before lowercase
letters.

ANALYSIS   As you can see the uppercase letters have been placed before the lowercase letters. The colors beginning with uppercase letters are alphabetically ordered, and the colors beginning with a lowercase letter are alphabetically ordered, but the two groups are separate. This is because in Unicode uppercase and lowercase letters are separate, with the uppercase letters placed before the lowercase letters. Most of the time we will not want to sort our arrays like this. We will probably prefer the words in an array to be ordered alphabetically regardless of the case of the letters. Later in this section we will see how this can be done. For the moment, let's continue with our look at the characteristics of the `sort()` method.

Sometimes the arrays we wish to sort will contain elements with numerical values. If we told you that numbers come before both uppercase *and* lowercase letters in the Unicode standard, you may think you know the order in which the elements in these types of arrays will end up. However, you may still be surprised. Let's look at another two examples, this time with some numerical elements. See Listing 14.12.

LISTING 14.12 Using the `sort()` Method to Sort Numbers and Strings (`SortStringsAndNumbers.htm`)

```
<!DOCTYPE html
PUBLIC "-//W3C//DTD XHTML 1.0 Transitional//EN"
"DTD/xhtml1-transitional.dtd">
<html>
<head>
<title>Using the sort() method on numbers and strings</title>
<script type="text/javascript" language="javascript">
<!-- //
function SortElements() {
var mixture = new Array("red",4,"blue",2,"green",9);
    mixture.sort();
var mj = mixture.join(", ");
alert("The sorted array contains: " + mj);
}
// -->
</script>
</head>
<body onload="SortElements()">

</body>
</html>
```

Figure 14.12 shows the results of running Listing 14.12.

OUTPUT

FIGURE 14.12

Using the `sort()` *method produces numbers before letters.*

14

ANALYSIS The numbers have been moved to the front of the array and are in the order that you most likely expected. The 2 is placed before the 4, which in turn is placed before the 9. However, as it happens, this is another deceptive example. The `sort()` method does not take the data type of the elements it is comparing into consideration (at least not in its unmodified form, as we are using it at the moment). The ordering is lexicographical based on the order of the characters in the Unicode standard. In the Unicode standard characters are just characters. They do not have a data type.

At this point you may be wondering why this matters. After all the characters seem to have been placed into the correct order. Well, let's look at another example where the array contains some different numbers. See Listing 14.13.

INPUT **LISTING 14.13**   A Second Example of Using `sort()` on Numbers and Strings (`SortStringsAndNumbers02.htm`)

```
<!DOCTYPE html
PUBLIC "-//W3C//DTD XHTML 1.0 Transitional//EN"
"DTD/xhtml1-transitional.dtd">
<html>
<head>
<title>Using the sort() method on numbers and strings</title>
<script type="text/javascript" language="javascript">
<!-- //
function SortElements() {
var myNums = new Array(9,4,"Bob",11,301);
    myNums.sort();
var mj = myNums.join(", ");
alert("The sorted array contains: " + mj);
}
// -->
</script>
</head>
<body onload="SortElements()">

</body>
</html>
```

Figure 14.13 shows the results of running Listing 14.13.

OUTPUT

FIGURE 14.13

Notice that the numbers have been sorted as strings by initial character, not by numerical value.

ANALYSIS At first the results of this sort may surprise you. With the 11 and 301 coming before 4 and 9, the elements of the array are most certainly not in numerical order. To understand why, let's look more closely at what happens when we order words alphabetically.

For this example, let's assume we have three words: "first," "second," and "third." To put these words into alphabetical order, the first thing we do is compare the first letters of the three words. If the first letter of one alphabetically comes before the first letter of another, then it is placed first. But if the first letter of one comes after the first letter of another, then it is placed later in the order. In the case of our three words, "f" comes before "s", so "first" is placed before "second," and "s" comes before "t" so "second" is placed before "third." The fact that status "first" comes before the status "second," and status "second" comes before the status "third" has nothing to do with it. This is just coincidence. It is the first letters on which our sort is based.

In the same way the fact that the numbers in the first of our two numerical examples were placed in the order they were in was also just a coincidence. When JavaScript made the comparison for the sort what it did was consider the numbers purely as characters. This time though its reference wasn't the alphabet; it was the Unicode standard. Because the character 2 comes before the character 4 in the Unicode standard, it was placed before 4; and because the character 4 comes before the character 9, it was placed before 9. It is not because the number 2 is before the number 4 numerically, nor because the number 4 comes before the number 9 numerically.

The difference between sorting numerically and sorting lexicographically using the Unicode standard is illustrated by Listing 14.13. JavaScript didn't look at the numbers as numbers but rather it compared the first character of each number (this is what lexicographically means). The first character of 11 is 1. Because in the Unicode standard the character "1" comes before the first character of 9 (just "9"), the first character of 4 ("4"), the first character of "Bob" ("B"), and the first character of 301 ("3"), the number 11 was placed first. In the same way the first character of 301 ("3") comes before the first character of 9, 4, and "hat," so it was placed next. This method of ordering was continued so that 4 was placed next, then the 9, and finally the string "Bob."

14

Of course most of the time the order of the characters in the Unicode standard will have nothing to do with the order in which we want to sort the elements of our arrays. Most likely we will want to do either a *case insensitive* alphabetical sort on strings, or a numerical sort where the order of our numbers is numerical and not lexicographical. To do this we need to define our own sort criteria.

Defining Our Own Sort Criteria

To define our own sort criteria, we need to understand a little more about how the Array object's sort() method works.

When we sort the elements of an array using the sort() method there are two processes that go on behind the scenes. One is the comparison of the data in an array's elements to determine the order in which they should be placed, and the other is the actual process of moving the data from element to element. It is the sort() method that moves the data from one element to another, but hidden away is a second function that does the data comparison. It is this function that tells the sort() method into which order it should move the data in an array's elements. Because of the task it performs, this second function is often called the *comparison function.*

The way these two functions work is that the sort() method sends the comparison function the data from two of the elements in the array it is working on, and asks the question, "should I swap the data in these elements?". The comparison function compares the two pieces of data and returns, telling the sort() method "yes" or "no". If the two pieces of data are the "wrong way around," then the comparison function tells the sort() method "Yes, you should swap them." It does this by returning the value 1, which you can think of as the numerical equivalent of the boolean value true (true to the question, "should the data be swapped?").

If the sort() method receives back the value 1 from the comparison function, then it swaps the data in the two elements and proceeds to send the comparison function another two pieces of data. Of course the pieces of data won't always be out of order and therefore won't always need to be swapped. When this is the case the comparison function returns a different value. When the two pieces of data it receives are in the "right" order, then the comparison function returns the value –1. This can be thought of as the numerical equivalent to the boolean value false, meaning "no", the data in the elements should not be swapped.

The third condition is of course that the two elements compared are exactly equal. In this case the elements need not be swapped, and the value returned by the comparison function is 0. This again tells the sort() method that it should not swap the data in the elements, and so is again effectively equivalent to the boolean value false.

By making use of the comparison function, the sort() method repeatedly cycles through an array's elements moving their data two at a time until no further changes need to be made. Once the contents of the array's elements have been completely rearranged the sort() method stops.

When we define our own sort criteria we do not need to worry about how to move the data in the elements of our arrays; the sort() method will do that for us. What we do need to concern ourselves with is the construction of a comparison function for the sort() method to use. The sort method will send this function two elements as arguments, which it should compare before returning the numerical value that tells the sort() method what it should do with the elements. To get a feel for what a comparison function should look like consider the following example. It is designed to cause the sort() method to order the elements of an array in a similar way to how it would sort them by default—lexicographically, based on the order of the characters in the Unicode standard:

```
function defaultSort(elementX, elementY)
{
    if (elementX < elementY) return -1;
    if (elementX > elementY) return  1;
    return 0;
}
```

To understand how this function works, recall from Chapter 2, "Working with Data," how the comparison operators behave when used with strings. They check to see if one of their operands comes before or after their other operand based on the order of the characters in the Unicode standard! For example,

```
x < y
```

returns true if x comes before y, but false otherwise. This characteristic of the comparison operators makes them ideal for creating a comparison function that will order the elements of an array according to the order of the characters in the Unicode standard.

In the comparison function above, called defaultSort(), we use the comparison operators as our means of checking the two elements that the function is sent. We have given the arguments of the function the names elementX and elementY to help make this clearer. The comparison function must return -1 if the first argument comes before the second by our ordering scheme. Therefore, in the first line of code in the function body we use the if statement coupled with the < operator to check for this condition and return -1 if it is true. We do not need to worry which elements the function has been sent. The sort() method will keep track of this.

14

If, on the other hand, the first argument (elementX) comes after the data in the second (elementY) by our ordering scheme, then we need to return the value 1 so that they are swapped. This condition is checked for by the second if statement in the function body. If the data in elementX comes after the data in elementY, then 1 is returned to the sort() method.

If neither of the first two return statements has been evaluated by the third line of the function body, then the data in the two elements must be identical. Therefore we include a last return statement to make the function return the value 0, indicating the data in the elements is the same.

We haven't yet seen how to tell the sort() method that it should use a comparison function, which we have defined, rather than its built-in default function. This is actually a lot easier than creating our function in the first place. You simply send the name of your comparison function to the sort() method as a parameter. For example, to tell the sort() method to use the function we have just been looking at, we would write the following:

```
arrayName.sort(defaultSort);
```

Note

> When telling the sort() method to use a function you have created, only give it the name of the function. You do not include a function call after this name (a pair of opening and closing parentheses). This means you would not write something like this:
>
> ```
> arrayName.sort(defaultSort());
> ```
>
> The function call after the function name will cause an error because you don't want to call the function. You only want to give the sort() method the function name so that it knows which function to use.

Let's look at an example of how to use this function we have created. See Listing 14.14.

INPUT

LISTING 14.14 Using the defaultSort() Function with the Array Object's sort() Method (SortStringsAndNumbers03.htm)

```
<!DOCTYPE html
PUBLIC "-//W3C//DTD XHTML 1.0 Transitional//EN"
"DTD/xhtml1-transitional.dtd">
<html>
<head>
<title>Using the sort() method on numbers and strings</title>
<script type="text/javascript" language="javascript">
<!-- //
```

LISTING 14.14   continued

```
function defaultSort(elementX, elementY)
{
    if (elementX < elementY) return -1;
    if (elementX > elementY) return  1;
    return 0;
}
function SortElements() {
var mixture = new Array("red",4,"blue",2,"green",9);
    mixture.sort(defaultSort);
var mj = mixture.join(", ");
alert("The sorted array contains: " + mj);
}
// -->
</script>
</head>
<body onload="SortElements()">

</body>
</html>
```

This brings up the alert box shown in Figure 14.14.

OUTPUT

FIGURE 14.14

A strange "sort." Not quite what we were looking for....

ANALYSIS It is at this point that we have to admit that the function above doesn't quite produce the same results as the internal default function used by the sort() method. The reason for this is that our function compares elements with the data type of the data in the array. The default comparison function on the other hand converts the data type of the elements it is sent with their data type set as a string (so that it can do a lexicographical sort).

There is a reason why having a mixture of data types causes problems for our function—it is a feature of the comparison operators that we haven't looked at before. When the operands of the comparison functions have different data types the value returned is (almost) always the value false. Therefore:

```
1 < "a"  // evaluates to false
"a" < 1  // evaluates to false
```

14

The result of this is that our comparison function can send the sort() method contradictory commands. Inevitably this results in ordering that at times can seem almost random. To prevent this problem from occurring, we need the elements that are sent to our comparison functions to be compared with the same data type. To do this for our previous function we might write it like this:

```
function defaultSort(elementX, elementY)
{
    var element1 = elementX.toString();
    var element2 = elementY.toString();
    if (element1 < element2) return -1;
    if (element1 > element2) return  1;
    return 0;
}
```

In this modified function, we have created two temporary variables called element1 and element2 (notice the slight change in name). To these variables we have assigned the data from the two arguments after converting their data to the datatype string using the toString() method. It is then these copies with the modified data type that we use for the comparison to decide which value to return to the sort() method. This allows us to have a mixture of data with the datatypes number, string and boolean in our arrays, and they will be ordered lexicographically. Listing 14.15 shows a revised example.

INPUT **LISTING 14.15** A Custom Function Produces the Same as the Default sort() Method (SortStringsAndNumbers04.htm)

```
<!DOCTYPE html
PUBLIC "-//W3C//DTD XHTML 1.0 Transitional//EN"
"DTD/xhtml1-transitional.dtd">
<html>
<head>
<title>Using the sort() method on numbers and strings</title>
<script type="text/javascript" language="javascript">
<!-- //

function defaultSort(elementX, elementY)
{
    var element1 = elementX.toString();
    var element2 = elementY.toString();
    if (element1 < element2) return -1;
    if (element1 > element2) return  1;
    return 0;
}

function SortElements() {
var mixture = new Array("red",4,"blue",2,"green",9);
    mixture.sort(defaultSort);
```

LISTING 14.15   continued

```
var mj = mixture.join(", ");
alert("The sorted array contains: " + mj);
}
// -->
</script>
</head>
<body onload="SortElements()">

</body>
</html>
```

When you run Listing 14.15 it will produce the alert box shown in Figure 14.15.

OUTPUT

FIGURE 14.15

The output of a modified `defaultSort()` *function.*

ANALYSIS   Although the functions we have seen so far have introduced us to the use of the comparison operators in comparison functions, and the need for conversion to a consistent data type, they are not really of much use. After all we don't need to create a function that will produce the same results as the `sort()` method produces by default. Far more useful would be functions that will produce a case-insensitive sort and a numerical sort. Let's go on now to create both of these.

Hopefully by now you have grasped the idea of the arguments of our comparison functions containing the data from two array elements. We will now drop the longer names we have been using and use the traditional shorter argument names for comparison function arguments: a and b.

The first function we are going to look at is one that causes a case-insensitive alphabetical sort. In the previous example, we converted the arguments of the function so that they had the datatype `string`. In this function we are going to make a slightly more significant modification to the data and convert it to lowercase letters. By comparing the arguments with all their letters reduced to lowercase, the case of the characters in the actual array elements doesn't play a part:

14

```
function alphabetical(a, b)
{
    var A = a.toLowerCase();
    var B = b.toLowerCase();
    if (A < B) return -1;
    if (A > B) return  1;
    return 0;
}
```

Notice that the temporary variables are uppercase, whereas the argument names are lowercase. Because JavaScript is case sensitive the arguments are not changed.

We could just as well have used the string method toUpperCase() rather than the method toLowerCase(); both would stop the uppercase letters from being separated from lower-case letters.

For example, if we wanted to make a case-insensitive sort of the colors we were using before, we would use code like that in Listing 14.16 (see Figure 14.16).

INPUT **LISTING 14.16**   An Alphabetical String Sort, Independent of Case
(SortStringsAndNumbers05.htm)

```
<!DOCTYPE html
PUBLIC "-//W3C//DTD XHTML 1.0 Transitional//EN"
"DTD/xhtml1-transitional.dtd">
<html>
<head>
<title>Using an alphabetical sort() method on strings</title>
<script type="text/javascript" language="javascript">
<!-- //

function alphabetical(a, b)
{
    var A = a.toLowerCase();
    var B = b.toLowerCase();
    if (A < B) return -1;
    if (A > B) return  1;
    return 0;
}

function SortElements() {
var colors = new Array("red","Red","blue","Blue","green","Green");
    colors.sort(alphabetical);
var cj = colors.join(", ");
alert("The sorted array contains: " + cj);
}
// -->
</script>
</head>
```

LISTING 14.16 continued

```
<body onload="SortElements()">

</body>
</html>
```

FIGURE 14.16

A case-independent, alphabetical string sort.

ANALYSIS As you can see from the alert box, this time color names have not been separated by the case of their initial letter—upper and lowercase characters have been treated equally.

Note

The ordering of words equal in a case-insensitive comparison will depend on their relative position in the initial ordering of the array.

Let's now look at how we can create a sort for numerical values. It is as simple as the following code:

```
function numerical(a, b) {
    return a - b;
}
```

There are two points to note about these two comparison functions. The case-insensitive comparison function will result in an error, if the array it is used on has any data that has a datatype other than a string. This is because the `toLowerCase()` method is a method belonging to the `String` object and therefore can't be used with other datatypes. This could be partially remedied by applying the `toString()` method prior to the `toLowerCase()` method. This is shown in the code below:

```
function alphabetical(a, b)
{
    var A = a.toString().toLowerCase();
    var B = b.toString().toLowerCase();
    if (A < B) return -1;
    if (A > B) return  1;
    return 0;
}
```

14

This will allow numerical and boolean values to be present in the array on which the function is used. Most of the time when you are doing a case-insensitive alphabetical sort, these values will not be present. But for completeness, you may want to use that form of the `alphabetical()` function.

The numerical comparison function may also result in an error (or at least unexpected results); but this time it would be because the array it is used on contains data that is not numerical. For example,

```
10 - "a"
```

evaluates to NaN. Again this isn't an issue if the array you will use the `numerical()` function with only contains numerical data.

Multidimensional Arrays

The arrays we have been working with so far have been single dimension arrays. By this we mean that you can think of them as a single column of data. There is another type of array that we may wish to work with that can be thought of as not only containing columns of data but also rows. These types of arrays are called two-dimensional arrays. In most full-programming languages, the syntax for these types of arrays is written as in the following example:

```
myElement[x,y]        // Not how it's done in JavaScript!!
```

This refers to an element y that can be thought of as belonging to x (where x and y are index numbers).

JavaScript doesn't directly support two-dimensional arrays but, with a clever little trick, we can simulate two-dimensional arrays in JavaScript. To do this we need to store arrays within the elements of another array. Effectively, we then have an array of arrays. This is probably easier to understand with an example, so let's take a look at one:

```
var TwoDArray    = new Array();
    TwoDArray[0] = new Array();
    TwoDArray[1] = new Array();
```

In the piece of code above we have created an array called TwoDArray in the normal way with the new operator and the Array() constructor function. However, instead of assigning a piece of data to its first and second elements, we have assigned them two new arrays. These arrays are effectively stored within the elements of TwoDArray. To see how this is similar to a two-dimensional array, let's give the two arrays stored within the elements of the array TwoDArray some data:

```
var TwoDArray     = new Array();
    TwoDArray[0] = new Array();
    TwoDArray[1] = new Array();

    TwoDArray[0][0] = "a";
    TwoDArray[0][1] = "b";
    TwoDArray[1][0] = "c";
    TwoDArray[1][1] = "d";
```

At first this may look a little complex, but if you take time to think it through hopefully you will see what's happening in the four new lines. In the first of these lines the part TwoDArray[0] is simply a reference to the array we stored in the first element of TwoDArray. Therefore, the extra [0] is a reference to the first element of the array stored in the first element of TwoDArray. It is this element of the array—stored in the first element of TwoDArray—that is assigned the value a.

The same happens for the second element of the array stored in the first element of the array TwoDArray, except that it is given the value b.

In the third line, we move to the second element of TwoDArray. Remember this element contains a different array from the one in the first element. First we assign its first element the value c, then in the next line we assign its second element the value d.

If it helps you to understand two-dimensional arrays, you can think of them as a table. The number in the first set of square brackets would represent the row number, and the number in the second set of square brackets would represent the column number. In the example we have just looked at, this would mean that row 1 would have the values a and b in columns 1 and 2 respectively, and row 2 would have the values c and d in columns 1 and 2 respectively.

The benefit of ordering our data in two-dimensional arrays is that it gives us an extra level of detail.

The idea of containing arrays in the elements of another array can be extended indefinitely. We are not limited simply to two dimensions. We can have as many levels of arrays stored in elements of arrays as needed for a given task. In general, when we store arrays in the elements of another array we call them *multidimensional* arrays. JavaScript multidimensional arrays are really just arrays where the indexes are references to other arrays.

Before we finish, let's look at a more involved example where multidimensional arrays are used in conjunction with the Array object's sort() method to order a list of e-mails. This example assumes that a server-side process has filled the arrays with the latest four e-mails. Take a look at Listing 14.17. The initial output is shown in Figure 14.17.

14

LISTING 14.17 Using Multidimensional Arrays and Sorting on Screen
(emailArray.htm)

INPUT

```html
<html>
<head>
<title>My Emails</title>

<style type="text/css">
th        {background-color: #999999}
tr.odd    {background-color: #cccccc}
tr.even   {background-color: #ffffff}
th, td    {padding: 0.1em 1em}
</style>

<script language="javascript" type="text/javascript">
<!--

var emails    = new Array();

for (var i=0; i<4; i++) {
    emails[i] = new Array();
}

    emails[0]["From"] = "Iain";
    emails[0]["Date"] = "2001-07-31";
    emails[0]["Subject"] = "TV Tonight";

    emails[1]["From"] = "Member's Services";
    emails[1]["Date"] = "2001-07-30";
    emails[1]["Subject"] = "Welcome";

    emails[2]["From"] = "Lottery";
    emails[2]["Date"] = "2001-07-29";
    emails[2]["Subject"] = "You've Won!!";

    emails[3]["From"] = "Unwanted Spam";
    emails[3]["Date"] = "2001-07-28";
    emails[3]["Subject"] = "Annoying Email";

function sortByFrom(a, b)
{
    var A = a["From"].toLowerCase();
    var B = b["From"].toLowerCase();
    if (A < B) return -1;
    if (A > B) return  1;
    return 0;
}

function sortByDate(a, b)
{
```

LISTING 14.17   continued

```
        var A = a["Date"];
        var B = b["Date"];
        if (A < B) return -1;
        if (A > B) return  1;
        return 0;
    }

    function sortBySubject(a, b)
    {
        var A = a["Subject"].toLowerCase();
        var B = b["Subject"].toLowerCase();
        if (A < B) return -1;
        if (A > B) return  1;
        return 0;
    }

    var sortCriteria = location.search.substr(1);

    if (sortCriteria) {
      emails.sort(eval(sortCriteria));
    }

    //-->
    </script>

    </head>
    <body>

    <h1>My Emails</h1>

    <table>
      <tr>
        <th><a href="?sortByFrom">From</a></th>
        <th><a href="?sortByDate">Date</a></th>
        <th><a href="?sortBySubject">Subject</a></th>
      </tr>

    <script language="javascript" type="text/javascript">
    <!--

    for (var i=0; i<emails.length; i++) {
      document.write("  <tr class='" + ((i%2)? "odd": "even") + "'>");

      document.write("    <td>" + emails[i]["From"] + "</td>");
      document.write("    <td>" + emails[i]["Date"] + "</td>");
      document.write("    <td>" + emails[i]["Subject"] + "</td>");

      document.write("  </tr>");
    }
```

14

LISTING **14.17**   continued

```
//-->
</script>

</table>

</body>
</html>
```

OUTPUT

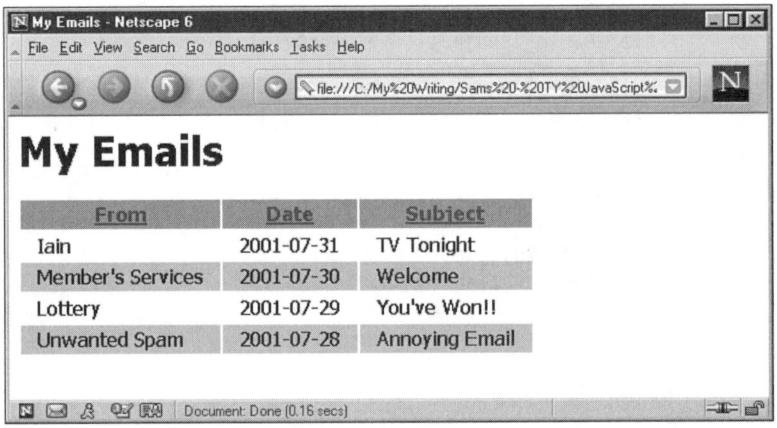

FIGURE 14.17

Sorting on screen using multidimensional arrays.

ANALYSIS On the very first line of JavaScript we created an array called `emails`. Each element of the `emails` array will contain information about an e-mail. However, because we want to have several pieces of information about each e-mail, such as who it's from and when it arrived, we can't just put pieces of data straight into this array. Instead we insert new arrays into each of the elements of the `emails` array (in this case we have used a `for` loop to do all four assignments). This allows us to associate several pieces of information with each e-mail entry.

The next four blocks of three lines each assign a piece of data to associate elements (remember, elements with a name instead of a number). We could have used numerical indexes but using names makes it easier to read for this example.

A piece of data is assigned to elements called `"From"`, `"Date"`, and `"Subject"` for each of our four e-mails.

For the moment ignore the rest of the code in the script block in the head and skip to the body. Here we create a table with three headings: one for each e-mail field. Note that these headings are wrapped with links with `href` attributes containing a short query string. When clicked on, these links will simply reload the document with the query string added to the end of the URL. We will see why shortly.

To write out the table's contents, we use a script block containing a `for` loop. This loop is set to loop through the array called `emails` and write the data for each e-mail into the table in its own row. The first line in the loop is probably the one you are least likely to understand, so let's take a closer look at it now:

```
document.write("  <tr class='" + ((i%2)? "odd": "even") + "'>");
```

The line writes a `<tr>` in the following form:

```
<tr class='xxx'>
```

The xxx part is determined by the modulo expression within the conditional operator. If `i` is even, then the expression evaluates to `0`; but if `i` is odd, then it evaluates to `1`. Because JavaScript understands `0` to be `false` and `1` to be `true` in logical contexts, the conditional operator alternates between evaluating as "odd" and "even" with each loop. By alternating the class of each row, we can assign a different background color to help each e-mail stand out.

The first time the page loads the e-mails are written into the table in the order in which they are contained within the array called `emails`. But if we click on one of the headers we can change this. To understand how this works, let's look at how the URL might change if we clicked on the `From` header:

```
http://www.xmml.com/email/index.htm?sortByFrom
```

Let's now look at the code contained within the document head that we missed earlier, at the last line to be more precise. As we said in an earlier chapter, by using the `location.search` property of the `window` object, we can obtain the query string from the URL. However, this returns the query string with the question mark still in place. To remove this, we use the `substr()` method. In effect the following line retrieves the query string and removes the question mark so that we can assign the rest of the query string to the variable `sortCriteria`, like so:

```
var sortCriteria = location.search.substr(1);
```

Notice that the query string values given to the three-header links correspond to the names of the three functions that precede the above line. When the value after the question mark in the query string has been assigned to the variable `sortCriteria`, an `if` statement checks to see whether the variable has any value. If it does the following line is executed:

```
emails.sort(eval(sortCriteria));
```

14

The `eval()` function is the first thing to evaluate in this statement. It takes the function name that is stored in the `sortCriteria` variable and interprets it as code. Therefore the function name is passed as a parameter to the `sort()` method, as it is applied to the array called `emails`. In the case of our example, where the From header is clicked, it is the name of the following function:

```
function sortByFrom(a, b)
{
    var A = a["From"].toLowerCase();
    var B = b["From"].toLowerCase();
    if (A < B) return -1;
    if (A > B) return  1;
    return 0;
}
```

This function tells the `sort()` method that rather than basing the sort on the contents of the elements of the array it is applied to, it should look at an element of the array contained within that element. In this case, the element it should base the sort on is the `"From"` element. The values of this field are also converted to lowercase for the check to make the sort case insensitive.

The conditions are then as we saw earlier in the chapter. If the first element comes before the other in the alphabet, then –1 is returned to indicate it should not be swapped. But if the first element comes after the other in the alphabet, then 1 is returned to indicate that it should be swapped. If neither of these conditions are met, then the elements must be identical and so 0 is returned to indicate they do not need swapped.

Note that in this case that when a swap does take place, then all that is contained within the two elements being compared is swapped. Therefore in the case of these elements containing arrays, the whole arrays are moved—not just parts of them. This will keep all of the information connected with one e-mail together.

Once the sort of the `emails` array has taken place the rest of the page finishes loading. This time when the table is generated from the array, it has already been sorted into the order that was selected by clicking on the header.

Of course if we are going to reload the page to restructure it, we might as well omit the JavaScript and get the server to order the e-mails and write them into a table itself. This isn't the point though. You will learn techniques elsewhere in the book that will enable you to restructure the page without reloading and hence have virtually instant ordering. The point of this example was to show how a multidimensional array can be useful, and as an added benefit, how the sort method can be used with multidimensional arrays.

Summary

Always look out for ways of using arrays to structure your data so that your scripts can run more efficiently. Whenever you have a script that performs a repeated operation on some data, ask yourself if this data wouldn't be better suited as an array so a loop statement could make this process easier. For example when you have elements of a form that must have the same check made, then give them all the same name so that you can treat them as an array. This will save you writing out individual lines of code for processing each one (hard-coding).

Workshop

In this workshop we will review what you have learned about advanced arrays in this chapter.

Q&A

Q. Are all the `Array` object's methods cross-browser?

A. No. Some methods, such as the `splice()` method are new to one browser. The `splice()` method was introduced in JScript 5.5, and with Internet Explorer 5.5, so you may want to avoid its use for a little time until most of the users of your site have upgraded to Internet Explorer 5.5 or higher. The `splice()` method has been available to Netscape since version 4.

Q. If you sort "100" and "85" as strings will "85" be less than "100"?

A. No. When sorted as strings the character "1" comes before the character "8". Therefore "100" is "less" than "85". Of course, if these two values were sorted as numbers, you would have the opposite result.

Q. Can you make a copy of an array by assigning the array to a new variable?

A. No. If you were to attempt this, the new variable would only contain a copy of a reference to the area in memory in which the array is stored. Any changes made to the array are also reflected if accessed using the new variable.

Quiz

1. Which method is used to concatenate two arrays?
2. Which method of the `Array` object allows array elements to be deleted, inserted, and/or replaced?
3. Which method is used to make a true copy of an array?

14

Quiz Answers

1. The `concat()` method is used to concatenate two arrays.

2. The `splice()` method. The second argument of the `splice()` method controls how many elements are deleted. If further arguments are present, then new elements are added to the array. Whether the `length` property increases, decreases, or stays the same depends on how many deletions and insertions are made.

3. The `concat()` method can be used to make a true copy of an array by concatenating that array with an empty array.

Exercises

1. Create an array that contains numerical values in each element of the array, and then sort the array by numerical value.

2. Create a two-dimensional array for two locations, with maximum daily temperature for each of seven days of the week. Sort the data by temperature value.

WEEK 3

Advanced Topics

WEEK 3

DAY 15

Debugging and Error Handling

The people who put together Web pages run the gamut from professional programmers, who are accustomed to working with computers and computer languages, to those whom a Web page is their first exposure to "programming." The HTML used to put together Web pages is, as the "ML" in HTML signifies, a "markup language" that is relatively straightforward to use.

When you leave the safe confines of HTML, however, and embark into JavaScript programming, you are using a real programming language. As an interpreted language, JavaScript is a lot easier to get into than languages such as C++ or Java, but as soon as you go beyond cutting and pasting "prefab" JavaScript directly into your pages, you are programming.

Like with all programming, you will quickly discover the "joy" of dealing with programming errors and bugs. There are not very many development tools specifically designed for debugging JavaScript, but there are a few. Additionally, there are a number of techniques that can be used to debug your own JavaScript programs.

This chapter will show you how to do the following:

- Use some good programming practices to cut down on errors
- Use `document.writeln()` to output debugging information
- Use alert boxes to step through JavaScript programs
- Add HTML form fields to display debugging information
- Use some dedicated script debugging tools

Preventing and Classifying JavaScript Errors

Ideally, the best way to "debug" JavaScript programs is to write error-free code. Unfortunately, this is nearly impossible to do on a consistent basis. It is possible, however, to develop coding practices and to become familiar with the different types of errors, and in doing so help make your JavaScript code run as desired.

The field of software engineering is concerned with many aspects of computer programming—including the development of coding practices that minimize programming errors. Obviously, in these few pages, these topics cannot be covered fully. However, some topics can be discussed and techniques can be shown that will give you the necessary tools for creating and debugging JavaScript code.

Commenting Code

If you've ever read any book on programming, one of the first recommendations is that you comment your code. Obviously, simply adding comments to your programs is not going to prevent errors, but it does mean that you will need to put some thought into how your programs are constructed, which may help you catch logic or other errors.

The real benefit of commenting code, though, happens when you come back to the code at a later time. It is a common practice in programming to start with an older program and then change it when doing something new, rather than starting from scratch. It is in a situation like this when you will be glad that you have commented your code. Well-commented and documented code makes it easier for you to remember what a given JavaScript does, and also will make it much easier for you to adapt your code for other uses.

Note

> The topic of commenting your code is usually one of those, "Do what I say, not what I do" sort of things. A lot of the examples in this book may not be commented as well as they should; still, it is a good practice.

Keeping Track of JavaScript Variables

A common source of errors in JavaScript programs comes from its fairly lax requirements concerning variables. JavaScript does not require variables to be strongly typed, so the same variable can be used to hold integers, floating-point numbers, Boolean values, and strings. JavaScript does a fairly good job of automatic conversion from one data type to another when performing various operations, but there is still the possibility of problems during conversion (particularly with the addition operator +, which is also used for string concatenation).

There are a number of techniques and approaches that can be used to minimize the potential pitfalls of JavaScript variable problems. These include the following:

- Explicit casting—Rather than relying on JavaScript's automatic data-type conversion, use explicit casting to convert values before operating on them. To convert to an integer or floating-point number, use the `int()` or `float()` functions, respectively. To convert a number to a string, you can use the `toString()` method of the `Math` object. The `eval()` function also can be used to turn numeric strings into numbers.

- Variable declaration—The JavaScript `var` statement is used to declare variables, but it is not required. Variables can be created on-the-fly by simply assigning a value to them. By explicitly using the `var` statement to declare each variable, you will be able to keep better track of them.

- Local versus global variables—Similar to the explicit use of the `var` statement, it is important to remember the scope of variables created. When declared with the `var` statement inside a function, a variable is local to that function and cannot be accessed elsewhere. When a variable is declared outside of a function, it is a global variable and can be accessed in any script. Conflicts between global and local variables are a common source of errors, particularly when outside scripts are loaded using the `src` attribute of the `<script>` tag.

- Variable-naming convention—By creating a variable naming convention, you can make it much easier to keep track of all of your variables, particularly when there are a lot of them. One way you can keep track of your variables is to use a given prefix to identify integers, floating-point numbers, Booleans, and strings. If you are including and using external JavaScripts, you also might consider prefixing all of your variables with a given prefix (such as your initials), in order to reduce the possibility of conflicts with any variables in the external script.

JavaScript Error Types

There are several different types of errors that are commonly encountered when creating any program, including JavaScript. How each type of error is found and dealt with is slightly different. The most common types of errors are the following:

- Syntax errors—In the initial creation of any program, the first type of error that you will encounter is a syntax error. This most commonly happens because of a typo you may have inserted into the program when typing a JavaScript statement, either in the spelling of the keyword itself or by mis-nesting braces or parentheses. As will be shown below, some browsers are able to help you pinpoint where these errors are, and once found they usually are not too hard to correct. Typically, syntax errors prevent a script from running.

- Logic errors—This catch-all classification covers the bulk of errors, and they are the hardest types of errors to discover. There are even cases where "syntax" type errors cause logic errors, since a typo in a variable name will not necessarily keep the program from running. Correcting the logic in a program to get it to run correctly is at the heart of computer programming.

- Browser-based errors—Each Web browser has slightly different capabilities, and supports different versions of JavaScript. It is quite possible that a JavaScript that works fine in one browser will not work well in another, either because of differences in the implementation of JavaScript or because of the differences in the capabilities of the underlying browser. The three most prominent browsers, Internet Explorer, Netscape Navigator 6.x, and Netscape Navigator 4.x, are largely compatible, but they also have significant differences from each other. Additionally, older versions of all of these browsers (as well as other JavaScript-enabled browsers such as Opera) also have some differences. There are strategies for programming multiple browsers to avoid these types of errors. These strategies were covered in Chapter 8, "The Browser Issue," and Chapter 11, "Dynamic HTML."

Finding Syntax Errors

In most computer languages, a syntax error will prevent a program from running. Often you will be informed of where the problem is, which generally makes finding and correcting syntax errors fairly simple. After writing a program, you continue trying to run it until it actually runs. At that point, the syntax errors (at least the syntax errors in the portion of the program that you have run) will have all been corrected.

In many cases, a JavaScript interpreter treats syntax errors the same way. The JavaScript interpreter that actually runs a JavaScript program is part of the Web browser used to load the HTML document that includes and calls it. The JavaScript interpreters in Netscape Navigator and Internet Explorer have different reactions to syntax errors, however.

Errors in Netscape Navigator

Figure 15.1 shows the reaction of Netscape Navigator 6 to an HTML document that contains JavaScript, which includes a syntax error that prevents correct execution. The example program is one shown in greater detail in the next section; if the program were working, though, there would be output between the two horizontal rules. As can be seen from the figure, however, there is no outward indication that there is a syntax error, other than the lack of output.

FIGURE 15.1

Syntax errors in Netscape Navigator are not always reported.

Netscape Navigator has a JavaScript console that can be displayed in order to get information about JavaScript errors. In order to display the console, type `javascript:` into the address line of the browser, and a window similar to that shown in Figure 15.2 will display.

FIGURE 15.2

Netscape's JavaScript console gives error information.

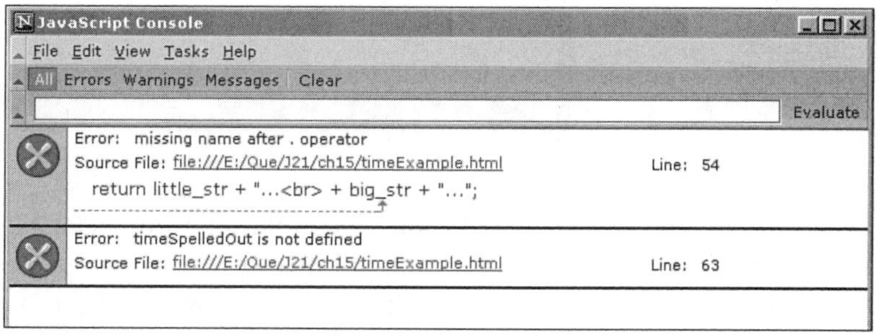

As shown, the JavaScript console gives information about the different types of errors that occurred. In this case, it is possible to pinpoint the syntax error (a missing close quotation mark on line 54) by looking at these error messages. It is interesting to note that a single syntax error caused both of the error messages shown in Figure 15.2. This is because the first error, the one listed as being in line 54, caused the definition of the timeSpelledOut function to be incomplete and undefined, causing the error from line 63.

Errors in Internet Explorer

Similar to Netscape Navigator, Internet Explorer also allows you to examine error messages caused by syntax errors in JavaScript programs. In fact, Internet Explorer makes it a little more obvious that an error has occurred, as shown in Figure 15.3. In addition to there not being any script output (as expected), Internet Explorer uses a small icon on the left side of the status bar to indicate an error. (Sometimes, a line such as "Done, but errors have occurred" will also appear in the status line.)

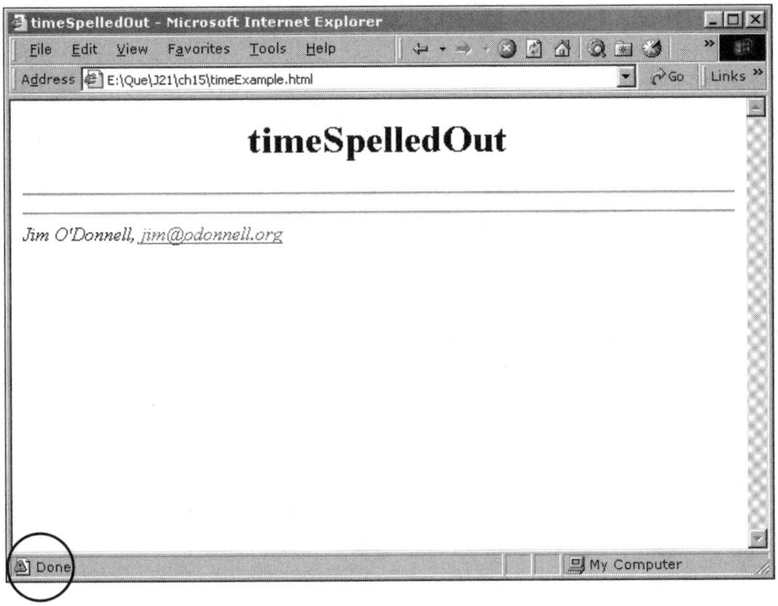

FIGURE 15.3

By default, Internet Explorer uses a small status bar icon to indicate a script error.

When the error icon appears, you can display an Error dialog box by double-clicking on the error icon. The Error dialog box will appear, as shown in Figure 15.4. The details of the error can be examined, as with Netscape's JavaScript console, to determine where the JavaScript error occurred. Note that the Previous and Next buttons (when enabled) on the bottom of the Error dialog box allow you to scroll through all of the error messages generated. As shown above, it is possible for a single error to generate more than one error message; in that case, it is important to scroll through all of the messages in order to find the exact source of the error.

FIGURE 15.4

Double-clicking the error icon will display the Error dialog box.

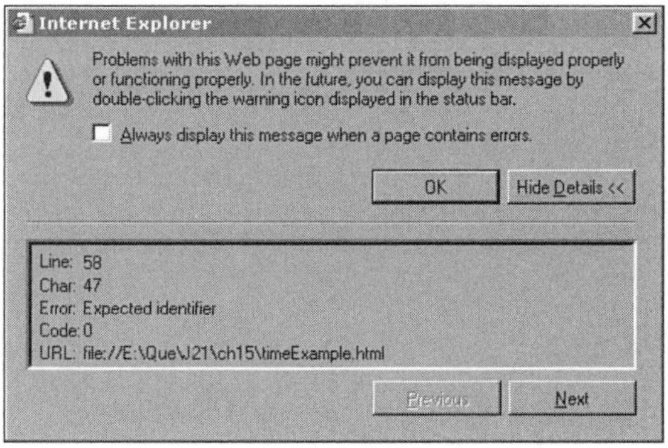

> **Note**
>
> Notice the check box in the Error dialog box shown in Figure 15.4, "Always display this message when a page contains errors." If you check this box, any JavaScript (or other Web page) errors in the future will automatically bring up the Error dialog box. This optional setting can also be made using the Advanced tab of the Internet Options, checking the box for "Display a notification about every script error."

Debugging Load-Time Errors

For the most part, in the rest of the chapter you will see different techniques that you can use to debug JavaScript errors. Different types of JavaScript require different approaches to debugging; in the next three sections, three different types of scripts will be discussed.

The first type of JavaScript that will be discussed is a load-time script. This is a JavaScript that is loaded and executed when the Web page first loads in the browser. Listing 15.1 shows an example of such a Web page and JavaScript program.

INPUT   **LISTING 15.1**   Load-Time Script for "Formatted" Time (`timeExample.html`)

```
<html>
<head>
<title>timeSpelledOut</title>
<script language="javascript" type="text/javascript">
function timeSpelledOut() {
   var now = new Date();
   var hour = now.getHours();
   var minute = now.getMinutes();
   var hourn,minuten,minute_frac,little_str,big_str;
/*
```

LISTING 15.1   continued

```
 * figure out what two numbers the little hand are between
 */
   if (hour >= 12) hour -= 12;
   if (hour == 0) {
      hour = 12;
      hourn = 1;
   }
   else
      hourn = hour + 1;
/*
 * figure out what two numbers the big hand are between
 */
   minute /= 5;
   minute_frac = minute - Math.floor(minute);
   minute = Math.floor(minute);
   if (minute == 0) {
      minute = 12;
      minuten = 1;
   }
   else
      minuten = minute + 1;
/*
 * spell out where the little and big hands are
 */
   if (minute == 12 && minute_frac < 0.1)
      little_str = "The little hand is on the " + hour;
   else if (minute == 11)
      little_str = "The little hand is almost on the " + hourn;
   else if (minute == 12 || minute == 1)
      little_str = "The little hand is just past the " + hour;
   else
      little_str = "The little hand is between the " + hour +
                   " and the " + hourn;
   if (minute_frac == 0.0)
      big_str = "The big hand is on the " + minute;
   else if (minute_frac > 0.7)
      big_str = "The big hand is almost on the " + minuten;
   else if (minute_frac < 0.3)
      big_str = "The big hand is just past the " + minute;
   else
      big_str = "The big hand is between the " + minute + " and the " + minuten;
/*
 * return time spelled out
 */
   return little_str + "...<br>" + big_str + "...";
}
</script>
</head>
<body>
```

15

LISTING 15.1   continued

```
<center>
<h1>timeSpelledOut</h1>
<hr>
<script language="javascript">
document.writeln("<h2>" + timeSpelledOut() + "</h2>");
</script>
<hr>
</center>
<em>Jim O'Donnell,
    <a href="mailto:jim@odonnell.org">jim@odonnell.org</a></em>
</body>
</html>
```

The JavaScript included in Listing 15.1 displays a formatted time when the Web page is loaded. This particular format, known as "time spelled out," gives the current time as it would be displayed on an analog clock. Figure 15.5 shows an example of the current time, "spelled out."

OUTPUT

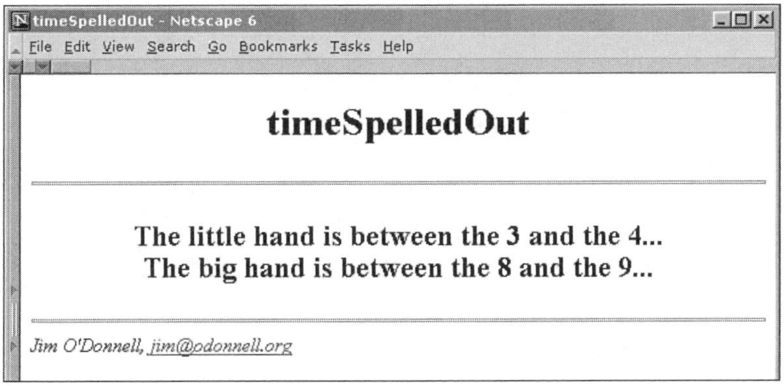

FIGURE 15.5

Load-time JavaScript that outputs "analog" time.

Using the `document.writeln()` Method

Because a load-time JavaScript executes while the Web page is writing out, the easiest way to get debugging information (to get some insight into the workings of the script), is to use the `document.writeln()` method to write out additional information directly into the page.

Listing 15.2 shows the same HTML document and JavaScript as that shown in Listing 15.1, only this time with additional debugging statements included to write out intermediate information from the script. JavaScript comments are used to highlight the debugging information included, so that the statements may be removed (or commented out easily when the script is working correctly). Figure 15.6 shows an example of the resulting Web page that shows both the intended output as well as the debug output that shows intermediate values.

INPUT   **LISTING 15.2**   Using `document.writeln()` to Write Debugging Information

```html
<html>
<head>
<title>timeSpelledOut</title>
<script language="javascript" type="text/javascript">
function timeSpelledOut() {
   var now = new Date();
   var hour = now.getHours();
   var minute = now.getMinutes();
   var hourn,minuten,minute_frac,little_str,big_str;
/*
 * figure out what two numbers the little hand are between
 */
   if (hour >= 12) hour -= 12;
   if (hour == 0) {
      hour = 12;
      hourn = 1;
   }
   else
      hourn = hour + 1;
/*
 * figure out what two numbers the big hand are between
 */
   minute /= 5;
   minute_frac = minute - Math.floor(minute);
   minute = Math.floor(minute);
   if (minute == 0) {
      minute = 12;
      minuten = 1;
   }
   else
      minuten = minute + 1;
/*
 * spell out where the little and big hands are
 */
   if (minute == 12 && minute_frac < 0.1)
      little_str = "The little hand is on the " + hour;
   else if (minute == 11)
      little_str = "The little hand is almost on the " + hourn;
   else if (minute == 12 || minute == 1)
      little_str = "The little hand is just past the " + hour;
```

LISTING 15.2   continued

```
    else
       little_str = "The little hand is between the " + hour +
                    " and the " + hourn;
    if (minute_frac == 0.0)
       big_str = "The big hand is on the " + minute;
    else if (minute_frac > 0.7)
       big_str = "The big hand is almost on the " + minuten;
    else if (minute_frac < 0.3)
       big_str = "The big hand is just past the " + minute;
    else
       big_str = "The big hand is between the " + minute +
                 " and the " + minuten;
  /*
   * DEBUG: output intermediate variables
   */
    document.writeln("now           = " + now         + "<br>");
    document.writeln("hour          = " + hour        + "<br>");
    document.writeln("hourn         = " + hourn       + "<br>");
    document.writeln("minute        = " + minute      + "<br>");
    document.writeln("minuten       = " + minuten     + "<br>");
    document.writeln("minute_frac = " + minute_frac + "<br>");
    document.writeln("little_str   = " + little_str  + "<br>");
    document.writeln("big_str      = " + big_str     + "<br>");
  /*
   * return time spelled out
   */
    return little_str + "...<br>" + big_str + "...";
}
</script>
</head>
<body>
<center>
<h1>timeSpelledOut</h1>
<hr>
<script language="javascript">
document.writeln("<h2>" + timeSpelledOut() + "</h2>");
</script>
<hr>
</center>
<em>Jim O'Donnell,
    <a href="mailto:jim@odonnell.org">jim@odonnell.org</a></em>
</body>
</html>
```

OUTPUT

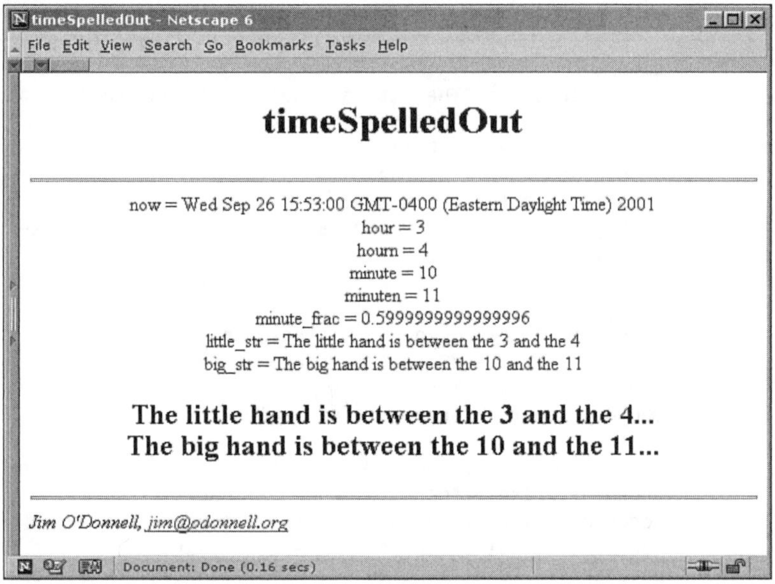

FIGURE 15.6

*Debugging informa-
tion can be written
directly into the Web
page.*

```
N timeSpelledOut - Netscape 6                                    _ □ x
 File  Edit  View  Search  Go  Bookmarks  Tasks  Help

                         timeSpelledOut
  ─────────────────────────────────────────────────────────────

         now = Wed Sep 26 15:53:00 GMT-0400 (Eastern Daylight Time) 2001
                              hour = 3
                              hourn = 4
                             minute = 10
                             minuten = 11
                    minute_frac = 0.5999999999999996
               little_str = The little hand is between the 3 and the 4
               big_str = The big hand is between the 10 and the 11

          The little hand is between the 3 and the 4...
          The big hand is between the 10 and the 11...

  ─────────────────────────────────────────────────────────────
   Jim O'Donnell, jim@odonnell.org

 N  🔍  📰   Document: Done (0.16 secs)
```

Using the Alternate Inputs

The `timeSpelledOut()` JavaScript function shown in Listings 15.1 and 15.2 indicates a
need for further techniques for debugging. Because the script is designed to print out a
formatted version of the current time, it would take 24 hours to test all of the necessary
combinations of times. Obviously, you don't want to have to wait all that time to test all
of the pertinent combinations.

Listing 15.3 shows another alternative approach, one that allows for full testing of the
function without requiring a great deal of time to hit all of the possibilities. As shown in
the function, it is accomplished by supplying alternative inputs to the `timeSpelledOut()`
function. When the function is called using these inputs, they are used in place of the
actual time, thereby allowing for times other than the current time to be used. When the
function is called without these inputs, the current time is used.

INPUT

LISTING 15.3 Supplying Alternate Inputs to Debug Different Cases
(`timeExampleDebug2.html`)

```
<html>
<head>
<title>timeSpelledOut</title>
<script language="javascript" type="text/javascript">
function timeSpelledOut(h_in,m_in) {
```

15

LISTING 15.3   continued

```
    var now = new Date();
    var hour = now.getHours();
    var minute = now.getMinutes();
    var hourn,minuten,minute_frac,little_str,big_str;
/*
 * DEBUG: use function inputs, if defined
 */
    document.writeln("h_in " + h_in + "<br>");
    h_in = Math.floor(h_in);
    if (h_in >= 0 && h_in <= 23)
        hour = h_in;
    document.writeln("m_in " + m_in + "<br>");
    h_in = Math.floor(m_in);
    if (m_in >= 0 && m_in <= 59)
        minute = m_in;
/*
 * figure out what two numbers the little hand are between
 */
    if (hour >= 12) hour -= 12;
    if (hour == 0) {
        hour = 12;
        hourn = 1;
    }
    else
        hourn = hour + 1;
/*
 * figure out what two numbers the big hand are between
 */
    minute /= 5;
    minute_frac = minute - Math.floor(minute);
    minute = Math.floor(minute);
    if (minute == 0) {
        minute = 12;
        minuten = 1;
    }
    else
        minuten = minute + 1;
/*
 * spell out where the little and big hands are
 */
    if (minute == 12 && minute_frac < 0.1)
        little_str = "The little hand is on the " + hour;
    else if (minute == 11)
        little_str = "The little hand is almost on the " + hourn;
    else if (minute == 12 || minute == 1)
        little_str = "The little hand is just past the " + hour;
    else
        little_str = "The little hand is between the " + hour +
                     " and the " + hourn;
```

LISTING 15.3   continued

```
    if (minute_frac == 0.0)
       big_str = "The big hand is on the " + minute;
    else if (minute_frac > 0.7)
       big_str = "The big hand is almost on the " + minuten;
    else if (minute_frac < 0.3)
       big_str = "The big hand is just past the " + minute;
    else
       big_str = "The big hand is between the " + minute +
                 " and the " + minuten;
/*
 * DEBUG: output intermediate variables
 */
    document.writeln("now         = " + now         + "<br>");
    document.writeln("hour        = " + hour        + "<br>");
    document.writeln("hourn       = " + hourn       + "<br>");
    document.writeln("minute      = " + minute      + "<br>");
    document.writeln("minuten     = " + minuten     + "<br>");
    document.writeln("minute_frac = " + minute_frac + "<br>");
    document.writeln("little_str  = " + little_str  + "<br>");
    document.writeln("big_str     = " + big_str     + "<br>");
/*
 * return time spelled out
 */
    return little_str + "...<br>" + big_str + "...";
}
</script>
</head>
<body>
<center>
<h1>timeSpelledOut</h1>
<hr>
<script language="javascript">
document.writeln("<h2>" + timeSpelledOut(11, 0) + "</h2>");
document.writeln("<h2>" + timeSpelledOut(11, 1) + "</h2>");
document.writeln("<h2>" + timeSpelledOut(11, 2) + "</h2>");
document.writeln("<h2>" + timeSpelledOut(11, 3) + "</h2>");
document.writeln("<h2>" + timeSpelledOut(11, 4) + "</h2>");
document.writeln("<h2>" + timeSpelledOut(11, 5) + "</h2>");
document.writeln("<h2>" + timeSpelledOut(11, 6) + "</h2>");
document.writeln("<h2>" + timeSpelledOut(11,54) + "</h2>");
document.writeln("<h2>" + timeSpelledOut(11,55) + "</h2>");
document.writeln("<h2>" + timeSpelledOut(11,56) + "</h2>");
document.writeln("<h2>" + timeSpelledOut(11,57) + "</h2>");
document.writeln("<h2>" + timeSpelledOut(11,58) + "</h2>");
document.writeln("<h2>" + timeSpelledOut(11,59) + "</h2>");
document.writeln("<h2>" + timeSpelledOut(12, 0) + "</h2>");
</script>
<hr>
```

LISTING 15.3   continued

```
</center>
<em>Jim O'Donnell,
    <a href="mailto:jim@odonnell.org">jim@odonnell.org</a></em>
</body>
</html>
```

Figure 15.7 displays the output of a debugged version of the Web page, showing the output from many different combinations of input times, which are spelled out on the page.

OUTPUT

FIGURE 15.7

Use debugging techniques to quickly test many output possibilities. Only a small part of the output is shown.

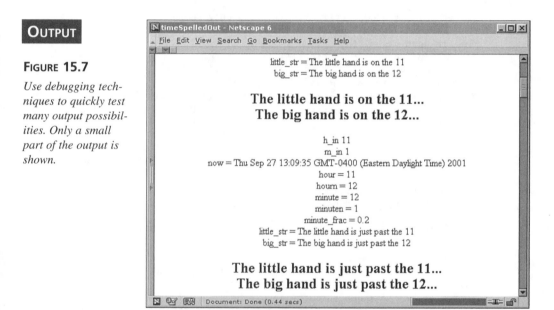

Debugging Run-Time Errors I: Discrete Events

Many JavaScript programs do not run at load-time, however. Using the document.writeln() method is not as appropriate for debugging those types of scripts, since the page is not currently open for writing. A prime example of such a run-time script—one that runs after the page has completely loaded and been displayed—is a script for performing validation of HTML form inputs. An example of such a script is shown in Listing 15.4. This script takes a telephone number as input, ensures that it is a valid U.S. telephone number (seven or ten digits, with an optional leading 1), and then reformats and displays it back in the form. (An example of its operation is shown in Figures 15.8 and 15.9.)

LISTING 15.4   JavaScript to Format U.S. Telephone Number
INPUT   (phoneExample.html)

```
<html>
<head>
<title>phoneNumberFormat</title>
<script language="javascript" type="text/javascript">
function phoneNumberFormat(obj) {
   var num_str = obj.phoneNumber.value;
   var xChars = new Array(" ","(",")","+","-",".",
                          "I","N","V","A","L","D","!");
/*
 * remove all extraneous characters leaving only numbers
 */
   num_str_save = num_str;
   for (i = 0;i < xChars.length;i++) {
      x = xChars[i];
      while (num_str.indexOf(x) > -1)
         num_str = num_str.substring(0,num_str.indexOf(x)) +
                     num_str.substring(num_str.indexOf(x) + 1,
                                  num_str.length)
   }
/*
 * remove leading 1, if present
 */
   if (num_str.indexOf("1") == 0)
      num_str = num_str.substring(1,num_str.length);
/*
 * verify length of number, if valid
 */
   if (num_str.length == 7)
      num_str = num_str.substring(0,3) + "-" + num_str.substring(3,7);
   else if (num_str.length == 10)
      num_str = "(" + num_str.substring(0,3) + ") " +
                  num_str.substring(3,6) + "-" + num_str.substring(6,10);
   else
      if (num_str_save.indexOf(" INVALID!") > -1)
         num_str = num_str_save;
      else
         num_str = num_str_save + " INVALID!";
/*
 * put formatted phone number back into the form
 */
   obj.phoneNumber.value = num_str;
}
</script>
</head>
<body>
<center>
<h1>phoneNumberFormat</h1>
<hr>
```

15

LISTING 15.4 continued

```
<form name="formInfo">
<b>Input Phone Number</b>
<input type="text" size="30" name="phoneNumber"
 onChange="phoneNumberFormat(document.formInfo)">
</form>
<hr>
</center>
<em>Jim O'Donnell,
    <a href="mailto:jim@odonnell.org">jim@odonnell.org</a></em>
</body>
</html>
```

OUTPUT

FIGURE 15.8

JavaScript is often used to validate and format forms input.

FIGURE 15.9

Using document.writeln() does not work as well because the page has completely loaded.

Using the `alert()` Method

The `alert()` method makes it very simple to output intermediate script values, which enables you to get insight into the workings of a script by looking at the intermediate values that were generated. If the answer is not what you expect, which is why you would need to perform the debugging in the first place, looking at intermediate values is the best way to figure out why things are not working. Using alert boxes also allows you to single step through a script.

Listing 15.5 shows the telephone-number formatting example, with a series of alert boxes used to show the intermediate values. When the script function is called by the onChange() event of the form text box, it formats the telephone number entered into the field. Now, at each step in the process, an alert box pops up to show the current state of the formatted output.

INPUT **LISTING 15.5**   Use Alert Boxes to Pop Up Important Debugging Information (phoneExampleDebug1.html)

```
<html>
<head>
<title>phoneNumberFormat</title>
<script language="javascript" type="text/javascript">
function phoneNumberFormat(obj) {
   var num_str = obj.phoneNumber.value;
   var xChars = new Array(" ","(",")","+","-",".",
                          "I","N","V","A","L","D","!");
/*
 * DEBUG: display num_str in alert box
 */
   alert("INPUT: num_str = " + num_str);
/*
 * remove all extraneous characters leaving only numbers
 */
   num_str_save = num_str;
   for (i = 0;i < xChars.length;i++) {
      x = xChars[i];
      while (num_str.indexOf(x) > -1)
         num_str = num_str.substring(0,num_str.indexOf(x)) +
                   num_str.substring(num_str.indexOf(x) + 1,
                                     num_str.length)
   }
/*
 * DEBUG: display num_str in alert box
 */
   alert("EXTRANEOUS CHARACTERS REMOVED: num_str = " + num_str);
/*
 * remove leading 1, if present
 */
   if (num_str.indexOf("1") == 0)
      num_str = num_str.substring(1,num_str.length);
/*
 * DEBUG: display num_str in alert box
 */
   alert("LEADING \"1\" REMOVED: num_str = " + num_str);
/*
 * verify length of number, if valid
 */
```

LISTING 15.5 continued

```
    if (num_str.length == 7)
        num_str = num_str.substring(0,3) + "-" + num_str.substring(3,7);
    else if (num_str.length == 10)
        num_str = "(" + num_str.substring(0,3) + ") " +
                    num_str.substring(3,6) + "-" + num_str.substring(6,10);
    else
        if (num_str_save.indexOf(" INVALID!") > -1)
            num_str = num_str_save;
        else
            num_str = num_str_save + " INVALID!";
/*
 * DEBUG: display num_str in alert box
 */
    alert("FORMATTED: num_str = " + num_str);
/*
 * put formatted phone number back into the form
 */
    obj.phoneNumber.value = num_str;
}
</script>
</head>
<body>
<center>
<h1>phoneNumberFormat</h1>
<hr>
<form name="formInfo">
<b>Input Phone Number</b>
<input type="text" size="30" name="phoneNumber"
 onchange="phoneNumberFormat(document.formInfo)">
</form>
<hr>
</center>
<em>Jim O'Donnell,
    <a href="mailto:jim@odonnell.org">jim@odonnell.org</a></em>
</body>
</html>
```

Figures 15.10 through 15.13 show the debugging alert boxes that popped up in the example from Listing 15.5. Note that, in addition to showing the current value of the formatted telephone number, explanatory text is included to detail where in the process the script is.

OUTPUT

FIGURE 15.10

Alert boxes can be used to show intermediate values.

FIGURE 15.11

Intermediate script values give insight into its operation.

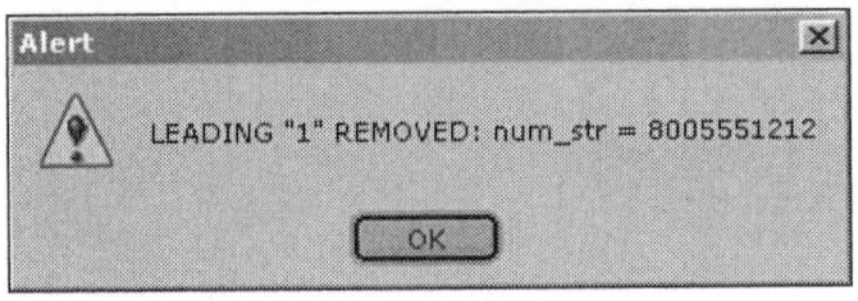

FIGURE 15.12

Use alert boxes to show how a script is progressing step by step.

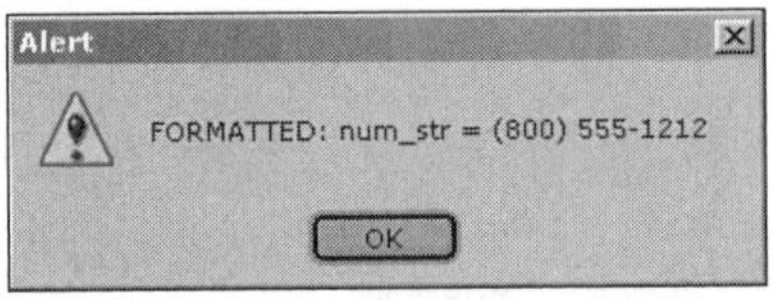

FIGURE 15.13

Alerts can be used to pinpoint script errors and show intermediate and final results.

ANALYSIS While alert boxes work pretty well for stepping through scripts, they can be a problem if there are many steps to go through. Even though you will remove the alert boxes after the script is fully debugged, it can still be a pain to get through a full script if there are too many alert boxes. In such a case, there is a way you can include all of the debugging input without requiring your input to display an alert box at each step.

Using HTML Form Elements

Another way to output debugging information during the operation of a script is to use HTML forms—in particular, text and text-area boxes. The text contents of each of these elements can be accessed and changed via JavaScript. Just as separate alerts were used in Listing 15.5 to display intermediate calculations and values in the script, the same information can be displayed in a text-area box.

Listing 15.6 shows another version of the telephone-number formatting example, this one using a text-area box to display debug information. Figure 15.14 shows the page before the script is run. Notice that the debug text-area box is included at the end of the Web page, after the "real" Web page content.

INPUT

LISTING 15.6   TEXTAREA Boxes Can Display Lots of Information
(phoneExampleDebug2.html)

```
<html>
<head>
<title>phoneNumberFormat</title>
<script language="javascript" type="text/javascript">
function phoneNumberFormat(obj) {
   var num_str = obj.phoneNumber.value;
   var xChars = new Array(" ","(",")","+","-",".",
                          "I","N","V","A","L","D","!");
/*
 * DEBUG: display num_str in alert box
 */
   textareaDebugWrite("INPUT: num_str = ",num_str);
/*
 * remove all extraneous characters leaving only numbers
 */
   num_str_save = num_str;
   for (i = 0;i < xChars.length;i++) {
      x = xChars[i];
      while (num_str.indexOf(x) > -1)
         num_str = num_str.substring(0,num_str.indexOf(x)) +
                   num_str.substring(num_str.indexOf(x) + 1,num_str.length)
   }
/*
 * DEBUG: display num_str in alert box
 */
   textareaDebugWrite("EXTRANEOUS CHARACTERS REMOVED: num_str = ",num_str);
/*
 * remove leading 1, if present
 */
   if (num_str.indexOf("1") == 0)
      num_str = num_str.substring(1,num_str.length);
/*
 * DEBUG: display num_str in alert box
 */
   textareaDebugWrite("LEADING \"1\" REMOVED: num_str = ",num_str);
/*
 * verify length of number, if valid
 */
   if (num_str.length == 7)
      num_str = num_str.substring(0,3) + "-" + num_str.substring(3,7);
```

LISTING 15.6   continued

```
      else if (num_str.length == 10)
         num_str = "(" + num_str.substring(0,3) + ") " +
                    num_str.substring(3,6) + "-" + num_str.substring(6,10);
      else
         if (num_str_save.indexOf(" INVALID!") > -1)
            num_str = num_str_save;
         else
            num_str = num_str_save + " INVALID!";
  /*
   * DEBUG: display num_str in alert box
   */
      textareaDebugWrite("FORMATTED: num_str = ",num_str);
  /*
   * put formatted phone number back into the form
   */
      obj.phoneNumber.value = num_str;
  }
  </script>
  </head>
  <body>
  <center>
  <h1>phoneNumberFormat</h1>
  <hr>
  <form name="formInfo">
  <b>Input Phone Number</b>
  <input type="text" size="30" name="phoneNumber"
   onchange="phoneNumberFormat(document.formInfo)">
  </form>
  <hr>
  </center>
  <em>Jim O'Donnell,
       <a href="mailto:jim@odonnell.org">jim@odonnell.org</a></em>
  <!-- DEBUG STUFF -->
     <hr>
     <form name="debugInfo">
     <textarea name="debugText" rows="8" cols="70">DEBUG INFO...</textarea>
     </form>
     <hr>
     <script language="javascript" type="text/javascript">
     function textareaDebugWrite(lbl,val) {
        document.debugInfo.debugText.value += "\n" + lbl + val;
     }
     </script>
  <!-- DEBUG STUFF -->
  </body>
  </html>
```

15

OUTPUT

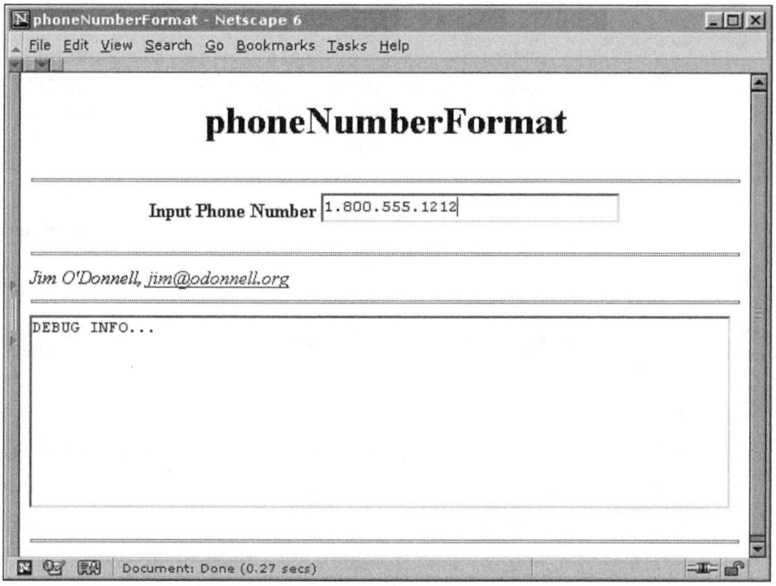

FIGURE 15.14

Text-area boxes can be used to display debugging information.

After the script is executed, Figure 15.15 shows the resulting output. As shown, the telephone number has been correctly formatted. Additionally, the intermediate information that you can use to debug the script is shown in the text-area box. If the script does not work, this information would allow you to pinpoint where the problem exists.

OUTPUT

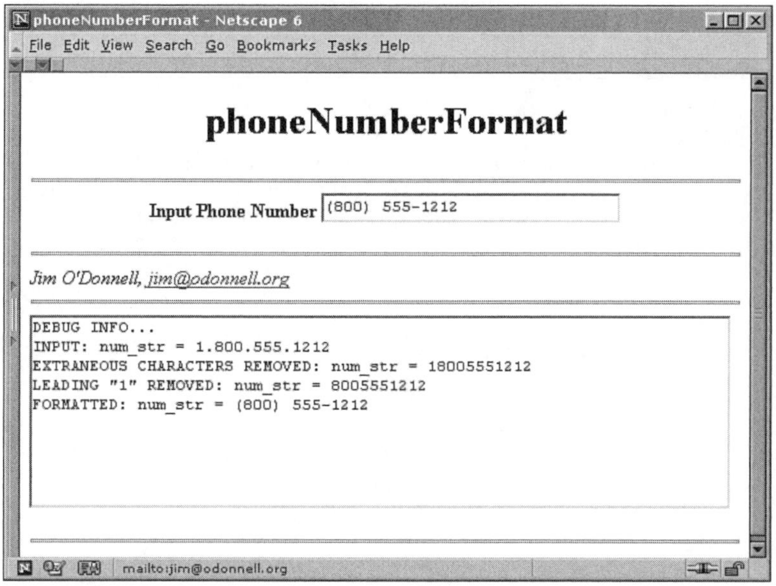

FIGURE 15.15

All intermediate calculations can be output onto page.

Note

> Before the advent of Dynamic HTML, you could only use form elements, such as text and text-area boxes, to dynamically change text content once a Web page was loaded. HTML forms were among the first elements for Web pages accessible through JavaScript as well. Now, there are other ways to add and change content on a Web page using Dynamic HTML, and these techniques also can be used to include debugging information. However, using HTML forms is still the most straightforward approach.

Debugging Run-Time Errors II: Continuous Events

Validation of HTML forms is a discrete event. When a form field is changed or a Submit button is clicked, a JavaScript runs once and performs its function (for example, validating and formatting the contents of a text box as in the example in the previous section). For this sort of script, the alert box and text-area methods shown in the previous section are appropriate.

What about "continuous" events, such as those generated by mouse and keyboard events? Listing 15.7 shows an example of this, which is a positioning example that runs in Internet Explorer or Navigator 4. In this example, Dynamic HTML techniques are used to allow a Web-page graphic to be dragged anywhere on the page.

INPUT   **LISTING 15.7**   Dynamic HTML Allows Objects to Be Dynamically Moved (positioningExample.html)

```
<html>
<head>
<title>Positioning with Cross-Browser Dynamic HTML</title>
<script language="JavaScript" src="dynlayer.js"></script>
<script language="JavaScript" src="mouseevents.js"></script>
<script language="JavaScript" src="drag.js"></script>
<script language="JavaScript">
function init() {
/*
 * initialize DynLayers
 */
  DynLayerInit();
/*
```

LISTING 15.7 continued

```
 * add the draggable layers to the drag object
 */
   drag.add(author);
/*
 * initialize mouse events
 */
   initMouseEvents();
}
</script>
</head>
<body onLoad="init()">
<center>
<h1>Positioning with<br>Cross-Browser Dynamic HTML</h1>
<hr>
<table>
<tr><td width="50%">
    This example uses the DynAPI JavaScript Library
    (<a href="http://www.dansteinman.com/dynduo/">
    http://www.dansteinman.com/dynduo/</a>) to create
    an example that will work in Internet
    Explorer and Netscape Navigator 4.</td>
<td> </td></tr>
</table>
<hr>
</center>
<em>Jim O'Donnell, <a href="mailto:jim@odonnell.org">jim@odonnell.org</a></em>
<div id="authorDiv"
 style="position:absolute;width:275;height:215;left:320;top:150">
   <table>
   <tr valign="BOTTOM">
       <td><img src="rbflag_ls.gif" width="50"  height="47"
               border="0" /></td>
       <td><img src="Author.jpg"    width="175" height="215"
               border="0" /></td>
       <td><img src="rbflag_rs.gif" width="50"  height="47"
               border="0" /></td></tr>
   </table>
</div>
</body>
</html>
```

Figure 15.16 shows the Web page, as it first appears when it is loaded. As shown in Figure 15.17, you can pick up and drag the image and move it around the Web page.

OUTPUT

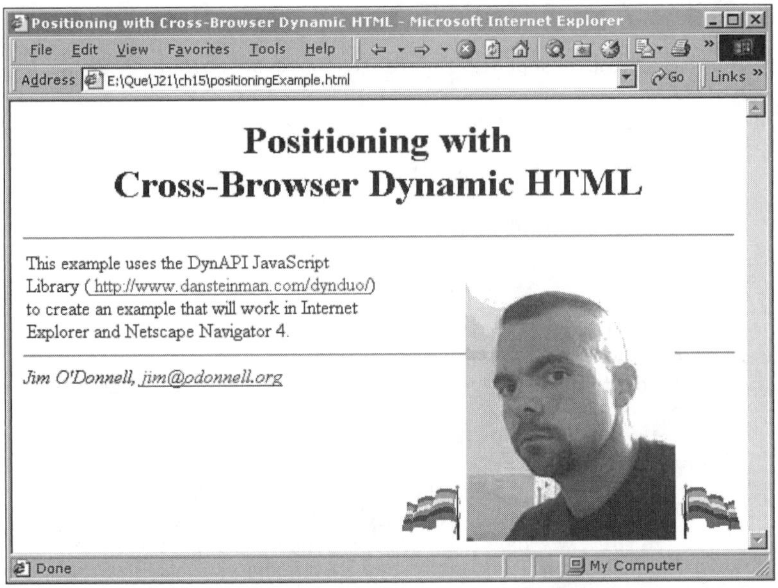

FIGURE 15.16

JavaScript and Dynamic HTML can be used to move objects.

FIGURE 15.17

Continuous events need a way of displaying debugging information that will not interrupt them.

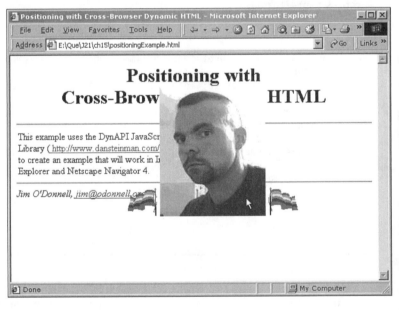

> **Note**
>
> The Dynamic Duo Web site, located at `http://www.dansteinman.com/` `dynduo/`, is a good example of what you can achieve using Dynamic HTML that is targeted for both Netscape Navigator and Microsoft Internet Explorer. The external JavaScripts loaded in this example are from this Web site. While this site is no longer being updated, it still has lots of good information, and links to more up-to-date content.

How do you debug scripts such as this? While the graphic is being dragged from one position to another, it is generating events continuously. Obviously, popping up an event box every time a script was called in this case would not be acceptable, as it would interrupt the dragging operation. Likewise, if a text-area box were used, as in the example in Listing 15.6, where information was appended to the box contents each time the script was called, the box would quickly fill up the text-area box and would not be useful. So, what is the answer?

In this case, a good way to display intermediate or internal script values while it is continually running is to use an HTML form text box. (Another way would be to use the status bar area.) Instead of appending new content, the contents of the box or boxes are replaced each time the script is called. So, in the positioning example, each time a mouse event calls the script, it is able to display new information from the script internals.

Listing 15.8 shows the example with debugging information included. In this case, a simple HTML table is used to format a collection of four text boxes, with each being used to show information about the object being dragged.

INPUT

LISTING 15.8   Text Boxes Can Be Updated On-The-Fly
(positioningExampleDebug.html)

```
<html>
<head>
<title>Positioning with Cross-Browser Dynamic HTML</title>
<script language="JavaScript" src="dynlayer.js"></script>
<script language="JavaScript" src="mouseevents.js"></script>
<script language="JavaScript" src="drag.js"></script>
<script language="JavaScript" type="text/javascript">
function init() {
/*
 * initialize DynLayers
 */
   DynLayerInit();
/*
 * add the draggable layers to the drag object
 */
```

LISTING 15.8 continued

```
   drag.add(author);
/*
 * set up supplemental event handlers
 */
   drag.onDragStart = dragStart;
   drag.onDragMove = dragMove;
   drag.onDragEnd = dragEnd;
/*
 * initialize mouse events
 */
   initMouseEvents();
}
function dragStart(x,y) {
       document.MyForm.ID.value = drag.obj.id
       document.MyForm.STATE.value = "moving"
       return false
}
function dragMove(x,y) {
       document.MyForm.X.value = drag.obj.x
       document.MyForm.Y.value = drag.obj.y
       return false
}
function dragEnd(x,y) {
       document.MyForm.STATE.value = "static"
       return false
}
</script>
</head>
<body onLoad="init()">
<center>
<h1>Positioning with<br>Cross-Browser Dynamic HTML</h1>
<hr>
<table>
<tr><td width="50%">
    This example uses the DynAPI JavaScript Library
    (<a href="http://www.dansteinman.com/dynduo/">
    http://www.dansteinman.com/dynduo/</a>) to create
    an example that will work in Internet
    Explorer and Netscape Navigator 4.</td>
<td> </td></tr>
</table>
<hr>
</center>
<em>Jim O'Donnell, <a href="mailto:jim@odonnell.org">jim@odonnell.org</a></em>
<form name="MyForm">
<table width="50%">
<tr><td>Drag Information</td>
    <td>ID   </td><td><input name="ID"    type="text" size="10" /></td></tr>
<tr><td> </td>
    <td>STATE</td><td><input name="STATE" type="text" size="10" /></td></tr>
```

15

LISTING 15.8 continued

```
<tr><td> </td>
    <td>X     </td><td><input name="X"     type="text" size="10" /></td></tr>
<tr><td> </td>
    <td>Y     </td><td><input name="Y"     type="text" size="10" /></td></tr>
</table>
</form>
<div id="authorDiv"
  style="position:absolute;width:275;height:215;left:320;top:150">
    <table>
    <tr valign="BOTTOM">
        <td><img src="rbflag_ls.gif" width="50"  height="47"
                 border="0" /></td>
        <td><img src="Author.jpg"    width="175" height="215"
                 border="0" /></td>
        <td><img src="rbflag_rs.gif" width="50"  height="47"
                 border="0" /></td></tr>
    </table>
</div>
</body>
</html>
```

Figure 15.18 shows this example when the page is loaded. As displayed, the debugging information can be found in the lower lefthand corner of the page. When the graphic is dragged with the mouse, as shown in Figure 15.19, the information in the text boxes is continuously updated to reflect the current position and state of the movement.

OUTPUT

FIGURE 15.18

Text boxes are ideal for the display of changing data.

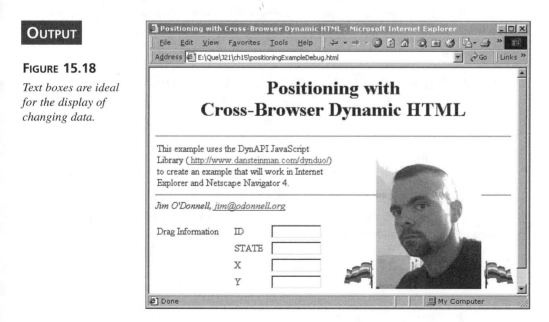

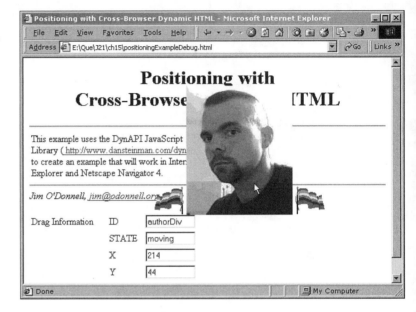

FIGURE 15.19

Information associated with continuous events can be displayed as the events unfold.

Advanced Debugging Techniques

In addition to the techniques shown above, which are designed to give you the ability to step through a script and look at some of the internal values and calculations, there are some other techniques that can be performed that are a bit more involved. In this section, a couple of these more advanced techniques will be briefly discussed. These techniques, when used with some of those described above, give you even more capabilities when debugging.

Creating a Run-Time JavaScript Interpreter

Your JavaScript-enabled browser, whether it is Netscape Navigator, Internet Explorer, or even Opera, has a built-in JavaScript interpreter. When a Web page is loaded that includes JavaScript, these scripts are interpreted and the results are output or displayed, or in some way acted upon by the Web browser. In essence, this is a "batch" process—where you write a bunch of JavaScript code and submit it to the browser to see if it runs.

In some cases, it would be nice to have the equivalent of a command-line interface to the JavaScript browser. This would allow you to type in a line of JavaScript and have it immediately evaluated and its output displayed. Fortunately, JavaScript has a function that gives you this ability.

Listing 15.9 shows a JavaScript file that implements a simple JavaScript interpreter using the prompt() method. When loaded and called from another JavaScript, a prompt box will display, which takes a line of JavaScript input, evaluates it, and shows the results.

INPUT

LISTING 15.9   JavaScript eval() Function Used as JavaScript Interpreter (debugInterpreter.js)

```
function debugInterpreter () {
   var pstr = "JAVASCRIPT INTERPRETER";
   while (true) {
      x = prompt(pstr);
      if (!x) break;
      pstr = "eval(" + x + ") = " + eval(x);
   }
}
```

ANALYSIS   The JavaScript interpreter shown in Listing 15.10 uses the JavaScript eval() function to interpret JavaScript expressions entered into the prompt box. It then redisplays a prompt box with the results of the previous line while ready to accept a new line of input. Clicking on the Cancel button of the prompt box exits the interpreter.

Listing 15.10 shows an application of the interpreter, as it is included in the telephone-number formatting example. By writing the interpreter as a separate function and calling it, as in Listing 15.10, you preserve the modularity of the code, thereby making it very simple to include in a script. The trade-off for doing it this way is that, while in the interpreter, you can access only JavaScript variables and browser properties that have global scope. You will notice in Listing 15.10 that a few of the variables have been made global by declaring them outside of the JavaScript function. Alternatively, you could actually include the debug interpreter while loop itself in your script, rather than as a separate function; this is a little messier, but gives access to all of the local variables in the script.

INPUT

LISTING 15.10   A Real-Time Interpreter Can Be Used for Debugging (phoneExampleDebug3.html)

```
<html>
<head>
<title>phoneNumberFormat</title>
<script language="javascript" src="debugInterpreter.js"></script>
<script language="javascript" type="javascript">
   var num_str,num_str_save;
function phoneNumberFormat(obj) {
   var xChars = new Array(" ","(",")","+","-",".",
                          "I","N","V","A","L","D","!");
```

LISTING 15.10   continued

```
/*
 * remove all extraneous characters leaving only numbers
 */
   num_str = obj.phoneNumber.value;
   num_str_save = num_str;
   for (i = 0;i < xChars.length;i++) {
      x = xChars[i];
      while (num_str.indexOf(x) > -1)
         num_str = num_str.substring(0,num_str.indexOf(x)) +
                   num_str.substring(num_str.indexOf(x) + 1,num_str.length)
   }
/*
 * remove leading 1, if present
 */
   if (num_str.indexOf("1") == 0)
      num_str = num_str.substring(1,num_str.length);
/*
 * verify length of number, if valid
 */
   if (num_str.length == 7)
      num_str = num_str.substring(0,3) + "-" + num_str.substring(3,7);
   else if (num_str.length == 10)
      num_str = "(" + num_str.substring(0,3) + ") " +
                num_str.substring(3,6) + "-" + num_str.substring(6,10);
   else
      if (num_str_save.indexOf(" INVALID!") > -1)
         num_str = num_str_save;
      else
         num_str = num_str_save + " INVALID!";
/*
 * DEBUG: call debug interpreter
 */
   debugInterpreter();
/*
 * put formatted phone number back into the form
 */
   obj.phoneNumber.value = num_str;
}
</script>
</head>
<body>
<center>
<h1>phoneNumberFormat</h1>
<hr>
<form name="formInfo">
<b>Input Phone Number</b>
<input type="text" size="30" name="phoneNumber"
 onchange="phoneNumberFormat(document.formInfo)">
</form>
```

LISTING 15.10   continued

```
<hr>
</center>
<em>Jim O'Donnell,
    <a href="mailto:jim@odonnell.org">jim@odonnell.org</a></em>
</body>
</html>
```

15

Figure 15.20 shows an example of the interpreter in action. It has already been used to print out the current contents of the num_str variable, and it is in the process of showing the contents of the HTML form text box.

OUTPUT

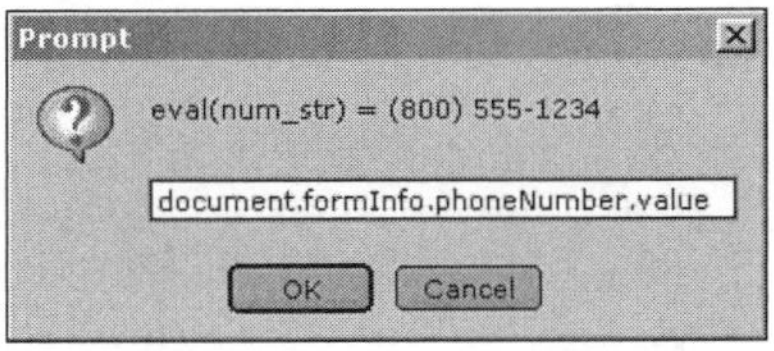

FIGURE 15.20

A simple script can be used as a real-time JavaScript interpreter.

Opening a Debug Browser Window

Another alternative that can be used to the text-area method shown in an earlier example is to use JavaScript to open a completely new window and to direct debug output into the new window. By opening a new window, you can use the document.writeln() method to write debug output into it. New windows can be opened using the document.open() method.

Using JavaScript Debuggers

In addition to the techniques shown in this chapter, there are a few tools available for debugging JavaScript. Both Microsoft and Netscape have JavaScript debuggers available. The Microsoft debugger is available at

http://msdn.microsoft.com/scripting/debugger/

The Netscape debugger can be downloaded from

http://developer.netscape.com/software/jsdebug.html

In this chapter, we are not going to go into any great depth into the operations of these debuggers. Most of the capabilities that they give are similar to the ones that were added to our own scripts using the techniques above. Each of the debuggers has its own strengths, weaknesses, and quirks, and will not be discussed fully. Instead, some of the capabilities of the debuggers will be shown with illustrations from Microsoft's Script Debugger.

Some of the capabilities that are present in the script debuggers are as follows:

- Entering a script upon error—Internet Explorer can be set up, using one of the check boxes under the Advanced tab of Internet Options, to enter the script debugger upon script errors. If this is done, then a script error will pop up an alert box similar to the one shown in Figure 15.21. One of the quirks of the script debugger is that you have to click on OK to enter the debugger; if you click on Cancel, the alert box will continue to pop up.

- Stepping through a script—Once you have entered a script, the script debugger enables you to proceed through it in a variety of ways. You can single step through it, or run until the next breakpoint (see below). As shown in Figure 15.22, Microsoft's Script Debugger indicates the current line with a yellow arrow along the left-hand side.

- Setting breakpoints—A breakpoint is something you can set within a program that causes the debugger to halt whenever it reaches that spot. In the case of a JavaScript, you might want to set a breakpoint just before a crucial operation, thus allowing yourself to use the debugger to check the values of the information used in that operation. In the Script Debugger, a breakpoint is denoted with a small stop-sign icon along the left side.

- Entering JavaScript commands—If a script debugger allows you to stop the script at a given point (or before each statement), in order for it to be useful you need to be able to get further information on the current state of the script. You can accomplish this by allowing JavaScript statements and expressions to be inputted and immediately evaluated. The small window in Figure 15.22 shows the Script Debugger command window; every other line in the window was typed in directly, followed by what it evaluated.

FIGURE 15.21

JavaScript errors give you the option to enter the debugger.

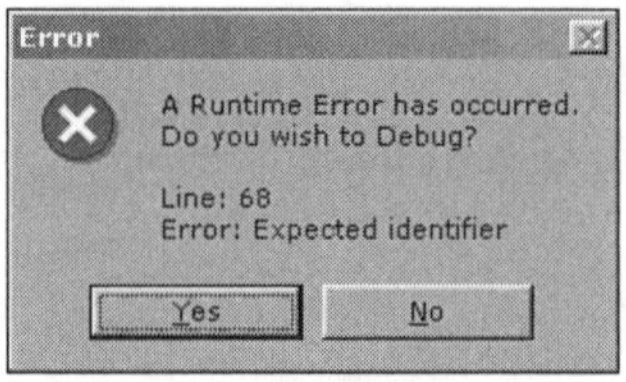

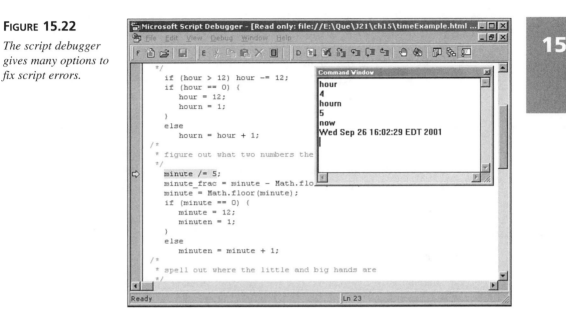

FIGURE 15.22

The script debugger gives many options to fix script errors.

15

Summary

As with programming in any other language, the process of programming in JavaScript often involves spending some time tracking down and fixing bugs in what you have written. Both Microsoft and Netscape have developed script debuggers which ideally would make this job easier, but neither of their offerings is terribly robust. This chapter has shown you a variety of ways that you can use some of JavaScript's own language elements to carefully step through your code and narrow down the location and cause of any errors.

Workshop

In this workshop we will review some of the debugging techniques you have learned in this chapter.

Q&A

Q. Where are two places you can display debugging information within a web page while other events are taking place?

A. Either in HTML form fields, normally text or text-area boxes, or in the status area of the browser window.

Q. Why aren't alert boxes appropriate for debugging JavaScripts that involve continuous events?

A. By their very nature, an alert box interrupts anything else that is happening in a web page or JavaScript. As soon as the continuous event began, such as one involving mouse movement or dragging, the alert box would pop up and stop it.

Quiz

1. If you had a JavaScript that looked at a preexisting cookie that gave a "last visited" time, in order to print out how long it had been since the last time the user accessed a given Web page, what type of script would that be?

2. What use could a confirm box (as opposed to the alert and prompt box uses shown above) be put to when debugging a JavaScript?

Quiz Answers

1. That sort of script would be a load-time script, using the `document.cookie` property.

2. An alert box allows you to display information and pause before continuing. With a little more logic, you could use a confirm box instead, but give the option to either continue or abort the script.

Exercise

Use `document.open()` and `document.writeln()` to create a separate debug window for information from a run-time, discrete event script.

DAY **16**

Cookies: Storing Persistent Data

Most Web servers have very short memories. When you request a page, the server usually doesn't really know who you are, what you entered on a form three pages ago, or whether this is your first visit to the site or your 75th visit. One of the challenges of using the Hypertext Transfer Protocol (HTTP) is that it doesn't track the state of your interactions with the server. *State* refers to any information about you or your visit to a Web site. It can be maintained as you move from page to page within the site, and it can be used by the Web server or a JavaScript program (or both) to customize your experience at the site. But if HTTP doesn't maintain the state, what does?

This chapter shows you how to get around HTTP's limitations by using cookies, which allow you to store persistent data about someone's visit to your web site. In addition to the material on cookies, you will also be introduced to a few other methods of preserving information from one Web page to the next, using URL query string parameters and hidden form variables.

This chapter will teach you

- How and why you would want to maintain state information
- What cookies are and how they work
- How to use cookies in your Web pages
- How to use other state maintenance options

Maintaining State

Maintaining state means remembering information while the user moves from page to page within a Web site. With this information at hand, you can set user preferences, fill in default form values, track visit counts, and do many other things that make browsing easier for users and that give you more information about how your pages are used.

You can maintain state information in a number of ways:

- Store it in cookies
- Encode it in URL links
- Send it in hidden form variables
- Store it in variables in other frames
- Store it on the Web server

Be aware, however, that some technical challenges regarding state maintenance can occur. While browsing a site, a user might suddenly zoom off to another Web site and return minutes, hours, or days later, only to find that any saved state information is out of date or has been erased. He or she might return by clicking the browser's Back button, by using a bookmark, or by typing in the URL directly, causing state information encoded in the URL to be overwritten or lost.

The Web developer must maintain state information regardless of whether the user navigates through the site using buttons on a form or a URL link on a page. This could mean adding information to both hidden form variables and every URL <a href…> tag that appears on the page.

With all these difficulties to overcome, these state maintenance mechanisms had better be useful. Luckily, they are. Many advantages exist to maintaining state both within a single site visit and from one visit to the next. Consider the following scenarios:

- **A shopping cart application**—Users could browse through the site while selecting and adding items to a virtual shopping cart. At any time, they can view the items in the cart, change the contents of their cart, or take the cart to the checkout counter for purchase. Keeping track of which user owns which shopping cart is essential.

- **Custom home pages**—Many Web sites have now set up home pages where users can customize what they see when they arrive. After giving the user a choice of layouts, color schemes, and favorite destinations, it stores the preferences on the user's own computer through the use of cookies. Some sites ask for your zip code and store this information in a cookie, and use it to provide you with local weather and news information. The user can return to the site any time and get the previously configured page.

- **Frequent visitor bonuses**—By storing information on the client computer, this application keeps track of how many times a browser has hit a particular page. When the user reaches a certain level of hits, he or she gets access to more or better services.

- **Change banners**—You can make the graphical banners and the text change each time the user hits a page. This technique is often used to cycle through a list of advertisements.

- **Bookmarks**—Remember where a user was when he last visited the site. Was he reading a story, filling out a questionnaire, or playing a game? Let him pick up where he left off.

- **Login information**—If your site requires users to log on, you can give the user the option of allowing your Web site to remember his or her username and/or password. This information can be stored in a cookie and therefore allow the user faster access to your site in the future.

- **Games**—Remember current or high scores, and hence present new challenges based on past answers and performance.

Cookies: An Introduction

Cookies—sometimes called magic cookies, but more formally known as persistent client-state HTTP cookies—enable you to store information on the client browser's computer for later retrieval. Although they have their drawbacks, cookies are the most powerful technique available for maintaining state within a Web site.

Netscape came up with the original cookie specification. There doesn't seem to be any good reason why Netscape chose that particular name. In fact, on its cookie specification page, Netscape admits "the state object is called a cookie for no compelling reason."

In their simplest form, cookies store data in the form of `name=value` pairs. You, the developer, can pick any name and value combination you want. More advanced cookie features include the capability to set an expiration date and to specify which Web pages can see the cookie information.

Advantages of Cookies

One of the most powerful aspects of cookies is its persistence. When a cookie is set on the user's browser, it can persist for days, months, or even years. This makes it easy to save user preferences and visit information, and to keep this information available every time the user returns to your site.

Cookies prove especially helpful when used in conjunction with JavaScript. Because JavaScript has functions for reading, adding, and editing cookies, your JavaScript programs can use them to store global information about a user as he surfs through your Web site.

Limitations of Cookies

Some limitations of cookies could prove problematic. Cookies are stored on the user's computer, usually in a special cookie file or, as with Internet Explorer, in a number of files. As with all files, this cookie file might be accidentally (or purposely) deleted, taking all the browser's cookie information with it. The cookie file could be write protected, thus preventing any cookies from being stored there. Browser software could impose limitations on the size and number of cookies that can be stored, and newer cookies might overwrite older ones.

Because cookies are associated with a particular browser, problems arise if users switch from one browser to another. If you usually use Netscape Navigator and have a collection of cookies, they will no longer be available for you to use if you decide to switch to Microsoft Internet Explorer.

Finally, if several people use the same computer and browser, they could find themselves using cookies that belong to someone else. The reason for this is that cookie information is stored in a file on the computer, and depending on how the computer is set up, the browser might have no way to distinguish between multiple users.

Disadvantages of Cookies

Some problems, both real and imagined, also occur with the use of cookies. Because many browsers store their cookie information in an unencrypted text file, you should never store sensitive information, such as a password, in a cookie. Anyone with access to the user's computer could read it.

Netscape Navigator and Microsoft Internet Explorer browsers have a feature that can alert the user every time an attempt is made to set a cookie. These browsers can even be configured to prevent cookies from being set at all. This sometimes results in confusion on the user's part when a dialog box informs her that something strange involving a cookie is happening to her computer. If cookies are disabled, your carefully designed

Web application might not run at all, unless you are careful to not rely on the cookie information being there.

Cookie Myths

The biggest problem facing cookies could be a psychological one. Some savvy Web users believe that cookies are used by "Big Brother" as a tool to violate their privacy. Considering the capabilities of cookies for storing information about where specifically they have visited on a Web site, how many times they have been there, which advertising banners they have viewed, and what they have selected and placed on forms, some people think their privacy is invaded whenever a cookie gets set on their computer.

16

In reality, cookies are seldom used for these purposes, although technically these things are possible. The most common use of cookies is to give developers an easy way to customize their Web sites for everyone that visits them. A site can ask you for your name or ask you about some other preference once, and then store this information in a cookie. That way, the next time you visit the site, it doesn't have to ask you for this same information again, assuming you are using the same browser.

Other users complain about Web sites that write information to their computers and take up space on their hard drives. This is somewhat true. Web browser software limits the total size of the cookies stored, as well as the amount of space that can go to the cookies of a particular Web site. Consider, however, that this limit probably is small when compared to the size of the pages and graphic images that Web browsers routinely store in their page caches.

Other users are concerned that cookies set by one Web site might be read by other sites. This is completely untrue. Your Web browser software prevents this from taking place by making cookies available only to the sites that created them.

If your users understand the usefulness of cookies, this "cookie backlash" shouldn't be a problem.

As mentioned previously, Netscape came up with the original cookie specification. You can find more information about cookies on the Netscape Web site at

```
http://www.netscape.com/newsref/std/cookie_spec.html
```

Using Cookies

By now you have considered the pros and cons of cookies and have decided that they are just what you need to make your JavaScript application a success.

This section discusses a number of handy functions for reading and setting cookies, which will help you make your Web sites smarter and more user-friendly. Also included are Internet references for finding additional information concerning cookies.

Retrieving Cookie Values

Cookie names and values are stored and set using the `cookie` property of the `document` object. To store the raw cookie string in a variable, you would use a JavaScript command such as the following:

```
var myCookie = document.cookie;
```

To display it on a Web page, use the following command:

```
document.write("Raw Cookies: " + document.cookie + "<br />");
```

JavaScript stores cookies in the following format:

```
name1=value1; name2=value2; name3=value3
```

Individual `name=value` pairs are separated by a semicolon and a blank space. No semicolon is used after the final value. To retrieve a particular cookie, you can use a JavaScript routine such as the one shown in Listing 16.1.

LISTING 16.1 JavaScript Function for Retrieving a Specific Cookie, `favoritesList.htm` (excerpted)

INPUT

```
//
// GetCookie - Returns the value of the specified cookie or null
//             if the cookie doesn't exist
//
function GetCookie(name) {
   var result = null;
   var myCookie = " " + document.cookie + ";";
   var searchName = " " + name + "=";
   var startOfCookie = myCookie.indexOf(searchName)
   var endOfCookie;
   if (startOfCookie != -1) {
      startOfCookie += searchName.length; // skip past cookie name
      endOfCookie = myCookie.indexOf(";",startOfCookie);
      result =
         unescape(myCookie.substring(startOfCookie,endOfCookie));
   }
   return result;
}
```

> **Note**
>
> Most of the listings that appear in this chapter are excerpts from the
> `favoritesList.htm` document discussed in the "A Cookie Example" section
> later in this chapter.

ANALYSIS In Listing 16.1, the `myCookie` string is created with a leading space and trailing semicolon; this helps cookie processing by making sure all cookie string names start and end similarly. From there, it is easy to find the start of the `name=` portion of the string, skip it, and retrieve everything from that point until the next semicolon.

Setting Cookie Values

The `name=value` combination is the minimum amount of information you need to set up a cookie. However, there can be more to cookies than just this. The complete list of parameters, which should be separated by a space and semicolon, that you can use to specify a cookie is as follows:

- `name=value`
- `expires=date`
- `path=path`
- `domain=domainname`
- `secure`

Choosing Meaningful Cookie Names and Values

The name and value can be anything you choose. In some cases, you might want it to be very explanatory, such as `FavoriteColor=Blue`. In other cases, it could just be code that the JavaScript program interprets, such as `CurStat=1:2:1:0:0:1:0:3:1:1`. In any case, the name and value are completely up to you.

Listing 16.2 shows the simplest way to create cookies. The function `SetCookieEZ()` is a routine to add a single `name=value` pair to a cookie.

INPUT **LISTING 16.2** Adding Cookies Is Easy with JavaScript, `favoritesList.htm` (excerpted)

```
//
// SetCookieEZ - Quickly sets a cookie which will last until the
//               user shuts down his browser
//
function SetCookieEZ(name,value) {
    document.cookie = name + "=" + escape(value);
}
```

ANALYSIS Notice that the value is encoded using the JavaScript `escape()` function. If there were a semicolon in the value string itself, it might prevent you from achieving the expected results. Using the `escape()` function eliminates this problem.

Also notice that the `document.cookie` property works rather differently from most other properties. In most other cases, using the assignment operator (=) causes the existing property value to be completely overwritten with the new value. This is not the case with the cookie property. With cookies, each new name you assign is added to the active list of cookies. If you assign the same name twice, the second assignment replaces the first.

Some exceptions exist to this last statement; these are explained in the "Path" section later in this chapter.

Setting a Cookie Expiration Date

The `expires=date` property tells the browser when the cookie will expire. The cookie specification page at Netscape states that dates are in the form of

```
Wdy, DD-Mon-YY HH:MM:SS GMT
```

Here's an example:

```
Mon, 08-Jul-96 03:18:20 GMT
```

This date format is based on Internet RFC 822, which you can find at `http://www.w3.org/hypertext/WWW/Protocols/rfc822/#z28`.

The only difference between RFC 822 and the Netscape implementation is that in Netscape Navigator, the expiration date must end with GMT (Greenwich Mean Time). The JavaScript language provides a function to do just that. By using the `toGMTString()` function, you can set cookies to expire in the near or distant future

> **Tip**
> Even though the date produced by the `toGMTString()` function doesn't match the Netscape specification, it still works under JavaScript.

If the expiration date isn't specified, the cookie remains in effect until the browser is shut down.

The following is a code segment that sets a cookie to expire in one week (where the number of milliseconds in one week equals 7 days/week × 24 hours/day × 60 minutes/hour × 60 seconds/minute × 1000 milliseconds/second):

```
var name="foo";
var value="bar";
var oneWeek = 7 * 24 * 60 * 60 * 1000;
var expDate = new Date();
expDate.setTime(expDate.getTime() + oneWeek);
document.cookie = name + "=" + escape(value) + "; expires=" +
                  expDate.toGMTString();
```

How to Delete a Cookie

To delete a cookie, set the expiration date to some time in the past—how far in the past doesn't generally matter. To be on the safe side, a few days prior should work fine. The following is a routine to delete a cookie, shown in Listing 16.3.

LISTING 16.3   Use the Cookie Expiration Date to Delete an Unwanted
INPUT   Cookie, `favoritesList.htm` (excerpted)

```
//
// ClearCookie  - Removes a cookie by setting an expiration date
//                three days in the past
//
function ClearCookie(name) {
   var ThreeDays = 3 * 24 * 60 * 60 * 1000;
   var expDate = new Date();
   expDate.setTime(expDate.getTime() - ThreeDays);
   document.cookie = name + "=NA; expires=" +
                     expDate.toGMTString();
}
```

When deleting cookies, it doesn't matter what you use for the cookie value—any value will do.

> **Caution**
>
> Some versions of Netscape do a poor job of converting times to GMT. Some common JavaScript functions for deleting a cookie consider the past to be 1 millisecond behind the current time. Although this is usually true, it doesn't work on all platforms. To be on the safe side, use a few days in the past to set the expiration for the cookies.

Using the Cookie Path to Adjust Its Accessibility

By default, cookies are available to other Web pages within the same directory as the page on which they were created. The `path` parameter enables a cookie to be made available to pages in other directories. If the value of the `path` parameter is a sub-string of a page's URL, cookies created with that path are available to that page. You could create a cookie, for example, with the following command:

```
document.cookie = "foo=bar1; path=/javascript";
```

This would make the cookie foo available to every page in the javascript directory and all those directories beneath it. If, instead, the command looked like this:

```
document.cookie = "foo=bar2; path=/javascript/sam";
```

the cookie would be available to sample1.html, sample2.html, sammy.exe, and so on, if they are located in the javascript directory or one of its subdirectories.

Finally, to make the cookie available to everyone on your server, use the following command:

```
document.cookie = "foo=bar3; path=/";
```

What happens when a browser has multiple cookies on different paths but with the same name? Which one wins?

Actually, they all do. When this situation arises, it is possible to have two or more cookies with the same name but with different values. If a page issued all the commands listed previously, for example, its cookie string would look like the following:

```
foo=bar3; foo=bar2; foo=bar1
```

To help be aware of this situation, you might want to write a routine to count the number of cookie values associated with a cookie name. It would look something like this:

```
function GetCookieCount(name) {
    var result = 0;
    var myCookie = " " + document.cookie + ";";
    var searchName = " " + name + "=";
    var nameLength = searchName.length;
    var startOfCookie = myCookie.indexOf(searchName)
    while (startOfCookie != -1) {
        result += 1;
        startOfCookie = myCookie.indexOf(searchName,startOfCookie + nameLength);
    }
    return result;
}
```

Of course, if a GetCookieCount function exists, a GetCookieNum function should be available to retrieve a particular instance of a cookie. That function would look like this:

```
function GetCookieNum(name,cookieNum) {
    var result = null;
    if (cookieNum >= 1) {
        var myCookie = " " + document.cookie + ";";
        var searchName = " " + name + "=";
        var nameLength = searchName.length;
        var startOfCookie = myCookie.indexOf(searchName);
        var cntr = 0;
        for (cntr = 1; cntr < cookieNum; cntr++)
            startOfCookie = myCookie.indexOf(searchName,
                                            startOfCookie + nameLength);
if (startOfCookie != -1) {
            startOfCookie += nameLength; // skip past cookie name
            var endOfCookie = myCookie.indexOf(";",startOfCookie);
            result = unescape(myCookie.substring(startOfCookie,endOfCookie));
        }
    }
    return result;
}
```

To delete a cookie, the name and the path must match the original name and path used when the cookie was set.

Using the Cookie Domain to Adjust Its Accessibility

Usually, after a page on a particular server creates a cookie, that cookie is accessible only to other pages on that server. Just as the path parameter makes a cookie available outside its home path, the domain parameter makes it available to other Web servers at the same site, as described in the next paragraph.

You can't create a cookie that anyone on the Internet can see. You can only set a path that falls inside your own domain. This is because the use of the domain parameter dictates that you must use at least two periods (for example, .mydomain.com) if your domain ends in .com, .edu, .net, .org, .gov, .mil, .int, or the newer root domains such as .info. Otherwise, if the domain ends in a two-letter country code, it must have at least three periods (.mydomain.ma.us). Your domain parameter string must match the tail of your server's domain name.

How to Use the Cookie secure Parameter

The final cookie parameter tells your browser that this cookie should be sent only under a secure connection with the Web server. This means that the server and the browser must support HTTPS security. (HTTPS is Netscape's Secure Socket Layer Web page encryption protocol.)

If the secure parameter is not present, cookies are sent unencrypted over the network.

Note

You can't set an infinite number of cookies on every Web browser that visits your site. The following list shows the number of cookies you can set and how large they can be:

- Cookies per server or domain: 20
- Total cookies per browser: 300
- Largest cookie: 4KB (including both the `name` and `value` parameters

If these limits are exceeded, the browser might attempt to discard older cookies by tossing out the oldest cookies first.

Now that you have seen all the cookie parameters, it would be helpful to have a JavaScript routine set cookies with all the parameters. The `SetCookie()` function shown in Listing 16.4 does just that.

INPUT

LISTING 16.4   JavaScript Routine to Add a Cookie, Including Any Optional Parameters, `favoritesList.htm` (excerpted)

```
//
// SetCookie - Adds or replaces a cookie. Use null for parameters
//             that you don't care about
//
function SetCookie(name,value,expires,path,domain,secure) {
   var expString =
      ((expires == null) ? "" : ("; expires=" + expires.toGMTString()))
   var pathString = ((path == null) ? "" : ("; path=" + path))
   var domainString =
      ((domain == null) ? "" : ("; domain=" + domain))
   var secureString = ((secure == true) ? "; secure" : "")
   document.cookie = name + "=" + escape(value) +
                     expString + pathString + domainString +
                     secureString;
}
```

To use this routine, you call it with whatever parameters you care about and use `null` in place of parameters that don't matter.

A Cookie Example

The JavaScript program in this example is in the HTML document `favoritesList.htm`. Excerpts of the program were shown in Listings 16.1 through 16.4; these showed the JavaScript functions used to create and manipulate the document cookies used in this example. The full listing of the document is shown in Listing 16.5, which enables the user to create a personalized Web page containing links to sites of general interest in a number of categories. The user's favorite links are stored in cookies.

LISTING 16.5   The <body> Section of the Cookie Example, favoritesList.htm (excerpted)

INPUT

16

```
<!DOCTYPE html PUBLIC "-//W3C//DTD XHTML 1.0 Transitional//EN"
    "http://www.w3.org/TR/xhtml1/DTD/xhtml1-transitional.dtd">
<html xmlns="http://www.w3.org/1999/xhtml">
<head>
<title>Cookie Example</title>
<script type="text/javascript" language="javascript">
<!-- Hide this script from incompatible Web browsers!
//
// This JavaScript code should run under Netscape Navigator 3.0
// and Microsoft Internet Explorer 3.0 and above. It will not run
// locally under Internet Explorer. If you use Internet Explorer,
// you must load this page from a Web server.
//
// STANDARD COOKIE ROUTINES
//
// GetCookie - Returns the value of the specified cookie or null
//             if the cookie doesn't exist
//
function GetCookie(name) {
   var result = null;
   var myCookie = " " + document.cookie + ";";
   var searchName = " " + name + "=";
   var startOfCookie = myCookie.indexOf(searchName)
   var endOfCookie;
   if (startOfCookie != -1) {
      startOfCookie += searchName.length; // skip past cookie name
      endOfCookie = myCookie.indexOf(";",startOfCookie);
      result =
         unescape(myCookie.substring(startOfCookie,endOfCookie));
   }
   return result;
}
//
// SetCookieEZ - Quickly sets a cookie which will last until the
//               user shuts down his browser
//
function SetCookieEZ(name,value) {
   document.cookie = name + "=" + escape(value);
}
//
// SetCookie - Adds or replaces a cookie. Use null for parameters
//             that you don't care about
```

LISTING **16.5**   continued

```
//
function SetCookie(name,value,expires,path,domain,secure) {
   var expString =
      ((expires == null) ? "" : ("; expires=" + expires.toGMTString()))
   var pathString = ((path == null) ? "" : ("; path=" + path))
   var domainString =
      ((domain == null) ? "" : ("; domain=" + domain))
   var secureString = ((secure == true) ? "; secure" : "")
   document.cookie = name + "=" + escape(value) +
                     expString + pathString + domainString +
                     secureString;
}
//
// ClearCookie  - Removes a cookie by setting an expiration date
//                three days in the past
//
function ClearCookie(name) {
   var ThreeDays = 3 * 24 * 60 * 60 * 1000;
   var expDate = new Date();
   expDate.setTime(expDate.getTime() - ThreeDays);
   document.cookie = name + "=NA; expires=" +
                     expDate.toGMTString();
}
//
// JAVASCRIPT OBJECT AND METHODS AND GLOBAL VARIABLES
//
// Here is our "favorite" object...
//
// Properties: fullName - The full descriptive name
//             cook     - The code used for the cookie
//             urlpath  - The full url (http://...) to the site
//     Methods: Enabled - Returns true if the link's cookie is
//                          turned on
//             Checked  - Returns the word "CHECKED" if the
//                          link's cookie is turned on
//             WriteAsCheckBox - Sends text to the document in a
//                                 checkbox control format
//             WriteAsWebLink  - Sends text to the document in a
//                                 <A HREF...> format
//
function favorite(fullName,cook,urlpath) {
   this.fullName = fullName;
   this.cook = cook;
   this.urlpath = urlpath;
   this.Enabled = Enabled;
   this.Checked = Checked;
   this.WriteAsCheckBox = WriteAsCheckBox;
   this.WriteAsWebLink = WriteAsWebLink;
}
```

LISTING **16.5**   continued

```
//
// Enabled - Checks to see if the cookie exists
//    returns true,  if the cookie exists
//             false, otherwise
//
function Enabled() {
   var result = false;
   var FaveCookie = GetCookie("Favorites");
   if (FaveCookie != null) {
      var searchFor = "<" + this.cook + ">";
      var startOfCookie = FaveCookie.indexOf(searchFor);
      if (startOfCookie != -1)
         result = true;
   }
   return result;
}
//
// Checked - Checks to see if the cookie exists (using Enabled)
//    returns "CHECKED ", if the cookie exists
//             "", otherwise
//
function Checked () {
   if (this.Enabled())
      return "CHECKED ";
   return "";
}
//
// WriteAsCheckBox - The favorite may be either a regular URL or
//                   a section title. If the urlpath is an empty
//                   string, then the favorite is a section title.
//                   The links will appear within a definition
//                   list, and are formatted appropriately.
//
function WriteAsCheckBox() {
//
// check to see if it's a title or regular link
//
   if (this.urlpath == "")
//
//    it's a section title
//
      result = '<dt /><strong>' + this.fullName + '</strong>';
   else
//
//    it's a regular link
//
      result = '<dd /><input type="checkbox" name="' +
               this.cook + '" ' +
               this.Checked() +
```

LISTING 16.5   continued

```
                    'onclick="SetFavoriteEnabled(this.name,this.checked);" />' +
                    this.fullName;
        document.writeln(result);
    }
    //
    // NextHeading - Sometimes we only want to print a heading if one
    //               its favorites is turned on. The NextHeading
    //               variable helps us to do this. See WriteAsWebLink.
    //
    var NextHeading = "";
    //
    // WriteAsWebLink - The favorite may be either a regular URL or
    //                  a section title. If the urlpath is an empty
    //                  string, then the favorite is a section title.
    //                  The links will appear within a definition
    //                  list, and are formatted appropriately.
    //
    function WriteAsWebLink() {
        var result = '';
        if (this.urlpath == "")
            NextHeading = this.fullName; // it must be a title
        else {
            if (this.Enabled() || (GetCookie("ViewAll") != "F")) {
                if (NextHeading != "") {
                    result = '<dt /><strong>' + NextHeading+ '</strong>';
                    NextHeading = "";
                }
                result = result + '<dd><a href="' + this.urlpath + '">' +
                         this.fullName + '</a>';
            }
        }
        document.writeln(result);
    }
    //
    // FaveList - Will be a list of all favorite objects, which are
    //            then declared below. favorites with an empty urlpath
    //            property are section headings.
    //
    var FaveList = new Array();
    //
    // Comics
    //
    FaveList[1] = new favorite("Comics","","");
    FaveList[2] = new favorite("Dilbert","cdilb",
        "http://www.unitedmedia.com/comics/dilbert/");
    FaveList[3] = new favorite("For Better of For Worse","cfbofw",
        "http://www.fbofw.com");
```

LISTING 16.5 continued

```
FaveList[4] = new favorite("The Boondocks","cboon",
    "http://www.boondocks.net");
//
// General News
//
FaveList[5] = new favorite("General News","","");
FaveList[6] = new favorite("CNN","ncnn","http://www.cnn.com/");
FaveList[7] = new favorite("NPR","nnpr",
    "http://www.npr.org/news/");
FaveList[8] = new favorite("Washington Blade","nblade",
    "http://www.washblade.com/");
//
// Computer Industry
//
FaveList[9] = new favorite("Computer Industry","","");
FaveList[10] = new favorite("ZDNet eWeek","ieweek",
    "http://www.zdnet.com/eweek/");
FaveList[11] = new favorite("Infoworld","iinfo",
    "http://www.infoworld.com/");
FaveList[12] = new favorite("CMP TechWeb","icmp",
    "http://www.techweb.com/");
//
// Search Engines
//
FaveList[13] = new favorite("Search Engines","","");
FaveList[14] = new favorite("Yahoo!","syah",
    "http://www.yahoo.com/");
FaveList[15] = new favorite("AltaVista","sav",
    "http://www.altavista.com/");
FaveList[16] = new favorite("Excite","sexc",
    "http://www.excite.com/");
//
// Miscellaneous
//
FaveList[17] = new favorite("Miscellaneous","","");
FaveList[18] = new favorite("Today in History","mtih",
    "http://www.thehistorynet.com/today/today.htm");
FaveList[19] = new favorite("Merriam-Webster's Word of the Day",
    "mwod","http://www.m-w.com/cgi-bin/mwwod.pl");
FaveList[20] = new favorite("Quotes of the Day","mquot",
    "http://www.quotationspage.com/qotd.html");
FaveList[21] = new favorite("The House of JOD","mjod",
    "http://jim.odonnell.org");
FaveList[22] = new favorite("Richard's World","mgunther",
    "http://richard.gunther.com");
FaveList[23] = new favorite("Damone Motton's Personal Webspace","mmotton",
    "http://www.damone.com");
```

16

LISTING 16.5 continued

```
//
// PAGE WRITING ROUTINES
//
// SendOptionsPage - Writes a page allowing the user to select
//                   her favorite preferences
//
function SendOptionsPage() {
   document.writeln('<h1>Select Favorites...</h1><hr />');
   document.writeln('<form method="POST">');
//
// here's the button for viewing the Favorites page
//
   document.writeln('<table><tr><td>');
   document.writeln('<input type="BUTTON" value="Show Favorites" ' +
                    'onclick="ReloadPage();" />');
   document.writeln('</td></tr></table>');
//
// the links will look nicer inside a definition list
//
   document.writeln('<dl>');
   for (var i = 1; i < FaveList.length; i++)
      FaveList[i].WriteAsCheckBox(); // Write each checkbox
   document.writeln('</dl>');
   SetCookieEZ("ViewAll","F");
   document.writeln('</form>');
}
//
// LoadOptions - Sets the ShowOptions cookie, which makes the
//               option selection page appear when the page is
//               then reloaded.
//
function LoadOptions() {
   SetCookieEZ("ShowOptions","T");
   window.open(document.location.href,"_top");
}
//
// ToggleView - Toggles ViewAll mode on and off. When on, all
//              links will be displayed. When off, only the
//              user's favorite selections will be displayed.
//
function ToggleView() {
   if (GetCookie("ViewAll") == "F")
      ClearCookie("ViewAll");
   else
      SetCookieEZ("ViewAll","F");
   window.open(document.location.href,"_top");
}
//
```

LISTING 16.5   continued

```
// ClearCookies - Clear the Favorites cookie and reload page
//
function ClearCookies() {
   ClearCookie("Favorites");
   ClearCookie("ViewAll");
   ClearCookie("ShowOptions");
   window.open(document.location.href,"_top");
}
//
// SendPersonalPage - Writes a page showing the categories and
//                    links which the user prefers. Only shows a
//                    heading if one of its favorites is enabled
//
function SendPersonalPage() {
   if (GetCookie("ViewAll") != "F")
      document.writeln('<h1>Links...</h1><hr />');
   else
      document.writeln('<h1>Your Favorites...</h1><hr />');
//
// here are the buttons for viewing the options or "View All" pages
//
   document.writeln('<form method="POST">');
   document.writeln('<table><tr><td>');
   if (GetCookie("ViewAll") != "F")
      document.writeln('<input type="BUTTON" value="View Favorites" ' +
                       'onclick="ToggleView();" />')
   else
      document.writeln('<input type="BUTTON" value="View All" ' +
                       'onclick="ToggleView();" />');
   document.writeln('<input type="BUTTON" ' +
                    'VALUE="Select Personal Favorites" ' +
                    'onclick="LoadOptions();">');
   if (GetCookie("Favorites") != null | GetCookie("ViewAll") != null |
      GetCookie("ShowOptions") != null)
      document.writeln('<input type="BUTTON" value="Clear Cookies" ' +
                       'onclick="ClearCookies();" />');
   document.writeln('</td></tr></table>');
   document.writeln('</form>');
//
// the links will look nicer inside a definition list
//
   document.writeln('<dl>');
   for (var i = 1;i < FaveList.length;i++)
      FaveList[i].WriteAsWebLink(); // write each link
   document.writeln('</dl>');
}
//
// HELPER FUNCTIONS
```

LISTING 16.5   continued

```
//
// isEnabled - Returns True if the favorite identified by the
//             name parameter is enabled.
//
function isEnabled(name) {
   var result = false;
   var FaveCookie = GetCookie("Favorites");
   if (FaveCookie != null) {
      var searchFor = "<" + name + ">";
      var startOfCookie = FaveCookie.indexOf(searchFor)
      if (startOfCookie != -1)
         result = true;
   }
   return result;
}
//
// AddFavorite - Enables the favorite identified by the name
//               parameter.
//
function AddFavorite(name) {
   if (!isEnabled(name)) {
      var fiveYears = 5 * 365 * 24 * 60 * 60 * 1000;
      var expDate = new Date();
      expDate.setTime (expDate.getTime() + fiveYears );
      SetCookie("Favorites",
                GetCookie("Favorites") + "<" + name + ">",
                expDate,null,null,false);
   }
}
//
// ClearFavorite - Disables the favorite identified by the name
//                 parameter.
//
function ClearFavorite(name) {
   if (isEnabled(name)) {
      var FaveCookie = GetCookie("Favorites");
      var searchFor = "<" + name + ">";
      var startOfCookie = FaveCookie.indexOf(searchFor);
      var NewFaves =
         FaveCookie.substring(0,startOfCookie) +
         FaveCookie.substring(startOfCookie+searchFor.length,
                              FaveCookie.length);
      var fiveYears = 5 * 365 * 24 * 60 * 60 * 1000;
      var expDate = new Date();
      expDate.setTime(expDate.getTime() + fiveYears );
      SetCookie("Favorites",NewFaves,expDate,null,null,false);
   }
}
```

LISTING 16.5   continued

```
//
// SetFavoriteEnabled - Turns the favorite identified by the name
//                      parameter on (SetOn=true) or off
//                      (SetOn=false).
//
function SetFavoriteEnabled(name,SetOn) {
   if (SetOn)
      AddFavorite(name);
   else
      ClearFavorite(name);
}
//
// ReloadPage - Reloads the page
//
function ReloadPage() {
   window.open(document.location.href,"_top");
}
//   Hide script from incompatible browsers! -->
</script>
</head>
<body bgcolor="#ffffff">
<script type="text/javascript" language="javascript">
<!-- Hide script from incompatible browsers!
//
// Here's where we select the page to send. Normally we send the
// personalized favorites page (by calling SendPersonalPage). However,
// If the cookie ShowOptions is set, we'll send the options selection
// page instead (by calling SendOptionsPage).
//
if (GetCookie("Favorites") != null)
   SetCookieEZ("ViewAll","F");
if (GetCookie("ShowOptions") == "T") {
   ClearCookie("ShowOptions");
   SendOptionsPage();
} else
   SendPersonalPage();
//   Hide script from incompatible browsers! -->
</script>
<hr />
<h3>Current Document Cookie Contents...</h3>
<center>
<form name="MyForm">
<textarea name="MyTextArea" rows="1" cols="60">
</textarea>
</form>
</center>
<script type="text/javascript" language="javascript">
<!-- Hide script from incompatible browsers!
```

16

LISTING 16.5   continued

```
document.MyForm.MyTextArea.value = document.cookie;
//   Hide script from incompatible browsers! -->
</script>
<hr />
<em>Jim O'Donnell, <a href="mailto:jim@odonnell.org">jim@odonnell.org</a></em>
</body>
</html>
```

ANALYSIS   As shown in Listing 16.5, when this page is loaded, one of two JavaScripts is
called to actually "fill" the page: either `SendOptionsPage()` or
`SendPersonalPage()`. The former enables the user to select from a list of sites to be
included as favorites; the latter is used to display those sites (or to display all the possible
sites). Figure 16.1 shows this page when it first loads, before the user has selected a list
of favorites (so all possible sites are shown).

OUTPUT

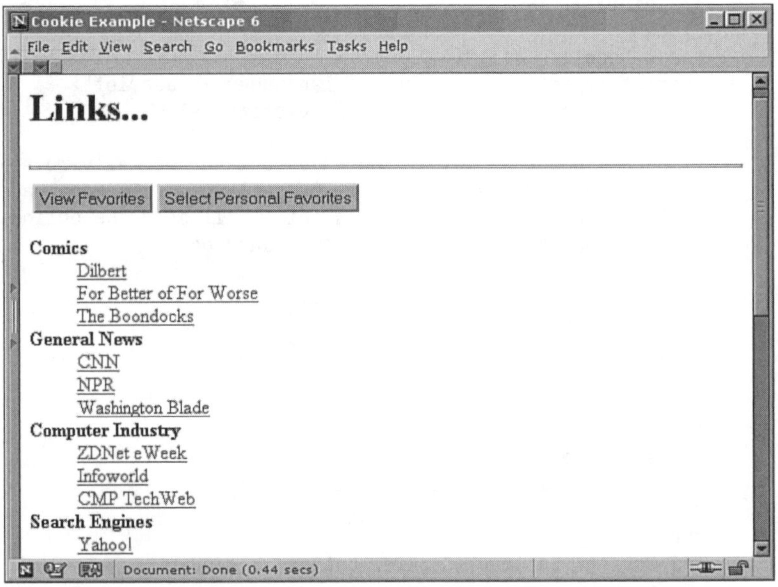

FIGURE 16.1

*The Favorites page
displays all possible
sites when first
loaded.*

Before JavaScript, a task such as this would have been handled at the server level. Each
hit would have involved having the server run some type of script or program to read the
user's cookies and generate his page on-the-fly. With JavaScript, all this processing takes
place in the client's browser. The server just downloads the static page—and it might
not even need to do that because the page might come from the client's local cache.

When the page loads, all the links, selected or not, are sent. The client, with the help of cookies and JavaScript, decides which ones to show the user.

This program makes use of three cookies: The Favorites cookie contains a unique code for each favored link. The ViewAll cookie toggles between showing the user's favorites and all possible links. The program can also display either of two pages: one for displaying the selected links, and the other for changing the configuration and options. When the ShowOptions cookie is set, the Options selection page is displayed. Otherwise, the regular page is shown.

When the screen shown in Figure 16.1 is displayed after the page loads for the very first time, the document cookie has not been set yet, so it is empty, which results in all links displaying. If View Favorites is clicked at this point, then the document cookie is set to

```
ViewAll=F
```

and the screen shown in Figure 16.2 is displayed—empty, because no favorites have been selected yet. Clicking the Select Personal Favorites button gets the screen shown in Figure 16.3, where favorites can be selected from the list of choices. One such selection might result in the Favorites list shown in Figure 16.4, which has the document cookie value of

```
ViewAll=F; Favorites=null%3Ccfbofw%3E%3Csyah%3E%3Cmjod%3E
```

which indicates a selection of the "For Better or For Worse", "Yahoo", and my home page as favorites.

Note

The %XX encoding, such as the %3C and %3E shown above, is used for such symbols as semicolons, commas, and whitespace.

Note

You might notice in Figures 16.2 and 16.4 that the current contents of the document cookie are displayed in a text-area box at the bottom of the page. This is done in this example so you can see the changes to the cookie as they occur; in an actual "production" page, you wouldn't include it. The Clear Cookies button shown in these two figures is also something you probably wouldn't include in the final page.

16

OUTPUT

FIGURE 16.2

An empty Favorites list doesn't yield a very exciting Web page.

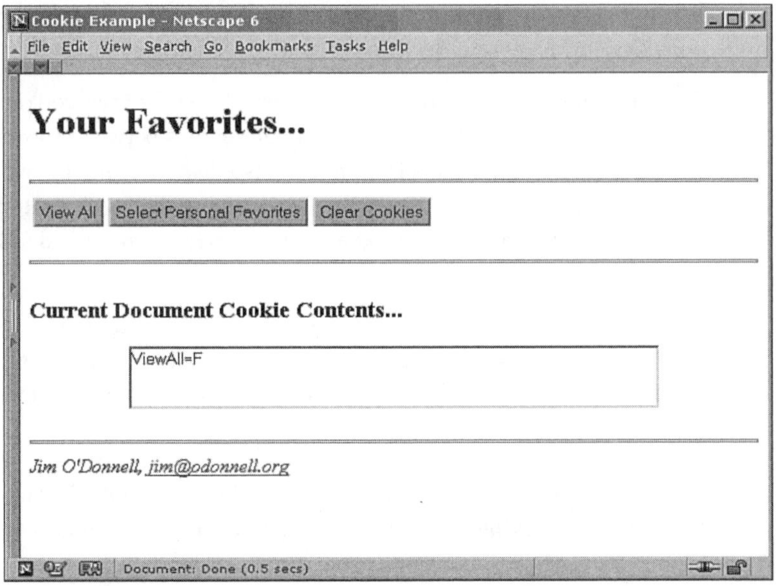

FIGURE 16.3

The Select Favorites page displays all the possible sites as checkboxes and enables the user to select and deselect which to use as favorites.

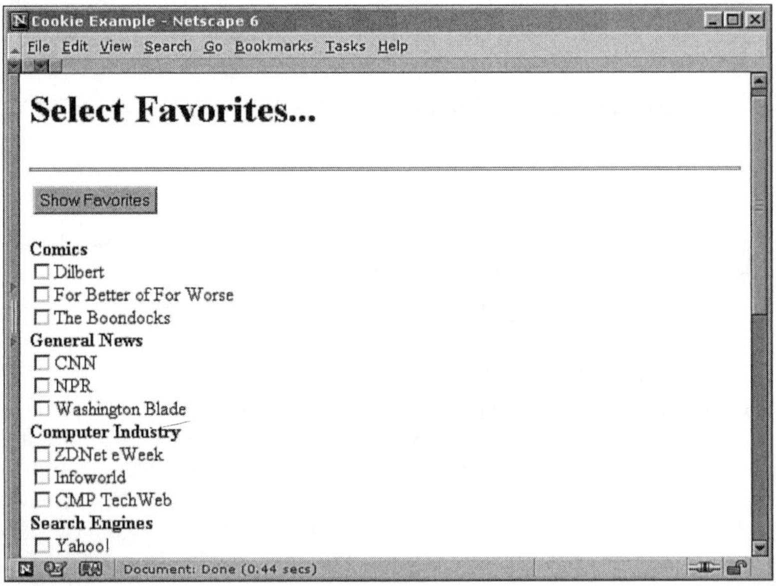

FIGURE 16.4

By enabling users to personalize their copy of your Web page, you allow a more personal experience without a greater burden on your server.

Once this list of favorites is created, any of them can be selected to load the corresponding Web page, as shown in Figure 16.5.

FIGURE 16.5

By using cookies to customize your site for your users, you can allow them to navigate through it more easily.

The program creates objects called *favorites*. Each favorite is, in essence, a Web link to another page. The favorite contains information on the link's URL, a user-friendly page description, and the code that identifies it in the Favorites cookie string. The favorite also knows how to print itself on a Web page as a regular link for the Favorites page, or in a checkbox format for the Options page. The functions used to manipulate the cookies in the `favoritesList.htm` example were shown in Listings 16.1 through 16.5. The other functions used in this example are summarized in the following list:

- **SendOptionsPage()**—Loads the Web browser with a page that enables the user to select which sites to be included as favorites.
- **SendPersonalPage()**—Loads the Web browser with a page that shows either the user's favorites or all the sites as hypertext links.
- **WriteAsCheckBox()**—Used by SendOptionsPage to display each potential favorite site as a check box, to enable the user to select or deselect it.
- **WriteAsWebLink()**—Used by SendPersonalPage to display each site as a hypertext link.
- **LoadOptions()**—This function is called to initiate the display of the options page.
- **ToggleView()**—This function is called to toggle the personal page between displaying favorites and all sites.
- **favorite()**—This function is used to create a JavaScript object that is used to store the information used to define a favorite site.
- **Enabled()**—This JavaScript function is used as a method by the favorite object; it returns true if the link corresponding to this object is enabled.
- **Checked()**—This JavaScript function is used as a method by the favorite object; it returns the string CHECKED if the link corresponding to this object is enabled.
- **isEnabled()**—Returns true if the favorite identified by the Name parameter passed to the function is enabled.
- **AddFavorite()**—Enables the favorite identified by the Name parameter passed to the function.
- **ClearFavorite()**—Disables the favorite identified by the Name parameter passed to the function.
- **ClearCookies()**—Clears the three cookies associated with this page.
- **SetFavoriteEnabled()**—Enables or disables the favorite identified by the Name parameter passed to the function by calling AddFavorite or ClearFavorite.
- **ReloadPage()**—Reloads the Web browser with the current page; what is displayed, however, changes according to the current state of the Document cookie.

Where Are Cookies Going?

As mentioned earlier, cookies were designed and first implemented by Netscape.
However, the Internet Engineering Task Force (IETF) has a committee—the Hypertext
Transfer Protocol (HTTP) Working Group—whose charter it is to examine, document,
and suggest ways to improve HTTP.

You can find a link to the HTTP Working Group's latest Internet Draft, called "HTTP
State Management Mechanism," at
`http://www.ietf.cnri.reston.va.us/rfc/rfc2109.txt`.

16

Although the specification resembles Netscape cookies in theory, if not in syntax, it does
have a few notable differences. It doesn't encourage having cookies around much longer
than the browser session. If the new specification is accepted, cookies will be given a
`Max-Age` lifetime rather than an `expires` date. All cookies still expire when their time
comes.

Reading the specification provides insight into the complexities that surround the inner
workings of cookies; it is well worth the read, regardless of whether the specification is
approved.

Where to Find More Information About Cookies

Although other ways of Web programming, such as CGI and special server interfaces,
require that the server as well as the browser understand cookies, only the browser matters to JavaScript. This means, in general, that you can use JavaScript with impunity as
long as you know your clients are JavaScript-capable, and they can run them with
JavaScript enabled.

Many JavaScript Web applications probably mix the language with other development
tools, however, which would require the server to understand cookies. Nowadays,
though, most clients and servers in use have both JavaScript and cookie support. You can
find cookie information at the following locations on the Web:

- Netscape cookie spec page (referenced previously in this chapter):

  `http://www.netscape.com/newsref/std/cookie_spec.html`

- Browsers supporting cookies:

  `http://www.research.digital.com/nsl/formtest/stats-by-test/NetscapeCookie.html`

- Cookie Central:

  `http://www.cookiecentral.com/`

- Robert Brooks' Cookie Taste Test:

  `http://www.geocities.com/SoHo/4535/cookie.html`

- Article about tracking cookies from the HotWired Web site:

  `http://www.arctic.org/~dgaudet/cookies`

Other State Maintenance Options

As mentioned earlier in this chapter, a few drawbacks exist to using cookies. Perhaps you would rather just avoid the controversy and find some other way to maintain state from one page to the next. Two ways of doing this are available. Which one you use depends on how you, the developer, will have your users get from one page to the next.

The main limitation of these methods is that they work only from one page to the page immediately following the previous page. If state information is to be maintained throughout a series of pages, these mechanisms must be used on every single page.

Using Query Strings to Send Information

If most of your navigation is done through hypertext links embedded in your pages, you can add extra information to the end of the URL. This is usually done by adding a question mark (?) to the end of your Web page URL, followed by information in an encoded form, such as that returned by the escape method. To separate one piece of information from another, place an ampersand (&) between them.

If you want to send the parameters color=blue and size=extra large along with your link, for example, you could use a link such as this:

```
<a href="MyPage.htm?color=blue&size=extra+large">XL Blue</a>
```

This format is the same as the format used when submitting forms using the get method. A succeeding page can read this information by using the search property of the location object. This property is called search because many Internet search engines use this part of the URL to store their search criteria.

The following is an example of how to use the location.search property. In this example, the name of the current page is sent as a parameter in a link to another page. The other page reads this property through the search property and states where the browser came from. Listing 16.6 shows the first page that contains the link.

INPUT

LISTING 16.6 You Can Include Extra Parameters in the href to Pass State Information, `whereOne.htm`

```
<!DOCTYPE html PUBLIC "-//W3C//DTD XHTML 1.0 Transitional//EN"
    "http://www.w3.org/TR/xhtml1/DTD/xhtml1-transitional.dtd">
<html xmlns="http://www.w3.org/1999/xhtml">
<head>
<title>Where Was I? (Page 1)</title>
</head>
<body>
<h1>Where Was I? (Page 1)</h1>
<hr />
This page sets information which will allow the page to which it is
linked to figure out where it came from. It uses values embedded in
the link URL in order to do this.
<p>
We'll assume that any URL parameters are separated by an ampersand.
</p>
<p>
Notice that there doesn't need to be any JavaScript code in this page.
</p>
<p>
And now...
<a href="whereTwo.htm?camefrom=whereOne.htm&more=needless+stuff">
   ON TO PAGE 2!!!
</a>
</p>
<hr />
<em>Jim O'Donnell, <a href="mailto:jim@odonnell.org">jim@odonnell.org</a></em>
</body>
</html>
```

Listing 16.7 shows the second page, which demonstrates how to use `location.search` to find where the browser came from.

INPUT

LISTING 16.7 Access href Information Using the `window.location.search` Property, `whereTwo.htm`

```
<!DOCTYPE html PUBLIC "-//W3C//DTD XHTML 1.0 Transitional//EN"
    "http://www.w3.org/TR/xhtml1/DTD/xhtml1-transitional.dtd">
<html xmlns="http://www.w3.org/1999/xhtml">
<head>
<title>Where Was I? (Page 2)</title>
</head>
<body>
<h1>Where Was I? (Page 2)</h1>
<hr />
This page reads information which allows it to figure out where it
came from.
```

LISTING 16.7 continued

```
<p>
<script type="text/javascript" language="JavaScript">
<!-- Hide script from incompatible browsers!
//
// WhereWasI - Reads the search string to figure out what link
//             brought it here.
//
function WhereWasI() {
//
// start by storing our search string in a handy place (so we don't
// need to type as much)
//
    var handyString = window.location.search;
//
// find the beginning of our special URL variable
//
    var startOfSource = handyString.indexOf("camefrom=");
//
// if it's there, find the end of it
//
    if (startOfSource != -1) {
        var endOfSource = handyString.indexOf("&",startOfSource + 9);
        var result = handyString.substring(startOfSource + 9,
                                           endOfSource);
    }
    else
        var result = "Source Unknown";
    return result;
}
if (WhereWasI() != "Source Unknown")
    document.write("You just came from <B>" + WhereWasI() + "</B>...")
else
    document.write("Unfortunately, we don't know where you came from...");
//   Hide script from incompatible browsers! -->
</script>
</p>
<hr />
<em>Jim O'Donnell, <a href="mailto:jim@odonnell.org">jim@odonnell.org</a></em>
</body>
</html>
```

Figures 16.6 and 16.7 show the two Web pages, demonstrating that the first was able to pass information to the second.

FIGURE 16.6

Extra information can be included in a hypertext link using the ? character.

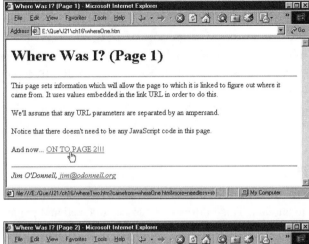

FIGURE 16.7

By including extra information in your hypertext links, you can enable some state information to be passed among pages in your Web site.

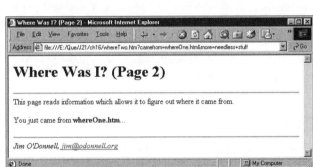

Note that the above techniques can also be used to send information from one Web page to another with query strings by using the # instead of the ? character. The method is the same, except that you use location.hash instead of location.search to look through the string.

How to Use Hidden Form Variables

The method used in the preceding section works fine as long as the user navigates from one page to another using links. To do the same thing with forms, you can use hidden form variables rather than the location.search parameter.

Hidden form variables have the following format:

```
<input type="HIDDEN" name="HiddenFieldName" value="HiddenFieldValue" />
```

You can specify whatever you like instead of *HiddenFieldName* and *HiddenFieldValue* for the values of the name and value attributes of the <input> element.

Using hidden fields does not necessarily require the use of JavaScript code. They are defined, instead, in the `<input/>` tag of normal HTML documents. You normally will need to have a server-based script, such as a CGI program or a server API program, to read the values of these hidden fields. The form containing the hidden variables is submitted to a server script, which can then process the information for subsequent pages. It is possible to avoid the need for server processing of hidden form fields if you include them in a hidden frame, as well. At this point, however—using hidden form fields in hidden frames—you're better off going ahead and using cookies.

Summary

It is often useful for a Web page to remember information about its different users from one visit to another. This information can be collected and maintained on the server, but an easier way to remember a few things is through the use of browser cookies. Cookies are stored on your users' computers, and allow your Web pages to remember information about them from one visit to another, which can enable you to customize and improve their experience on your page.

Workshop

In this workshop we will review what you have learned about cookies in today's chapter.

Q&A

Q. How can you set up a cookie so that it can be accessed from Web pages on other parts of your Web site?

A. By setting the cookie `Path` and/or `Domain` parameters, the cookies can still be accessed from other locations within your domain; but they still are not accessible from other domains.

Q. Can you set a cookie equal to more than one value?

A. Yes, by using a character such as an ampersand to append separate cookie values, and then by using JavaScript's string functions to split the string apart.

Quiz

1. What are the two ways to clear a cookie that has been set with no expiration date?

2. In addition to using the `location.search` property, what is one other way of implementing an URL-based, state maintenance technique?

Quiz Answers

1. Within JavaScript, the cookie can be cleared by setting a cookie with the same name with an expiration date in the past. Another way to clear a cookie set with no expiration date is for the user to close the browser.

2. By using the `location.hash` property. Just as `location.search` is set equal to the part of a URL after the ?, `location.hash` is set equal to the part after the hash mark symbol #.

Exercise

Create a Web page with a cookie that keeps track of the amount of time since the last time a user viewed the page, and prints the time out at the bottom of each page. Here's a tip: To make this time as accurate as possible, you can use the `onUnload` event to set the last viewed time when the page is exited.

16

DAY **17**

Privacy and Security

This chapter will look at the privacy and security issues you could face with visitors to your Web page and dealing with JavaScript code. Internet security issues have become a hot topic these days, and Web users have become more leery about where they visit and the type of information they provide to those sites they do visit. By the same token, corporations have had to become more vigilant in their efforts to secure the information on their own corporate sites. Quite often the information provided on a Web page is not intended for all potential visitors. Because of this, you need to look at methods to secure the content, such as password protection.

This chapter will teach you:

- Privacy for Web users
- Privacy for Webmasters
- The impact on JavaScript

Privacy for Web Users

Security issues for Web users have become a major concern—everyone is concerned about their personal information falling into the wrong hands, and this concern is well founded. Other concerns arise from the fact that there were security holes in the early browsers that allowed scripts to access files on an individual user's computer.

Many of these Web user security issues originally surfaced when Netscape first introduced JavaScript. As you remember from our discussions in Chapter 8, "The Browser Issue," JavaScript was originally introduced as a scripting language for interacting with Java. With both Java and scripting support added to the browser, bright programmers quickly figured out how to access client information on each Web user's machine when they visited a particular site. Of course it didn't take long for news of these security issues to spread.

As security-related issues have become obvious, each Web browser has been updated with various security fixes to correct potential holes. Of course, correcting these "holes" has created more limitations on the capabilities of your JavaScript code. These issues, with respect to the user's browser, deal with cookies, file access, and browser-window access.

File Restrictions

In general, browsers prevent JavaScript code from executing or performing on the user's machine any file input or output without the user's permission. This security restriction was established to eliminate the risk of unwanted access to file directories and other personal information available on the machine. So overall, users can be fairly confident that no changes are occurring on their local computers outside of what they are viewing in their browser windows. Yet there are still issues to be aware of.

Often, especially in an intranet environment, scripts may be loaded directly onto a user's machine. These scripts may be designed to allow access to a corporate site, or other related areas. If you load JavaScript code that resides on your machine, the script has the ability to actually read, write, and create files as long as that function is allowed by the machine. Typically, the browser will still display a warning message indicating that this action is occurring and allowing the user to cancel out of the function, as illustrated in Figure 17.1, though how the browser ultimately reacts is determined by security settings.

FIGURE 17.1

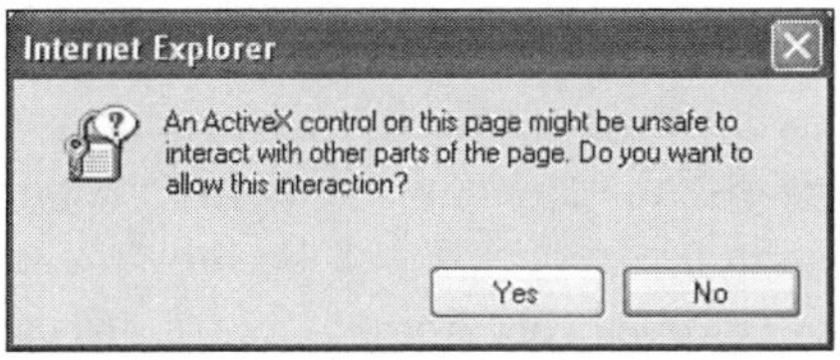

Browsers detect suspicious file access attempts and allow the user to stop the activity.

Messages will display similar to the one in Figure 17.1 when JavaScript, or any other code, attempts to perform file access commands outside of the browser (as shown in Listing 17.1), which if allowed by the user creates a text file on the C-drive of the user's machine. Again, this type of access can only occur if the script is opened on the user's machine and allowed to run.

INPUT   **LISTING 17.1**   File Access on User Machine (`fileaccess.htm`)

```
<html>
<head>
<script language="JavaScript" type = "text/javascript">
<!--
var newfile = new ActiveXObject("Scripting.FileSystemObject");
var createfile = newfile.CreateTextFile("c:\\test.txt", true);
createfile.WriteLine("This is a test message created in a text file.");
createfile.Close();
//..>
</script>
</head>
<body>
</body>
</html>
```

ANALYSIS   Keep in mind, the code in Listing 17.1 only works on Internet Explorer by using the `File` and `FileSystemObject` objects to create a new text file. There is similar functionality available in Netscape, but it requires interaction with Java and LiveConnect. Again, with Netscape the user must agree to allow the script to execute, as shown in Figure 17.2.

FIGURE 17.2

Netscape also requires user interaction before scripts requesting File I/O can execute.

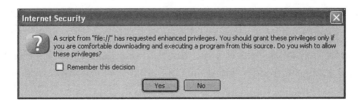

Cookies

Cookies have become a concern for many Web users primarily because of their concern about the ability of someone else to store unwanted information on their machine. Most cookie concerns are unwarranted, as you will see, because the access a site may have to your machine, by way of a cookie, is very limited. As we discussed in Chapter 16, "Cookies: Storing Persistent Data," cookies provide a means for storing user-specific information on the user's machine that can be accessed the next time the user visits your site. The cookies are tagged with the URL of the Web site that created the cookie so only that particular Web site has access to the information in that particular cookie.

Cookies can store information about the user (for example, the number of visits to a site). But personal information about the user cannot be stored in a cookie without the user's acknowledgment. For example, cookies can be used to store form information for sites the user frequents. If a cookie is used, the next time the user visits the site, the form information can be pulled from the cookie and used to auto-fill the form. Keep in mind though, the cookie file stores the data in plain text; therefore, any personal information stored in a cookie, such as a credit card number or password, can be read by anyone who has access to the machine. Therefore, sensitive information is typically encrypted or encoded in the cookie, making it difficult to read. For example, the following illustrates a sample cookie file contents:

```
uniqueUserId %2A0AF A567B%2D1F91%4122D8%12C3CB4DA%31D2F839A51BF%8E jstest.com/
35448444887922553694551245084014324637686*RMID de9123357433bf7f5e30 jstest.com/
70051367567040373071437821445252564254424000029455*
```

As you can see, by using encryption techniques you can make it difficult for others to interpret the information you store in the cookie file. Keep in mind other Web sites cannot access the cookie files that you create—only those individuals with access to the actual machine can view the cookies on the machine.

There are some general restrictions placed on cookies by browsers to protect the user. For example, in Netscape, your Web site domain cannot create more than 20 cookies. If you attempt to create more, one of your existing cookies will be discarded when you add cookie number 21. Although this restriction does not exist in Internet Explorer, to eliminate potential errors you will not want to create more than 20 cookies. To avoid this problem, I would recommend creating only a couple of cookies and storing all necessary information in them.

Keep in mind that there is a size limitation on the cookie description of 4096 bytes. Finally, there cannot be more than 300 total cookies on each computer system.

Note   For more specific information about creating and accessing cookies, refer to Chapter 16.

Browser Window Access

As we discussed in Chapter 12, "Windows and Frames," through the use of objects, specifically the Window object, you have the ability to access the browser window and associate elements from your JavaScript code. By doing so, your JavaScript code is capable of writing new content to the browser window and changing the appearance of the window by adding and removing window chrome.

As you probably already know, you can have multiple browser windows open or view multiple URLS in one browser window if you are using frames. Although the browser window allows you to open multiple URLs on one page or even in multiple windows, you can only manipulate the content from pages on the same URL of the JavaScript code that is executing. We will look at this concept more in the next section when we discuss the same origin policy.

Computer Resource Limitations

Another important security step that has been taken is to limit the computer resources available for execution of the script by the browser. These limitations help ensure that a script does not overuse any of the resources on the user's machine.

Some limitations are actually specified by the user within the browser. For example, the user can specify the amount of cache that the browser can use to load an HTML page or image. Although cookies can be created by a Web site the user visits, Netscape limits the size of each cookie file to 80 kilobytes. This forces the Web designers to limit the amount of information they can store in a cookie.

One restriction that Web developers need to keep in mind is the limit on the number of instructions (or statements) that can be executed for a JavaScript script, which is one million. This is to keep a script from executing and essentially locking up a user's machine. Typically this is not an issue, as there are not too many situations where you would need to have a script execute over 1 million statements. However, if you ever need to do complex calculations, this could become an issue. Consider the following code:

```
var totalsum = 1;
for (var x = 1; x < 1100000; x++)
{
 totalsum = totalsum + x
}
```

This code would not complete its calculation because 1,100,000 is greater than 1 million. In order to perform a complex calculation such as this, you would have to break it into smaller calculations. Doing so would keep the browser from rendering the system unavailable to execute the script.

Privacy for Webmasters

Although a lot of steps have been taken in the browser world to protect the Web user, very little security exists for the code you write. In fact, because JavaScript is a scripted, and not a compiled language, everyone has the ability to see exactly what your code does.

Yes, unfortunately the JavaScript code that you create is not secure. As you have probably learned by now, you can pretty much view all the source code used on pages on the Internet by simply selecting the View Code option in your browser for a Web page. So, you know those cool JavaScript functions you create, they can be copied by anyone.

There are some who would tell you that you simply need to create a separate .js file in which to store your JavaScript code. That way, when the user views your HTML source, they simply see a reference call to the .js file that contains the corresponding JavaScript code.

```
<script src="myjavascript.js"></script>
```

As we have previously discussed, if you place JavaScript code in a .js file the source does not display when the user selects View Source for the HTML page. But they do see the src= statement indicating the name of the file on your Web site that contains the JavaScript code. This file is not protected or hidden, so a curious Web user simply needs to type in the name of that file with the URL and they will have access to the source. Keep in mind, the use of the separate JavaScript file was never designed for security or privacy purposes, it simply cuts down on your development work by placing frequently used code in one central location.

There are methods that can make your code a little more difficult to interpret; but, quite frankly, most methods just cause more grief than they are worth. However, if you are really concerned about the privacy of your code, you may want to consider using a different method. One way to make your JavaScript code more obscure is to place the entire script on one line within your browser. I am going to attempt to illustrate how this looks, in Listing 17.2. Unfortunately there is a limit to how long a line of text can be in a book, so the code will appear on several lines even though it would be one continuous line.

INPUT   **LISTING 17.2**   Obscuring JavaScript Code (`oneline.htm`)

```
<html><head><script language="javascript" type = "text/javascript">
<!--
function selectlink(sellink,linkdesc){ sellink.style.background='yellow';
 if (document.getElementById)
document.getElementById("selectdesc").innerHTML=linkdesc;
 else selectdesc.innerHTML=html; } function
leavelink(sellink){ sellink.style.background='blue';
 if (document.getElementByI d)
document.getElementById("selectdesc").innerHTML=' ';
 else selectdesc.innerHTML=' '; }
//-->
</script></head><body>
<table bgcolor="blue" border="1" bordercolor="white" cellpadding="2"
 cellspacing="0"><tr>
<td class="menu" bordercolor="black" id="choice1"
 onmouseover="selectlink(this,'Developers of IE')"
onmouseout="leavelink(this)"">
<a href="http://www.microsoft.com">Microsoft</a></td></tr>
<td class="menu" bordercolor="black" id="choice2"
 onmouseover="selectlink(this,'Developers of Netscape Navigator')"
 onmouseout="leavelink(this)"><a
href="http://www.netscape.com">Netscape</a></td></tr>
<td class="menu" bordercolor="black" id="choice3"
 onmouseover="selectlink(this,'Responsible for W3C DOM')"
onmouseout="leavelink(this)"><a href="http://www.w3.org/">W3C</a></td></tr>
<td class="menu" bordercolor="black" id="choice4"
 onmouseover="selectlink(this,'Publisher of Computer Books')"
onmouseout="leavelink(this)">
<a href="http://www.samspublishing.com">Sams Publishing</a></td></tr>
<tr><td bordercolor="black" bgcolor="white" height="18">
 <font id="selectdesc" size="2"></font></td></tr>
</table>
</body></html>
```

ANALYSIS   If you look at the code above, the JavaScript portion of the code is crammed together, making it more difficult to read. (Although, any astute Web developer can figure out how to space it all out again.)

Another method you can consider is not only placing the code on one line, but also changing the names of variables and functions so that they do not relate to their actual functionality. For example, instead of having a function called `selectlink`, why not call it `feedthedog`? Okay, now you can really have some fun. Although keep in mind, you will have to maintain this code, so don't make it too difficult for yourself to figure out. You should actually keep an unaltered version for yourself.

If you are really concerned about protecting your code, you can consider using a code-shrouding program. These programs read your code and translate it to source similar to the original source by removing all of the formatting and then using randomly generated variable names. Again this code still can be deciphered, but it does take some work.

Finally, you can add copyright statements to your code. Although this does not inhibit someone from copying your code, it does give you some legal grounds if you need to prove it was copied. Of course, you will have to determine if it is really worth your time and effort to pursue.

> **Note**
>
> The issues we have discussed so far have dealt with the user's ability to view and copy your JavaScript code—that is,the code that runs on the client-side. Server-side scripting—JavaScript code that runs on the server—is never passed to the Web browser. Therefore, this code remains unseen by the user.

Same Origin Policy

In an effort to ensure that another site cannot manipulate your own content, the same origin policy was added to browsers. What exactly does that mean? As you know, you can have documents from multiple locations open simultaneously in a browser window using frames (as we discussed in Chapter 12). These documents can come from any valid URL. You also may remember from that chapter how a script in one frame can interact with the contents of another frame. This will work fine if the documents are from the same URL, but if they are different the interaction is not allowed.

The origin of a document is determined by the protocol (that is, http or ftp) and domain. If these values match for both frames, then the script in one frame is allowed to interact with the other frame's contents. If you attempt to modify a document from a different origin, an error message such as "access disallowed" or "permission denied" will display in the frame.

Okay, this may not sound like such a big deal. After all, this ensures that someone cannot alter your Web site content . But, imagine your organization has multiple URLs, or is using different protocols on the Web site (for example, in a situation with an Ecommerce site where the order form is secured and the protocol is https:. Because the rest of the site has an http: protocol, you will have a difficult time interacting between frames, even though both pages are on the same server.

To allow for the fact that you may need to access different portions of your site using different protocols, you can set the document.domain property to match. In order to use this property, both pages must exist on the same domain, but they can be from different servers or have different protocols. To do this, you simply need to set the property to match for each document:

```
document.domain = "www.testdomain.com"
```

Keep in mind, you can only set the domain value to match your current domain. In other words, the domain value cannot be modified from another domain.

Of course, the document origin is not the only check performed by the browser. The document object model for windows or frames that do not have the same origin cannot be accessed. Essentially any object, property, or method that either grants access to the user's local system or provides information about Web browsing activity, such as the Location object, cannot be accessed if the origin does not match.

Privacy Impact on JavaScript

Based on our discussion so far, you can see that although security measures have been taken for JavaScript, there are still things for the developer to consider. For starters, all documents on your Web server are accessible if the user knows the name of the file. In order to keep users from accessing sensitive files, you need to have some type of security established for the documents that you do not want all Web visitors to view. The best method for doing this is to employ some form of password protection for the documents with content you want to restrict. We will discuss password protection options in the next section.

Another issue you may want to look at is creating signed scripts. As Web users become more leery about running scripts on Web sites, many of them are opting to disable the running of scripts within their browsers. In an effort to gain the user's trust in your site and the script that is running on it, you may want to look at signing your script. Unfortunately this ability is not supported equally by Netscape and Microsoft. In fact, Netscape is the only one that offers the ability to truly sign your script. Microsoft offers a capability called Authenticode, but it cannot be used directly to sign scripts. Since Netscape's object signing options work well for signing your JavaScript code, we are going to discuss the process of setting this up in this section below.

Password Protection

Depending upon the type of Web site you are creating, more than likely you do not want all of your content accessible to everyone. You may want to restrict certain documents so that only users with a valid username and password can access them. There are multiple methods that you can use to password protect your site, and the methods you can use ultimately are based upon the capabilities of the location where you are hosting your site. There are three general types of password protection: using the operating system, a CGI Program, or JavaScript coding.

Using Operating System Security

Each networking system has security that can be used to limit the access to particular directories. This same security can be used to limit access to a particular Web directory. For example, with Windows NT/XP as your Web server, you or your network administrators can create a sub-directory for your Web site where only certain users have access. When a user attempts to access a document from that directory, they are requested to specify network login information in order to access that directory. Once they have specified the appropriate login information they can access any files within that directory.

This type of security can be specified for multiple users, and is probably one of the more effective methods of security because the login is required in order to access any documents within the corresponding directory.

If the documents you want to secure are sensitive, you definitely want to consider using either this type or CGI security options outlined in the next section. You can contact your Network Administrator to determine the feasibility of incorporating this type of security. Again, if your site is being hosted, this type of security is probably not available.

Security with CGI Scripts

If the server that hosts your Web site supports CGI scripts, this is probably the best method for securing your documents. But if you select this method, you also need to either create the CGI script that verifies the username and password information or find one that you can use on the Internet.

Unfortunately with the complexity of CGI, it is not feasible to look at creating a CGI script within this chapter. If you decide to pursue this path, there are several resources available for learning more about CGI, including CGI scripts that you can download from other sites. You can find CGI resources listed in Appendix D. Another great source for information on CGI is *Sams Teach Yourself CGI in 24 Hours* by Rafe Colburn.

Password Protection with JavaScript

Let's look at some options for performing password protection within JavaScript scripts. Keep in mind, as with any type of programming you do, there are many options when determining the best method for accomplishing the task. With JavaScript, you can even create encrypted passwords. Potentially the user will be able to view your code, so you will want to use a method that is least obvious. For example, look at the code in Listing 17.3; although it provides a method for specifying a password, if users view the source code they immediately can see that they simply need to open the file named pswdfile.htm.

LISTING 17.3 Simple Password Protection (password1.htm)

```
<html>
<head>
<script language="javascript" type = "text/javascript">
<!--
function verify_password()
{
 var docpwrd = prompt("Specify the password for this document:", "");
 if (docpwrd == "pwrdfile")
 {
 self.location = docpwrd + ".htm";
 }
 else
 {
 alert("That is not the correct password.");
 }
}
//-->
</script>
</head>
<body>
<form>
  <input type="button" value="Open Password Protected File."
 name="OpenFile" onclick="verify_password()"></p>
</form>
</body>
</html>
```

17

ANALYSIS The code for password protecting a file in Listing 17.3 provides a quick and simple method to request a password from the user with the prompt() method as shown in Figure 17.3. If you examine the code closely, you will see that the user must specify the name of the HTML document as the password. This works well except for the fact that you must verify that a valid password was entered in order to open the file. Therefore, if you view the code you can quickly see that the password is specified in the if statement. With this code, the user only gets to see the document if the correct password pwrdfile is specified. Otherwise, an alert box displays indicating the password was not correct and the current document remains displayed in the browser window.

> **Tip**
>
> Another way to make the code even more secure is to remove the `if (docpwrd == "pwrdfile")` statement. This eliminates the inclusion of the password from your code if the user decides to view the source. Again, the only way the appropriate file is opened is if the proper password or file name is specified.

FIGURE 17.3

Using the `prompt()` *method, you can require that a specific password be entered before a document can be opened.*

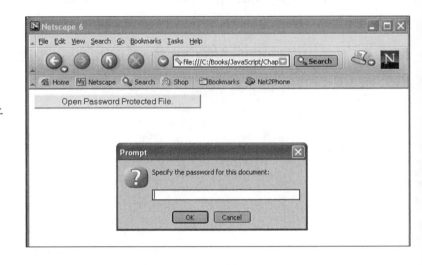

> **Note**
>
> We discussed the `prompt()` method in Chapter 12 when we talked about popup windows.

As I mentioned earlier, JavaScript coding works well for the general protection of your documents, but it does not ensure that sensitive documents could not be accessed by an ambitious visitor. Another method you can use to limit file access is to distinguish (encode) the password, as shown in Listing 17.4.

INPUT   **LISTING 17.4**   Encoding the Password (`password2.htm`)

```
<html>
<head>
<script language="javascript" type = "text/javascript">
<!--
var checkpwrd = 1121191141001 02105108101;
var enterpwrd = " ";
function verify_password()
```

LISTING 17.4   continued

```
{
 var docpwrd = prompt("Specify the password for this document:", "");
 for(i =0; i < docpwrd.length; i++)
 {
  enterpwrd += docpwrd.charCodeAt(i);
 }
 if (enterpwrd == checkpwrd)
 {
 self.location = docpwrd + ".htm";
 }
 else
 {
 alert("That is not the correct password.");
 }
}
//-->
</script>
</head>
<body>
<form>
  <input type="button" value="Open Password Protected File."
 name="OpenFile" onclick="verify_password()"></p>
</form>
</body>
</html>
```

17

The code in Listing 17.4 is very similar to the previous password code in Listing 17.3. The only difference is that we used an encryption method that converts the password entered by the user to a numeric value. That numeric value is compared to the stored numeric value of the password. If they match, the code opens the file, as we did in Listing 17.3. We are creating the numeric value by simply converting each character in the specified password to its two-digit numeric value with the charCodeAt() method of the String object. Of course this method is still not totally secure, but it requires some work to determine the password.

There are actually several different methods that you can use to encode values within your JavaScript code. In fact, there are several different examples of methods that can be used on the Internet. Many of the sites referenced in Appendix D have samples of encryption methods.

Creating Signed Scripts in Netscape

As we mentioned earlier, Netscape provides the capability to digitally sign your scripts. Digital signatures assure a user of the reliability of the script(s) that reside on your Web site. When you have a digital signature attached to your script it essentially tells the user that your script can be trusted because it has a valid signature attached. By the same token, allowing a signed script access to the user permits elements of the browser that are not typically accessible by your JavaScript code; specifically, you no longer need to worry about the "same origin" policy we discussed earlier in this chapter.

Note

Keep in mind the concepts related to signing scripts discussed in this section are only relevant to Netscape. Although Microsoft has a version for digitally signing called Authenticode, it is not available for signing your JavaScript code. For more information about Authenticode, visit the Microsoft Web site.

In order to sign your script, you first create the JavaScript code that you want to sign. Once your code is complete you run a signing tool (such as the Netscape signing tool) to create the digital signature. The signing tool creates and associates a digital signature with the script you want to sign. The digital signature is placed in a Java Archive (JAR) file. Once you create your digital signature you cannot alter the script code. The signature stands to confirm the validity of the code, if the code is altered then it is no longer valid.

Also, remember the user may refuse to allow your code to run, even though it has a digital signature. Or the user may be running a non-Netscape browser meaning the signed script is not valid. You need to allow for both of these situations when designing your script.

Obtaining a Digital Certificate

In order to sign your JavaScript code, or any other code that you develop, you must first obtain a digital certificate. The digital certificate, or digital id, is a code that is assigned to your organization that identifies you as a trusted source. When your JavaScript code is downloaded to the user's machine, the digital certificate is also downloaded. When the HTML document containing the digital certificate is loaded, the user is notified that JavaScript code has been loaded and it is requesting additional access; the user has the option of either allowing or rejecting the request.

Each digital certificate is issued by an organization called a certificate authority. The digital certificate is issued when you provide specific information identifying you as a valid certificate holder. There are various organizations on the Internet where you can purchase a digital certificate. The most popular is VeriSign Inc.(www.verisign.com). There is a fee required to obtain a digital certificate in addition to the submission of documents to prove your identity. Once you have obtained the digital certificate you can assign it to the scripts that you want to sign, as outlined in the next section.

Signing a Script

Once you have your digital certificate, you are ready to sign your scripts. In order to sign your script, you will need to obtain another program from Netscape called SignTool. This utility allows you to sign your JavaScript for NetScape. You can find this utility at `http://developer.netscape.com/software/signedobj/jarpack.html`. This page includes the information you need to not only acquire this utility but also the steps you will need to take to package and sign your scripts. This file creates a Java Archive file, `.jar`. A `.jar` file is a compressed file format required to work with Netscape Navigator security. The `.jar` file contains a file that lists the files within the `.jar` file, the certificate information, and the contents of the file when it was signed. This is how the digital certificate ensures the JavaScript code is secure. If the JavaScript code has been altered, then it does not match the contents of the `.jar` file.

In order to specify which script should be signed, you need to add two additional attribute values to your Script tags: the `Archive` and `id` attributes.

The Archive attribute must be added to the first Script tag that you want to sign. If the Script tag is not near the top of your HTML document, you need to create a Script tag to specify the attribute value. This attribute specifies the name of the `.jar` file you want to associate with the HTML document. For example, if the `.jar` file was `securejs.jar` you would specify the following:

```
<script language="javascript" type = "text/javascript" archive="securejs.jar"
id="sec1">
```

When you run the SignTool utility it assigns the attribute specified by the Archive attribute to the `.jar` file. When the user loads the HTML document, the attribute serves to point to the corresponding `.jar` file.

As I mentioned earlier, the other attribute that must be specified is the `id` attribute. This attribute must be unique for each script associated with a particular `.jar` file. When the SignTool assigns the `.jar` file it generates a unique value (hash value) and associates it with the particular script. Once the user loads the document in his browser, the `id` attribute is again used to compare the hash value with the `.jar` file. The value of the `id` attribute can be any valid string, as long as it is unique for the corresponding `.jar` file.

17

Summary

This chapter discussed the various security issues you need to be aware of when developing JavaScript code for your Web site. Security is a concern for site visitors and hosts alike.

Because of security "holes" that were exposed in early versions of browsers that allowed scripting, measures were put in place by Netscape and Microsoft to create a more secure environment for the browser user. These security measures were related to cookie access, file access, and browser window access. All three elements were discussed in the chapter.

Ensuring privacy for the site you are hosting is a bit more difficult than simply protecting browser users. For the most part, the entire contents of an HTML page, including your JavaScript code, can be accessed and read by anyone.

In order to mitigate this security risk, we discussed how you can secure documents through the operating system on the Web server by using a CGI script or by creating JavaScript code to password protect the page.

Finally, in this chapter we looked at the exclusive Netscape method of signing scripts to allow you to have additional access to the user's browser.

Workshop

In the workshop today we will use the questions to review what you have learned in this chapter about privacy and security when working with JavaScript.

Q&A

Q. How secure is a file if I password protect it by requiring the file name to be specified?

A. Within the chapter we looked at a couple of examples that illustrated methods for password protecting a particular file by requiring the filename to be specified in order to open the file. If you use this method the only real security is the fact that the user needs to know the file name in order to open it. But keep in mind, if they just type that file name in as part of the URL, it will open anyhow. This method only serves to help hide the file from most visitors. Also, be sure that the file name is not hidden within your script. If you really want to ensure that specific files are secured from unauthorized access, your best method is to use a CGI script or use the security of the operating system running the Web site to secure the files.

Q. How do you use the operating system to secure a file?

A. If you have access to the computer that is hosting your Web site, operating system security is a good option. In order to use this method you would place the files that you want to secure in a separate folder within the Web site. Once you do this, you can set the security for the folder to only allow specific usernames and passwords for access. This method requires you to have Administrative privileges for setting security.

Q. How does the Same Origin Policy affect my Web site?

A. The Same Origin Policy simply means that if multiple documents are open, they must be from the same original URL in order for one document to interact with the elements of another document. This does not inhibit you from opening documents on other sites from your Web site, but you will not be able to interact with those sites.

Quiz

1. What are the cookie limitations imposed on cookies?

2. Does a separate .js file help to secure your JavaScript code from the prying visitor?

3. What is the advantage of creating a signed script?

Quiz Answers

1. Within Netscape Navigator, a Web site domain cannot create more than 20 cookies. If you attempt to create 21, an existing cookie will be deleted. There cannot be more than 300 total cookies on the system, with a maximum size of 4096 kilobytes for each cookie.

2. Only a little. Although the JavaScript code you create does not appear directly within the HTML page when a user selects to view the source, it still indicates the name of the .js file. The user can view that source by simply typing the name of the .js file as the path for the browser. This method is intended to be used to place frequently used JavaScript functions in one location so they do not need to be specified on each page.

3. Signed scripts allow you to identify yourself to the visitor as a trusted source. By doing so, you also request that the user allow you to have additional access to his system. He has the option of allowing or rejecting your request. This capability is really only available within Netscape, so you need to code not only for other browsers that don't provide signing, but also for the situation where the user rejects your request.

17

Exercises

1. Create a page that successfully executes over a million mathematical calculations without being stopped by the browser. Keep in mind, you need to break the calculations into smaller steps.

2. Create a page that requests a password before allowing the user to view a specific file. The user should only have three attempts to enter the password. Once the maximum number of attempts has been tried, an Alert box displays a message.

3. Create a page you can use to create your encrypted passwords. Basically you just want a page where you can type the desired password and it returns the encrypted version.

Plugins and Applets

With all of the capabilities of JavaScript, there are many additional features that can be used to enhance the capabilities of your Web page. You can enhance your Web site by using different Java applets and plugins.

Java applets are essentially Java programs that have been designed to run from a Web page. You can use JavaScript to interface with the applet (for example, starting and stopping) and change its properties and methods.

Plugins are similar to applets in that they allow you to add additional capabilities to your Web site. A plugin, however, is not necessarily developed within Java. There are many commonly used plugins that are available for use within your Web site. Typically these plugins are available for viewing multimedia type files. For example, Adobe provides a plugin that allows Web users to view Adobe Acrobat files within their browsers.

This chapter looks at plugins and how you can detect their existence. Of course with some file types, you may not be as concerned about the existence of a particular plugin as just knowing whether or not the file type is supported by the browser. We will also look at how to determine if the browser supports a particular file type. Finally, we will show how to work with Java applets and how they can be incorporated into your Web page.

This chapter will teach you about:

- Plugins versus applets
- Detecting plugin installation
- Working with plugin objects
- Working with applets

Plugins Versus Applets

Plugins and applets are terms that are frequently used interchangably, giving a novice user the impression that they both refer to the same thing. However, in fact, they are two different things—although, browsers treat each similarly.

An *applet* is essentially a mini-application created within Java that will run on any Java-Enabled browser. Once called, a Java applet is capable of interacting with the user without any interaction from your HTML or JavaScript code. Although, ideally, you want to use JavaScript to create an interface between your Web page and the embedded Java applet. By doing so, as the Web developer you have control over the interaction with the Java applet.

Plugins on the other hand have a much broader scope. A plugin is essentially an add-on to the browser that allows the user to work with additional types of data within the browser. Typically, browsers enable the playing of sound files, video clips, or the ability to view specific file types. For example, Adobe Acrobat files are frequently available on Web sites to provide copies of standard printed documents, as illustrated in Figure 18.1. By loading the Adobe Acrobat plugin, a user can view these files in the same format and layout in which they were designed.

FIGURE 18.1

Plugins allow you to incorporate other file types into your Web site.

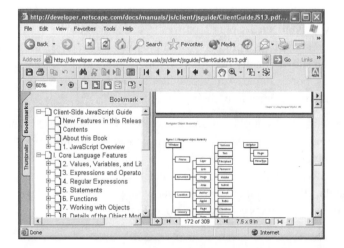

Plugins and applets were both originally introduced by Netscape with the use of JavaScript to communicate with them. This technology was originally called LiveConnect and was first implemented in Netscape Navigator 3.0. Microsoft followed suit by adding the capability to Internet Explorer also in 4.0, although they were not able to use the LiveConnect name that was trademarked by Netscape. The `Applet` and `Plugin` objects are now part of the document object model (DOM) maintained by the W3C, which we covered in Chapter 8, "The Browser Issue."

The `Applet` object is a child object of the `Document` object. In HTML, the code for the applet is enclosed in the `<applet>` tags. But you can reference an applet directly from your JavaScript code by using the corresponding properties and methods for the object, as we will discuss later in this chapter.

Netscape Navigator provides a child object to the Navigator object called `plugins`. This object is actually an array of all the plugins that are installed on the browser. Using the properties associated with the `plugins` object you can determine specific information about a particular plugin, such as its name or description. When working with Internet Explorer, the `plugins` object associated with the `Navigator` object is not supported. Internet Explorer treats plugins like ActiveX controls and therefore you will need to use the `Embeds` object. We will look at this in more detail in the chapter, but it is important to realize that each browser handles plugins differently.

Detecting Plugin Installation

18

As we have already discussed, plugins allow you to add multimedia capabilities to your Web page by adding the ability to play sound, video, or just display specific file types. However, in order to use these types of files, the plugin must be installed on the user's browser. Therefore, you need to determine whether the plugin, or at least support for the desired file type, exists before attempting to load it on the page.

There are a multitude of plugins available for incorporating this type of capability into your Web page. Some plugins allow you to interact with them, as we will discuss in the next section, while other plugins simply perform a specific task with the only interaction being the specification of which file to open. Typically as the Web developer it becomes your responsibility to ensure that the files are saved in the appropriate format for use with the selected plugins. For example, in order to open a PDF file you must have the appropriate file saved in that format. Although the plugins are generally free to download by the Web user, the software to create the file formats typically needs to be purchased. Table 18.1 lists some of the most common plugins used and the Web sites where you can gather more information about using the particular plugin.

TABLE 18.1   Commonly Used Plugins

Plugin	Description
Adobe Acrobat Reader	`www.adobe.com` Allows the Web site visitor to view files stored in a .PDF file format. Storing a file in a PDF format allows you to preserve all formatting.
Windows Media Player	`windowsmedia.com/download/download.asp` Allows you to view multimedia files. Available as default player on most versions of Windows.
Apple QuickTime	`www.apple.com` Typically used to play animation and video files.
Netscape LiveAudio	`home.netscape.com` Provides the ability to play AIFF, AU, MIDI, and WAV files within Netscape Navigator.
RealPlayer	`www.real.com` Provides the ability to play streaming audio and video.
Flash	`www.macromedia.com/flash` Macromedia's premier plugin that allows users to view animations, presentations, and any other interactive Web content created using Macromedia Flash.
Shockwave	`www.macromedia.com/shockwave` Provides the ability to view animations, play games, and run interactive demos.

As you can see by the list of plugins in Table 18.1, there are several multimedia players available to play audio and video files. For example, current versions of Microsoft Windows come with Windows Media Player installed, but the user can choose to load another player, such as RealPlayer, as their selected multimedia player. Because of this, you may not always check for the availability of a specific plugin but the support of a specific file type by the browser. We are going to look at both techniques to determine if a plugin is loaded and to see if a file type is supported. Depending on what you are trying to accomplish, you can determine which type of testing works best for your Web page.

Of course, the type of checking you are going to be able to perform is constrained by the user's browser. While both Netscape and Internet Explorer support the use of plugins, the way each browser handles plugins is different.

Plugin Handling by Browsers

As we briefly mentioned earlier, each browser provides the `Navigator` object which contains specific information that describes the specific browser being used by the user. If you remember, we used the properties related to this object in Chapter 8 to determine which browser the user was using to view your Web site. This object also contains two child objects, shown in Figure 18.2, `plugins` and `mimeType`, that provide information about the specific plugins that are installed within the browser. As shown in the figure, these objects are actually part of `plugins` and `mimeTypes` arrays that contain corresponding objects for the browser. Unfortunately, only Netscape makes use of these plugin-related child objects.

FIGURE 18.2

The Navigator object provides child objects for handling plugins.

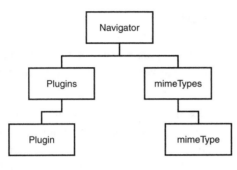

> **Note**
>
> Multipurpose Internet Mail Extensions (MIME) is the standard used to classify different types of files and to transmit them over the Internet. Each type of file is called a *MIME type*. By default, most browsers have a very limited number of mime types that they support (for example, HTML, GIF, JS). As you add additional plugins to your browser, the number of MIME types supported within the browser increases. Because some multimedia plugins support multiple MIME types it is highly likely that users may be able to view a particular file type even though they are lacking a particular plugin.

18

As you will see in the next section, within Netscape it is quite simple to check the `plugins` array to determine if a particular plugin has been installed on the user's machine. If a corresponding `Plugin` object does not exist, you can then inform the user of the need to load the required plugin.

Although within Internet Explorer, the `Navigator` object also includes the `Plugin` and `mimeType` objects, they are not supported in the same fashion as in Netscape. Microsoft uses a different methodology for dealing with plugins when working in the Microsoft Windows environment. Internet Explorer treats all plugins as ActiveX controls. Although they are actually an ActiveX control, plugin type controls are still commonly referred to as plugins, even in Internet Explorer.

Because plugins are handled as ActiveX controls, they are added to a page using the `<object>` tag in Internet Explorer; whereas, plugins are added using the `<embed>` tag in Netscape Navigator. The `Object` element has an attribute called `classid`, which can be used to determine if a particular plugin is loaded. We will look at this attribute more closely in the next section when we figure out how to determine if the plugin you need is installed on the user's machine. As we will discuss later, it requires the combination of both the `<embed>` and `<object>` tags to add a particular plugin.

Checking for a Plugin

Before you attempt to load a file in a user's browser that requires a specific plugin, it is important to verify that the required plugin exists on the user's machine. This verification helps to avoid potential errors due to lack of support for the file type, giving visitors to your site a more pleasing experience.

If you determine that the user's browser does not have the appropriate plugin loaded, you can either display a link to download the appropriate plugin, or you can display a non-plugin required version of the page. In most cases, it is important to provide an option that does not require loading a plugin. Some users may choose not to load the specific plugin on their machine, or they may be in a corporate environment that prohibits the loading of software from the Internet. Because of this situation, you do not want to build a Web site that relies on the existence of a particular plugin.

> **Caution**
>
> Many of today's Web sites have utilized Macromedia Flash for the creation of dynamic menus. Because of the animation capabilities of Flash, the developer can create effects that are often much flashier than those created with standard DHTML; or at least, Flash requires fewer programming capabilities to accomplish similar effects. Keep in mind that if you choose to make your site reliant on this type of multimedia plugin, you run the risk of encountering browsers which do not have the ability to load the required plugin. Therefore, you should also provide a non-plugin-required option for your Web site.

Of course detection of the plugin is actually easier than it sounds—as you will soon find out. Unfortunately browsers are not consistent in their support of plugin object information. The easiest method to employ when you want to use a particular plugin is to inform users that the site uses the plugin and allow users to load the plugin into their browsers before proceeding, as illustrated in Listing 18.1.

INPUT   **LISTING 18.1**   Informing User of Plugin Use (informuser.htm)

```
<html>
<head>
</head>
<body>
<p>This site uses Macromedia Flash. </p>
<p>Click here to download the Flash plugin
<a href="http://www.macromedia.com/go/getflashplayer/">
<img border="0" src="flash.bmp" width="88" height="31">
</a> for your browser.</P>
</body>
</html>
```

Although this code notifies the user of the use of the particular plugin on your site, as shown in Figure 18.3, it does not verify that the plugin is actually installed. You are at the whim of the user to download the particular plugin from the specified link before proceeding with your site.

OUTPUT

This site uses Macromedia Flash.

Click here to download the Flash plugin [GET macromedia FLASH PLAYER] for your browser.

FIGURE 18.3

It is a good practice to notify the user of the use of a plugin, even if your code checks for its existence.

18

Ideally your code verifies that the plugin exists on the user's browser before loading the code that references the plugin. But in order to do this, you need to access the properties for the browser. As we discussed earlier, Netscape and Internet Explorer each have different methods for handling of plugins, making the process of checking for plugins a little more tedious. Therefore, even if you are checking for the plugin, it is still a good idea to inform the user of a use of the plugin, as in Listing 18.1, to allow them to download it on their own, in case your code is not able to verify its existence.

Netscape makes the detection of the browser quite simple by allowing you to check the plugins collection to determine if a `Plugin` object exists for the specified browser. Unfortunately, Internet Explorer does not support this. For example, you can use code like Listing 18.2 to determine if Macromedia Flash is running on the user's browser.

INPUT   **LISTING 18.2**   Checking Netscape for a Plugin (netscapeplugin.htm)

```
<html>
<head>
<script language="JavaScript" type = "text/javascript">
<!--
for (i = 0; i < navigator.plugins.length; i++)
{
 if (navigator.plugins[i].name.indexOf("Flash") >=0)
  {
     alert("You have the Macromedia Flash Plug-in installed!")
  }
}
//..>
</script>
</head>
<body>
</body>
</html>
```

ANALYSIS   As you can see the code is simply for checking the existence of a plugin within Netscape. The for loop cycles through the list of plugins. If a plugin containing the string "Flash" in the name is encountered, the code determines that the appropriate plugin exists on the user's machine.

Because the Internet Explorer document object model includes the plugins object collection it does not return an error when this script is executed. But since the plugins collection is not activated, the code is ignored. Although, older browsers and some other current browsers may still have a problem with that code, if they do not recognize the plugins collections. Therefore, it is a good idea to add the following if statement to the beginning of the code to ensure that only browsers that recognize the plugins collection execute the specified code:

```
if (navigator.plugins)
```

By placing the if statement around the code in Listing 18.2 you ensure that the code only executes on browsers that recognize the plugins collection. Because Internet Explorer recognizes the object it will also execute the code, but it will be ignored because the plugins object collection is not activated within Internet Explorer.

Checking for a plugin within Internet Explorer requires a slightly different approach. As we have previously discussed, Internet Explorer treats all of the plugin objects as ActiveX controls. Therefore, if you want to determine if a particular plugin is installed, you need to actually look for it as an ActiveX control. The easiest method for doing this is to create an object of the specified plugin type. If the object exists, the `IsObject` function returns a value of `true`, as illustrated in the code in Listing 18.3. Since Internet Explorer was designed to use VBScript to interact with ActiveX controls, it is the best method for us to use with our code. We are using a `Document.Writeln` statement to create the VBScript code within your JavaScript code. Within the Internet Explorer browser, the code is written to the browser and executed.

INPUT   **LISTING 18.3**   Checking Internet Explorer for a Plugin (`ieplugin.htm`)

```
<html>
<head>
<script language="Javascript" type = "text/javascript">
<!--
if ((navigator.userAgent.indexOf('MSIE') != -1) &&
 (navigator.userAgent.indexOf('Win') != -1)){
  document.writeln('<script language="VBscript">');
  document.writeln('Function IEPluginDetect(pluginname)');
  document.writeln('  on error resume next');
  document.writeln('     IEPluginDetect = False');
  document.writeln('     IEPluginDetect = IsObject(CreateObject(pluginname))');
  document.writeln('     If (err) then');
  document.writeln('        IEPluginDetect = False');
  document.writeln('     End If');
  document.writeln('End Function');
  document.writeln('</script>');
}
//-->
</script>
</head>
<body>
<script>
<!--
    document.write('<b>Macromedia Flash Plugin: </b>'  +
 IEPluginDetect('ShockwaveFlash.ShockwaveFlash'));
// -->
</script>
</body>
</html>
```

18

This code executes and displays a value of `true` if the specified plugin exists on the user's browser or `false` if it does not exist. See Figure 18.4.

OUTPUT

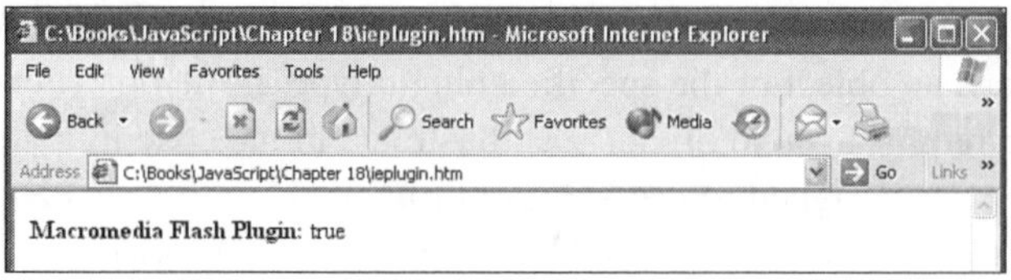

FIGURE 18.4

You can check to see if a plugin is installed in Internet Explorer by looking for the corresponding ActiveX control.

ANALYSIS   As you can see, it is a little more complicated to determine if a particular plugin is available within Internet Explorer. But it is still possible. In order to do so though, you need to know the ActiveX control name assigned to the plugin. For example, in Listing 18.3 the name of the ActiveX control for Flash is "ShockwaveFlash. ShockwaveFlash". Table 18.2 provides a list of common control names. You can replace the "ShockwaveFlash.ShockwaveFlash" code in Listing 18.3 with one of the names in the table.

TABLE 18.2   Internet Explorer Plugin Control Names

Plugin Name	Description
Adobe.SVGCtl	Adobe SVG Viewer
PDF.PdfCtrl.5	Adobe Acrobat Reader
SWCtl.SWCtl.1	Shockwave Director
ShockwaveFlash.ShockwaveFlash	Flash
Rmocx.RealPlayer G2 Control.1	RealPlayer
QuickTimeCheckObject.QuickTimeCheck.1	QuickTime
MediaPlayer.MediaPlayer.1	Windows Media Player

Determining Browser Support for a File Type

As we have previously discussed, many multimedia file types are supported by multiple plugins. For example, if you want to play a MP3 file there are a multitude of different plugins available for playing that file type. Typically, it becomes less important to determine whether a particular plugin exists, when what you are really most concerned with is the user's ability to access the specific file type. For example, you don't really care if they prefer to listen to MP3 files on RealPlayer, or Windows Media Player, you just want to make sure they can play it.

Unfortunately, the ability to check for support of a specific file type is only available with Netscape, using the mimeType object. Although the Internet Explorer DOM supports the mimeType object, the object is ignored within the browser. Therefore, what we are going to look at in this section is only valid for Netscape Navigator.

The mimeType object represents a file type that is transmitted over the Internet. You can use the mimeTypes collection of the Navigator object to determine if that specific file type is supported by the browser. The code in Listing 18.4 illustrates how to use the mimeTypes collection to check for a specific file type supported by the browser. The code in Listing 18.4 illustrates how to create a list of the file types supported by the browser.

INPUT   **LISTING 18.4**   Checking for a File Type (checkmimetype.htm)

```
<html>
<head>
</head>
<body>
<Table Border="1">
<tr><th>MIME Type</th><th>Description</th><th>Extensions</th><th>Plugin</th>
</tr>
<script language="javascript" type = "text/javascript">
<!--
for (var i = 0; i < navigator.mimeTypes.length ; i++) {
  document.write("<td>", navigator.mimeTypes[i].type, "</td>")
  document.write("<td>", navigator.mimeTypes[i].description, "</td>")
  if (navigator.mimeTypes[i].suffixes != "")
    document.write("<td>", navigator.mimeTypes[i].suffixes, "</td>")
  else
    document.write("<td>", navigator.mimeTypes[i].suffixes + " * ", "</td>");
  if (navigator.mimeTypes[i].enabledPlugin)
    document.write("<td>", navigator.mimeTypes[i].enabledPlugin.name,
"</TD></TR>");
  else
    document.write("<td>", "None", "</td></tr>");
}
//-->
</script>
</table>
</body>
</html>
```

The code in Listing 18.4 creates a table that lists the various file types supported by the browser, as shown in Figure 18.5.

OUTPUT

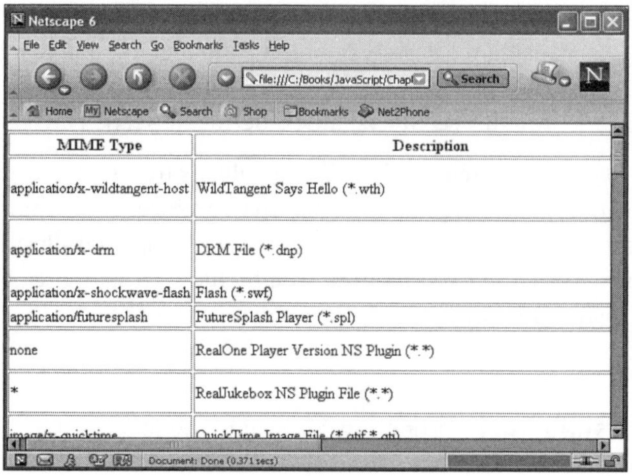

FIGURE 18.5

You can use the
`mimeTypes` *collection*
of the `Navigator`
object to determine
the file types sup-
ported by Netscape
Navigator.

You will notice that we used the properties associated with the `mimeType` object to provide information about each file type supported by the browser. The `mimeType` object has
four different properties that you can access, as outlined in Table 18.3.

TABLE 18.3   `mimeType` Object Properties

Property	Description
`type`	Indicates the name of the MIME file type
`description`	Provides a description of the MIME file type
`suffixes`	Indicates the file extensions for the MIME type
`enabledPlugin`	Indicates the plugin that has been assigned to display data for that MIME type (This property is NULL when there is no plugin assigned to that MIME type.)

Again, although the `mimeType` object provides some very useful information, you can
only rely on it with Netscape Navigator, since Internet Explorer does not support it.

Working with Plugin Objects

Once you determine the existence of the particular plugin, you are ready to work with
the actual plugin. Most plugins run by embedding the appropriate file type. For example,
to play a MIDI file called `sample.mid` you would use the HTML `<embed>` tag as follows:

```
<embed src="sample.mid">
```

Of course the actual player used to play the specified MIDI file varies based upon which plugin is loaded for playing that file type.

As with any other object, when you embed a plugin object on your HTML page there are various properties and methods associated with that object. The actual properties and methods vary based on the specific object that you have embedded. For example, nearly every plugin object has an `src` property that identifies the specific file to open. If you are unfamiliar with the properties and methods for the selected plugin, refer to the plugin's documentation.

For example, you may only want an audio file to play when a specific button is pressed. In this case, you still use the `<embed>` tag to load the file, but you load it with the `Hidden` property set to `true`. When the corresponding button is pressed, the associated `.wav` file plays as illustrated in Listing 18.5.

INPUT   **LISTING 18.5**   Specifying Plugin Properties (`pluginprops.htm`)

```
<html>
<head>
<script language="javascript" type = "text/javascript">
<!--
var sound1 = "ding.wav"
var sound2 = "chord.wav"
function playsound(x)
{
 document.write('<embed src='+'"'+x+'"'+'hidden="true" autostart="true">');
}
//-->
</script>
</head>
<body>
  <input type="button" value="Sound 1" onclick="playsound(sound1);">
          
     
<input type="button" value="Sound 2" onclick="playsound(sound2);">
</body>
</html>
```

18

Again, there is much that can be accomplished using plugins. Of course, the most common use of plugins is to add multimedia effects to a page, as illustrated in Listing 18.5.

Working with Applets

Java applets are simply programs written in Java that are designed to be embedded on a Web page, in much the same fashion as a plugin.

As we have previously discussed, JavaScript was originally introduced by Netscape as a means for creating scripts to interact with Java applets. With the use of JavaScript you can pass values into a Java applet to specify how the applet performs on your page.

> **Note**
>
> Developers that are well versed in Java may choose to have the Java applet contain all of the code for interacting with the page, thereby eliminating the need for the JavaScript code. Although this is totally feasible, it requires more work in the long run. The beauty of using JavaScript is that changes generally can be made on-the-fly to the settings for the Java applet. If you have all of the settings specified within the applet, the applet code must be recompiled each time you make a change.

Just like plugins, there are various applets available on the Internet that you can download and incorporate into your Web pages. Of course, applets also allow the flexibility of developing your own Java applets for use on a Web page (although this type of development is beyond the scope of this book). I am, however, going to provide a brief overview of Java so that you can understand a little more about the language and how JavaScript can interact with a particular Java applet.

Java Basics

Just like JavaScript, Java deals heavily with objects. In fact, objects are actually the basis of the Java language, making it one of the commonly referenced object-oriented languages. Objects are used for all tools, such as screen interaction. Every object in Java is referred to as a class. Actually when you compile a Java applet it becomes a class and it is referenced on your Web page with a `.class` file extension, as follows:

```
<applet code="javaapplet.class">
```

Since JavaScript has a lot in common with Java, such as strings, arrays, numbers, and so forth, you will find that the code is fairly easy to interpret based on your JavaScript knowledge at this point. For example, Listing 18.6 provides some basic code for creating a simple Java applet. Again, don't be too concerned if you don't understand the Java code, I am only providing it to give you a sampling of what Java looks like compared to JavaScript.

INPUT **LISTING 18.6** Simple Java Applet (`Ch18Applet.class`)

```
import java.applet.Applet;
import java.awt.Label;

public class Ch18Applet extends Applet {

  public void init() {
   Label applabel = new Label("Java Applet");
   add(applabel);
  }
}
```

ANALYSIS We are going to call the applet defined in Listing 18.6 from our Web page. As we mentioned earlier, one major difference between Java and JavaScript is the fact that all Java code is compiled, whereas JavaScript is not. This means that the code must be recompiled each time you make modifications to it. Because of this inconvenience Java applets are typically created for tasks that cannot be easily coded within JavaScript.

There are several different Web sites available that provide extensive information about creating Java applets, the most popular being Sun's Web site at www.sun.com. You can find more Java resources sites listed in Appendix D.

Calling a Java Applet

Java applets are historically embedded into an HTML page using the `<applet>` tag. But in HTML 4.0, the `<applet>` tag has been replaced with the `Object` tag for applets. This was done to create a standard tag that could be used to embed all types of objects on the page. There are several properties that you can set for the applet when you embed it on the page, as outlined in Table 18.4. You must always specify the `code` property because that identifies the location of the applet that you are placing on the Web page.

TABLE 18.4 Object Tag Properties

Property	Description
archive	Specifies the URL of archives with components that are relevant to the applet
code	Indicates the URL of the applet's class
codebase	Indicates the URL of the applet's implementation
height	Specifies the height in pixels that the applet should appear on the page
hspace	Indicates the left and right padding that should be applied around the applet (The measurement is in pixels.)
name	Identifies a name for the applet (This makes it easier for other portions of the Web page to reference the applet.)

TABLE 18.4   continued

Property	Description
tabindex	Indicates the tab order that should be applied to the applet (This is only available in Internet Explorer.)
vspace	Indicates the top and bottom padding that should be applied to the applet (The measurement is in pixels.)
width	Specifies the width in pixels that the applet should appear on the page

Calling the applet from within your HTML page is fairly simple. You use the object tag with the code property.

INPUT

```
<object code="Ch18Applet.class" name="newapp" height=100 width=100>
</object>
```

You will notice in this line of code, we also used the Height and Width properties to specify the size that the Java applet appears on the page. With these settings, the applet would display in a box that is 100 pixels wide by 100 pixels high, as shown in Figure 18.6.

OUTPUT

FIGURE 18.6

You can use the Object *tag properties to specify the size of the Java applet on the HTML page.*

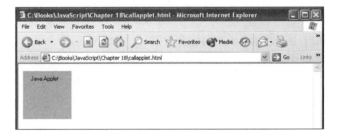

Interfacing with Java Applets

As we mentioned, JavaScript was originally developed to provide the ability to interact with the Java applets, making it possible to change properties of the applet when the page is viewed. In order to do this, you need access to the properties and methods defined for the applet. If you are the one that is creating the applet, you simply need to define public properties and methods that can be changed. Methods and properties are made public using the public keyword, as shown here:

```
public stopApplet()
{
 thread.stop;
}
```

Within your JavaScript code, you simply need to know the name of the properties or methods that you want to access. They are accessed in the same fashion in which we called the properties and methods for other objects. For example, if the Java applet is named `newapplet` you would access the method as follows:

```
document.newapplet.stopApplet();
```

Of course you will quickly recognize that you need to have information about the applet you are adding to your Web page in order to know what properties and methods you can script to. If you acquire the Java applet from another source, this information is typically provided.

Summary

This chapter has allowed you to explore the differences between Java applets and plug-ins. Although they are both add-ons for the browser, they are actually quite different.

Plugins allow the user to work with additional file types, and applets are Java programs that are developed to run on a Web page.

We looked at methods for checking to see if a particular plugin exists on a user's machine prior to loading a file type that requires the plugin.

We also covered the basics of working with Java applets.

Finally, we discussed the fact that there are many Java applets and plugins that are available on the Web to download and incorporate into your site. By doing this you can incorporate the additional functionality of these plugins and applets.

Workshop

In the workshop today we will use the questions to review what you have learned in this chapter about plugins and Java applets when working with JavaScript.

Q&A

Q. How do I make sure the appropriate plugin gets installed on a user's machine?

A. Although both Netscape and Internet Explorer provide methods for determining if a particular plugin exists on a user's browser there is no method for automatically loading the plugin. If you determine that the plugin does not exist, you can provide the option for the user to download the plugin and install it on his machine. Place a link to the vendor's site on the page for the user to download and install the plugin.

Q. So do I check for file type support or a specific plugin?

A. As we discussed in this chapter, you have the option with Netscape of checking either for the existence of a particular plugin or for file type support. When dealing with common file types, such as .mp3, .wav, and so on, the file types are supported by multiple plugins. Because the plugin loaded for a particular file type is a personal preference, in those cases you don't want to force them to load a particular plugin. Instead, you can use the `mimeTypes` collection to determine if the specific file type you want to open is supported by the browser.

Q. Which tag should I use to place an applet on a page?

A. As you are probably aware, HTML provides both the `<applet>` and `<object>` tags that can be used to place a Java applet on a Web page. Although the original design of HTML provided the `<applet>` tag for the purpose of adding Java applets to an HTML page, HTML 4.0 was updated to use the `<object>` tag for applets too. Therefore, while browsers will allow the use of either tag, the preferred method is to use the `<object>` tag.

Quiz

1. How do you detect the existence of a plugin on the user's browser?
2. Is it necessary to detect a specific plugin if I want to play a .wav file on my Web site?
3. How do I determine which plugin is being used to support a particular `mimeType`?

Quiz Answers

1. The process of detecting a plugin varies based on the browser that the user is using. Netscape makes the process quite easy by allowing you to use the `plugins` collection. You can simply search through the list of plugins and try to locate one with the name of the desired plugin. If the plugin is located, then that plugin exists on the user's browser. With Internet Explorer you have to take a different approach. Internet Explorer treats plugins as ActiveX controls. You need to use VBScript to determine if an object exists with the specified name.

2. No, you can look for the support of the file type by using the `mimeTypes` collection on Netscape. You can use the `type` property to determine if the support exists for that plugin.

3. The `enabledPlugin` property of the `mimeTypes` collection keeps track of the plugin that has been assigned for that particular file type. You can use that property to determine if the file type is being supported by the desired plugin. If you prefer the file to display with a different plugin, you can notify the user that current plugin is not what you anticipated.

Exercises

1. Write code to determine if a particular plugin is installed on both Netscape Navigator and Microsoft Internet Explorer. Remember to make the code browser specific (as we discussed in Chapter 8).

2. Create code that executes on Netscape Navigator to check whether a plugin is enabled for a specific mimeType, such as MP3 files. Display that plugin information for the user.

18

DAY **19**

Creating Your Own Objects

As already discussed, JavaScript provides access to several objects that you can use to change the content of your page. More than likely, though, you are going to reach a point where you will want to create your own custom objects to contain specific properties and methods. Custom objects can be very useful especially when creating e-commerce applications.

This chapter discusses the process of creating custom objects that can be used to store related values. Because custom objects store values as properties, we will discuss how to create and modify property values for a custom object. We also will look at how to instantiate these objects once they have been created, as well as how to create custom methods for each object. Finally, we will look at how you can customize the built-in JavaScript objects by adding additional properties and methods.

This chapter will teach you

- What a custom object is
- How to use the constructor function to create an object
- How to create an instance of a custom object
- How to create object methods

What Is a Custom Object?

JavaScript is designed to work with objects. Until this point, the objects that we have worked with have been either the built-in JavaScript objects or the objects associated with the browser (DOM). As you have learned, by working with an object you are able to make modifications to the properties associated with that object and so alter the appearance of a Web page.

Not only does JavaScript work well with existing JavaScript and DOM objects, but it also provides you the option of creating your own objects for storing data. Your first inclination may be to wonder why you need to create a custom object—after all JavaScript already provides variables and arrays that are quite versatile in the way they allow you to store data. Although the use of variables and arrays work well for most types of data, you may find that you need a more complex structure for storing the data.

Probably the most common use of a custom object in JavaScript is creating a database type of structure. For example, if you are creating an e-commerce site (as we will look at in the next chapter), you may want to create a customer object that stores custom information about your customer. By doing this, the information is stored in one location.

Of course customer information can also be easily stored with variables and arrays, but it would require several different arrays to store the same information that you can place in one object. For example, if you wanted to store name, address, phone number, and e-mail address, you would typically use a separate array for each type of information. Whereas, if you were to create a custom object, you would have one object for each customer that would contain each of the data types.

Once you create your custom object, you can have properties for each object. In our case, our customer object would have properties for Name, Address, Phone, and E-mail. Besides creating properties for your custom object you can also create custom methods. For example, you may want to create a custom method to display the customer information.

Therefore a custom object greatly expands the potential you have for working with custom data.

Combine Multiple Data Elements into One Object

Without the use of an object you will likely use multiple data elements, such as variables and arrays, to represent multiple elements of data. Additionally, you will need a separate variable for each element of information stored about a customer, for example, a `name` variable, `address` variable, and so forth. With the use of a custom object, you only create one object and then add properties to represent each data element.

Using this process will greatly simplify your code because you are only dealing with one object. For example, the following code illustrates how you would assign data to each property of our customer object:

```
this.name = name;
this.address = address;
this.phone = phone;
this.email = email;
```

We will look at the process of creating custom objects in detail later in this chapter; for now, notice that values are assigned to each property of the object in basically the same fashion.

Create Methods and Properties Specific for the Custom Object

As discussed in the previous chapters, each object you work with in JavaScript has its own assortment of custom properties and methods. The properties contain specific information that you want to access (for example, the URL property of the `Document` object, which specifies the location of the document displayed in the Web browser).

19

Typically most objects also have different methods that you can use with the object. These methods allow you to make modifications to properties of the object. For example, the `window.alert()` method creates an alert window that displays on top of the browser window.

Just like built-in objects, you can also create properties and methods for your custom object. In fact, all objects that you create will have properties that represent the data you want to assign to the object. You can also create methods, as we will discuss in depth later in this chapter.

Use of the Constructor to Create Objects

As with any other data element that you use, you must create a custom object before you can use it. Custom objects are created using a function. Functions that create objects are referred to as the *constructor* for the object. A constructor function is structured in basically the same as any other function that you create, with the name of the object you are going to create used as the function name, like so:

```
function customerObj (parameters) {
}
```

When you create a custom object with the constructor function, the use of parameters is actually optional. However, typically you will want to use these parameters to allow values to be passed to the object. For example, if you use the built-in `document.writeln` method to write text to the screen, the text that you specify is the parameter that is passed to the `Document` object. By this same token, if you want to pass values to your object, you will need to specify parameters for the object; for example, to receive the parameters for name, address, phone, and e-mail, the parameter statement would appear as follows:

```
function customerObj (name, address, phone, email) {
}
```

Okay, now we know how to create the constructor function, but this is only part of the process. Passing the parameters into the constructor function requires that properties are created to receive the parameter values, as we will discuss in the next section.

Adding Properties to the Object

Of course you are creating a custom object for the purpose of storing data. In order to do so, you will need to define these values. With a custom object the data values are stored as properties of the object. When you create a custom object you do so by defining the properties of the new object. For example, our customer object would have the following properties representing each data element stored in the object:

- name

- address

- telephone

- emailaddress

Typically, you would pass in a separate parameter for each property you are creating for your object. For example, when we created the `customerObj` object using the constructor function, we specified four different parameters, each of which should be assigned to a separate property within your object. To assign these parameter values to properties within our custom object, we would add the following property assignment code:

```
function customerObj (name, address, phone, email) {
this.name = name;
this.address = address;
this.telephone = phone;
this.emailaddress = email;
}
```

If you examine the code for the constructor function used to create our `CustomerObj` object, you will notice that the keyword `this` is used for each property assignment statement. The `this` keyword is always used when you create a property assignment statement. The `this` keyword refers to the current object. In the instant case, the keyword is referring to the custom object that we are creating called `customerObj`.

Keep in mind, you do not have to pass in parameter values for the properties, as we stated previously. If you want to have constant values for only some properties, you can simply assign those values to the property within your constructor function. For example, we can add a property for the salesperson to our `customerObj` object. If the orders are generated by the Web site, the salesperson can be referred to as `"Web"`. Our object constructor function would look like this:

```
function customerObj (name, address, phone, email) {
this.name = name;
this.address = address;
this.telephone = phone;
this.emailaddress = email;
this.salesperson = "Web";
```

NEW TERM So now we have specified how to create the custom object. Of course, once you create the object, it is useless until you actually use it. An object is used by creating an object instance. In order to create an object instance, or use a custom object, you will need to use a process referred to as *instantiating*. We will discuss how to go about instantiating an object in the next section.

19

Note

> **The this Keyword**
>
> As referred to in the text, the this keyword is used as a reference to the receiving object, which means that it refers to the corresponding object based on the location of the keyword. Within this chapter, we are illustrating the use of this keyword in two different types of locations: within an object constructor function and within a method function.
>
> When the this keyword is used within an object constructor function the keyword is a reference to the object created by the function. For example, if you have a function creating an object called newBook, the this keyword refers to the newBook object whenever used within the function.
>
> When the this keyword is used within a method function the keyword references the object that the method belongs to. This can be a little confusing if there are multiple objects within the code, but the keyword references the object that has a statement defining the method.
>
> Finally, the this keyword can also be used outside of any functions. This location is commonly referred to as global code. In this instance, the this keyword refers to the Window object.

Creating an Instance of a Custom Object

Once you have defined the custom object, of course you are going to want to use it. In order to use a custom object, you must first create an instance of, or instantiate it. Instantiating an object is similar to declaring a variable. In fact, what you are doing is creating an instance of the custom object by creating an object variable and assigning it the new custom object. You will recognize this process as it is the same as that used to create instances of built-in objects.

In order to instantiate the object, you will need to use the new keyword to assign an instance of custom object to the new object variable. Listing 19.1 illustrates how to instantiate our customerObj object, created in the previous section.

INPUT   **LISTING 19.1**   Instantiating the Custom Object (newobject.htm)

```
<html>
<head>
<script language="Javascript" type = "text/javascript">
<!--
function customerObj (name, address, phone, email) {
this.name = name;
this.address = address;
this.telephone = phone;
this.emailaddress = email;
```

LISTING 19.1 continued

```
}
var newCust = new customerObj("Tom Jones", "Dallas, Texas", "214-555-5555",
"tom@jones.com");
alert("Hello " + newCust.name);
//-->
</script>
</head>
<body>
</body>
</html>
```

ANALYSIS The customerObj object is instantiated when we declare the new object variable:

```
var newCust = new customerObj("Tom Jones", "Dallas, Texas", "214-555-5555",
"tom@jones.com");
```

Notice we declared a new variable called newCust, which is an instance of the customerObj object. You will notice that we are passing four different values to the customerObj object Constructor function. This is because the function is expecting four different parameter values. Keep in mind these values can be actual values, as we have in Listing 19.1, or other variables containing the appropriate values. In other words, you create an instance of an object in the same fashion that you can any other function—by passing it the appropriate values.

Of course, it is not necessary to specify the values for the properties when you create the object instance with the new keyword. You can also create the object instance and then assign property values after the fact. For example, we could revise the creation of the object instance, shown in Listing 19.1, as follows:

```
var newCust = new customerObj();
newCust.name = "Tom Jones";
newCust.address = "Dallas, Texas";
newCust.telephone = "214-555-5555";
newCust.emailaddress = "tom@jones.com";
```

This method of assigning values to the properties of the object works best for instances when the custom object has several different properties. By assigning each property individually, it makes your code easier to read because you can quickly determine what value was assigned to each property.

Keep in mind, you can create multiple instances of the same object within your code. For example, if you wanted to work with information from two different customers, you could create two instances of the customerObj object, as follows:

19

```
<script language="Javascript" type = "text/javascript">
<!--
function customerObj (name, address, phone, email) {
this.name = name;
this.address = address;
this.telephone = phone;
this.emailaddress = email;
}
var newCust1 = new customerObj("Tom Jones", "Dallas, Texas", "214-555-5555",
"tom@jones.com");
var newCust2 = new customerObj("Sam Smith", "Austin, Texas", "703-555-5555",
sam@smith.com");
```

With this scenario, we now have two different object instances, newCust1 and newCust2. Each object instance is based on the properties and methods associated with the customerObj object. This means that they each have the same properties, but they each have different values for those same properties. As you can see, we are passing in different values for the properties when the object is created. For example, newCust1 has a value of "Tom Jones" for the name property and newCust2 has a value of "Sam Smith" for the same property.

Accessing Properties of a Custom Object

Once an instance of the object has been created, you can access any of the object properties in the same fashion that we accessed properties from other objects. To do so, you simply specify the object name, a period, and the name of the property that you want to access. For example, in Listing 19.1, the alert() method contains a reference to the name property for the object:

INPUT

```
alert("Hello " + newCust.name);
```

When this statement executes, the contents of the name property of the object display in the Alert dialog box as shown in Figure 19.1.

OUTPUT

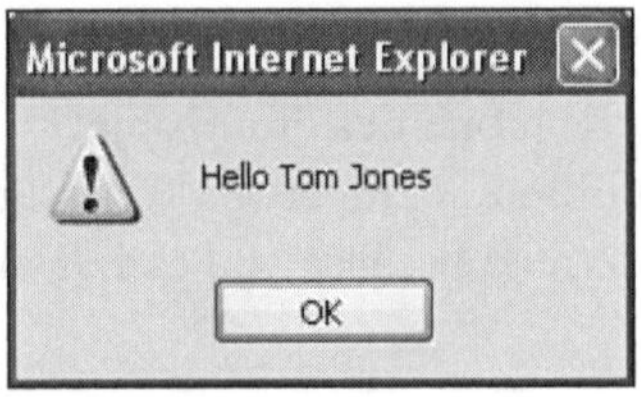

FIGURE 19.1

You can access properties of a custom object in much the same fashion as you do with built-in JavaScript objects.

Microsoft Internet Explorer

! Hello Tom Jones

OK

ANALYSIS So essentially what occurs is that you have created an instance of the `customerObj` called `newCust`. The new object instance has all of the properties that are assigned to the custom object. Therefore, since `customerObj` has the properties `name`, `address`, `telephone`, and `emailaddress`, those properties are associated with the object instance, `newCust`. You can now reference any of those properties for your new object instance. Therefore, properties would be referenced using the standard object property notation of object name, a period, and the property name, as follows:

```
newCust.name
newCust.address
newCust.telephone
newCust.emailaddress
```

Once you have created the object instance, the properties of the object instance can be used anywhere within your code. Keep in mind, you must use the properties of the object instance, and not the actual object.

Changing the Value of an Object Property

Of course, you are not always going to want to keep the values that you initially assigned to the properties of the object. Just like built-in objects, you can change the values of the properties for your custom object at any point within your code. You can accomplish this in the same manner in which we assigned individual values to each property of the object.

To change the value of the property for a custom object, you will need to specify the object instance name, a period, and the name of the property that you want to change. For example, if we look back at the `newCust` object instance that we created earlier, we could change the value of the `name` property by typing the following line of code:

```
newCust.name = "Tom Thompson"
```

This would allow you to receive values from the visitor to your Web site, and then assign them to the properties for the object. For example, we may want to receive the customer information in a Web form and assign the values to the object, as outlined in the code in Listing 19.2.

INPUT   **LISTING 19.2**   Changing the Object Properties (`setprops.htm`)

```
<html>
<head>
<script language="Javascript" type = "text/javascript">
<!--
function customerObj() {
this.name = "";
```

19

LISTING 19.2   continued

```
this.address = "";
this.telephone = "";
this.emailaddress = "";
}
var newCust = new customerObj();
function createCust() {
newCust.name = custform.name.value;
newCust.address = custform.address.value;
newCust.telephone = custform.phone.value;
newCust.emailaddress = custform.email.value;
alert("Hello " + newCust.name);
}
//-->
</script>
</head>
<body>
<form name="custform">
  <u><b>Customer Information</b></u></p>
  <p><b>Name:   </b>   
  <input type="text" name="name" size="20"></p>
  <p><b>Address: </b>   <input type="text" name="address"
size="55"></p>
  <p><b>Telephone:</b> <input type="text" name="phone" size="20"></p>
  <p><b>Email:  </b>      
  <input type="text" name="email" size="20"></p>
  <p><input type="submit" value="Submit" onclick="createCust()"></p>
</form>
</body>
</html>
```

ANALYSIS   As you can see from the code in Listing 19.2, you can pass values from an HTML form to the custom object as values for the associated properties. When the page first loads, the values of the properties are empty strings. As soon as the user clicks the submit button, the values typed into the form become the values of the properties for the object instance, as shown here:

```
function createCust() {
newCust.name = custform.name.value;
newCust.address = custform.address.value;
newCust.telephone = custform.phone.value;
newCust.emailaddress = custform.email.value;
alert("Hello " + newCust.name);
}
```

The createCust() function is called when the submit button is clicked by the user. In this instance, the function is not directly associated with the custom object instance; so, instead of using the this keyword as we did earlier to reference the object, you will need to actually state the object instance name. In this case, the object instance that was created is newCust. The function also contains a statement containing the alert() method. This method displays an alert() popup message that contains a message for the user that submitted the form, as shown in Figure 19.2.

OUTPUT

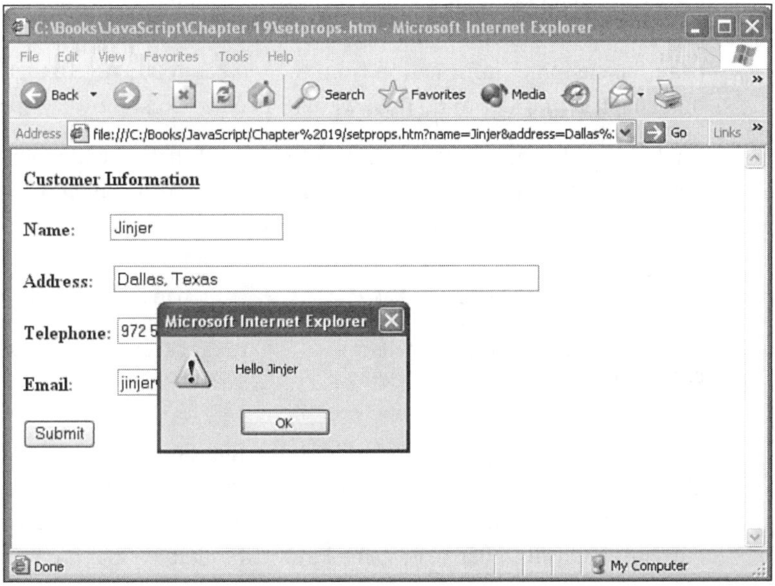

FIGURE 19.2

You can use JavaScript to change the properties of a custom object in the same fashion as built-in objects.

You can change the values of properties for an object at any point within your Web page. Remember though, you need to reference the object instance, and not the actual object, when you want to change the value of an object property.

Creating Object Methods

You may remember that nearly all of the built-in objects that we have worked with have had properties as well as associated methods. As discussed in Chapter 4, "JavaScript Is Object-Based," methods provide a means for working with the properties associated with an object. For example, one method that we have used repeatedly throughout this book is the alert() method that is associated with the Window object. We often forget that it is actually a method of a built-in object because we do not have to specify the object name when we use properties and methods associated with the Window object. Consequently, this method, shown below, allows us to specify any text to display in an alert() popup window that displays on top of the current browser window:

```
window.alert("Display text");
```

By the same token, you may have a method designed for displaying the properties of
your custom object. Custom methods have the same capabilities as any other JavaScript
functions that you can create.

Defining methods for a custom object is a little more complicated than defining properties. You create methods for an object by defining a function for each method, and then
associating the function with the object function. For example, we can create a method to
print the customer information from the CustomerObj object that we created earlier in
this chapter. In order to do this, we will need to do some very specific things.

First, we will need to create a custom method function called printCust that indicates
how the customer information should print. This is a standard JavaScript function with
the name of the desired method being used as the function name, as shown below:

```
function printCust() {
document.write("Customer Name:     " + this.name + "<br>\n");
document.write("Address:           " + this.address + "<br>\n");
document.write("Telephone Number: " + this.telephone + "<br>\n");
document.write("Email Address:     " + this.emailaddress);
}
```

You will notice that within the printCust function that we have defined, it is using the
this keyword to reference the current object. Each property of the object is also referenced. This is because the function is designed to be a method function related to the
current object. In other words, the keyword indicates that the property specified is associated with the current object.

The next task to be accomplished is to make this method part of the function definition.
This is accomplished in a similar fashion as that used to define a property of the
function:

```
function customerObj (name, address, phone, email) {
this.name = name;
this.address = address;
this.telephone = phone;
this.emailaddress = email;
this.printCust = printCust;
}
```

You will notice that this object definition looks the same as earlier in the chapter when
we first defined the customerObj constructor function. The only difference is the line
that was added to link the printCust method function to the object, as shown here:

```
this.printCust = printCust;
```

This is a very crucial step in the process of defining methods for a custom object. You
must link the method to the appropriate object in order to have the method function

behave like a standard object method. You will notice that this added statement looks like the other property definitions. The difference is that instead of referencing a parameter passed to the constructor function, the statement refers to the method function we created.

Once you have created a method function and added the method reference to the object constructor function, you can call the method in the same fashion as other methods. For example, if we have created an object instance called newCust, you can reference the method by stating the object reference name, a period, and the name of the method, as follows:

```
newCust.printCust();
```

We can combine the new method with our custom object to print the customer information on the page, as showns in Listing 19.3.

INPUT   **LISTING 19.3**   Using a Custom Method (newmethod.htm)

```
<html>
<head>
<script language="Javascript" type = "text/javascript">
<!--
function customerObj (name, address, phone, email) {
this.name = name;
this.address = address;
this.telephone = phone;
this.emailaddress = email;
this.printCust = printCust;
}
function printCust() {
document.write("Customer Name:    " + this.name + "<br>\n");
document.write("Address:          " + this.address + "<br>\n");
document.write("Telephone Number: " + this.telephone + "<br>\n");
document.write("Email Address:    " + this.emailaddress);
}
var newCust = new customerObj("Tom Jones", "Dallas, Texas", "214-555-5555",
"tom@jones.com");
newCust.printCust();
//-->
</script>
</head>
<body>
</body>
</html>
```

19

The code in Listing 19.3 creates the custom object and associated method. The method is called and it prints the contents of the custom object to the screen, as shown in Figure 19.3.

FIGURE **19.3**

You can create custom methods to use with custom objects.

Linking Objects Together

So far we have seen how to create custom objects with the associated properties and methods. But what happens when the value of the property is another object? JavaScript allows you to create objects with property values that are actually references to other custom objects. Sound a little confusing? Well let's explore this issue a little further.

Suppose we have two different custom objects. The first object (as shown earlier) contains the customer information such as name, address, telephone number, and e-mail address. The second object contains company information, such as company name, address, and phone number, like so:

```
function companyObj (cname, caddress, cphone) {
this.name = cname;
this.address = caddress;
this.telephone = cphone;
}
```

Once you have created the object for the company information, you can still create the company object instance using the new keyword:

```
var newComp = new companyObj("ABC Corp.", "Dallas, Texas", "214-444-5555");
```

You can link a customer to the company information by linking the two objects together. By doing this the newComp instance of the companyObj actually becomes a property of the customerObj object:

```
function customerObj (name, address, phone, email) {
this.name = name;
this.address = address;
this.telephone = phone;
```

```
this.emailaddress = email;
this.companyObj = newComp;
}
```

Once you have created the company object, you can assign values to the customer object with one statement:

```
var newCust = new customerObj("Jane Smith", "Dallas, Texas", "972-555-5555",
 "jane@smith.com", newComp);
```

Notice we simply passed the contents of the newComp object instance as the final parameter value when creating the newCust object. The values specified for the object instance are assigned to our objects, as illustrated in Listing 19.4.

INPUT   **LISTING 19.4**   Linking Custom Objects (linkobjects.htm)

```
<html>
<head>
<script language="Javascript" type = "text/javascript">
<!--
function companyObj (cname, caddress, cphone) {
this.cname = cname;
this.caddress = caddress;
this.ctelephone = cphone;
}
var newComp = new companyObj("ABC Corp", "Dallas, Texas", "214-444-5555");
function customerObj (name, address, phone, email) {
this.name = name;
this.address = address;
this.telephone = phone;
this.emailaddress = email;
this.compObj = newComp;
}
var newCust = new customerObj("Jane Smith", "Dallas, Texas", "972-555-5555",
 "jane@smith.com", newComp);
document.write("Customer Name:    " + newCust.name + "<br>\n");
document.write("Address:          " + newCust.address + "<br>\n");
document.write("Telephone Number: " + newCust.telephone + "<br>\n");
document.write("Email Address:    " + newCust.emailaddress + "<br>\n");
document.write("Company Name:     " + newCust.compObj.cname + "<br>\n");
document.write("Company Address:  " + newCust.compObj.caddress + "<br>\n");
document.write("Telephone Number: " + newCust.compObj.ctelephone);
//-->
</script>
</head>
<body>
</body>
</html>
```

19

You will notice that when we referenced properties from the newComp object instance, we also had to reference the name of the property in the customerObj object that corresponds to the object as well as the corresponding property in the companyObj object. You need to do this in order to capture the companyObj object that corresponds to the customerObj object you are referencing. The customer and company information are written to the screen, as shown in Figure 19.4.

OUTPUT

FIGURE 19.4

You can link custom objects together.

```
Customer Name: Jane Smith
Address: Dallas, Texas
Telephone Number: 972-555-5555
Email Address: jane@smith.com
Company Name: ABC Corp
Company Address: Dallas, Texas
Telephone Number: 214-444-5555
```

ANALYSIS As you can probably imagine, the possibilities of things that you can accomplish with the use of custom objects is tremendous. By linking different objects together you can access not only other objects' properties, but also the corresponding methods of that object. What is even more cool, is that multiple objects can be linked to the same object. For example, you can have both a customer and vendor object that are both linked to a company object.

The process of linking multiple objects together can become quite complex, and can start to resemble relational databases. However, you've learned there are many ways to combine objects and methods.

Summary

This chapter has provided a stepping stone for creating and working with custom objects in your JavaScript code. You were able to see how quickly you can create a custom object that can be used anywhere within your code for the current page.

We learned that in order to create a custom object you need to create an object constructor function. This function closely resembles a standard JavaScript function. Each property of a custom object is defined using the this keyword. The this keyword always refers to the current object. Once you create a custom object, you must create an instance of the object. This process is commonly referred to as *instantiating* the object. To create the new instance of the object, you need to use the new keyword as part of the variable definition. You can also create custom methods that can be assigned to the custom objects. These methods give you the same capabilities available with built-in objects. Finally, we looked at how you can create even more complex objects by linking multiple objects together. This allows you to link related objects easily (for example, multiple customers from the same company). This requires just one company object by a separate customer object for each customer. Each of those customer objects can link to the same company object.

As we have discussed, the capabilities are enormous when dealing with custom objects in JavaScript.

Workshop

In the workshop today, we will use the Q&A, questions, and exercises to review what you have learned in this chapter about creating custom objects and defining properties and methods for the objects used within your JavaScript code.

Q&A

Q. **Why should I use a custom object?**

A. A custom object allows you to combine multiple data types. For example, you can store a string, numeric value, and a Boolean value, all within the same custom object. By doing so, you can group common data together. Custom objects also allow you to create methods specific to that object. These methods can be customized to work only with the data stored in the custom object.

Q. **Can I really link an object to more than one other object?**

A. Yes, you can link an object to several different objects on the same page. For example, in this chapter we created a customer object and a company object, so if you have several customers that work for the same company, each one of the customers would have the same company object linked to them. You can even take it a step further and create a salesperson object that is linked to either the customer of the salesperson, or perhaps the company that is within the salesperson's territory.

Q. **When can I use the `this` keyword?**

A. The this keyword is used to refer to the current object. Of course the location where you use the this keyword dictates the actual object that it is referring to.

19

If the this keyword is used within an object constructor function, it refers to the object being created by the function. If the this keyword is used within a method function, it refers to the object that is linked to the method function. Finally, if the this keyword appears outside of any functions, it refers to the Window object. Therefore, be careful when using this keyword to ensure that you achieve the appropriate results.

Quiz

1. What keyword is used to "instantiate" an object?
2. If you have a customer object called Book with a property of Name and you create an object instance of Book1, how would you set the Name property to "Teach Yourself JavaScript in 21 Days"?
3. What statement do I add to the Book object to link it to the bookInfo method?

Quiz Answers

1. To "instantiate" or create an instance of a custom object, you need to use the new keyword when you create your variable definition defining the object instance. For example, var newbook = new book(); creates a new object instance called newbook of the object Book.
2. In order to change the property for the Book1 object, you would need to type the following statement: Book1.Name = "Teach Yourself JavaScript in 21 Days".
3. In order to link a method to an object, you will need to add a statement to the object indicating the name of the method. To add this to the Book object you would type the following statement: this.bookInfo = bookInfo;.

Exercises

1. Write the code to create an object that gathers customer information from a form, and another object that gets the company information from the same form. This information should include name, address, zip code, phone number, e-mail address, and customer number. The company information should be name, address, and phone number. Display a welcome message to the user with the information gathered from the form.
2. Create a custom method to display the contents of your customer object.

Day 20

JavaScript in E-Commerce

As you are probably aware, the Internet has become a Mecca for both buyers and sellers of different products. In fact it is difficult to visit a Web site these days without encountering something for sale. Therefore, if you haven't already encountered the need to develop this type of site, your day will likely come.

E-commerce applications can be very involved and this chapter will demonstrate how you can use JavaScript when creating an online store. As we work through this chapter, you are going to recognize the limitations of using JavaScript to meet the requirements for creating an e-commerce site. We will look at the process involved in creating an online catalog and shopping basket. Finally, we will look at how the order is sent back to the e-commerce site for processing.

This chapter will teach you

- Requirements for an e-commerce site
- Shop structure
- The online catalog
- Shopping carts

Requirements for an E-Commerce Site

As with any type of programming that you do either in JavaScript or another programming language, there are many ways to design your e-commerce site. No matter how you ultimately decide to design your Web site, there are some basic requirements that you must meet in order to have a successful e-commerce Web site:

- Online store—As with any store, you will need a location where visitors come to locate the desired items.
- Database—You will need to create an online catalog (or database) that contains specific information about each product available for purchase.
- Shopping cart—This is a list of the items that the visitor would like to purchase.
- Order desk—This is the location for receiving the order, along with pertinent customer information for processing it.

These four items may seem fairly obvious; after all, you would need to have some type of catalog of the items that can be purchased. Of course, there are various methods that can be used to create each of these items, but in this chapter let's focus on creating these items using JavaScript and HTML. We will also discuss any limitations that exist with this method of development.

As mentioned, e-commerce sites can be created using a wide variety of technologies. The technologies you actually use will depend on the sophistication that you want to achieve with your site. There are other technologies, besides JavaScript and HTML, that you should consider incorporating when creating an e-commerce site. For example, as we will discuss later in this chapter, you will want to use a database program if you have a large number of items to sell on your site. Also, CGI provides a good interface between the Web servers and your Web page that runs on the user's page.

Shop Structure

Before you start coding, you need to decide the type of structure you want to use for your e-commerce site. At the bare minimum you need to have a place where the customers can select the items they want and where you can provide the ordering information. Of course this could potentially be accomplished all on one page, but it is typically done with multiple Web pages. Essentially you want to make sure your Web site has each of the four things specified in the previous section: an online store, database, shopping cart, and order desk.

In this chapter, we are going to create an e-commerce bookstore site that has each of these items. This site is going to incorporate the technology that we have discussed in the previous chapters by making use of cookies, custom objects, forms, and event handling. Therefore, we are assuming you have a thorough understanding of the technology already discussed in each of those chapters before proceeding with the creation of the Web site in this chapter.

Our bookstore site is going to consist of two HTML pages. The first page is our online store. This page provides a list of all items available at our e-commerce site, as shown in Figure 20.1.

FIGURE 20.1

Your site must contain at least one page that lists the items that are available for ordering.

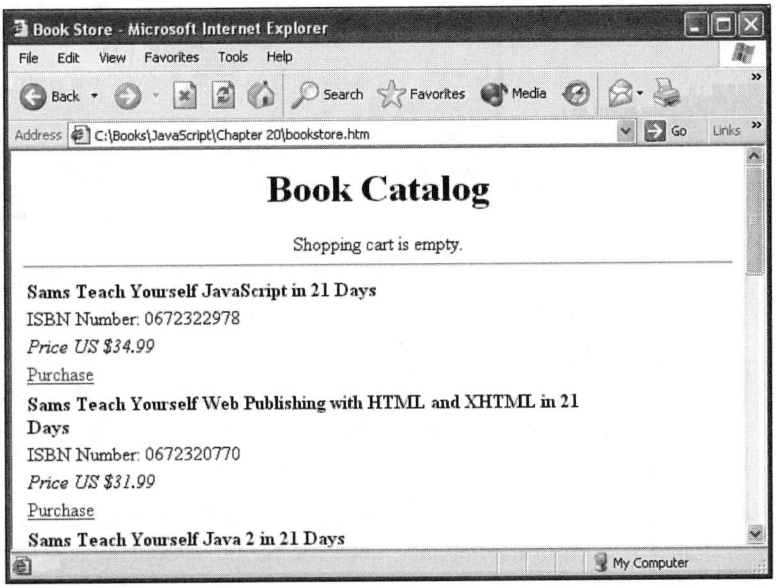

As you can see in Figure 20.1, we have a catalog of the available items and each one can be ordered by selecting the Purchase link associated with the desired item. (We will discuss the creation of this online catalog in detail in the following section.)

The second page of our e-commerce site is our shopping cart page. This page will list the items ordered and will give the user the ability to remove items from the cart. We will collect the personal information for the order on this page, as illustrated in Figure 20.2.

20

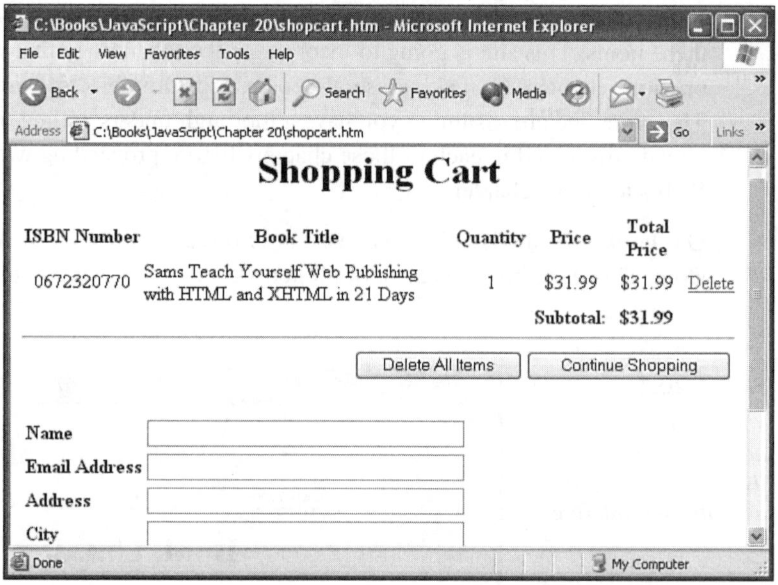

FIGURE 20.2

Create a shopping cart page to provide the user with a list of items that have been ordered.

Next for our bookstore project, we will use a custom object to track the different books that are available for purchase on our Web site.

Finally, we are going to use a simplistic method for the order desk of sending a message containing the order. This type of method for placing orders is used quite frequently, especially with smaller companies. We will look at this process in more detail when we discuss the creation of the shopping cart page.

All of the code used to create the e-commerce bookstore is available on the Web site outlined in the Introduction. The code for the site is contained in three files, as outlined in Table 20.1.

TABLE 20.1 Files Used to Create the E-Commerce Web Site

File	Contents
bookstore.htm	Contains the HTML and JavaScript code required to create the bookstore page.
shopcart.htm	Contains the HTML and JavaScript code needed to create the shopping cart page. It also contains the code needed to capture the user information and send the order for processing.
books.js	Contains functions needed by both the bookstore.htm and shopcart.htm pages. This includes the functions for creating the book custom object and the bookDB array.

The Online Catalog

It stands to reason that if you are going to create an e-commerce site you must have something to sell. Typically most e-commerce sites have multiple items for sale, but a site can have as few as one single item. The page or pages that list the items you have for sale constitute your online catalog. When creating your online catalog there are really only two requirements you need to keep in mind: you need to list the items for sale, and you need to provide a method to select the items for purchase.

There are multiple methods that you can use to create an online catalog, and the method that you choose is governed by factors such as the number of items you have for sale, how frequently your list changes, and even whether or not you want to allow visitors to search for items that match specific criteria.

For our bookstore site, the online catalog consists of two major pieces: the online catalog page that displays the items for sale, and the actual database of items for sale. Of course, it may seem that they would both be the same thing, but it will become evident why you will need these to be two separate elements of the Web site.

Creating the Custom Database

Since we are creating an online bookstore, our online catalog will contain a list of books that are available for purchase. Because the list of books is fairly short, and we do not intend to change it, we will use a custom JavaScript object for our database of items. Perhaps you remember from the last chapter, custom objects allow us to group multiple related data types together. Our custom object is going to be made up of four different data values that describe a book, as listed below and shown in Listing 20.1.

Note

Keep in mind that we want to place this code in the books.js file so that the object can be accessed by both the shopcart.htm and bookstore.htm pages.

20

- Title—This value will be a string that contains the title of the book.

- Number—This value will be a string that contains the ISBN number assigned to the book. Because ISBN numbers are all unique, this provides a good field for locating the desired book.

- Price—This is a numeric value that indicates the price of the book.

- Quantity—This value indicates the number of units ordered for the corresponding book, which was ordered by the user. We initially assign a value of zero to this field.

LISTING 20.1   Creating a Book Object

```
function book(title, number, price, quantity)
{
    this.title = title;
    this.number = number;
    this.price = price;
    this.quantity = quantity;
}
```

As you are aware, the custom object would only represent one book in our bookstore.
Therefore we need to have a separate object for each book. Instead of creating different
objects for each book, we will create one array that contains all of the book objects.

```
var bookDB = new Array();
```

Once we have our array of books created, we need to assign values for each book. We
will accomplish this by creating 10 array elements that create separate book objects, as
illustrated in Listing 20.2. Again, place this code in the books.js file.

LISTING 20.2   Assigning the Book Information to the Book Database Array

```
function createBookDB()
{
    bookDB[0] = new book("Sams Teach Yourself JavaScript in 21 Days",
                         "0672322978", 34.99, 0);
    bookDB[1] = new book("Sams Teach Yourself Web Publishing with
HTML and XHTML in 21 Days",  "0672320770", 31.99, 0);
    bookDB[2] = new book("Sams Teach Yourself Java 2 in 21 Days",
                         "0672319586", 26.99, 0);
    bookDB[3] = new book("Sams Teach Yourself XSLT in 21 Days",
                         "0672323184", 35.99, 0);
    bookDB[4] = new book("Sams Teach Yourself Ruby in 21 Days",
                         "0672322528", 35.99, 0);
    bookDB[5] = new book("Sams Teach Yourself Mozilla Programming in 21 Days",
                         "0672321726", 35.99, 0);
    bookDB[6] = new book("Sams Teach Yourself Cisco Routers in 21 Days",
                         "067232296X", 35.99, 0);
    bookDB[7] = new book("Sams Teach Yourself Access 2002 in 21 Days",
                         "0672321033", 35.99, 0);
    bookDB[8] = new book("Sams Teach Yourself Perl in 21 Days",
                         "0672320355", 31.99, 0);
    bookDB[9] = new book("Sams Teach Yourself .NET Windows Forms in 21 Days",
                         "0672323206", 35.99, 0);
}
```

You will notice that as we create each array element, we are actually calling the book() function to create a separate book object for each element of the array. Again, if you want more information about creating custom objects, you can refer back to Chapter 19, "Creating Your Own Objects."

Using an Actual Database

If you have a more complex online store than the one we are creating, you will need to seriously consider the use of a real database package for maintaining your list of items. There are several different database options to consider. For smaller stores, you might consider using a Microsoft Access database. More complex databases should be created using database programs such as Microsoft SQL Server, or MySQL. These database applications are designed to handle larger databases and are also better designed for handling a lot of traffic.

Unfortunately, dealing with these different databases is beyond the scope of this book, but there are several great resources available. Check out *Sams Teach Yourself MySQL in 24 Hours* and *Sams Teach Yourself Access 2002 in 21 Days* for more information on dealing with other types of databases.

Designing Your Catalog

We already have designed a custom object array to contain the items in the bookstore, now we need to capture the data from the array to list on the online catalog page. Of course, you can just as easily create a static HTML page that lists the items for sale, but by pulling the data from the custom object array (if you do decide to modify the online catalog), you only need to change the data in your array and it will be updated on the catalog page.

We are going to create a table of the items in the catalog. Since we are going to be getting the items for the table from our array of custom objects, we need to use JavaScript to accomplish this, as you can see in Listing 20.3.

20

INPUT   **LISTING 20.3**   Creating the Online Catalog

```
for (var n = 0; n < bookDB.length; n++)
{
    document.writeln('<table width=500>');
    document.writeln('<tr><td><b>' + bookDB[n].title + '</b></td></tr>');
    document.writeln('<tr><td>'+ 'ISBN Number: ' + bookDB[n].number +
    '</td></tr>');
    document.writeln('<tr><td><i>'+ 'Price US $' + bookDB[n].price +
 '</i></td></tr>');
    document.writeln('<tr><td><a href="javascript:addBook(\'' +
bookDB[n].number + '\')">' +  'Purchase</a></td></tr></table>');
}
```

ANALYSIS In Listing 20.3 you probably noticed that we are creating a `for` loop that executes as long as there are items in our array. It determines how many times to execute by evaluating the array length with the `bookDB.length` statement.

Finally, if you examine the code in Listing 20.3, you will notice that the last `document.writeln` statement creates a call to the JavaScript function `addBook()`. We are going to create this JavaScript function to add the books selected by the user to the shopping cart. The `addBook()` function is called by passing it the ISBN number for the selected book as an identifier for the book that the user would like to purchase. As mentioned earlier, ISBN numbers are all unique so this value makes a good identifier for locating a book in our custom object array.

The `addBook()` function will accomplish two goals. First we will use the book's ISBN number to determine which book the user wants to purchase. We will change the `number` property of the array element to reflect the selection. The next step in this function is to create a cookie string that contains the purchase selections. We then will use this cookie to maintain a list of the books that the user wants to order. That way, if the user leaves the site for any reason, when she returns the order can continue to be placed because the cookie remembers which items have been selected. Finally, as you can see in Listing 20.4, the function calls our shopping cart page.

INPUT   **LISTING 20.4**   Creating the Selection of Books

```
<script language="JavaScript" type="text/javascript">
<!--
function addBook(isbn_number)
{
    for (var n = 0; n < bookDB.length; n++)
    {
        if (bookDB[n].number == isbn_number)
        {
          var numOrdered = bookDB[n].quantity;
          numOrdered++;
          bookDB[n].quantity = numOrdered;
          break;
        }
    }
    var ordered = " ";
    for (var n = 0; n < bookDB.length; n++) {
       ordered += bookDB[n].quantity;
       if (n < bookDB.length - 1) {
           ordered += "+";
       }
    }
    var ordercookie = "orders = " + ordered;
```

Listing 20.4   continued

```
        document.cookie = ordercookie;
        window.location = "shopcart.htm";
    }
    //-->
    </script>
```

ANALYSIS   If you look at the last part of the function, you will see the code that creates the cookie. First, we create a string of the orders for the user and place the string in the ordered variable. In this case we are using an addition symbol (+) to separate the number quantities. Essentially, though, if the user were to order the first, third, and seventh books in the custom array, the ordered variable would have a value of "1+0+1+0+0+0+1+0+0+0". This value is stored in the cookie called orders so it can be retrieved later.

Note

> For more information on working with cookies in JavaScript refer to Chapter 16, "Cookies: Storing Persistent Data."

The Bookstore Code

So far we have looked at the pieces of the code required to create our online bookstore page. This page is actually fairly simple, as you will see in Listing 20.5.

INPUT   **LISTING 20.5**   Creating the Online Bookstore (bookstore.htm)

```
<html>
<head>
<title>Book Store</title>
<script language="JavaScript" type="text/javascript" src="books.js"></script>

<script language="JavaScript" type="text/javascript">
<!--
function addBook(isbn_number)
{
    for (var n = 0; n < bookDB.length; n++)
    {
        if (bookDB[n].number == isbn_number)
        {
         var numOrdered = bookDB[n].quantity;
         numOrdered++;
         bookDB[n].quantity = numOrdered;
         break;
```

20

LISTING 20.5 continued

```
                }
            }
        var ordered = " ";
        for (var n = 0; n < bookDB.length; n++) {
            ordered += bookDB[n].quantity;
            if (n < bookDB.length - 1) {
                ordered += "+";
            }
        }
        var ordercookie = "orders = " + ordered;
        document.cookie = ordercookie;
        window.location = "shopcart.htm";
    }
//-->
</script>
</head>
<body>
<h1 align="center">Book Catalog</h1>
<p align="center">
<script language="JavaScript" type="text/javascript">
<!--
createBookDB();
if (total_ordered > 0) {
    document.writeln('<a href=shopcart.htm>' + 'view shopping cart</a>');
}
else {
    document.writeln('Shopping cart is empty.');
}
document.writeln('<hr>');
for (var n = 0; n < bookDB.length; n++)
{
    document.writeln('<table width=500>');
    document.writeln('<tr><td><b>' + bookDB[n].title + '</b></td></tr>');
    document.writeln('<tr><td>'+ 'ISBN Number: ' + bookDB[n].number +
'</td></tr>');
    document.writeln('<tr><td><i>'+ 'Price US $' + bookDB[n].price +
'</i></td></tr>');
    document.writeln('<tr><td><a href="javascript:addBook(\'' +
bookDB[n].number + '\')">' +  'Purchase</a></td></tr></table>');
}
//-->
</script>
</body>
</html>
```

ANALYSIS In Listing 20.5, you more than likely noticed that there are a few additional lines of code that we have not covered yet.

As mentioned earlier in the book, we are using the books.js file to store functions that are needed by each page of our Web site. Of course, if you have this page, you need to specify its location, as we did at the beginning of the file. This statement directs that that file be looked in for any functions that are not found in the current file.

```
<script language="JavaScript" type="text/javascript" src="books.js"></script>
```

We make use of the code in the books.js file when we make a call to create the custom book database with the statement createBookDB(). This line of code calls the function in that file, and the book database is created and loaded with the initial values as shown in Listings 20.1 and 20.2.

There is one more piece of the code that we have not discussed. We need to provide a method for the users to quickly view the contents of their shopping carts. Of course if the cart is empty, there is no reason to view it. Therefore, we can create code to check to see if any items have been ordered by checking the contents of a global variable called total_ordered. If this variable is greater than zero, we provide a link to the shopping cart. Otherwise, we provide a message indicating the cart is empty, as shown in Listing 20.6.

INPUT   **LISTING 20.6**   Linking to the Shopping Cart

```
if (total_ordered > 0) {
    document.writeln('<a href=shopcart.htm>' + 'view shopping cart</a>');
}
else {
    document.writeln('Shopping cart is empty.');
}
```

As mentioned, if the user has selected any books to order, the link "view shopping cart" displays under the page title, as shown in Figure 20.3. By clicking on that link, the shopping cart page displays with a list of the books that have been selected.

Creation of the Books.js File

So far there have been a lot of references made to the books.js file that the e-commerce site uses to maintain functions that are used by both Web pages. Keep in mind, this file is not necessary, but without it all of these functions would need to exist in both the shopcart.htm and bookstore.htm files. By creating this include file, you are able to clean up your code and eliminate any redundant functions. Also, if you decide to modify a function, you only have to make the changes in one location.

20

User has selected 1 or more books.

FIGURE 20.3

You can display a different message depending on whether or not the user has placed an order for any books.

> **Book Store - Microsoft Internet Explorer**
>
> File   Edit   View   Favorites   Tools   Help
>
> Back ·   ·   Search   Favorites   Media
>
> Address C:\Books\JavaScript\Chapter 20\bookstore.htm   Go   Links
>
> # Book Catalog
>
> view shopping cart
>
> ---
>
> **Sams Teach Yourself JavaScript in 21 Days**
> ISBN Number: 0672322978
> *Price US $34.99*
> Purchase
> **Sams Teach Yourself Web Publishing with HTML and XHTML in 21 Days**
> ISBN Number: 0672320770
> *Price US $31.99*
> Purchase
> **Sams Teach Yourself Java 2 in 21 Days**
>
> Done   My Computer

Meanwhile, we have created two functions that exist in the books.js file, the book() and createBookDB() functions. There are a couple of other functions that we are going to place in this file—as you can see in Listing 20.7.

INPUT   **LISTING 20.7**   Creating the Common Functions (books.js)

```javascript
var bookDB = new Array();
var total_ordered = 0;
function book(title, number, price, quantity)
{
    this.title = title;
    this.number = number;
    this.price = price;
    this.quantity = quantity;
}
function createBookDB()
{
    bookDB[0] = new book("Sams Teach Yourself JavaScript in 21 Days",
                        "0672322978", 34.99, 0);
    bookDB[1] = new book("Sams Teach Yourself Web Publishing with
HTML and XHTML in 21 Days",
                        "0672320770", 31.99, 0);
    bookDB[2] = new book("Sams Teach Yourself Java 2 in 21 Days",
                        "0672319586", 26.99, 0);
```

LISTING 20.7   continued

```
        bookDB[3] = new book("Sams Teach Yourself XSLT in 21 Days",
                             "0672323184", 35.99, 0);
        bookDB[4] = new book("Sams Teach Yourself Ruby in 21 Days",
                             "0672322528", 35.99, 0);
        bookDB[5] = new book("Sams Teach Yourself Mozilla Programming in 21 Days",
                             "0672321726", 35.99, 0);
        bookDB[6] = new book("Sams Teach Yourself Cisco Routers in 21 Days",
                             "067232296X", 35.99, 0);
        bookDB[7] = new book("Sams Teach Yourself Access 2002 in 21 Days",
                             "0672321033", 35.99, 0);
        bookDB[8] = new book("Sams Teach Yourself Perl in 21 Days",
                             "0672320355", 31.99, 0);
        bookDB[9] = new book("Sams Teach Yourself .NET Windows Forms in 21 Days",
                             "0672323206", 35.99, 0);
        checkQuantity();
}
function checkQuantity()
{
    var ordersCookie = findOrder("orders");
    if (!ordersCookie) {return}
    var userOrders = ordersCookie.split("+");
    for (var n = 0; n < userOrders.length; n++)
    {
        var orderNum = userOrders[n];
        bookDB[n].quantity = orderNum;
        if (orderNum > 0)
        {
            total_ordered++;
        }
    }
}
function findOrder(findName)
 {
    var entireCookie;
    var cookieName;
    var cookieValue;
    var cookieArray = document.cookie.split("; ");
    for (var n = 0; n < cookieArray.length; n++)
    {
        entireCookie = cookieArray[n].split("=");
        cookieName = entireCookie[0];
        cookieValue = entireCookie[1];
        if (cookieName == findName)
        {
            return unescape(cookieValue);
        }
    }
    return null;
}
```

20

ANALYSIS At the beginning of the books.js file you need to declare two different global variables; both have been mentioned earlier in the chapter. The bookDB variable is an array used to create the array of custom objects (book database). The total_ ordered variable keeps track of the total number of books that have been ordered.

You probably also noticed that there are two additional functions that we have not looked at, checkQuantity() and FindOrder(). The checkQuantity() function is called from the createBookDB() function to determine how many of each book has been ordered. You will notice that the createBookDB() function first sets the quantity of each book to zero, and then the checkQuantity() function checks for the cookie. If the cookie exists, the number of orders for each book is updated by changing the quantity property of the bookDB array element.

The findOrder() function is also used by another function in the books.js file. This function is called by the checkQuantity() function to determine if a cookie exists on the user's machine. If the specified cookie, in this case the "orders" cookie, exists, it is returned to the checkQuantity() function so that the function can determine the number of orders.

Note When you use include files to store your common JavaScript functions it typically helps to clean up your code. You can include as many different .js files as you want. You just need to add a separate line of code for each filename.

Include files work great for commonly used functions. Not only do you eliminate code redundancy by only having a function appear in one location in your source code, but you also eliminate errors caused by updating a function and forgetting to update it on all pages of the site.

Also, by placing JavaScript functions in .js files you can greatly simplify your actual HTML page. As discussed in Chapter 17, "Privacy and Security," these files can make your code a little more secure because the visitor to your site must open each .js file to see your JavaScript code.

In this case our .js file is actually rather small. While we could have placed most of our JavaScript code in this file to simplify the HTML pages, it is your own personal preferences that determine how you use the .js file.

Shopping Carts

I am sure you have visited a multitude of different e-commerce sites on the Web. Although each site has a different look and feel, they are all quite similar when it comes to the shopping cart page. This page always lists the items that have been ordered. Our shopping cart lists the ordered items and allows a book order to be removed from the cart by selecting the Delete link, as shown in Figure 20.4.

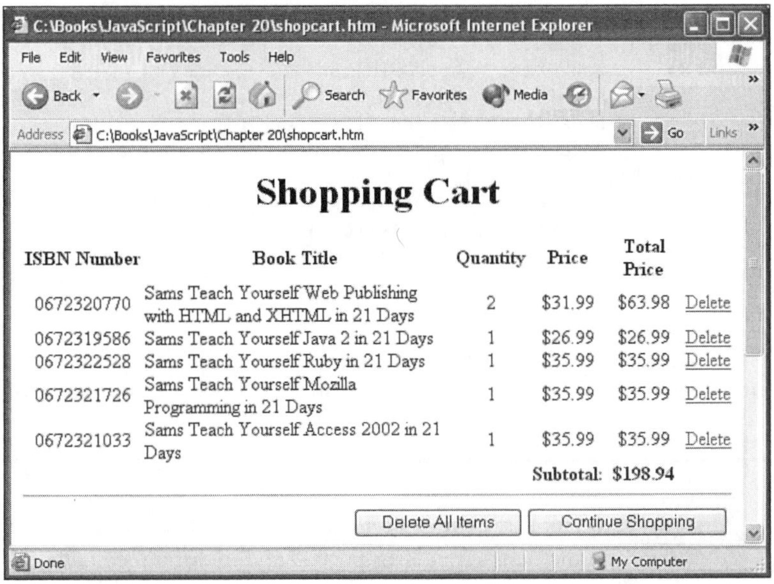

FIGURE 20.4

The shopping cart provides the ability to remove unwanted items.

To create the items in the shopping cart, we will use a method similar to the one we used to create the online catalog by pulling the items from the bookDB array. The main difference is that on the shopping cart page we only want to display the items, or books, that the user has selected for purchase. To accomplish this, we are only going to display book objects with a quantity property value greater than zero, as shown in Listing 20.8.

20

| INPUT | **LISTING 20.8** Viewing Ordered Items |

```
var orderTotal = 0;
document.writeln('<tr><th>ISBN Number</th>');
document.writeln('<th>Book Title</th>');
document.writeln('<th>Quantity</th>');
document.writeln('<th>Price</th>');
document.writeln('<th>Total Price</th>');
document.writeln('<th> </th></tr>');
```

LISTING 20.8   continued

```
for (var n = 0; n < bookDB.length; n++)
   {
    bookNum = bookDB[n].quantity;
    if (bookNum > 0)
       {
        document.writeln('<td width="110" align="center">' +
bookDB[n].number + '</td>');
        document.writeln('<td width="320">' + bookDB[n].title + '</td>');
        document.writeln('<td width="75" align="center">' +
bookDB[n].quantity + '</td>');
        bookPrice = bookDB[n].price;
        bookTotal = bookNum * bookPrice;
        orderTotal += parseFloat(bookTotal);
        document.writeln('<td width="65" align="center">' + '$' +
bookPrice + '</td>');
        document.writeln('<td width="75" align="center">' + '$' +
fixFloat(bookTotal, 2) + '</td>');
        document.writeln('<td><a href="javascript:deleteOrder(\'' +
                         n + '\')">' + 'Delete</a></td></tr>');
       }
   }
document.writeln('<tr><td colspan="4" align="right"><b>Subtotal:</b></td>');
document.writeln('<td align="center"><b>$' + fixFloat(orderTotal, 2) +
'</b></td></tr>');
document.close();
```

ANALYSIS   Again, this code is quite similar to the code used to display the book information on the `bookstore.htm` page. The big difference is the `if` statement that checks to see whether any books have been ordered, ensuring that only books ordered are displayed in the shopping cart. We calculate the total price for each book title by multiplying the number of books ordered by the price for that particular book.

Finally we need to total the cost of purchasing the selected books. This is done by adding up the individual costs for each book title. You will notice that we are calling a `fixFloat()` function with each of the total values that we are displaying. This function solves the math errors that occur when dealing with floating-point numbers, as outlined in the following section.

Solving Floating-Point Math Errors

Because of floating-point math errors that can exist when performing calculations with floating-point numbers, it is necessary to ensure that these errors are not displayed on the Web site. Floating-point math errors occur because of the method that computers use to represent numeric values. As you are aware, our math system is based on a base-10 system (i.e., 1, 2, 3, 4, 5, 6, 7, 8, 9, 10, and so forth). Computers, on the other hand, store all values as binary numbers. This means that the number 2 is represented as 10, 3 is 11, and so on.

The problems with this type of math occur when dealing with floating-point numbers. All integer numbers can be represented exactly as a binary value, but this is not true with floating-point numbers. Because of this, a simple addition of two floating-point values can produce some odd results.

To counteract this problem let's create a function called `fixFloat()` to make sure each floating-point value is properly formatted, as shown in Listing 20.9.

INPUT   **LISTING 20.9**   Fixing Floating-Point Errors

```
function fixFloat(numValue, decimals)
{
    var roundVal = Math.round(numValue * Math.pow(10, decimals));
    var convertVal = roundVal / Math.pow(10, decimals);
    var stringVal = convertVal.toString();
    var decimalLoc = stringVal.indexOf(".");
    if (decimalLoc == -1)
      {
        numDecimals = 0;
        stringVal += ".";
      }
    else
      {
        numDecimals = stringVal.length - decimalLoc - 1;
      }
    var padAmt = decimals - numDecimals;
    if (padAmt > 0)
    {
    for (var n = 1; n <= padAmt; n++)
        stringVal += "0";
    }
  return stringVal;
}
```

20

ANALYSIS   Essentially this function takes the numeric value and multiplies it by 10 raised to the power represented by the decimals variable, in this case 100. Then the value is rounded and divided by the same value again. Next we convert the numeric value to a string and if necessary, insert a decimal at the end of the string, and then pad with zeros (if needed) to make sure there are two decimal places.

Deleting Orders

If you look at Figure 20.4 again you will see that there are actually two ways that users can remove contents from the cart. They can either delete individual book titles from the cart or remove the entire contents of the cart. Therefore, we will need to create the two functions required to delete orders.

Our first function called `deleteOrder()` is called when the user selects the Delete link next to a particular book. This function, shown in Listing 20.10, receives the ISBN number of the book that should be removed from the shopping list. The function simply changes the quantity property associated with that bookDB array element to zero and then recreates the orders cookie.

INPUT   **LISTING 20.10**   Deleting an Item from the Shopping Cart

```
function deleteOrder(bookID)
{
    bookDB[bookID].quantity = 0;
    total_ordered--;
    var ordered = "";
    for (var n = 0; n < bookDB.length; n++)
    {
        ordered += bookDB[n].quantity;
        if (n < bookDB.length - 1)
        {
            ordered += "+";
        }
    }
    var ordercookie = "orders = " + ordered;
    document.cookie = ordercookie;
    location.reload();
}
```

ANALYSIS   Notice that once we have changed the quantity for a particular element of the BookDB array we reload the Web page with the `location.reload()` statement. When this happens, the shopping cart is recreated by loading the orders from the orders array giving the appearance of deleting the book order from the shopping cart. This also causes the amounts to be re-totaled for the order.

The other function that we will need to create will delete all the items from the shopping cart when the user selects the Delete All Items button. This `deleteAll()` function, shown in Listing 20.11, works similarly to the `deleteOrder()` function discussed earlier. The main difference is that the quantity property is set to zero for all elements of the bookDB array, indicating that there are no orders for the particular user.

INPUT   **LISTING 20.11**   Deleting All Items from the Shopping Cart

```
function deleteAll()
  {
    for (var n = 0; n < bookDB.length; n++)
    {
      bookDB[n].quantity = 0;
    }
     var ordered = "";
    for (var m = 0; m < bookDB.length; m++)
    {
       ordered += bookDB[m].quantity;
       if (m < bookDB.length - 1)
       {
           ordered += "+";
       }
    }
    var ordercookie = "orders = " + ordered;
    document.cookie = ordercookie;
    window.location = "shopcart.htm";
    location.reload();
  }
```

ANALYSIS   As with `deleteOrder()`, the `deleteAll()` function also ends with the
`location.reload();` statement to reload the Web page. An interesting thing
happens though when we reload the page. Since there are no longer any book orders the
`bookstore.htm` page loads. This is because we have the code in Listing 20.12 that
checks to see whether there are any book orders each time the `shopcart.htm` page loads.
If there are no orders, there is no reason to load the `shopcart.htm` page, and therefore
we load the `bookstore.htm` page.

INPUT   **LISTING 20.12**   Checking Whether Orders Exist

```
if (total_ordered == 0)
{
    location.replace("bookstore.htm");
}
```

20

Gathering User Information

Finally, in order to send the order to the user you need to capture specific user information. Typically this consists of the user's name, address, telephone number, and credit
card information. There are different methods that can be used to capture this information. For our bookstore site, let's place fields at the bottom of the shopping cart page to

gather the user information before they select the Checkout button, as shown in
Figure 20.5.

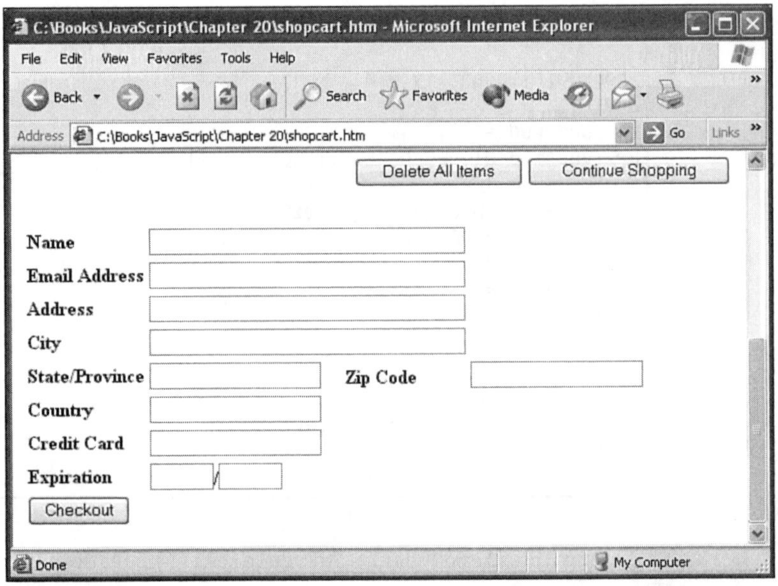

FIGURE 20.5

*You need to capture
information about the
user to complete the
order.*

Let's capture this information and use the user's e-mail program to send the order to be
processed. As you can see in Listing 20.13, the order is sent to the address entered in the
e-mail address line on the form. (Obviously you would not send the order to the user, but
in this instance we did in order to test the code to see how an order would arrive within
an e-mail message.)

INPUT **LISTING 20.13** Sending Order Information

```
function mailOrder()
{
   who=document.order.Email.value;
   what="order";
   var mess = "";
   for (var n = 0; n < bookDB.length; n++)
   {
    bookNum = bookDB[n].quantity;
    if (bookNum > 0)
      {
      mess += "ISBN: " + bookDB[n].number + "   ";
      mess += "Book Name: " + bookDB[n].title + "   ";
      mess += "Quantity Ordered: " + bookDB[n].quantity +
```

LISTING 20.13   continued

```
"   ";
        mess += "Book Price: " + bookDB[n].price + "   ";
        mess += " ***************************************************** ";
        }
    }
    mess +="Customer Name: " + document.order.Name.value + "   ";
    mess +="Email Address: " + document.order.Email.value + "   ";
    mess +="Address: " + document.order.Address.value + "   ";
    mess +="City: " + document.order.City.value + "   ";
    mess +="State: " + document.order.State.value + "   ";
    mess +="Zip Code: " + document.order.ZipCode.value + "   ";
    mess +="Country: " + document.order.Country.value + "   ";
    parent.location.href='mailto:'+who+'?subject='+what+'&body='+mess;
}
```

This code creates a message string by concatenating the entire order and the user information. When the Checkout button is selected an e-mail message is created to send for the order to be processed, as shown in Figure 20.6.

OUTPUT

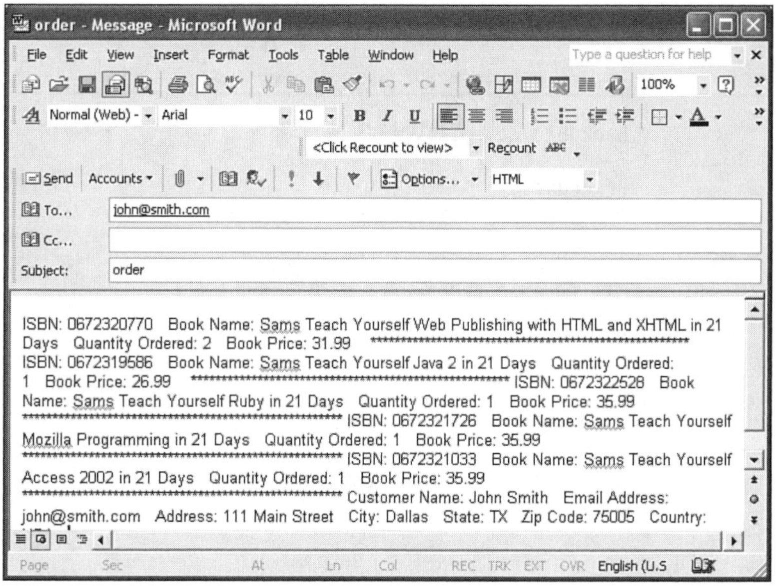

FIGURE 20.6

You can use e-mail to send an order for processing.

20

Coding for the Shopping Cart Page

We already have created several different functions for our shopcart.htm page. Now let's look at how they come together on the page, as shown in Listing 20.14.

INPUT **LISTING 20.14** The Shopping Cart Page (shopcart.htm)

```html
<html>
<script language="JavaScript" type="text/javascript" src="books.js"></script>
<script language="JavaScript" type="text/javascript">
<!--
function deleteOrder(bookID)
{
    bookDB[bookID].quantity = 0;
    total_ordered--;
    var ordered = "";
    for (var n = 0; n < bookDB.length; n++)
    {
       ordered += bookDB[n].quantity;
       if (n < bookDB.length - 1)
       {
           ordered += "+";
       }
    }
    var ordercookie = "orders = " + ordered;
    document.cookie = ordercookie;
    location.reload();
}
function deleteAll()
  {
    for (var n = 0; n < bookDB.length; n++)
    {
      bookDB[n].quantity = 0;
    }
     var ordered = "";
    for (var m = 0; m < bookDB.length; m++)
    {
       ordered += bookDB[m].quantity;
       if (m < bookDB.length - 1)
        {
            ordered += "+";
        }
    }
    var ordercookie = "orders = " + ordered;
    document.cookie = ordercookie;
    window.location = "shopcart.htm";
    location.reload();
  }
function fixFloat(numValue, decimals)
{
    var roundVal = Math.round(numValue * Math.pow(10, decimals));
    var convertVal = roundVal / Math.pow(10, decimals);
    var stringVal = convertVal.toString();
    var decimalLoc = stringVal.indexOf(".");
    if (decimalLoc == -1)
      {
```

LISTING 20.14   continued

```
            numDecimals = 0;
            stringVal += ".";
          }
        else
          {
            numDecimals = stringVal.length - decimalLoc - 1;
          }
        var padAmt = decimals - numDecimals;
        if (padAmt > 0)
        {
        for (var n = 1; n <= padAmt; n++)
            stringVal += "0";
        }
    return stringVal;
}
function mailOrder()
{
    who=document.order.Email.value;
    what="order";
    var mess = "";
    for (var n = 0; n < bookDB.length; n++)
    {
     bookNum = bookDB[n].quantity;
     if (bookNum > 0)
        {
        mess += "ISBN: " + bookDB[n].number + "   ";
        mess += "Book Name: " + bookDB[n].title + "   ";
        mess += "Quantity Ordered: " + bookDB[n].quantity +
"   ";
        mess += "Book Price: " + bookDB[n].price + "   ";
        mess += " *************************************************** ";
        }
    }
    mess +="Customer Name: " + document.order.Name.value + "   ";
    mess +="Email Address: " + document.order.Email.value +
"   ";
    mess +="Address: " + document.order.Address.value + "   ";
    mess +="City: " + document.order.City.value + "   ";
    mess +="State: " + document.order.State.value + "   ";
    mess +="Zip Code: " + document.order.ZipCode.value + "   ";
    mess +="Country: " + document.order.Country.value + "   ";
    parent.location.href='mailto:'+who+'?subject='+what+'&body='+mess;
}
//-->
</script>
</head>
<body>
<h1 align = "center">Shopping Cart</h1>
<table cellpadding="0" cellspacing="0">
```

20

LISTING 20.14 continued

```
<script language="JavaScript" type="text/javascript">
<!--
createBookDB();
if (total_ordered == 0)
{
    location.replace("bookstore.htm");
}
var orderTotal = 0;
document.writeln('<tr><th>ISBN Number</th>');
document.writeln('<th>Book Title</th>');
document.writeln('<th>Quantity</th>');
document.writeln('<th>Price</th>');
document.writeln('<th>Total Price</th>');
document.writeln('<th> </th></tr>');
for (var n = 0; n < bookDB.length; n++)
   {
    bookNum = bookDB[n].quantity;
    if (bookNum > 0)
       {
        document.writeln('<td width="110" align="center">' +
bookDB[n].number + '</td>');
        document.writeln('<td width="320">' + bookDB[n].title + '</td>');
        document.writeln('<td width="75" align="center">' +
bookDB[n].quantity + '</td>');
        bookPrice = bookDB[n].price;
        bookTotal = bookNum * bookPrice;
        orderTotal += parseFloat(bookTotal);
        document.writeln('<td width="65" align="center">' + '$' +
bookPrice + '</td>');
        document.writeln('<td width="75" align="center">' + '$' +
fixFloat(bookTotal, 2) + '</td>');
        document.writeln('<td><a href="javascript:deleteOrder(\'' +
                        n + '\')">' + 'Delete</a></td></tr>');
       }
   }
document.writeln('<tr><td colspan="4" align="right"><b>Subtotal:</b></td>');
document.writeln('<td align="center"><b>$' + fixFloat(orderTotal, 2) +
'</b></td></tr>');
document.close();
//-->
</script>
</table>
<hr>
<table align="right">
<tr><td><input type="button" value="Delete All Items"
onClick="deleteAll()"></td>
<td><input type="button" value="Continue Shopping"
onClick="location='bookstore.htm'"></td></tr>
</table>
```

LISTING 20.14 continued

```
<form METHOD="post" Name="order">
<p> </p>
<table border="0">
<tr><td><b>Name</b></td><td><input type="text" name="Name" size="40"></td></tr>
<tr><td><b>Email Address</b></td><td><input type="text" name="Email"
size="40"></td></tr>
<tr><td><b>Address </b></td><td><input type="text" name="Address"
size="40"></td></tr>
<tr><td><b>City</b></td><td><input type="text" name="City" size="40"></td></tr>
<tr><td><b>State/Province</b></td><td><input type="text" name="State"
size="20">    
<b>Zip Code</b></td><td><input type="text" name="ZipCode" size="20"></td></tr>
<tr><td><b>Country</b></td><td><input type="text" name="Country"
size="20"></td></tr>
<tr><td><b>Credit Card</b></td><td><input type="text" name="Credit" size="20">
</td></tr>
<tr><td><b>Expiration</b></td><td><input type="text" name="Month" size="5">/
<input type="text" name="Year" size="5"> </td></tr>
<tr><td><input type="button" value="Checkout" onClick="mailOrder()"></td></tr>
</table>
</form>
</body>
</html>
```

Keep in mind, as with the `bookstore.htm` page, the `createBookDB()` function also needs to be called when this page loads. This function creates the `bookDB()` array so that the code on this page can determine which orders exist.

Issues to Consider

This e-commerce example was designed to use the existing e-mail of the user to enable the creation of this Web site with the use of existing tools, including JavaScript and HTML. Unfortunately this is not always the ideal situation. As you probably noticed, the use of this method typically requires the user to select the Send button on the e-mail message before the order will be submitted. Also, it is possible that your code may not be able to access an e-mail program on the user's computer to send the message with. Because of this issue there are other methods available on the market for submitting orders. You can incorporate CGI scripts to process and submit your order. There also are several other products available for capturing user orders.

Another issue to keep in mind is the security risk of e-mailing credit card numbers. As you are aware, an e-mail message is not secure, so it is typically not recommended to e-mail credit card information without encrypting it. There are different encryption methods that you can use to encrypt a credit card number so that it can be sent securely.

20

If you are using e-mail to process your orders you will probably want to use the telephone to gather credit card information. There are also several server-side options available for processing credit cards.

Summary

This chapter has provided a look at the basic elements needed to create a successful e-commerce site. As illustrated, you can create a fairly sophisticated e-commerce site boasting an online store, database (catalog), shopping cart, and order desk—all accomplished with just JavaScript and HTML.

Workshop

In the workshop today, we will look at some Q&A issues dealing with an e-commerce site and use the questions and exercises to review what you have learned in this chapter about creating an e-commerce site with JavaScript.

Q&A

Q. Why do I need to use the `fixFloat()` function? My code works fine without it.

A. As mentioned within the chapter, the method used by your computer to store numeric, actually all values, is binary or a series of 1's and 0's. This works fine for integer values, but not all floating-point values can be accurately represented in a binary form. Therefore, when you add two simple numbers together you may end up with a number with more digits than anticipated. For example, if you have your computer add these values: 53.98, 35.99, 35.99 it will return a value of 125.96000000000001. This math error will not be apparent until you perform a calculation that cannot be accurately represented. To avoid errors, you need to use `fixFloat()` or another similar function.

Q. What if I want to allow the quantity to be modified on the shopping cart page?

A. Rather than making the user return to the bookstore page to select another copy of a book, you can make the Quantity field on your form editable. To do this you need to make the field into a textbox. Keep in mind that if you do this, you also need to devise a method to recalculate the form after the quantity is modified. You can consider using event handling to determine when the field has been modified. For more information refer to Chapter 10, "Events and Events Handling," and Chapter 6, "HTML Forms and the `String` Object."

Q. **Is there a way to store the user information so they don't have to re-enter it each time?**

A. If you are using cookies you can contain any of the values from your site. For example, you can store the information that the user enters on the shopping cart form in a cookie that is placed on his machine. When the page opens again you can redisplay the values from the cookie. For more information on cookies, refer to Chapter 16, "Cookies: Storing Persistent Data."

Quiz

1. Why do you use cookies for an e-commerce site?

2. What value is gained by creating a .js file for the Web site?

3. How do we switch between pages within our JavaScript code?

Quiz Answers

1. Cookies allow you to store the order selections so that they can be accessed on other pages. With our site we created in this chapter, the "orders" cookie contains a string of numbers that indicates the number of each book that has been ordered. This cookie can be accessed on either page of our site.

2. By creating an include file with the .js file extension, you are able to place code that is needed by each page in one central location. This eliminates the need to recreate the same code on each page. For example, with our e-commerce site, the books.js page contains the code for creating our bookDB custom object array that stores the book information. This also reduces chances for errors when you update the code because you only need to make the changes in one location.

3. You can have the code switch to another page by changing the replace property for the location object. When you set this property the specified page is loaded.

Exercises

1. Modify the bookstore.htm page to indicate the number of items that have been placed in the user's shopping cart. Keep in mind that since users can order multiple copies of each book you need to count the number of actual books ordered, not just the book titles that have been selected.

2. Add code to the shopcart.htm page to make sure the user information is entered in the fields before allowing the order to be submitted.

20

WEEK 3

DAY 21

JavaScript and SVG

Throughout this book you have looked at the use of JavaScript with HTML or XHTML Web pages. However, JavaScript can be used with many other technologies. This chapter will introduce you to one of the exciting emerging Web technologies, Scalable Vector Graphics (SVG), and how it can be used with JavaScript.

In the space available here, we can only introduce you to the fundamentals of using JavaScript and SVG. The SVG specification itself is over 600 pages long and, in addition, references other W3C documents such as those for the Document Object Model (DOM), and the JavaScript Bindings for the SVG DOM. To give you a flavor of how you can use JavaScript with SVG, this chapter will introduce you to the use of SVG with some relatively simple SVG graphics; then it will show you some techniques for manipulating or creating those shapes using JavaScript.

In this chapter you will learn

- A brief introduction to SVG
- Potential uses of SVG on the Web
- How JavaScript can be used productively with SVG

Overview of Scalable Vector Graphics

Scalable Vector Graphics, typically referred to as SVG, is a recently finalized, XML-based vector graphics specification from the World Wide Web Consortium (W3C). The full text of the SVG 1.0 Recommendation is located at `http://www.w3.org/TR/2001/REC-SVG-20010904/`.

SVG provides a powerful multi-capable vector graphics language for the display of 2D vector graphics, text, and bitmap graphics. SVG includes powerful animation syntax by "borrowing" elements from SMIL (Synchronized Multimedia Integration Language) 2.0 (see the specification located at `http://www.w3.org/TR/2001/REC-smil-animation-20010904/`). SVG images can be embedded in HTML/XHTML Web pages(we will show you how in a moment). SVG also provides the syntax to create free-standing "all-SVG" Web pages (see `www.SVGSpider.com/default.svg` for an example site).

SVG is an application language of the Extensible Markup Language, XML, just as HTML is an application language of the Standard Generalized Markup Language, SGML. Since XML has many similarities to SGML the general form of an XML, and therefore a SVG document will be familiar—it uses markup tags which look similar to those in HTML/XHTML—but the details of XML syntax differ from those of HTML. One important difference is that XML start tags, such as <svg>, must be balanced by a closing end tag, </svg>. If you omit the end tag your code will be in error and likely part or all of your SVG image won't display.

Note

> XHTML is HTML written to comply with XML syntax rules. XHTML tags, unlike HTML ones, do require an end tag for every start tag.

Why SVG?

You might be asking why W3C added a new graphics format since we already have bitmap graphics such as GIFs and JPEGs and a widely used vector format, Macromedia Flash.

Let's suppose you want to search for Web pages which have information contained in their graphics; no search engine will ever be able to find those since the "information" is now simply a pattern of pixels. With SVG, although the information can be incorporated in attractive graphics, the source code remains searchable since it is held as text in XML format.

As you will see later in this chapter, it is possible to create rollover images using SVG alone which reduce file size and network usage. Since many users will be restricted to 56K modems or slower for some time to come, such bandwidth savings are worthwhile. In addition, if you master SVG you can create sophisticated rollovers without the need to invest in expensive bitmap graphics software.

The source code for all SVG images is accessible to the visitor to a Web page, so the understanding of SVG is expected to snowball in a way similar to the way that HTML knowledge exploded a few years back. If you can see exactly the SVG techniques used in an attractive Web page or image, then you can learn the new techniques much faster.

Why SVG and JavaScript?

If SVG on its own can do all these clever things, why do we need to use JavaScript with it?

One important functionality that JavaScript can add to SVG is to give you the ability to make decisions based on testing for a particular existing situation. In other words, adding control logic is a key advantage of combining JavaScript with SVG.

For example, imagine an SVG map of a locality with information on, say, roads, buildings, and utility supplies. It may be very helpful to be able to selectively hide certain parts of the map so that information, which is of particular interest, can be selectively displayed. Using JavaScript by clicking on a control button can conceal certain parts of the map if they are already displayed, or display them if they are currently concealed.

Equally, if you were using a multi-step SVG diagram in a Web page as a teaching aid to describe some process, then clicking on a control could take the display forward step by step, or allow the user to "rewind" the diagram to gain a better grasp of the sequence of events. Similarly, a control could allow the user to zoom out or zoom in to see more detail of what is being displayed or to take a broader view.

The combination of SVG and JavaScript allows user control of the display of SVG image—limited only by the imagination and skills of the JavaScript programmer.

Basic SVG Tools

To use SVG you will need two types of tools—something to create SVG with, and something that will render SVG on screen. SVG is XML, which means that an SVG image is also a text document that you can type character by character in a text editor, if you prefer to do that.

21

SVG Creation Tools

A plain text editor such as Windows Notepad is adequate for the creation of simple SVG files. If you are going to hand code SVG, then an XML-aware editor is useful since it will automatically color code the syntax as you type, and it may be able to check what you have typed for "well-formedness," an XML term which means essentially that you have followed the syntax rules correctly. Such color coding will save you a lot of time trying to find an omitted quote mark or other syntax error in your code. One useful XML Editor is XMLWriter, which is available as a free time-limited evaluation version from http://www.xmlwriter.net. Its color highlighting and checking for well-formedness is straightforward to use.

If you prefer to create SVG more visually, then a number of currently available commercial vector graphics tools can now export drawings that you produce as SVG files. Among the big names which have that capability are Adobe Illustrator 10 and CorelDraw 10. At the time of writing, Macromedia Freehand has no SVG export facility.

A powerful vector drawing tool dedicated to SVG is WebDraw from Jasc. At the time of writing, WebDraw is unique in that it lets you create SVG visually as well as tweak the source code by hand. WebDraw has a tabbed interface that you use to create SVG images by drawing (on the Canvas tab) or by editing SVG code directly (on the Source tab). Figures 21.1 and 21.2 show the Canvas and Source tabs on a pre-release version of WebDraw. Further information is located at http://www.jasc.com/products/webdraw/. At the time of writing version 1.0 of WebDraw has been released and a preview version is available for download from http://www.jasc.com/products/webdraw/wdrawdl.asp.

FIGURE 21.1

The Canvas tab of WebDraw enables you to draw on screen.

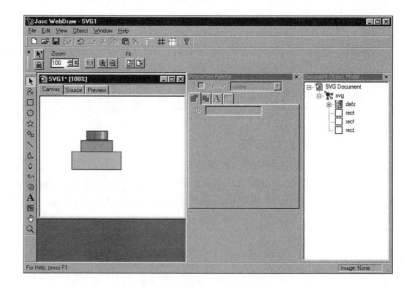

Notice in Figure 21.1 that on the left side of the image there is the three-tabbed pane with Canvas, Source, and Preview tabs. On the right, you can see a representation of the Document Object Model of the SVG image.

FIGURE 21.2

The Source tab of WebDraw, showing the code generated by creating the graphic shown in Figure 21.1.

```
01 <?xml version="1.0" standalone="no"?>
02 <!DOCTYPE svg PUBLIC "-//W3C//DTD SVG 1.0//EN"
03    "http://www.w3.org/TR/2001/REC-SVG-20010904/DTD/svg10.dtd">
04 <svg width="300" height="250">
05    <defs>
06       <linearGradient id="electric-stripe" x1="0%" y1="0%" x2="100%" y2="0%
07          spreadMethod="pad" gradientUnits="objectBoundingBox">
08          <stop offset="0%" style="stop-color:rgb(128,0,128);stop-opacity:0
09          <stop offset="25%" style="stop-color:rgb(255,0,255);stop-opacity:
10          <stop offset="50%" style="stop-color:rgb(104,0,192);stop-opacity:
11          <stop offset="75%" style="stop-color:rgb(0,255,255);stop-opacity:
12          <stop offset="100%" style="stop-color:rgb(0,0,192);stop-opacity:0
13       </linearGradient>
14    </defs>
15    <rect x="66" y="115" width="103" height="37"
16       style="fill:rgb(192,192,255);stroke:rgb(0,0,128);stroke-width:1"/>
17    <rect x="85" y="92" width="66" height="23"
18       style="fill:rgb(255,128,128);stroke:rgb(0,0,128);stroke-width:1"/>
19    <rect x="97" y="72" width="44" height="18"
20       style="fill:url(#electric-stripe);stroke:rgb(0,0,128);stroke-width:1
21 </svg>
22
```

When seen on screen you can see that the code shown in Figure 21.2 is color-coded to help you when editing, if you want to tweak an image that you created earlier. WebDraw also allows you to import existing SVG images for further drawing or coding.

Whichever technique you choose to use to create SVG, you will also need a rendering engine, often called a viewer, to interpret the SVG source code and display the SVG image on screen.

SVG Viewers

At the time of writing, none of the popular Web browsers can natively display more than a very little of SVG. Mozilla (http://www.mozilla.org) and Amaya (http://www.w3.org/Amaya) are the only Web browsers that currently have even limited native SVG rendering capabilities.

To display SVG in most Web browsers and script that SVG using JavaScript, you will need to download and install the Adobe SVG Viewer which is a browser plugin, similar to the one for Macromedia Flash. At the time of writing, the Adobe Viewer is at Version 3.0 and is already a very powerful implementation of SVG.

To download the Adobe SVG Viewer go to http://www.adobe.com/svg/viewer/install/main.html. The viewer is intended for use on Internet Explorer 4.0 and above, and Netscape Navigator 4.0–4.7x, and is therefore officially supported only on those browsers. Officially the Adobe SVG Viewer is not supported on Netscape 6.x or on Mozilla or Opera. In practice you can install the Adobe Viewer if you have a supported browser to which the viewer can first be installed.

21

Note

To install the Adobe SVG Viewer, version 3.0, to Netscape 6.x, Mozilla 0.9.3 or above, or Opera 5.x, first install the Adobe Viewer on an officially supported browser. On the Windows 98SE platform you will then find the key file in the `c:\Windows\System\Adobe\SVG Viewer 3.0` directory. In that directory you will find a file named `NPSVG3.dll`. Copy that file to the plugin directory of the browser(s) to which you want to add SVG support.

Once you have the Adobe SVG Viewer installed, then you can access SVG Web pages or HTML/XHTML Web pages that contain SVG images in the normal way. Simply type in a URL such as `http://www.svgspider.com/default.svg` and the page will display.

The Adobe Viewer supports most of the W3C SVG Recommendation including animations, transformations, and scripting. At the time of writing, all other SVG implementations are more limited in the scope of the SVG Recommendation which is implemented. Therefore, at the present time, the Adobe Viewer is the SVG viewer of choice.

If you want to create your own SVG images and display them on the Web you, or your ISP, will need to adjust the server settings so that SVG images are served as type "image/svg+xml".

Example SVG Code

To help you gain an impression of what an SVG document (without JavaScript) might look like, let's take a look at a simple SVG document that describes how three basic SVG graphics shapes should be rendered. This is shown in Listing 21.1.

INPUT   **LISTING 21.01**   Three Basic SVG Shapes (SimpleShapes.svg)

```
<?xml version="1.0" standalone="no"?>
<!DOCTYPE svg PUBLIC "-//W3C//DTD SVG 20010904//EN"
"http://www.w3.org/TR/2001/REC-SVG-20010904/DTD/svg10.dtd">
<svg width="300" height="250">
<line x1="10" y1="25" x2="200" y2="25" style="stroke:#FF0000" />
<rect x="30" y="50" width="150" height="75"
 style="stroke:#FF0000; fill:#999999" />
<ellipse cx="150" cy="180" rx="90" ry="25"
style="stroke:#FF6600; stroke-width:4; fill:#00FF00; fill-opacity:0.3" />
</svg>
```

ANALYSIS   The first line of the code

```
<?xml version="1.0" standalone="no"?>
```

is called the "XML declaration." It tells the SVG rendering engine which syntax (XML 1.0) the document contains. The DOCTYPE declaration, as shown here

```
<!DOCTYPE svg PUBLIC "-//W3C//DTD SVG 20010904//EN"
"http://www.w3.org/TR/2001/REC-SVG-20010904/DTD/svg10.dtd">
```

indicates the vocabulary that is allowable and the URL where the Document Type Definition, DTD, which defines that vocabulary is located. Taken together the XML declaration and the DOCTYPE declaration tell any SVG rendering engine that the syntax rules to be followed are those of XML 1.0, and that the vocabulary to be used in accordance with those syntax rules is that of SVG 1.0.

Following the DOCTYPE declaration there is an <svg> element which is the *document element* for all SVG documents. Nested within the <svg> element are three elements which describe some of the basic SVG shapes: in this case a line, a rectangle, and an ellipse. The visual appearance of this simple code is shown in Figure 21.3. Mozilla is not one of the officially supported browsers for the Adobe SVG Viewer but, as you can see, the SVG displays using it once the necessary file has been copied to the plugins directory, as described earlier.

FIGURE 21.3

Simple SVG shapes seen using the Adobe SVG Viewer in Mozilla version 0.9.3.

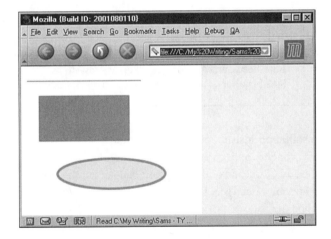

In order to use JavaScript with SVG, you need to have some understanding of both the DOM (to which you were introduced in Chapter 8) and the SVG Document Object Model, as well as several other SVG elements.

21

The SVG Document Object Model

Throughout much of this book you have been manipulating or accessing the Document Object Model (DOM) for an XHTML or HTML document. Just as each element and attribute of an XHTML document has a corresponding node in the XHTML DOM, so for each element and attribute of an SVG document there is a corresponding node in the SVG DOM. In other words, the XHTML DOM and the SVG DOM are different because each reflects the details of the structure of an XHTML document and an SVG document respectively which, clearly, differ significantly.

Batik DOM Viewer

One of the SVG viewers that is used without a normal HTML browser is Batik. Batik includes an SVG viewer that also allows you to directly see the DOM for an SVG document which you are viewing.

Batik is a Java-based application. It can be downloaded from `http://xml.apache.org/batik`. It also needs a Java 1.3 Runtime Environment, which you can download, if you don't already have one, from `http://java.sun.com`.

> **Caution**
>
> The Java Virtual Machine, JVM, installed automatically on Windows 32-bit platforms, is not compliant with Java 1.3, due to the long-running legal dispute between Microsoft and Sun Microsystems. To make use of the Batik SVG browser you will need the Sun Java 1.3 download.

Detailed installation instructions are located at `http://xml.apache.org/batik/install.html`. Once you have downloaded and installed the Java Runtime and Batik, you can access the Batik SVG Viewer using a command-line interface (MS DOS Window on some Windows platforms). In the Batik directory type the following:

```
java -jar batik-svgbrowser.jar
```

and, if everything is installed correctly, the Batik browser will open.

If we have a simple SVG document as shown in Listing 21.2, we can use Batik to display the DOM hierarchy (as shown in Figure 21.4).

LISTING 21.2   A Simple SVG Document (WelcomeToSVG.svg)

```
<?xml version="1.0" standalone="no"?>
<!DOCTYPE svg PUBLIC "-//W3C//DTD SVG 20010904//EN"
"http://www.w3.org/TR/2001/REC-SVG-20010904/DTD/svg10.dtd">
<svg width="400px" height="200px">
<style type="text/css">
<![CDATA[
rect {fill:red; opacity:0.5; stroke:none;}
text {font-family:Arial, sans-serif; font-size:14;}
]]>
</style>
<rect x="20" y="20" width="360px" height="160px" />
<text x="40" y="50" >Welcome to SVG!</text>
</svg>
```

OUTPUT

FIGURE 21.4

*The SVG image is
displayed in the
Batik browser. The
Tools menu and the
option to display the
DOM Viewer are
highlighted.*

> Batik:WelcomeToSVG.svg
>
> File Edit View Processing Go **Tools** ?
>
> Location: file:/C:/My Writing/Sams
>
> Memory Monitor Ctrl-M
> DOM Viewer   Ctrl-D
>
> Welcome to SVG!
>
> w: 400.0   h: 200.0

With the image opened in the Batik browser, select the Tools menu, and then the DOM
Viewer option within it to open the DOM Viewer. The DOM Viewer shows the hierarchy
of objects in the object model of the SVG document. The hierarchy can be expanded or
collapsed to allow you to focus on the part of the DOM tree which is of interest to you.
Figure 21.5 shows the DOM hierarchy for the SVG document displayed in Figure 21.4.
The object corresponding to the <rect> element is highlighted. Notice the x, y, width,
and height attributes as well as, in the lower part of the right pane, a host of CSS
properties (mostly default values) for that object.

21

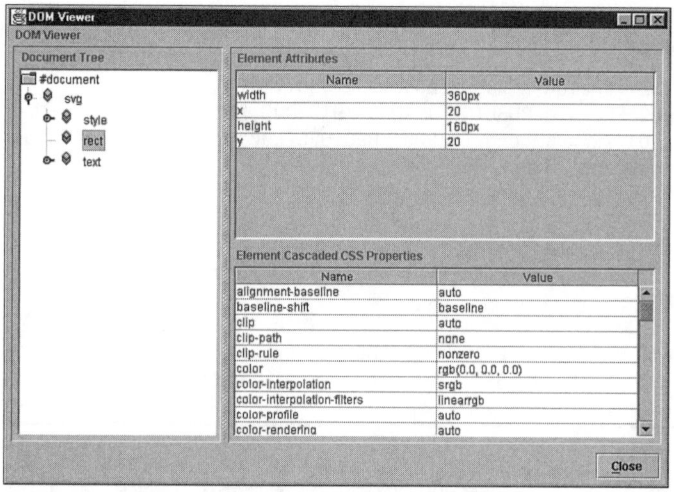

FIGURE 21.5

*The DOM hierarchy
of the image shown
in Figure 21.4 dis-
played in Batik's
DOM Viewer.*

As you want to examine and understand the structure of an SVG document and its associated DOM, you can expand or collapse parts of the tree to allow for study of the parts
which are of interest to you. The ability to see the structure of the DOM for a particular
object can be very useful as you are learning the SVG DOM.

If you want to view SVG primarily in a Web browser, then the Adobe Viewer is likely
best. However, Batik includes much more SVG functionality than simply an SVG
viewer. Batik also allows you to embed SVG display functionality in a Java program.

SVG DOM Basics

The SVG DOM is based on the W3C DOM specification. The full Recommendations for
DOM Level 1 and Level 2 Core are located, respectively, at
http://www.w3.org/TR/1998/REC-DOM-Level-1-19981001 and
http://www.w3.org/TR/2000/REC-DOM-Level-2-Core-20001113. In addition the DOM
Level 2 Events Recommendation (http://www.w3.org/TR/2000/REC-DOM-Level-2-
Events-20001113) and DOM Level 2 Style Recommendation
(http://www.w3.org/TR/2000/REC-DOM-Level-2-Style-20001113) are also relevant to
the SVG DOM.

In order to use the SVG DOM from JavaScript, an SVG document must exist. Thus there
must be an <svg> element present, typically preceded by an XML declaration and a
DOCTYPE declaration, as you saw earlier. The DOCTYPE declaration shown below is
the declaration for the SVG 1.0 Recommendation of September, 2001:

```
<?xml version="1.0" standalone="no"?>
<!DOCTYPE svg PUBLIC "-//W3C//DTD SVG 20010904//EN"
"http://www.w3.org/TR/2001/REC-SVG-20010904/DTD/svg10.dtd">
<svg width="250" height="250" >
```

The `<svg>` element has optional width and height attributes. If you omit those, then the SVG image defaults to 100% of the browser window's width and height.

Later in the document, of course, there is an end `</svg>` tag to match the `<svg>` start tag; otherwise the SVG rendering engine will report an error and likely refuse to render any image on screen.

So how do elements like this translate into the DOM, and how do we access them using JavaScript?

Using JavaScript in SVG

Strictly speaking the default scripting language for use with SVG is ECMAScript, rather than JavaScript. As you are already aware, the differences between the two allow us to often, although not totally correctly, think of JavaScript and ECMAScript as almost interchangeable terms.

The `<script>` Element in SVG Documents

JavaScript code in an SVG document is, as in HTML, nested between a `<script>` start tag and a `</script>` end tag. However, you should be aware that a `<script></script>` tag pair in SVG is referring to the SVG `<script>` element, not the similar HTML/XHTML `<script>` element. In XML jargon, they are in different namespaces.

SVG is XML, therefore an XML parser will attempt to parse any content contained between the `<script>` and `</script>` tags. If, for example, it comes across a less-than sign, the parser (since an SVG parser is an XML parser) would signify an error. It would interpret the less-than sign as the opening character of a tag, and then would try to interpret the following JavaScript code as a tag name. Unless you were remarkably lucky you wouldn't have a corresponding greater-than sign and therefore an error would result.

To avoid that type of problem, JavaScript or ECMAScript code is contained within what is called a CDATA section within the `<script></script>` tag pair, like so:

```
<script>
<![CDATA[
// Your code goes here
]]>
</script>
```

21

The CDATA section begins with `<![CDATA[` and ends with the character sequence `]]>`. It signifies to the SVG parser that the content of the CDATA section is character data, which the parser should not attempt to treat as SVG. The JavaScript interpreter sees the `<script>` tag, ignores the `<![CDATA[` and `]]>` lines, and is happy if we write correct JavaScript syntax.

Specifying the Scripting Language

SVG provides two methods for us to declare the scripting language that is being used. In the `<svg>` element which is the element root, we can use a `contentScriptType` attribute to define the default scripting language. Typically we will set the `contentScriptType` attribute to a value of `"text/ecmascript"`. By setting the `contentScriptType`, we set the default scripting language for the whole document. Thereafter, for example, we do not need to specify a type attribute on any subsequent `<script>` start tags:

```
<svg contentScriptType="text/ecmascript" ...>
```

However, if we wish to make unambiguous which scripting language we are using in a particular piece of scripting code, we can add a type attribute to a `<script>` start tag as shown below:

```
<script type="text/ecmascript">
```

The `<script>` start tag also allows us to reference external JavaScript files, like so:

```
<script type="text/ecmascript" xlink:href="MyJavaScript.js" />
```

> **Note**
>
> In XML syntax, an empty element can be written either as `<someTag>` `</someTag>` or using a shorthand syntax `<someTag />`. If you are referencing an external JavaScript file, it is often convenient to use that shorthand syntax for the `<script />` tag.

Of course, if you want to use an HTML script you would use the following code, for example:

```
<script type="text/javascript" src="MyJavaScript.js" ></script>
```

in the normal way. Remember too that although a `<script />` tag is acceptable for an SVG viewer, some traditional browsers will choke on that if you use it in an HTML page.

A Skeleton SVG Document with JavaScript

An SVG document has to be written according to the rules of XML 1.0 syntax. Clearly, JavaScript and ECMAScript lack the start tags and end tags required in XML syntax. If an XML or SVG processor were to attempt to parse JavaScript directly, then an error, or many errors, would quickly occur. XML provides a technique that indicates to an XML or SVG processor that a defined block of text in the document is not to be parsed as XML. To embed JavaScript within an SVG document, we use the CDATA section. A skeleton document using the CDATA section is shown in Listing 21.3.

INPUT

LISTING 21.3 A Skeleton Document for Using JavaScript (SkeletonJavaScript.svg)

```
<?xml version="1.0" standalone="no"?>
<!DOCTYPE svg PUBLIC "-//W3C//DTD SVG 20010904//EN"
"http://www.w3.org/TR/2001/REC-SVG-20010904/DTD/svg10.dtd">
<svg width="250" height="250" >
    <script type="text/javascript">
    <![CDATA[
    // JavaScript code would go here.
    ]]>
    </script>
</svg>
```

ANALYSIS Let's look at each line of the code which is nested within the <svg> element. The first line,

```
<script type="text/javascript">
```

consists of the <script> element. The <script> element in SVG has the same element type name as the <script> element in HTML. However, unlike the HTML <script> element, the SVG <script> element has no language attribute but does have a type attribute.

Let's move on now and create some simple JavaScript code. In the examples which follow, you will see the SVG code we are trying to produce, and then in the accompanying example how we can use JavaScript to achieve that.

Adding a Title to an SVG Image

If you are using an SVG document as a standalone image or Web page, you can apply a title to the image or page, which is displayed in the title bar of the browser.

Using declarative syntax, we can add a title as shown in Listing 21.4.

21

INPUT

LISTING 21.4   Adding a Title Using Declarative Syntax

INPUT   (AddTitleDeclar.svg)

```
<?xml version="1.0" standalone="no"?>
<!DOCTYPE svg PUBLIC "-//W3C//DTD SVG 20010904//EN"
"http://www.w3.org/TR/2001/REC-SVG-20010904/DTD/svg10.dtd">
<svg width="300" height="150">
<title>JavaScript works well with SVG!</title>
<rect x="0" y="0" width="300" height="150" style="fill:red; stroke:none;"/>
</svg>
```

The code simply adds a title to the browser title bar, as shown in Figure 21.6.

OUTPUT

FIGURE 21.6

Adding a title to the browser window using declarative syntax.

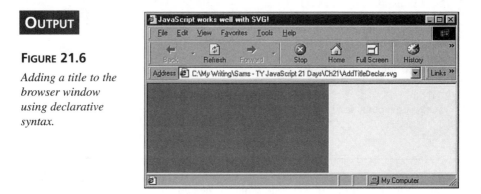

To achieve the same appearance in the browser window using JavaScript, you will need to create an SVG <title> element and some content for it. An SVG image with embedded simple JavaScript is shown in Listing 21.5.

LISTING 21.5   Adding a Title to an SVG Image Using JavaScript

INPUT   (AddTitle.svg)

```
<?xml version="1.0" standalone="no"?>
<!DOCTYPE svg PUBLIC "-//W3C//DTD SVG 20010904//EN"
"http://www.w3.org/TR/2001/REC-SVG-20010904/DTD/svg10.dtd">
<svg width="300" height="150" onload="AddTitle(evt)" >
    <script type="text/javascript">
    <![CDATA[
    function AddTitle(evt){
     var SVGDoc = evt.getTarget().getOwnerDocument();
     var SVGRoot = SVGDoc.getDocumentElement();
     var myTitleData, myTitle;
     myTitleData = SVGDoc.createTextNode('JavaScript works well with SVG!');
```

LISTING 21.5   continued

```
      myTitle = SVGDoc.createElement("title");
      myTitle.appendChild(myTitleData);

      SVGRoot.appendChild(myTitle);
      }
   ]]>
   </script>
<rect x="0" y="0" width="300" height="150" style="fill:red; stroke:none;"/>
</svg>
```

ANALYSIS The JavaScript code does exactly the same visually as the declarative code shown in Listing 21.4.

The start tag of the <svg> element includes an onload attribute which calls the AddTitle() function. We create an SVGDoc variable to identify the SVG image. Having identified the SVG document, we then create the SVGRoot variable using the getDocumentElement() method of the SVGDoc object. The variable myTitleData is assigned the text string "JavaScript works well with SVG!" using the createTextNode() method of the SVGDoc object. The SVGDoc.createElement() method is used to create a node representing a <title> element.

The variables we need are created, but we need to add them to the document element. First we add MyTitleData to the myTitle object using the appendChild() method. Finally we add the myTitle object (with its new property myTitleData) to the SVGRoot object.

If you download or type in the code in AddTitle.svg and display it in a browser window, you will see that it is identical to that shown in Figure 21.6.

Of course we could have achieved the same result by using an external JavaScript file. Listing 21.6 shows an SVG document with a reference to an external JavaScript script.

INPUT **LISTING 21.6**   An SVG Document Referencing an External JavaScript Script (AddTitle02.svg)

```
<?xml version="1.0" standalone="no"?>
<!DOCTYPE svg PUBLIC "-//W3C//DTD SVG 20010904//EN"
"http://www.w3.org/TR/2001/REC-SVG-20010904/DTD/svg10.dtd">
<svg width="300" height="150" onload="AddTitle(evt)" >
    <script type="text/javascript" xlink:href="AddTitle02.js" />

<rect x="0" y="0" width="300" height="150" style="fill:red; stroke:none;"/>
</svg>
```

21

Notice in Listing 21.6 that there is an `xlink:href` attribute to identify the location of the external script. This functions similarly to the familiar `href` attribute in the HTML `script` tag but uses the XML Linking Language (XLink) to provide the linking functionality. Listing 21.7 shows the script.

LISTING 21.7   A Simple JavaScript to Add a `<title>` Element to an SVG

INPUT   Image (`AddTitle02.js`)

```
function AddTitle(evt){
  var SVGDoc = evt.getTarget().getOwnerDocument();
  var SVGRoot = SVGDoc.getDocumentElement();
  var myTitleData, myTitle;
  myTitleData = SVGDoc.createTextNode('JavaScript works well with SVG!');

  myTitle = SVGDoc.createElement("title");
  myTitle.appendChild(myTitleData);

  SVGRoot.appendChild(myTitle);
}
```

Creating a Simple Shape Using JavaScript

In Chapter 4 you saw how `document.write()` can be used to add new, or dynamic, content to an HTML document which had not completed loading. Similarly, it is possible to create a new SVG shape using JavaScript and then to write that to the SVG canvas. In the next JavaScript example, we will do something similar by using the `onload` event of the SVG document.

Our aim is to use JavaScript to create an ellipse on screen. If we wanted to do that without JavaScript, we could do it using the code in Listing 21.8.

INPUT   **LISTING 21.8**   Declaring an Ellipse Without JavaScript (`DeclareEllipse.svg`)

```
<?xml version="1.0" standalone="no"?>
<!DOCTYPE svg PUBLIC "-//W3C//DTD SVG 20010904//EN"
"http://www.w3.org/TR/2001/REC-SVG-20010904/DTD/svg10.dtd">
<svg width="250" height="250" >
 <ellipse cx="125" cy="125" rx="90" ry="40" style="fill:#CCCCCC;
stroke:#FF0000"/>
</svg>
```

To create an ellipse using JavaScript which exactly matches the one in Listing 21.8, we could use the code in Listing 21.9. In a moment, we will examine each part of the code to see what it does.

LISTING 21.9 Creating an Ellipse Using JavaScript (CreateEllipse.svg)

```
<?xml version="1.0" standalone="no"?>
<!DOCTYPE svg PUBLIC "-//W3C//DTD SVG 20010904//EN"
"http://www.w3.org/TR/2001/REC-SVG-20010904/DTD/svg10.dtd">
<svg width="250" height="250" onload="createShape(evt)" >
    <script type="text/javascript">
    <![CDATA[
        function createShape(evt) {
            var SVGDoc  = evt.getTarget().getOwnerDocument();
            var SVGRoot = SVGDoc.getDocumentElement();
            var myShape;

            myShape = SVGDoc.createElement("ellipse");
            myShape.setAttribute("cx", 125);
            myShape.setAttribute("cy", 125);
            myShape.setAttribute("rx",  90);
            myShape.setAttribute("ry",  40);
            myShape.setAttribute("style", "fill: #CCCCCC; stroke:#FF0000");

            SVGRoot.appendChild(myShape);
            }

    ]]>
    </script>
</svg>
```

ANALYSIS The first three lines of the code, shown here, should be familiar:

```
<?xml version="1.0" standalone="no"?>
<!DOCTYPE svg PUBLIC "-//W3C//DTD SVG 20010904//EN"
"http://www.w3.org/TR/2001/REC-SVG-20010904/DTD/svg10.dtd">
```

The first line is the XML declaration. The second and third lines, which form the DOC-TYPE declaration, specify that the document is an SVG 1.0 document. The <svg> element has changed slightly from those you have seen up to now:

```
<svg width="250" height="250" onload="createShape(evt)" >
```

The <svg> element has an onload attribute which calls the createShape() JavaScript function, like so:

```
<script type="text/javascript">
    <![CDATA[
```

We need the <script> element with a type attribute to specify that the contained script is JavaScript. The JavaScript does not comply with XML syntax rules, so we need to inform the SVG rendering engine of that by indicating the start of a CDATA section.

Then we come to the definition of the `createShape()` function itself:

```
function createShape(evt) {
        var SVGDoc  = evt.getTarget().getOwnerDocument();
        var SVGRoot = SVGDoc.getDocumentElement();
        var myShape;

        myShape = SVGDoc.createElement("ellipse");
        myShape.setAttribute("cx", 125);
        myShape.setAttribute("cy", 125);
        myShape.setAttribute("rx",  90);
        myShape.setAttribute("ry",  40);
        myShape.setAttribute("style", "fill: #CCCCCC; stroke:#FF0000");

        SVGRoot.appendChild(myShape);
            }
```

We declare three variables: The SVGDoc variable represents the SVG document itself. The SVGRoot variable represents the root node of the SVG document. And, we will use SVGRoot later to add our new node representing the ellipse.

Finally we create a variable called myShape. We use the `createElement()` method of the SVGDoc object to create a node corresponding to an `ellipse` element. As created, it is empty and lacks any attribute values, so we need to add those. We use the `setAttribute()` method to, respectively, define the values of the cx, cy, rx, ry, and style attributes of the `ellipse` element with values that correspond to those you saw earlier in Listing 21.8.

We now have created an object that represents an `<ellipse>` element but it is not connected to anything. So we use the `appendChild()` method to add the newly created node to the root of the SVG document. This is equivalent to nesting the newly created `<ellipse>` element within the `<svg>` element of Listing 21.8, as shown here:

```
SVGRoot.appendChild(myShape);
}
    ]]>
    </script>
```

Having defined the work which the function is to carry out, you must remember the curly brace to correctly end the function, add the `]]>` to indicate the end of the CDATA section and indicate to the SVG rendering engine, by means of the `</script>` end tag, that the content of the `<script>` element has been completed.

Adding Text Using JavaScript

In SVG to create text, you must use a `<text>` element. You have additional options in SVG to use `<tspan>` elements, which we won't consider further here. To use the `<text>`

element, you must specify where in the SVG image the text is to be located. That is done using x and y attributes. At the top left of the screen the value of both the x and y attributes is zero. Additionally you will typically specify the style to be applied to the text. There are four techniques to add style: using an external style sheet, an internal `style` element, a `style` attribute, or a series of individual attributes each of which represents a CSS property.

To create a simple text message using declarative syntax, you can use a listing like the one shown in Listing 21.10.

INPUT   **LISTING 21.10**   A Simple Text Message in SVG (`SimpleText.svg`)

```
<?xml version="1.0" standalone="no"?>
<!DOCTYPE svg PUBLIC "-//W3C//DTD SVG 20010904//EN"
"http://www.w3.org/TR/2001/REC-SVG-20010904/DTD/svg10.dtd">
<svg width="400" height="400">
<text x="30" y="50"
  style="opacity:0.8; font-size:20;
  font-family:Arial, sans-serif; fill:red">
Hello SVG
</text>
</svg>
```

Again, we can use a simple JavaScript script to create the `text` element, its attributes, and its content, as shown in Listing 21.11.

INPUT   **LISTING 21.11**   Using JavaScript to Create a Simple Text Message
(`CreateText.svg`)

```
<?xml version="1.0" standalone="no"?>
<!DOCTYPE svg PUBLIC "-//W3C//DTD SVG 20010904//EN"
"http://www.w3.org/TR/2001/REC-SVG-20010904/DTD/svg10.dtd">
<svg width="400" height="300" onload="CreateText(evt)">
<script type="text/javascript">
<![CDATA[
function CreateText(evt)
{
var myText="Hello SVG";
var SVGDoc = evt.getTarget().getOwnerDocument();
var SVGRoot = SVGDoc.getDocumentElement();
textElement = SVGDoc.createElement("text");
textElement.setAttribute("x","30");
textElement.setAttribute("y","50");
textElement.setAttribute("style","opacity:0.8;
   ➥font-size:20; font-family:Arial, sans-serif; fill:red");
textElement.setAttribute("id","MyText");
```

21

LISTING 21.11   continued

```
textNode = SVGDoc.createTextNode(myText);
textElement.appendChild(textNode);
SVGRoot.appendChild(textElement);
}

]]>
</script>
</svg>
```

In Listing 21.11 we have used JavaScript to create the text element dynamically. The techniques are very similar to those we used in Listing 21.9, so if anything is unclear refer back to the detailed description given earlier for Listing 21.9.

A Timed Animation Using JavaScript

SVG allows us to create timed animations using a number of animation elements "borrowed" from the SMIL 2.0 Recommendation (SMIL is another XML-application language). Using those animation elements alone, it is possible to create timed animations of part or all of a SVG image.

Let's animate the simple text message created in Listing 21.10. We can do that using SVG declarative animation, which is shown in Listing 21.12.

INPUT

LISTING 21.12   Animating a Text Message by Declarative Animation (AnimSimpleText.svg)

```
<?xml version="1.0" standalone="no"?>
<!DOCTYPE svg PUBLIC "-//W3C//DTD SVG 20010904//EN"
"http://www.w3.org/TR/2001/REC-SVG-20010904/DTD/svg10.dtd">
<svg width="400" height="400">
<text x="30" y="50"
  style="opacity:0.8; font-size:16; font-family:Arial, sans-serif; fill:red">
  <animate begin="2s" dur="1.5s" attributeName="font-size" from="16" to="36"
repeatCount="indefinite"/>
Hello SVG
</text>
</svg>
```

ANALYSIS   Listing 21.12 shows the syntax that we will want to create using JavaScript. Note that there is, nested within the text element, an animate element which has several attributes. The begin attribute of the animate element tells us that the animation is to begin 2 seconds after the document loads. The dur attribute tells us that the animation is to last 1.5 seconds. The attributeName attribute tells us that it is the font-size property that is to be animated. The `from` attribute tells us the value which the font size is to be animated from, and the `to` attribute tells the value which the font size is to be animated to. The `repeatCount` attribute has the value indefinite which tells us that the animation, once started (2 seconds after the document loads) is to continue indefinitely.

Listing 21.13 shows how, using JavaScript, we can create an animation that is visually identical to that shown in Listing 21.12.

LISTING 21.13   Using JavaScript to Animate a Simple Text Message
(AnimFontSize.svg)

INPUT

```
<?xml version="1.0" standalone="no"?>
<!DOCTYPE svg PUBLIC "-//W3C//DTD SVG 20010904//EN"
"http://www.w3.org/TR/2001/REC-SVG-20010904/DTD/svg10.dtd">
<svg width="400" height="300" onload="AnimateFontSize(evt)">
<script type="text/javascript">
<![CDATA[
function AnimateFontSize(evt)
{
var myText="Hello SVG";
var SVGDoc = evt.getTarget().getOwnerDocument();
var SVGRoot = SVGDoc.getDocumentElement();

textElement = SVGDoc.createElement("text");
textElement.setAttribute("x","30");
textElement.setAttribute("y","50");
textElement.setAttribute("style", "opacity:0.8; font-size:16;
➥ font-family:Arial, sans-serif; fill:red");
textElement.setAttribute("id","MyText");
var textNode = SVGDoc.createTextNode(myText);
textElement.appendChild(textNode);


var animElement = SVGDoc.createElement("animate");
animElement.setAttribute("begin", "2s");
animElement.setAttribute("dur", "1.5s");
animElement.setAttribute("attributeName", "font-size");
animElement.setAttribute("from", "16");
animElement.setAttribute("to", "36");
animElement.setAttribute("repeatCount", "indefinite");

textElement.appendChild(animElement);

SVGRoot.appendChild(textElement);
}

]]>
</script>
</svg>
```

21

ANALYSIS First, let's create a `<text>` element using techniques similar to those you have seen before. Then we create an `animate` element and set the values of the attributes of the `animElement` object to values corresponding to those which we want.

> **Caution**
>
> Be careful to avoid splitting code lines at a point where they end with a semicolon, for example, part way through the values of a complex style attribute. The JavaScript interpreter will think you have finished the JavaScript statement without closing the quote marks. So do not split the lines in your source code. In this chapter, of course, lines need to be split for presentation on the page.

Finally we must remember to add the objects we have created as children of the `SVGRoot` object, which represents the document element of the SVG document.

Creating a Shape That Responds to Events

SVG natively allows you to do things with graphic objects which, using HTML, *require* the use of JavaScript. In SVG you can just describe how you want the object to respond to certain events. In this section, you will see how using native SVG alone you can create rollover effects, and then you will see how to use JavaScript to produce the same visual effect.

Listing 21.14 shows a simple rollover of a rectangle.

INPUT **LISTING 21.14** A Rollover Using Declarative Animation and a Gradient Fill (`SimpleRollover.svg`)

```
<?xml version="1.0" standalone="no"?>
<!DOCTYPE svg PUBLIC "-//W3C//DTD SVG 20010904//EN"
"http://www.w3.org/TR/2001/REC-SVG-20010904/DTD/svg10.dtd">
<svg width="250" height="150">
<defs>
<linearGradient id="MyGradient" gradientUnits="objectBoundingBox"
  x1="0%" y1="0%" x2="0%" y2="100%">
<stop offset="1%" style="stop-color:#FF0000"/>
<stop offset="50%" style="stop-color:#FFFF00"/>
<stop offset="100%" style="stop-color:#FF00FF"/>
</linearGradient>
</defs>
<rect x="10" y="20" rx="5" ry="15" width="150" height="40"
 style="opacity:0.3; fill:red; stroke:none">
 <set begin="mouseover" end="mouseout" attributeName="fill"
 from="red" to="url(#MyGradient)"/>
</rect>
</svg>
```

ANALYSIS The <rect> element uses two attributes, rx and ry, which you haven't seen before. They allow you to create rounded corners on a rectangle.

The code in Listing 21.14 also introduces three SVG elements which you haven't met yet. The <defs> element is used to contain definitions which we will use later in an SVG document. In this case the definition is of a linear gradient which, not surprisingly, is created using an SVG linearGradient element. In this case, the linear gradient is a vertical gradient starting red at the top, changing to yellow in the middle, and to magenta at the bottom.

Notice too that we use an SVG set animation element. The set element is activated on mouse-over and causes the fill of the rectangle to be changed from plain red (modified by the opacity which we will describe in a moment) to the linear gradient called "MyGradient". Notice that in the to attribute of the first <set> element that we see the value "url(#MyGradient)". The "url" indicates that we are referencing some fill that is defined elsewhere (in this case within the <defs> element of the same document). The "#MyGradient" tells us that the fill being referenced has an id attribute of "MyGradient"—in this case our vertical linear gradient.

Notice how much simpler this is than using two bitmap images and JavaScript to produce a rollover. Of course we can add text to the button using SVG text elements to produce a full rollover button.

Again JavaScript can produce the same effect in response to a mouse-over event. Code using JavaScript to produce this is shown in Listing 21.15.

INPUT **LISTING 21.15** Using JavaScript with SVG to Create a Rollover (JSRollover.svg)

```
<?xml version="1.0" standalone="no"?>
<!DOCTYPE svg PUBLIC "-//W3C//DTD SVG 20010904//EN"
"http://www.w3.org/TR/2001/REC-SVG-20010904/DTD/svg10.dtd">
<svg width="250" height="150" onload="CreateJSRollover(evt)">
<script type="text/javascript">
<![CDATA[
function CreateJSRollover(evt)
{
var SVGDoc = evt.getTarget().getOwnerDocument();
var SVGRoot = SVGDoc.getDocumentElement();

var MyRect = SVGDoc.createElement("rect");
MyRect.setAttribute("x", 10);
MyRect.setAttribute("y", 20);
MyRect.setAttribute("rx", 5);
MyRect.setAttribute("ry", 15);
MyRect.setAttribute("width", 150);
```

21

LISTING 21.15   continued

```
MyRect.setAttribute("height", 40);
MyRect.setAttribute("style", "opacity:0.3; fill:red; stroke:none");

var Set1 = SVGDoc.createElement ("set");
Set1.setAttribute("begin", "mouseover");
Set1.setAttribute("end", "mouseout");
Set1.setAttribute("attributeName", "fill");
Set1.setAttribute("from", "red");
Set1.setAttribute("to", "url(#MyGradient)");
MyRect.appendChild(Set1);

SVGRoot.appendChild(MyRect);
}
]]>
</script>
<defs>
<linearGradient id="MyGradient" gradientUnits="objectBoundingBox"
  x1="0%" y1="0%" x2="0%" y2="100%">
<stop offset="1%" style="stop-color:#FF0000"/>
<stop offset="50%" style="stop-color:#FFFF00"/>
<stop offset="100%" style="stop-color:#FF00FF"/>
</linearGradient>
</defs>

</svg>
```

ANALYSIS   When the rectangle is not moused, it is plain red and partly transparent (controlled by the opacity property which is 0 for fully transparent and 1 for fully opaque). When it is moused, the fill for the rectangle uses the linear gradient defined within the <linearGradient> element.

Figure 21.7 shows the rectangle displaying the linear gradient on mouse-over.

OUTPUT

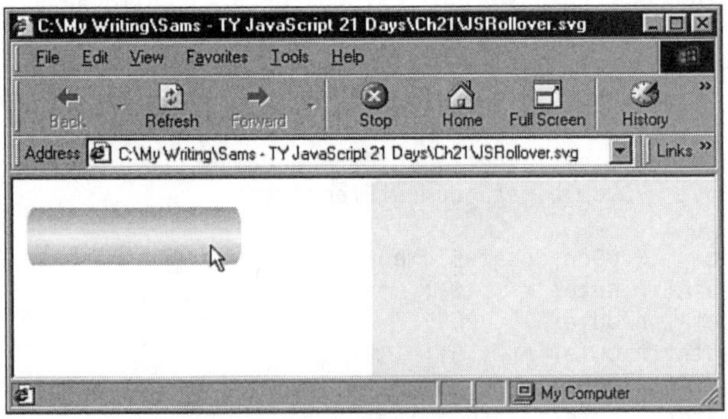

FIGURE 21.7

When moused the rectangle displays a linear gradient.

Events Available Using JavaScript with SVG

In this section we will briefly examine some of the events available using JavaScript.

Using `mouseover` and `mouseout` Events

First we will use SVG to define an ellipse which changes the color of its fill when we mouse over the ellipse. The fill will change from gray to bright green. Don't worry too much about the detail of the syntax of the animation; it is there simply to show you what SVG can do. See Listing 21.16.

 INPUT
LISTING 21.16   A Mouseover Effect Using Only SVG
(`DeclareEllipseAnimation.svg`)

```
<?xml version="1.0" standalone="no"?>
<!DOCTYPE svg PUBLIC "-//W3C//DTD SVG 20010904//EN"
"http://www.w3.org/TR/2001/REC-SVG-20010904/DTD/svg10.dtd">
<svg width="250" height="250" >
 <ellipse cx="125" cy="125" rx="90" ry="40"
 style="fill:#CCCCCC; stroke:#FF0000">
  <set attributeName="fill" begin="mouseover"
 end="mouseout" from="#CCCCCC" to="#00FF00" />
 </ellipse>
</svg>
```

ANALYSIS When we mouse over the ellipse the fill color changes instantly from gray to green. Notice within the set element that the animation from gray to green is set to begin on the mouseover event and to end on the mouseout event.

Listing 21.17 uses JavaScript to produce the same visual effect.

INPUT
LISTING 21.17   A Mouseover Effect Using JavaScript with SVG
(`JSEllipseAnimation.svg`)

```
<?xml version="1.0" standalone="no"?>
<!DOCTYPE svg PUBLIC "-//W3C//DTD SVG 20010904//EN"
"http://www.w3.org/TR/2001/REC-SVG-20010904/DTD/svg10.dtd">
<svg width="250" height="250" xmlns="http://www.w3.org/2000/svg">
   <script type="text/javascript">
    <![CDATA[
    function ellipseMouse(evt) {
    var ellipse = evt.target;
    ellipse.style.setProperty("fill", "#00FF00");
    }
    function ellipseMouse2(evt) {
    var ellipse = evt.target;
    ellipse.style.setProperty("fill", "#CCCCCC");
```

21

LISTING 21.17   continued

```
      }
      ]]>
    </script>
    <ellipse cx="125" cy="125" rx="90" ry="40"
  style="fill:#CCCCCC; stroke:#FF0000"
      onmouseover="ellipseMouse(evt)"
      onmouseout="ellipseMouse2(evt)"
      />
  </svg>
```

ANALYSIS   In Listing 21.17 we change an individual property within the values of the style attribute. The ellipse object accesses its style property and uses the `setProperty()` method to alter the value of the fill of the ellipse when the ellipse is moused over.

Notice in the `ellipse` element that the attributes are called `onmouseover` and `onmouseout`; whereas when we use the same events within an `animate` element, for example, the value of the attributes would be called `mouseover` and `mouseout` (without the "on" prefix).

Using Click Events

One of the most basic interactive functions is the response of an object to a mouse click. In SVG we can program such responses using either declarative animation or using JavaScript. On this occasion, in Listing 21.18, you will be introduced to two JavaScript techniques that respond to a mouse click. Both listings cause a simple message to be displayed in the status bar of the browser window when the rectangle is clicked.

LISTING 21.18   One Syntax to Capture and Process a Click Event Using
INPUT   JavaScript (`WindowStatus.svg`)

```
<?xml version="1.0" standalone="no"?>
<!DOCTYPE svg PUBLIC "-//W3C//DTD SVG 20010904//EN"
"http://www.w3.org/TR/2001/REC-SVG-20010904/DTD/svg10.dtd">
<svg width="300px" height="200px" onload="Initialize(evt)">
<defs>
<script type="text/ecmascript">
<![CDATA[
var SVGDoc;

function Initialize (evt) {
SVGDoc = evt.getTarget().getOwnerDocument();

SVGDoc.getElementById("MyRect").addEventListener("click", ChangeStatus,
false);
}
```

LISTING 21.18 continued

```
function ChangeStatus(evt){
var StatusInfo = "You clicked over the rectangle";
window.status = StatusInfo;
}

]]>
</script>
</defs>
<rect id="MyRect" x="20" y="20" rx="10" ry="15" width="150" height="40"
  style="fill:#CCCCCC; stroke:none;"/>
</svg>
```

ANALYSIS In Listing 21.18 the Initialize() function is called by the onload event, as specified by the onload attribute of the svg element. We first create an SVGDoc element. We then can use the getElementById() and addEventListener() methods to create an event listener for the rectangle. The event listener specifies that the ChangeStatus() function is called when the rectangle is clicked. Listing 21.19 uses an alternate syntax which will be explained following the listing.

INPUT **LISTING 21.19** An Alternate Syntax to Capture and Process Click Events Using JavaScript (WindowStatus02.svg)

```
<?xml version="1.0" standalone="no"?>
<!DOCTYPE svg PUBLIC "-//W3C//DTD SVG 20010904//EN"
"http://www.w3.org/TR/2001/REC-SVG-20010904/DTD/svg10.dtd">
<svg width="300px" height="200px" >
<defs>
<script type="text/ecmascript">
<![CDATA[

function ChangeStatus(evt){
var StatusInfo = "You clicked over the rectangle";
window.status = StatusInfo;
}
]]>
</script>
</defs>
<rect id="MyRect" x="20" y="20" width="150"
height="40" onclick="ChangeStatus(evt)"/>
</svg>
```

ANALYSIS In Listing 21.19, we add an onclick attribute which calls the ChangeStatus() function directly.

21

Figure 21.8 shows the output from Listing 21.18. Running Listing 21.19 would produce the same appearance.

FIGURE 21.8

Displaying a message in the browser status bar in response to a mouse click.

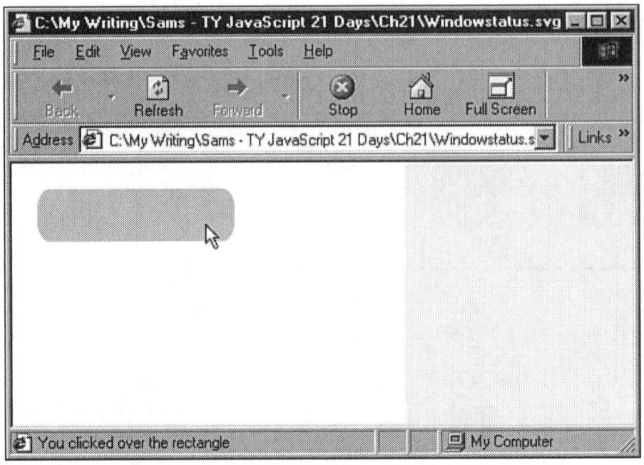

Caution

The Adobe SVG Viewer version 3.0 seems to ignore the "`mouseover`" event when using syntax similar to that shown in Listing 21.18 or 21.19, although it responds correctly to a mouse click.

JavaScript Beyond Declarative Animation

The examples we have looked at to this point have shown you JavaScript techniques that mimic what is already available in SVG using declarative syntax. However, JavaScript can carry out programming tasks in SVG, which SVG alone cannot perform.

For example, if we have the simple animation shown below in Listing 21.20, we can use declarative animation to create the visual effect of "curtains" opening and closing, but we can't—using declarative syntax—provide any conditional processing. We can't, for example, ensure that if the curtains are already closed that they don't go through the closing animation again.

INPUT

LISTING 21.20   Declarative Animation to Open and Close "Curtains" (`CurtainsDeclar.svg`)

```
<?xml version="1.0" standalone="no"?>
<!DOCTYPE svg PUBLIC "-//W3C//DTD SVG 20010904//EN"
"http://www.w3.org/TR/2001/REC-SVG-20010904/DTD/svg10.dtd">
<svg width="800px" height="600px">

<rect style="fill:black" x="50" y="60" height="100" width="150"/>
```

LISTING 21.20   continued

```
<rect style="fill:white" x="55" y="65" height="90" width="140"/>
<text style="font-family:Arial; font-size:12; fill:red; stroke:red" x="75"
y="80">SVGSpider.com</text>
<text style="font-family:Arial; font-size:12; fill:red; stroke:red" x="60"
y="110">
Do you like my curtains?
</text>
<rect style="fill:red" x="55" y="65" height="90" width="1" >
<animate attributeName="width" values="1; 75; 1" dur="5s" begin="0s" />
<animate id="close3" attributeName="width" attributeType="XML" values="1; 75"
dur="2.5s"
        begin="button2.click" fill="freeze"/>
<animate id="open" attributeName="width" attributeType="XML" values="75; 1"
dur="2.5s"
        begin="button1.click" fill="freeze"/>
</rect>

<rect style="fill:red" x="194" y="65" height="90" width="1">
<animate attributeName="width" values="1; 75; 1" dur="5s" begin="0s"/>
<animate attributeName="x" values="194; 122; 194" attributeType="XML" dur="5s"
begin="0s"/>
<animate id="close1" attributeName="width" attributeType="XML" values="1; 75"
dur="2.5s"
        begin="button2.click" fill="freeze"/>
<animate id="close2" attributeName="x" attributeType="XML" values="194; 122"
dur="2.5s"
        begin="button2.click" fill="freeze" />
<animate id="open" attributeName="width" attributeType="XML" values="75; 1"
dur="2.5s"
        begin="button1.click" fill="freeze"/>
<animate id="open" attributeName="x" attributeType="XML" values="122; 194"
dur="2.5s"
        begin="button1.click" fill="freeze" />
</rect>

<g id="controls">

<g id="button1">
    <ellipse cx="58" cy="210" rx="34" ry="12" style="fill:red;" />
    <text pointer-events="none" x="42" y="214" style="fill:white;
font-weight:bold;">Open</text>
</g>

<g id="button2">
    <ellipse cx="195" cy="210" rx="34" ry="12" style="fill:red "/>
    <text pointer-events="none" x="179" y="214" style="fill:white;
font-weight:bold;">Close</text>
</g>
</g>
</svg>
```

21

ANALYSIS The animation of the rectangles that form the "curtains" depends on one or another of the controls being clicked. So, in order to create a JavaScript-based solution, we will need to capture the click event. The logic we want to express is "If the curtain is open when the Close control is clicked, then close the curtains; but if it is already closed, do nothing." Listing 21.21 shows us the JavaScript-based solution.

INPUT **LISTING 21.21** Using JavaScript to Add Intelligence to the Opening and Closing of the "Curtains" (`CurtainsJS.svg`)

```
<?xml version="1.0" standalone="no"?>
<!DOCTYPE svg PUBLIC "-//W3C//DTD SVG 20010904//EN"
"http://www.w3.org/TR/2001/REC-SVG-20010904/DTD/svg10.dtd">
<svg width="800px" height="600px" onload="Initialize(evt)">
<script type="text/javascript">
<![CDATA[
var SVGDoc;
var SVGRoot;
var LeftCurtain;
var RightCurtain;
var NewLeftWidth = 1;
var NewRightWidth = 1;
var NewRightX = 194;

var open;
var closed;
var TimeNow = 0;
var TimerIncrement = 67;
var MaxTime = 5000;

function Initialize(evt){
SVGDoc = evt.getTarget().getOwnerDocument();
SVGRoot = SVGDoc.getDocumentElement();
LeftCurtain = SVGDoc.createElement("rect");
RightCurtain = SVGDoc.createElement("rect");
open = true;
closed = false;
CreateCurtains();
InitialMovements();
// Set values for open and close at end of the initial animation
open = true;
closed = false;
} // End function Initialize()


function CreateCurtains(){
// Create left "curtain"
LeftCurtain.setAttribute("id", "MyLeftCurtain");
LeftCurtain.setAttribute("style", "fill:red; stroke:none");
LeftCurtain.setAttribute("x", "55px");
```

LISTING 21.21   continued

```
LeftCurtain.setAttribute("y", "65px");
LeftCurtain.setAttribute("width", "1px");
LeftCurtain.setAttribute("height", "90px");
SVGRoot.appendChild(LeftCurtain);

// Create right "curtain"
RightCurtain.setAttribute("id", "MyRightCurtain");
RightCurtain.setAttribute("x", "194px");
RightCurtain.setAttribute("y", "65px");
RightCurtain.setAttribute("width", "1px");
RightCurtain.setAttribute("height", "90px");
RightCurtain.setAttribute("style", "fill:red; stroke:none");
SVGRoot.appendChild(RightCurtain);
} // End function CreateCurtains()


function InitialMovements(){
//Left Initial Movement - only width needs to be changed
var InitialAnim1;
InitialAnim1 = SVGDoc.createElement("animate");
InitialAnim1.setAttribute("attributeName", "width");
InitialAnim1.setAttribute("values", "1; 75; 1");
InitialAnim1.setAttribute("dur", "5s");
InitialAnim1.setAttribute("begin", "0s");
LeftCurtain.appendChild(InitialAnim1);

// Right Initial Movements - both width and x need to
// be altered in a synchronized way
var InitialAnim2;
var InitialAnim3;
InitialAnim2 = SVGDoc.createElement("animate");
InitialAnim2.setAttribute("attributeName", "width");
InitialAnim2.setAttribute("values", "1; 75; 1");
InitialAnim2.setAttribute("dur", "5s");
InitialAnim2.setAttribute("begin", "0s");
RightCurtain.appendChild(InitialAnim2);

InitialAnim3 = SVGDoc.createElement("animate");
InitialAnim3.setAttribute("attributeName", "x");
InitialAnim3.setAttribute("values", "194; 122; 194");
InitialAnim3.setAttribute("dur", "5s");
InitialAnim3.setAttribute("begin", "0s");
RightCurtain.appendChild(InitialAnim3);
} // end function InitialMovements()


function Open(evt)
{
```

21

LISTING 21.21 continued

```
TimeNow = 0;
OpenCurtains();
} // end function Open()


function Close(evt)
{
TimeNow = 0;
CloseCurtains();
} // end function Close()


function CloseCurtains(){
TimeNow = TimeNow + TimerIncrement;
if (TimeNow > MaxTime) {
  closed = true;
  open = false;
  TimeNow = 0;
  return;
  } // End if statement
if (NewLeftWidth < 75){
  ++NewLeftWidth;
  ++NewRightWidth;
  --NewRightX;
  LeftCurtain.setAttribute("width", NewLeftWidth);
  RightCurtain.setAttribute("width", NewRightWidth);
  RightCurtain.setAttribute("x", NewRightX);
  } // End if statement

setTimeout("CloseCurtains()", TimerIncrement);
window.CloseCurtains = CloseCurtains;
} // end CloseCurtains() function

function OpenCurtains(){
TimeNow = TimeNow + TimerIncrement;
if (TimeNow > MaxTime) {
  closed = false;
  open = true;
  TimeNow = 0;
  return;
  } // End if statement
if (NewLeftWidth > 1){
  --NewLeftWidth;
  --NewRightWidth;
  ++NewRightX;
  LeftCurtain.setAttribute("width", NewLeftWidth);
  RightCurtain.setAttribute("width", NewRightWidth);
  RightCurtain.setAttribute("x", NewRightX);
  } // End if statement
```

LISTING 21.21   continued

```
setTimeout("OpenCurtains()", TimerIncrement);
window.OpenCurtains = OpenCurtains;
} // end OpenCurtains() function


]]>
</script>


<rect style="fill:black" x="50" y="60" height="100" width="150"/>
<rect style="fill:white" x="55" y="65" height="90" width="140"/>
<text style="font-family:Arial; font-size:12; fill:red; stroke:red" x="75"
y="80">SVGSpider.com</text>
<text style="font-family:Arial; font-size:12; fill:red; stroke:red" x="60"
y="110">
Do you like my curtains?
</text>

<g id="controls">
 <g id="button1" onclick="OpenCurtains(evt)">
    <ellipse cx="58" cy="210" rx="34" ry="12" style="fill:red;" />
    <text pointer-events="none" x="42" y="214" style="fill:white;
    font-weight:bold;">Open</text>
 </g>

 <g id="button2" onclick="CloseCurtains(evt)">
    <ellipse cx="195" cy="210" rx="34" ry="12" style="fill:red "/>
    <text pointer-events="none" x="179" y="214" style="fill:white;
    font-weight:bold;">Close</text>
 </g>
</g>
</svg>
```

ANALYSIS   The code should be pretty familiar to you, if you have followed the techniques used in earlier examples with the exception of the techniques used in the CloseCurtains() and OpenCurtains() functions. Let's look at the CloseCurtains() function in more detail, as shown here:

```
function CloseCurtains(){
TimeNow = TimeNow + TimerIncrement;
if (TimeNow > MaxTime) {
  closed = true;
  open = false;
  TimeNow = 0;
  return;
  } // End if statement
if (NewLeftWidth < 75){
  ++NewLeftWidth;
```

21

```
++NewRightWidth;
--NewRightX;
LeftCurtain.setAttribute("width", NewLeftWidth);
RightCurtain.setAttribute("width", NewRightWidth);
RightCurtain.setAttribute("x", NewRightX);
} // End if statement
```

We enter the `CloseCurtains()` function through the `Close()` function which resets the timer. The variables used in `CloseCurtains()` have been declared as global variables earlier in the script, since they will also be used within the `OpenCurtains()` function. First we test if more time has elapsed than the maximum allowed by the `MaxTime` variable. If so, then the function sets the values of the closed and open variables appropriately and then returns. If the function hasn't timed out, it checks whether the width of the curtains is still less than 75 and, if so, the width of each curtain is adjusted by one, and the right curtain is moved by one pixel—since the top left corner of a rectangle is what SVG refers to. We then change the values of the relevant attributes of the left and right curtain.

Finally, the `setTimeout()` function is called, which again calls the `CloseCurtains()` function recursively:

```
setTimeout("CloseCurtains()", TimerIncrement);
window.CloseCurtains = CloseCurtains;
```

This progressively increases the width of the curtains until the width is 75 (in which case the width doesn't increase any more) and the timeout takes place.

Note
You may find that you need a "long" click—that is, hold the mouse button down for slightly longer than usual—to get the code in Listing 21.21 to operate correctly.

Interaction Between the HTML and SVG DOM

Often when you use an SVG image it will be embedded within an HTML or XHTML Web page. An HTML page may contain one or more Document Object Models. In the situation where you have a simple HTML/XHTML Web page with a single SVG image embedded within it, then you will have two separate DOMs—one for the HTML page, and the other (an SVG DOM) for the SVG image.

Listing 21.22 shows a modification of Listing 21.18, which allows for the situation where the SVG image is embedded in an HTML page.

LISTING 21.22 An SVG Event That Affects the Containing HTML/XHTML
Web page (`WindowStatus.htm`)

```
<!DOCTYPE HTML PUBLIC "-//W3C//DTD HTML 4.0 Transitional//EN"
"http://www.w3.org/TR/REC-html40/loose.dtd">
<html>
<head>
<title>SVG Events affecting the browser window</title>
<script type="text/javascript">
<!-- //
// Your JavaScript to script the HTML/XHTML parts of a Web page can go here.

//-->
</script>
</head>
<body>
<embed src="WindowStatus.svg" type="image/svg+xml"
 width="300px" height="200px">
</body>
</html>
```

ANALYSIS Notice that the embed tag has been used to display the SVG image. The W3C
recommends the object tag but in practice this will cause real difficulties. Use
the embed tag to avoid cross-browser problems. Details are discussed in Chapter 10,
"Events and Events Handling."

When you click on the rectangle embedded within the WindowStatus.htm file, the event
in the SVG DOM is able, given the code you saw in Listing 21.18, to alter values in the
HTML DOM. Figure 21.9 shows the result.

OUTPUT

FIGURE 21.9

*Altering the content
of the status bar of
an HTML Web page
window by using an
SVG DOM event.*

21

Finding Out More About SVG

In this chapter, it has been possible only to introduce SVG which is an extensive, powerful, and flexible graphics technology. In this section you will see a number of places where you can get further information on SVG, and what you can do with it in your Web pages.

SVG is only five months old at the time of writing; therefore, there are few SVG books available. The first SVG book published, *Designing SVG Web Graphics*, provides a broad introduction to SVG for someone who is new to the topic. By the time this book is in print, the *Sams Teach Yourself SVG in 24 Hours* will be available as an alternate introduction to SVG.

The main general mailing list for SVG developers is located on YahooGroups.com. Further information is available at `http://www.adobe.com/svg/viewer/install/main.html`. To subscribe, simply send an e-mail to `svg-developers-subscribe@yahoogroups.com`.

There are a number of Web sites where you can either see SVG in use or access online SVG tutorials.

The Adobe.com Web site, at `http://www.adobe.com/svg/`, has a significant amount of introductory material. Two individual sites that are useful are `http://www.kevlindev.com/` and `http://www.pinkjuice.com/`. A very useful SVG and JavaScript site is located at `http://pilat.free.fr/english/`. Another useful site with an engineering bias, but which includes JavaScript examples, is located at `http://www.mecxpert.de/`. Finally, if you want to see how SVG can be used in Web page layout, including simple declarative animations, take a look at `http://www.svgspider.com/default.svg` or `http://www.xmml.com` and the linked pages.

Summary

This chapter introduced you to Scalable Vector Graphics and has shown you the element and attribute structure of simple SVG graphics. You have been introduced to the JavaScript techniques to carry out simple manipulations of the SVG DOM, in order to give you an impression of the potential of SVG combined with JavaScript.

Workshop

In this workshop, questions and exercises will be used to review what you have learned in this chapter about using JavaScript with Scalable Vector Graphics.

Q&A

Q. **I have lots of bitmap graphics and I would like to continue to use them with SVG. Is that possible?**

A. Yes, it's straightforward to use bitmap graphics, such as GIFs or PNGs, with SVG. The SVG `image` element allows an image to be imported into an SVG image or Web page.

Q. **I heard that Flash is a vector graphics format and can use XML too. Why is SVG any better?**

A. One big difference between SVG and Flash is that SVG *is* XML. So, if you are planning to use SVG with an XML data store or with some of the many other XML-based languages, you can use one set of XML tools and your growing XML knowledge with all the XML languages you want to work with.

Q. **Can I create effects like drop shadows in SVG?**

A. Yes, SVG provides a range of "filter" effects. One of the simpler SVG *filter primitives* can be used to create Gaussian blurs, a typical technique that creates drop shadows.

Q. **Does it matter which order I put elements in an SVG document?**

A. Yes, it is important that you place objects you want at the back of a graphic early in an SVG document. To place an object at the front of an SVG graphic, you need to place the corresponding SVG element last in the source code. Think of it like a "painter's model" using oil paint. You paint the first object, and then if you paint a second object on top of it the first one is likely to be no longer visible. In SVG you can use semi-transparent effects which allow some "paint" further back to show through, but if the SVG object is fully opaque then the corresponding area behind it is no longer visible.

Quiz

1. What is the document element for all SVG documents?
2. Is the `script` element in SVG the same as the `script` element in HTML?
3. Which special syntax do you need to use to protect your JavaScript code from being interpreted as SVG?

Quiz Answers

1. Each SVG document always has an `svg` element as the document element. Notice that the technology, SVG, is written all in uppercase letters. The name of the `svg` element is always written only in lowercase letters. SVG, like XML and JavaScript, is case sensitive.

21

2. No. The name of the element is "script" in each case but there are important differences. Refer back, for example, to the different attributes used to reference an external JavaScript file.

3. The CDATA section is nested within an SVG script element. Any JavaScript code within that section is treated by the SVG processor as text. The JavaScript interpreter processes the JavaScript code nested within a CDATA section in the normal way.

Exercises

1. You were shown simple techniques to place SVG text and a rectangle on the page. To create a rollover button with text, combine the techniques to place the text over the button.

2. After you have added text to the rectangle (hint: the text element must come after the rect element in document order), add set elements to each object so that the fill of the rectangle and the color of the text both change when you mouse over the button.

Appendixes

Appendix A

New Features in JavaScript 1.5

Just as with a programming language, each version of JavaScript provides not only fixes for any existing problems but also updated features that you can use. This appendix provides a brief overview of the additions that were made to JavaScript 1.5.

Number Formatting Additions

Number formatting was enhanced in JavaScript 1.5 to provide three additional methods that can be used. Three additional methods have been added to the Number object.

toExponential Method

The toExponential method returns a string representing a Number object in exponential notation. The string has one digit before the decimal point, and the number of digits after the decimal are determined by the value specified for the argument, described in Table A.1. The digits are rounded to the nearest number.

TABLE A.1   toExponential() Arguments

Argument	Description
fractionDigits	An integer value specifying the number of digits to display after the decimal point

Number.prototype.toExponential(fractionDigits)

toFixed Method

The toFixed method returns a string representing a Number object in fixed-point notation. The string is rounded to the number of digits after the decimal specified for the argument, described in Table A.2. For example, toFixed(2) is a good way to format U.S. currency.

TABLE A.2   toFixed() Arguments

Argument	Description
fractionDigits	An integer value specifying the number of digits to display after the decimal point

Number.prototype.toFixed(fractionDigits)

toPrecision Method

The toPrecision method returns a string representing a Number object in exponential or fixed-point notation. The string has one digit before the decimal point and the number of digits after the decimal are determined by the value specified for the argument, described in Table A.3. The digits are rounded to the nearest number.

TABLE A.3   toPrecision() Arguments

Argument	Description
precision	An integer value specifying the number of digits to display after the decimal point

Number.prototype.toPrecision(fractionDigits)

Runtime Error Messages

In JavaScript 1.5 runtime errors are reported as exceptions.

Regular Expressions

The following enhancements have been made to regular expressions in JavaScript 1.5.

Greedy Quantifiers

The ? character can now be used after any of the greedy quantifiers, *, +, ? and {}, to make them non-greedy. This means that instead of matching the maximum number of times (greedy) the ? character follows the qualifier, it will match the minimum number of times.

Non-Capturing Parentheses

You can keep a captured expression from being available as a back-reference by using ?: before the variable. For example, (?:x) matches x but does not remember the match.

Support for Positive and Negative Lookahead Assertions

Lookahead assertions are supported with the addition of the ? to the statement. For example, x(?=y) makes a match if x is followed by y. Therefore, if you have the statement Java(?=Script), it will match statements where Java is followed by Script.

JavaScript 1.5 also supports negative assertions, x(?!y), where the match only occurs if x is not followed by y. Therefore, with the example Java(?!Script), it matches all cases where Java is not followed by Script.

The Multiple-Line Flag with RegExp

By using the m flag you can now specify that the regular expression should match over multiple lines.

```
RegExp(stringtomatch, "m")
```

Conditional Function Declarations

You can declare functions within an if clause. By doing so, the function only gets declared if the if statement evaluates to true. For example, in the following code the function addnumbers() is only declared if x is greater than 5.

```
If (x > 5)
{
 function addnumbers()
  {
   x = x + y;
  }
}
```

Functions Can Be Declared Within an Expression

You can declare a function within any expression:

```
var a = function(b) {return b*5};
```

Multiple Catch Clauses

JavaScript 1.5 allows you to place multiple catch clauses in a `try...catch` statement. This allows you to have more than one conditional catch block to handle specific exceptions. For example, the following code sample catches either the `RangeError` or `EvalError` exceptions.

```
Try {
  Runcode ();
}
catch (e if e instance of RangeError)
{
 rangeErrorCode();
}
catch (e if e instance of EvalError)
{
 evalErrorCode();
}
catch (e)
{
 nonSpecifiedError()
}
```

When working with the `try ... catch` statement, make sure you always provide a catch block for situations when you do not specify an exception. In our code segment, we did this by creating a `catch (e)` block of code.

APPENDIX B

Color Codes

One area of Web development that can cause some frustration is the display of different colors. Color allows you to add more interest to your site, but you have to be careful to ensure that the colors you select display properly on each user's monitor.

The color palette available for the user's browser typically ranges from 8-bit (256 colors) to 32-bit, which allows the display of millions of colors. If a particular color does not exist on the user's browser, the color palette finds a different color within the palette to display. With this is mind, it is advisable to use the generic palette of 216 colors that Netscape uses for all 8-bit systems. By using only these colors, you can be fairly certain that your colors will display properly when viewed on Netscape Navigator, Internet Explorer, or another browser.

There are essentially three different methods that can be used to specify the color you want to use:

- Color name specified as plain-language
- Hexadecimal value representing the desired color
- RGB color code specified using the RGB() function

Color Names Specified as Plain-Language

Netscape originally developed a list of plain-language color names that are now accepted by most browsers. These color names, found in Table B.1, can be used to set the color for most objects. However, not all of the colors are considered Web safe and therefore may not always produce the desired results. I have placed an asterisk (*) next to the color names that can be safely used with the `<font>` HTML tag or in Cascading Style Sheets.

TABLE B.1   Plain-Language Color Names

antiquewhite	darkmagenta	honeydew	*magenta
*aqua	darkolivegreen	hotpink	maroon
aquamarine	darkorange	indianred	mediumaquamarine
azure	darkorchid	indigo	mediumblue
beige	darkred	ivory	mediumorchid
bisque	darksalmon	khaki	mediumpurple
*black	darkseagreen	lavender	mediumseagreen
blanchedalmond	darkslateblue	lavenderblush	mediumslateblue
*blue	darkslategray	lawngreen	mediumspringgreen
blueviolet	darkturquoise	lemonchiffon	medium turquoise
brown	darkviolet	lightblue	mediumvioletred
burlywood	deeppink	lightcoral	midnightblue
cadetblue	deepskyblue	lightcyan	mintcream
chartreuse	dimgray	lightgoldenrodyellow	mistyrose
chocolate	dodgerblue	lightgreen	moccasin
coral	firebrick	lightgrey	navajowhite
cornflowerblue	floralwhite	lightpink	navy
cornsilk	forestgreen	lightsalmon	oldlace
crimson	*fuchsia	lightseagreen	olive
*cyan	gainsboro	lightskyblue	olivedrab
darkblue	ghostwhite	lightslategray	orange
darkcyan	gold	lightsteelblue	orangered
darkgoldenrod	goldenrod	lightyellow	orchid
darkgray	gray	*lime	palegoldenrod
darkgreen	green	limegreen	palegreen
darkkhaki	greenyellow	linen	paleturquoise

TABLE B.1   continued

palevioletred	rosybrown	skyblue	tomato
papayawhip	royalblue	slateblue	turquoise
peachpuff	saddlebrown	slategray	violet
peru	salmon	snow	wheat
pink	sandybrown	springgreen	*white
plum	seagreen	steelblue	whitesmoke
powderblue	seashell	tan	*yellow
*purple	sienna	*teal	yellowgreen
*red	silver	thistle	

B

Hexadecimal Color Value

Although many browsers support the color names specified in the previous section, their interpretations of the color names often vary. To ensure the desired colors display, it is advisable to use a numeric value to represent the desired color. One common method is to use the hexadecimal value of the corresponding color value. A hexadecimal color code is comprised of six different characters (0-9 and A-F) with each code preceded by a # (number sign). When you use a hexadecimal value for a color, the first two digits represent the red value; the next two digits are the green value; and the last two digits are the blue value. Table B.2 lists the hexadecimal color codes that you can use. Again, with these hexadecimal color values not all of the colors are considered Web safe and therefore may not always produce the desired results. I have placed an asterisk (*) next to the color names that can be safely used. However, there is a trick that can be used with hexadecimal values to determine a Web safe color: If the color has pairs of digits in each position the color is Web safe. For example, #009933 is a Web safe color but #019933 is not because the first two digits are not a pair.

TABLE B.2   Hexadecimal Values

Hexadecimal Code	Color	Hexadecimal Code	Color
*#000000	Black	#008000	Green
#000080	Navy	#008080	Teal
#00008B	Dark blue	#008B8B	Dark cyan
#0000CD	Medium blue	#00BFFF	Deep sky blue
*#0000FF	Blue	#00DED1	Dark turquoise
#006400	Dark green	#00FA9A	Medium spring green

TABLE B.2   continued

Hexadecimal Code	Color	Hexadecimal Code	Color
*#00FF00	Lime	#808080	Gray
#00FF7F	Spring green	#87CEEB	Sky blue
*#00FFFF	Aqua	#87CEFA	Light sky blue
*#00FFFF	Cyan	#8A2BE2	Blue violet
#191970	Midnight blue	#8B0000	Dark red
#1E90FF	Dodger blue	#8B008B	Dark magenta
#20B2AA	Light seagreen	#8B4513	Saddle brown
#228B22	Forest green	#8DBC8F	Dark seagreen
#2E8B57	Sea green	#90EE90	Light green
#2F4F4F	Dark slate gray	#9370DB	Medium purple
#32CD32	Lime green	#9400D3	Dark violet
#3CB371	Medium sea green	#98FB98	Pale green
#40E0D0	Turquoise	#9932CC	Dark orchid
#4169E1	Royal blue	#9ACD32	Yellow green
#4682B4	Steel blue	#A0522D	Sienna
#483D8B	Dark slate blue	#A52A2A	Brown
#48D1CC	Medium turquoise	#A9A9A9	Dark gray
#4B0082	Indigo	#ADD8E6	Light blue
#556B2F	Dark olive green	#ADFF2F	Green yellow
#5F9EA0	Cadet blue	#AFEEEE	Pale turquoise
#6495ED	Cornflower blue	#B0C4DE	Light steel blue
#66CDAA	Medium aquamarine	#B0E0E6	Powder blue
#696969	Dim gray	#B22222	Firebrick
#6A5ACD	Slate blue	#B8860B	Dark goldenrod
#6B8E23	Olive drab	#BA55D3	Medium orchid
*#778899	Light slate gray	#BC8F8F	Rosy brown
#7B68EE	Medium slate blue	#BDB76B	Dark khaki
#7CFC00	Lawn green	#C0C0C0	Silver
#7FFF00	Chartreuse	#C71585	Medium violet red
#7FFFD4	Aquamarine	#CD5C5C	Indian red
#800000	Maroon	#CD853F	Peru
#800080	Purple	#D2691E	Chocolate

TABLE B.2 continued

Hexadecimal Code	Color	Hexadecimal Code	Color
#D2B48C	Tan	*#FF0000	Red
#D3D3D3	Light grey	*#FF00FF	Fuchsia
#D8BFD8	Thistle	*#FF00FF	Magenta
#DA70D6	Orchid	#FF1493	Deep pink
#DAA520	Goldenrod	#FF4500	Orange red
#DB7093	Pale violet red	#FF6347	Tomato
#DC143C	Crimson	#FF69B4	Hot pink
#DCDCDC	Gainsboro	#FF7F50	Coral
#DDA0DD	Plum	#FF8C00	Dark orange
#DEB887	Burlywood	#FFA07A	Light salmon
#E0FFFF	Light cyan	#FFA500	Orange
#E6E6FA	Lavender	#FFB6C1	Light pink
#E9967A	Dark salmon	#FFC8CB	Pink
#EE82EE	Violet	#FFD700	Gold
#EEE8AA	Pale goldenrod	#FFDAB9	Peach puff
#F08080	Light coral	#FFDEAD	Navajo white
#F0E68C	Khaki	#FFE4B5	Moccasin
#F0F8FF	Alice blue	#FFE4C4	Bisque
#F0FFF0	Honeydew	#FFE4E1	Misty rose
#F0FFFF	Azure	#FFEBCD	Blanched almond
#F4A460	Sandy brown	#FFEFD5	Papaya whip
#F5DEB3	Wheat	#FFF0F5	Lavender blush
#F5F5DC	Beige	#FFF5EE	Sea shell
#F5F5F5	White smoke	#FFF8DC	Cornsilk
#F5FFFA	Mint cream	#FFFACD	Lemon chiffon
#F8F8FF	Ghost white	#FFFAF0	Floral white
#FA8072	Salmon	#FFFAFA	Snow
#FAEBD7	Antique white	*#FFFF00	Yellow
#FAF0E6	Linen	#FFFFE0	Light yellow
#FAFAD2	Light goldenrod yellow	#FFFFF0	Ivory
#FDF5E6	Old lace	*#FFFFFF	White

B

RGB Color Values

The other method for specifying color values with JavaScript is to use the RGB() function. When you use this function you are specifying a color as defined by combining a specific combination of red, green, and blue. You must specify a value for each color component either as a numeric value between 0 and 255 or a percentage of color. The most commonly used method is the numeric value, as illustrated in Table B.3 which shows the RGB values for the most commonly used colors. When you use the RGB() function you must specify the three-color values in the order red, green, blue. For example, to display blue you would specify:

```
rgb(0, 0, 255);
```

Notice, the red and green values are 0 when you want to display blue. If you wanted to use the percentage method you would specify the color value as follows:

```
rgb(0%, 0%, 100%);
```

TABLE B.3   RGB Combinations for Common Colors

Color	Red	Green	Blue
Aqua	0	255	255
Black	0	0	0
Blue	0	0	255
Green	0	255	0
Magenta	255	0	255
Orange	255	153	0
Pink	255	0	204
Silver	204	204	204
Red	255	0	0
White	255	255	255
Yellow	255	255	0

APPENDIX C

Functions Reference

JavaScript provides several different built-in functions for your use. Some of these functions are actually associated with specific objects, such as the math functions that are associated with the Math object. This simply means that the appropriate object name must be specified as part of the function reference. When a function is associated with an object, it is also referred to as the method for that object.

abs()

The abs() function returns the absolute value of the argument. This function has one argument, outlined in Table C.1, and is associated with the Math object.

TABLE C.1   abs() Argument

Argument	Description
numValue	Any expression that returns a numeric value
Math.abs(numValue)	

acos()

The acos() function returns the inverse cosine or arccosine value of the argument. This function has one argument, outlined in Table C.2, and is associated with the Math object.

TABLE C.2   acos() Argument

Argument	Description
numValue	Any expression that returns a numeric value (This value should be between -1 and 1.)
Math.acos(numValue)	

asin()

The asin() function returns the inverse sine or arcsine of the argument. This function has one argument, outlined in Table C.3, and is associated with the Math object.

TABLE C.3   asin() Argument

Argument	Description
numValue	Any expression that returns a numeric value (The value should be between -1 and 1.)
Math.asin(numValue)	

atan()

The atan() function returns the inverse tangent of the argument. This function has one argument, outlined in Table C.4, and is associated with the Math object.

TABLE C.4   atan() Argument

Argument	Description
numValue	Any expression that returns a numeric value
Math.atan(numValue)	

atan2()

The `atan2()` function returns the inverse tangent or arctangent of the slope of two arguments, outlined in Table C.5. The function first computes the quotient of `numValue2/numValue1`, and then determines the arc tangent of the result. This function also takes into account the quadrant that the value falls into based upon the signs of the arguments. This function is associated with the `Math` object.

TABLE C.5   `atan2()` Arguments

Argument	Description
numValue1	Any expression that returns a numeric value
numValue2	Any expression that returns a numeric value
Math.abs(numValue1, numValue2)	

atob()

The `atob()` function decodes a base-64 encoded value which represents the encoded form of binary data. The value is decoded and converted to a block of binary data. This function has one argument, outlined in Table C.6, and is associated with the `Window` object.

TABLE C.6   `atob()` Argument

Argument	Description
b64Value	A string that contains base-64 encoded data
Window.atob(b64Value)	

Boolean()

The `Boolean()` function converts the specified argument to a Boolean value of either `true` or `false`. This function has one argument, outlined in Table C.7, but if the argument is omitted it returns a value of `false`.

TABLE C.7   `Boolean()` Argument

Argument	Description
bValue	Any expression
Boolean(bValue)	

C

The `Boolean()` function converts the specified argument as outlined in Table C.8.

TABLE C.8   `Boolean()` Function Results

Value	Result
0	false
null	false
no value	false
undefined	false
NaN	false
"" (zero length string)	false
false (Boolean)	false
true (Boolean)	true
Non-zero number	true
Non-zero length string	true
Object	true

btoa()

The `btoa()` function encodes the specified value into base-64 form. Base-64 is typically used to convert binary data into a format that transmits better across a network. This function has one argument, outlined in Table C.9, and is associated with the `Window` object.

TABLE C.9   btoa() Argument

Argument	Description
bValue	Any binary expression
Window.btoa(bValue)	

captureEvents()

The `captureEvents()` function is only available within Netscape. This function is used to route events to other event handlers, or the receiving `Document`, `Layer`, or `Window` objects. The function has one argument, as outlined in Table C.10, and is associated with the `Document`, `Layer`, and `Window` objects.

TABLE C.10   captureEvents() Argument

Argument	Description
eventMask	An event mask, such as Event.KEYPRESS
Document.captureEvents(eventMask)	
Layer.captureEvents(eventMask)	
Window.captureEvents(eventMask)	

catch()

The catch() function is used with the try ... catch... error-handling method to trap errors. This function has one argument, outlined in Table C.11.

TABLE C.11   catch() Argument

Argument	Description
errorVal	An instance of the Error object
catch(errorVal)	

ceil()

The ceil() function rounds up the specified value to the next integer value. This function has one argument, outlined in Table C.12, and is associated with the Math object.

TABLE C.12   ceil() Argument

Argument	Description
numValue	Any expression that returns a numeric value
Math.ceil(numValue)	

cos()

The cos() function returns the cosine of the specified argument. This function has one argument, outlined in Table C.13, and is associated with the Math object.

TABLE C.13   cos() Argument

Argument	Description
numValue	Any expression that returns a numeric value
Math.cos(numValue)	

Date()

The Date() function returns the current date. This function has no arguments.

Date()

decodeURI()

The decodeURI() function decodes a URI value. This function has one argument, shown in Table C.14.

TABLE C.14   decodeURI() Argument

Argument	Description
URIValue	An encoded URI value
decodeURI(URIValue)	

decodeURIComponent()

The decodeURIComponent() function decodes a URI component. This function has one argument, shown in Table C.15.

TABLE C.15   decodeURIComponent() Argument

Argument	Description
URIComp	An encoded URI component
decodeURIComponent(URIComp)	

encodeURI()

The encodeURI() function encodes a URI value. The function encodes the string by replacing in certain characters with hexadecimal escape sequences to conform with the UTF-8 profile. This function has one argument, shown in Table C.16.

TABLE C.16   encodeURI() Argument

Argument	Description
URIValue	An unencoded URI value
encodeURI(URIValue)	

encodeURIComponent()

The encodeURIComponent() function encodes a URI component. This function has one argument, shown in Table C.17.

TABLE C.17   encodeURIComponent() Argument

Argument	Description
URIComp	An unencoded URI component
enecodeURIComponent(URIComp)	

Error()

The Error() function creates and initializes a new Error object. For example, you can use this to create a user-defined error. This function has two arguments, as shown in Table C.18.

TABLE C.18   Error() Arguments

Argument	Description
errNumber	An error number
errText	A text description of the error
Error(errNumber, errText)	

escape()

The escape() function computes a new version of the string. It is passed by replacing certain characters with hexadecimal escape sequences. All character codes between zero and 32 are escaped. For example, a shape is escaped as %20. This function has two arguments, as outlined in Table C.19.

TABLE C.19   escape() Arguments

Argument	Description
inputString	A string of un-escaped characters
switch	A switch that indicates whether the plus signs should be escaped
escape(inputString, switch)	

eval()

The eval() function evaluates and executes the code in the specified string. This function has one argument, as outlined in Table C.20.

TABLE C.20   eval() Argument

Argument	Description
sourceText	A string that contains a syntactically correct script source code
eval(sourceText)	

exp()

The exp() function returns the exponential value of the specified argument (e raised to the specified power). This function has one argument, outlined in Table C.21, and is associated with the Math object.

TABLE C.21   exp() Argument

Argument	Description
numValue	Any expression that returns a numeric value
Math.exp(numValue)	

floor()

The floor() function rounds down the specified value to the next integer value. This function has one argument, outlined in Table C.22, and is associated with the Math object.

TABLE C.22 floor() Argument

Argument	Description
numValue	Any expression that returns a numeric value
Math.floor(numValue)	

Function()

The Function() function creates and initializes a new function object. This function can have any number of arguments, outlined in Table C.23.

TABLE C.23 Function() Arguments

Argument	Description
argumentlist	Formal parameters and script code
Function(argumentlist)	

GetObject()

The GetObject() function returns a reference to an object representing a file that belongs to an application on your system. This is a Jscript-only function and, therefore, only works in Internet Explorer. This function has three arguments, outlined in Table C.24.

TABLE C.24 GetObject() Arguments

Argument	Description
ObjectType	The application type and object class type to create
Location	The path or URL of the object to instantiate
SubObject	A fragment identifier for a subobject within the file
GetObject(ObjectType, Location, SubObject)	

handleEvent()

The handleEvent() function is only available in Netscape Navigator. This function handles the specified event object. This function has one argument, outlined in Table C.25. This function can be used alone, or associated with the Document, Layer, or Window objects.

TABLE C.25   handleEvent() Arguments

Argument	Description
EventObj	Any event object
handleEvent(EventObj)	
Document.handleEvent(EventObj)	
Layer.handleEvent(EventObj)	
Window.handleEvent(EventObj)	

isFinite()

The isFinite() function checks the specified value for the infinity value. This function has one argument, outlined in Table C.26.

TABLE C.26   isFinite() Argument

Argument	Description
numValue	Any expression that returns a numeric value
isFinite(numValue)	

isNaN()

The isNaN() function tests the specified value to determine whether it is a valid numeric value. If the value is not numeric (not-a-number), the function returns a value of false; otherwise it returns a value of true. This function has one argument, outlined in Table C.27.

TABLE C.27   isNaN() Argument

Argument	Description
numValue	Any expression that returns a numeric value
isNaN(numValue)	

log()

The log() function returns the natural logarithm for the specified value. This function has one argument, outlined in Table C.28, and is associated with the Math object.

TABLE C.28 log() Argument

Argument	Description
numValue	Any expression that returns a numeric value
Math.log(numValue)	

max()

The max() function determines the maximum of two specified values. This function has two arguments, outlined in Table C.29, and is associated with the Math object.

TABLE C.29 max() Arguments

Argument	Description
numValue1	Any expression that returns a numeric value
numValue2	Any expression that returns a numeric value
Math.max(numValue1, numValue2)	

min()

The min() function determines the minimum of two specified values. This function has two arguments, outlined in Table C.30, and is associated with the Math object.

TABLE C.30 min() Arguments

Argument	Description
numValue1	Any expression that returns a numeric value
numValue2	Any expression that returns a numeric value
Math.min(numValue1, numValue2)	

Number()

The Number() function converts the specified expression to a numeric value. This function has one argument as outlined in Table C.31.

TABLE C.31   Number() Argument

Argument	Description
Value1	Any valid expression
Number(Value1)	

The Number() function returns a different result based on the type of value passed to the function, as outlined in Table C.32.

TABLE C.32   Number() Function Results

Value	Result
Number	Number
No value	0
Null	0
Undefined	NaN
Non-numeric string	NaN
Boolean true	1
Boolean false	0
Numeric string	Equivalent numeric string
Object	Internal conversion causes either a number or NaN to be returned based on the specified object

Object()

The Object() function converts the specified expression to an object. This function has one argument as outlined in Table C.33.

TABLE C.33   Object() Argument

Argument	Description
Value1	Any valid expression
Object(Value1)	

The Object() function returns a different result based on the type of value passed to the function, as outlined in Table C.34.

TABLE C.34   Object() Function Results

Value	Result
Number	Number object with a default value of specified number
No value	Empty object
Null	Empty object
Undefined	Empty object
String	String object with the default value of the specified string
Boolean	Boolean object with a default value of the specified Boolean value
Object	Object is returned as specified

parseFloat()

The parseFloat() function extracts a floating point number from the specified string. This function has one argument as outlined in Table C.35.

TABLE C.35   parseFloat() Argument

Argument	Description
numValue	Any valid expression
parseFloat(numValue)	

parseInt()

The parseInt() function extracts an integer value from the specified string. This function has one argument as outlined in Table C.36.

TABLE C.36   parseInt() Argument

Argument	Description
numValue	Any valid expression
parseInt(numValue)	

pow()

The pow() function returns the result of raising a value to the specified power. The function always raises the first argument to the power of the second. This function has two arguments as outlined in Table C.37 and is associated with the Match object.

TABLE C.37   pow() Argument

Argument	Description
numValue1	Any expression that returns a numeric value
numValue2	Any expression that returns a numeric value
Math.pow(numValue1, numValue2)	

random()

The random() function returns randomly generated value between 0 and 1 inclusive. This function has no arguments.

Math.random()

releaseEvents()

The releaseEvents() function is only available within Netscape. This function is used to specify the events that no longer need to be captured. The function has one argument, as outlined in Table C.38, and is associated with the Document, Layer, and Window objects.

TABLE C.38   releaseEvents() Argument

Argument	Description
eventMask	An event mask, such as Event.KEYPRESS
Document.releaseEvents(eventMask)	
Layer.releaseEvents(eventMask)	
Window.releaseEvents(eventMask)	

rgb()

The rgb() function defines a color value by combining specified amounts of blue, red, and green. This function has three arguments as outlined in Table C.39.

TABLE C.39 rgb() Arguments

Argument	Description
redValue	Integer value specifying red intensity
greenValue	Integer value specifying green intensity
blueValue	Integer value specifying blue intensity
rgb(redValue, greenValue, blueValue)	

round()

The round() function rounds the specified value to the nearest integer value. This function has one argument, outlined in Table C.40, and is associated with the Math object.

TABLE C.40 round() Argument

Argument	Description
numValue	Any expression that returns a numeric value
Math.round(numValue)	

routeEvents()

The routeEvents() function is only available within Netscape. This function is used to specify the events to route to other event handlers, other than the defaults. The function has one argument, as outlined in Table C.41, and is associated with the Document, Layer, and Window objects.

TABLE C.41 routeEvents() Argument

Argument	Description
eventMask	An event mask, such as Event.KEYPRESS
Document.routeEvents(eventMask)	
Layer.routeEvents(eventMask)	
Window.routeEvents(eventMask)	

C

ScriptEngine()

The ScriptEngine() function is only available in Internet Explorer. It returns a value of JScript, VBA, or VBScript indicating the currently installed scripting engine. This function has no arguments.

```
ScriptEngine()
```

sin()

The sin() function returns the sine of the value. This function has one argument, outlined in Table C.42, and is associated with the Math object.

TABLE C.42   sin() Argument

Argument	Description
numValue	Any expression that returns a numeric value
Math.sin(numValue)	

sqrt()

The sqrt() function returns the square root of the specified value. This function has one argument, outlined in Table C.43, and is associated with the Math object.

TABLE C.43   sqrt() Argument

Argument	Description
numValue	Any expression that returns a numeric value
Math.sqrt(numValue)	

tan()

The tan() function returns the tangent of the specified value. This function has one argument, outlined in Table C.44, and is associated with the Math object.

TABLE C.44   tan() Argument

Argument	Description
numValue	Any expression that returns a numeric value
Math.tan(numValue)	

toString()

The toString() function returns a string representation of the associated object. This function has one argument as outlined in Table C.45 and is associated with the Object object.

TABLE C.45   toString() Argument

Argument	Description
radix	Radix conversion to be applied when the receiving object is a number
Object.toString(radix)	

unescape()

The unescape() function converts a string back after the escape() function has been applied. This function has one argument as outlined in Table C.46.

TABLE C.46   unescape() Argument

Argument	Description
inputString	Any expression string expression
unescape(inputString)	

unwatch()

The unwatch() function is only available with Netscape Navigator. The function unsets a watch point for the property of an object. This function has one argument as outlined in Table C.47.

TABLE C.47   unwatch() Argument

Argument	Description
objProp	Any valid object property
unwatch(objProp)	

watch()

The watch() function is only available with Netscape Navigator. The function sets a watch point for the property of an object. This function has one argument as outlined in Table C.48.

TABLE C.48 watch() Argument

Argument	Description
objProp	Any valid object property
watch(objProp)	

APPENDIX D

Resources Online

One of the great aspects of working with JavaScript is that there are many resources available online. There are several sites that provide additional tips about working with JavaScript along with good examples on how to perform different tasks. There are also good sites for CGI, Java, HTML, and Java Applets which we have discussed in this book. Many of these sites are outlined in this appendix.

JavaScript

These sites provide good information about using JavaScript on your Web pages.

CNET Builder.COM

This site provides not only tutorials and examples for JavaScript, but also for other Web technologies such as HTML, XML, and DHTML.

```
http://builder.cnet.com/
```

Dynamic Drive

Dynamic Drive's site provides a lot of great DHTML examples that are created using JavaScript.

```
http://www.dynamicdrive.com/
```

JavaScript Kit

This is another great site for finding sample code to use on your own Web pages. The site also includes some good DHTML and CSS examples.

```
http://wsabstract.com/
```

The JavaScript Source

This site is loaded with different JavaScript source examples that you can copy and use on your own site.

```
http://javascript.internet.com/
```

JavaScript World

This site provides tutorials and sample scripts for working with JavaScript.

```
http://www.jsworld.com
```

Microsoft JScript Reference

This site provides a language reference and user guide for JScript, which is Microsoft's version of JavaScript.

```
http://msdn.microsoft.com/library/default.asp?url=/library/en-us/script56/
html/js56jsoriJScript.asp
```

Netscape JavaScript Developer Central

This site provides some good JavaScript resource information, which includes a newsgroup, articles, and sample code.

```
http://developer.netscape.com/tech/javascript/index.html
```

Netscape Plugin Guide

This site provides online documentation for working with plugins.

```
http://developer.netscape.com/docs/manuals/communicator/plugin/index.htm
```

W3C World Wide Web Consortium

This site contains the guidelines and standards that have been developed for HTML, CSS, and other Web technologies.

`http://www.w3.org/`

W3Schools.com

This site provides a good tutorial and examples for using JavaScript. It also provides tutorials for HTML, CSS, XML, DHTML, VBScript, SQL, and ASP.

`http://www.w3schools.com/default.asp`

WebReference.com

This site provides valuable tips for working with JavaScript and several other Web technologies including DHTML, HTML, XML, and Perl.

`http://webreference.com/`

Java and Java Applets

These sites provide good information about using Java and Java Applets.

FreewareJava.com

This site provides links to some good resources on the Internet for Java applets, Java tutorials, and even JavaScript.

`http://www.freewarejava.com`

The Java Boutique

This site provides different Java Applets that can be used on your site.

`http://www.javaboutique.internet.com/`

Java Technology Tutorials

IBM provides some good tutorials for working with Java.

`http://www-105.ibm.com/developerworks/education.nsf/dw/java-onlinecourse-bytitle`

Javalobby

This site provides a lot of good resources on Java technologies. It also provides the ability to chat with other Java developers.

`http://www.javalobby.org/`

D

JavaWorld

This site provides reference and tips for working with Java.

`http://www.javaworld.com/`

The Source for Java Technology

As the developers of Java, Sun's site provides a good resource for learning about the latest Java technology.

`http://java.sun.com`

ZDNet Developer

This site provides Java applets that you can use on your Web site. This site also provides information on other Web technologies including HTML, CSS, JavaScript, DHTML, XMP, and ActiveX.

`http://www.zdnet.com/devhead/resources/scriptlibrary/applets/`

HTML

The following sites provide some good resources for working with HTML.

HTML Writers Guild

This site provides an international organization of Web authors. By becoming part of this organization you have access to a support network of other Web developers.

`http://www.hwg.org/`

NCSA Beginners Guide to HTML

This site provides a good resource for working with HTML by describing each of the HTML tags.

`http://archive.ncsa.uiuc.edu/General/Internet/WWW/HTMLPrimer.html`

Website Tips

This site provides tips and tutorials for building HTML pages. It also contains tips for other Web technologies, such as JavaScript.

`http://www.websitetips.com/index.html`

CGI

The following sites provide good information about working with CGI scripts.

CGI 101

This site provides beginner-level training and tutorials for CGI.

`http://www.cgi101.com/`

CGI City

This site provides several CGI scripts that you can use on your site.

`http://www.icthus.net/CGI-City/`

The CGI Resource Index

This site provides access to over 2,600 different CGI resources.

`http://www.cgi-resources.com/`

The Common Gateway Interface

This site provides detailed information about CGI.

`http://hoohoo.ncsa.uiuc.edu/cgi/`

D

APPENDIX E

A Short History of JavaScript

JavaScript has become a fairly widely accepted scripting language that you can use to perform tasks not available with standard HTML. In fact, JavaScript has become the most popular scripting language for performing the following tasks:

- Working with Java applets and plugins
- Detecting the user's browser version, and determining content for that browser
- Changing the messages within the status line
- Validating form content
- Displaying messages to the user
- Creating mouse-over effects

Evolution of the Internet

Amazingly enough, the Internet can actually trace its origin back to the 1960s. The Internet concept was actually conceived in the 1960s under the direction of the Department of Defense, Advanced Research Projects Agency (ARPA).

Therefore, the first small network of computers that was created was called ARPANET with the intention of sharing supercomputers among researchers in the United States.

Although originally intended for sharing of computer resources, e-mail capabilities were added and ARPANET became the first digital post office as researchers learned to collaborate on projects. By 1971, ARPANET had grown to 23 hosts, connecting universities and government research centers around the United States.

In 1972, the government formed the InterNetworking Working Group as a standard-setting group to govern the expanding network. Vinton Cerf was elected as the first chairman of the group, and later became known as the "father of the Internet."

The first public exposure to the network came in 1974 when Telenet was introduced as the first commercial version of ARPANET. In 1979, the first USENET groups were created, allowing users from around the world to join discussion groups on all sorts of topics.

By 1981, the ARPANET hosts had grown to 213, with a new host being added about every 20 days. In the mid-1980s, Bob Kahn and Vinton Cerf were members of a team that developed TCP/IP—the communication language still used today for Internet computers. During that time, the network of computers that made up ARPANET were seen as an "internet," thus coining the term used to refer to the network today.

Also during the 1980s, personal computer sales soared, making the Internet a great communication tool for corporations. By 1987, the number of Internet hosts exceeded 10,000.

The first "Internet worm" was released in November 1988, temporarily disabling 6,000 of the 60,000 Internet hosts. This prompted the development of the Computer Emergency Response Team (CERT) to address security concerns of the Internet.

The Internet has grown in leaps and bounds from its very limited beginnings in the 1960s. As the network grew, the demand for technologies to display and capture content grew as well, dramatically causing an increased interest in JavaScript and other Web development technologies.

Internet Programming Revolution

As previously mentioned, when the Internet (or ARPANET as it was called), first came into existence it was used as a method for sharing files among researchers. From that point, different individuals created their own versions of a "hypertext" type of system that could be used globally for sharing information. The first popular hypertext system was actually developed in 1987 by Bill Atkinson, and was called HyperCard. HyperCard simplified the process of creating graphical hypertext applications. This system spanned other hypertext systems running on large scale systems.

In 1989, the Hypertext Markup Language (HTML) was actually conceived as a system that could be accessed across a wide range of computer systems by individuals working at CERN. HTML was conceived as a simple solution that matched tags with simple network protocol HTTP. HTML was created based on SGML (Standard Generalized Markup Language), which was widely used at that time.

In fall of 1990, the first text-only browsers were implemented providing access to hypertext files created using HTML. Popularity of HTML grew making it the standard for displaying dynamic content on the Internet. Because of the vast growth of HTML, the World Wide Web Consortium (W3C) gained responsibility for developing standards for Web developers.

As you are probably aware, HTML provided a good vehicle for displaying static content; but it was, and still is unable to interact with the visitor. HTML is also unable to make decisions, or automate repetitive tasks. Because of these constraints, and the demands to create more dynamic content, other Web technologies were developed.

New technologies, such as Java, were used to create dynamic content on Web pages. Although use of Java applets created a more dynamic page, it did not allow for interaction between your HTML code and the Java applet. This being the case, Netscape recognized the need for a programming language that would allow for the interface with Java applets.

JavaScript Introduction

E

As Web development evolved, Netscape determined that a method was needed as a means for communicating among the HTML code and the embedded objects on the page. That being the case, Netscape decided to create a scripting language that would accomplish this task, along with other tasks that could not be accomplished with the existing tools, such as allowing Web server administrators to manage the Web server and connect its pages to other services, providing Web-page authors the ability to create scripts to run on a Web page and perform tasks such as verifying a value typed in a field, and finally creating an interface for communicating with Java applets placed on an HTML page.

As mentioned, JavaScript originally got its start as a scripting language for Netscape Navigator. This scripting language was originally titled "LiveScript." It was designed to be released as part of Netscape Navigator 2.

Before the release of Navigator 2, Netscape and Sun formed an agreement to call the new scripting language JavaScript. When Navigator 3 was released, it included an updated version of JavaScript, titled "JavaScript 1.1."

At the same time Netscape was releasing Navigator 3, Microsoft released Internet Explorer 3 with it own version of JavaScript named JScript. Because the Java name was trademarked by Sun, Microsoft chose to call it JScript to avoid the need to license the name from Sun. Although JScript was intended to parallel the capabilities of JavaScript 1.1, available with Navigator 3, its functionality more closely resembled that available in the original version of JavaScript released with Navigator 2.

Finally with the release of Navigator 4 and Internet Explorer 4 the versions of JavaScript and JScript essentially matched core functionalities. Although Microsoft continued to call its version JScript, Internet Explorer Script tags recognized both JScript and JavaScript, allowing for both types of scripting. Of course, that was not true of Netscape Navigator, which only recognized JavaScript Script tags. But since the tags are essentially the same for both JavaScript and JScript, if the developer uses JavaScript as the language reference the code will run on both browsers.

In an effort to create a more standardized core language, the European Computer Manufacturers Association (ECMA) met with Microsoft, Netscape, and other organizations with JavaScript interests. Formal language specifications were published as standards for the language. Because of the licensing issues with the name JavaScript, the new language was named ECMAScript.

Currently the ECMA maintains the standards for the core language. The core language typically maintains the most compatible features consistent between Netscape Navigator and Microsoft Internet Explorer. Therefore, you can typically feel confident that everything within the ECMA standard will work on the current browser versions for both Netscape and Microsoft, but may not work on previous browser versions, or any of the many other browsers available.

Unfortunately, the ECMA standard does not include all the fun and exciting features that you will find on various Web sites that you visit today. Most of these extended features are built in to particular browsers by Microsoft and Netscape. In order to take advantage of these features, you potentially limit your audience of visitors capable of viewing your site in all its glory. One good example of this would be when Navigator 3 provided additional objects that allowed Web developers to create rollover button effects like those you see on the most current sites today. Microsoft was slower to add this type of feature. Meaning the Internet Explorer users did not see the rollover effects when visiting sites that had incorporated that feature. Of course this functionality was later incorporated into the Internet Explorer Document Object Model.

As I mentioned earlier, the ECMA maintains the standards for the core JavaScript language, called ECMAScript because of licensing issues with Sun. Both Netscape Navigator and Microsoft Internet Explorer maintain that they are ECMA-compliant, meaning that they include all of the core language features as outlined by the EMCA standard. The ECMA standards body maintains a document called ECMA-262, which contains all core language standards. You can find the latest version of this document on `http://www.ecma.ch`.

It is important to recognize that the ECMA only provides core-language standards. But it is important to be familiar with some of these standards so that you can quickly determine whether the JavaScript functionality you want is supported by all current browsers.

Browser Support of JavaScript Versions

As mentioned, new versions of JavaScript were developed to add additional functionality. Each version was released with a new version of the Web browser. Table E.1 illustrates the versions of JavaScript that were supported by each browser version.

TABLE E.1 JavaScript Version Support

JavaScript Version	Browser Support
JavaScript 1.1	Netscape 3.01
JavaScript 1.2	Netscape 4.05, Internet Explorer 4.01
JavaScript 1.3	Netscape 4.61, Internet Explorer 5.0
JavaScript 1.4	Mozilla 5.0 Alpha Pre-Release
JavaScript 1.5	Netscape 6, Internet Explorer 5.5

As you can see from the table, JavaScript 1.5 features were supported beginning with Netscape Navigator 6 and Internet Explorer 5.5.

As discussed in Chapter 8, "The Browser Issue," JavaScript is supported by most current browsers on the market today (with the exception of Internet devices, such as cellular phones, that have recently come to market and that have very limited scripting capabilities). But you always run the risk that someone may access your site with an older browser that does not support JavaScript. Therefore, it is always a good idea to check for browser support of JavaScript on your page, to avoid any potential errors. For more information about doing this, refer to Chapter 8.

INDEX

Symbols

; (semicolons), 22

A

abs()
 function, 699
 method, 271
absolute values, 271
access
 arguments, 85-86
 arrays, 168-173
 browser windows, 569
 cookies, 539-541
 elements
  HTML forms, 205-206
  by ID, 301
  by tag names, 302
 external files, 27
 nodes, 300-302

N

X-Y-Z

Hey, you've got enough worries.

Don't let IT training be one of them.

Get on the fast track to IT training at InformIT,
your total Information Technology training network.

 | **www.informit.com** | *SAMS*

■ Hundreds of timely articles on dozens of topics ■ Discounts on IT books
from all our publishing partners, including Sams Publishing ■ Free, unabridged
books from the InformIT Free Library ■ "Expert Q&A"—our live, online chat
with IT experts ■ Faster, easier certification and training from our Web- or
classroom-based training programs ■ Current IT news ■ Software downloads
■ Career-enhancing resources

InformIT is a registered trademark of Pearson. Copyright ©2001 by Pearson.
Copyright ©2001 by Sams Publishing.